Nonlinear Statistical Modelin

T0328788

This collection brings together important contributions by leading econometricians on (i) parametric approaches to qualitative and sample selection models, (ii) nonparametric and semiparametric approaches to qualitative and sample selection models, and (iii) nonlinear estimation of cross-sectional and time series models. The advances achieved here can have important bearing on the choice of methods and analytical techniques in applied research. The collection is dedicated to Professor Takeshi Amemiya in honor of his path-breaking contributions to econometrics and statistics.

Cheng Hsiao is Professor of Economics at the University of Southern California and Hong Kong University of Science and Technology. He is the author of *Analysis of Panel Data* (Econometric Society Monograph 11, Cambridge University Press, 1986), a coauthor of *Econometric Models, Techniques, and Applications, Second Edition* (Prentice-Hall, 1996, with M. Intriligator and R. Bodkin), and a coeditor of *Analysis of Panels and Limited Dependent Variable Models* (Cambridge University Press, 1999, with K. Lahiri, L. F. Lee, and M. H. Pesaran). Professor Hsiao is a Fellow of the Econometric Society and coeditor and Fellow of the *Journal of Econometrics*.

Kimio Morimune is a professor at the Kyoto Institute of Economic Research, Kyoto University. He has also served as visiting professor at Fuddan University, China, the University of Western Australia, and Stanford University. Professor Morimune is a coeditor of the *Journal of Economic Research*, a recent coeditor of the *Japanese Economic Review*, and an advisory board member of the *Journal of Economic Surveys*. Professor Morimune is the author of three texts in Japanese: *Statistical Inference in Econometrics*, *Introductory Statistics*, and *Econometrics*.

James L. Powell is Professor of Economics at the University of California, Berkeley. He is a Fellow of the Econometric Society, a Fellow and former Associate Editor of the *Journal of Econometrics*, and a former associate editor of *Econometrica*. Professor Powell is also a coeditor of *Nonparametric and Semiparametric Methods in Econometrics and Statistics: Proceedings of the Fifth International Symposium in Economic Theory and Econometrics* (Cambridge University Press, 1991, with W. Barnett and G. Tauchen).

ISET (International Symposia in Economic Theory and Econometrics)

Editor
William A. Barnett, *Washington University in St. Louis*

Other edited books in the series

William A. Barnett and A. Ronald Gallant
*New approaches to modeling, specification selection, and
   econometric inference*

William A. Barnett and Kenneth J. Singleton
New approaches to monetary economics

William A. Barnett, Ernst R. Berndt, and Halbert White
Dynamic econometric modeling

William A. Barnett, John Geweke, and Karl Shell
Econometric complexity

William A. Barnett, James Powell, and George E. Tauchen
Nonparametric and semiparametric methods in econometrics and statistics

William A. Barnett, Bernard Cornet, Claude D'Aspremont,
Jean J. Gabszweicz, and Andreu Mas-Colell
Equilibrium theory and applications

William A. Barnett, Herve Moulin, Maurice Salles, and
Norman J. Schofield
Social choice, welfare, and ethics

William A. Barnett, Giancarlo Gandolfo, and Claude Hillinger
Dynamic disequilibrium modeling

William A. Barnett, Alan P. Kirman, and Mark Salmon
Nonlinear dynamics and economics

William A. Barnett, David F. Hendry, Svend Hylleberg, Timo Teräsvirta,
Dag Tjøstheim, and Allan Würtz
Nonlinear econometric modeling in time series analysis

William A. Barnett, Carl Chiarella, Steve Keen, Robert Marks,
and Hermann Schnabl
*Commerce, complexity, and evolution: Topics in economics, finance,
   marketing, and management*

Nonlinear statistical modeling

Proceedings of the Thirteenth International Symposium
in Economic Theory and Econometrics:
Essays in Honor of Takeshi Amemiya

Edited by

CHENG HSIAO
University of Southern California

KIMIO MORIMUNE
Kyoto University

JAMES L. POWELL
University of California, Berkeley

CAMBRIDGE
UNIVERSITY PRESS

CAMBRIDGE UNIVERSITY PRESS
Cambridge, New York, Melbourne, Madrid, Cape Town, Singapore,
São Paulo, Delhi, Dubai, Tokyo, Mexico City

Cambridge University Press
The Edinburgh Building, Cambridge CB2 8RU, UK

Published in the United States of America by Cambridge University Press, New York

www.cambridge.org
Information on this title: www.cambridge.org/9780521169264

First published 2001
First paperback edition 2010

A catalogue record for this publication is available from the British Library

Library of Congress Cataloguing in Publication data
International Symposium in Economic Theory and Econometrics (13th)
    Nonlinear statistical modeling : proceedings of the thirteenth International Symposium
in Economic Theory and Econometrics : essays in honor of Takeshi Amemiya / edited by
Cheng Hsiao, Kimio Morimune, James L. Powell.
        p.   cm. – (International symposia in economic theory and econometrics)
    "Bibliography of Takeshi Amemiya."
    Includes bibliographical references.
    ISBN 0-521-66246-x
    1. Econometric models – Congresses.   2. Nonlinear theories – Congresses.   3. Parameter
estimation – Congresses.   4. Sampling (Statistics) – Congresses.   I. Amemiya, Takeshi.   II.
Hsiao, Cheng, 1943–   III. Morimune, Kimio.   IV. Powell, James, 1955–   V. Title.   VI.
Series.
HB141 .I57   2000
519.5 – dc21
                                                                              00-031289

ISBN 978-0-521-66246-8 Hardback
ISBN 978-0-521-16926-4 Paperback

Contents

Contents

Series editor's introduction

This volume is the thirteenth in a series, called *International Symposia in Economic Theory and Econometrics*. The series is under the general editorship of William A. Barnett. Individual volumes in the series generally have editors, who differ for each volume, since the topics of the volumes change each year. The editors of this volume are Cheng Hsiao, Kimio Morimune, and James L. Powell.

The primary focus of this book is "Nonlinear Statistical Inference," which is the book's title. But the volume's breadth extends beyond that topic, since the volume was produced in honor of Takeshi Amemiya, whose influence in econometrics extends to the many areas of econometrics and statistics in which he has dramatically increased the level of sophistication, rigor, and depth. The inspiration provided by Amemiya's work to that of other leading econometricians is reflected by the chapters contained in this book, which includes recent advances in (i) the parametric approach to qualitative response and sample selection models, (ii) the nonparametric and semiparametric approaches to qualitative response and sample selection models, and (iii) nonlinear estimation of cross-sectional and time series models.

Many of the prior volumes in this series were sponsored by the IC^2 Institute at the University of Texas at Austin, and some have been cosponsored by the RGK Foundation. The first conference in this Cambridge series was co-organized by William Barnett and Ronald Gallant, who also co-edited the proceedings volume. That volume has appeared as the volume 30, October/November 1985 issue of the *Journal of Econometrics* and has been reprinted as a volume in this Cambridge University Press monograph series. The topic was "New Approaches to Modeling, Specification Selection, and Econometric Inference."

Beginning with the second symposium in the series, the proceedings of the symposia appear exclusively as volumes in this Cambridge University Press monograph series. The co-organizers of the second symposium and co-editors of its proceedings volume were William Barnett and Kenneth Singleton. The topic was "New Approaches to Monetary Economics." The co-organizers of the third symposium, which was on "Dynamic Econometric Modeling," were William Barnett and Ernst Berndt; and the co-editors of that proceedings volume were William Barnett, Ernst Berndt, and Halbert White. The co-organizers of the fourth symposium and co-editors of its proceedings volume, which was on "Economic Complexity: Chaos, Sunspots, Bubbles, and Nonlinearity," were William Barnett, John Geweke, and Karl Shell. The co-organizers of the fifth symposium and co-editors of its proceedings volume, which was on "Nonparametric and Semiparametric Methods in Econometrics and Statistics," were William Barnett, James Powell, and George Tauchen. The co-organizers and proceedings coeditors of the sixth symposium, which was on "Equilibrium Theory and Applications," were William Barnett, Bernard Cornet, Claude d'Aspremont, Jean Gabszewicz, and Andreu Mas-Colell. The co-organizers of the seventh symposium, which was on "Political Economy," were William Barnett, Melvin Hinich, Douglass North, Howard Rosenthal, and Norman Schofield. The co-editors of that proceedings volume were William Barnett, Melvin Hinich, and Norman Schofield.

The eighth symposium was part of a large scale conference on "Social Choice, Welfare, and Ethics." That conference was held in Caen, France in June 9–12, 1993. The organizers of the conference were Maurice Salles and Herve Moulin. The co-editors of that proceedings volume were William Barnett, Herve Moulin, Maurice Salles, and Norman Schofield. The ninth volume in the series was on "Dynamic Disequilibrium Modeling: Theory and Applications," and was organized by Claude Hillinger at the University of Munich, Giancarlo Gandolfo at the University of Rome "La Sapienza," A. R. Bergstrom at the University of Essex, and P. C. B. Phillips at Yale University. The co-editors of the proceedings volume were William Barnett, Claude Hillinger, and Giancarlo Gandolfo.

Much of the contents of the tenth volume in the series comprises the proceedings of the conference, "Nonlinear Dynamics and Economics," held at the European University Institute in Florence, Italy, on July 6–17, 1992. But the volume also includes the related, invited chapters presented at the annual meetings of the American Statistical Association held in San Francisco on August 8–12, 1993. The organizers of the Florence conference, which produced part of the tenth volume, were Mark Salmon and Alan Kirman at the European University Institute in Florence, and David Rand and Robert MacKay from the Mathematics Department at Warwick University in England, while the organizer of the invited American Statistical Association sessions, which produced the other chapters in the volume, was William Barnett, who was Program Chair in Economic and Business Statistics of the American Statistical Association during that year.

The eleventh volume was the proceedings of a conference held at the University of Aarhus, Denmark, on December 14–16, 1995. In addition to being the eleventh in this series, that volume was the proceedings of the Sixth Meeting of the European Conference Series in Quantitative Economics and Econometrics, $(EC)^2$. The organizer of the Aarhus conference was Svend Hylleberg at the University of Aarhus. The editors of the proceedings volume were William A. Barnett, David F. Hendry, Svend Hylleberg, Timo Teräsvirta, Dag Tjøstheim, and Allan Würtz. The topic of the conference and focus of that book was "Nonlinear Econometric Modeling," with an emphasis on nonlinear time series.

The twelfth volume was the proceedings of a conference held at the University of New South Wales in Sydney, Australia, in 1996. The organizers of the Sydney conference were Carl Chiarella, Steve Keen, Bob Marks, and Hermann Schnabl. The editors of the proceedings volume were William Barnett, Carl Chiarella, Steve Keen, Bob Marks, and Hermann Schnabl. The topic of the conference and focus of that book was "Commerce, Complexity, and Evolution: Complexity and Evolutionary Analysis in Economics, Finance, Marketing, and Management," with an emphasis on the new evolutionary approach to analyzing and modeling commercial systems. The research in that volume straddles economics, finance, marketing, and management.

The intention of the volumes in this series is to provide *refereed* journal-quality collections of research chapters of unusual importance in areas of currently highly visible activity within the economics profession. Most of the volumes in the series are proceedings of conferences. Because of the refereeing requirements associated with the editing of the volumes, they do not necessarily contain all of the chapters presented at the corresponding symposia or submitted to the editors of the volume.

William A. Barnett
Washington University in St. Louis

Editors' introduction

The chapters presented in this volume are dedicated to Takeshi Amemiya in honor of his sixty-fifth birthday. Takeshi Amemiya stands out among econometricians as distinctive in the rigor and breadth in his contributions. He has done path-breaking work in areas as diverse as limited dependent variables, discrete choice, nonlinear estimation, duration analysis, panel data, and dynamic models and simultaneous equation models. He has contributed to raising the general analytical and methodological level of econometrics. He has shown the advantages of strict formalization of the analytical techniques, thereby setting the style of generations of econometricians. In spite of the high level of abstraction of much of his work, the advances in the theory achieved have had important bearing on the choice of methods and analytical techniques in applied research. He has been an inspiration to econometricians all over the world.

Besides being a scientist and a scholar, above all, Takeshi Amemiya is a gentleman. He gives generously of himself and is always willing to help the cause of econometrics. We edit this volume on behalf of Takeshi Amemiya's students and colleagues to highlight a small part of his outstanding contribution to the profession. The collection in this volume put together important recent advances in (i) parametric approaches to qualitative response and sample selection models, (ii) nonparametric and semiparametric approaches to qualitative response and sample selection models, and (iii) nonlinear estimation of cross-sectional and time series models.

The chapter by J. J. Heckman and E. J. Vytlacil unites the treatment effect literature and the latent variable literature. It uses the local instrumental variable (LIV) parameters and the Roy model as a unifying concept and a classificatory model, respectively. The LIV can be viewed as a marginal relative of the local average treatment effect (LATE) proposed by Imbens and Angrist (1994), and the chapter shows its close mathematical relation to other causal parameters of interest, the average treatment effect (ATE) and effect of treatment on the treated (TT). The chapter applies these various treatment effect concepts to a particular model of economic interest, the Roy model of self-selection, and illustrates how the LIV parameter can be used to identify normalized versions of the cost and benefit functions for that model. It also discusses the relative merits of the various treatment effect concepts in traditional cost–benefit analysis of social policy, and give bounds for the treatment parameters when the support of the distribution of propensity scores is not sufficiently rich to identify them exactly.

The chapter by N. E. Savin and A. H. Würtz compares the properties of hypothesis tests for limited dependent variable models that use critical values based on first order asymptotic approximations with tests that use critical values calculated by the bootstrap. The authors argue persuasively that critical values based on first order asymptotic approximations sometimes get the size wrong. They find that for several permutations of a probit and tobit model in a sample of fifty observations, the tests that use the bootstrap critical values have more accurate size.

The chapter by L.-F. Lee considers simulation estimation of sample selection models. Simulation estimation techniques are useful when sample selection criteria are complicated with polychotomous choice alternatives and correlated disturbances. Simulated likelihood and two-stage estimation methods are considered. For two-stage estimation, possible simulation estimation of outcome regression equations based on Gibbs sampler and variance-reduction techniques are considered. Monte Carlo results are provided for finite sample comparison on performance of various simulation methods. Issues of sensitivity of parameter estimates to distributional assumptions are investigated. Semiparametric estimation methods with simulation are also studied in Monte Carlo experiments. A useful decomposition of the finite sample variances of the estimators into their simulation-based and sample-variation-based components is also provided.

The chapter by K. Ryu proposes a new approach to tackling attrition problems in panel studies. Panel data sets are often unbalanced due to attrition. Over time, cross-sectional units are dissipated, possibly in a nonrandom fashion, thus negating the initial randomization. If the variables of interest are stochastically related to the factors governing the attrition process, then the attrition is called *nonrandom*, and is said to cause *attrition bias*. This chapter proposes three different ways of accounting for attrition problem in unbalanced panel data. They key element of the Ryu's approach is to identify the nature of selection arising from panel attrition. Using grouped duration techniques with heterogeneity, the author proposes to estimate the attrition process. Once the nature of attrition is identified, Hausman–Wise–Ridder joint maximum likelihood estimation, sequential maximum likelihood estimation, and Heckman (1976, 1979) sequential estimation are proposed.

The chapter by F. Goto discusses estimation of parametric duration models which are subject to left-censoring and in which the distribution of starting times is not parametrically specified. The authors shows that if one has a sample of the completed spells, sampled from the spells that are in progress at a point in time, then the semiparametric maximum likelihood estimator (MLE) that takes this sampling scheme into account is efficient. This is true for both the parametric and nonparametric components.

The chapter by J. L. Powell proposes semiparametric estimators of a class of bivariate latent dependent variable models, including the censored sample selection model and the disequilibrium regression model. Estimation proceeds in two steps. In the first step, consistent semiparametric estimates of the coefficients of the "selection" or "regime" equation are obtained for the *single index* variables characterizing the selectivity bias in the equation of interest. In the second step a weighted instrumental variables method is applied to the pairwise differences of the equation of interest. The chapter proves the root-n consistency and asymptotic normality of the proposed estimator and proposes consistent estimators of its asymptotic covariance matrix.

The chapter by Y. Nishiyama and P. M. Robinson considers semiparametric estimates, up to scale, of single index models. A valid Edgeworth expansion is established for the limiting distribution of density-weighted semiparametric averaged derivative estimates, which depends on the choice of bandwidth and kernel order.

The epidemiological literature has devoted much attention to relative risks and attributable risks, that is, to ratios and differences of conditional response probabilities at distinct covariate values. The chapter by C. F. Manski provides interesting bounds on these measures using auxiliary distributional information. Under the less stringent assumptions that only the marginal distribution of the response, $P(y)$, is known, but not the marginal distribution of the covariate, $P(z)$, or that $P(z)$ is known, but not $P(y)$, Manski proves that the available information implies informative sharp bounds on response probabilities, relative risks, and attributable risks.

A common problem in applied regression analysis is to select the variables that enter a regression model. It is often computationally convenient to estimate such models by least squares, with variables selected from possible candidates by enumeration, grid search, or Gauss–Newton iteration to maximize their conventional least squares significance level; this method is termed *pre-screened least squares* (PLS). D. McFadden shows that PLS in equivalent to direct estimation by nonlinear least squares, and thus provides a practical computational shortcut that shares the statistical properties of the nonlinear least squares solution. However, standard errors and test statistics produced by least squares software are biased by variable selection. The chapter also gives consistent estimators for covariance and test statistics and shows in examples that kernel-smoothing or bootstrap methods appear to give adequate approximation in samples of moderate size.

The chapter by T. E. MaCurdy develops new estimators for regression and simultaneous equations that make use of the second and higher moments of the disturbances of the equation under consideration. The estimator are in general asymptotically strictly efficient relative to the conventional least squares and two-stage least squares procedures, except when these latter procedures correspond directly to the application of maximum likelihood methods. The small scale Monte Carlo findings suggest that substantial efficiency gains may be attainable by implementing these estimation procedures.

In proving the weak convergence of the standardized empirical spectral distribution function of a stationary process to a Gaussian process, Grenander and Rosenblatt (1952) assumed that the eighth moment of the process is finite. T. W. Anderson and L. You's chapter gives a neat and direct proof that the existence of the second moment is sufficient for weak convergence of the standardized spectral distribution when the process consists of independently identically distributed variables.

The chapters by H. Lütkepohl, C. Müller, and P. Saikkonen and by K. Morimune and M. Nakagawa consider unit root tests. These tests are important because the trending properties of a set of time series determine to some extent which model and statistical procedures are suitable for analyzing their relationship. When the breakpoint is known, this is useful information which should be taken into account in testing for unit roots. Lütkepohl, Müller, and Saikkonen propose a framework in which the shift is modeled as part of the intercept term of the stationary part of the data-generating process, which is separated from the unit root part. In this framework simple shift functions result in a smooth transition from one state to another, both under the null hypothesis of a unit root and under the alternative hypothesis of stationarity. A major advantage of their approach is that for conducting a standard unit root test, e.g. of the Dickey-Fuller type, the estimation of the nuisance parameters reduces to a fairly simple nonlinear least squares problem. Moreover, their asymptotic null distribution is known from the unit root literature, and tables of critical values exist.

Morimune and Nakagawa's chapter proposes a unified framework for the unit root tests that allows for multiple breaks in both the intercepts and trend coefficients. They derive the asymptotic expressions for the t-test statistics. The small-sample power of the Dickey–Fuller test (1981) and Perron (1989) tests are compared by simulations, and the Dickey–Fuller test is found to be more powerful.

The chapter by N. Kunitomo and S. Sato introduces a simultaneous switching autoregressive model (SSAR) as a generalization of the Tobit model. The distinction between the structural form and the reduced form SSAR is stressed. The reduced form SSAR is shown as a nonlinear Markovian time series model. This type of time series modelling can be useful for the analysis of financial time series data. The chapter has given some conditions for the geometrical ergodicity and proposes maximum likelihood and instrumental variable estimators that are consistent and asymptotically normally distributed.

One of the issues in panel data analysis is to control the effect of unobserved heterogeneity on inference about characteristics of the population. When cross-sectional dimension is large and the time series dimension is finite, the presence of individual specific effects introduces the classical incidental parameter problem (Neyman and Scott 1948). If the model is linear in individual specific effects (incidental parameters), one can difference out the individual specific effects and obtain, from the differenced equation, consistent estimators of the parameters that are common across individuals and over time (structural parameters). If the model is nonlinear in the effects, this differencing method does not work. The structural parameters usually cannot be consistently estimated, because of the presence of incidental parameters. The chapter by T. Lancaster proposes a novel approach of orthogonal reparameterization of the fixed effect for each individual to a new fixed effect which is independent of the structural parameters in the information matrix sense. The chapter shows how we can derive consistent estimators of structural parameters for a duration model using two consecutive uncensored spelled lengths for many people.

The chapter by S. J. Yhee, J. B. Nugent, and C. Hsiao uses a censored switching regression approach to evaluate the effect of sunk costs and firm level disequilibrium on export performance using panel data on South Korean small and medium sized enterprises. The effect of sunk costs is captured as the difference between the technology capability and the marketing capability, each depending on the characteristics of the individual firm, and the results are used to measure the firm-specific effectiveness of export support systems.

Takeshi Amemiya has had a lasting influence on nearly every field of econometrics. Clearly no single volume can do justice to the wide variety of topics to which he has made pioneering contributions. Nevertheless, the included chapters provide a rich selection of techniques and applications that are inspired by Amemiya's work.

Finally, we would like to thank the economics editor of the Cambridge University Press, Scott Parris, for his support of this project. We are also grateful to a number of our colleagues who have acted as anonymous referees. Their comments have led to the improvement of the chapters published in this volume.

REFERENCES

Dickey, D. A. and Fuller, W. A. (1981), "Likelihood Ratio Statistics for Autoregressive Time Series with a Unit Root," *Econometrica*, **49**, 1057–1072.

Grenander, U. and Rosenblatt, M. (1952), "On Spectral Analysis of Stationary Time Series," *Proceedings of the National Academy of Sciences*, **38**, 519–521.

Heckman, J. (1976), "The Common Structure of Statistical Models of Truncation, Sample Selection, and Limited Dependent Variables and a Simple Estimator for such Models," *Annals of Economics and Social Measurement*, **5**, 474–492.

(1979), "Sample Selection Bias as a Specification Error," *Econometrica*, **47**, 153–161.

Imbens, G. and Angrist, J. (1994), "Identification and Estimation of Local Average Treatment Effects," *Econometrica*, **62**, 467–476.

Neyman, J. and Scott, E. (1948), "Consistent Estimates Based on Partially Consistent Observations," *Econometrica*, **16**, 1–32.

Perron, P. (1989), "The Great Crash, the Oil Price Shock, and the Unit Root Hypothesis," *Econometrica*, **57**, 1361–1401.

Contributors

T. W. Anderson
Stanford University

Fumihiro Goto
Aoyama Gakuin University

James J. Heckman
University of Chicago

C. Hsiao
University of Southern California
    and Hong Kong University
    of Science and Technology

Naoto Kunitomo
University of Tokyo

Tony Lancaster
Brown University

Lung-fei Lee
Hong Kong University of Science
    and Technology

Helmut Lütkepohl
Humboldt University

Thomas E. MaCurdy
Stanford University

Charles F. Manski
Northwestern University

Daniel McFadden
University of California, Berkeley

Kimio Morimune
Kyoto University

Christian Müller
Humboldt University

Mitsuru Nakagawa
Osaka City University

Y. Nishiyama
Nagoya University

J. B. Nugent
University of Southern
    California

James L. Powell
University of California, Berkeley

P. M. Robinson
London School of Economics

Keunkwan Ryu
Seoul National University
    and Hong Kong University
    of Science and Technology

Pentti Saikkonen
University of Helsinki

Seisho Sato
Institute of Statistical Mathematics,
  Tokyo

N. E. Savin
University of Iowa

Edward J. Vytlacil
Stanford University

Allan H. Würtz
University of Aarhus

Seung-Jae Yhee
American Express

L. Y. You
Salomon Smith Barney

CHAPTER 1

Local instrumental variables

James J. Heckman and Edward J. Vytlacil

1   Introduction

Takeshi Amemiya made basic contributions to the econometrics of discrete choice and limited dependent variable models. His fundamental 1973 paper on the censored normal regression model was the first systematic application in econometrics of the uniform law of large numbers and the central limit theorems required to establish consistency and asymptotic normality of nonlinear econometric models. That paper and his later work on nonlinear least squares are summarized in his magisterial text *Advanced Econometrics* (1985). His research and his text set the standard for a generation of econometricians, and provided the framework for modern structural econometric analysis of index models or latent variable models.

Latent variable models of the type analyzed by Amemiya arise in well-posed economic problems. The latent variables can be utilities, potential wages (or home wages as in Gronau 1974 and Heckman 1974) or potential profitability. This class of models, which originates in psychology in the work of Thurstone (1930, 1959), has been widely developed in the econometrics of discrete choice (see McFadden 1981, and the survey of index models in labor economics presented by Heckman and MaCurdy 1985). Amemiya provided

James J. Heckman is Henry Schultz Distinguished Service Professor of Economics at the University of Chicago and a Senior Fellow at the American Bar Foundation. Edward Vytlacil is a Sloan Fellow at the University of Chicago. We would like to thank Arild Aakvik, Jaap Abbring, Victor Aguirregabiria, Lars Hansen, Justin Tobias, two anonymous referees, and especially Cheng Hsiao for close and helpful readings of this manuscript. We thank participants in the Canadian Econometric Studies Group (September, 1998), The Midwest Econometrics Group (September, 1998), the University of Upsalla (November, 1998), the University of Chicago (December, 1998), University College London (December, 1998), the University of California, Berkeley (April, 1999), and the North American Summer Meetings of the Econometric Society (June, 1999). This research was supported by NIH:R01-HD3498-01, NIH:R01-HD3208-03, NSF97-09-873, and the Donner Foundation.

1

the econometric foundations for the application of these methods to numerous economic problems.

This paper uses the latent variable or index model of econometrics and psychometrics to impose structure on the model of Neyman (1923)–Fisher (1935)–Cox (1958)–Rubin (1978) of potential outcomes used to define treatment effects. That model is isomorphic to the Roy model (1951) as summarized by Heckman and Honoré (1990) and to Quandt's (1972, 1988) switching regression model. For a comprehensive discussion of these models, see Heckman and Vytlacil (2000b).

A major development in econometrics since the publication of Amemiya's text has been an emphasis on the estimation of certain features of economic models under weaker assumptions about functional forms of estimating equations and error distributions than are conventionally maintained in estimating structural econometric models. The recent treatment effect literature is the most agnostic in this regard, focusing on the estimation of certain treatment effects that can be nonparametrically identified under general conditions. Two major limitations of this literature are (a) that the economic questions answered by the estimated treatment effects are usually not clearly stated and (b) that the connection of this literature with the traditional parametric index function literature is not well established. The parameters estimated in the classical parametric discrete choice literature can be used to answer a variety of policy questions. In contrast, the parameters in the modern treatment effect literature answer only narrowly focused questions, but typically under weaker conditions than are postulated in the parametric literature.

This paper unites the treatment effect literature and the latent variable literature. The economic questions answered by the commonly used treatment effect parameters are considered. We demonstrate how the marginal treatment effect (MTE) parameter introduced in Heckman (1997) can be used in a latent variable framework to generate the average treatment effect (ATE), the effect of treatment on the treated (TT) and the local average treatment effect (LATE) of Imbens and Angrist (1994), thereby establishing a new relationship among these parameters. The method of local instrumental variables (LIV) introduced in Heckman and Vytlacil (1999b) directly estimates the MTE parameter, and thus can be used to estimate all of the conventional treatment effect parameters when the index condition holds and the parameters are identified. When they are not, LIV can be used to produce bounds on the parameters with the width of the bounds depending on the width of the support for the index generating the choice of the observed potential outcome.

As a consequence of the analysis of Vytlacil (1999a), the latent variable framework used in this paper is more general than might at first be thought. He establishes that the assumptions used by Imbens and Angrist (1994) to identify LATE using linear instrumental variables both imply and are implied by the latent variable set up used in this paper. Thus our analysis applies to the entire class of models estimated by LATE.

LATE analysis focuses on what linear instrumental variables can estimate. LIV extends linear IV analysis and estimates (or bounds) a much wider class of treatment parameters. Under conditions presented in this paper, suitably weighted versions of LIV identify the average treatment effect (ATE) and treatment on the treated (TT) even in the general case where responses to treatment are heterogeneous and agents participate in the program being evaluated at least in part on the basis of this heterogeneous response. Heckman (1997) shows that in this case the linear instrumental variable estimator does not identify ATE or TT. We establish conditions under which LIV identifies those parameters.

The plan of this chapter is as follows. Section 2 presents a model of potential outcomes in a latent variable framework. Section 3 defines four different mean treatment parameters within the latent variable framework. Section 4 establishes a new relationship among the parameters, using MTE as a unifying device. Section 5 presents conditions for identification of treatment effect parameters, and presents bounds for them when they are not identified. The LIV estimator is introduced as the empirical analog to MTE that operationalizes our identification analysis. Section 6 compares the LIV estimator with the linear IV estimator. Weighted versions of LIV identify the treatment on the treated parameter (TT) and the average treatment effect (ATE) in cases where the linear instrumental variable estimator does not. The leading case where this phenomenon arises is the additively separable correlated random coefficient model which is developed in this section. Section 7 extends the analysis of the additively separable case and applies it to classical results in the selection bias literature. Section 8 concludes the chapter. Appendix A explores the sensitivity of the analysis presented in the text to the assumptions imposed on the latent index model.

2   Models of potential outcomes in a latent variable framework

For each person i, assume two potential outcomes (Y_{0i}, Y_{1i}) corresponding, respectively, to the potential outcomes in the untreated and treated states. Our methods generalize to the case of multiple outcomes, but in this paper we consider only two.[1] Let $D_i = 1$ denote the receipt of treatment; $D_i = 0$ denotes nonreceipt. Let Y_i be the measured outcome variable so that

$$Y_i = D_i Y_{1i} + (1 - D_i)Y_{0i}.$$

---

[1] See Heckman and Vytlacil (2000b) for the multi-outcome extension.

This is the Neyman–Fisher–Cox–Rubin model of potential outcomes. It is also the switching regression model of Quandt (1972) and the Roy model of income distribution (Roy 1951; Heckman and Honoré 1990).

This paper assumes that a latent variable model generates the indicator variable D_i. Specifically, we assume that the assignment or decision rule for the indicator is generated by a latent variable D_i^*:

$$D_i^* = \mu_D(Z_i) - U_{Di}$$
$$D_i = 1 \quad \text{if} \quad D_i^* \geq 0, \quad = 0 \text{ otherwise,} \tag{1}$$

where Z_i is a vector of observed random variables and U_{Di} is an unobserved random variable. D_i^* is the net utility or gain to the decision-maker from choosing state 1. The index structure underlies many models in econometrics (see the survey in Amemiya 1985) and in psychometrics (see, e.g., Junker and Ellis 1997).

The potential outcome for the program participation state is

$$Y_{1i} = \mu_1(X_i, U_{1i}),$$

and the potential outcome for the nonparticipation state is

$$Y_{0i} = \mu_0(X_i, U_{0i}),$$

where X_i is a vector of observed random variables and (U_{1i}, U_{0i}) are unobserved random variables. No assumptions are imposed restricting the joint distribution of (U_{0i}, U_{1i}) beyond the regularity conditions presented below.[2] It is assumed that Y_{0i} and Y_{1i} are defined for everyone and that these outcomes are independent across persons so that there are no interactions among agents.[3] Important special cases include models with (Y_{0i}, Y_{1i}) generated by latent variables. These models include $\mu_j(X_i, U_{ji}) = \mu_j(X_i) + U_{ji}$ if Y is continuous and $\mu_j(X_i, U_{ji}) = 1(X_i\beta_j + U_{ji} \geq 0)$ if Y is binary, where X_i is independent of U_{ji} and where $1(A)$ is the indicator function that takes the value 1 if the event A is true and takes the value 0 otherwise. We do not restrict the functions (μ_1, μ_0) except for the regularity conditions noted below. Let Δ_i denote the treatment effect for individual i:

$$\Delta_i = Y_{1i} - Y_{0i}. \tag{2}$$

---

[2] A common restriction is that $U_{0i} = U_{1i}$. If U_{1i}, U_{0i} are additively separable from X_i, this restriction generates a common treatment effect model (Heckman and Robb 1986; Heckman 1997). The restriction $U_{0i} = U_{1i}$ also aids in identification of treatment effects in nonseparable models if at least one instrument is continuous (Vytlacil, 1999b). We do not impose these restrictions in this paper.

[3] The problem of interactions among agents in the analysis of treatment effects was extensively discussed by Lewis (1963) although he never used the term "treatment effect." See the papers by Davidson and Woodbury (1993) and Heckman, Lochner and Taber (1998) for empirical demonstrations of the importance of these social interaction effects, and the general discussion of general equilibrium treatment effects in Heckman, LaLonde and Smith (1999).

The treatment effect is a person-specific counterfactual. For person i it answers the question, what would be the outcome if the person received the treatment compared to the case where the person had not received the treatment? For notational convenience, we will henceforth suppress the subscript i.

In this chapter we assume that:

   (i) $\mu_D(Z)$ is a nondegenerate random variable conditional on X.
   (ii) U_D is absolutely continuous with respect to Lebesgue measure.
   (iii) U_D is independent of X, (U_1, U_0, U_D) is independent of Z conditional on X.
   (iv) Y_1 and Y_0 have finite first moments.
   (v) $1 > \Pr(D = 1 \mid X = x) > 0$ for every $x \in \mathrm{Supp}(X)$.

Assumption (i) requires an exclusion restriction: there exists a variable that determines the treatment decision but does not directly affect the outcome. Variables that satisfy these conditions are commonly called instrumental variables. Assumption (ii) is imposed for convenience, both to simplify the notation and to impose smoothness on certain conditional expectations; it can readily be relaxed. The first part of assumption (iii), that X is independent of U_D, can be removed. We include this assumption only to simplify the notation. The modifications required for the more general case are trivial. Assumption (v) guarantees that for each $x \in X$, we obtain observations in both the treated and untreated states. An analogous assumption is made in matching. (See Rosenbaum and Rubin 1983). If assumption (v) is relaxed so that $\Pr(D = 1 \mid X = x) = 1$ or 0 for some x values, then the analysis of this paper will still hold for any x value for which $1 > \Pr(D = 1 \mid X = x) > 0$.

For any random variable A, let F_A denote the variable's distribution function, and let a denote a possible realization of A. Let $P(z)$ denote the probability of receiving treatment conditional on the observed covariates,

$$P(z) \equiv \Pr(D = 1 \mid Z = z) = F_{U_D}(\mu_D(z)). \tag{3}$$

$P(z)$ is sometimes called the "propensity score" by statisticians following Rosenbaum and Rubin (1983) and is called a "choice probability" by economists.[4]

Without loss of generality, we assume that $U_D \sim \mathrm{Unif}[0, 1]$, in which case $\mu_D(z) = P(z)$. To see that there is no loss of generality, note that if the underlying index is $D^* = \nu(Z) - V$, with assumptions (ii) and (iii) satisfied for V, taking $\mu(Z) = F_V(\nu(Z))$ and $U = F_V(V)$ equates the two models. This transformation is innocuous, since any CDF is left-continuous and nondecreasing and

---

[4] Heckman and Robb (1986) present a discussion of how the propensity score is used differently in selection models and in matching models for program evaluation. See also Heckman, LaLonde and Smith (1999) and Heckman and Vytlacil (2000b).

thus $\mu(z) \geq U_D \Leftrightarrow v(z) \geq V$.[5] In addition, since U_D is distributed Unif[0, 1] and independent of Z, we have $\mu(z) = P(z)$.

Note that the latent variable assumption (given by equation (1) and conditions (i)–(v)) does not impose testable restrictions on choice behavior, i.e., on the distribution of (D, Z, X).[6] If we take Z to include all observed covariates, and define $\mu(z) = \Pr(D = 1 \mid Z = z)$ and $U_D \sim \text{Unif}[0, 1]$, the latent index assumption imposes no restrictions on the observed choice behavior.[7] However, it does impose two restrictions on counterfactual outcomes. First, consider the following hypothetical intervention. If we take a random sample of individuals, and externally set Z at level z, with what probability will they have $D = 1$ after the intervention? Using the assumption that U_D is independent of Z, the answer is $\Pr(D = 1 \mid Z = z)$, that is, the probability that $D = 1$ among those individuals who were observed to have $Z = z$. Second, if we instead took individuals with $Z = z$ and externally set their Z characteristics to z', where $\Pr(D = 1 \mid Z = z) < \Pr(D = 1 \mid Z = z')$, then the threshold-crossing model implies that some individuals who would have had $D = 0$ with the $Z = z$ characteristic will now have $D = 1$ with the $Z = z'$ characteristics, but that no individual who would have had $D = 1$ with the $Z = z$ characteristics will have $D = 0$ with the $Z = z'$ characteristics.[8] These two properties are the *only* restrictions imposed on the choice behavior, i.e., on the distribution of (D, Z), by the threshold-crossing model as we have defined it (by equation (1) and conditions (i)–(v)).[9] Under these conditions on counterfactual outcomes, there is no loss of generality in imposing a threshold-crossing model (Vytlacil 1999a).

[5] More precisely, $v(z) \geq V \Rightarrow F_V(v(z)) \geq F_V(V)$ and $F_V(v(z)) \geq F_V(V) \Rightarrow v(z) \geq V$ for any $V \in \text{Supp}(V)$, so that the equivalence holds w.p.1.

[6] The one exception to this statement is the trivial restriction given by assumption (v), that $1 > \Pr[D = 1 \mid X = x] > 0$ for every $x \in \text{Supp}(X)$. This assumption is not an intrinsic feature of the selection model.

[7] This argument is also used in Das and Newey (1998).

[8] Following Imbens and Angrist (1994), these two restrictions can be expressed as follows. Let D_z denote the counterfactual choice that would have been observed if Z had been externally set to z. The two conditions can then be expressed as: (1) Z is independent of (U_1, U_0, D_z) for each $z \in \mathcal{Z}$ (Independence); (2) For any z, z' in the support of Z, either $D_z \geq D_{z'}$ everywhere (for all individuals) or $D_z \leq D_{z'}$ everywhere (for all individuals) (Monotonicity).

[9] The threshold-crossing model (defined by equation (1) and conditions (i)–(v)) imposes two testable restrictions on the full distribution of the observed data, (Y, D, X, Z). First, it imposes the index sufficiency restriction that, for any set A, $\Pr(Y_j \in A \mid Z = z, D = j) = \Pr(Y_j \in A \mid P(Z) = P(z), D = j)$. See Heckman, Ichimura, Smith and Todd (1998) for a nonparametric test of this restriction. Second, if (Y_0, Y_1) are bounded from below conditional on X, i.e., there exists $y_x^l > -\infty$ such that $\Pr[Y_j \geq y_x^l \mid X = x] = 1$ for $j = 0, 1$, then $E((Y_1 - y_x^l) D \mid X = x, P(Z) = p)$ is increasing in p and $E((Y_0 - y_x^0)(1 - D) \mid X = x, P(Z) = p)$ is decreasing in p. Thus, while the threshold-crossing model defined by equation (1) and conditions (i)–(v) does not impose any testable restrictions on the distribution of (D, Z, X), it does impose testable restrictions on (Y, D, Z, X). In addition, trivially, condition (iv) imposes the restriction that Y_0, Y_1 have finite first moments.

Imbens and Angrist (1994) invoke these two properties of independence and monotonicity in their LATE analysis. Thus our latent variable model is equivalent to the LATE model. If we remove the assumption that U_D is independent of Z, while leaving the assumptions otherwise unchanged, then the monotonicity property continues to hold but not the independence property. If instead we remove the assumption that U_D is additively separable from Z (i.e., we consider $\mu_D(Z, U_D)$ instead of $\mu_D(Z) - U_D$), while leaving the model otherwise unchanged, then the independence property will hold but not in general, the monotonicity property.[10] If we remove both assumptions, while imposing no additional restrictions, then the threshold-crossing model becomes completely vacuous, imposing no restrictions on the observed outcomes or counterfactual outcomes.

Appendix A investigates the sensitivity of the analysis presented in the text to the index assumption by alternatively dropping the independence or the monotonicity assumption (allowing U_D and Z to be dependent or allowing U_D and Z to be additively nonseparable in the latent index in a general way). We show that the definition of the parameters and the relationships among them as described below in Sections 3 and 4 generalize with only minor modifications to the case where U_D and Z are additively nonseparable or are stochastically dependent. The separability and independence assumptions allow us to define the parameters in terms of $P(z)$ instead of z and allow for slightly simpler expressions, but are not crucial for the definition of parameters or the relationship among them. However, the assumptions of independence and monotonicity *are* essential for establishing the connection between the LATE or LIV estimators and the underlying parameters as described in Section 5, and *are* essential to the identification analysis that accompanies that discussion.

3   Definition of parameters

A major shift in econometric research since the time Amemiya wrote his influential textbook has been toward estimating features of a model, rather than estimating the full model as is emphasized in structural econometrics. In the context of the program evaluation problem, this comes down to estimating parameters like ATE, TT, LATE and MTE directly, rather than estimating all the ingredients of the underlying structural model separately that can be built up to estimate these parameters. In general, these special parameters can be identified

---

[10] Note that monotonicity is implied by additive separability, but additive separability is not required; supermodular $\mu_D(Z, U_D)$ is all that is required. Thus in the differentiable case a uniform positive (or negative) cross partial of μ_D with respect to Z and U_D is all that is required. However, Vytlacil (1999a) shows that any latent index that satisfies the monotonicity condition will have an additively separable representation, so that having an additively separable representation is required.

under weaker conditions than are required to estimate the full structural parameters, but at the same time, they cannot generate the complete array of policy counterfactuals produced from estimates of the full model. The weaker identifying assumptions make estimators based on them more widely accepted. At the same time, the estimates produce answers to more narrowly focused questions.

In this chapter, we consider four different mean treatment parameters within this framework: the average treatment effect (ATE), the effect of treatment on the treated (TT), the marginal treatment effect (MTE), and the local average treatment effect (LATE). ATE and TT are the traditional parameters. Each of these parameters is a mean of the individual treatment effect, $\Delta = Y_1 - Y_0$, but with different conditioning sets.

The average treatment effect is defined as[11]

$$\Delta^{\text{ATE}}(x) \equiv E(\Delta \mid X = x).$$

The mean effect of treatment on the treated is the most commonly estimated parameter for both observational data and social experiments (see Heckman and Robb 1985, 1986, and Heckman, LaLonde and Smith 1999). It is defined as[12]

$$\Delta^{\text{TT}}(x, D = 1) \equiv E(\Delta \mid X = x, D = 1).$$

It will be useful for the analysis of this paper to define a version of $\Delta^{\text{TT}}(x, D = 1)$ that conditions on the propensity score, $P(z)$, defined in equation (3):[13]

$$\Delta^{\text{TT}}(x, P(z), D = 1) \equiv E(\Delta \mid X = x, P(Z) = P(z), D = 1)$$

so that

$$\Delta^{\text{TT}}(x, D = 1) = \int_0^1 \Delta^{\text{TT}}(x, p, D = 1) \, dF_{P(Z)\mid X, D}(p \mid x, 1). \qquad (4)$$

The third parameter that we analyze is the marginal treatment parameter introduced in Heckman (1997) and defined in the context of a latent variable model as

$$\Delta^{\text{MTE}}(x, u) \equiv E(\Delta \mid X = x, U_D = u).[14]$$

The final parameter we analyze is the LATE parameter of Imbens and Angrist (1994) defined by an instrumental variable. Using $P(Z)$ as the instrument, we

---

[11] From assumption (iv), it follows that $E(\Delta \mid X = x)$ exists and is finite a.e. F_X.

[12] From assumption (iv), $\Delta^{\text{TT}}(x, D = 1)$ exists and is finite a.e. $F_{X \mid D=1}$, where $F_{X \mid D=1}$ denotes the distribution of X conditional on $D = 1$.

[13] From our assumptions, $\Delta^{\text{TT}}(x, P(z), D = 1)$ exists and is finite a.e. $F_{X, P(Z)\mid D=1}$.

[14] From our assumptions, $\Delta^{\text{MTE}}(x, u)$ exists and is finite a.e. F_{X, U_D}.

obtain

$$\Delta^{\text{LATE}}(x, P(z), P(z'))$$
$$\equiv \frac{E(Y \mid X = x, P(Z) = P(z)) - E(Y \mid X = x, P(Z) = P(z'))}{P(z) - P(z')}$$

We require that $P(z) \neq P(z')$ for any (z, z') where the parameter is defined. We will assume that $P(z) > P(z')$, with no loss of generality given the restriction that $P(z) \neq P(z')$. This definition of the treatment parameter, while consistent with that used by Imbens and Angrist, is somewhat peculiar in that it is based on an estimator rather than a property of a model. An alternative, more traditional, definition is given below.

A more general framework defines the parameters in terms of Z. As a consequence of the latent variable or index structure, defining the parameters in terms of Z or $P(Z)$ results in equivalent expressions.[15] In the index model, Z enters the model only through the index, so that for any measurable set A,

$$\Pr(Y_j \in A \mid X = x, Z = z, D = 1) = \Pr(Y_j \in A \mid X = x, U_D \leq P(z))$$
$$= \Pr(Y_j \in A \mid X = x, P(Z) = P(z), D = 1)$$
$$\Pr(Y_j \in A \mid X = x, Z = z, D = 0) = \Pr(Y_j \in A \mid X = x, U_D > P(z))$$
$$= \Pr(Y_j \in A \mid X = x, P(Z) = P(z), D = 0).$$

4   Relationship among parameters using the index structure

Given the index structure, a simple relationship exists among the four parameters. From the definition it is immediate that

$$\Delta^{\text{TT}}(x, P(z), D = 1) = E(\Delta \mid X = x, U_D \leq P(z)). \tag{5}$$

Next consider $\Delta^{\text{LATE}}(x, P(z), P(z'))$. Note that

$$E(Y \mid X = x, P(Z) = P(z))$$
$$= P(z)[E(Y_1 \mid X = x, P(Z) = P(z), D = 1)]$$
$$+ (1 - P(z))[E(Y_0 \mid X = x, P(Z) = P(z), D = 0)]$$
$$= \int_0^{P(z)} E(Y_1 \mid X = x, U_D = u) \, du$$
$$+ \int_{P(z)}^1 E(Y_0 \mid X = x, U_D = u) \, du, \tag{6}$$

---

[15] As discussed in the Appendix A, we can equivalently define the parameters in terms of Z or $P(Z)$ because of both our additive separability and independence assumptions.

so that

$$E(Y \mid X = x, P(Z) = P(z)) - E(Y \mid X = x, P(Z) = P(z'))$$

$$= \int_{P(z')}^{P(z)} E(Y_1 \mid X = x, U_D = u)\,du - \int_{P(z')}^{P(z)} E(Y_0 \mid X = x, U_D = u)\,du,$$

and thus

$$\Delta^{\mathrm{LATE}}(x, P(z), P(z')) = E(\Delta \mid X = x, P(z') \leq U_D \leq P(z)).$$

Notice that this expression could be taken as an alternative definition of LATE. We can rewrite these relationships in succinct form in the following way:

$$\Delta^{\mathrm{MTE}}(x, u) = E(\Delta \mid X = x, U_D = u)$$

$$\Delta^{\mathrm{ATE}}(x) = \int_0^1 E(\Delta \mid X = x, U_D = u)\,du$$

$$P(z)[\Delta^{\mathrm{TT}}(x, P(z), D = 1)] = \int_0^{P(z)} E(\Delta \mid X = x, U_D = u)\,du \qquad (7)$$

$$(P(z) - P(z'))[\Delta^{\mathrm{LATE}}(x, P(z), P(z'))] = \int_{P(z')}^{P(z)} E(\Delta \mid X = x, U_D = u)\,du.$$

Each parameter is an average value of MTE, $E(\Delta \mid X = x, U_D = u)$, but for values of U_D lying in different intervals and with different weighting functions. MTE defines the treatment effect more finely than do LATE, ATE, or TT.[16]

$\Delta^{\mathrm{MTE}}(x, u)$ is the average effect for people who are just indifferent between participation in the program $(D = 1)$ or not $(D = 0)$ if the instrument is externally set so that $P(Z) = u$. For values of u close to zero, $\Delta^{\mathrm{MTE}}(x, u)$ is the average effect for individuals with unobservable characteristics that make them the most inclined to participate in the program $(D = 1)$, and for values of u close to one it is the average treatment effect for individuals with unobserved (by the econometrician) characteristics that make them the least inclined to participate. ATE integrates $\Delta^{\mathrm{MTE}}(x, u)$ over the entire support of U_D (from $u = 0$ to $u = 1$). It is the average effect for an individual chosen at random from the entire population. $\Delta^{\mathrm{TT}}(x, P(z), D = 1)$ is the average treatment effect for persons who chose to participate at the given value of $P(Z) = P(z)$; it integrates $\Delta^{\mathrm{MTE}}(x, u)$ up to $u = P(z)$. As a result, it is primarily determined by the MTE

---

[16] As suggested by a referee, the relationship between MTE and LATE or TT conditional on $P(z)$ is analogous to the relationship between a probability density function and a cumulative distribution function. The probability density function and the cumulative distribution function represent the same information, but for some purposes the density function is more easily interpreted. Likewise, knowledge of TT for all $P(z)$ evaluation points is equivalent to knowledge of the MTE for all u evaluation points, so it is not the case that knowledge of one provides more information than knowledge of the other. However, in many choice-theoretic contexts it is often easier to interpret MTE than the TT or LATE parameters. It has the interpretation as a measure of willingness to pay on the part of people on a specified margin of participation in the program.

parameter for individuals whose unobserved characteristics make them the most inclined to participate in the program. LATE is the average treatment effect for someone who would not participate if $P(Z) \leq P(z')$ and would participate if $P(Z) \geq P(z)$. The parameter $\Delta^{\text{LATE}}(x, P(z), P(z'))$ integrates $\Delta^{\text{MTE}}(x, u)$ from $u = P(z')$ to $u = P(z)$.

Using the third expression in equation (7) to substitute into equation (4), we obtain an alternative expression for the TT parameter as a weighted average of MTE parameters:

$$\Delta^{\text{TT}}(x, D=1) = \int_0^1 \frac{1}{p} \left[\int_0^p E(\Delta \mid X = x, U_D = u) du \right] dF_{P(Z) \mid X, D}(p \mid x, 1).$$

Using Bayes' rule, it follows that

$$dF_{P(Z) \mid X, D}(p \mid x, 1) = \frac{\Pr(D=1 \mid X=x, P(Z)=p)}{\Pr(D=1 \mid X=x)} dF_{P(Z) \mid X}(p \mid x). \qquad (8)$$

Since $\Pr(D=1 \mid X=x, P(Z)=p) = p$, it follows that

$$\Delta^{\text{TT}}(x, D=1) = \frac{1}{\Pr(D=1 \mid X=x)}$$
$$\times \int_0^1 \left[\int_0^p E(\Delta \mid X=x, U_D=u) du \right] dF_{P(Z) \mid X}(p \mid x). \qquad (9)$$

Note further that since $\Pr(D=1 \mid X=x) = E(P(Z) \mid X=x) = \int_0^1 (1 - F_{P(Z) \mid X}(t \mid x)) dt$, we can reinterpret (9) as a weighted average of local IV parameters where the weighting is similar to that obtained from a length-biased, size-biased, or P-biased sample:

$$\Delta^{\text{TT}}(x, D=1) = \frac{1}{\Pr(D=1 \mid X=x)}$$
$$\times \int_0^1 \left[\int_0^1 1(u \leq p) E(\Delta \mid X=x, U_D=u) du \right] dF_{P(Z) \mid X}(p \mid x)$$
$$= \frac{1}{\int (1 - F_{P(Z) \mid X}(t \mid x)) dt}$$
$$\times \int_0^1 \left[\int_0^1 E(\Delta \mid X=x, U_D=u) 1(u \leq p) dF_{P(Z) \mid X}(p \mid x) \right] du$$
$$= \int_0^1 E(\Delta \mid X = x, U_D = u) \left[\frac{1 - F_{P(Z) \mid X}(u \mid x)}{\int (1 - F_{P(Z) \mid X}(t \mid x)) dt} \right] du$$
$$= \int_0^1 E(\Delta \mid X = x, U_D = u) g_x(u) du$$

where $g_x(u) = \frac{1 - F_{P(Z) \mid X}(u \mid x)}{\int (1 - F_{P(Z) \mid X}(t \mid x)) dt}$. Thus $g_x(u)$ is a *weighted distribution* (Rao 1985). Since $g_x(u)$ is a nonincreasing function of u, we have that drawings from

$g_x(u)$ oversample persons with low values of U_D, i.e., values of unobserved characteristics that make them the most likely to participate in the program no matter what their value of $P(Z)$. Since

$$\Delta^{\text{MTE}}(x, u) = E(\Delta \mid X = x, U_D = u)$$

it follows that

$$\Delta^{\text{TT}}(x, D = 1) = \int_0^1 \Delta^{\text{MTE}}(x, u)g_x(u)\,du.$$

The TT parameter is thus a weighted version of MTE, where $\Delta^{\text{MTE}}(x, u)$ is given the largest weight for low u values and is given zero weight for $u \geq p_x^{\text{max}}$, where p_x^{max} is the maximum value in the support of $P(Z)$ conditional on $X = x$.

Figure 1 graphs the relationship between $\Delta^{\text{MTE}}(u)$, Δ^{ATE} and $\Delta^{\text{TT}}(P(z),$ $D = 1)$, assuming that the gains are the greatest for those with the lowest U_D values and that the gains decline as U_D increases. The curve is the MTE parameter as a function of u, and is drawn for the special case where the outcome variable is binary so that MTE parameter is bounded between -1 and 1. The ATE parameter averages $\Delta^{\text{MTE}}(u)$ over the full unit interval (i.e., is the area under A minus the area under B and C in the figure). $\Delta^{\text{TT}}(P(z), D = 1)$ averages $\Delta^{\text{MTE}}(u)$ up to the point $P(z)$ (is the area under A minus the area under B in the figure). Because $\Delta^{\text{MTE}}(u)$ is assumed to be declining in u, the TT parameter for any given $P(z)$ evaluation point is larger than the ATE parameter.

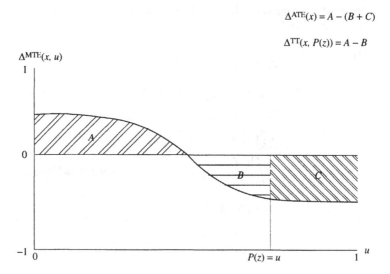

Figure 1.1. MTE integrates to ATE and TT under full support (for dichotomous outcome).

Equation (7) relates each of the other parameters to the MTE parameter. One can also relate each of the other parameters to the LATE parameter. This relationship turns out to be useful later on in this chapter when we encounter conditions where LATE can be identified but MTE cannot. MTE is the limit form of LATE:

$$\Delta^{\text{MTE}}(x, p) = \lim_{p' \to p} \Delta^{\text{LATE}}(x, p, p').$$

Direct relationships between LATE and the other parameters are easily derived. The relationship between LATE and ATE is immediate:

$$\Delta^{\text{ATE}}(x) = \Delta^{\text{LATE}}(x, 0, 1).$$

Using Bayes' rule, the relationship between LATE and TT is

$$\Delta^{\text{TT}}(x, D=1) = \int_0^1 \Delta^{\text{LATE}}(x, 0, p) \frac{p}{\Pr(D=1 \mid X=x)} dF_{P(Z) \mid X}(p \mid x). \qquad (10)$$

5 Identification and bounds for the treatment effect parameters

Assume access to an infinite i.i.d. sample of (D, Y, X, Z) observations, so that the joint distribution of (D, Y, X, Z) is known. Let $\mathcal{P}_x$ denote the closure of the support of $P(Z)$ conditional on $X = x$, and let $\mathcal{P}_x^c = (0, 1) \setminus \mathcal{P}_x$. Let $p_x^{\max}$ and $p_x^{\min}$ be the maximum and minimum values in $\mathcal{P}_x$. We show that the identification of the treatment parameters and the width of the bounds on the unidentified parameters depend critically on $\mathcal{P}_x$.[17]

We define the Local IV (LIV) estimand to be

$$\Delta^{\text{LIV}}(x, P(z)) \equiv \frac{\partial E(Y \mid X = x, P(Z) = P(z))}{\partial P(z)}.$$

LIV is the limit form of the LATE expression as $P(z) \to P(z')$.[18] In equation (6), $E(Y_1 \mid X = x, U_D)$ and $E(Y_0 \mid X = x, U_D)$ are integrable with respect to dF_U

[17] Heckman, Ichimura, Smith and Todd (1996, 1998), and Heckman, Ichimura, and Todd (1998) emphasize that the identification of treatment parameters critically depends on the support of the propensity score and present empirical evidence that failure of a full support condition is a major source of evaluation bias.

[18] The limit form of LATE was introduced in this context by Heckman (published 1997; first draft 1995) and Heckman and Smith (published 1998; first draft, 1995). Those authors introduced the limit form of LATE within the context of a selection model as a way to connect the LATE parameter to economic theory and to policy analysis. Angrist, Graddy and Imbens (1995) also develop a limit form of LATE within the context of a model of supply and demand, but use it only as a device for interpreting the linear IV estimand and place no direct economic interpretation on the limit LATE parameter. Bjorklund and Moffitt (1987) consider a parametric version of this parameter for the Roy model. These papers do not develop the relationships among the parameters or the identification analysis that are the primary concerns of this paper and of Heckman and Vytlacil (1999b, 2000a).

a.e. F_X. Thus, $E(Y_1 \mid X = x, P(Z) = P(z))$ and $E(Y_0 \mid X = x, P(Z) = P(z))$ are differentiable a.e. with respect to $P(z)$, and thus $E(Y \mid X = x, P(Z) = P(z))$ is differentiable a.e. with respect to $P(z)$ with the derivative given by

$$\frac{\partial E(Y \mid X = x, P(Z) = P(z))}{\partial P(z)} = E(Y_1 - Y_0 \mid X = x, U_D = P(z)), \,^{19} \qquad (11)$$

and thus

$$\Delta^{\text{LIV}}(x, P(z)) = \Delta^{\text{MTE}}(x, P(z)).$$

Note that while $\Delta^{\text{LIV}}(x, P(z))$ is defined for individuals with a given value of $P(Z)$, $P(Z) = P(z)$, it gives the marginal effect for individuals with a given value of U_D, $U_D = P(z)$. In other words, it is estimated conditional on an observed $P(Z) = P(z)$ but defines a treatment effect for those with a given unobserved proclivity to participate that is equal to the evaluation point, $U_D = P(z)$.

LATE and LIV are defined as functions (Y, X, Z), and are thus straightforward to identify. $\Delta^{\text{LATE}}(x, P(z), P(z'))$ is identified for any $(P(z), P(z')) \in \mathcal{P}_x \times \mathcal{P}_x$ such that $P(z) \neq P(z')$. The estimand $\Delta^{\text{LIV}}(x, P(z))$ is identified for any $P(z)$ that is a limit point of $\mathcal{P}_x$. The larger the support of $P(Z)$ conditional on $X = x$, the bigger the set of LIV and LATE parameters that can be identified.

ATE and TT are not defined directly as functions of (Y, X, Z), so a more involved discussion of their identification is required. We can use LIV or LATE to identify ATE and TT under the appropriate support conditions:

(i) If $\mathcal{P}_x = [0, 1]$, then $\Delta^{\text{ATE}}(x)$ is identified from $\{\Delta^{\text{LIV}}(x, p) : p \in [0, 1]\}$. If $\{0, 1\} \in \mathcal{P}_x$, then $\Delta^{\text{ATE}}(x)$ is identified from $\Delta^{\text{LATE}}(x, 0, 1)$.

(ii) If $[0, P(z)] \subset \mathcal{P}_x$, then $\Delta^{\text{TT}}(x, P(z), D = 1)$ is identified from $\{\Delta^{\text{LIV}}(x, p) : p \in [0, P(z)]\}$. If $\{0, P(z)\} \in \mathcal{P}_x$, then $\Delta^{\text{TT}}(x, P(z), D = 1)$ is identified from $\Delta^{\text{LATE}}(x, 0, P(z))$.

(iii) If $\mathcal{P}_x = [0, p_x^{\max}]$, then $\Delta^{\text{TT}}(x, D = 1)$ is identified from $\{\Delta^{\text{LIV}}(x, p) : p \in [0, p_x^{\max}]\}$. If $\{0\} \in \mathcal{P}_x$, then $\Delta^{\text{TT}}(x, D = 1)$ is identified from $\{\Delta^{\text{LATE}}(x, 0, p) : p \in \mathcal{P}_x\}$. (see equation 10).

Note that TT (not conditional on $P(z)$) is identified under weaker conditions than is ATE. To identify TT, one needs to observe $P(z)$ arbitrarily close to 0 ($p_x^{\min} = 0$) and to observe some positive $P(z)$ values, while to identify ATE one

<hr/>

[19] See, e.g., Kolmogorov and Fomin (1970), Theorem 9.8 for one proof. From assumption (iv), the derivative in (11) is finite a.e. F_{X, U_D}. The same argument could be used to show that $\Delta^{\text{LATE}}(x, P(z), P(z'))$ is continuous and differentiable in $P(z)$ and $P(z')$.

needs to observe $P(z)$ arbitrarily close to 0 and also $P(z)$ arbitrarily close to 1 ($p_x^{\max} = 1$ and $p_x^{\min} = 0$).

5.1 *Bounds for the parameters*

When the preceding support conditions do not hold, it is still possible to construct bounds for the treatment parameters if Y_1 and Y_0 are known to be bounded w.p.1. To simplify the notation, assume that Y_1 and Y_0 have the same bounds, so that

$$\Pr\left(y_x^l \le Y_1 \le y_x^u \mid X = x\right) = 1$$

and

$$\Pr\left(y_x^l \le Y_0 \le y_x^u \mid X = x\right) = 1.^{20}$$

For example, if Y is an indicator variable, then the bounds are $y_x^l = 0$ and $y_x^u = 1$ for all x. One set of bounds follows directly from the fact that MTE can be integrated up to the other parameters. For example, for ATE

$$\Delta^{\text{ATE}}(x) = \int_{\mathcal{P}_x} \Delta^{\text{LIV}}(x, p)\, dp + \int_{\mathcal{P}_x^c} \Delta^{\text{LIV}}(x, p)\, dp.$$

Since $\Delta^{\text{LIV}}(x, P(z))$ is bounded by $(y_x^l - y_x^u)$ and $(y_x^u - y_x^l)$, we obtain

$$\Delta^{\text{ATE}}(x) \le \int_{\mathcal{P}_x} \Delta^{\text{LIV}}(x, p)\, dp + \left(y_x^u - y_x^l\right) \int_{\mathcal{P}_x^c} dp$$

$$\Delta^{\text{ATE}}(x) \ge \int_{\mathcal{P}_x} \Delta^{\text{LIV}}(x, p)\, dp + \left(y_x^l - y_x^u\right) \int_{\mathcal{P}_x^c} dp. \tag{12}$$

A similar analysis applies to the expressions for TT.

Figures 2 and 3 present a graphical analysis of these bounds for ATE, drawn for the same assumptions about MTE as is used in Figure 1. As before the outcome variable is assumed binary so that $y_x^l = 0$ and $y_x^u = 1$. Figures 2 and 3 are drawn assuming that the support of the propensity score is an interval, with the vertical dotted lines denoting the end points of the interval. Figure 2 is drawn to represent the lower bound on ATE, with the lower bound being the area under the curve after its value has been set to $y_x^l - y_x^u = 0 - 1 = -1$ for u outside the support. Figure 3 is drawn to represent the upper bound on ATE, with the upper bound being the area under the curve after its value has been set to $y_x^u - y_x^l = 1 - 0 = 1$ for u outside the support.

These bounds can be tightened substantially by virtue of the following argument. We do not identify $E(Y_1 \mid X = x, P(Z) = p)$ or $E(Y_0 \mid X = x, P(Z) = p)$

---

[20] The modifications required to analyze the more general case are straightforward.

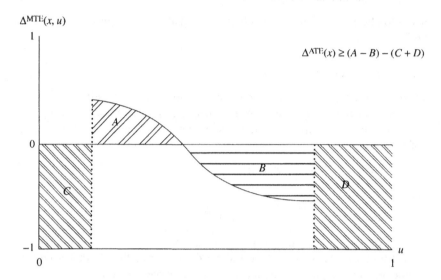

Figure 1.2. Lower bound on ATE under limited support (for dichotomous outcome).

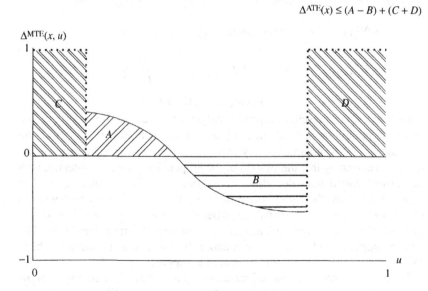

Figure 1.3. Upper bound on ATE under limited support (for dichotomous outcome).

pointwise for $p < p_x^{\min}$ or $p > p_x^{\max}$, and thus cannot use LIV to identify $\Delta^{\mathrm{MTE}}(x, u)$ for $u < p_x^{\min}$ or $u > p_x^{\max}$. However, it turns out that the latent index structure allows us to identify an averaged version of $E(Y_1 \mid X = x, U = u)$ for $u < p_x^{\min}$ and averaged version of $E(Y_0 \mid X = x, U = u)$ for $u > p_x^{\max}$, and we can use this additional information to construct tighter bounds. Our argument is of interest in its own right, because it shows how to use information on $E(Y_0 \mid X = x, P(Z) = p, D = 0)$, something we can observe within the proper support, to attain at least partial information on $E(Y_0 \mid X = x, P(Z) = p, D = 1)$, an unobserved, counterfactual quantity.

To apply this type of reasoning, note that $DY = DY_1$ is an observed random variable, and thus for any $x \in \mathrm{Supp}(X)$, $P(z) \in \mathcal{P}_x$, we identify the expectation of DY_1 given $X = x$, $P(Z) = P(z)$:

$$E(DY_1 \mid X = x, P(Z) = P(z)) = E(Y_1 \mid X = x, D = 1, P(Z) = P(z))P(z)$$

$$= E(Y_1 \mid X = x, P(z) \geq U_D)P(z)$$

$$= \int_0^{P(z)} E(Y_1 \mid X = x, U_D = u)\, du. \tag{13}$$

By similar reasoning,

$$E((1 - D)Y_0 \mid X = x, P(Z) = P(z)) = \int_{P(z)}^1 E(Y_0 \mid X = x, U_D = u)\, du. \tag{14}$$

We can evaluate (13) at $P(z) = p_x^{\max}$ and evaluate (14) at $P(z) = p_x^{\min}$. The distribution of (D, Y, X, Z) contains no information on $\int_{p_x^{\max}}^1 E(Y_1 \mid X = x, U_D = u)\, du$ and $\int_0^{p_x^{\min}} E(Y_0 \mid X = x, U_D = u)\, du$, but we can bound these quantities:

$$\left(1 - p_x^{\max}\right)y_x^l \leq \int_{p_x^{\max}}^1 E(Y_1 \mid X = x, U_D = u)\, du \leq \left(1 - p_x^{\max}\right)y_x^u$$

$$p_x^{\min}y_x^l \leq \int_0^{p_x^{\min}} E(Y_0 \mid X = x, U_D = u)\, du \leq p_x^{\min}y_x^u. \tag{15}$$

We can thus bound $\Delta^{\mathrm{ATE}}(x)$ by

$$\Delta^{\mathrm{ATE}}(x) \leq p_x^{\max}\left[E(Y_1 \mid X = x, P(Z) = p_x^{\max}, D = 1)\right] + \left(1 - p_x^{\max}\right)y_x^u$$

$$- \left(1 - p_x^{\min}\right)\left[E(Y_0 \mid X = x, P(Z) = p_x^{\min}, D = 0)\right] - p_x^{\min}y_x^l$$

$$\Delta^{\mathrm{ATE}}(x) \geq p_x^{\max}\left[E(Y_1 \mid X = x, P(Z) = p_x^{\max}, D = 1)\right] + \left(1 - p_x^{\max}\right)y_x^l$$

$$- \left(1 - p_x^{\min}\right)\left[E(Y_0 \mid X = x, P(Z) = p_x^{\min}, D = 0)\right] - p_x^{\min}y_x^u.$$

The width of the bounds is thus

$$\left[\left(1 - p_x^{\max}\right) + p_x^{\min}\right]\left(y_x^u - y_x^l\right).$$

If $\mathcal{P}_x$ is an interval, then the width of these bounds is half the width of the bounds given by equation (12). If $\mathcal{P}(x)$ is not an interval, then the width of these bounds is less than half the width of the bounds given by equation (12). We show that these bounds are tight in Appendix B.

The width of the bounds is linearly related to the distance between $p_x^{\max}$ and 1 and the distance between $p_x^{\min}$ and 0. These bounds are directly related to the identification at infinity results of Heckman (1990) and Heckman and Honoré (1990). Such identification at infinity results require the condition that $\mu_D(Z)$ takes arbitrarily large and arbitrarily small values if the support of U_D is unbounded. This type of identifying condition is sometimes criticized as not being credible. However, as is made clear by the width of the bounds just presented, the proper metric for measuring how close one is to identification at infinity is the distance between $p_x^{\max}$ and 1 and the distance between $p_x^{\min}$ and 0. It is credible that these distances may be small. In practice, semiparametric econometric methods that use identification at infinity arguments to identify ATE implicitly extrapolate $E(Y_1 \mid X = x, U_D = u)$ for $u > p_x^{\max}$ and $E(Y_0 \mid X = x, U_D = u)$ for $u < p_x^{\min}$. These bounds are related to work by Manski (1990), Robins (1989) and Balke and Pearl (1997), but are distinct. We connect our work with that in the literature in Appendix B.

We can construct analogous bounds for $\Delta^{\mathrm{TT}}(x, P(z), D = 1)$ for $P(z) \in \mathcal{P}_x$ in terms of observed objects in an analogous fashion. Recall that

$$
\begin{aligned}
\Delta^{\mathrm{TT}}(x, P(z), D = 1) &= E(Y_1 - Y_0 \mid X = x, P(Z) = P(z), D = 1) \\
&= E(Y_1 \mid X = x, P(Z) = P(z), D = 1) \\
&\quad - E(Y_0 \mid X = x, P(Z) = P(z), D = 1).
\end{aligned}
$$

We know the first term for $P(z) \in \mathcal{P}(x)$. The second term is the missing counterfactual, which we can rewrite as

$$E(Y_0 \mid X = x, P(Z) = P(z), D = 1) = \frac{1}{P(z)} \int_0^{P(z)} E(Y_0 \mid X = x, U = u)\, du.$$

For $P(z) \in \mathcal{P}_x$, we identify

$$E(Y_0 \mid X = x, P(Z) = P(z), D = 0) = \frac{1}{1 - P(z)} \int_{P(z)}^1 E(Y_0 \mid X = x, U = u)\, du,$$

and we identify

$$E\left(Y_0 \mid X = x, P(Z) = p_x^{\min}, D = 0\right) = \frac{1}{1 - p_x^{\min}} \int_{p_x^{\min}}^1 E(Y_0 \mid X = x, U = u)\, du.$$

We therefore identify

$$\left(1 - p_x^{\min}\right) E\left(Y_0 \mid X = x, P(Z) = p_x^{\min}, D = 0\right)$$
$$- (1 - P(z)) E\left(Y_0 \mid X = x, P(Z) = p_x^{\min}, D = 0\right)$$
$$= \int_{p_x^{\min}}^{P(z)} E(Y_0 \mid X = x, U = u) \, du.$$

We do not identify $\int_0^{p_x^{\min}} E(Y_0 \mid X = x, U = u) \, du$. However, we can bound it by

$$y_x^l p_x^{\min} \le \int_0^{p_x^{\min}} E(Y_0 \mid X = x, U = u) \, du \le y_x^u p_x^{\min}.$$

We thus have that

$$E(Y_0 \mid X = x, P(Z) = P(z), D = 1)$$
$$\le \frac{1}{P(z)} \Big[p_x^{\min} y_x^l + \left(1 - p_x^{\min}\right) E\left(Y_0 \mid X = x, P(Z) = p_x^{\min}, D = 0\right)$$
$$- (1 - P(z)) E(Y_0 \mid X = x, P(Z) = P(z), D = 0) \Big]$$
$$E(Y_0 \mid X = x, P(Z) = P(z), D = 1)$$
$$\ge \frac{1}{P(z)} \Big[p_x^{\min} y_x^u + \left(1 - p_x^{\min}\right) E\left(Y_0 \mid X = x, P(Z) = p_x^{\min}, D = 0\right)$$
$$- (1 - P(z)) E(Y_0 \mid X = x, P(Z) = P(z), D = 0) \Big].$$

Using these inequalities, we can bound $\Delta^{\mathrm{TT}}(x, P(z), D = 1)$ as follows:

$$\Delta^{\mathrm{TT}}(x, P(z), D = 1) \le E(Y_1 \mid X = x, P(Z) = P(z), D = 1)$$
$$- \frac{1}{P(z)} \Big[p_x^{\min} y_x^l + \left(1 - p_x^{\min}\right) E\left(Y_0 \mid X = x, P(Z) = p_x^{\min}, D = 0\right)$$
$$- (1 - P(z)) E(Y_0 \mid X = x, P(Z) = P(z), D = 0) \Big]$$
$$\Delta^{\mathrm{TT}}(x, P(z), D = 1) \ge E(Y_1 \mid X = x, P(Z) = P(z), D = 1)$$
$$- \frac{1}{P(z)} \Big[p_x^{\min} y_x^u + \left(1 - p_x^{\min}\right) E\left(Y_0 \mid X = x, P(Z) = p_x^{\min}, D = 0\right)$$
$$- (1 - P(z)) E(Y_0 \mid X = x, P(Z) = P(z), D = 0) \Big].$$

The width of the bounds for $\Delta^{\mathrm{TT}}(x, P(z), D = 1)$ is thus

$$\frac{p_x^{\min}}{P(z)} \left(y_x^u - y_x^l\right).$$

As in the analysis of ATE, the width of the bounds is linearly decreasing in the distance between $p_x^{\min}$ and 0. Note that the bounds are tighter for larger $P(z)$ evaluation points, because the higher the $P(z)$ evaluation point, the less weight is placed on the unidentified quantity $\int_0^{p_x^{\min}} E(Y_0 \mid X = x, U_D = u) \, du$.

We can integrate the bounds on $\Delta^{TT}(x, P(z), D = 1)$ to bound $\Delta^{TT}(x, D = 1)$:

$$\Delta^{TT}(x, D = 1) \leq \int_0^{p_x^{max}} \Bigg[E(Y_1 \mid X = x, P(Z) = p, D = 1)$$
$$- \frac{1}{p} \left(p_x^{min} y_x^l + \left(1 - p_x^{min}\right) \right)$$
$$\times E\left(Y_0 \mid X = x, P(Z) = p_x^{min}, D = 0\right)$$
$$- (1 - p)E(Y_0 \mid X = x, P(Z) = p, D = 0)) \Bigg]$$
$$\times dF_{P(Z) \mid X, D}(p \mid x, 1)$$

$$\Delta^{TT}(x, D = 1) \geq \int_0^{p_x^{max}} \Bigg[E(Y_1 \mid X = x, P(Z) = p, D = 1)$$
$$- \frac{1}{p} \left(p_x^{min} y_x^u + \left(1 - p_x^{min}\right) \right)$$
$$\times E\left(Y_0 \mid X = x, P(Z) = p_x^{min}, D = 0\right)$$
$$- (1 - p)E(Y_0 \mid X = x, P(Z) = p, D = 0)) \Bigg]$$
$$\times dF_{P(Z) \mid X, D}(p \mid x, 1).$$

The width of the bounds on $\Delta^{TT}(x, D = 1)$ is thus

$$p_x^{min} \left(y_x^u - y_x^l\right) \int_{p_x^{min}}^{p_x^{max}} \frac{1}{p} dF_{P(Z) \mid X, D}(p \mid x, 1).$$

Using (8), we obtain

$$p_x^{min} \left(y_x^u - y_x^l\right) \int_{p_x^{min}}^{p_x^{max}} \frac{1}{p} dF_{P(Z) \mid X, D}(p \mid x, 1)$$
$$= p_x^{min} \left(y_x^u - y_x^l\right) \int_{p_x^{min}}^{p_x^{max}} \frac{1}{\Pr(D = 1 \mid X = x)} dF_{P(Z) \mid X}(p \mid x)$$
$$= p_x^{min} \left(y_x^u - y_x^l\right) \frac{1}{\Pr(D = 1 \mid X = x)}.^{[21]}$$

Unlike the bounds on ATE, the bounds on TT depend on the distribution of $P(Z)$, in particular, on $\Pr(D = 1 \mid X = x) = E(P(Z) \mid X = x)$. The width of the bounds is linearly related to the distance between p_x^{min} and 0, holding $\Pr(D = 1 \mid X = x)$ constant. The larger $\Pr(D = 1 \mid X = x)$, the tighter the

[21] Recall that, by the definition of p_x^{max} and p_x^{min}, we have that the support of $P(Z)$ is a subset of the interval $[p_x^{min}, p_x^{max}]$.

bounds, since the larger $P(Z)$ is on average, the less probability weight is being placed on the unidentified quantity $\int_0^{p_x^{\min}} E(Y_0 \mid X = x, U_D = u) \, du$.

6 Linear IV vs. local IV

Our analysis differs from that of Imbens and Angrist (1994) because we use a local version of instrumental variables and not linear instrumental variables. This section compares these two approaches. As before, we condition on X, and use the propensity score, $P(Z)$, as the instrument.

The linear IV estimand is

$$\Delta^{IV}(x) = \frac{\text{Cov}(Y, P(Z) \mid X = x)}{\text{Cov}(D, P(Z) \mid X = x)}.$$

Using the law of iterated expectations, we obtain

$$\frac{\text{Cov}(Y, P(Z) \mid X = x)}{\text{Cov}(D, P(Z) \mid X = x)} = \frac{\text{Cov}(Y, P(Z) \mid X = x)}{\text{Var}(P(Z) \mid X = x)}.$$

The linear IV estimand can thus be interpreted as the slope term on p from the linear least squares approximation to $E(Y \mid P(Z) = p, X = x)$, holding x fixed. The local IV estimand can be interpreted in the following way. Take a Taylor series expansion of $E(Y \mid P(Z) = p, X = x)$ for a fixed x in a neighborhood of $p = p_0$:

$$
\begin{aligned}
E(Y \mid P(Z) = p, X = x) &= E(Y \mid P(Z) = p_0, X = x) + (p - p_0) \\
&\quad \times \left. \frac{\partial E(Y \mid X = x, P(Z) = p)}{\partial p} \right|_{p=p_0} \\
&\quad + o(|p - p_0|) \\
&= E(Y \mid P(Z) = p_0, X = x) \\
&\quad + (p - p_0) \Delta^{LIV}(x, p_0) + o(|p - p_0|).
\end{aligned}
$$

Local IV evaluated at the point p_0 estimates the slope term from a linear approximation to $E(Y \mid P(Z) = p, X = x)$ for p in a neighborhood of the point p_0, conditional on $X = x$. Linear IV is the slope term from a global (but conditional on X), linear least squares approximation to $E(Y \mid P(Z) = p, X = x)$, while local IV is the slope term from a local, linear approximation to $E(Y \mid P(Z) = p, X = x)$ at a prespecified point. If the treatment effect, $\Delta = Y_1 - Y_0$, does not vary over individuals conditional on X, then it can easily be shown that[22]

$$E(Y \mid P(Z) = p, X = x) = E(Y_0 \mid X = x) + E(Y_1 - Y_0 \mid X = x)p.$$

---

[22] Thus $Y = Y_0 + D(Y_1 - Y_0)$, $E(Y \mid X = x, P(Z) = p) = E(Y_0 \mid X = x) + E(Y_1 - Y_0 \mid X = x, P(Z) = p, D = 1)p$, and the result follows using that $E(Y_1 - Y_0 \mid X = x, P(Z) = p, D = 1) = E(Y_1 - Y_0 \mid X = x)$ from the assumption that the treatment effect does not vary over individuals conditional on X.

Thus, if the treatment effect does not vary over individuals, $E(Y \mid P(Z) = p,$ $X = x)$ will be a linear function of p with slope given by $E(Y_1 - Y_0 \mid X = x)$ and the linear IV estimand and the local IV estimand coincide. If the treatment effect varies over individuals, then in the general case

$$
\begin{aligned}
E(Y \mid P(Z) &= p, X = x) \\
&= E(Y_0 \mid X = x) + E(Y_1 - Y_0 \mid X = x, Z = z, D = 1)p \\
&= E(Y_0 \mid X = x) + E(Y_1 - Y_0 \mid X = x, P(Z) = p, D = 1)p.
\end{aligned}
$$

Then, if $Y_1 - Y_0$ is not mean independent of $P(Z)$ conditional on (X, D), we have that $E(Y \mid P(Z) = p, X = x)$ will not be a linear function of p and the linear IV estimand and the local IV estimand will not coincide. We present an economic interpretation of this condition later on in this section.

By estimating the slope term locally, LIV is able to identify the MTE parameter pointwise:

$$
\Delta^{\mathrm{LIV}}(x, p) = \Delta^{\mathrm{MTE}}(x, p).
$$

In contrast, linear IV identifies a weighted average of the LIV estimands, and thus a weighted average of the MTE parameter. Using the law of iterated expectations, and assuming that the relevant second moments exist and are finite, one can show that

$$
\Delta^{\mathrm{IV}}(x) = \int_0^1 \Delta^{\mathrm{LIV}}(x, u) h_x(u)\, du = \int_0^1 \Delta^{\mathrm{MTE}}(x, u) h_x(u)\, du, \quad (16)
$$

where

$$
h_x(u) = \frac{(E(P(Z) - E(P(Z) \mid X = x) \mid P(Z) \geq u, X = x)) \Pr(P(Z) \geq u, X = x)}{\mathrm{Var}[P(Z) \mid X = x]},
$$

$$(17)$$

and

$$
\int_0^1 h_x(u)\, du = 1.^{23} \tag{18}
$$

As shown by Imbens and Angrist (1994), linear IV converges to some weighted average of treatment effects. However, the implicit weighting of the MTE parameter implied by linear IV does not in general equal the weighting corresponding to the parameters defined in Section 3. One can show that the IV weighting equals the weighting corresponding to LATE only if the support of $P(Z)$ conditional on $X = x$ only contains two values, $\mathcal{P}_x = \{p', p\}$. The linear

---

[23] This result is essentially the same as Theorem 2 of Imbens and Angrist (1994) except that it is explicitly based on the latent index representation.

IV weighting equals the weighting of MTE corresponding to TT in the special case where $\mathcal{P}_x = \{0, p\}$, and equals the weighting corresponding to ATE in the special case where $\mathcal{P}_x = \{0, 1\}$. The IV weighting cannot correspond to the MTE parameter at a given evaluation point. Linear IV is a global approach (conditional on X) which estimates a weighted average of the MTE parameters. Local IV is a form of instrumental variables, conditional on $X = x_0$ and within a neighborhood of $P(Z) = p_0$, that estimates a given MTE parameter, which when suitably weighted and integrated, produces both TT and ATE.

To summarize the discussion of this section and to link the treatment effect parameters defined and discussed in the previous section to the familiar switching regression model, or correlated random coefficient model, it is useful to consider the following separable version of it. Let

$$Y_1 = \mu_1(X) + U_1,$$
$$Y_0 = \mu_0(X) + U_0,$$

and define D as arising from a latent index crossing a threshold as before. Assume $E(U_1) = 0$ and $E(U_0) = 0$.[24] Assume (Z, X) are independent of (U_1, U_0). We maintain assumptions (i)–(v). Let F denote the distribution function of U_D, and let $\tilde{U}_D = F(U_D)$. In this case, we can write the outcome equation as a random coefficient model:

$$\begin{aligned} Y &= DY_1 + (1 - D)Y_0 \\ &= \mu_0(X) + [\mu_1(X) - \mu_0(X) + U_1 - U_0]D + U_0, \end{aligned}$$

where the coefficient of D is a random or variable coefficient. From the definition, it follows that

$$\begin{aligned} E(Y_1 \mid X = x, Z = z, D = 1) &= \mu_1(X) + E(U_1 \mid X = x, Z = z, D = 1) \\ &= \mu_1(X) + E(U_1 \mid U_D \leq \mu_D(z)) \\ &= \mu_1(X) + K_{11}(P(z)), \end{aligned}$$

and

$$\begin{aligned} E(Y_0 \mid X = x, Z = z, D = 0) &= \mu_0(X) + E(U_0 \mid X = x, Z = z, D = 0) \\ &= \mu_0(X) + E(U_1 \mid U_D > \mu_D(z)) \\ &= \mu_0(X) + K_{00}(P(z)), \end{aligned}$$

where $K_{ij}(P(z)) = E(U_i \mid Z = z, D = j)$ is a control function (see Heckman 1980 and Heckman and Robb 1985, 1986).

---

[24] Because of the additive separability assumption, it is more natural to consider (Y_0, Y_1) to be continuous variables in this example.

In this setup,

$$\Delta^{ATE}(x) = E(Y_1 - Y_0 \mid X = x) = \mu_1(x) - \mu_0(x)$$
$$\Delta^{TT}(x, z, D = 1) = E(Y_1 - Y_0 \mid X = x, Z = z, D = 1)$$
$$= \mu_1(x) - \mu_0(x) + E(U_1 - U_0 \mid X = x, Z = z, D = 1)$$
$$= \mu_1(x) - \mu_0(x) + E(U_1 - U_0 \mid U_D \le \mu_D(z)).$$

We develop these expressions further in the next section.

Again consider the relationship between the LIV and linear IV estimators. Using the additive separability assumption, we obtain

$$\Delta^{LIV}(x, p) = \Delta^{MTE}(x, p) = \mu_1(x) - \mu_0(x) + E(U_1 - U_0 \mid \tilde{U}_D = p),$$

and using equation (16),

$$\Delta^{IV}(x) = \mu_1(x) - \mu_0(x) + \int_0^1 E(U_1 - U_0 \mid \tilde{U}_D = u) h_x(u) \, du, \quad (19)$$

where $h_x(u)$ is defined in equation (17).

To compare what LIV and the linear instrumental variable estimator identify, it is useful to follow Heckman (1997) in comparing three cases. Case 1 (C-1) is the homogeneous response model:

$$U_1 = U_0. \tag{C-1}$$

In this case, $\Delta^{MTE}(x, u) = \mu_1(x) - \mu_0(x)$ for all u. The effect of treatment does not vary over individuals given X. Using equation (19) and the fact that $h_x(u)$ integrates to one, we obtain $\Delta^{IV}(x) = \Delta^{ATE}(x) = \Delta^{TT}(x, D = 1)$. Because $\Delta^{MTE}(x, u)$ does not vary with u, this is a case where linear IV will identify the parameters of interest even though the implicit weighting of MTE implied by linear IV will not generally equal the weighting corresponding to the parameters of interest.

In the case of heterogeneous responses, $U_1 \ne U_0$, it is useful to distinguish two further cases: (C-2) where agent enrollment into the program does not depend on $U_1 - U_0$ and case (C-3) where it does. Case (C-2) is (C-2a) plus (C-2b) or (C-2b'):

$$U_1 \ne U_0 \tag{C-2a}$$

and

$$E(U_1 - U_0 \mid X = x, Z = z, D = 1) = E(U_1 - U_0 \mid X = x, D = 1) \tag{C-2b}$$

for z a.e. $F_{Z \mid X = x}$ s.t. $P(z) \ne 0$, or

$$E(U_1 - U_0 \mid X = x, Z = z, D = 1) = M \tag{C-2b'}$$

for z a.e. $F_{Z \mid X=x}$ s.t. $P(z) \neq 0$, for some constant M. Under (C-2a) and (C-2b), $\Delta^{IV}(x) = \Delta^{TT}(x, D = 1)$; under (C-2a) and (C-2b'), $\Delta^{IV}(x) = \Delta^{ATE}(x)$ (see Heckman 1997; Heckman and Smith 1998; and Heckman, LaLonde and Smith 1999). From assumption (iii), $((U_D, U_1)$ and (U_D, U_0) are independent of $(Z, X))$, we obtain that $U_1 - U_0$ is mean independent of X conditional on (D, Z), and thus (C-2b) can be rewritten as

$$E(U_1 - U_0 \mid Z = z, D = 1) = E(U_1 - U_0 \mid X = x, D = 1)$$

and (C-2b') can be rewritten as

$$E(U_1 - U_0 \mid Z = z, D = 1) = M.^{25}$$

Although we impose assumption (iii) to simplify the argument, it can be weakened substantially. Since all the IV analysis is performed conditional on $X = x$, assumption (iii) can be weakened to allow U_1, U_0 to depend on X (see Heckman 1997; Heckman and Smith 1998; Heckman, LaLonde and Smith 1999).

A sufficient condition for both (C-2b) and (C-2b') is that $\Pr(D = 1 \mid X, Z, U_1 - U_0) = \Pr(D = 1 \mid X, Z)$, i.e., U_D is independent of $U_1 - U_0$. This condition implies that $\Delta^{MTE}(x, u) = \mu_1(x) - \mu_0(x)$ for all u, and thus $\Delta^{IV}(x) = \Delta^{ATE}(x) = \Delta^{TT}(x, D = 1)$. This is another case where the implicit weighting of MTE implied by linear IV need not equal the weighting corresponding to ATE or TT and linear IV still identifies the parameters of interest since $\Delta^{MTE}(x, u)$ does not vary with u. In this case, the treatment effect varies over individuals conditional on X, but individuals do not participate in the program being evaluated on the basis of this variation.

The conditions under which (C-2b) and (C-2b') hold, and whether these conditions are equivalent to each other or not, depend on the support of $P(Z)$ conditional on $X = x$ ($\mathcal{P}_x$). First consider the case where the support of $P(Z)$ conditional on $X = x$ is the full unit interval ($\mathcal{P}_x = [0, 1]$). Then both conditions are equivalent to the assumption that $U_1 - U_0$ is mean independent of U_D. To see this, note that the left hand side of (C-2b) can be rewritten as

$$E(U_1 - U_0 \mid X = x, Z = z, D = 1) = E(U_1 - U_0 \mid Z = z, D = 1)$$

$$= E(U_1 - U_0 \mid U_D \leq \mu_D(z)).$$

By assumption, the support of $\mu_D(Z)$ contains the support of U_D conditional on $X = x$, so we have that (C-2b) is equivalent to assuming that $U_1 - U_0$ is

---

[25] Conditioning on X is necessary on the right hand side of assumption (C-2b) since, in general, $U_1 - U_0$ will be mean dependent on X conditional on D even though $U_1 - U_0$ are mean independent of X conditional on (D, Z).

mean independent of U_D. Now consider the left hand side of (C-2b'),

$$E(U_1 - U_0 \mid X = x, Z = z, D = 1) = E(U_1 - U_0 \mid Z = z, D = 1)$$
$$= E(U_1 - U_0 \mid U_D \leq \mu_D(z)).$$

Again using the fact that the support of $\mu_D(Z)$ contains the support of U_D conditional on $X = x$, we have that condition (C-2b') is equivalent to assuming that $U_1 - U_0$ is mean independent of U_D. This is another case where the implicit weighting of MTE implied by linear IV will not equal the weighting corresponding to ATE or TT but linear IV still identifies these parameters since $\Delta^{\text{MTE}}(x, u)$ does not vary with u.

Next consider the case where the support of $P(Z)$ conditional on $X = x$ is a set of two values, p' and p (i.e., $\mathcal{P}_x = \{p', p\}$). We then have that $\Delta^{\text{IV}}(x) = \Delta^{\text{LATE}}(x, p', p)$. Following the analysis of Section 5, if $p' = 0$, $p = 1$, we have that $\Delta^{\text{IV}}(x) = \Delta^{\text{LATE}}(x, 0, 1) = \Delta^{\text{ATE}}(x) = \Delta^{\text{TT}}(x, D = 1)$, and both conditions (C-2b) and (C-2b') are satisfied allowing $\Delta^{\text{MTE}}(x, u)$ to vary freely with u (i.e., allowing arbitrary dependence between $U_1 - U_0$ and U_D). In this special case, the implicit weighting of MTE implied by linear IV equals the weighting corresponding to ATE and TT, so that the parameters are equal even though $\Delta^{\text{MTE}}(x, u)$ varies freely with u.

Next consider the case where $p' = 0$ and $0 < p < 1$. The implicit weighting implied by linear IV equals the weighting corresponding to TT, $\Delta^{\text{IV}}(x) = \Delta^{\text{LATE}}(x, 0, p) = \Delta^{\text{TT}}(x, D = 1)$, and condition (C-2b) is satisfied, even though $\Delta^{\text{MTE}}(x, u)$ may vary arbitrarily with u, thus allowing $U_1 - U_0$ to be arbitrarily dependent on U_D.[26] However, in this case, the weighting implied by $\Delta^{\text{IV}}(x)$ is not the same as the weighting corresponding to $\Delta^{\text{ATE}}(x)$. Thus $\Delta^{\text{IV}}(x) = \Delta^{\text{ATE}}(x)$ and condition (C-2b') is satisfied iff $\Delta^{\text{ATE}}(x) = \Delta^{\text{TT}}(x, D = 1)$, i.e., iff $\frac{1-p}{p} \int_0^p E(U_1 - U_0 \mid U_D = u) \, du = \int_p^1 E(U_1 - U_0 \mid U_D = u) \, du$. This will not be satisfied in general. Imposing this condition is equivalent to imposing a particular restriction on the dependence of $U_1 - U_0$ on U_D. This restriction does not require mean independence, but is implied by mean independence. Thus, in the case where the support of $P(Z)$ conditional on $X = x$ is the set of two values, 0 and p ($\mathcal{P}_x = \{0, p\}$), conditions (C-2b) and (C-2b') differ with (C-2b) satisfied without restrictions on the dependence of $U_1 - U_0$ on U_D but (C-2b') is satisfied only if a peculiar restriction is imposed on this dependence. Finally, consider the case where $0 < p' < p < 1$. In this case, $\Delta^{\text{IV}}(x) = \Delta^{\text{LATE}}(x, p', p)$, and the implicit weighting produced by linear IV will not equal the weighting corresponding to TT or ATE, and conditions (C-2b) and (C-2b') will not hold, unless a particular restriction is imposed on the dependence between

---

[26] Arbitrary subject to the maintained assumption (ii) in Section 2.

$U_1 - U_0$ and U_D, with the restriction being weaker than a mean independence assumption.

We have thus considered two extreme cases. First, where the support of $P(Z)$ conditional on $X = x$ is the full unit interval ($\mathcal{P}_x = [0, 1]$), in which case (C-2b) and (C-2b') are both equivalent to the assumption that $U_1 - U_0$ is mean independent of U_D. Second, we have also considered the case where the support of $P(Z)$ conditional on $X = x$ is a set of two points ($\mathcal{P}_x = \{p', p\}$), in which case (C-2b) and (C-2b') will generally be different assumptions and will require restrictions on the dependence of $U_1 - U_0$ on U_D weaker than a mean independence assumption. Following the same arguments, we can consider any other support for the propensity score. In general, (C-2b) is a weaker condition than (C-2b'). Both conditions will be satisfied under a condition weaker than mean independence of $U_1 - U_0$ on U_D if the support of $P(Z)$ conditional on $X = x$ is a strict subset of the unit interval ($\mathcal{P}_x \subset [0, 1]$). Both conditions will impose some restriction on the dependence of $U_1 - U_0$ on U_D except in the extreme case where the support of $P(Z)$ conditional on $X = x$ is only two points, one of the two points being 0 ($\mathcal{P}_x = \{0, p\}$) for (C-2b) or only two points, one point being 0 and one point being 1 ($\mathcal{P}_x = \{0, 1\}$) for (C-2b').

In the general case of a correlated random coefficient model where agents select into the program partly based on $U_1 - U_0$, or information correlated with it, we have

$$U_1 \neq U_0 \tag{C-3a}$$

and

$$E(U_1 - U_0 \mid Z = z, D = 1) \neq E(U_1 - U_0 \mid X = x, D = 1) \tag{C-3b}$$

for a set of z values having positive probability ($F_{Z \mid X = x}$), or

$$E(U_1 - U_0 \mid Z = z, D = 1) = M(z), \tag{C-3b'}$$

where $M(z)$ is a nondegenerate function of z for z in the support of Z conditional on $X = x$. In this case the linear instrumental variable estimator does not identify TT if (C-3b) holds or ATE if (C-3b') applies (Heckman 1997). These cases arise in the Roy model discussed in the next section.

Even though the linear instrumental variable estimator breaks down for identifying TT or ATE in the third case, it still identifies LATE if the support of $P(Z)$ conditional on $X = x$ only contains two elements. In this general case, LIV can be used to identify all three treatment parameters. Under the support conditions presented in Section 5, suitably reweighted and integrated versions of LIV identify or bound TT and ATE while linear IV does not.

We now show how to relate this analysis to the familiar case of the Roy model.

7   Additive separability and the Roy model

Pursuing the additively separable case further, we obtain the following representation:

$$\Delta^{\text{TT}}(x, z, D = 1) = \mu_1(x) - \mu_0(x) + K(P(z)), \text{[27]}$$

where $K(P(z)) = E(U_1 - U_0 \mid \tilde{U}_D \le P(z)) = K_{11}(P(z)) - K_{01}(P(z))$.

Integrating out over the support of Z given $X = x$ and $D = 1$,

$$\Delta^{\text{TT}}(x, D = 1) = E(Y_1 - Y_0 \mid X = x, D = 1)$$

$$= \int \Delta^{\text{TT}}(x, z, D = 1) dF_{Z \mid X, D}(z \mid x, 1)$$

$$= \mu_1(x) - \mu_0(x) + \int K(p) dF_{P(Z) \mid X, D}(p \mid x, 1)$$

$$= \mu_1(x) - \mu_0(x) + \int K(p) \frac{p}{E(P(Z) \mid X = x)} dF_{P(Z) \mid X}(p \mid x),$$

$$(20)$$

where $\int K(p) \frac{p}{E(P(Z) \mid X = x)} dF_{P(Z) \mid X}(p \mid x) = E(U_1 - U_0 \mid \tilde{U}_D \le P(Z))$.

For a fixed X, and two distinct values of Z,

$$\Delta^{\text{LATE}}(x, P(z), P(z')) = \mu_1(x) - \mu_0(x) + \frac{P(z)K(P(z)) - P(z')K(P(z'))}{P(z) - P(z')}$$

In the limit as $z' \to z$,

$$\lim_{z' \to z} \Delta^{\text{LATE}}(x, P(z), P(z')) = \mu_1(x) - \mu_0(x) + K(P(z)) \frac{\partial P(z)}{\partial z} + P(z) \frac{\partial K(P(z))}{\partial z}$$

This limit exists as a consequence of our assumptions. Working directly with limit $P(z') \to P(z)$,

$$\lim_{P(z') \to P(z)} \Delta^{\text{LATE}}(x, P(z), P(z')) = \mu_1(x) - \mu_0(x) + K(P(z)) + \frac{\partial K(P(z))}{\partial P(z)} P(z)$$

$$= \mu_1(x) - \mu_0(x) + K(P(z))[1 + \eta],$$

where $\eta = \frac{\partial \ln K(P(z))}{\partial \ln P(z)}$ is the elasticity of the conditional mean of the unobservables with respect to the propensity score. The above is LIV as previously defined, and since $\Delta^{\text{LIV}}(x, P(z)) = \Delta^{\text{MTE}}(x, P(z))$, we obtain

$$\Delta^{\text{MTE}}(x, u) = \mu_1(x) - \mu_0(x) + K(u)[1 + \eta].$$

---

[27] This representation is from Heckman (1980), and Heckman and Robb (1985, 1986).

As noted by Heckman (1997) and Heckman and Smith (1998), $\Delta^{\text{MTE}}(x, u)$ is the "treatment on the treated" parameter for those with characteristics $X = x$ who would be indifferent between sector 1 and sector 0 if the instrument were externally set so that $P(Z) = u$. This is the parameter required for evaluating the marginal gross gain (exclusive of any costs of making the move) for persons of characteristics $P(Z) = u$ at the margin of indifference between sector 1 and sector 0. It is also the parameter required for evaluating the effect of a marginal change in Z on the persons induced into (or out) of the program by the change. It is *one* of the three parameters required in a cost-benefit analysis of the change.[28]

For the case of the classical selection model, (U_0, U_1, U_D) are mean zero joint normal random variables, independent of (Z, X). In this case, we obtain the following expressions for $P(z)$ and the treatment parameters:

$$P(z) = \Phi\left(\frac{\mu_D(z)}{\sigma_{DU}}\right)$$

$$K(P(z)) = \left[\frac{\sigma_{1U} - \sigma_{0U}}{\sigma_U}\right] \frac{\exp\{-\frac{1}{2}[\Phi^{-1}(P(z))]^2\}}{P(z)}$$

$$\Delta^{\text{ATE}}(x) = \mu_1(x) - \mu_0(x)$$

$$\Delta^{\text{TT}}(x, P(z), D = 1) = \mu_1(x) - \mu_0(x) + \left[\frac{\sigma_{1U} - \sigma_{0U}}{\sigma_U}\right]$$

$$\times \frac{1}{\sqrt{2\pi}} \frac{\exp\left\{-\frac{1}{2}[\Phi^{-1}(P(z))]^2\right\}}{P(z)}$$

$$\Delta^{\text{LATE}}(x, P(z), P(z')) = \mu_1(x) - \mu_0(x) + \left[\frac{\sigma_{1U} - \sigma_{0U}}{\sigma_U}\right] \frac{1}{\sqrt{2\pi}}$$

$$\times \left[\frac{\exp\left\{-\frac{1}{2}[\Phi^{-1}(P(z))]^2\right\} - \exp\left\{-\frac{1}{2}[\Phi^{-1}(P(z'))]^2\right\}}{P(z) - P(z')}\right]$$

$$\Delta^{\text{MTE}}(x, u) = \mu_1(x) - \mu_0(x) - \left[\frac{\sigma_{1U} - \sigma_{0U}}{\sigma_{DU}}\right] \Phi^{-1}(u),$$

where $\sigma_{jU} = [\text{Var}(U_j)]^{\frac{1}{2}}$. The expression for $\Delta^{\text{TT}}(x, D = 1)$ is obtained from Equation (20) and depends on the distribution of $P(Z)$. Observe that in the normal case, $\Delta^{\text{MTE}}(x, \frac{1}{2}) = \Delta^{\text{ATE}}(x)$ and $\Delta^{\text{LATE}}(x, p, 1 - p) = \Delta^{\text{ATE}}(x)$ as a result of the symmetry of the normal distribution.[29]

---

[28] The other parameters are the cost of the change $C'(Z)$ (where $C(Z)$ is the cost function) and the effects of the change in Z on the outcomes of persons who are not affected by the change in Z. For the complete definition, see Heckman (1997) and Heckman and Smith (1998) or see the discussion in Heckman and Vytlacil (2000b).

[29] These equalities will hold for any distribution such that (U_D, U_1) and (U_D, U_0) are jointly symmetric around their means. As in the work of Powell (1987) and Chen (1999), symmetry is one assumption that can be exploited to achieve identification without large support assumptions.

7.1   *The Roy model*

Next consider the special case of a Roy model with sector-specific costs. In particular, consider a case where

$$D^* = (Y_1 - Y_0) - \varphi(W) - V$$
$$= [(\mu_1(x) - \mu_0(x)) - \varphi(W)] + [(U_1 - U_0) - V],$$

and

$$D = 1 \quad \text{if } D^* \geq 0, \quad = 0 \text{ otherwise,}$$

where $\varphi(W) + U_D$ is the cost of being in sector 1, $Y_1 - Y_0$ is the gross benefit of being in sector 1, and D^* is the net benefit of being in sector 1. The agent will choose to be in sector 1 if the gross benefit exceeds the cost, i.e., if $Y_1 - Y_0 \geq \varphi(W) + U_D$. This model is similar to models used to analyze labor supply, unionism and educational and occupational choice. Taking $Z = (W, X)$, $U_D = U_1 - U_0 - V$, and $\mu_D(z) = \mu_1(x) - \mu_0(x) - \varphi(w)$, this model is a special case of the model previously developed. If we continue to maintain assumptions (i)–(v) from Section 2, then all analysis of section 5 continues to hold.[30] Recall assumption (i), that $\mu_D(Z)$ be a nondegenerate random variable conditional on $X = x$. In the Roy model considered here, $\mu_D(Z) = \mu_1(X) - \mu_0(X) - \varphi(W)$, so that this assumption requires that $\varphi(W)$ be a nondegenerate random variable conditional on X. In other words, we require variables that do not affect the outcome equations but that affect the cost of selecting into treatment. The requirement for $\varphi(W)$ to be a nondegenerate random variable conditional on X rules out the special case of the original Roy model with no costs. To analyze such a model, restrict $\varphi(W) = 0$ and $V = 0$, so $D^* = Y_1 - Y_0 = \mu_1(X) - \mu_0(X) + U_1 - U_0$ and $U_D = -(U_1 - U_0)$. Assumption (i) no longer holds, but we impose conditions (ii)–(v).

The treatment parameters are still well defined, the relationship between the parameters continues to hold, but we are no longer able to identify the parameters from LIV. To establish these claims, note that

$$\Delta^{\text{MTE}}(x, u) = \mu_1(x) - \mu_0(x) + E(U_1 - U_0 \mid U_1 - U_0 = -u)$$
$$= \mu_1(x) - \mu_0(x) - u$$
$$\Delta^{\text{ATE}}(x, u) = \mu_1(x) - \mu_0(x) = \int \Delta^{\text{MTE}}(x, u) \, dF_U$$
$$\Delta^{\text{TT}}(x, D = 1) = \mu_1(x) - \mu_0(x)$$
$$\qquad + E(U_1 - U_0 \mid -(U_1 - U_0) \leq \mu_1(x) - \mu_0(x))$$
$$= \frac{1}{\Pr(D = 1 \mid X = x)} \int_{-\infty}^{\mu_1(x) - \mu_0(x)} \Delta^{\text{MTE}}(x, u) \, dF_U,$$

---

[30] In addition, by imposing the Roy model structure, one can identify the average cost of treatment parameters without observing any direct information on the cost of treatment. See Heckman and Vytlacil (2000b).

so that the same relationships exist among the parameters as established in the case when exclusion restrictions are present. However, there is no longer a well defined LIV estimator, since it is no longer possible to shift the index for the decision rule while holding X constant. Hence the instrumental variable argument breaks down in this case.

8   Conclusion

This chapter uses an index model or latent variable model to model selection variable D to impose structure on a model of potential outcomes that originates with Neyman (1923), Fisher (1935), and Cox (1958). We introduce the marginal treatment effect (MTE) parameter and its sample analog, the local IV (LIV) estimator, as devices for unifying different treatment parameters. Different treatment effect parameters are averaged versions of the marginal treatment parameter which differ according to how they weight the marginal parameter. ATE weights all marginal parameters equally. LATE gives equal weight to the marginal treatment parameters within a given interval. TT gives a larger weight to those marginal treatment parameters corresponding to the treatment effect for individuals who have larger values of the unobserved proclivity to participate in the program. The weighting of the marginal treatment parameter for the treatment on the treated parameter is like that obtained in length-biased or sized-biased samples.

The local IV estimator identifies the marginal treatment effect under conditions (i)–(v). Identification of LATE and LIV depends on the support of the propensity score, $P(Z)$. The larger the support of $P(Z)$, the larger the set of LATE and LIV parameters that are identified. Identification of ATE depends on observing $P(Z)$ values arbitrarily close to 1 and $P(Z)$ values arbitrarily close to 0. When such $P(Z)$ values are not observed, ATE can be bounded and the width of the bounds is linearly related to the distance between 1 and the largest $P(Z)$ and to the distance between 0 and the smallest $P(Z)$ value. For TT, identification requires that one observe $P(Z)$ values arbitrarily close to 0. If this condition does not hold, then the TT parameter can be bounded and the width of the bounds will be linearly related to the distance between 0 and the smallest $P(Z)$ value, holding $\Pr(D = 1 \mid X)$ constant.

Under full support conditions, the local IV estimator, when suitably weighted, can be used to estimate LATE, TT, and ATE in cases where linear IV cannot estimate these parameters. When support conditions fail, local IV can be use to bound LATE, TT, and ATE. Local IV is thus a more general and flexible estimation principle than linear IV, which, in the case of heterogeneous response to treatment, at most identifies LATE.

Appendix A: Relaxing additive separability and independence

There are two central assumptions that underlie the latent index representation used in this chapter: that U_D is independent of Z, and that U_D and Z are additively separable in the index. The latent index model with these two restrictions implies the independence and monotonicity assumptions of Imbens and Angrist (1994) and the latent index model implied by those assumptions implies a latent index model with a representation that satisfies both the independence and the monotonicity assumptions. In this appendix, we consider the sensitivity of the analysis presented in the text to relaxation of either of these assumptions.

First, consider allowing U_D and Z to be nonseparable in the treatment index:

$$D^* = \mu_D(Z, U_D),$$
$$D = 1 \quad \text{if } D^* \geq 0, \quad = 0 \text{ otherwise}$$

while maintaining the assumption that Z is independent of (U_D, U_1, U_0). We do not impose any restrictions on the cross partials of μ_D. The monotonicity condition of Imbens and Angrist (1994) is that for any (z, z') pair, $\mu_D(z, u) \geq \mu_D(z', u)$ for all u, or $\mu_D(z, u) \leq \mu_D(z', u)$ for all u.[31] Vytlacil (1999a) shows that monotonicity always implies one representation of μ_D as $\mu_D(z, u) = \mu(z) + u$. We now reconsider the analysis in the text without imposing the monotonicity condition by considering the latent index model without additive separability. Since we have imposed no structure on the $\mu_D(z, u)$ index, one can easily show that this model is equivalent to imposing the independence condition of Imbens and Angrist (1994) without imposing their monotonicity condition. A random coefficient discrete choice model with $\mu_D = Z\beta + \varepsilon$ where β and ε are random, and β can assume positive or negative values is an example of this case, i.e., $U_D = (\beta, \varepsilon)$.

We impose the regularity condition that, for any $z \in \text{Supp}(Z)$, $\mu_D(z, U_D)$ is absolutely continuous with respect to Lebesgue measure.[32] Let

$$\Omega(z) = \{u : \mu_D(z, u) \geq 0\},$$

so that

$$P(z) \equiv \Pr(D = 1 \mid Z = z) = \Pr(U_D \in \Omega(z)).$$

Under additive separability, $P(z) = P(z') \Leftrightarrow \Omega(z) = \Omega(z')$. This equivalence enables us to define the parameters in terms of the $P(z)$ index instead of the full z vector. In the more general case without additive separability, it is possible to

---

[31] Note that the monotonicity condition is a restriction across u. For a given fixed u, it will always trivially have to be the case that either $\mu_D(z, u) \geq \mu_D(z', u)$ or $\mu_D(z, u) \leq \mu_D(z', u)$.

[32] We impose this condition to ensure that $\Pr(\mu_D(z, U_D) = 0) = 0$ for any $z \in \text{Supp}(Z)$.

have (z, z') s.t. $P(z) = P(z')$ and $\Omega(z) \neq \Omega(z')$. In this case, we can no longer replace $Z = z$ with $P(Z) = P(z)$ in the conditioning sets.

Define as before:

$$\Delta^{\mathrm{MTE}}(x, u) = E(\Delta \mid X = x, U_D = u).$$

For ATE, we obtain the same expression as before:

$$\Delta^{\mathrm{ATE}}(x) = \int_0^1 E(\Delta \mid X = x, U_D = u) \, du.$$

For TT, we obtain a similar but slightly more complicated expression:

$$\begin{aligned}
\Delta^{\mathrm{TT}}(x, z, D = 1) &\equiv E(\Delta \mid X = x, Z = z, D = 1) \\
&= E(\Delta \mid X = x, U_D \in \Omega(z)) \\
&= \frac{1}{P(z)} \int_{\Omega(z)} E(\Delta \mid X = x, U_D = u) \, du.
\end{aligned}$$

Because it is no longer the case that we can define the parameter solely in terms of $P(z)$ instead of z, it is possible to have (z, z') such that $P(z) = P(z')$ but $\Delta^{\mathrm{TT}}(x, z, D = 1) \neq \Delta^{\mathrm{TT}}(x, z', D = 1)$.

Following the same derivation as used in the text for the TT parameter not conditional on Z,

$$\begin{aligned}
\Delta^{\mathrm{TT}}(x, D = 1) &\equiv E(\Delta \mid X = x, D = 1) \\
&= \int E(\Delta \mid X = x, Z = z, D = 1) \, dF_{Z \mid X, D}(z \mid x, 1) \\
&= \frac{1}{\Pr(D = 1 \mid X = x)} \\
&\quad \times \int \left[\int_0^1 \mathbf{1}[u \in \Omega(z)] E(\Delta \mid X = x, U_D = u) \, du \right] dF_{Z \mid X}(z \mid x) \\
&= \frac{1}{\Pr(D = 1 \mid X = x)} \\
&\quad \times \int_0^1 \left[\int \mathbf{1}[u \in \Omega(z)] E(\Delta \mid X = x, U_D = u) \, dF_{Z \mid X}(z \mid x) \right] du \\
&= \int_0^1 E(\Delta \mid X = x, U_D = u) g_x(u) \, du,
\end{aligned}$$

where

$$g_x(u) = \frac{\int \mathbf{1}[u \in \Omega(z)] \, dF_{Z \mid X}(z \mid x)}{\Pr(D = 1 \mid X = x)} = \frac{\Pr(D = 1 \mid U_D = u, X = x)}{\Pr(D = 1 \mid X = x)}.$$

Thus the definitions of the parameters and the relationships among them that are developed in the main text of this chapter generalize in a straightforward way to the nonseparable case. Separability allows us to define the parameters in terms of $P(z)$ instead of z and allows for slightly simpler expressions, but is not crucial for the definition of parameters or the relationship among them.

Separability is, however, crucial to the form of LATE when we allow U_D and Z to be additively nonseparable in the treatment index. For simplicity, we will keep the conditioning on X implicit. This analysis essentially replicates the analysis of Imbens of Angrist (1994) using a latent index representation. Define the following sets:

$$A(z, z') = \{u : \mu_D(z, u) \geq 0, \mu_D(z', u) \geq 0\}$$
$$B(z, z') = \{u : \mu_D(z, u) \geq 0, \mu_D(z', u) < 0\}$$
$$C(z, z') = \{u : \mu_D(z, u) < 0, \mu_D(z', u) < 0\}$$
$$D(z, z') = \{u : \mu_D(z, u) < 0, \mu_D(z', u) \geq 0\}.$$

Monotonicity implies that either $B(z, z')$ or $D(z, z')$ is empty. Suppressing the z, z' arguments, we have:

$$E(Y \mid Z=z) = \Pr(A \cup B)E(Y_1 \mid A \cup B) + \Pr(C \cup D)E(Y_0 \mid C \cup D)$$
$$E(Y \mid Z=z') = \Pr(A \cup D)E(Y_1 \mid A \cup D) + \Pr(B \cup C)E(Y_0 \mid B \cup C),$$

so that

$$\frac{E(Y \mid Z=z) - E(Y \mid Z=z')}{\Pr(D = 1 \mid Z=z) - \Pr(D = 1 \mid Z = z')} = \frac{E(Y \mid Z=z) - E(Y \mid Z=z')}{\Pr(A \cup B) - \Pr(A \cup D)}$$
$$= \frac{\Pr(B)E(Y_1 - Y_0 \mid B) - \Pr(D)E(Y_1 - Y_0 \mid D)}{\Pr(B) - \Pr(D)}$$
$$= w_B E(\Delta \mid B) - w_D E(\Delta \mid D)$$

with

$$w_B = \frac{\Pr(B \mid B \cup D)}{\Pr(B \mid B \cup D) - \Pr(D \mid B \cup D)}$$
$$w_D = \frac{\Pr(D \mid B \cup D)}{\Pr(B \mid B \cup D) - \Pr(D \mid B \cup D)}.$$

Under monotonicity, either $\Pr(B) = 0$ and LATE identifies $E(\Delta \mid D)$ or $\Pr(D) = 0$ and LATE identifies $E(\Delta \mid B)$. Without monotonicity, the IV estimator used as the sample analog to LATE converges to the above weighted difference in the two terms, and the relationship between LATE and the other treatment parameters presented in the text no longer holds.

Consider what would happen if we could condition on a given u. For $u \in A \cup C$, the denominator is zero and the parameter is not well defined. For $u \in B$, the parameter is $E(\Delta \mid U_D = u)$, for $u \in D$, the parameter is $E(\Delta \mid U_D = u)$. If we could restrict conditioning to $u \in B$ (or $u \in D$), we would obtain monotonicity within the restricted sample.

Now consider LIV. For simplicity, assume z is a scalar. Assume $\mu_D(z, u)$ is continuously differentiable in (z, u), with $\mu^j(z, u)$ denoting the partial derivative with respect to the jth argument. Assume that $\mu_D(z, U_D)$ is absolutely continuous with respect to Lebesgue measure. Fix some evaluation point, z_0. One can show that there may be at most a countable number of u points s.t. $\mu_D(z_0, u) = 0$. Let $j \in \mathcal{J} = \{1, ..., L\}$ index the set of u evaluation points s.t. $\mu_D(z_0, u) = 0$, where L may be infinity, and thus write: $\mu_D(z_0, u_j) = 0$ for all $j \in \mathcal{J}$. (Both the number of such evaluation points and the evaluation points themselves depend on the evaluation point, z_0, but we suppress this dependence for notational convenience.) Assume that there exists

$$\{B_k\}_{k \in \mathcal{J}}, \sum_{k \in \mathcal{J}} B_k < \infty,$$

such that

$$\left| \frac{\mu^1(z, u_k)}{\mu^2(z, u_k)} \right| \le B_k$$

for $k \in \mathcal{J}$, and all z in some neighborhood of z_0. One can show that

$$\frac{\partial}{\partial z}[E(Y \mid Z = z_0)] = \sum_{k=1}^{L} \frac{\mu^1(z_0, u_k)}{|\mu^2(z_0, u_k)|} E(\Delta \mid U_D = u_k)$$

and

$$\frac{\partial}{\partial z}[\Pr(D = 1 \mid Z = z)] = \sum_{k=1}^{L} \frac{\mu^1(z, u_k)}{|\mu^2(z, u_k)|}.$$

LIV is the ratio of these two terms, and does not in general equal the MTE. Thus, the relationship between LIV and MTE breaks down in the nonseparable case.

As an example, take the case where L is finite and $\left| \frac{\mu^1(z, u_k)}{\mu^2(z, u_k)} \right|$ does not vary with k. Using the fact that U_D is distributed unit uniform, we have

$$\begin{aligned}
\Delta^{\mathrm{LIV}}(z_0) &= \Pr(\mu^1(z_0, U_D) > 0 \mid \mu(z_0, U_D) = 0) \\
&\quad \times E(\Delta \mid \mu_D(z_0, U_D) = 0, \mu^1(z_0, U_D) > 0) \\
&\quad - \Pr(\mu^1(z_0, U_D) < 0 \mid \mu(z_0, U_D) = 0) \\
&\quad \times E(\Delta \mid \mu_D(z_0, U_D) = 0, \mu^1(z_0, U_D) < 0).
\end{aligned}$$

Thus, while the definition of the parameters and the relationship among them does not depend crucially on the additive separability assumption, the connection between the LATE or LIV estimators and the underlying parameters crucially depends on the additive separability assumption.

Next consider the assumption that U_D and Z are separable in the treatment index while allowing them to be stochastically dependent:

$$D^* = \mu_D(Z) - U_D,$$
$$D = 1 \quad \text{if } D^* \geq 0, \quad = 0 \text{ otherwise}$$

with Z independent of (U_1, U_0), and U_D distributed unit uniform, but allowing Z and U_D to be stochastically dependent. The analysis of Vytlacil (1999a) can be easily adapted to show that the latent index model with separability but without imposing independence is equivalent to imposing the monotonicity assumption of Imbens and Angrist without imposing their independence assumption.[33]

We have

$$\Omega(z) = \{u : \mu(z) \leq u\}$$

and

$$P(z) \equiv \Pr(D = 1 \mid Z = z) = \Pr(U \in \Omega(z) \mid Z = z).$$

Note that $\Omega(z) = \Omega(z') \Rightarrow \mu_D(z) = \mu_D(z')$, but $\Omega(z) = \Omega(z')$ does not imply $P(z) = P(z')$ since the distribution of U conditional on $Z = z$ need not equal the distribution of U conditional on $Z = z'$. Likewise, $P(z) = P(z')$ does not imply $\Omega(z) = \Omega(z')$. As occurred in the nonseparable case, we can no longer replace $Z = z$ with $P(Z) = P(z)$ in the conditioning sets.[34]

Consider the definition of the parameters and the relationship among them. The definition of MTE and ATE in no way involves Z, nor does the relationship between them, so that both their definition and their relationship remains unchanged by allowing Z and U_D to be dependent. Now consider the TT parameter:

$$\Delta^{\mathrm{TT}}(x, z, D = 1) = E(\Delta \mid X = x, Z = z, U_D \leq \mu_D(z))$$

$$= \frac{1}{P(z)} \int_0^{\mu_D(z)} E(\Delta \mid X = x, U_D = u) \, dF_{U \mid Z, X}(u \mid z, x)$$

$$= \frac{1}{P(z)} \int_0^{\mu_D(z)} E(\Delta \mid X = x, U_D = u) \frac{f_{Z \mid U, X}(z \mid u, x)}{f_{Z \mid X}(z \mid x)} \, dF_U(u),$$

---

[33] To show that the monotonicity assumption implies a separable latent index model, one can follow the proofs of Vytlacil (1999a) with the sole modification of replacing $P(z) = \Pr(D = 1 \mid Z = z)$ with $\Pr(D_z = 1)$, where D_z is the indicator variable for whether the agent would have received treatment if Z had been externally set to z.

[34] However, we again have equivalence between the alternative conditioning sets if we assume index sufficiency, i.e., that $F_{U \mid Z}(u \mid z) = F_{U \mid P(Z)}(u \mid P(z))$.

where $f_{Z|X}$ and $f_{Z|U,X}$ denote the densities corresponding to $F_{Z|X}$ and $F_{Z|U,X}$ with respect to the appropriate dominating measure. We thus obtain

$$\Delta^{TT}(x, D = 1) = E(\Delta \mid X = x, U_D \leq \mu_D(Z))$$

$$= \frac{1}{\Pr(D = 1 \mid X = x)} \int \left[\int \int_0^{\mu_D(z)} E(\Delta \mid X = x, U_D = u) \right.$$

$$\left. \times \frac{f_{Z|U,X}(z \mid u, x)}{f_{Z|X}(z \mid x)} dF_U(u) \right] dF_{Z|X}(z \mid x)$$

$$= \frac{1}{\Pr(D = 1 \mid X = x)} \int \left[\int \mathbf{1}[u \leq \mu_D(z)] \right.$$

$$\left. \times E(\Delta \mid X = x, U_D = u) \frac{f_{Z|U,X}(z \mid u, x)}{f_{Z|X}(z \mid x)} dF_{Z|X}(z \mid x) \right]$$

$$= \frac{1}{\Pr(D = 1 \mid X = x)} \int \left[\int \mathbf{1}[u \leq \mu_D(z)] \right.$$

$$\left. \times E(\Delta \mid X = x, U_D = u) dF_{Z|U,X}(z \mid u, x) \right] dF_U(u)$$

$$= \int_0^1 E(\Delta \mid X = x, U_D = u) g_x(u) \, du,$$

where again

$$g_x(u) = \frac{\Pr(D = 1 \mid U_D = u, X = x)}{\Pr(D = 1 \mid X = x)}.$$

We thus have that the definitions of parameters and the relationships among the parameters that are developed in the text generalize naturally to the case where Z and U_D are stochastically dependent. Independence (combined with the additive separability assumption) allows us to define the parameters in terms of $P(z)$ instead of z and allows for slightly simpler expressions, but is not crucial for the definition of parameters or the relationship among them.

We next investigate LATE when we allow U_D and Z to be stochastically dependent. We have

$$E(Y \mid X = x, Z = z)$$

$$= P(z)[E(Y_1 \mid X = x, Z = z, D = 1)]$$

$$+ (1 - P(z))[E(Y_0 \mid X = x, Z = z, D = 0)]$$

$$= \int_0^{\mu_D(z)} E(Y_1 \mid X = x, U_D = u) \, dF_{U|X,Z}(u \mid x, z)$$

$$+ \int_{\mu_D(z)}^0 E(Y_0 \mid X = x, U_D = u) \, dF_{U|X,Z}(u \mid x, z).$$

For simplicity, take the case where $\mu_D(z) > \mu_D(z')$. Then

$$
\begin{aligned}
E(Y \mid X = x, Z = z) &- E(Y \mid X = x, Z = z') \\
= &\left[\int_{\mu_D(z')}^{\mu_D(z)} E(Y_1 \mid X = x, U_D = u) \, dF_{U \mid X,Z}(u \mid x, z) \right. \\
&\left. - \int_{\mu_D(z')}^{\mu_D(z)} E(Y_0 \mid X = x, U_D = u) \, dF_{U \mid X,Z}(u \mid x, z') \right] \\
&+ \int_0^{\mu_D(z')} E(Y_1 \mid X = x, U_D = u)[dF_{U \mid X,Z}(u \mid x, z) - dF_{U \mid X,Z}(u \mid x, z')] \\
&+ \int_{\mu_D(z)}^1 E(Y_0 \mid X = x, U_D = u)[dF_{U \mid X,Z}(u \mid x, z) - dF_{U \mid X,Z}(u \mid x, z')]
\end{aligned}
$$

and thus

$$
\begin{aligned}
\Delta^{\text{LATE}}(x, z, z') \\
= &\, \delta_0(z) E(Y_1 \mid X = x, Z = z, \mu_D(z') \le U_D \le \mu_D(z)) \\
&- \delta_0(z') E(Y_0 \mid X = x, Z = z', \mu_D(z') \le U_D \le \mu_D(z)) \\
&+ [\delta_1(z) E(Y_1 \mid X = x, Z = z, U_D \le \mu_D(z')) - \delta_1(z') \\
&\quad \times E(Y_1 \mid X = x, Z = z', U_D \le \mu_D(z'))] \\
&+ [\delta_2(z) E(Y_0 \mid X = x, Z = z, U_D > \mu_D(z)) - \delta_2(z') \\
&\quad \times E(Y_1 \mid X = x, Z = z', U_D > \mu_D(z))]
\end{aligned}
$$

with

$$
\delta_0(t) = \frac{\Pr(\mu_D(z') \le U_D \le \mu_D(z) \mid Z = t)}{\Pr(U_D \le \mu_D(z) \mid Z = z, X = x) - \Pr(U_D \le \mu_D(z') \mid Z = z', X = x)}
$$

$$
\delta_1(t) = \frac{\Pr(U_D \le \mu_D(z') \mid Z = t)}{\Pr(U_D \le \mu_D(z) \mid Z = z, X = x) - \Pr(U_D \le \mu_D(z') \mid Z = z', X = x)}
$$

$$
\delta_2(t) = \frac{\Pr(U_D > \mu_D(z) \mid Z = t)}{\Pr(U_D \le \mu_D(z) \mid Z = z, X = x) - \Pr(U_D \le \mu_D(z') \mid Z = z', X = x)}
$$

Note that $\delta_0(z) = \delta_0(z') = 1$ and the two terms in the preceding expression are zero in the case where Z and U_D are independent. In the more general case, δ_0 may be bigger or smaller than 1, and the terms in brackets are of unknown sign. In general, LATE may be negative even when Δ is positive for all individuals.

Now consider LIV. For simplicity, take the case where Z is a continuous scalar r.v. Let $f_{U|Z}(u|z)$ denote the density of U_D conditional on $Z = z$, and assume that this density is differentiable in z. Then, using equation (21), we have

$$\frac{\partial E(Y \mid X = x, Z = z)}{\partial z} = E(\Delta \mid X = x, U_D = \mu_D(z))\mu_D'(z)$$

$$+ \left[\int_0^{\mu_D(z)} E(Y_1 \mid X = x, U_D = u) \frac{\partial f_{U \mid Z}(u \mid z)}{\partial z} \, du \right.$$

$$\left. + \int_{\mu_D(z)}^1 E(Y_0 \mid X = x, U_D = u) \frac{\partial f_{U \mid Z}(u \mid z)}{\partial z} \, du \right],$$

and

$$\frac{\partial \Pr(D = 1 \mid Z = z)}{\partial z} = \mu_D'(z) + \int_0^{\mu_D(z)} \frac{\partial f_{U \mid Z}(u \mid z)}{\partial z} \, du.$$

LIV is the ratio of the two terms. Thus, without the independence condition, the relationship between LIV and the MTE breaks down.

Appendix B: Comparison with previous literature on bounds under IV assumptions.

The bounds constructed in this paper are related to previous literature on bounding the average treatment effect under instrumental variable assumptions. We first compare our bounding analysis with that of Manski (1990) and then with the analysis of Balke and Pearl (1997). All analysis in this section assumes that the outcomes are bounded. In particular, we assume that there exists $y_x^u < \infty$, $y_x^l > -\infty$, such that $\Pr[y_x^u \geq Y_j \geq y_x^l \mid X = x] = 1$ for $j = 0, 1$. Without loss of generality, assume $\Pr[D = 1 \mid X, Z] = \Pr[D = 1 \mid Z]$.[35]

First consider the analysis of Manski (1990). Manski considers the mean-independence form of the IV assumption: $E(Y_j \mid X, Z) = E(Y_j \mid X)$ for $j = 0, 1$. Let $\mathcal{Z}_x$ denote the support of Z conditional on $X = x$. Using the law of iterated expectations and the assumption that $E(Y_1 \mid X, Z) = E(Y_1 \mid X)$, we have for any x in the support of X and $z \in \mathcal{Z}_x$,

$$P(z)E(Y_1 \mid D = 1, X = x, Z = z) + (1 - P(z))y_x^l$$

$$\leq E(Y_1 \mid X = x) \leq P(z)E(Y_1 \mid D = 1, X = x, Z = z) + (1 - P(z))y_x^u.$$

Since these bounds hold for all $z \in \mathcal{Z}_x$, we have

$$\sup_{z \in \mathcal{Z}_x} \left\{ P(z)E(Y_1 \mid D = 1, X = x, Z = z) + (1 - P(z))y_x^l \right\}$$

$$\leq E(Y_1 \mid X = x) \leq \inf_{z \in \mathcal{Z}_x} \left\{ P(z)E(Y_1 \mid D = 1, X = x, Z = z) + (1 - P(z))y_x^u \right\}.$$

---

[35] To see that this is without loss of generality, note that we can always include each element of X in Z without affecting the analysis since all analysis is done conditional on X.

Following the parallel argument for $E(Y_0 \mid X = x)$, Manski derives the following sharp bounds under the mean independence assumption:

$$B_x^L \le E(Y_1 - Y_0 \mid X = x) \le B_x^U,$$

with

$$
\begin{aligned}
B_x^U &= \inf_{z \in \mathcal{Z}_x} \left\{ P(z)E(Y_1 \mid D = 1, X = x, Z = z) + (1 - P(z))y_x^u \right\} \\
&\quad - \sup_{z \in \mathcal{Z}_x} \left\{ (1 - P(z))(E(Y_0 \mid D = 0, X = x, Z = z) + P(z)y_x^l \right\}, \\
B_x^L &= \sup_{z \in \mathcal{Z}_x} \left\{ P(z)E(Y_1 \mid D = 1, X = x, Z = z) + (1 - P(z))y_x^l \right\} \\
&\quad - \inf_{z \in \mathcal{Z}_x} \left\{ (1 - P(z))(E(Y_0 \mid D = 0, X = x, Z = z) + P(z)y_x^u \right\}.
\end{aligned}
$$

Our analysis imposes the nonparametric selection model. Our assumptions imply the mean independence conditions of Manski, so that his bounds hold given our assumptions. We now show that, under our assumptions, our bounds on the average treatment effect coincide with those of Manski.

Claim 1. *Impose the nonparametric selection model defined by equation (1) and conditions (i)–(v). The Heckman–Vytlacil bounds coincide with the Manski mean-independence bounds.*

Proof: We first show that the first term of the Heckman–Vytlacil upper bound coincides with the first term of the Manski upper bound,

$$
\inf_{z \in \mathcal{Z}_x} \left\{ P(z)E(Y_1 \mid D = 1, X = x, Z = z) + (1 - P(z))y_x^u \right\}
$$
$$
= p_x^{\max} E\left(Y_1 \mid D = 1, X = x, P(Z) = p_x^{\max}\right) + \left(1 - p_x^{\max}\right)y_x^u.
$$

Fix any $x \in \text{Supp}(X)$, fix any $z \in \mathcal{Z}_x$.

$$
\begin{aligned}
&\left[p_x^{\max} E\left(Y_1 \mid D = 1, X = x, P(Z) = p_x^{\max}\right) + \left(1 - p_x^{\max}\right)y_x^u \right] \\
&\quad - \left[P(z)E(Y_1 \mid D = 1, X = x, Z = z) + (1 - P(z))y_x^u \right] \\
&= \left[\int_0^{p_x^{\max}} E(Y_1 \mid X = x, U_D = u)\, du + \left(1 - p_x^{\max}\right)y_x^u \right] \\
&\quad - \left[\int_0^{P(z)} E(Y_1 \mid X = x, U_D = u)\, du + (1 - P(z))y_x^u \right] \\
&= \int_{P(z)}^{p_x^{\max}} E(Y_1 \mid X = x, U_D = u)\, du - \left(p_x^{\max} - P(z)\right)y_x^u \\
&= \int_{P(z)}^{p_x^{\max}} \left[E(Y_1 \mid X = x, U_D = u) - y_x^u \right] du \\
&\le 0.
\end{aligned}
$$

Since this inequality holds for any $z \in \mathcal{Z}_x$, we have

$$p_x^{\max} E\left(Y_1 | D = 1, X = x, P(Z) = p_x^{\max}\right) + \left(1 - p_x^{\max}\right) y_x^u$$

$$\leq \inf_{z \in \mathcal{Z}_x} \left\{ P(z) E(Y_1 | D = 1, X = x, Z = z) + (1 - P(z)) y_x^u \right\}.$$

Using that $E(Y_1 | X = x, U_D = u) - y_x^u$ is bounded and the definition of $p_x^{\max}$, we have that

$$p_x^{\max} E\left(Y_1 | D = 1, X = x, P(Z) = p_x^{\max}\right) + \left(1 - p_x^{\max}\right) y_x^u$$

$$\geq \inf_{z \in \mathcal{Z}_x} \left\{ P(z) E(Y_1 | D = 1, X = x, Z = z) + (1 - P(z)) y_x^u \right\},$$

and thus

$$p_x^{\max} E\left(Y_1 | D = 1, X = x, P(Z) = p_x^{\max}\right) + \left(1 - p_x^{\max}\right) y_x^u$$

$$= \inf_{z \in \mathcal{Z}_x} \left\{ P(z) E(Y_1 | D = 1, X = x, Z = z) + (1 - P(z)) y_x^u \right\}.$$

By the parallel argument, all other terms of the two sets of bounds coincide.

□

Thus, our bounds on ATE derived from the index structure coincide with the Manski bounds derived from a mean independence assumption. Imposing the nonparametric selection model allows a much simpler form for the bounds, and evaluating the bounds does not require evaluating the conditional expectations at every value in the support of Z, but only at $P(Z) = p_x^{\max}$ and $P(Z) = p_x^{\min}$. In contrast, the Manski bounds do not simplify under his assumptions if no further structure is imposed.

While the Manski bounds are tight under mean-independence, our analysis imposes additional conditions. We now discuss the question of whether our bounds are tight given that a nonparametric selection model has been imposed. This issue arises in relating our analysis to that of Balke and Pearl (1997). For the case where Y and Z are binary, Balke and Pearl consider bounds that impose stronger restrictions than are imposed in the Manski analysis. In particular, Balke and Pearl impose the same statistical independence condition as Imbens and Angrist (1994):

$$(Y_1, Y_0, D_0, D_1) \perp\!\!\!\perp Z | X,$$

where $\perp\!\!\!\perp$ denotes statistical independence and D_z denotes the counterfactual choice that would have been observed if Z had been externally set to z. Note that this independence condition strengthens the Manski assumptions not only by imposing statistical independence of potential outcomes from Z instead of mean-independence from Z, but also by imposing independence of the counterfactual choices from Z. When Z and Y are binary, Balke and Pearl show that the sharp bounds under their statistical independence condition are narrower in general than the Manski bounds, although their bounds and the Manski bounds coincide for some distributions of the observed data. In the context of binary Z and Y, Balke and Pearl discuss the LATE monotonicity condition: either $D_1 \geq D_0$ everywhere or $D_1 \leq D_0$ everywhere. They show that this assumption imposes constraints on the observed data which imply that their bounds and the Manski mean-independence bounds will coincide.[36]

Our analysis imposes the nonparametric selection model. As demonstrated by Vytlacil (1999), imposing a nonparametric selection model is equivalent to imposing the independence and monotonicity conditions of LATE analysis. Thus, for the nonparametric selection model, we have from the analysis of Balke and Pearl that the tight bounds when Y and Z are binary are the Manski mean-independence bounds, and thus our bounds are tight when Y and Z are binary. Since we do not require that either Y or Z be binary in our analysis, the question arises of whether our bounds are tight under the nonparametric selection model when Y or Z is not binary. We demonstrate the following claim.

Claim 2. *Impose the nonparametric selection model defined by equation (1) and conditions (i)–(v). Then the Heckman–Vytlacil bounds on ATE are tight.*

Proof: The logic of the proof is as follows. We show that the Heckman–Vytlacil upper bound is tight by showing there exists a distribution with the following properties: (i) the distribution is consistent with the observed data; (ii) the distribution is consistent with all of the Heckman–Vytlacil assumptions; and (iii) $E(Y_1 - Y_0 \mid X)$ evaluated under the distribution equals the Heckman–Vytlacil upper bounds. Thus, no smaller upper bound can be constructed and therefore the Heckman–Vytlacil upper bound is tight. By the parallel argument, the Heckman–Vytlacil lower bound is tight. We prove the existence of such a distribution by constructing one that conforms to conditions (i)–(iii).

For any random variable A, let F_A^0 denote the "true" CDF of A, and let $F_{A|B}^0(\cdot \mid b)$ denote the true CDF of A conditional on $B = b$. For $(u, x) \in$ Supp(U, X), define

$$F_{Y_1 \mid U_D, X}(y_1 \mid u, x) = \begin{cases} F_{Y_1 \mid U_D, X}^0(y_1 \mid u, x) & \text{if } u \leq p_x^{\max} \\ 1[y_1 \geq y_x^u] & \text{if } u > p_x^{\max} \end{cases},$$

$$F_{Y_0 \mid U_D, X}(y_0 \mid u, x) = \begin{cases} F_{Y_0 \mid U_D, X}^0(y_0 \mid u, x) & \text{if } u \geq p_x^{\min} \\ 1[y_0 \geq y_x^l] & \text{if } u < p_x^{\min} \end{cases}.$$

Note that this is implicitly defining a (not necessarily unique) distribution for

---

U_1 and U_0 conditional on U_D, X. Define

$$F_{Y_0,Y_1,U_D,X,Z}(y_0, y_1, u, x, z)$$

$$= \int \left[\int_0^u F_{Y_0 \mid U_D,X}(y_0 \mid t_u, t_x) F_{Y_1 \mid U_D,X}(y_1 \mid t_u, t_x) \, dF^0_{U_D}(t_u) \right]$$

$$\times 1[t_x \leq x, t_z \leq z] \, dF^0_{X,Z}(t_x, t_z).$$

Where $F^0_{X,Z}$ and $F^0_{U_D}$ are the "true" distributions of (X, Z) and U_D. Note that F is a proper CDF and that F is a distribution satisfying Y_1, Y_0 bounded conditional on X, satisfying Z independent of (Y_0, Y_1, U_D) conditional on X, and satisfying X independent of U_D. By construction, $F_{X,Z,U_D}(x, z, u) = F^0_{X,Z,U_D}(x, z, u)$ so that $F_{X,Z,D}(x, z, d) = F^0_{X,Z,D}(x, z, d)$. In addition, using that $F_{Y_1 \mid U_D,X}(y_1 \mid u, x) = F^0_{Y_1 \mid U_D,X}(y_1 \mid u, x)$ for $u \leq p_x^{\max}$, we have

$$F_{Y_1 \mid X,Z,D}(y_1 \mid x, z, 1) = \int_0^{P(z)} F^0_{Y_1 \mid U_D,X}(y_1 \mid u, x) \, dF^0_{U_D,X}(u, x)$$

$$= F^0_{Y_1 \mid X,Z,D}(y_1 \mid x, z, 1)$$

for $(x, z) \in \text{Supp}(X, Z \mid D = 1)$. By a parallel argument,

$$F_{Y_0 \mid X,Z,D}(y_0 \mid x, z, 0) = F^0_{Y_0 \mid X,Z,D}(y_0 \mid x, z, 0)$$

for $(x, z) \in \text{Supp}(X, Z \mid D = 0)$. Combining these results, we have

$$F_{Y,X,Z,D}(y, x, z, d) = F^0_{Y,X,Z,D}(y, x, z, d).$$

We thus have that F is observationally equivalent to the true F^0.

The expected value of $Y_1 - Y_0$ under F equals the Heckman–Vytlacil upper bound:

$$E(Y_1 - Y_0 \mid X) = \int \left[\int y_1 \, dF_{Y_1 \mid U_D,X}(y_1 \mid u, x) \right] dF^0_{U_D}(u)$$

$$- \int \left[\int y_0 \, dF_{Y_0 \mid U_D,X}(y_0 \mid u, x) \right] dF^0_{U_D}(u)$$

$$= \Pr\left[U_D \leq p_x^{\max}\right] \int \left[\int_0^{p_x^{\max}} y_1 \, dF^0_{Y_1 \mid U_D,X}(y_1 \mid u, x) \right]$$

$$\times dF^0_{U_D}(u) + \Pr\left[U_D > p_x^{\max}\right] y_x^u$$

$$- \Pr\left[U_D > p_x^{\min}\right] \int \left[\int_{p_x^{\min}}^1 y_0 \, dF^0_{Y_0 \mid U_D,X}(y_0 \mid u, x) \right]$$

$$\times dF^0_{U_D}(u) - \Pr\left[U_D \leq p_x^{\min}\right] y_x^l$$

$$= p_x^{\max} E\left(Y_1 \mid X, P(Z) = p_x^{\max}, D = 1\right) + p_x^{\max} y_x^u$$

$$- p_x^{\min} E\left(Y_0 \mid X, P(Z) = p_x^{\min}, D = 0\right) - p_x^{\min} y_x^l.$$

Since the expected value of $Y_1 - Y_0$ under F equals the Heckman–Vytlacil upper bound, and since F satisfies all of the required properties of the nonparametric selection model and is observationally equivalent to the true F^0, we have that the Heckman–Vytlacil upper bound is tight. By the parallel argument, we have that the Heckman–Vytlacil lower bound is tight.   □

Thus, the results of this paper can be seen as an extension of the Balke and Pearl results for binary Y and Z under the LATE conditions. While they show that the tight bounds for binary Y and Z under the LATE conditions coincide with the Manski mean-independence bounds, our analysis shows that the tight bounds for Y and Z having any support under the LATE conditions coincide with the Manski mean-independence bounds while having a much simpler form than the Manski mean-independence bounds.

REFERENCES

Amemiya, T. (1973), "Regression Analysis When the Dependent Variable is Truncated Normal," *Econometrica*, **41**, 997–1016.

(1985), *Advanced Econometrics* (Cambridge MA: Harvard University Press).

Angrist, J., Graddy, K., and Imbens, G. (1995), "Non-Parametric Demand Analysis with an Application to the Demand for Fish," NBER working paper No. T0178.

Angrist, J., Imbens, G., and Rubin, D. (1996), "Identification of Causal Effects Using Instrumental Variables," *Journal of the American Statistical Association*, **91**, 444–455.

Balke, A. and Pearl, J. (1997), "Bounds on Treatment Effects From Studies with Imperfect Compliance," *Journal of the American Statistical Association*, **92**, 1171–1176.

Bjorklund, A. and Moffitt, R. (1987), "The Estimation of Wage Gains and Welfare Gains in Self-Selection Models," *Review of Economics and Statistics*, **69**, 42–49.

Boadway, R. and Bruce, N. (1984), *Welfare Economics* (Oxford: U.K. Blackwell).

Chen, S. (1999), "Distribution-Free Estimation of the Random Coefficient Dummy Endogenous Variable Model," *Journal of Econometrics*, **91**, 171–199.

Chipman, J. and Moore, J. (1976), "Why an Increase in GNP Need Not Imply an Improvement in Potential Welfare," *Kylos*, **29**, 391–418.

Cox, D. R. (1958), *The Planning of Experiments* (New York: Wiley).

Das, M. and Newey, W. (1998), "Non-parametric Estimation of the Sample Selection Model," unpublished working paper, Massachusetts Institute of Technology.

Davidson, C. and Woodbury, S. (1993), "The Displacement Effect of Reemployment Bonus Programs," *Journal of Labor Economics*, **11**(4), 575–607.

Fisher, R. A. (1935), *Design of Experiments* (London: Oliver and Boyd).

Gronau, R. (1974), "Wage Comparisons: A Selectivity Bias," *Journal of Political Economy*, **82**, 1119–1143.

Harberger, A. (1971), "Three Basic Postulates for Applied Welfare Economics: An Interpretive Essay," *Journal of Economic Literature*, **9**, 785–797.

Heckman, J. (1974), "Shadow Prices, Market Wages and Labor Supply," *Econometrica*, **42**, 679–694.

(1980), "Addendum to Sample Selection Bias as a Specification Error," in G. Farkas, ed., *Evaluation Studies Review Annual, Vol. 5* (Sage Publications).

(1990), "Varieties of Selection Bias," *American Economic Review*, **80**, 313–318.

(1992), "Randomization and Social Policy Evaluation," in C. Manski and I. Garfinkel, eds., *Evaluating Welfare and Training Programs* (Cambridge, MA: Harvard University Press).

(1997, first draft 1995), "Instrumental Variables: A Study of Implicit Behavioral Assumptions Used in Making Program Evaluations," *Journal of Human Resources* **32**, 441–462.

Heckman, J. and Honoré, B. (1990), "The Empirical Content of the Roy Model," *Econometrica*, **58**, 1121–1149.

Heckman, J., Ichimura, H., Smith, J., and Todd, P. (1996), "Sources of Selection Bias in Evaluating Social Programs: An Interpretation of Conventional Measures and Evidence on the Effectiveness of Matching as a Program Evaluation Method," *Proceedings of the National Academy of Sciences, 93*, 13416–13420.

Heckman, J., Ichimura, H., Smith, J., and Todd, P. (1998), "Characterizing Selection Bias Using Experimental Data," *Econometrica*, **66**, 1017–1098.

Heckman, J., Ichimura, H., and Todd, P. (1998), "Matching As An Econometric Evaluation Estimator," *Review of Economic Studies*, **65**, 261–294.

Heckman, J., LaLonde, R., and Smith, J. (1999), "The Economics and Econometrics of Active Labor Market Programs," in O. Ashenfelter and D. Card, eds., *Handbook of Labor Economics, Volume 3* (Amsterdam: Elsevier), 1865–2097.

Heckman, J., Lochner, L., and Taber, C. (1998), "General Equilibrium Treatment Effects: A Study of Tuition Policy," *American Economic Review*, **88**, 381–386.

Heckman, J. and MaCurdy, T. (1985), "A Simultaneous Equations Linear Probability Model," *Canadian Journal of Economics*, **18**, 28–37.

Heckman, J. and Robb, R. (1985), "Alternative Methods for Estimating the Impact of Interventions," in J. Heckman and B. Singer, eds., *Longitudinal Analysis of Labor Market Data* (New York: Cambridge University Press), 156–245.

(1986), "Alternative Methods for Solving the Problem of Selection Bias in Evaluating the Impact of Treatments on Outcomes," in H. Wainer, ed., *Drawing Inference From Self-Selected Samples* (NY: Springer-Verlag), 63–107.

Heckman, J. and Smith, J. (1998, first draft 1995), "Evaluating The Welfare State," in S. Strom, ed., *Econometrics and Economic Theory in the 20th Century: The Ragnar Frisch Centennial*, Econometric Society Monograph Series (Cambridge, UK: Cambridge University Press).

Heckman, J. and Vytlacil, E. (1999a), "Identifying and Estimating Correlated Random Coefficient Models of the Impact of Schooling and Training on Earnings," unpublished working paper, University of Chicago.

(1999b), "Local Instrumental Variables and Latent Variable Models for Identifying and Bounding Treatment Effects," *Proceedings of the National Academy of Sciences*, **96**, 4730–4734.

(2000a) "The Relationship Between Treatment Parameters within a Latent Variable Framework," *Economic Letters*, **66**, 33–39.

(2000b), "Econometric Evaluations of Social Programs," forthcoming in J. Heckman and E. Leamer, eds., *Handbook of Econometrics, Volume 5* (North-Holland: Amsterdam).

Imbens, G. and Angrist, J. (1994), "Identification and Estimation of Local Average Treatment Effects," *Econometrica*, **62**, 467–476.

Junker, B. and Ellis, J. (1997), "A Characterization of Monotone Unidimensional Latent Variable Models," *Annals of Statistics*, **25**, 1327–1343.

Kolmogorov, A. N. and Fomin, S. V. (1970), *Introductory Real Analysis*, R. Silverman, trans. (Mineola, NY: Dover Publications).

Laffont, J. J. (1989), *Fundamentals of Public Economics* (Cambridge, MA: MIT Press).

Lewis, H. G. (1963), *Unionism and Relative Wages* (Chicago: University of Chicago Press).

McFadden, D. (1981), "Econometric Models of Probabilistic Choice," in D. McFadden and C. Manski, eds., *Structural Analysis of Discrete Data* (Cambridge, MA: MIT Press).

Manski, C. (1990), "Nonparametric Bounds on Treatment Effects," *American Economic Review*, **80**, 319–323.

Moffitt, R. (1992), "Evaluation of Program Entry Effects," in C. Manski and I. Garfinkel, eds., *Evaluating Welfare and Training Programs* (Cambridge, MA: Harvard University Press).

Neyman, J. (1923), "Statistical Problems in Agricultural Experiments," Supplement to the *Journal of Royal Statistical Society*, **2**(2), 107–180.

Powell, J. L. (1987), "Symmetrically Trimmed Least Squares Estimation for Tobit Models," *Econometrica*, **54**, 1435–1460.

Quandt, R. (1972), "Methods for Estimating Switching Regressions," *Journal of The American Statistical Association*, **67**(338), 306–310.

(1988), *The Econometrics of Disequilibrium* (Oxford: Blackwell).

Rao, C. R. (1985), "Weighted Distributions," in A. Atkinson, and S. Feinberg, eds., *A Celebration of Statistics: The ISI Centenary Volume* (Berlin: Springer-Verlag), 543–569.

Robins, J. (1989), "The Analysis of Randomized and Non-randomized AIDS Treatment Trials Using a New Approach to Causal Inference in Longitudinal Studies," in L. Sechrest, H. Freeman and A. Mulley, eds., *Health Service Research Methodology: A Focus on AIDS* (U.S. Public Health Service, Washington, DC), 113–159.

Rosenbaum, P. and Rubin, D. (1983), "The Central Role of the Propensity Score in Observational Studies for Causal Effects," *Biometrika*, **70**, 41–55.

Roy, A. (1951), "Some Thoughts on the Distribution of Earnings," *Oxford Economic Papers*, **3**, 135–146.

Rubin, D. (1978), "Bayesian Inference for Casual Effects: The Role of Randomization," *Annals of Statistics*, **6**, 34–58.

Thurstone, L. (1930), *The Measurement of Values* (Chicago: University of Chicago Press).

(1959), "A Law of Comparative Judgement," *Psychological Review*, **34**, 273–286.

Vytlacil, E. (1999a), "Independence, Monotonicity, and Latent Variable Models: An Equivalence Result," working paper, University of Chicago.

(1999b), "Semiparametric Identification of the Average Treatment Effect in Nonseparable Models," working paper, University of Chicago.

CHAPTER 2

Empirically relevant power comparisons for limited-dependent-variable models

Nathan E. Savin and Allan H. Würtz

1   Introduction

Most hypotheses in limited dependent variable (LDV) models are composite, meaning that the null hypothesis H_0 does not completely specify the data-generating process (DGP). In this case, the null specifies only that the DGP belongs to a given set. As a consequence, the sampling distribution of a test statistic under H_0 is unknown except in special cases, because it depends on the true DGP in the set specified by H_0. The problem is how to test the null hypothesis in this situation. In this chapter, the bootstrap is used to solve the hypothesis-testing problem.

The LDV models considered in this chapter are the simple binary probit model and the simple censored normal linear regression model. For these models, a typical null hypothesis H_0 is that the slope coefficient is zero. This null is composite, the remaining parameters being nuisance parameters. This null is tested using the Lagrange multiplier (LM), likelihood ratio (LR), and Wald test statistics. In our Monte Carlo experiments, we compare the powers of the competing tests when the tests use bootstrap-based critical values. We argue that the powers of the tests with bootstrap-based critical values are empirically relevant because these critical values can be calculated in applications.

There are two basic approaches to obtaining critical values for testing a composite null hypothesis. One approach employs the concept of the size of a test. The size is the supremum of the test's rejection probability over all DGPs contained in H_0. The α-level *size-corrected critical value* is the critical value that makes the size equal to α. In principle, the exact size-corrected critical value can be calculated if it exists, but this is rarely done in applications, possibly because doing so typically entails very difficult computations.

We gratefully acknowledge discussions with Joel Horowitz, Hidehiko Ichimura, and George R. Neumann and the comments of Jim Powell and two referees.

In addition to the difficulty of computing size-corrected critical values, size-corrected tests (that is, tests based on size-corrected critical values) have two fundamental problems. First, the size-corrected critical value may be infinite, in which case a test based on the size concept has no power. Second, even if the size-corrected critical value is finite, the power of the test may be less than or equal to its size. Dufour (1997) gives several examples of the first problem. Bahadur and Savage (1956) demonstrate the second for the case of testing a hypothesis about a population mean. Savin and Würtz (1999a) consider testing the hypothesis that the slope parameter is zero in a binary logit model with one explanatory variable. In their example, the size-corrected critical value of the outer product LM test exists, but it is sensitive to the interval of admissible values for the intercept. If this interval is large, then the power of the test is zero for empirically relevant sample sizes.

A second approach to dealing with a composite H_0 is to base the test on an estimator of the *Type I critical value*. Horowitz and Savin (2000) define this critical value as the one that would be obtained if the exact finite-sample distribution of the test statistic under the true DGP were known. In general, the true Type I critical value is unknown because the exact finite-sample distribution of the test statistic depends on population parameters that are not specified by H_0. Thus, an approximation to the Type I critical value is required to implement the second approach.

An approximation to the Type I critical value often can be obtained by using the (first-order) asymptotic distribution of the test statistic to approximate its finite-sample distribution. This approximation is useful because most test statistics in econometrics are asymptotically pivotal: their asymptotic distributions do not depend on unknown population parameters when the hypothesis being tested is true. Thus, an approximate Type I critical value can be obtained from asymptotic distribution theory without knowledge of the true DGP. Critical values obtained from asymptotic distribution theory are widely used in applications. However, Monte Carlo experiments have shown that first-order asymptotic theory often gives a poor approximation to the exact distributions of test statistics with the sample sizes available in applications. As a result, the true and nominal probabilities that a test makes a Type I error can be very different when an asymptotic critical value is used.

Under certain conditions, the bootstrap provides an approximation to the Type I critical value that is more accurate than the approximation of first-order asymptotic theory. These conditions are satisfied for the test statistics considered in this chapter. Given that the LDV models in this chapter are fully parametric, the Type I critical value can be estimated by the parametric bootstrap. Our Monte Carlo results show that the parametric bootstrap estimates of the Type I critical values provide good control over the probability of making a Type I error. Thus, for the examples we consider, the bootstrap provides a way to obtain empirically relevant critical values for the purpose of making power comparisons. As consequence, the powers of tests with bootstrap-based critical values are empirically relevant because these critical values can be calculated in actual applications.

By contrast, conventional Monte Carlo studies comparing the finite-sample powers of tests usually take a different approach to obtaining critical values. Most studies report powers based on critical values that are called "size corrected," but are really Type I critical values for essentially arbitrary chosen simple null hypotheses. These Type I critical values ignore the uncertainty about the values of the nuisance parameters; they implicitly assume that the values of the nuisance parameters are known. Therefore, conventional Monte Carlo studies compare tests using powers that can be misleading in empirical research. In short, the Type I critical values used by conventional Monte Carlo studies are both misnamed and irrelevant in empirical research.

The organization of this chapter is as follows. The Type I critical value is defined in Section 2. The bootstrap critical value when H_0 is true is developed in Section 3. Section 4 considers the Type I critical value when H_0 is false and its bootstrap estimate. Monte Carlo results on the numerical performance of the bootstrap are presented in Section 5 for a simple binary probit model and in Section 6 for a simple censored normal linear regression model. Section 7 concludes the chapter.

2   Type I critical values

Let the data be a random sample of size n from a probability distribution whose cumulative distribution function (CDF) is F. Denote the data by $\{X_i, i = 1, \ldots, n\}$. For the purpose of this chapter, F is assumed to belong to a family of CDFs that is indexed by the finite-dimensional parameter θ whose population value is θ^*. We write $F(x, \theta^*)$ for $P(X \leq x)$ and $F(\cdot, \theta)$ for a general member of the parametric family. The unknown parameter θ is restricted to a parameter set Θ. The null hypothesis H_0 restricts θ to a subset Θ_0 of Θ. If H_0 is composite, then Θ_0 contains two or more points.

Let $T_n = T_n(X_1, \ldots, X_n)$ be a statistic for testing H_0. Let $G_n[\tau, F(\cdot, \theta)] \equiv P(T_n \leq \tau \mid \theta)$ be the exact finite-sample CDF of T_n when the CDF of the sampled distribution is $F(\cdot, \theta)$. Consider a symmetrical, two-tailed test of H_0. This is the kind of test typically used to test the parameters of LDV models. H_0 is rejected by such a test if $|T_n|$ exceeds a suitable critical value and accepted otherwise. For θ^* in Θ_0, the exact, α-level Type I critical value of $|T_n|$, $z_{n\alpha}$, is defined as the solution to the equation $G_n[z_{n\alpha}, F(\cdot, \theta^*)] - G_n[-z_{n\alpha}, F(\cdot, \theta^*)] = 1 - \alpha$. A test based on this critical value rejects H_0 if $|T_n| > z_{n\alpha}$. Such a test makes a Type I error with probability α. However, $z_{n\alpha}$ can be calculated in applications only in special cases. If H_0 is simple so that Θ_0 contains only one point, then

θ^* is specified by H_0, and $z_{n\alpha}$ can be calculated or estimated with arbitrary accuracy by Monte Carlo simulation.

If, as usually happens in econometrics, H_0 is composite, then θ^* is unknown and $z_{n\alpha}$ cannot be evaluated unless $G_n[\tau, F(\cdot, \theta)]$ does not depend on θ when H_0 is true. In this special case, T_n is said to be *pivotal*. The Student t statistic for testing a hypothesis about the mean of a normal population or a slope coefficient in a normal linear regression model is pivotal. However, pivotal test statistics are generally not available in most econometric applications, and, in particular, for LDV models. When T_n is not pivotal, its Type I critical value $z_{n\alpha}$ can be very different at different points in Θ_0. This is illustrated by the examples in Sections 5 and 6.

When H_0 is composite and T_n is not pivotal, it is necessary to replace the true Type I critical value with an approximation or estimator. First-order asymptotic distribution theory provides one approximation. Most test statistics in econometrics are asymptotically pivotal. Indeed, the asymptotic distributions of most commonly used test statistics are standard normal or chi-square under H_0, regardless of the details of the DGP. If n is sufficiently large and T_n is asymptotically pivotal, then $G_n[\cdot, F(\cdot, \theta^*)]$ can be approximated accurately by the asymptotic distribution of T_n. The asymptotic distribution is the same for any θ in H_0 (including θ^*) when T_n is asymptotically pivotal, so approximate critical values for T_n can be obtained from the asymptotic distribution without having to know θ^*.

Critical values obtained from asymptotic distribution theory are widely used in applications of LDV models. However, Monte Carlo experiments have shown that first-order asymptotic theory often gives a poor approximation to the distributions of test statistics with the sample sizes available in applications. As a result, the true and nominal probabilities that a test makes a Type I error can be very different when an asymptotic critical value is used. Davidson and MacKinnon (1984) have documented such distortions for the case of logit and probit models.

3   Bootstrap critical values when the null hypothesis is true

The bootstrap provides a way to obtain approximations to the Type I critical value of a test that are more accurate than the approximations of first-order asymptotic distribution theory. The bootstrap does this by using the information in the sample to estimate θ and, thereby, $G_n[\cdot, F(\cdot, \theta^*)]$. The estimator of $G_n[\cdot, F(\cdot, \theta^*)]$ is $G_n(\cdot, F_n)$, where $F_n(x) = F(x, \theta_n)$ and θ_n is an $n^{1/2}$-consistent estimator of θ^* when $\theta^* \in \Theta_0$. The idea is that θ_n has a high probability of being close to θ^* when H_0 is true. Therefore, F_n is close to $F(\cdot, \theta^*)$. The bootstrap estimator of the α-level Type I critical value for $|T_n|$, $z_{n\alpha}^*$, solves $G_n(z_{n\alpha}^*, F_n) - G_n(-z_{n\alpha}^*, F_n) = 1 - \alpha$. Thus, the bootstrap estimator of the Type I critical value is, in fact, the exact Type I critical value at θ_n.

Usually, $G_n(\cdot, F_n)$ and $z^*_{n\alpha}$ cannot be evaluated analytically. They can, however, be estimated with arbitrary accuracy by carrying out a Monte Carlo experiment in which random samples are drawn from F_n. Although the bootstrap is usually implemented by Monte Carlo simulation, its essential characteristic is the use of F_n to approximate F in $G_n[\cdot, F(\cdot, \theta^*)]$, not the method that is used to evaluate $G_n(\cdot, F_n)$. From this perspective, the bootstrap is an analog estimator in the sense of Manski (1988); it simply replaces the unknown F with the sample analog F_n.

The bootstrap provides a good approximation to $G_n[\cdot, F(\cdot, \theta^*)]$ and $z_{n\alpha}$ if n is sufficiently large. This is because under mild regularity conditions, $\sup_x |F_n(x) - F(x, \theta^*)|$ and $\sup_\tau |G_n(\tau, F_n) - G_n[(\tau, F(\cdot, \theta^*)]|$ converge to zero in probability or almost surely. Of course, first-order asymptotic distribution theory also provides a good approximation if n is sufficiently large. It turns out, however, that if T_n is asymptotically pivotal and certain technical conditions are satisfied, the bootstrap approximations are more accurate than those of first-order asymptotic theory. See Beran (1988) and Hall (1992) for the details.

In particular, the bootstrap is more accurate than first-order asymptotic theory for estimating the distribution of a "smooth" asymptotically pivotal statistic. It can be shown that

$$P(|T_n| > z^*_{n\alpha}) = \alpha + O(n^{-2})$$

when H_0 is true and regularity conditions hold. (The bootstrap does not achieve the same accuracy for one-tailed tests.) Thus, with the bootstrap critical value, the difference between the true and nominal probabilities that a symmetrical test makes a Type I error is $O(n^{-2})$ if the test statistic is asymptotically pivotal. In contrast, when a critical value based on first-order asymptotic theory is used, the difference is $O(n^{-1})$. This ability to improve upon first-order asymptotic approximations makes the bootstrap an attractive method for estimating Type I critical values. Horowitz (1997) presents results of Monte Carlo experiments showing that the use of bootstrap critical values can dramatically reduce the difference between the true and nominal probability that a test makes a Type I error.

4   Bootstrap critical values when the null hypothesis is false

The discussion of Type I critical values up to this point has assumed that H_0 is true so that there is a $\theta^* \in \Theta_0$ corresponding to the true DGP. The exact, α-level Type I critical value of a symmetrical test based on the statistic T_n is the $1 - \alpha$ quantile of the distribution of $|T_n|$ that is induced by the DGP corresponding to $\theta = \theta^*$. When H_0 is false, θ^* is not in Θ_0, and so there is no Type I critical value corresponding to θ^*. To obtain a Type I critical value, we follow Horowitz and Savin (2000) and propose using the Type I critical value corresponding to a specific θ under H_0 called the *pseudo-true value*. The bootstrap estimates the exact Type I critical value at the pseudo-true value of θ. Therefore, when H_0 is false, the bootstrap provides an empirical analog of a test based on the exact Type I critical value evaluated at the pseudo-true value of θ.

The problem of choosing a critical value when H_0 is false does not arise with size-corrected critical values or asymptotic critical values for asymptotically pivotal test statistics. This is because size-corrected critical values and asymptotic critical values for asymptotically pivotal statistics do not depend on θ, that is, do not vary over the θ values in H_0. Thus, the problem discussed in this section arises only in connection with higher-order approximations to the Type I critical value such as that provided by the bootstrap.

When H_0 is false, the true parameter value θ^* is in the complement of Θ_0 in Θ. There is no $\theta \in \Theta_0$ that corresponds to the true DGP. What value of θ should then be used to define the Type I critical value? If H_0 is simple, Θ_0 consists of a single point, and this point can be used to define the Type I critical value. If H_0 is composite, however, there are many points in Θ_0, and it is not clear which of them should be used to define the Type I critical value. We now review the solution to this problem proposed by Horowitz and Savin (2000).

As has already been explained, the bootstrap estimator of the Type I critical value is obtained from the distribution whose CDF is $G_n[\cdot, F(\cdot, \theta_n)]$, where θ_n is an estimator of θ. Under regularity conditions (see, e.g., White 1982 and Amemiya 1985), θ_n converges in probability or almost surely as $n \to \infty$ to a nonstochastic limit θ^0, and $n^{1/2}(\theta_n - \theta^0) = O_p(1)$. The pseudo-true value is the limit θ^0 of θ_n when θ_n is restricted to Θ_0. If H_0 is true, then $\theta^0 = \theta^*$. Regardless of whether H_0 is true, the bootstrap computes the distribution of T_n at a point θ_n that is a consistent estimator of θ^0. It can be shown that when H_0 is false, the bootstrap provides a higher-order approximation to the Type I critical value based on θ^0 (Horowitz 1994). For the LDV models considered in this chapter, the bootstrap samples are generated imposing the constraint of H_0 and replacing the nuisance parameters by their constrained estimates.

There are two important considerations when selecting the parameter point used to calculate the Type I critical value. The first is that the θ value used to obtain the Type I critical value coincides with θ^* when H_0 is true and has an empirical analog that can be implemented in applications regardless of whether H_0 is true. Second, the resulting test has good power in comparison to alternatives when H_0 is false. As already explained, θ^0 satisfies the first of these conditions. Moreover, convergence of the Type I critical value based on θ^0 to the asymptotic critical value insures that a test based on this Type I critical value inherits any asymptotic optimality properties of a test based on the asymptotic critical value.

5   Binary probit model

This section reports the numerical performance of the bootstrap for tests of the null hypothesis that the slope parameter is zero in a simple binary probit model.

The binary probit model is

$$P(Y = 1 \mid X = x) = \Phi(\beta' x),$$

where $X = (X_1, X_2)'$ is a vector of explanatory variables, $\beta = (\beta_1, \beta_2)'$ is a vector of parameters, and Φ is the standard normal CDF; see Amemiya (1985). Here X consists of an intercept X_1 and one covariate X_2. The composite null hypothesis is $H_0 : \beta_2 = 0$, β_1 being the nuisance parameter, that is, the parameter not specified by H_0.

The null hypothesis is tested using the LM, LR, and Wald test statistics. The LM and Wald test statistics require an estimator of the asymptotic covariance matrix of the maximum likelihood (ML) estimator of β. Three consistent estimators can be constructed from the expected Hessian (EX), the observed Hessian (HS), and the outer product (OP) matrix of the score vectors, respectively. Hence, there are seven test statistics in total.

The test statistics defined as t statistics are asymptotically distributed as standard normal. In this and the following section, it is more convenient to consider the squares of the t statistics, that is, T_n^2, all of which are distributed asymptotically as a chi-square with one degree of freedom when H_0 is true. Hence, the asymptotic approximation to the $\alpha = 0.05$-level Type I critical value is 3.84. Moreover, the tests have the same asymptotic noncentral chi-square distribution under sequences of local alternatives. Although the test statistics are asymptotically pivotal, they are not pivotal: their finite-sample distributions depend on the value of the intercept β_1 under H_0.

The test statistics are calculated using the ML estimator. The ML estimate is not finite for some samples, that is, the ML estimator is not defined for certain points in the sample space; see Albert and Anderson (1984), or, for a brief discussion, Amemiya (1985). We call these sample points *bad* points. The LR statistic uses both a constrained and an unconstrained ML estimator. The value of the LR statistic, however, can be calculated for all sample points, because the value of the likelihood function is defined at the bad points; again see Albert and Anderson (1984).

The situation is different for the LM and Wald statistics. To calculate the LM statistic, only the ML estimator of β_1 subject to the constraint $\beta_2 = 0$ is needed. For the constrained ML estimator there are only two bad points; one is $y = (0, 0, \ldots, 0)'$ and the other is $y = (1, 1, \ldots, 1)'$. For finite n, these bad points have a positive probability of occurring. If a bad point occurs in the Monte Carlo experiments, it is deleted and not replaced. We note that the probability of a bad point goes to zero at an exponential rate in n when H_0 is true.

The Wald statistic employs the unconstrained ML estimator. For this estimator there are many bad points. The procedure for detecting bad points is fairly straightforward for ungrouped designs with one covariate plus intercept. A bad point can be detected by sorting the observations by the values of the covariate. A sample point is a bad point if the first i observations are all 0's and the remaining $n - i$ are all 1's, or the first i observations are all 1's and the remaining $n - i$ are all 0's. Under the alternative there are $2n$ bad points out of 2^n sample points. If a bad point occurs in the experiment, it is deleted and not replaced. It is important to note that each sample has to be checked *before* calculating the ML estimate. A misleading procedure is to delete points only when the ML estimation routine fails: standard estimation routines often produce finite estimates for bad points; see Hughes and Savin (1994).

The Monte Carlo experiment consists of repeating the following steps 1,000 times for each test statistic:

(1) Generate an estimation dataset of size $n = 50$ by random sampling from the model with $\beta_2 = 0$, with X fixed in repeated samples. Estimate the parameters of the model by the relevant ML method(s), and compute the test statistic.

(2) Generate a bootstrap sample of size $n = 50$ by random sampling from the model with $\beta_2 = 0$, using the constrained ML estimate β_1 instead of its true value. Using this bootstrap sample, compute the test statistic.

(3) Repeat step (2) above 1000 times. Estimate the 0.05 Type I critical value by the 0.95 quantile of the empirical distribution of the each test statistic. Let $z^*_{n0.05}$ denote the estimated Type I critical value.

(4) Reject H_0 at the nominal $\alpha = 0.05$ level if the value of the test statistic exceeds $z^*_{n0.05}$. The powers of the tests with bootstrap-based critical values are estimated by carrying out the same steps except that the value of β_2 is set equal to a nonzero number in step (1). Note that the estimate of the Type I critical value is R/G, where R is the number of rejections of H_0 in G nondeleted samples.

The experiment can also be used to estimate the rejection probability of the test based on the asymptotic critical value. In this case, H_0 is rejected at the nominal $\alpha = 0.05$ level if the test statistic exceeds the 0.95 quantile of a chi-square distribution with one degree of freedom, namely 3.84.

The Monte Carlo experiment is carried out for two designs.

Design 1: In the first design, β_1 ranges over the interval $[-1.5, 0]$ and β_2 over the interval $[0, 0.8]$. The values of X_2 are generated using a perfect standard normal $N(0, 1)$: $x_i = \Phi^{-1}(i/(n + 1)), i = 1, 2, \ldots, n$. For this design, the probability of a bad point is negligible.

Table 2.1. *Empirical rejection probabilities: probit with normal regressor X_2 (Design 1)*

Test	β_1	Probability (%)				
		$\beta_2 = 0.00$	0.20	0.40	0.60	0.80
EX LM	−1.5	(4.4) 4.6	8.8	24	50	77
	−1.0	(5.8) 5.5	14	38	70	91
	−0.50	(5.7) 5.8	20	50	81	96
	0.00	(5.0) 4.7	20	55	87	98
HS LM	−1.5	(3.1*) 4.6	9.4	25	50	77
	−1.0	(5.3) 5.8	14	38	70	91
	−0.50	(5.7) 5.8	19	51	82	96
	0.00	(5.1) 4.8	20	55	86	98
OP LM	−1.5	(27*) 2.1*	3.1	12	30	56
	−1.0	(9.8*) 4.2	12	34	64	87
	−0.50	(6.5) 5.2	19	49	82	96
	0.00	(5.2) 4.5	19	54	86	97
EX Wald	−1.5	(1.9*) 5.3	10	27	52	78
	−1.0	(4.5) 6.0	15	39	70	91
	−0.50	(5.5) 5.7	19	51	82	97
	0.00	(4.7) 4.7	20	55	87	98
HS Wald	−1.5	(1.9*) 4.6	10	26	53	78
	−1.0	(4.4) 5.9	14	39	70	91
	−0.50	(5.4) 5.7	19	51	82	96
	0.00	(4.8) 4.8	20	55	87	98
OP Wald	−1.5	(0.93*) 4.1	8.5	20	42	66
	−1.0	(3.2*) 6.0	13	36	66	88
	−0.50	(4.9) 5.6	19	49	81	95
	0.00	(4.8) 4.9	20	53	81	97
LR	−1.5	(6.3) 5.5	9.0	24	50	76
	−1.0	(6.3) 5.6	14	38	70	91
	−0.50	(6.0) 5.7	19	51	82	96
	0.00	(5.3) 4.7	20	55	86	98

Notes: Nominal .05 symmetric tests of $H_0 : \beta_2 = 0$ using bootstrap-based critical values; $n = 50$. The number of Monte Carlo replications is 1,000, and the number of bootstrap replications is 1,000. The numbers in parentheses are the empirical rejection probabilities for a nominal 0.05 test using the asymptotic critical value. An asterisk denotes rejection of the null that the nominal rejection probability is 0.05 using a 0.05 symmetric asymptotic test.

The second column of Table 2.1 reports the estimated probabilities (in parentheses) of making a Type I error when the tests are based on the 0.05 asymptotic critical value 3.84. Note that the estimated rejection probabilities tend to be sensitive to the value of the nuisance parameter β_1. The largest distortions in the rejection probabilities under H_0 occur for the asymptotic OP LM and OP Wald tests; for $\beta_1 = -1.5$, the OP LM test massively over-rejects, and the OP Wald substantially under-rejects. The asymptotic critical value works satisfactorily for the EX LM and LR tests. For the remaining tests, the asymptotic critical works satisfactorily except when $\beta_1 = -1.5$.

The remaining columns of Table 1 report the empirical rejection probabilities of the tests with bootstrap-based critical values, both under H_0 and under the alternative hypotheses. The bootstrap eliminates the distortions in the rejection probabilities under H_0 except for the OP LM test when $\beta_1 = -1.5$. Hence, the bootstrap provides good control over the probability of making a Type I error.

The empirical powers are very sensitive to the value of the nuisance parameter; the power tends to be largest when $\beta_1 = 0.0$ and smallest when $\beta_1 = -1.5$. The powers are similar for all the tests, except for the OP LM test and the OP Wald test. In particular, when $\beta_1 = -1.5$, the estimated powers of these two OP-based tests are lower than that of the LR test. This is due, at least in part, to the fact that the bootstrap does not fully correct the distortions in the rejection probabilities under H_0 of these OP-based tests. For example, when $\beta_1 = -1.5$, the estimated rejection probability under H_0 is 0.021 for the OP LM test and 0.055 for the LR test. The estimated power functions of the OP LM and LR tests are shown in Figure 2.1. The figure shows the lower power of the OP LM test compared with the LR test when $\beta_1 = -1.5$.

Table 2.2 reports the average bootstrap critical value for the 1000 Monte Carlo samples for each pair of parameter values. The average bootstrap critical values for the OP LM and OP Wald tests are very sensitive to the true parameter values. Under H_0, the average critical value depends on the value of the intercept; the average critical value ranges from about 3.9 to 23 for the OP LM test and from about 2.3 to 3.7 for the OP Wald test. When H_0 is false, the average critical value varies across the values of the slope, for a given value of the intercept. For example, for the OP LM test, the average critical value ranges from 12 to 22 when $\beta_1 = -1.5$. This is in sharp contrast to the behavior of the Type I critical value used in a conventional Monte Carlo study: for a given value of β_1, the Type I critical value is constant across alternative values of β_2.

In the introduction, we noted that the powers produced by the conventional Monte Carlo study could differ substantially from those produced by a study that uses bootstrap-based critical values. This is now illustrated for the case of the OP LM test. Assuming that the value of β_1 is known, the Type I critical value can be calculated. The Type I critical value is 25 for the OP LM test when $\beta_1 = -1.5$. Using this critical value, the power of the test increases from 0.050 to 0.066 as the alternative β_2 increases from 0.0 to 0.8. Using bootstrap-based critical values, the power of the test increases from 0.021 to 0.56 as β_2 increases from 0.0 to 0.8. For this example, the powers of the bootstrap-based OP LM test

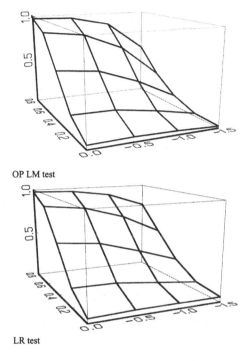

OP LM test

LR test

Figure 2.1. Powers of nominal 0.05 OP LM and LR tests in the probit model: Design 1.

are dramatically higher than those produced by the conventional Monte Carlo study.

The behavior of the average bootstrap critical values for the LR test differs markedly from those of the OP LM test. This is shown graphically in Figure 2.2. For the LR test, the average bootstrap critical values are close to 4.0, both when H_0 is true and when it is false. This reflects the fact that for Design 1 the LR test statistic is almost pivotal. Hence, for the LR test, the powers produced by the conventional Monte Carlo study are very close to those obtained using bootstrap-based critical values.

Design 2: In the second design, β_1 ranges over the interval $[-1.5, 0]$ and β_2 over the interval $[0, 0.8]$. The values of X_2 are now generated using a perfect uniform$[2, 4]$: $x_i = 2 + 2(i - 1)/(n - 1)$, $i = 1, 2, \ldots, n$. For this design, the power functions of the test statistics are nonmonotonic; in particular, the power first increases and then decreases as the value of β_2 increases. Savin and Würtz (1999b) show that the power function is nonmonotonic for a large class of tests when all values of X_2 are positive.

Table 2.2. *Average bootstrap critical values: probit with normal regressor X_2 (Design 1)*

Test	β_1	Critical value				
		$\beta_2 = 0.0$	0.20	0.40	0.60	0.80
EX LM	−1.5	3.8	3.8	3.8	3.8	3.8
	−1.0	3.9	3.9	3.9	3.9	3.9
	−0.50	3.9	3.9	3.9	3.9	3.9
	0.00	3.9	3.9	3.9	3.9	3.9
HS LM	−1.5	3.5	3.5	3.5	3.6	3.6
	−1.0	3.7	3.8	3.8	3.8	3.8
	−0.50	3.9	3.9	3.9	3.9	3.9
	0.00	3.9	3.9	3.9	3.9	3.9
OP LM	−1.5	23	22	19	16	12
	−1.0	7.4	7.1	6.3	5.5	4.9
	−0.50	4.2	4.2	4.1	4.1	4.1
	0.00	3.9	3.9	3.9	3.9	3.9
EX Wald	−1.5	3.0	3.0	3.2	3.3	3.4
	−1.0	3.6	3.6	3.6	3.7	3.7
	−0.50	3.8	3.8	3.8	3.8	3.8
	0.00	3.8	3.8	3.8	3.8	3.8
HS Wald	−1.5	2.9	2.9	3.1	3.2	3.2
	−1.0	3.5	3.5	3.6	3.6	3.7
	−0.50	3.8	3.8	3.8	3.8	3.8
	0.00	3.8	3.8	3.8	3.8	3.8
OP Wald	−1.5	2.3	2.3	2.5	2.7	2.8
	−1.0	3.1	3.2	3.2	3.3	3.4
	−0.50	3.6	3.6	3.6	3.6	3.6
	0.00	3.7	3.7	3.7	3.7	3.7
LR	−1.5	4.3	4.3	4.3	4.3	4.2
	−1.0	4.1	4.1	4.1	4.1	4.1
	−0.50	4.0	4.0	4.0	4.0	4.0
	0.00	4.0	4.0	4.0	4.0	4.0

Notes: See Table 2.1.

The second column of Table 2.3 reports the estimated probabilities of making a Type I error for the tests with asymptotic critical values. Again, the asymptotic critical value of 3.84 does not work satisfactorily for most of the tests when $\beta_1 = -1.5$. In particular, for Design 2, the LR test signficantly over-rejects when $\beta_1 = -1.5$. As in the case of Design 1, the largest distortions in the rejection probabilities under H_0 occur for the OP LM and OP Wald tests.

The estimated rejection probabilities of the bootstrap tests are also given in Table 2.3. The bootstrap eliminates the distortions in the rejection probabilities

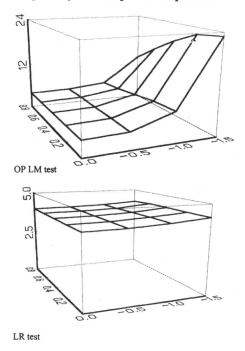

OP LM test

LR test

Figure 2.2. Average bootstrap critical values of nominal 0.05 OP LM and LR tests in the probit model: Design 1.

under H_0 except for OP LM and OP Wald tests when $\beta_1 = -1.5$. In contrast to Design 1, the power tends to be largest when $\beta_1 = -1.5$ and smallest when $\beta_1 = 0$. In general, the powers tend to be much lower for Design 2 than for Design 1. This is partly due to the nonmonotonicity of the power functions. The estimated power functions of the OP LM and LR tests are shown in Figure 2.3. The non-monotonicity is most clearly seen in the figure when $\beta_1 = 0$. Comparing the powers across the tests, the OP-based tests have lower powers than the other tests at $\beta_2 = 0.60$ and 0.80 when $\beta_1 = 0$. The EX and HS Wald tests also have non-monotonic powers at $\beta_2 = 0.80$ when $\beta_1 = 0$.

Table 2.4 presents the average bootstrap critical values. As the case of the Design 1, there is substantial variation in the average critical value for the OP LM test. But in contrast to Design 1, the average bootstrap critical values do not always decrease as β_2 increases from 0.0 to 0.8. For example, the average bootstrap critical value for the OP LM test increases from 3.9 to 35 as β_2 increases from 0.0 to 0.8 when $\beta_1 = 0$. This dramatic increase is shown in Figure 2.4. This is because the distribution of the OP LM test statistic evaluated at the estimate of the pseudo-true value is shifting rapidly to the right as β_2

Nathan E. Savin and Allan H. Würtz

Table 2.3. *Empirical rejection probabilities: probit with uniform regressor X_2 (Design 2)*

		Probability (%)				
Test	β_1	$\beta_2 = 0.00$		0.20	0.40	0.60	0.80
EX LM	-1.5	(4.0)	4.9	8.1	27	49	63
	-1.0	(5.4)	5.6	11	26	42	42
	-0.50	(5.7)	5.1	11	23	28	27
	0.00	(5.0)	5.0	9.1	18	17	13
HS LM	-1.5	(3.5)	5.3	8.1	27	49	63
	-1.0	(5.6)	5.8	11	26	43	42
	-0.50	(5.7)	5.1	11	23	28	27
	0.00	(5.1)	4.8	9.1	19	17	12
OP LM	-1.5	(28*)	2.0*	7.2	26	49	59
	-1.0	(9.9*)	4.1	11	25	40	26
	-0.50	(7.1*)	4.9	11	22	17	11
	0.00	(5.0)	5.1	8.0	10	6.1	12
EX Wald	-1.5	(1.0*)	4.6	8.8	27	49	64
	-1.0	(5.1)	6.1	11	25	43	43
	-0.50	(5.7)	5.3	11	23	29	22
	0.00	(4.8)	4.9	8.9	20	13	5.3
HS Wald	-1.5	(0.93*)	4.4	8.8	27	49	64
	-1.0	(4.5)	6.3	11	26	44	42
	-0.50	(5.5)	5.1	11	24	29	21
	0.00	(4.9)	4.8	9.0	20	13	4.7
OP Wald	-1.5	(0.41*)	2.8*	9.6	28	50	58
	-1.0	(3.2)	6.0	11	26	40	27
	-0.50	(4.9)	5.6	12	22	21	11
	0.00	(4.9)	5.2	9.7	14	7.8	2.8
LR	-1.5	(8.0*)	5.5	7.6	26	49	62
	-1.0	(6.5)	5.5	11	26	42	40
	-0.50	(5.9)	5.0	11	23	26	24
	0.00	(5.3)	4.8	9.1	18	14	11

Note: See Table 2.1.

increases; see Savin and Würtz (1999a). By comparison, the average bootstrap critical value for the LR tests increases only from 4.0 to 4.6 as β_2 increases from 0.0 to 0.8 when $\beta_1 = 0$. Again see Figure 2.4.

From the behavior average bootstrap critical values for the OP LM test, it is clear that the conventional Monte Carlo study will produce substantially different powers from a study using bootstrap-based critical values. Note further that in the case of Design 2, there is also substantial variation in the average bootstrap critical value for all the Wald tests, though the variation is not as pronounced as in the case of the OP LM test.

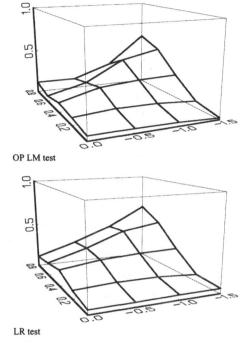

OP LM test

LR test

Figure 2.3. Powers of nominal 0.05 OP LM and LR tests in the probit model: Design 2.

6   Censored normal linear regression model

This section reports the numerical performance of the bootstrap for tests of the null hypothesis that the slope parameter is zero in a simple censored normal linear regression model.

The censored regression model is

$$Y = \max(0, X'\beta + U),$$

where $X = (X_1, X_2)'$ is a vector of explanatory variables, $\beta = (\beta_1, \beta_2)'$ is a vector of parameters, and U is $N(0, \sigma^2)$; this is the standard Tobit model in Amemiya (1985). Here X consists of an intercept X_1 and one covariate X_2. The composite null hypothesis is $H_0 : \beta_2 = 0$, β_1 and σ^2 being the nuisance parameters.

Design 3: In this design, the intercept varies, but not the variance: β_1 ranges over the interval $[-0.75, 0.75]$, β_2 over $[0, 0.8]$, and $\sigma^2 = 1$. The values of X_2 are generated using a perfect standard normal $N(0, 1)$: $x_i = \Phi^{-1}(i/(n + 1))$, $i = 1, 2, \ldots, n$.

Nathan E. Savin and Allan H. Würtz

Table 2.4. *Average bootstrap critical values: probit with uniform regressor X_2 (Design 2)*

		Critical value				
Test	β_1	$\beta_2 = 0.0$	0.20	0.40	0.60	0.80
EX LM	−1.5	3.5	3.9	3.9	3.9	3.9
	−1.0	3.8	3.9	3.9	3.9	3.7
	−0.50	3.9	3.9	3.9	3.7	3.3
	0.00	3.9	3.9	3.8	3.3	3.0
HS LM	−1.5	3.4	3.8	3.9	3.9	3.8
	−1.0	3.8	3.9	3.9	3.9	3.6
	−0.50	3.9	3.9	3.9	3.6	3.1
	0.00	3.9	3.9	3.7	3.1	3.8
OP LM	−1.5	25	6.6	4.0	4.0	5.5
	−1.0	8.6	4.1	4.0	5.1	17
	−0.50	4.2	3.9	4.7	15	31
	0.00	3.9	4.4	13	31	35
EX Wald	−1.5	2.7	3.6	3.8	3.8	3.7
	−1.0	3.5	3.8	3.8	3.7	3.1
	−0.50	3.8	3.8	3.8	3.2	2.4
	0.00	3.9	3.8	3.3	2.4	2.1
HS Wald	−1.5	2.6	3.6	3.8	3.8	3.7
	−1.0	3.4	3.8	3.8	3.7	3.0
	−0.50	3.8	3.8	3.7	3.1	2.3
	0.00	3.8	3.8	3.2	2.3	2.0
OP Wald	−1.5	2.0	3.3	3.8	3.8	3.4
	−1.0	3.1	3.7	3.8	3.5	2.5
	−0.50	3.7	3.8	3.5	2.6	1.6
	0.00	3.8	3.6	2.7	1.6	1.2
LR	−1.5	4.6	4.2	4.0	4.0	4.1
	−1.0	4.2	4.0	4.0	4.1	4.5
	−0.50	4.0	4.0	4.1	4.4	4.7
	0.00	4.0	4.0	4.4	4.7	4.6

Note: See Table 2.1.

The experiment with Design 3 was carried out for six of the seven tests. Under the alternative it often happens that the Hessian matrix evaluated at the constrained estimate is not positive definite. Bera and McKenzie (1986) also encountered this problem. For this reason, we do not consider the HS LM test further in the censored normal regression model.

The estimated rejection probabilities in the second column of Table 2.5 show that the asymptotic critical value does not work satisfactorily for the OP-based tests when $\beta_1 = -0.75$ and -0.50 or for the EX Wald test when $\beta_1 = -0.75$.

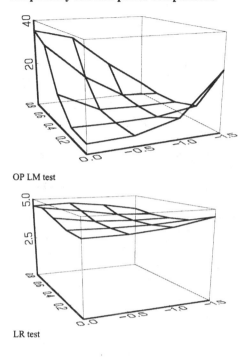

OP LM test

LR test

Figure 2.4. Average bootstrap critical values of nominal 0.05 OP LM and LR tests in the probit model: Design 2.

The largest distortions in the rejection probabilities under H_0 occur for the OP LM and OP Wald tests. Recall that this was also true for Design 2.

The results in Table 5 also show that the bootstrap eliminates the distortions in the rejection probabilities under H_0 except in the case of the OP Wald test. The powers of the tests are sensitive to the value of β_1. The power against the alternative $\beta_2 = 0.40$ varies from about 0.32 to 0.70 as β_1 varies from -0.75 to 0.75. For Design 3, the powers of the EX Wald and OP Wald tests are lower than the powers of the other tests when $\beta_1 = -0.75$. Aside from this case, the power functions of the tests are similar.

Table 2.6 presents the average bootstrap critical values. For each of the test, there is relatively little variation in the average critical value, except for the OP LM and OP Wald tests. Figure 2.5 shows the average critical values for the OP LM test. The same figure also shows that there is relatively little variation in the case of the LR test.

For Design 3, the powers produced by the conventional Monte Carlo study are not very different from those using bootstrap-based critical values, even for the OP LM and OP Wald tests. For example, the Type I critical value is 5.1 for

Table 2.5. *Empirical rejection probabilities: censored model with* $\sigma^2 = 1$ *(Design 3)*

Test	β_1	$\beta_2 = 0.00$	0.20	0.40	0.60	0.80
		Probability (%)				
EX LM	−.75	(5.1) 5.4	16	46	81	97
	−.50	(5.9) 6.1	20	53	87	99
	.00	(5.9) 5.7	23	63	94	100
	.50	(6.7*) 6.2	24	70	96	100
	.75	(5.8) 5.7	25	70	97	100
OP LM	−.75	(10*) 5.2	14	43	76	96
	−.50	(8.5*) 5.7	18	51	84	98
	.00	(7.8*) 5.2	22	61	92	100
	.50	(7.9*) 6.2	23	67	95	100
	.75	(7.5*) 6.0	23	68	96	100
EX Wald	−.75	(6.8*) 5.7	11	32	65	90
	−.50	(4.9) 5.7	16	50	83	97
	.00	(5.9) 5.7	23	63	94	100
	.50	(6.6*) 6.2	24	69	96	100
	.75	(6.6*) 6.0	25	70	97	100
HS Wald	−.75	(4.0) 5.5	16	46	81	97
	−.50	(4.9) 6.1	19	53	86	98
	.00	(5.9) 5.6	23	63	94	100
	.50	(6.7*) 6.2	24	69	96	100
	.75	(6.4) 6.0	25	70	97	100
OP Wald	−.75	(2.7*) 6.0	14	39	68	90
	−.50	(3.2*) 6.6*	18	48	80	96
	.00	(4.5) 5.7	23	59	92	99
	.50	(4.9) 5.3	23	67	96	100
	.75	(5.7) 5.8	24	69	96	100
LR	−.75	(6.3) 5.1	16	47	81	97
	−.50	(6.4) 5.8	20	53	86	98
	.00	(6.0) 5.8	23	63	94	100
	.50	(6.7*) 6.2	24	69	96	100
	.75	(6.1) 5.8	24	70	97	100

Note: See Table 2.1.

the OP LM test when $\beta_1 = -0.75$. Using this critical value, the powers of the OP LM test are 0.05, 0.18, 0.52, 0.82, and 0.96 as β_2 increases from 0.0 to 0.8. These are somewhat higher than the powers reported in Table 2.5 for this case.

Design 4: The intercept is fixed and the variance varies: $\beta_1 = -0.25$, β_2 ranges over the interval [0, 0.8], and σ^2 over the interval [0.25, 2]. The values of X_2 are generated using a perfect normal $N(0.5, 1)$: $x_i = \Phi^{-1}(i/(n + 1)) + 0.5$,

Table 2.6. *Average bootstrap critical values: censored model with $\sigma^2 = 1$ (Design 3)*

Test	β_1	Critical value				
		$\beta_2 = 0.00$	0.20	0.40	0.60	0.80
EX LM	−.75	3.8	3.8	3.8	3.8	3.9
	−.50	3.9	3.9	3.9	3.9	3.9
	.00	4.0	4.0	4.0	4.0	4.0
	.50	4.0	4.0	4.0	4.0	4.0
	.75	4.0	4.0	4.0	4.0	4.0
OP LM	−.75	6.3	6.2	5.8	5.5	5.2
	−.50	5.0	5.0	4.9	4.9	4.8
	.00	4.5	4.5	4.5	4.5	4.5
	.50	4.4	4.4	4.4	4.4	4.4
	.75	4.5	4.5	4.5	4.5	4.5
EX Wald	−.75	4.3	4.3	4.1	3.9	3.8
	−.50	3.7	3.7	3.7	3.7	3.7
	.00	4.0	4.0	4.0	4.0	4.0
	.50	4.1	4.1	4.1	4.1	4.1
	.75	4.1	4.1	4.1	4.1	4.1
HS Wald	−.75	3.4	3.4	3.4	3.5	3.5
	−.50	3.6	3.6	3.7	3.7	3.7
	.00	3.9	3.9	3.9	3.9	3.9
	.50	4.1	4.1	4.1	4.1	4.1
	.75	4.1	4.1	4.1	4.1	4.1
OP Wald	−.75	2.8	2.8	2.9	2.9	3.0
	−.50	3.1	3.1	3.2	3.2	3.3
	.00	3.5	3.5	3.6	3.6	3.6
	.50	3.7	3.7	3.7	3.7	3.7
	.75	3.8	3.8	3.8	3.8	3.8
LR	−.75	4.1	4.1	4.1	4.1	4.1
	−.50	4.1	4.1	4.1	4.1	4.1
	.00	4.0	4.0	4.0	4.0	4.0
	.50	4.0	4.0	4.0	4.0	4.0
	.75	4.0	4.0	4.0	4.0	4.0

Note: See Table 2.1.

$i = 1, 2, \ldots, n$, to avoid too high a degree of censoring. The experiment with Design 4 was carried out for six of the seven tests. Again, the HS LM test was not considered, for the reason discussed under Design 3.

Column 2 of Table 2.7 reports the estimated probabilities of making a Type I error with asymptotic critical values. The effect of the nuisance parameter σ^2 is different for different tests. The asymptotic critical value does not work

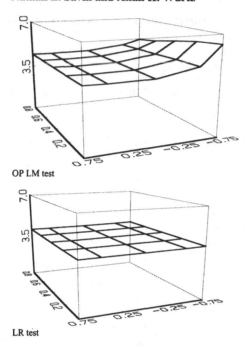

OP LM test

LR test

Figure 2.5. Average bootstrap critical values of nominal 0.05 OP LM and LR tests in the censored model: Design 3.

satisfactorily for the OP LM test and the Wald tests when $\sigma^2 = 0.25$, or for the LM tests and the LR test when $\sigma^2 = 2.0$. Note that for Design 4, the LR test over-rejects when $\sigma^2 = 1.0$ and 2.0. The largest distortions in the rejection probabilities under H_0 occur for the OP LM and OP Wald tests. Recall that this also true for Design 2.

The estimated rejection probabilities of the bootstrap tests are also given in Table 2.7. The bootstrap eliminated the distortions in the rejection probabilities under H_0 except for $\sigma^2 = 2.0$. The powers are very sensitive to the value of σ^2. The power against the alternative $\beta_2 = 0.20$ varies from about 1 to 0.1 as σ^2 varies from 0.25 to 2.0. For Design 4, all the tests have very similar power functions.

Table 2.8 presents the average bootstrap critical values. There is substantial variation in the average critical value for the OP LM test and the HS and OP Wald tests when H_0 is true. Figure 2.6 shows the average bootstrap critical values for the OP LM and LR tests. Note that for both tests there is relatively little variation in the average critical value when H_0 is false; the latter is true for the other tests as well.

Table 2.7. *Empirical rejection probabilities: censored model with $\beta_1 = -0.25$ (Design 4)*

Test	σ^2	Probability (%) $\beta_2 = 0.00$	0.20	0.40	0.60	0.80
EX LM	0.25	(5.0) 5.7	98	100	100	100
	0.50	(5.9) 6.1	58	100	100	100
	1.0	(6.9*) 5.9	22	62	94	100
	2.0	(6.9*) 6.7*	9.3	23	42	64
OP LM	0.25	(14*) 3.9	98	100	100	100
	0.50	(8.5*) 5.7	56	100	100	100
	1.0	(8.1*) 5.9	21	60	92	100
	2.0	(8.6*) 5.8	9.6	22	41	63
EX Wald	0.25	(6.9*) 4.6	96	100	100	100
	0.50	(4.9) 5.7	58	100	100	100
	1.0	(6.2) 6.1	23	62	94	100
	2.0	(6.6*) 6.5*	9.8	23	42	64
HS Wald	0.25	(2.6*) 6.4	98	100	100	100
	0.50	(4.9) 6.1	58	100	100	100
	1.0	(6.1) 6.1	22	62	94	100
	2.0	(6.4) 6.3	9.8	23	41	64
OP Wald	0.25	(1.6*) 5.6	94	100	100	100
	0.50	(3.2*) 6.6*	53	99	100	100
	1.0	(4.6) 6.0	21	58	92	100
	2.0	(5.0) 6.5*	9.1	22	38	62
LR	0.25	(6.4) 5.4	98	100	100	100
	0.50	(6.4) 5.8	58	100	100	100
	1.0	(7.0*) 6.1	22	62	94	100
	2.0	(7.2*) 6.5*	9.4	23	42	64

Note: See Table 2.1.

We note that for the OP LM test, the Type I critical value is 7.4 when $\sigma^2 = 0.25$. This implies that the conventional Monte Carlo study will produce somewhat lower powers than a study using bootstrap-based critical values.

7   Discussion

For the simple LDV models considered in this chapter, the bootstrap provides better estimates of the Type I critical values of LM, LR, and Wald tests than first-order asymptotic theory. The bootstrap substantially reduces or essentially eliminates the distortions in the probability of making a Type I error. The bootstrap estimates of the Type I critical values are empirically relevant, since

Nathan E. Savin and Allan H. Würtz

Table 2.8. *Average bootstrap critical values: censored model with $\beta_1 = -0.25$ (Design 4)*

| Test | σ^2 | Critical value | | | | |
		$\beta_2 = 0.0$	0.20	0.40	0.60	0.80
EX LM	0.25	3.7	3.9	4.0	4.0	4.0
	0.50	3.9	3.9	4.0	4.0	4.0
	1.0	4.0	4.0	4.0	4.0	4.0
	2.0	4.0	4.0	4.0	4.0	4.0
OP LM	0.25	11	4.9	4.5	4.4	4.4
	0.50	5.0	4.7	4.5	4.5	4.4
	1.0	4.6	4.5	4.5	4.5	4.4
	2.0	4.5	4.5	4.5	4.5	4.4
EX Wald	0.25	5.6	3.7	3.9	4.0	4.1
	0.50	3.7	3.8	3.9	4.0	4.1
	1.0	3.8	3.9	4.0	4.0	4.0
	2.0	3.9	3.9	4.0	4.0	4.0
HS Wald	0.25	3.0	3.7	3.9	4.0	4.0
	0.50	3.6	3.8	3.9	4.0	4.0
	1.0	3.8	3.9	3.9	3.9	4.0
	2.0	3.9	3.9	3.9	3.9	4.0
OP Wald	0.25	2.3	3.2	3.5	3.6	3.7
	0.50	3.1	3.3	3.5	3.6	3.6
	1.0	3.4	3.4	3.5	3.6	3.6
	2.0	3.5	3.5	3.5	3.6	3.6
LR	0.25	4.2	4.1	4.0	4.0	4.0
	0.50	4.1	4.0	4.0	4.0	4.0
	1.0	4.0	4.0	4.0	4.0	4.0
	2.0	4.0	4.0	4.0	4.0	4.0

Note: See Table 2.1.

they can be calculated in empirical applications. The same is not true for the so-called size-corrected critical values calculated in most Monte Carlo studies, which are in fact Type I critical values for simple null hypotheses. The Type I critical value for a composite hypothesis depends on the value of the parameter vector θ, both when the null is true (except if the test statistic is pivotal) and when the alternative is true. This is mirrored by the behavior of the bootstrap estimate of the Type I critical value: the estimate also depends on the value of θ under the null and the alternative. This point is illustrated by showing that the average bootstrap critical value depends on the value of θ in our Monte Carlo results. This behavior is in sharp contrast to that of size-corrrected critical values, which are invariant to the value of θ for a given value of the nuisance parameter.

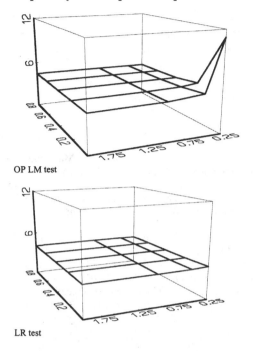

OP LM test

LR test

Figure 2.6. Average bootstrap critical values of nominal 0.05 OP LM and LR tests in the censored model: Design 4.

We noted in the introduction that size-corrected tests have two fundamental problems. Both problems are the consequence of having a null-hypothesis set Θ_0 that is too large. Dufour (1997) has shown that this happens in a wide variety of settings that are important in applied econometrics. Thus, even if computation of a size-corrected critical value is not an issue, size-corrected tests are available only when Θ_0 is a sufficiently small set. Usually, this is accomplished by restricting $F(\cdot, \theta)$ to a suitably small, finite-dimensional family of functions. In applications, however, there is usually little justification for assuming such restrictions. This is reflected in the recent emphasis on semiparametric and nonparametric models and methods in econometrics, especially in the case of LDV models; for example, see Horowitz (1998a) and Powell (1994). Hence, we believe it is unlikely that size-corrected tests will play an important role in the future in testing of LDV models.

As also noted in the introduction, the parametric LDV models considered in this chapter satisfy the standard conditions under which the bootstrap provides improved estimates of the critical values. In particular, the test statistics can be approximated as smooth functions of sample moments. This is generally not the case for semiparametric and nonparametric models. The estimators and test statistics for these models typically depend on a bandwidth that decreases to zero as the sample size increases. Developing bootstrap methods for statistics that are not smooth functions of sample moments, even approximately, is a current area of research (Horowitz 1998b). This research promises to provide improved estimates of critical values and hence empirically relevant power comparisons for semiparametric and nonparametric models.

REFERENCES

Albert, A. and Anderson, J. A. (1984), "On the Existence of Maximum Likelihood Estimates in Logistic Regression Models," *Biometrika*, **71**, 1–10.

Amemiya, T. (1985), *Advanced Econometrics* (Cambridge: Harvard University Press).

Bahadur, R. R. and Savage, L. J. (1956), "The Nonexistence of Certain Statistical Procedures in Nonparametric Problems," *Annals of Mathematical Statistics*, **27**, 1115–1122.

Bera, A. K. and McKenzie, C. (1986), "Alternative Forms and Properties of the Score Test," *Journal of Applied Statistics*, **13**, 13–25.

Beran, R. (1988), "Prepivoting Test Statistics: A Bootstrap View of Asymptotic Refinements," *Journal of the American Statistical Association*, **85**, 687–697.

Davidson, R. and MacKinnon, J. G. (1984), "Convenient Specification Tests for Logit and Probit Models," *Journal of Econometrics*, **25**, 241–262.

Dufour, J.-M. (1997), "Some Impossibility Theorems in Econometrics with Applications to Structural and Dynamic Models," *Econometrica*, **65**, 1365–1387.

Hall, P. (1992), *The Bootstrap and Edgeworth Expansion* (New York: Springer-Verlag).

Horowitz, J. L. (1994), "Bootstrap-Based Critical Values for the Information Matrix Test," *Journal of Econometrics*, **61**, 395–411.

(1997), "Bootstrap Methods in Econometrics: Theory and Numerical Performance," In: D. M. Kreps, K. F. Wallis, eds., *Advances in Economics and Econometrics: Theory and Applications*, vol. 3, pp. 188–222 (New York: Cambridge University Press).

1998a. "The Bootstrap," In: J. J. Heckman, E. E. Leamer, eds., *Handbook of Econometrics*, vol. 5 (Amsterdam: Elsevier Science, forthcoming).

1998b. "Bootstrap Methods for Median Regression Models," *Econometrica*, **66**, 1327–1352.

Horowitz, J. L. and Savin, N. E. (2000), "Empirically Relevant Critical Values for Hypothesis Tests: A Bootstrap Approach," *Journal of Econometrics*, **95**, 375–389.

Hughes, G. A. and Savin, N. E. (1994), "Is the Minimum Chi-Square Estimator the Winner in Logit Regression?," *Journal of Econometrics*, **61**, 345–366.

Manski, C. F. (1988), *Analog Estimation Methods in Econometrics* (New York: Chapman and Hall).

Powell, J. L. (1994), "Estimation of Semiparametric Models," In: R. F. Engle, D. L. McFadden, eds., *Handbook of Econometrics*, vol. 4 (Amsterdam: Elsevier Science).

Savin, N. E. and Würtz, A. H. (1999a), "The Power of LM Tests in Logit Models: Size-Corrected Versus Type I Critical Values," Department of Economics, University of Iowa, Iowa City, Iowa.

1999b. "Power of Tests in Binary Response Models," *Econometrica*, **67**, 413–421.

White, H. (1982), "Maximum Likelihood Estimation of Misspecified Models," *Econometrica*, **50**, 1–26.

CHAPTER 3

Simulation estimation
of polychotomous-choice sample
selection models

Lung-fei Lee

1   Introduction

This chapter considers the estimation of sample selection (SEL) models with
polychotomous choices or multiple selection criteria.The focus is on the
estimation of models which require estimation via simulation techniques. An
example of such models is a model with multivariate normal disturbances.
SEL models with polychotomous choices have been considered in Dubin and
McFadden (1984), Lee (1983), and others, under extreme-value distributions.
Schmertmann (1994) discussed limitations of these model specifications. In
some empirical studies, in order to achieve simplicity, researchers imposed
restrictive and unrealistic assumptions such as independence across disturbances of equations. Such practices resulted in controversies and debates
(e.g., Duan et al. 1984, Hay and Olsen 1984). In many circumstances with
complex selection criteria, multivariate normal disturbances may be the
preferred specification (Amemiya 1974, Hausman and Wise 1978). With
the development of simulation estimation methods, complex models can, in
principle, be estimated (McFadden 1989, Pakes and Pollard 1989). Methods
of simulated moments (MSM), simulated pseudolikelihood (SPL), and simulated maximum likelihood (SML) have been proposed in the literature (see
McFadden 1989, Pakes and Pollard 1989, Lee 1992, Gourieroux and Monfort
1993, and Borsch-Supan and Hajivassiliou 1993). Parameter estimates may,
however, be sensitive to simulators used (McFadden and Ruud 1994). The
GHK simulator introduced by Geweke (1991), Borsch-Supan and Hajivassiliou
(1993), and Keane (1994) provides an adequate probability simulator for
the multinomial probit model. Monte Carlo results on comparing various
simulation methods and simulators have mostly focused on discrete choice

Financial support from the Research Grant Council of Hong Kong under grant no. HKUST595/96H
for my research is gratefully acknowledged. I appreciate having valuable comments from Professor
Jim Powell and an anonymous referee.

71

(DC) models (Hajivassiliou, McFadden, and Ruud 1996, Borsch-Supan and Hajivassiliou 1993, Geweke, Keane, and Runkle 1994, 1997).

This chapter considers simulation estimation of SEL models. Two-stage estimation methods can be generalized for the estimation of outcome equations. Both biased and unbiased simulators for observed outcome equations are proposed. The same methods can be used for simulating other conditional outcome equations, such as opportunity costs of unchosen alternatives (Heckman 1990, Lee 1995a). A two-stage simulation estimation method (TSSM) is essentially MSM. SML methods can be more efficient. Various ways to generalize the GHK simulator to SEL models are possible. We investigate the performance of the various SML and TSSM methods in their finite-sample performance by Monte Carlo studies. The studies provide numerical evidence on the feasibility and accuracy of various simulation approaches for the estimation of SEL models. Estimates of parameters in limited dependent variable (LDV) models may be sensitive to distributional specifications (see, e.g., surveys by Maddala 1983 and Amemiya 1984). A polychotomous-choice sample selection (P-SEL) model will be subject to the same criticism. We provide Monte Carlo results to demonstrate how sensitive the SML estimators (SMLEs) will be when the disturbances are skew-distributed or have bimodal distributions. Finally, we investigate a possible semiparametric MLE method originated by Gallant and Nychka (1987). The likelihood function of the semiparametric P-SEL model can be simulated. The simulated semiparametric likelihood (SSL) function can be used for estimation and the construction of specification error test of normality. Monte Carlo experiments are designed to investigate the finite sample properties of the semiparametric estimates. The finite-sample levels of significance and power of SML tests are also investigated.

2   Sample selection models, selected outcomes, and opportunity costs

There are several broadly applicable SEL models with different choice processes or selection criteria.

A general P-SEL model with m alternatives and a continuous outcome equation is

$$y = x\beta + \varepsilon, \tag{3.2.1}$$

and

$$U_j = z_j\gamma + u_j, \qquad j = 1, \ldots, m, \tag{3.2.2}$$

where the subscript j refers to the alternative j for an individual. A subscript i for an individual has been suppressed. The U_j represents the utility of the alternative j, and the outcome y can be observed only if the first alternative is chosen by the individual. In a utility-maximization framework, the alternative j will be chosen if $U_j > U_l$ for all $l \neq j$, $l = 1, \ldots, m$. As a normalization on the utility function, $U_m = 0$ for the alternative m for all individuals. Let $I_j = 1$ if the alternative j is chosen by the individual; $I_j = 0$ otherwise. A popular but theoretically restrictive specification of the choice component assumes that the u's in (3.2.2) are i.i.d. Gumbel distributed. This specification results in logistic choice probabilities. A more general specification may assume normally distributed and correlated disturbances. For the latter specification, simulation estimation techniques are required, because implied choice probabilities involve multiple integrals which do not have a closed-form expression.

Another SEL model allows multiple selection criteria. In such a model, an outcome can be observed only if several selection criteria are satisfied. Let $U_j = z_j \gamma + u_j$, $j = 1, \ldots, m$, be m selection criteria, and let $y = x\beta + \varepsilon$ be an outcome equation. The outcome y for an individual can be observed only if $U_j > 0$ for all $j = 1, \ldots, m$. This model can also be a sequential decision model with selectivity if the decision process is sequential. A simple but restrictive specification imposes an independence assumption on the distributions of the u's. More general specifications with correlated disturbances, such as those with a multivariate normal distribution, will require simulation estimation.

Simulation techniques can be useful for estimating unknown parameters in these models. In addition, one may be interested in the computation of observed or potential outcome equations conditional on choice status. Heckman (1990) and Lee (1995a) discuss opportunity costs for unchosen alternatives in SEL models. In a polychotomous-choice model, the expected-outcome equation is $E(y \mid x, I_1 = 1) = x\beta + E(\varepsilon \mid x, U_1 > U_l, l = 2, \ldots, m)$. In a multiple-selection-criteria model, the conditional outcome equation is $E(y \mid x, U_1 > 0, \ldots, U_m > 0) = x\beta + E(\varepsilon \mid x, U_1 > 0, \ldots, U_m > 0)$. For an individual who has chosen the alternative l, the expected opportunity cost for the potential outcome of the alternative 1 is $E(y \mid x, I_l = 1) = x\beta + E(\varepsilon \mid x, U_l > U_r, r = 1, \ldots, l - 1, l + 1, \ldots, m)$. These equations under a multivariate distribution, such as the multivariate normal distribution, for disturbances may involve multiple integrals which need to be evaluated by simulation techniques.

3   Two-stage estimation with simulation

Unknown parameters of the SEL model can be estimated by two-stage methods. With simulation, a TSSM is similar to the MSM. Unknown parameters and regressors of a model are suppressed for simplicity in the following presentations if that does not lead to confusion. The choice model that will be explicitly analyzed is the polychotomous-choice model. Generalizations of simulation methods to models with multiple selection criteria are similar. In the first stage, the DC equations in (3.2.2) are estimated. The likelihood function of the DC model of a single observation is

$$L(\bar{I}) = \prod_{j=1}^{m} \left[\int g(\bar{U}_{m-1}, I_j = 1) d\bar{U}_{m-1} \right]^{I_j}, \tag{3.3.1}$$

where $\bar{U}_{m-1} = (U_1, \ldots, U_{m-1})$ and $\bar{I} = (I_1, \ldots, I_m)$. This likelihood function can be simulated with the GHK probability simulator. The probabilities of $U_j - U_l > 0$ for $l = 1, \ldots, m$ but $l \neq j$, are determined by the multivariate normal distribution of $v_j = (u_1 - u_j, \ldots, u_{j-1} - u_j, u_{j+1} - u_j, \ldots, u_m - u_j)$. Denote $w_j = (z_j - z_1, \ldots, z_j - z_{j-1}, z_j - z_{j+1}, \ldots, z_j - z_m)$. The variance matrix of v_j can be decomposed by the Cholesky decomposition $H_j H_j'$ where H_j is a lower triangular matrix. It follows that $v_{jl} = \sum_{k=1}^{l} h_{jlk} \eta_{jk}$, where v_{jl} is the lth component of v_j, h_{jlk} is the (l, k) entry of H_j, and $\eta_j = (\eta_{j1}, \ldots, \eta_{j,m-1})$ is a standard normal vector (with zero mean and an identity variance matrix), i.e., $v_j = H_j \eta_j$. Define $L_{j1} = w_{j1} \gamma / h_{j11}$ and $L_{jl} = [w_{jl} \gamma - \sum_{k=1}^{l-1} h_{jlk} \eta_k] / h_{jll}$ for $l = 2, \cdots, m - 1$. It follows that

$$P(I_j = 1) = \int_{-\infty}^{L_{j,m-1}} \cdots \int_{-\infty}^{L_{j1}} \prod_{l=1}^{m-1} \phi(\eta_{jl}) \, d\eta_{jl}$$

$$= \int_{-\infty}^{\infty} \cdots \int_{-\infty}^{\infty} \prod_{l=1}^{m-1} \Phi(L_{jl}) \phi_{(-\infty, L_{jl}]}(\eta_{jl}) \, d\eta_{jl}, \tag{3.3.2}$$

where ϕ and Φ are, respectively, the standard normal density and distribution, and $\phi_{(a,b]}$ is a truncated standard normal density with support on $(a, b]$. The GHK sampler is to generate sequentially truncated standard normal variables from $\prod_{l=1}^{m-1} \phi_{(-\infty, L_{jl}]}(\eta_{jl})$. With S simulation runs, the GHK likelihood simulator of the DC model is

$$\hat{L}_S^C(\bar{I}) = \prod_{j=1}^{m} \left\{ \frac{1}{S} \sum_{s=1}^{S} \prod_{l=1}^{m-1} \Phi(L_{jl}^{(s)}) \right\}^{I_j} \tag{3.3.3}$$

The parameter γ of (3.2.2) can be estimated by the maximum likelihood (ML) method applied to the simulated likelihood (SL) function (3.3.3). The consistency of the SMLE requires that S go to infinity as the sample size n tends to infinity. For asymptotic efficiency, S needs to go to infinity at a rate faster than $\sqrt{n}$ (see, e.g., Lee 1992, Hajivassiliou and McFadden 1998). If S goes to infinity at a rate not faster than $\sqrt{n}$, the SML estimator may converge at a slow rate and an asymptotic bias will be present (Lee 1995b). The GHK simulator for multivariate normal probabilities has advantages over many other simulators. The simulated likelihood function based on the GHK simulator is smooth in parameters, so popular gradient-based optimization methods can be used for effective implementation of the SL approach (Borsch-Supan and Hajivassiliou

1993). It is extensively demonstrated in Hajivassiliou, McFadden, and Ruud (1996) that the GHK simulator can have smaller simulation variances than other available simulators. The bias of the SMLE is related to the degree of variance of a simulator as shown by an asymptotic expansion in Lee (1995b).

With the first-stage estimate $\hat{\gamma}$, the outcome equation can be estimated in the second stage by MSM. Simulated moment equations can be derived from observed outcome equations. The common random draws can be either the same or independent draws for the first-stage estimation of (3.3.3). As there is no particular reason for using the same random draws for both the first- and the second-stage simulation estimation, in subsequent discussions the random draws for the second-stage simulation of the outcome equation are assumed to be independent of those of the first-stage estimation. For independent draws, the number of draws S can be different from that for (3.3.3). TSSM may be of special interest for the case where $E(\varepsilon \mid \bar{U}_{m-1}) = \delta \psi(\bar{U}_{m-1}, \gamma)$ for some function $\psi(\bar{U}_{m-1}, \gamma)$ involving only parameters of the DC equations. This general specification will include the linear expectation specification of Dubin and McFadden (1984) and its possible generalization with an Edgeworth expansion in Lee (1982), and the specification based on order statistics in Lee (1983). Unknown parameters of the observed outcome equation,

$$E(y \mid I_1 = 1) = x\beta + \delta E(\psi(\bar{U}_{m-1}, \gamma) \mid I_1 = 1), \qquad (3.3.4)$$

can be estimated by an instrumental variable (IV) procedure after $E(\psi(\bar{U}_{m-1}, \gamma) \mid I_1 = 1)$ is replaced by a simulated function $\hat{E}_S(\psi(\bar{U}_{m-1}, \gamma))$ evaluated at $\hat{\gamma}$. Simulators of $E(\psi(\bar{U}_{m-1}, \gamma) \mid I_1 = 1)$ can be derived in various ways. We consider first the recursive simulation technique underlying the GHK simulator. This technique does not provide an unbiased simulator. Unbiased simulators are then derived. Variance reduction based on conditioning may also be useful.

Consider the estimation of $E(y \mid I_1 = 1) = x\beta + E(\varepsilon \mid I_1 = 1)$ given values of unknown parameters and x. Let $f(\varepsilon \mid v_1)$ be the conditional density of ε conditional on v_1, where v_1 has the Cholesky decomposition $v_1 = H_1 \eta_1$. It follows that

$E(\varepsilon \mid I_1 = 1)$

$$= \frac{1}{P(I_1=1)} \int_{-\infty}^{\infty} \int_{-\infty}^{L_{1,m-1}} \cdots \int_{-\infty}^{L_{11}} \varepsilon f(\varepsilon \mid v_1 = H_1 \eta_1) \prod_{l=1}^{m-1} \phi(\eta_{1l}) \, d\eta_{1l} \cdot d\varepsilon$$

$$= \frac{1}{P(I_1=1)} \int_{-\infty}^{L_{1,m-1}} \cdots \int_{-\infty}^{L_{11}} E(\varepsilon \mid v_1 = H_1 \eta_1) \prod_{l=1}^{m-1} \phi(\eta_{1l}) \, d\eta_{1l}$$

$$= \frac{1}{P(I_1=1)} \int_{-\infty}^{\infty} \cdots \int_{-\infty}^{\infty} E(\varepsilon \mid v_1 = H_1 \eta_1) \prod_{l=1}^{m-1} \Phi(L_{1l}) \phi_{[-\infty, L_{1l}]}(\eta_{1l}) \, d\eta_{1l}.$$

$$(3.3.5)$$

The GHK sampler $\prod_{l=1}^{m-1} \phi_{[-\infty, L_{1l}]}(\eta_{1l})$ can be used simultaneously to simulate both the numerator and denominator in (3.3.5). With S simulation runs from the GHK sampler, (3.3.5) can be simulated as

$$\hat{E}_S(\varepsilon \mid I_1 = 1) = \frac{1}{S} \sum_{s=1}^{S} E\left(\varepsilon \mid v_1 = H_1 \eta_1^{(s)}\right) \prod_{l=1}^{m-1} \Phi\left(L_{1l}^{(s)}\right) \bigg/ \frac{1}{S} \sum_{s=1}^{S} \prod_{l=1}^{m-1} \Phi\left(L_{1l}^{(s)}\right)$$

$$= \sum_{s=1}^{S} E\left(\varepsilon \mid v_1 = H_1 \eta_1^{(s)}\right) \omega^{(s)}, \qquad (3.3.6)$$

where $\omega^{(s)} = \prod_{l=1}^{m-1} \Phi(L_{1l}^{(s)}) / \sum_{r=1}^{S} \prod_{l=1}^{m-1} \Phi(L_{1l}^{(r)})$. Here $\hat{E}_S(\varepsilon \mid I_1 = 1)$ is a consistent estimator of $E(\varepsilon \mid I_1 = 1)$ as S goes to infinity. But, as a ratio of simulated functions, this simulator is biased when S is fixed and finite.

If we are interested in unbiased simulators for $E(\varepsilon \mid I_1 = 1)$ at a given value of the parameter vector, the Gibbs sampler (GS) may be useful (Geman and Geman 1984, Tanner and Wong 1987). Since $E(\varepsilon \mid I_1 = 1) = \int \int \varepsilon f(\varepsilon, \bar{U}_{m-1} \mid I_1 = 1) d\varepsilon \, d\bar{U}_{m-1}$, the density $f(\varepsilon, \bar{U}_{m-1} \mid I_1 = 1)$ of ε and $\bar{U}_{m-1}$ conditional on $I_1 = 1$ is naturally a density for simulation draws. An attractive approach for drawing random variables from $f(\varepsilon, \bar{U}_{m-1} \mid I_1 = 1)$ is GS. GS is based on random variables drawn from full conditional marginal densities $f(\varepsilon \mid I_1 = 1, \bar{U}_{m-1})$ and $g(U_j \mid I_1 = 1, \varepsilon, \bar{U}_{(m-1,-j)})$, where $\bar{U}_{(m-1,-j)}$ denotes the subvector of $\bar{U}_{(m-1)}$ with U_j deleted. It makes use of Markov-chain simulation. It is a popular approach for drawing random variables from a posterior density in the Bayesian methodology (see, for examples, Albert and Chib 1993; Geweke, Keane, and Runkle 1994, 1997; McCulloch and Rossi 1994). It can also be useful in the sampling approach (Hajivassiliou, McFadden, and Ruud 1996, Hajivassiliou and McFadden 1998). With $(\varepsilon^{(s)}, \bar{U}_{m-1}^{(s)})$ drawn from $f(\varepsilon, \bar{U}_{m-1} \mid I_1 = 1)$, a simulator for $E(\varepsilon \mid I_1 = 1)$ is

$$\hat{E}_{1,S}(\varepsilon \mid I_1 = 1) = \frac{1}{S} \sum_{s=1}^{S} \varepsilon^{(s)}. \qquad (3.3.7)$$

This simulator is unbiased, as it is a sample average of random draws.

It is possible to have unbiased simulators with smaller variances than that in (3.3.7) under some circumstances. Because $E(\varepsilon \mid I_1 = 1, \bar{U}_{m-1}) = E(\varepsilon \mid \bar{U}_{m-1})$, we have $E(\varepsilon \mid I_1 = 1) = \int E(\varepsilon \mid \bar{U}_{m-1}) g(\bar{U}_{m-1} \mid I_1 = 1) d\bar{U}_{m-1}$. If $\bar{U}_{m-1}$ can be drawn from $g(\bar{U}_{m-1} \mid I_1 = 1)$ and $E(\varepsilon \mid \bar{U}_{m-1})$ is computationally tractable, a simulator will be

$$\hat{E}_{2,S}(\varepsilon \mid I_1 = 1) = \frac{1}{S} \sum_{s=1}^{S} E\left(\varepsilon \mid \bar{U}_{m-1}^{(s)}\right). \qquad (3.3.8)$$

GS is a feasible approach if random variables can be drawn from full conditional marginal densities of $g(\bar{U}_{m-1} \mid I_1 = 1)$. The simulator in (3.3.8) is unbiased. It has a smaller simulation or Monte Carlo variance (MCV) than that of (3.3.7). This can be shown as follows. For any two random vectors w and z, the identity $\operatorname{var}(w) = E[\operatorname{var}(w \mid z)] + \operatorname{var}[E(w \mid z)]$ implies that $\operatorname{var}[E(w \mid z)] \leq \operatorname{var}(w)$. The MCV of $\hat{E}_{1,S}(\varepsilon \mid I_1 = 1)$ is $\operatorname{var}[\varepsilon \mid I_1 = 1]$, and that of $\hat{E}_{2,S}(\varepsilon \mid I_1 = 1)$ is $\operatorname{var}[E(\varepsilon \mid I_1 = 1, \bar{U}_{m-1})]$. Because $\operatorname{var}[E(\varepsilon \mid I_1 = 1, \bar{U}_{m-1})] \leq \operatorname{var}(\varepsilon \mid I_1 = 1)$, $\hat{E}_{2,S}(\varepsilon \mid I_1 = 1)$ has a smaller MCV than that of $\hat{E}_{1,S}(\varepsilon \mid I_1 = 1)$.

Further variance reduction of simulators may be feasible. The conditional expectation can be rewritten as $E(\varepsilon \mid I_1 = 1) = \int E[\varepsilon \mid I_1 = 1, \bar{U}_{(m-1,-j)}] g(\bar{U}_{(m-1,-j)} \mid I_1 = 1) d\bar{U}_{(m-1,-j)}$ for $j = 1, \ldots, m - 1$. With $j = 1$,

$$
\begin{aligned}
E\left[\varepsilon \mid I_1 = 1, \bar{U}_{(m-1,-1)}\right] &= E\left[\varepsilon \mid \bar{U}_{(m-1,-1)}, U_1 > \bar{U}_{(m,-1)}\right] \\
&= \int E(\varepsilon \mid \bar{U}_{m-1}) g\left(U_1 \mid \bar{U}_{(m-1,-1)}, U_1 > \bar{U}_{(m,-1)}\right) dU_1.
\end{aligned}
$$

This function can be computationally tractable for some models as it involves only a single integration of $E(\varepsilon \mid \bar{U}_{m-1})$ with respect to a univariate truncated conditional density of U_1. Similarly, for $j = 2, \ldots, m - 1$,

$$
E\left[\varepsilon \mid I_1 = 1, \bar{U}_{(m-1,-j)}\right] = \int E(\varepsilon \mid \bar{U}_{m-1}) g\left(U_j \mid \bar{U}_{(m-1,-j)}, U_1 > U_j\right) dU_j.
$$

These suggest that any of the following simulators can be an unbiased simulator of $E(\varepsilon \mid I_1 = 1)$:

$$
\hat{E}_{3,S}^{(j)}(\varepsilon \mid I_1 = 1) = \frac{1}{S} \sum_{s=1}^{S} E\left[\varepsilon \mid I_1 = 1, \bar{U}_{(m-1,-j)}^{(s)}\right], \qquad j = 1, \ldots, m - 1,
$$

(3.3.9)

where $\bar{U}_{m-1}^{(s)}$, $s = 1, \ldots, S$ represent random draws from $g(\bar{U}_{m-1} \mid I_1 = 1)$. Each of these simulators can have smaller MCV than that of $\hat{E}_{2,S}(\varepsilon \mid I_1 = 1)$. This is so because

$$
E\left(\varepsilon \mid I_1 = 1, \bar{U}_{(m-1,-j)}\right) = E\left[E(\varepsilon \mid \bar{U}_{m-1}) \mid I_1 = 1, \bar{U}_{(m-1,-j)}\right];
$$

therefore $\operatorname{var}[E(\varepsilon \mid I_1 = 1, \bar{U}_{(m-1,-j)})] \leq \operatorname{var}[E(\varepsilon \mid \bar{U}_{m-1})]$.

Remarks. The $m - 1$ simulators can be combined into a weighted average. Let $\omega = (\omega_1, \ldots, \omega_{m-1})$, where $\omega_j \geq 0$ for all $j = 1, \ldots, m - 1$ and $\sum_{j=1}^{m-1} \omega_j = 1$, be a vector of weights. A weighted simulator with ω is

$$
\hat{E}_{\omega,S}(\varepsilon \mid I_1 = 1) = \sum_{j=1}^{m-1} \omega_j \hat{E}_{3,S}^{(j)}(\varepsilon \mid I_1 = 1).
$$

This weighted simulator with arbitrary weights can have smaller MCV than that of $\hat{E}_{2,S}(\varepsilon \mid I_1 = 1)$. For any random variable z with finite second moment, $E^2(z) \leq E(z^2)$. This inequality implies that

$$\left[\sum_{j=1}^{m-1} \omega_j \hat{E}_{3,S}^{(j)}(\varepsilon \mid I_1 = 1) - E(\varepsilon \mid I_1 = 1)\right]^2$$

$$\leq \sum_{j=1}^{m-1} \omega_j \left[\hat{E}_{3,S}^{(j)}(\varepsilon \mid I_1 = 1) - E(\varepsilon \mid I_1 = 1)\right]^2;$$

hence,

$$E\left[\sum_{j=1}^{m-1} \omega_j \hat{E}_{3,S}^{(j)}(\varepsilon \mid I_1 = 1) - E(\varepsilon \mid I_1 = 1)\right]^2$$

$$\leq \sum_{j=1}^{m-1} \omega_j E\left[\hat{E}_{3,S}^{(j)}(\varepsilon \mid I_1 = 1) - E(\varepsilon \mid I_1 = 1)\right]^2$$

$$\leq \text{var}[\hat{E}_{2,S}(\varepsilon \mid I_1 = 1)],$$

that is, $\text{var}[\hat{E}_{\omega,S}(\varepsilon \mid I_1 = 1)] \leq \text{var}[\hat{E}_{2,S}(\varepsilon \mid I_1 = 1)]$. From these inequalities, it can be seen that the weighted simulator can have smaller MCV than some $\hat{E}_{3,S}^{(j)}(\varepsilon \mid I_1 = 1)$, but it may not have smaller MCV than all of them. The latter issue is similar to the estimation of a common mean when samples are not i.i.d. A simulator that takes into account possible heteroskedastic variances and autocorrelations among $\hat{E}_{3,S}^{(j)}(\varepsilon \mid I_1 = 1)$ for $j = 1, \ldots, m - 1$ by a proper generalized least-squares formulation can be relatively efficient. The latter will be computationally involved, as heteroskedastic variances and autocovariances need to be simulated independently of $\hat{E}_{3,S}^{(j)}(\varepsilon \mid I_1 = 1)$ to maintain the unbiasedness property of the generalized least-squares simulator.

With a simulated bias-correction term $\hat{E}_S(\psi(\bar{U}_{m-1}, \gamma))$ evaluated at $\hat{\gamma}$, the TSSM can estimate the outcome equation (3.3.4). Let $\hat{z}_S = (x, \hat{E}_S(\psi(\bar{U}_{m-1}, \hat{\gamma})))$, and w be a vector of IVs. Then $\alpha = (\beta', \delta')'$ can be estimated as

$$\hat{\alpha} = \left[\sum_{i=1}^n I_{1i} w_i \hat{z}'_{S,i}\right]^{-1} \sum_{i=1}^n I_{1i} w_i y_i, \tag{3.3.10}$$

where the subscript i refers to an individual and n is the sample size. IVs for the bias-correction term can be derived by using another independent simulator of this term. This TSSM is a simulated IV (SIV) procedure. The TSSM estimates (TSSMEs) with any simulators in (3.3.6)–(3.3.9) are consistent as both n and S

go to infinity. The TSSMEs with any unbiased simulators in (3.3.7)–(3.3.9) are consistent for a fixed finite S (conditional on $\hat{\gamma}$ being consistent). The TSSME with the recursive simulator (3.3.6) is consistent only when S goes to infinity. The recursive simulation approach with a finite fixed S can still be useful if the following moment equation implied by the model is used for estimation:

$$I_1 y = I_1 x\beta + \delta E(I_1 \psi(\bar{U}_{m-1}, \gamma)) + \varepsilon_1, \tag{3.3.11}$$

where ε_1 is a disturbance term with zero mean. The GHK sampler can provide an unbiased simulator for $E(I_1 \psi(\bar{U}_{m-1}, \gamma))$, and x can be used as an IV for $I_1 x$. The asymptotic distributions and variances of these TSSMEs can be derived as in the MSM approach (McFadden 1989, Pakes and Pollard 1989) and by a Taylor expansion taking into account the influence of the asymptotic distribution of $\hat{\gamma}$ (Amemiya 1978).

4　Simulated maximum-likelihood estimation

Instead of the TSSM method, SML methods can be constructed to estimate the whole model. The likelihood function for an observation in the SEL model is

$$L(x, \bar{I}, y) = \left[\int f(\varepsilon, \bar{U}_{m-1}, I_1 = 1)\, d\bar{U}_{m-1} \right]^{I_1}$$
$$\times \prod_{j=2}^{m} \left[\int g(\bar{U}_{m-1}, I_j = 1)\, d\bar{U}_{m-1} \right]^{I_j}, \tag{3.4.1}$$

where $\varepsilon = y - x\beta$. It can be simulated without bias by simulating each likelihood components. The GHK simulator of choice probability can be generalized for the simulation. There are two possible ways to simulate the likelihood function in (3.4.1).

Based on the factorization $f(\varepsilon, \bar{U}_{m-1}, I_1 = 1) = f(\varepsilon \mid \bar{U}_{m-1})g(\bar{U}_{m-1}, I_1 = 1)$,

$$\int f(\varepsilon, \bar{U}_{m-1}, I_1 = 1)\, d\bar{U}_{m-1}$$

$$= \int_{-\infty}^{L_{1,m-1}} \cdots \int_{-\infty}^{L_{11}} f(\varepsilon \mid v_1 = H_1 \eta_1) \prod_{l=1}^{m-1} \phi(\eta_{1l})\, d\eta_{1l}$$

$$= \int_{-\infty}^{\infty} \cdots \int_{-\infty}^{\infty} f(\varepsilon \mid v_1 = H_1 \eta_1) \prod_{l=1}^{m-1} \Phi(L_{1l})\phi_{(-\infty, L_{1l}]}(\eta_{1l})\, d\eta_{1l}. \tag{3.4.2}$$

The likelihood function in (3.4.1) can thus be simulated as

$$\tilde{L}_S(\bar{I}, y) = \left\{ \frac{1}{S} \sum_{s=1}^{S} f\left(\varepsilon \mid v_1 = H_1 \eta_1^{(s)}\right) \prod_{l=1}^{m-1} \Phi\left(L_{1l}^{(s)}\right) \right\}^{I_1}$$

$$\times \prod_{j=2}^{m} \left\{ \frac{1}{S} \sum_{s=1}^{S} \prod_{l=1}^{m-1} \Phi\left(L_{jl}^{(s)}\right) \right\}^{I_j}, \qquad (3.4.3)$$

where the random variables are drawn from $\prod_{l=1}^{m-1} \phi_{(-\infty, L_{jl}]}(\eta_{jl})$ for each $j = 1, \ldots, m$.

The second approach depends on the factorization $f(\varepsilon, \bar{U}_{m-1}, I_1) = g(\bar{U}_{m-1}, I_1 \mid \varepsilon) f(\varepsilon)$. Let CC' be the Cholesky decomposition of the variance matrix of (ε, v_1'). It follows that $(\varepsilon, v_1')' = C\zeta$, where ζ is an m-dimensional standard normal vector. With this Cholesky representation, $\varepsilon = C_{11}\zeta_1$ and $v_{1k} = \sum_{l=1}^{k+1} C_{k+1,l}\zeta_l$ for each $k = 1, \ldots, m-1$. Define $K_k = [w_{1k}\gamma - \sum_{l=1}^{k} C_{k+1,l}\zeta_l]/C_{k+1,k+1}$ for $k = 1, \ldots, m-1$. It follows that

$$\int f(\varepsilon, \bar{U}_{m-1}, I_1)\, d\bar{U}_{m-1} = \int g(\bar{U}_{m-1}, I_1 \mid \varepsilon)\, d\bar{U}_{m-1} \cdot f(\varepsilon)$$

$$= \int_{-\infty}^{K_{m-1}} \cdots \int_{-\infty}^{K_1} \prod_{l=2}^{m} \phi(\zeta_l)\, d\zeta_l \cdot f(\varepsilon)$$

$$= \int_{-\infty}^{\infty} \cdots \int_{-\infty}^{\infty} \prod_{l=1}^{m-1} \Phi(K_l)\phi_{(-\infty, K_{l}]}(\zeta_{l+1})\, d\zeta_{l+1} \cdot f(\varepsilon),$$

$$(3.4.4)$$

where $\zeta_1 = \varepsilon/C_{11}$. With S simulation runs from $\prod_{l=1}^{m-1} \phi_{(-\infty, K_{l}]}(\zeta_{l+1})$ for $j = 1, \ldots, m_1$, (3.4.4) can be simulated and the SL is

$$\hat{L}_S(\bar{I}, y) = \left\{ \frac{1}{S} \sum_{s=1}^{S} \prod_{l=1}^{m-1} \Phi\left(K_l^{(s)}\right) \cdot f(\varepsilon) \right\}^{I_1} \prod_{j=2}^{m} \left\{ \frac{1}{S} \sum_{s=1}^{S} \prod_{l=1}^{m-1} \Phi\left(L_{jl}^{(s)}\right) \right\}^{I_j}.$$

$$(3.4.5)$$

Asymptotic properties of the SMLE can be found in Lee (1992, 1995b) and Gourieroux and Monfort (1993), among others. The difference between the two SLs in (3.4.3) and (3.4.5) is in the likelihood components of the observed outcomes. The accuracy of these SLs in a finite sample will be compared by Monte Carlo studies. The variance of a log SL is due to two sources of variation – simulation and sample. An SL is a function of sample observation z and simulated draws ξ, say, $\hat{L}^S(z, \xi)$. The variance of $\hat{L}^S$ is a sum of two terms:

$$\text{var}(\hat{L}^S(z, \xi)) = E[\text{var}(\hat{L}^S(z, \xi) \mid z)] + \text{var}[E(\hat{L}^S(z, \xi) \mid z)]. \qquad (3.4.6)$$

The $\text{var}(\hat{L}^S(z, \xi) \mid z)$ is the MCV conditional on a sample. The first term of (3.4.6) is the mean of MCVs over sample. For an unbiased SL, the second term captures the sample variation of the likelihood function. As the second term is the same for all unbiased SLs, the comparison of unbiased SLs can be based on the average of MCVs. For the two SLs in (3.4.3) and (3.4.5), we expect that the MCV of (3.4.5) can be smaller than that of (3.4.3). Some intuition is provided in Appendix B for this possibility.

5   Semiparametric maximum-likelihood estimation

For the estimation of LDV models, because a parametric distribution will impose specific probability and regression functions of choices and outcomes, estimates of parameters may not be robust to a distributional assumption. A large body of literature on semiparametric methods exists. In this section, we consider the semiparametric ML (SEML) method by Gallant and Nychka (1987). Related two-stage methods for the estimation of outcome equations can be found in Lee (1982) and Newey, Powell, and Walker (1990). The SEML method is based on a modified Hermite expansion of an unknown multivariate density around a multivariate normal density. Consider a scalar random variable w first. Let $f(w)$ be the (unknown) density of w. Gallant and Nychka (1987) have shown that, under some regularity conditions, f can be expanded with respect to a normal density of $N(\mu, \sigma^2)$ as

$$f(w) = \left[\sum_{j=0}^{\infty} c_j H_j \left(\frac{w - \mu}{\sigma} \right) \right]^2 \frac{1}{\sigma} \phi \left(\frac{w - \mu}{\sigma} \right) \bigg/ \sum_{j=0}^{\infty} j! c_j^2, \quad (3.5.1)$$

where $c_0 = 1$ and the H_j's are the univariate Hermite polynomials, where

$$H_j(w) = w^j - \frac{j^{[2]}}{2 \times 1!} w^{j-2} + \frac{j^{[4]}}{2^2 \times 2!} w^{j-4} - \frac{j^{[6]}}{2^3 \times 3!} w^{j-6} + \cdots, \tag{3.5.2}$$

and $j^{[r]} = j(j - 1) \cdots (j - (r - 1))$. In practice, a finite-order expansion will be used for estimation. An rth-order approximation is

$$f_r(w) = \left[\sum_{j=0}^{r} c_j H_j \left(\frac{w - \mu}{\sigma} \right) \right]^2 \frac{1}{\sigma} \phi \left(\frac{w - \mu}{\sigma} \right) \bigg/ \sum_{j=0}^{r} j! c_j^2. \quad (3.5.3)$$

This $f_r(w)$ is a proper density function, as its integral with respect to w is unity. It will reduce to a normal density with mean μ and variance σ^2 when $c_j = 0$ for all $j = 1, \ldots, r$. If w is an m-dimensional random vector, its density can be expanded with respect to a multivariate normal density of $N(\mu, \Sigma)$ as

$$f(w) = \frac{\left\{ \sum_{j_1=0}^{\infty} \cdots \sum_{j_m=0}^{\infty} c_{j_1 \cdots j_m} \prod_{l=1}^{m} H_{j_l}([P^{-1}(w - \mu)]_l) \right\}^2}{\sum_{i_1=0}^{\infty} \cdots \sum_{i_m=0}^{\infty} c_{i_1 \cdots i_m}^2 \prod_{l=1}^{m} i_l!}$$

$$\times \frac{|\Sigma|^{-1/2}}{(2\pi)^{m/2}} \exp\{-\tfrac{1}{2}(w - \mu)'\Sigma^{-1}(w - \mu)\}, \tag{3.5.4}$$

where $c_{0\cdots0} = 1$, $PP' = \Sigma$, and $[b]_l$ denotes the lth component of a vector b. Equivalently, write $w = \mu + P\bar{s}_m$. The density of $f(\bar{s}_m)$ of $\bar{s}_m = (s_1, \ldots, s_m)$ has the expansion

$$f(\bar{s}_m) = S_m(\bar{s}_m) \prod_{l=1}^{m} \phi(s_l), \tag{3.5.5}$$

where

$$S_m(\bar{s}_m) = \frac{\left\{ \sum_{j_1=0}^{\infty} \cdots \sum_{j_m=0}^{\infty} c_{j_1 \cdots j_m} \prod_{l=1}^{m} H_{j_l}(s_l) \right\}^2}{\sum_{i_1=0}^{\infty} \cdots \sum_{i_m=0}^{\infty} c_{i_1 \cdots i_m}^2 \prod_{l=1}^{m} i_l!}. \tag{3.5.6}$$

The marginal density of $\bar{s}_{m-1} = (s_1, \ldots, s_{m-1})$ implied by (3.5.5) is

$$f(\bar{s}_{m-1}) = S_{m-1}(\bar{s}_{m-1}) \prod_{l=1}^{m-1} \phi(s_l), \tag{3.5.7}$$

and

$$S_{m-1}(\bar{s}_{m-1}) = \frac{\sum_{j_m=0}^{\infty} j_m! \left\{ \sum_{j_1=0}^{\infty} \cdots \sum_{j_{m-1}=0}^{\infty} c_{j_1 \cdots j_m} \prod_{l=1}^{m-1} H_{j_l}(s_l) \right\}^2}{\sum_{i_m=0}^{\infty} i_m! \sum_{i_1=0}^{\infty} \cdots \sum_{i_{m-1}=0}^{\infty} c_{i_1 \cdots i_m}^2 \prod_{l=1}^{m-1} i_l!}$$

$$= \sum_{j_m=0}^{\infty} \omega_{j_m} \frac{\left\{ \sum_{j_1=0}^{\infty} \cdots \sum_{j_{m-1}=0}^{\infty} c_{j_1 \cdots j_m} \prod_{l=1}^{m-1} H_{j_l}(s_l) \right\}^2}{\sum_{j_1=0}^{\infty} \cdots \sum_{j_{m-1}=0}^{\infty} c_{j_1 \cdots j_m}^2 \prod_{l=1}^{m-1} j_l!}, \tag{3.5.8}$$

and

$$\omega_{j_m} = \frac{j_m! \sum_{j_1=0}^{\infty} \cdots \sum_{j_{m-1}=0}^{\infty} c_{j_1 \cdots j_m}^2 \prod_{l=1}^{m-1} j_l!}{\sum_{i_m=0}^{\infty} i_m! \sum_{i_1=0}^{\infty} \cdots \sum_{i_{m-1}=0}^{\infty} c_{i_1 \cdots i_m}^2 \prod_{l=1}^{m-1} i_l!}, \qquad j_m = 0, 1, \ldots. \tag{3.5.9}$$

The implied marginal density is a weighted mixture of Hermite expanded densities. It can be a single Hermite expanded density if independence of s_m and $\bar{s}_{m-1}$ is imposed on (3.5.5).

To expand the densities of disturbances v_j's and (ε, v_1') with Hermite expansion, one may proceed as follows. Let

$$(\bar{u}_{m-1}', \varepsilon)' = B_m \bar{\xi}_m, \tag{3.5.10}$$

where B_m is a lower diagonal $m \times m$ matrix, and the density of $\bar{\xi}_m$ has a Hermite expansion density in (3.5.5)–(3.5.6), i.e., $f(\bar{\xi}_m) = S_m(\bar{\xi}_m) \prod_{l=1}^{m} \phi(\xi_l)$. Let B_{m-1} be the matrix B_m with its mth row and column deleted. It follows from (3.5.10) that $\bar{U}_{m-1} = B_{m-1} \bar{\xi}_{m-1}$. The implied marginal density of $\bar{\xi}_{m-1}$ is the one in (3.5.7)–(3.5.9), i.e., $f(\bar{\xi}_{m-1}) = S_{m-1}(\bar{\xi}_{m-1}) \prod_{l=1}^{m-1} \phi(\xi_l)$. Let R_j be the transformation matrix such that $R_j \bar{u}_{m-1} = v_j$. Let H_j be the lower diagonal matrix in a Cholesky decomposition $H_j H_j' = R_j B_{m-1} B_{m-1}' R_j'$. Thus $v_j = H_j \eta_j$. The density of η_j can be derived from that of $\bar{\xi}_{m-1}$. The identity $H_j H_j' = R_j B_{m-1} B_{m-1}' R_j'$ implies that $B_{m-1}^{-1} R_j^{-1} H_j$ is an orthonormal matrix. Therefore, $H_j' R_j'^{-1} B_{m-1}'^{-1} B_{m-1}^{-1} R_j^{-1} H_j = I$ and $| B_{m-1}^{-1} R_j^{-1} H_j | = 1$. Since $\eta_j = H_j^{-1} R_j B_{m-1} \bar{\xi}_{m-1}$, it follows that

$$f(\eta_j) = \left| H_j R_j^{-1} B_{m-1}^{-1} \right| \cdot S_{m-1}\left(B_{m-1}^{-1} R_j^{-1} H_j \eta_j \right)$$

$$\times \frac{1}{(2\pi)^{(m-1)/2}} \exp\left\{ -\tfrac{1}{2} \eta_j' H_j' R_j'^{-1} B_{m-1}'^{-1} B_{m-1}^{-1} R_j^{-1} H_j \eta_j \right\}$$

$$= S_{m-1}\left(B_{m-1}^{-1} R_j^{-1} H_j \eta_j \right) \prod_{l=1}^{m-1} \phi(\eta_{jl}). \tag{3.5.11}$$

This implies that

$$P(I_j = 1) = \int_{-\infty}^{L_{j,m-1}} \cdots \int_{-\infty}^{L_{j1}} S_{m-1}\left(B_{m-1}^{-1} R_j^{-1} H_j \eta_j \right) \prod_{l=1}^{m-1} \phi(\eta_{jl}) \, d\eta_{jl}$$

$$= \int_{-\infty}^{\infty} \cdots \int_{-\infty}^{\infty} S_{m-1}\left(B_{m-1}^{-1} R_j^{-1} H_j \eta_j \right)$$

$$\times \prod_{l=1}^{m-1} \Phi(L_{jl}) \phi_{(-\infty, L_{jl}]}(\eta_{jl}) \, d\eta_{jl}. \tag{3.5.12}$$

It remains that $\int f(\varepsilon, \bar{U}_{m-1}, I_1 = 1) \, d\bar{U}_{m-1}$ should be considered with the Hermite expansion. Let Q be the transformation matrix such that $Q(\bar{u}_{m-1}', \varepsilon)' = (\varepsilon, v_1')'$. Let C be the lower diagonal matrix of the Cholesky decomposition $CC' = QB_m B_m' Q'$. Let $(\varepsilon, v_1')' = C\zeta$. It follows that $\zeta = C^{-1} Q B_m \bar{\xi}_m$ and

$$f(\zeta) = S_m\left(B_m^{-1} Q^{-1} C\zeta \right) \prod_{l=1}^{m} \phi(\zeta_l). \tag{3.5.13}$$

This implies that

$$\int f(\varepsilon, \bar{U}_{m-1}, I_1 = 1) d\bar{U}_{m-1}$$

$$= \int_{-\infty}^{K_{m-1}} \cdots \int_{-\infty}^{K_1} S_m \left(B_m^{-1} Q^{-1} C \zeta\right) \prod_{l=2}^{m} \phi(\zeta_l) d\zeta_l \cdot \frac{1}{C_{11}} \phi\left(\frac{\varepsilon}{C_{11}}\right)$$

$$= \int_{-\infty}^{\infty} \cdots \int_{-\infty}^{\infty} S_m \left(B_m^{-1} Q^{-1} C \zeta\right) \prod_{l=1}^{m-1} \Phi(K_l) \phi_{(-\infty, K_l]}(\zeta_{l+1}) d\zeta_{l+1}$$

$$\times \frac{1}{C_{11}} \phi\left(\frac{\varepsilon}{C_{11}}\right), \tag{3.5.14}$$

where $\zeta_1 = \varepsilon / C_{11}$.

The GHK samplers $\prod_{l=1}^{m-1} \phi_{(-\infty, L_{jl}]}(\eta_{jl})$ and $\prod_{l=1}^{m-1} \phi_{(-\infty, K_l]}(\zeta_{l+1})$ can be used for simulating the likelihood in (3.4.1) as

$$\tilde{L}_S(\bar{I}, y) = \left\{ \frac{1}{S} \sum_{s=1}^{S} S_m \left(B_m^{-1} Q^{-1} C \zeta^{(s)}\right) \prod_{l=1}^{m-1} \Phi(K_l^{(s)}) \cdot \frac{1}{C_{11}} \phi\left(\frac{\varepsilon}{C_{11}}\right) \right\}^{I_1}$$

$$\times \prod_{j=2}^{m} \left\{ \frac{1}{S} \sum_{s=1}^{S} S_{m-1} \left(B_{m-1}^{-1} R_j^{-1} H_j \eta_j^{(s)}\right) \prod_{l=1}^{m-1} \Phi(L_{jl}^{(s)}) \right\}^{I_j}. \tag{3.5.15}$$

The simulated SEML estimate (SSMLE) can be derived by maximizing the semiparametric SL (SSL) in (3.5.15) with respect to all the parameters, including those of the c's in (3.5.6).

Gallant and Nychka (1987) showed that the SEML estimator and the unknown density itself can be estimated consistently provided that the length r of the series expansion increases with sample size n. Subsequently, Fenton and Gallant (1996) obtained rates of convergence of their semiparametric density estimator in the L_1 norm. The density estimate achieves its best rate of order $n^{-2/5+\delta}$ for every small $\delta > 0$ when $r \approx n^{1/5}$. The rate of convergence and asymptotic distribution of the SEML estimates of the model remain unknown. The recent development of sieve estimates by Shen (1997) and Chen and Shen (1998) may shed light on such issues. With simulation, one may also be interested in knowing at what rates r and S should increase as a function of n in order that the SSMLE can possess desirable asymptotic properties. All these issues remain open for future research.

6   Monte Carlo experiments

This section will report Monte Carlo results on the finite-sample performance of various simulators.

6.1   *Experimental designs*

In the Monte Carlo experiment, a trichotomous-choice SEL model is studied. The utility equations are

$$U_j = z_j \gamma + u_j, \qquad j = 1, 2, \tag{3.6.1}$$

and $U_3 = 0$ as a normalization. The outcome for alternative 1 can be observed when it is chosen, which is

$$y = x\beta + \varepsilon. \tag{3.6.2}$$

u_1, u_2, and ε in (3.6.1)–(3.6.2) are jointly normally distributed. To impose the positive-definiteness of the covariance matrix of disturbances, a Cholesky decomposition can be used: $u_1 = b_{11}\xi_1$, $u_2 = b_{21}\xi_1 + b_{22}\xi_2$, and $\varepsilon = \delta_1\xi_1 + \delta_2\xi_2 + \delta_3\xi_3$, where ξ_1, ξ_2, and ξ_3 are independent standard normal variables. To impose a scale normalization, $b_{11} = 1$ is assumed. In the experiment, the true parameters are $\beta = 1$, $\gamma = 1$, $(b_{21}, b_{22}) = (0.6, 0.8)$, and $(\delta_1, \delta_2, \delta_3) = (1, 0, 1)$. Here u_1, u_2, and ε are correlated with each other. The implied marginal distributions of u_1, u_2, and ε are, respectively, $N(0, 1)$, $N(0, 1)$, and $N(0, 2)$, and the covariances of u_1 and u_2, u_1 and ε, and u_2 and ε are, respectively, 0.6, 1, and 0.6. x is generated from an $N(0, \frac{4}{3})$ distribution. This specification implies that the regression equation (3.6.2) has an $R^2 = 0.4$ for the underlying population before selection. For the utility functions in (3.6.1), $z_1 = w_1 + w_3$ and $z_2 = w_2 + w_3$, where the w's are independently $N(0, \frac{1}{2})$-distributed. Thus, z_1 and z_2 are both $N(0, 1)$, but are correlated with a covariance 0.5. In this model (model 1), x in (3.6.2) is independent of z_1 and z_2 in (3.6.1).

To investigate whether possible correlations between x and z_1 and z_2 have important effects on parameter estimates, two additional models will be estimated. In model 2, x is generated as $x = (\frac{4}{3})^{1/2}[w_3 + w_4]$, where w_4 is an $N(0, \frac{1}{2})$ independent of w_1, w_2, and w_3. The resulting x in model 2 is an $N(0, \frac{4}{3})$, as in model 1, but is correlated with z_1 and z_2 with a 0.5 correlation coefficient for each. To impose stronger correlation, model 3 is specified with $x = (\frac{4}{3})^{1/2}z_1$, which implies that x and z_1 are perfectly correlated and x is correlated with z_2 with a correlation coefficient of 0.5.

The TSSMEs of the outcome equations (3.6.2) based on the recursive simulator in (3.3.6) and unbiased GS simulators in (3.3.8) and (3.3.9) will be compared. They will also be compared with SMLEs based on (3.4.3) or (3.4.5). The optimization subroutine used for SML estimation is the DFP algorithm from the package GQOPT, version 6.08. The programs are written in Fortran and were run in both Sun Sparc and IBM RISC/6000 workstations. For two-stage methods, simulation draws for the estimation of the choice equation are independent of those for the estimation of the outcome equation. Estimates with various sample size n and simulation runs S will be reported. For each case, the number of replications is 400. There are a few cases with a slightly smaller number of replications because of nonconvergence. For these cases, we report the number of successful convergent replications (con#). Summary statistics on the empirical mean and empirical standard deviation (SD) based on the replications are reported. For SMLEs, estimated standard errors (Est. SD) will also be reported. The Est. SD of SMLE is calculated from the reciprocal of the negative numerical second-order derivative of a log SL from GQOPT. For some estimates, the average CPU time in seconds (T) per replication is reported for reference. These times are based on an IBM RISC/6000 model 580 single-processor workstation.

6.2   *Monte Carlo results on TSSM estimation*

The TSSMEs are reported in Tables 3.1 and 3.2. The first-stage estimates of the DC model (Table 3.1) are SMLEs derived with the GHK simulator for choice probabilities. The second column of Table 3.1 reports estimates when unit-variance restrictions are imposed on disturbances, i.e., $b(2, 1)^2 + b(2, 2)^2 = 1$. Estimates for the model without this variance restriction are reported in the first column of Table 3.1. The SMLEs of γ and all parameter estimates in the unrestricted model have small biases. A slightly larger bias in the restricted

Table 3.1. *SML estimation of discrete choice models*

n	S	Estimand	No restriction			Unit-variance restriction		
			Mean	SD	Est. SD	Mean	SD	Est. SD
200	30	γ	1.0326	0.1738	0.1613	1.0182	0.1384	0.1279
		$b(2, 1)$	0.5917	0.1796	0.1808	0.5736	0.1467	0.1430
		$b(2, 2)$	0.8087	0.1901	0.1815	—		
			$F = -151.062$			$F = -151.779, T = 4.27$		
	60	γ	1.0321	0.1738	0.1610	1.0190	0.1392	0.1263
		$b(2, 1)$	0.5922	0.1811	0.1806	0.5738	0.1492	0.1432
		$b(2, 2)$	0.8059	0.1906	0.1809	—		
			$F = -150.972$			$F = -151.699, T = 8.38$		
	100	γ	1.0317	0.1731	0.1609	1.0187	0.1388	0.1279
		$b(2, 1)$	0.5929	0.1816	0.1804	0.5750	0.1470	0.1429
		$b(2, 2)$	0.8050	0.1884	0.1806	—		
			$F = -150.964$			$F = -151.670, T = 13.88$		
500	50	γ	1.0121	0.0939	0.0993	1.0017	0.1023	0.0828
		$b(2, 1)$	0.5970	0.1103	0.1116	0.5853	0.0964	0.0899
		$b(2, 2)$	0.8067	0.1074	0.1121	—		
			$F = -380.859$			$F = -382.256, T = 18.51$		

True parameters: $\gamma = 1$, $b(2, 1) = 0.6$, and $b(2, 2) = 0.8$.

Table 3.2. *Two-stage simulation estimation of sample selection equations*

Method	S	c	β Mean	β SD	δ_1 Mean	δ_1 SD	δ_2 Mean	δ_2 SD	T
SIV-1	30		0.9930	0.1382	1.0084	0.4020	−0.0066	0.6405	0.16
	60		0.9960	0.1377	1.0154	0.3925	0.0017	0.6030	0.28
	100		0.9931	0.1389	1.0188	0.3768	0.0157	0.5893	0.44
SIV-2	30		0.9961	0.1545	1.0306	0.6222	0.0111	1.0789	0.28
	60		0.9942	0.1530	1.0028	0.5473	−0.0207	0.8877	0.51
	100		0.9957	0.1530	1.0108	0.4993	−0.0114	0.8079	0.82
SOLS	30		0.9948	0.1402	0.9280	0.3142	−0.1027	0.4553	0.10
	60		0.9943	0.1379	0.9586	0.3303	−0.0661	0.4933	0.16
	100		0.9942	0.1384	0.9837	0.3488	−0.0307	0.5199	0.24
SIV-Gibbs-1	30	5	0.9926	0.1389	1.0435	0.4345	0.0571	0.6728	0.92
	30	15	0.9959	0.1404	1.0111	0.4258	0.0040	0.6852	2.85
	30	30	0.9924	0.1403	1.0120	0.4054	0.0158	0.6653	5.65
	60	10	0.9940	0.1394	1.0296	0.3954	0.0364	0.6059	3.73
	100	10	0.9949	0.1367	1.0228	0.3673	0.0189	0.5653	6.34
SIV-Gibbs-2	30	5	0.9923	0.1388	1.0385	0.4342	0.0413	0.6748	0.95
	30	15	0.9955	0.1398	1.0088	0.4164	−0.0002	0.6661	2.87
	30	30	0.9923	0.1393	1.0133	0.4059	0.0174	0.6613	5.71
	60	10	0.9940	0.1388	1.0267	0.3970	0.0297	0.6072	3.82
	100	10	0.9940	0.1370	1.0202	0.3662	0.0176	0.5673	6.44

True parameters: $\beta = 1$, $\delta_1 = 1$, and $\delta_2 = 0$; sample size before selection $n = 200$.
Note: The sample size for the alternative 1 after selection is, on average, 65.65 with a minimum of 50 and a maximum of 83 observations.

estimate is observed for the estimate of $b(2, 1)$. There are some slight improvements in the maximized log SL value (F) when S increases from 30 to 100, but the SMLEs are not sensitive to S. As the restriction is correctly imposed, the SDs of restricted estimates are smaller than those of unrestricted estimates. As n increases from 200 to 500, the SDs decrease with a rate on average compatible to the theoretical $\sqrt{n}$ rate. These results provide additional Monte Carlo evidence of the good performance of the GHK simulator for the estimation of DC multinomial probit models (Hajivassiliou, McFadden, and Ruud 1996, Borsch-Supan and Hajivassiliou 1993, Keane 1994, and Geweke, Keane, and Runkle 1994).

Table 3.2 reports the TSSMEs of the outcome equation. Equation (3.6.2) implies that $y = x\beta + \delta_1\xi_1 + \delta_2\xi_2 + \delta_3\xi_3$. Conditional on samples with $I_1 = 1$, ξ_1 and ξ_2 are simulated. The SIV method SIV-1 is based on the recursive simulator (3.3.6), SIV-Gibbs-1 is based on $\hat{E}_{2,S}$ of (3.3.8), and SIV-Gibbs-2 is based on $\hat{E}_{3,S}^{(1)}$ of (3.3.9). IVs for the bias-correction term are independently simulated through a similar procedure in each approach. The IV procedure based on (3.3.11) by simulating $E(I_1\xi_1)$ and $E(I_1\xi_2)$ by the recursive simulator and using

x as IV for $I_1 x$ is reported as SIV-2 in Table 3.2. Finally, we report an ordinary least squares (SOLS) estimator of the bias-corrected simulated outcome equation conditional on $I_1 = 1$ with the recursive simulator. This SOLS estimator is consistent if S goes to infinity, but would be inconsistent if a constant S were used. The inconsistency comes from the correlation of the simulators' errors with the simulators themselves in the simulated bias-corrected equation. All the samples before selection are based on $n = 200$. The subsamples for individuals who choose the first alternative are, on average, about one third. Draws S vary from 30 to 100. The first-stage estimate for each case corresponds to the SMLE of DC with the same n and S. For the GS approach, the deterministic components, $z_1 \hat{\gamma}$ and $z_2 \hat{\gamma}$, are used as starting points for the Markov chain simulation via the Gibbs sampler. A more thorough description of the Gibbs sampler and its cycles is provided in Appendix A for reference. We have done some preliminary inspection on the stability of the Markov chain by monitoring the convergence of several quartiles of simulation runs as suggested in Tanner and Wong (1987); the sampler seems to have rapid convergence after a couple of iterations, as demonstrated in Figure 3.1. For the results in Table 3.2, we have tried different Gibbs cycles c from 5 to 30. All the TSSMEs of β hardly have any bias. Except for the SOLS approach with small S's, the estimates of δ_1

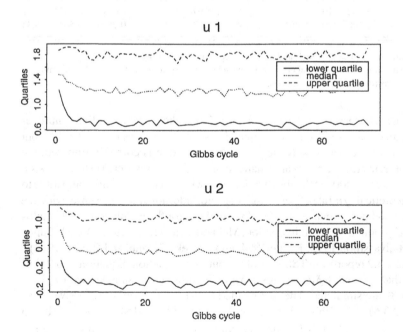

Figure 3.1. The Gibbs sampler and its convergence.

and δ_2 have very small biases. These estimates are sensitive to neither S nor c. The estimates of δ_1 from the SOLS approach show some biases with $S = 30$ or 60. As we have pointed out before, the SOLS approach will not give consistent estimates with a fixed finite S, which translates into small S in this context. For the SIV-1 approach, even though the simulator for the bias correction term is biased, the Monte Carlo results show that small $S = 30$ does not create a substantial bias for these TSSMEs. Estimates from the SIV-2 approach have the largest SD among all five approaches. The estimates from SIV-1, SIV-Gibbs-1, and SIV-Gibbs-2 have similar SDs. But the computing time for SIV-1 can be much less than for SIV-Gibbs-1 and SIV-Gibbs-2. Among the TSSMEs, the SIV-1 approach is preferable.

6.3 *Monte Carlo results on SML estimation*

Tables 3.3 and 3.4 report SMLEs for model 1 where x is independent of z_1 and z_2. Table 3.3 reports results (SML-1) for the SL (3.4.5). Results (SML-2) with the other SL (3.4.3) are reported in Table 3.4. Models with or without restrictions on parameters are estimated. A model with one restriction refers to one where unit-variance restrictions are imposed, and a model with two restrictions refers to one where both unit variances and $\delta_2 = 0$ are assumed known. All these SMLEs with various n's and S's provide unbiased estimates of β, γ, and b's.

There are downward biases in the SML-1 estimates of δ_3 with the unrestricted model. Such biases are relatively small in the SML-2 estimates. But the latter approach has relatively large biases for δ_1 with small $S = 30$. Those biases become small when the constraint $\delta_2 = 0$ is imposed. They also decrease as n increases.

Overall, these two different SLs are compatible with each other in mean and SD statistics with a moderate $S = 60$ or 100. The SMLEs do not seem to be very sensitive to S, except for the SML-2 approach for some of the δ's. There are some changes in mean and SD of the SML-2 estimates of δ_1 and δ_3 when S is increased from 30 to 60. The time cost is approximately linear in S or n. The estimated SDs are underestimated in some cases but, overall, are not too far off. The SMLEs of the SEL model are expected to be efficient relative to the SMLEs of the choice model. Comparing the SMLEs in Tables 3.3 and 3.4 with the SMLEs of the choice model in Table 3.1 and the TSSMEs of the outcome equation in Table 3.2, we find some slight improvements in the SMLEs of parameters of utility functions, but not much difference in the estimates of β. The major improvements are in the precision of estimates of δ_1 and δ_2. The SDs of the SMLEs of δ_1 and δ_2 in Tables 3.3 and 3.4 are much smaller than those of the TSSMEs in Table 3.2. That is expected, as the SML methods can be asymptotically efficient.

Table 3.3. *SML estimation of sample selection models – SML-1*

n	S	Estimand	No restriction			One restriction			Two restrictions		
			Mean	SD	Est. SD	Mean	SD	Est. SD	Mean	SD	Est. SD
200	30	β	0.9959	0.1364	0.1288	0.9945	0.1362	0.1302	0.9941	0.1340	0.1341
		δ_1	0.9978	0.2975	0.2306	0.9975	0.2981	0.2315	1.0206	0.1996	0.1877
		δ_2	-0.0287	0.4641	0.3494	-0.0259	0.4478	0.3510	—		
		δ_3	0.8098	0.2825	0.1958	0.8187	0.2784	0.1962	0.9352	0.1779	0.1535
		γ	1.0299	0.1705	0.1385	1.0202	0.1296	0.1149	1.0203	0.1262	0.1197
		$b(2,1)$	0.5902	0.1779	0.1639	0.5726	0.1472	0.1358	0.5743	0.1439	0.1407
		$b(2,2)$	0.8087	0.1897	0.1679	—			—		
			$F = -256.329$, con # 398			$F = -256.761$			$F = -257.312$, $T = 10.26$		
	60	β	0.9924	0.1459	0.1307	0.9948	0.1356	0.1322	0.9941	0.1339	0.1334
		δ_1	1.0018	0.2923	0.2367	0.9989	0.2904	0.2348	1.0200	0.2002	0.1872
		δ_2	-0.0128	0.4605	0.3669	-0.0282	0.4411	0.3619	—		
		δ_3	0.8048	0.2932	0.2032	0.8282	0.2582	0.2059	0.9358	0.1778	0.1536
		γ	1.0257	0.1766	0.1395	1.0197	0.1279	0.1164	1.0208	0.1267	0.1195
		$b(2,1)$	0.5779	0.2179	0.1659	0.5746	0.1466	0.1369	0.5756	0.1457	0.1404
		$b(2,2)$	0.8251	0.4016	0.1743	—			—		
			$F = -256.754$, con # 395			$F = -256.753$, con # 397			$F = -257.229$, $T = 20.20$		

100	β	0.9944	0.1441	0.1335	0.9939	0.1347	0.1325	0.9942	0.1339	0.1338
	δ_1	1.0035	0.2926	0.2384	0.9997	0.2908	0.2363	1.0200	0.2001	0.1875
	δ_2	−0.0150	0.4612	0.3698	−0.0230	0.4445	0.3660	—		
	δ_3	0.8126	0.2703	0.2106	0.8284	0.2499	0.2112	0.9357	0.1783	0.1532
	γ	1.0248	0.1745	0.1399	1.0194	0.1278	0.1171	1.0205	0.1264	0.1201
	$b(2,1)$	0.5903	0.1819	0.1657	0.5769	0.1446	0.1377	0.5764	0.1437	0.1405
	$b(2,2)$	0.8038	0.1866	0.1713						
		$F = -256.614$, con # 395			$F = -256.648$, con # 398			$F = -257.225$, $T = 33.66$		
500	β	0.9970	0.0899	0.0853	0.9971	0.0901	0.0856	0.9964	0.0897	0.0853
30	δ_1	0.9838	0.1760	0.1550	0.9845	0.1741	0.1574	1.0014	0.1208	0.1189
	δ_2	−0.0312	0.2764	0.2455	−0.0307	0.2686	0.2447	—		
	δ_3	0.9459	0.1418	0.1189	0.9480	0.1444	0.1199	0.9767	0.1068	0.0969
	γ	1.0113	0.0920	0.0875	1.0062	0.0729	0.0737	1.0065	0.0728	0.0754
	$b(2,1)$	0.5956	0.1103	0.1062	0.5874	0.0882	0.0863	0.5867	0.0880	0.0873
	$b(2,2)$	0.8075	0.1081	0.1075						
		$F = -646.527$, $T = 36.19$			$F = -647.035$, $T = 30.412$			$F = -647.543$, $T = 25.62$		

True parameters: $\beta = 1$, $\delta_1 = 1$, $\delta_2 = 0$, $\delta_3 = 1$, $\gamma = 1$, $b(2,1) = 0.6$, and $b(2,2) = 0.8$.

Notes: One restriction: unit variance for choice-equation disturbances; two restrictions: unit variance for all choice-equation disturbances and $\delta_2 = 0$.

Table 3.4. *SML estimation of sample selection models – SML-2*

n	S	Estimand	No restriction			One restriction			Two restrictions		
			Mean	SD	Est. SD	Mean	SD	Est. SD	Mean	SD	Est. SD
200	30	β	0.9935	0.1407	0.1333	0.9919	0.1398	0.1342	0.9943	0.1350	0.1353
		δ_1	0.9253	0.3028	0.2355	0.9298	0.2970	0.2325	0.9840	0.2049	0.1927
		δ_2	−0.1240	0.4333	0.3233	−0.1204	0.4289	0.3183	—		
		δ_3	0.9220	0.2169	0.1629	0.9260	0.2098	0.1666	0.9931	0.1600	0.1457
		γ	1.0304	0.1720	0.1431	1.0182	0.1288	0.1177	1.0188	0.1264	0.1208
		$b(2, 1)$	0.5908	0.1835	0.1692	0.5719	0.1509	0.1404	0.5728	0.1463	0.1429
		$b(2, 2)$	0.8112	0.1936	0.1758	—			—		
			$F = -256.606, T = 17.41$			$F = -257.178$			$F = -257.903$		
	60	β	0.9932	0.1391	0.1307	0.9947	0.1387	0.1301	0.9953	0.1345	0.1334
		δ_1	0.9655	0.2874	0.2274	0.9688	0.2922	0.2236	1.0039	0.2054	0.1871
		δ_2	−0.0629	0.4360	0.3298	−0.0555	0.4419	0.3245	—		
		δ_3	0.8734	0.2515	0.1697	0.8710	0.2581	0.1685	0.9614	0.1745	0.1478
		γ	1.0278	0.1706	0.1403	1.0199	0.1291	0.1160	1.0201	0.1271	0.1208
		$b(2, 1)$	0.5908	0.1799	0.1676	0.5726	0.1513	0.1385	0.5750	0.1466	0.1420
		$b(2, 2)$	0.8057	0.1929	0.1722	—			—		
			$F = -256.160, T = 35.65$			$F = -256.772$			$F = -257.479$		
	100	β	0.9961	0.1393	0.1299	0.9937	0.1423	0.1269	0.9942	0.1339	0.1332
		δ_1	0.9749	0.2899	0.2316	0.9817	0.2838	0.2247	1.0063	0.2014	0.1885
		δ_2	−0.0569	0.4483	0.3440	−0.0337	0.4704	0.3298	—		
		δ_3	0.8518	0.2710	0.1773	0.8407	0.2864	0.1750	0.9579	0.1741	0.1500
		γ	1.0264	0.1703	0.1380	1.0175	0.1281	0.1141	1.0198	0.1264	0.1201
		$b(2, 1)$	0.5924	0.1804	0.1650	0.5713	0.1526	0.1359	0.5761	0.1440	0.1413
		$b(2, 2)$	0.8039	0.1883	0.1700	—			—		
			$F = -256.054, T = 61.28$			$F = -256.660$			$F = -257.486$		
500	30	β	0.9971	0.0904	0.0853	0.9970	0.0904	0.0851	0.9969	0.0900	0.0852
		δ_1	0.9013	0.1809	0.1518	0.9040	0.1792	0.1539	0.9637	0.1222	0.1227
		δ_2	−0.1409	0.2543	0.2134	−0.1358	0.2525	0.2152	—		
		δ_3	1.0247	0.1068	0.0968	1.0249	0.1073	0.1024	1.0289	0.0993	0.0920
		γ	1.0132	0.0921	0.0886	1.0055	0.0725	0.0720	1.0055	0.0729	0.0750
		$b(2, 1)$	0.5988	0.1107	0.1068	0.5872	0.0883	0.0861	0.5854	0.0890	0.0883
		$b(2, 2)$	0.8120	0.1089	0.1087	—			—		
			$F = -647.799, T = 41.97$			$F = -648.306$			$F = -649.022$		

True parameters: $\beta = 1$, $\delta_1 = 1$, $\delta_2 = 0$, $\delta_3 = 1$, $\gamma = 1$, $b(2, 1) = 0.6$, and $b(2, 2) = 0.8$.

To investigate whether asymptotic normal distributions provide accurate approximations to finite-sample distributions of the SMLEs for $n = 200$ and 500, Figures 3.2 to 3.5 are graphical presentations of normal probability plots (Q-Q plots) for the SMLEs. These plots are derived from the statistical package S-Plus. When the sampling distribution is close to a normal distribution, the plotted quantiles should mostly lie on a straight line (Chambers et al. 1983). Figure 3.2 shows that for $n = 200$, except for the SML-1 estimate of δ_3,

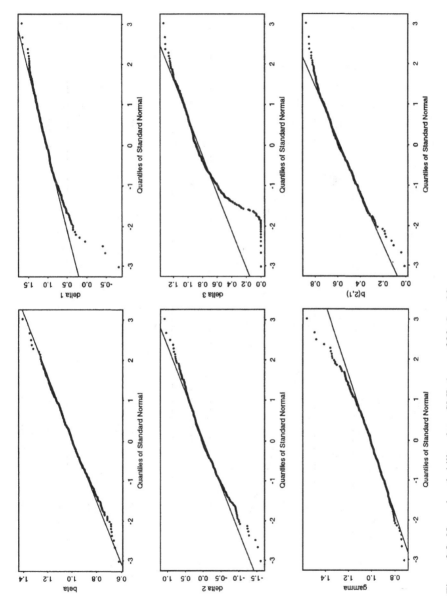

Figure 3.2. Normal probability plot – SML-1; $n = 200$, $S = 30$.

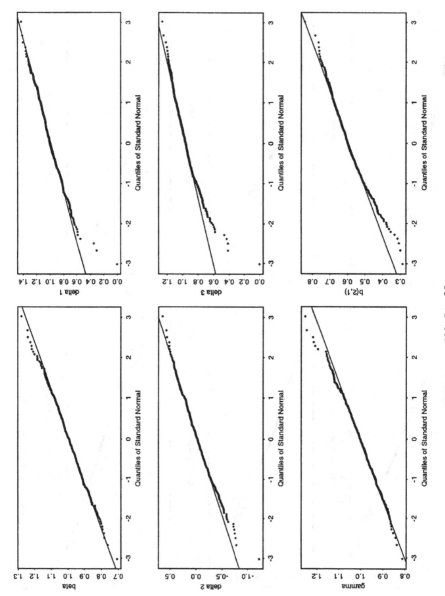

Figure 3.3. Normal probability plot – SML-1; $n = 500$, $S = 30$.

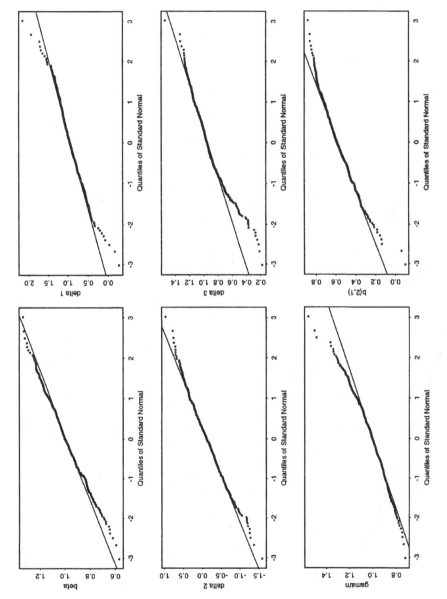

Figure 3.4. Normal probability plot – SML-2; $n = 200$, $S = 30$.

95

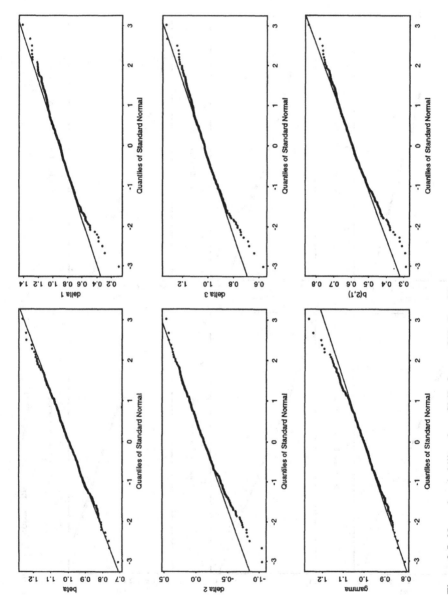

Figure 3.5. Normal probability plot – SML_2; $n = 500$, $S = 30$.

finite-sample distributions seem to be approximately normal. For the SML-1 estimate of δ_3, its finite-sample distribution has a thicker right-hand tail. This might be due to the fact that the δ_3 is a positive parameter in a Cholesky decomposition and its estimates have been restricted to be nonnegative in estimation. The estimates of δ_3 in some replications are very close to zero. For the SML-2 estimates in Figure 3.3, the corresponding distribution of the estimate of δ_3 is better approximated than that of the SML-1 estimate. For larger sample size, $n = 500$, normality approximates seem reasonably adequate.

To investigate effects of correlated regressors, Table 3.5 reports results for the SML estimation of model 2 and model 3. x and z_1 are perfectly correlated in model 3. The results in Table 3.5 can be compared with corresponding SMLEs in Tables 3.3 and 3.4. For both alternative models, the SMLEs of β in Table 3.5 have larger SDs, but the SDs of the SMLEs of γ can be slightly smaller. The SDs of β for model 2 turn out to be larger than those for model 3. But the reduction of SD for β in model 3 is accompanied by increased SDs for the SMLEs of δ_2 and $b(2, 1)$. Overall, stronger correlation among regressors in the outcome equation and utility functions does not have substantial effects on SMLEs for P-SEL models.

More detailed comparisons of the two different SLs in (3.4.3) and (3.4.5) will investigate their variances due to sample variation and due to simulation. Related plots in Figure 3.6 provide numerical evidence of the better performance of (3.4.5) over (3.4.3). The graphs are drawn for one sample of size $n = 200$ of model 1 and are derived from 100 replications of simulation runs with $S = 30$ at each value of a parameter vector. Each graph reports the mean and two SDs due to simulation variations from a cross section of an SL with respect to a single parameter while remaining parameters are fixed at their true values. The slk-1 refers to the log SL in (3.4.5) and the slk-2 refers to that in (3.4.3). The axes beta, gamma, b21, b22, d1, d2, and d3 refer, respectively, to the parameters β, γ, b_{21}, b_{22}, δ_1, δ_2, and δ_3. It is apparent that the log SL in (3.4.5) has much smaller simulation errors than that in (3.4.3).

Further evidence is provided in Table 3.6 in terms of variance decomposition. The variance of a log SL is due to two sources of variation – simulation and sample variations. The results in Table 3.6 are based on SLs for 100 sample sets, of which each has $n = 200$. For each sample of size 200, the likelihood is simulated by (3.4.5) and (3.4.3), which are referred to, respectively, as SL-1 and SL-2. The number of simulation runs is $S = 30$. The likelihood is evaluated at the true parameter vector. For each n, 100 independent sets of simulation runs with $S = 30$ are replicated. This allows us to investigate the variance of an SL due to both its MCV and sample variation.

In Table 3.6, results are reported for log SLs instead of SLs in (3.4.6). This is because the SL values are numerically too small for convenient tabulation. The log SL function involves a nonlinear transformation of the SL, however,

Table 3.5. *SML estimation of sample selection models – strongly correlated regressors*

Model	Method	Estimand	No restriction			One restriction			Two restrictions		
			Mean	SD	Est. SD	Mean	SD	Est. SD	Mean	SD	Est. SD
2	SMLE-1	β	1.0014	0.1626	0.1403	1.0013	0.1623	0.1427	0.9964	0.1496	0.1390
		δ_1	0.9836	0.2847	0.2477	0.9857	0.2783	0.2520	1.0157	0.2018	0.1885
		δ_2	−0.0607	0.4743	0.3695	−0.0543	0.4645	0.3818	—		
		δ_3	0.8145	0.2967	0.1971	0.8245	0.2865	0.2055	0.9396	0.1674	0.1527
		γ	1.0097	0.1517	0.1355	0.9995	0.1172	0.1129	0.9989	0.1153	0.1183
		$b(2,1)$	0.6096	0.1691	0.1613	0.5890	0.1309	0.1313	0.5884	0.1298	0.1379
		$b(2,2)$	0.8024	0.1791	0.1665	—			—		
			$F = -256.815$, con # 399			$F = -257.279$, $T = 13.64$			$F = -257.927$, $T = 10.27$		
	SMLE-2	β	1.0095	0.1644	0.1421	1.0119	0.1643	0.1446	0.9945	0.1523	0.1401
		δ_1	0.9010	0.2833	0.2356	0.8967	0.2809	0.2389	0.9804	0.2046	0.1951
		δ_2	−0.1604	0.4500	0.3248	−0.1712	0.4381	0.3341	—		
		δ_3	0.9243	0.2218	0.1603	0.9338	0.2120	0.1647	0.9939	0.1531	0.1464
		γ	1.0087	0.1494	0.1397	0.9975	0.1176	0.1155	0.9976	0.1159	0.1183
		$b(2,1)$	0.6061	0.1655	0.1663	0.5885	0.1303	0.1357	0.5872	0.1306	0.1394
		$b(2,2)$	0.8034	0.1786	0.1733	—			—		
			$F = -257.205$, $T = 17.81$			$F = -257.723$, $T = 14.63$			$F = -258.505$, $T = 12.21$		

3		A Est	A SD	A SD	B Est	B SD	B SD	C Est	C SD	C SD
SMLE-1	β	1.0007	0.1495	0.1437	0.9975	0.1465	0.1416	1.0020	0.1339	0.1374
	δ_1	1.0016	0.2785	0.2379	0.9987	0.2802	0.2351	1.0187	0.2009	0.1880
	δ_2	-0.0298	0.4938	0.3693	-0.0347	0.4931	0.3664	—		
	δ_3	0.8103	0.2767	0.2061	0.8167	0.2678	0.2088	0.9500	0.1581	0.1523
	γ	1.0229	0.1657	0.1437	1.0113	0.1249	0.1164	1.0115	0.1238	0.1216
	$b(2, 1)$	0.5935	0.1925	0.1630	0.5758	0.1507	0.1336	0.5766	0.1500	0.1384
	$b(2, 2)$	0.8051	0.1881	0.1704	—			—		
		$F = -258.552$			$F = -259.094$			$F = -259.713$		
SMLE-2	β	0.9984	0.1550	0.1416	0.9965	0.1507	0.1431	1.0115	0.1364	0.1389
	δ_1	0.9387	0.2896	0.2254	0.9360	0.2896	0.2312	0.9851	0.2034	0.1949
	δ_2	-0.1190	0.4634	0.3138	-0.1174	0.4574	0.3211	—		
	δ_3	0.9118	0.2144	0.1630	0.9162	0.2153	0.1664	1.0007	0.1472	0.1476
	γ	1.0209	0.1714	0.1468	1.0096	0.1259	0.1201	1.0114	0.1237	0.1220
	$b(2, 1)$	0.5949	0.1955	0.1665	0.5750	0.1526	0.1378	0.5753	0.1509	0.1391
	$b(2, 2)$	0.8051	0.1918	0.1759	—			—		
		$F = -258.930$			$F = -259.476$			$F = -260.269$		

True parameters: $\beta = 1, \delta_1 = 1, \delta_2 = 0, \delta_3 = 1, \gamma = 1, b(2, 1) = 0.6$, and $b(2, 2) = 0.8$. Sample size $n = 200, S = 30$.

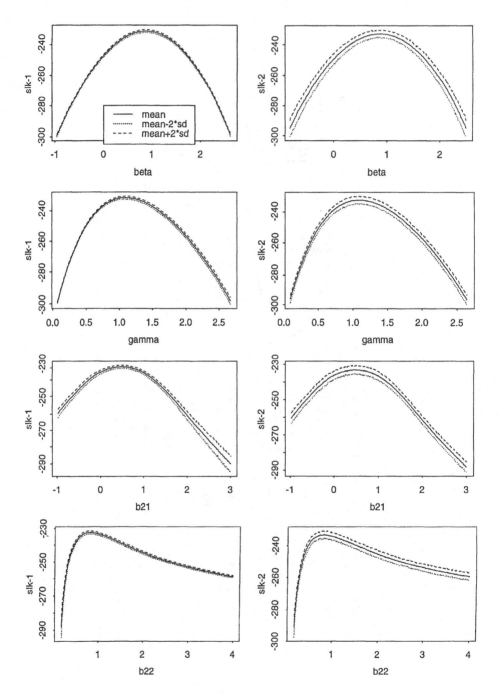

Figure 3.6. Simulated likelihood.

100

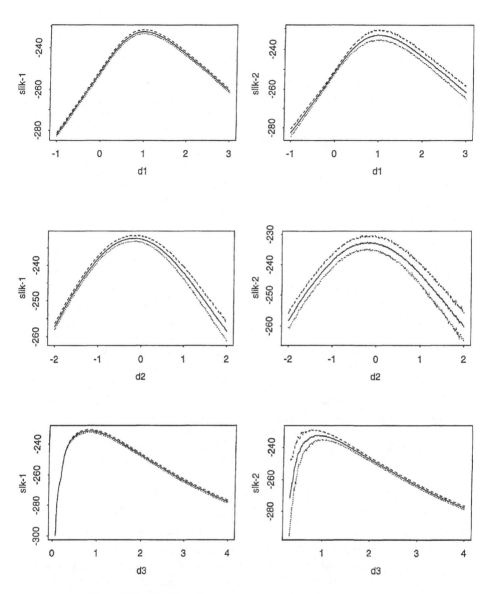

Figure 3.6. (*Continued*)

Table 3.6. *Variance decomposition of simulated likelihood functions*

Function	Model	Mean	sdcm1	sdcm2	SD
SL-1	1	−261.3	0.4759	13.55	13.56
	2	−262.4	0.4784	13.92	13.93
	3	−263.1	0.4727	14.53	14.54
SL-2	1	−261.9	1.238	13.72	13.78
	2	−263.0	1.239	14.01	14.07
	3	−263.8	1.272	14.66	14.71

Notes: Number of samples = 100; simulation replications, 100/sample; $n = 200; S = 30$.

and will no longer be unbiased. For this reason, the second variance term in (3.4.6) may be slightly different for various unbiased likelihood simulators.

Table 3.6 reports sample evaluations of the two variance components of log SLs for all three models at the true parameter vector. The sdcm1 refers to the empirical SD of the first variance term on the right-hand side of (3.4.6), the sdcm2 refers to the SD of the second variance term, and the SD refers to the overall SD. The mean refers to the overall mean of SL value for a model. The sdcm1 due to simulation for the SL (3.4.3) is three times larger than for the SL (3.4.5). This evidence confirms the intuition described in Appendix B. The sdcm1 component is, however, a small fraction of the sdcm2 component for these two SLs for all three models. The overall means and SDs are similar in magnitude for these two SLs, though those of (3.4.3) are slightly larger than those of (3.4.5).

6.4   *Finite-sample variance decomposition of TSSM and SML estimates*

A superior likelihood simulator with a relatively small MCV component in (3.4.6) does not necessarily imply that its corresponding SMLE of an unknown parameter will have smaller variance in a finite-sample setting. The variance of a parameter estimator (without simulation) is determined by the randomness of sample observations. In simulation estimation, it depends also on the randomness of simulation draws. It is known that the SMLE is asymptotically efficient only if S increases at a rate faster than $\sqrt{n}$ (see, e.g., Lee 1992, Gourieroux and Monfort 1993). Thus, under the latter design, the asymptotic variance of an SMLE may be determined solely by the randomness of sample observation. However, the randomness of simulation draws may still have an important effect on the overall variance of a simulated parameter estimator in a finite sample with a moderate S. Let $\hat{\theta}(y, \xi)$ be an estimator of an unknown parameter θ, where y is a sample vector and ξ is a vector of random draws. The variance of $\hat{\theta}$ is a sum of two terms:

$$\text{var}(\hat{\theta}(y, \xi)) = E[\text{var}(\hat{\theta}(y, \xi) \mid y)] + \text{var}[E(\hat{\theta}(y, \xi) \mid y)]. \tag{3.6.3}$$

Here $\text{var}(\hat{\theta}(y, \xi) \mid y)$ is the MCV of the estimator conditional on a sample. The first term in (3.6.3) is the mean of MCVs over sample sets. The second term captures, in general, not only the variance due to sample variation but also an effect due to simulation. As $\theta(y, \xi)$ depends on ξ nonlinearly in a complex implicit form, $E(\hat{\theta}(y, \xi) \mid y)$ of y may be different with various unbiased SLs. As SLs may have different shapes from various simulation approaches, the second term may also be different. Unless the conditional mean functions of y are the same, the comparison of MCVs does not necessarily provide the adequate ranking of simulation approaches in parameter estimation.

To evaluate the two effects of simulation, we report results on variance decomposition in Table 3.7. The reported results are the sample average of the conditional SD due to random draws (sdcm1), i.e., $E[\text{var}(\hat{\theta}(y, \xi) \mid y)]^{1/2}$, the sample SD of the conditional mean function (sdcm2), i.e., $\text{var}^{1/2}[E(\hat{\theta}(y, \xi) \mid y)]$, and the overall SD, based on 100 sets of random draws with $S = 30$ for each $n = 200$ and a total number of sample sets of 100. Compare first the TSSMEs of the outcome equation. In order of descending sdcm1, the ranking is SIV-2, SIV-1, SIV-Gibbs-1 (Gib-1), SIV-Gibbs-2 (Gib-2), and SOLS. In order of sdcm2, the corresponding ranking is SIV-2, Gib-1, Gib-2, SIV-1, and SOLS. The SIV-2 has the largest variance. The rankings among the SIV-1, Gib-1, and Gib-2 should not be exaggerated, since their differences on these variance components are very small. Overall, these three approaches are compatible with each other.

The SOLS turns out to have smaller variance components than the various SIV estimates. This may be due to the additional independent simulation of IVs for bias-correction terms with the various SIV approaches. In comparison, the SML-1 approach with the SL (3.4.5) has smaller sdcm1's than those of the SML-2 approach for all parameters in the model. This means that MCVs are smaller when the SML-1 approach is used. However, it is interesting to note that for the estimation of δ's, the SML-2 estimates have smaller sdcm2's than those of the SML-1 estimates. This means that the corresponding conditional mean functions of SML-2 estimators have smaller variance. For the latter, the reduction of the sdcm2 for δ_3 is large enough that its overall SD can even be smaller than the corresponding SD of the SML-1 approach. The shares of the sdcm1 over the SD for the β, γ and b's of both SML approaches are very small. The SML-1 and SML-2 estimates with parameter constraints imposed

Table 3.7. *Finite-sample variance decomposition of coefficient estimates*

Method	Statistic	β	δ_1	δ_2	δ_3	γ	$b(2, 1)$	$b(2, 2)$
SML-1	sdcm1	0.0083	0.0393	0.1046	0.1049	0.0163	0.0284	0.0240
	sdcm2	0.1392	0.2456	0.3980	0.2415	0.1330	0.1532	0.1780
	SD	0.1394	0.2487	0.4115	0.2633	0.1340	0.1558	0.1796
SML-1R	sdcm1	0.0010	0.0048	—	0.0043	0.0066	0.0159	—
	sdcm2	0.1473	0.2014	—	0.1873	0.1160	0.1349	—
	SD	0.1473	0.2014	—	0.1873	0.1162	0.1359	—
SML-2	sdcm1	0.0371	0.1729	0.2964	0.1506	0.0329	0.0500	0.0564
	sdcm2	0.1480	0.2116	0.2887	0.1529	0.1411	0.1591	0.1781
	SD	0.1525	0.2733	0.4138	0.2146	0.1448	0.1668	0.1868
SML-2R	sdcm1	0.0237	0.0581	—	0.0585	0.0111	0.0180	—
	sdcm2	0.1463	0.1950	—	0.1541	0.1156	0.1377	—
	SD	0.1482	0.2034	—	0.1648	0.1161	0.1389	—
SIV-1	sdcm1	0.0222	0.2136	0.3821				
	sdcm2	0.1501	0.3175	0.5001				
	SD	0.1517	0.3827	0.6294				
SIV-2	sdcm1	0.0228	0.4096	0.7512				
	sdcm2	0.1646	0.4138	0.6710				
	SD	0.1662	0.5822	1.0070				
SOLS	sdcm1	0.0174	0.1457	0.2494				
	sdcm2	0.1497	0.2520	0.3525				
	SD	0.1507	0.2911	0.4318				
Gib-1	sdcm1	0.0219	0.2100	0.3790				
	sdcm2	0.1503	0.3261	0.5170				
	SD	0.1519	0.3879	0.6410				
Gib-2	sdcm1	0.0185	0.2053	0.3671				
	sdcm2	0.1502	0.3258	0.5169				
	SD	0.1513	0.3851	0.6340				

Notes: Number of samples $= 100$; simulation replications, 100/sample; $n = 200$; $S = 30$; $c = 10$.

(SML-1R and SML-2R, respectively) have similar properties. Comparing the SMLEs of the outcome equation with TSSMEs, the SMLEs have smaller variance components than those of TSSMEs.

6.5   *Effects of distributional misspecification on SMLEs*

To investigate whether the SMLEs are sensitive to misspecified distributions, model 1 in Section 6.1 is used, except that ξ_1, ξ_2, and ξ_3 in the Cholesky decomposition are no longer normally distributed. The normal distribution is symmetric around zero and has a unique mode. To investigate possible effects of skewness and bimodals, we considered several alternatives. The Gumbel design refers to the case that ξ's are independent Gumbel-distributed random variables and are normalized to have zero means and unit variances. The second design, mixture 1, refers to the case that each of ξ's is a 50–50 mixture of two normal variables $N(-3, 1)$ and $N(3, 1)$. These ξ's are independent and normalized to have zero means and unit variances. Since $u_1 = b_{11}\xi_1$, $u_2 = b_{21}\xi_1 + b_{22}\xi_2$, and $\varepsilon = \delta_1\xi_1 + \delta_2\xi_2 + \delta_3\xi_3$, ε is a linear combination of three normal mixtures while u_1 is a single normal mixture. On the contrary, for the third design, mixture 2, ε is a single normal mixture and both u_1 and u_2 are linear combinations of normal mixtures. To be specific, permute (u_1, u_2, ε) to (ε, u_1, u_2). Let CC' be the Cholesky decomposition of the variance matrix of (ε, u_1, u_2). Given the true values of b's and δ's, they determine the variance of (ε, u_1, u_2) and hence C. With C, one has the representation that $\varepsilon = c_{11}\zeta_1^*$, $u_1 = c_{21}\zeta_1^* + c_{22}\zeta_2^*$, and $u_2 = c_{31}\zeta_1^* + c_{32}\zeta_2^* + c_{33}\zeta_3^*$. The ζ^*'s are designed to be independently distributed standardized 50–50 mixtures of $N(-3, 1)$ and $N(3, 1)$.

Table 3.8 reports SMLEs based on (3.4.5) under the normal disturbance specification when data are generated by a Gumbel, a mixture-1, or a mixture-2 design. These results should be compared with those in Table 3.3 (last column), where the SL is correctly specified. For the Gumbel samples, the SMLEs of γ and b_{21} are similar to those of the correctly specified normal SL. The estimate of β shows no bias. Only the estimates of δ's show relatively large biases. So the SMLE with normal SL is not very sensitive to the Gumbel misspecification. For samples generated from mixture-1 disturbances, the SMLE of γ has shown obvious downward bias. The bias does not change with a larger S (200 or 400). It cannot be reduced even when n increases from 200 to 500. On the contrary, the estimates of β and δ_1 are not biased. The downward bias in the SMLE of δ_3 is larger than that in Table 3.3.

In conclusion, the SMLEs of the coefficients in the utility functions, but not the coefficients of the outcome equation, are sensitive to the mixture-1 distribution. When samples are generated from mixture-2 disturbances, all the parameters show small biases. Comparing the latter SMLEs with those in Table 3.3, we find that the biases of both estimates of γ are only about 2 percent. The bias in Table 3.3 is upward, but that in Table 3.8 is downward.

6.6   *Monte Carlo results on semiparametric estimation*

The density of (ξ_1, ξ_2, ξ_3) in the Cholesky decomposition $u_1 = b_{11}\xi_1$, $u_2 = b_{21}\xi_1 + b_{22}\xi_2$ and $\varepsilon = \delta_1\xi_1 + \delta_2\xi_2 + \delta_3\xi_3$ is expanded in finite-order Hermite polynomials. The case called Hermite refers to the SL formulated with the

Table 3.8. *SMLE of misspecified sample selection models*

			Gumbel			Mixture-1			Mixture-2		
n	S	Estimand	Mean	SD	Est. SD	Mean	SD	Est. SD	Mean	SD	Est. SD
200	30	β	0.9962	0.1488	0.1410	0.9888	0.1314	0.1296	0.9884	0.1381	0.1349
		δ_1	1.2279	0.2108	0.1950	0.9984	0.1567	0.1768	0.9712	0.1351	0.1872
		δ_3	0.8908	0.1985	0.1795	0.9130	0.1252	0.1458	0.9669	0.1408	0.1422
		γ	1.0256	0.1219	0.1200	0.8998	0.1033	0.1100	0.9774	0.1192	0.1139
		$b(2,1)$	0.5760	0.1383	0.1336	0.6015	0.1310	0.1374	0.5490	0.1413	0.1471
			$F = -260.039$			$F = -262.866$			$F = -259.700$		
	60	β	0.9962	0.1487	0.1408	0.9888	0.1313	0.1295	0.9885	0.1381	0.1354
		δ_1	1.2275	0.2106	0.1962	0.9982	0.1571	0.1774	0.9708	0.1347	0.1874
		δ_3	0.8912	0.1985	0.1819	0.9130	0.1253	0.1462	0.9671	0.1406	0.1418
		γ	1.0262	0.1225	0.1200	0.9000	0.1029	0.1101	0.9782	0.1196	0.1143
		$b(2,1)$	0.5752	0.1405	0.1347	0.6022	0.1305	0.1374	0.5493	0.1399	0.1472
			$F = -259.995$			$F = -262.828$			$F = -259.648$		
	100	β	0.9962	0.1488	0.1412	0.9889	0.1313	0.1299	0.9884	0.1381	0.1351
		δ_1	1.2268	0.2106	0.1955	0.9982	0.1570	0.1775	0.9704	0.1347	0.1878
		δ_3	0.8916	0.1986	0.1814	0.9131	0.1252	0.1463	0.9674	0.1405	0.1416
		γ	1.0265	0.1222	0.1200	0.9004	0.1033	0.1102	0.9782	0.1198	0.1138
		$b(2,1)$	0.5749	0.1409	0.1346	0.6019	0.1308	0.1375	0.5501	0.1391	0.1471
			$F = -259.955$			$F = -262.788$			$F = -259.588$		

			Mixture-1								
			$S = 200$			$S = 400$					
200		β	0.9889	0.1312	0.1294	0.9889	0.1313	0.1296			
		δ_1	0.9980	0.1568	0.1771	0.9979	0.1567	0.1771			
		δ_3	0.9132	0.1252	0.1465	0.9133	0.1251	0.1461			
		γ	0.9006	0.1032	0.1107	0.9007	0.1029	0.1102			
		$b(2,1)$	0.6015	0.1308	0.1379	0.6020	0.1305	0.1377			
			$F = -262.787$			$F = -262.756$					
			$S = 60$			$S = 100$					
500		β	0.9946	0.0805	0.0822	0.9945	0.0805	0.0822			
		δ_1	1.0083	0.1019	0.1123	1.0083	0.1020	0.1120			
		δ_3	0.9332	0.0795	0.0932	0.9332	0.0795	0.0932			
		γ	0.8995	0.0643	0.0690	0.8995	0.0645	0.0693			
		$b(2,1)$	0.6056	0.0867	0.0872	0.6063	0.0869	0.0870			
			$F = -660.418$			$F = -660.294$					

True parameters: $\beta = 1$, $\delta_1 = 1$, $\delta_2 = 0$, $\delta_3 = 1$, $\gamma = 1$, $b(2,1) = 0.6$, and $b(2,2) = 0.8$.

density expansion

$$f(\xi) = \frac{(1 + c_{100}\xi_1 + c_{010}\xi_2 + c_{001}\xi_3)^2}{1 + c_{100}^2 + c_{010}^2 + c_{001}^2} \prod_{l=1}^{3} \phi(\xi_l). \qquad (3.6.4)$$

This expansion uses the first-order Hermite polynomial. However, because the Hermite expansion involves a square, it has implicitly utilized some second-order polynomial terms. This expansion has introduced three additional free parameters (c's) in addition to the original parameters. The formulation Hermite-ind-1 has the SL formulated with

$$f(\xi) = \frac{(1 + c_{100}\xi_1)^2}{1 + c_{100}^2} \frac{(1 + c_{010}\xi_2)^2}{1 + c_{010}^2} \frac{(1 + c_{001}\xi_3)^2}{1 + c_{001}^2} \prod_{l=1}^{3} \phi(\xi_l). \qquad (3.6.5)$$

This expansion has also three additional parameters. It differs from the Hermite case in that independence of ξ_1, ξ_2, and ξ_3 is imposed. The Hermite-ind-2 case extends the latter case to have a higher-order expansion:

$$f(\xi) = \frac{(1 + c_{100}\xi_1 + c_{200}(\xi_1 - 1)^2)^2}{1 + c_{100}^2 + 2c_{200}^2} \frac{(1 + c_{010}\xi_2 + c_{020}(\xi_2 - 1)^2)^2}{1 + c_{010}^2 + 2c_{020}^2}$$
$$\times \frac{(1 + c_{001}\xi_3 + c_{002}(\xi_3 - 1)^2)^2}{1 + c_{001}^2 + 2c_{002}^2} \prod_{l=1}^{3} \phi(\xi_l). \qquad (3.6.6)$$

This expansion has introduced a total of six more parameters.

Tables 3.9 and 3.10 report the SSMLEs based on (3.6.4)–(3.6.6). The interesting parameters in a semiparametric model are β and γ. Table 3.9 reports results where sample data are generated from model 1 with either normal or Gumbel disturbances. When sample data are generated by the normal distribution, the SSMLEs of β are unbiased and the biases of γ have magnitudes similar to those in Table 3.3. As all the three SSLs contain explicitly the normal SL as a special case, the SSLs correspond to unconstrained estimation for the normally distributed sample. For the latter, as expected, the SDs of the SSMLEs can be larger than those of Table 3.3. The SDs of Hermite-ind-2 SSMLEs γ are two times larger than those in Table 3.3. However, except for that, SDs for the others are not much larger. For data generated by Gumbel disturbances, the SSMLEs are similar to those in Table 3.8. Table 3.10 reports results where sample data are generated by either mixture-1 or mixture-2 disturbances. For the mixture-1 sample, neither Hermite nor Hermite-ind-1 improves the bias of the SMLE of γ in Table 3.8 (column 2). The 10-percent estimated bias remains. Only Hermite-ind-2 appears to have corrected some of the biases in γ. For the mixture-2 sample, the Hermite-ind-2 SSMLEs of β

Table 3.9. *SSML estimation of sample selection models*

n	S	Estimand	Hermite Mean	SD	Hermite-ind-1 Mean	SD	Hermite-ind-2 Mean	SD
			Normal disturbances					
200	30	β	0.9947	0.1371	0.9947	0.1371	0.9969	0.1420
		γ	1.0250	0.1377	1.0244	0.1380	0.9993	0.2293
			$F = -255.724$		$F = -255.729$		$F = -253.808$	
	60	β	0.9938	0.1383	0.9936	0.1386	0.9928	0.1415
		γ	1.0242	0.1407	1.0233	0.1399	1.0145	0.2559
			$F = -255.676$		$F = -255.675$		$F = -253.807$	
	100	β	0.9935	0.1378	0.9933	0.1377	0.9949	0.1423
		γ	1.0226	0.1398	1.0231	0.1394	1.0453	0.2828
			$F = -255.622$		$F = -255.629$		$F = -253.821$	
			Gumbel disturbances					
200	30	β	0.9947	0.1490	0.9954	0.1493	0.9957	0.1447
		γ	1.0235	0.1347	1.0197	0.1321	1.0115	0.2205
			$F = -257.662$		$F = -257.759$		$F = -255.409$	
	60	β	0.9945	0.1477	0.9947	0.1475	0.9957	0.1478
		γ	1.0255	0.1361	1.0189	0.1337	1.0371	0.2331
			$F = -257.539$		$F = -257.602$		$F = -255.424$, con # 399	
	100	β	0.9959	0.1470	0.9962	0.1475	0.9956	0.1468
		γ	1.0252	0.1386	1.0175	0.1371	1.0609	0.2552
			$F = -257.309$		$F = -257.402$		$F = -255.196$, con # 398	

True parameters: $\beta = 1$, $\delta_1 = 1$, $\delta_2 = 0$, $\delta_3 = 1$, $\gamma = 1$, $b(2, 1) = 0.6$, and $b(2, 2) = 0.8$.

have some smaller SDs, but those of γ are much larger than those in Table 3.8 (column 3).

6.7   *Test for normality – finite-sample level of significance and power*

The SLs formulated in (3.6.4)–(3.6.6) may also be valuable for testing normality in disturbances. Since the SL of the normal distribution is nested in any of the SSLs, we may investigate the possible use of SL ratio test statistics. Table 3.11 reports the level of significance and power of those statistics. The nominal levels of significance are based on the chi-square distribution with three degrees of

Table 3.10. *SSML estimation of sample selection models*

n	S	Estimand	Hermite		Hermite-ind-1		Hermite-ind-2	
			Mean	SD	Mean	SD	Mean	SD
					Mixture-1			
200	30	β	0.9895	0.1335	0.9894	0.1334	0.9916	0.1309
		γ	0.9044	0.1171	0.9046	0.1171	0.9197	0.2670
			$F = -261.040$		$F = -261.048$		$F = -258.325$	
	60	β	0.9894	0.1334	0.9894	0.1335	0.9903	0.1201
		γ	0.9051	0.1172	0.9029	0.1166	1.0077	0.3367
			$F = -260.918$		$F = -260.933$		$F = -257.641$, con # 399	
	100	β	0.9894	0.1331	0.9896	0.1335	0.9901	0.1214
		γ	0.9088	0.1196	0.9050	0.1163	1.0843	0.3991
			$F = -260.859$		$F = -260.888$		$F = -257.238$, con # 397	
500	60	β					0.9964	0.0711
		γ					0.9690	0.2838
							$F = -653.506$, con # 398	
	100	β					0.9974	0.0691
		γ					1.0520	0.3649
							$F = -651.885$, con # 398	
					Mixture-2, Hermite-ind-2			
200			$S = 30$		$S = 60$		$S = 100$	
		β	1.0001	0.0946	0.9963	0.0861	0.9965	0.0840
		γ	0.9551	0.2806	1.0170	0.3502	1.0809	0.3934
			$F = -239.638$, con # 398		$F = -239.092$, con # 398		$F = -238.507$, con # 399	

True parameters: $\beta = 1$, $\delta_1 = 1$, $\delta_2 = 0$, $\delta_3 = 1$, $\gamma = 1$, $b(2, 1) = 0.6$, and $b(2, 2) = 0.8$.

freedom for the Hermite and Hermite-ind-1 expansions. For the Hermite-ind-2 expansion, the chi-square distribution with six degrees of freedom is used. The Gumbel, mixture-1, and mixture-2 distributions are used to investigate the power of the test statistics.

The exact levels of significance of the three test statistics tend to be larger than the nominal ones. But they are not too much larger. Instead of a nominal level of 5 percent, the exact level of significance of the Hermite-ind-2 statistic is, on average, about 8 percent. The Hermite and Hermite-ind-1 statistics are slightly more accurate than the Hermite-ind-2 statistic. However, the Hermite and Hermite-ind-1 statistics have weaker power against the mixture-1 alternative. They have also only moderate power against the Gumbel alternative. The Hermite-ind-2 statistic tends to have better power. In particular, it has good power to test against the mixture-2 alternative.

Table 3.11. *Likelihood-ratio test – level of significance and power* (*H_0 normal*)

True distribution	Formulation	N	S	Power			
				10%	5%	2%	1%
Normal	Hermite	200	30	13.00	6.25	3.50	2.00
		200	60	12.00	6.50	3.00	1.75
		200	100	13.00	6.75	2.50	1.25
	Hermite-ind-1	200	30	12.75	5.75	3.50	2.00
		200	60	11.00	6.50	3.00	1.75
		200	100	13.25	7.00	2.75	1.50
	Hermite-ind-2	200	30	15.50	6.75	3.75	2.25
		200	60	15.75	9.50	4.75	2.50
		200	100	14.75	8.00	3.75	2.75
Gumbel	Hermite	200	30	23.75	16.75	9.75	7.00
		200	60	24.81	17.04	10.03	6.77
		200	100	30.75	22.00	13.75	9.00
	Hermite-ind-1	200	30	24.00	15.50	7.50	4.75
		200	60	24.75	16.50	9.25	6.00
		200	100	28.75	21.25	12.25	7.25
	Hermite-ind-2	200	30	30.50	22.75	14.50	10.25
		200	60	30.08	20.80	13.53	9.27
		200	100	33.17	23.62	14.82	9.30
Mixture 1	Hermite	200	30	17.00	8.75	3.50	1.75
		200	60	18.75	9.50	4.75	3.00
		200	100	18.25	9.50	5.75	3.75
	Hermite-ind-1	200	30	16.50	8.75	4.00	1.75
		200	60	18.50	9.25	4.00	3.00
		200	100	17.75	8.50	5.50	4.00
	Hermite-ind-2	200	30	28.00	18.75	10.50	7.50
		200	60	41.85	27.57	16.04	12.53
		200	100	44.58	33.00	23.68	16.62
		500	60	55.28	46.73	35.18	28.39
		500	100	66.58	55.53	45.73	41.21
Mixture 2	Hermite-ind-2	200	30	67.59	66.08	64.07	63.82
		200	60	75.88	72.86	69.35	67.84
		200	100	80.20	76.19	71.43	69.42

7   Conclusions

Simulation estimation of SEL models with a finite number of choice alternatives are considered. Conditional outcome equations can be simulated by various biased or unbiased simulators. A recursive simulator that generalizes the GHK approach for the DC model to the SEL model is possible. Unbiased simulators can be derived via GS. A variation reduction simulation technique based on conditioning can also be used. The outcome equation can be estimated by SIV methods, which are essentially MSM. The likelihood function can also be simulated with various generalizations of the GHK simulator.

To compare the finite-sample performance of various simulators and simulation estimation procedures, Monte Carlo experiments are reported. Monte Carlo experiments demonstrate that the TSSMEs derived with various biased or unbiased simulators for the outcome equation provide similar finite-sample properties. Unbiased simulators via the Gibbs sampler are not difficult to use, but they are computationally expensive compared to the recursive simulator, which however may be biased. The SMLEs based on different density factorizations are also similar, even though variance decompositions in finite samples show interesting differences. They are efficient compared to TSSMEs. Limited Monte Carlo results show that SMLEs based on the normal distributional specification may not be very sensitive to certain distributional misspecifications. But for certain normal-mixture cases, some parameters may have substantial downward biases. SSL generalization based on series expansions with second-order Hermite polynomials can have some use for reducing biases. But the semiparametric estimates may have much larger variances. The SSL ratio test based on second-order Hermite polynomials has good power against some nonnormal alternatives.

Appendix A: The Gibbs sampler and Gibbs cycles

This appendix provides descriptions of operational aspects of the Gibbs sampler and its cycles that are specific to the sample selection model with normal disturbances. For a clear illustration, the described procedures are for a sample selection model relevant to our Monte Carlo study. The outcome equation is $y = x\beta + \varepsilon$, which is observed only when the alternative 1 is chosen, and the utility functions for the choice component are $U_j = z_j\gamma + u_j$, $j = 1, \ldots, m - 1$, and $U_m = 0$. The disturbances ε and the u's are normally distributed with the following Cholesky factorization: $u_j = b_{j1}\xi_1 + \cdots + b_{jj}\xi_j$ for $j = 1, \ldots, m - 1$, and $\varepsilon = \delta_1\xi_1 + \cdots + \delta_m\xi_m$, where the ξ's are independent standard normal variables. Let Λ be the $m \times m$ lower triangular matrix consisting of the b's and δ's of this Cholesky decomposition. Let B_1 be the $(m - 1) \times (m - 1)$ lower triangular submatrix consisting only of the b's. Denote $Z = (z'_1, \cdots, z'_{m-1})'$, and let Φ be the standard normal distribution function. Let $\{e_j^{(s)}\}$, $j = 1, \cdots, m - 1$ and $s = 1, \ldots, S$, be a set of random draws from a uniform random number generator. This set of uniform random numbers is invariant with respect to unknown parameters of the model and is kept fixed during estimation (common draws in the terminology of McFadden 1989).

A.1   *The Gibbs sampler for the discrete choice component*

Let R_l be the permutation matrix which permutes $(u_1, \ldots, u_{m-1})$ to $(u_1, \ldots, u_{l-1}, u_{l+1}, \ldots, u_{m-1}, u_l)$. The variance matrix of $(u_1, \ldots, u_{l-1}, u_{l+1}, \ldots, u_{m-1}, u_l)$ is $R_l B_1 B_1' R_l'$. Let H_l be the lower triangular matrix from the Cholesky decomposition such that $H_l H_l' = R_l B_1 B_1' R_l'$. The (j, k)th entry of H_l will be denoted by $H_{l,jk}$. Denote $\bar{U}^{(l)}_{m-1} = R_l U_{m-1}$ and $Z^{(l)} = R_l Z$. Let $\bar{U}^{(0)}_{m-1}$ be an initial value or a simulated random utility vector.

(1) The simulation of U_1 from $g(U_1 \mid \bar{U}^{(0)}_{(m,-1)}, U_1 > \bar{U}^{(0)}_{(m,-1)})$ is equivalent to the simulation of $U^{(1)}_{m-1}$ from $g(U^{(1)}_{m-1} \mid \bar{U}^{(1),(0)}_{m-2}, U^{(1)}_{m-1} > \max\{\bar{U}^{(1),(0)}_{m-2}, 0\})$. This can be done with the following steps:

   (i) Given $\bar{U}^{(1),(0)}_{m-1}$, compute recursively the components of ξ via the Cholesky decomposition formulation as $\xi_j = (U^{(1),(0)}_j - z^{(1)}_j \gamma - H_{1,j,1}\xi_1 - \cdots - H_{1,j,j-1}\xi_{j-1})/H_{1,j,j}$ for $j = 1, \ldots, m-2$. Let $a_1 = [\max\{\bar{U}^{(1),(0)}_{m-2}, 0\} - (z^{(1)}_{m-1}\gamma + H_{1,m-1,1}\xi_1 + \cdots + H_{1,m-1,m-2}\xi_{m-2})]/H_{1,m-1,m-1}$.

   (ii) Simulate a truncated standard normal variable ξ_{m-1} on $[a_1, \infty)$, i.e., $\xi_{m-1} = -\Phi^{-1}[e^{(s)}_1 \Phi(-a_1)]$.

   (iii) Compute $U^{(1),(1)}_{m-1} = z^{(1)}_{m-1}\gamma + H_{1,m-1,1}\xi_1 + \cdots + H_{1,m-1,m-1}\xi_{m-1}$ and set $U^{(1)}_1 = U^{(1),(1)}_{m-1}$.

(2) Given $U^{(1)}_1, \cdots, U^{(1)}_{l-1}, U^{(0)}_{l+1}, \cdots, U^{(0)}_{m-2}$, simulate U_l from $g(U_l \mid U^{(1)}_1, \cdots, U^{(1)}_{l-1}, U^{(0)}_{l+1}, \cdots, U^{(0)}_{m-1}, U^{(1)}_1 > U_l)$. Equivalently, simulate $U^{(l)}_{m-1}$ from $g(U^{(l)}_{m-1} \mid U^{(l),(1)}_1, \cdots, U^{(l),(1)}_{l-1}, U^{(l),(0)}_{l+1}, \cdots, U^{(l),(0)}_{m-2}, U^{(l),(1)}_1 > U^{(l)}_{m-1})$.

   (i) Solve ξ_j recursively as $\xi_j = (U^{(l),(1)}_j - z^{(l)}_j \gamma - H_{l,j,1}\xi_1 - \cdots - H_{l,j,j-1}\xi_{j-1})/H_{l,j,j}$ for $j = 1, \ldots, l$, and $\xi_j = (U^{(l),(0)}_j - z^{(l)}_j \gamma - H_{l,j,1}\xi_1 - \cdots - H_{l,j,j-1}\xi_{j-1})/H_{l,j,j}$ for $j = l, \ldots, m-2$. Denote $a_l = (U^{(l),(1)}_1 - z^{(l)}_{m-1}\gamma - H_{l,m-1,1}\xi_1 - \cdots - H_{l,m-1,m-2}\xi_{m-2})/H_{l,m-1,m-1}$.

   (ii) Simulate a truncated standard normal variable ξ_{m-1} truncated on $(-\infty, a_l]$, i.e., $\xi_{m-1} = \Phi^{-1}[e^{(s)}_l \Phi(a_l)]$.

   (iii) Compute $U^{(l),(1)}_{m-1} = z^{(l)}_{m-1}\gamma + H_{l,m-1,1}\xi_1 + \cdots + H_{l,m-1,m-1}\xi_{m-1}$, and update $U^{(1)}_l = U^{(l),(1)}_{m-1}$.

One cycle of the Gibbs sampler with (i)–(iii) for $l = 1, \ldots, m - 1$ simulates $\bar{U}_{m-1}^{(1)}$. With $\bar{U}_{m-1}^{(1)}$ replacing $\bar{U}_{m-1}^{(0)}$, the recursion starts a new cycle.

A.2   *Likelihood simulation*

The following steps illustrate the simulation of the likelihood function (3.4.5). The simulation of that in (3.4.3) will be similar with a slight modification.

(1) For the $I_1 = 1$ likelihood component, permute $(u_1, \ldots, u_{m-1}, \varepsilon)$ to $(\varepsilon, u_1, \ldots, u_{m-1})$. Let Q be the corresponding permutation matrix. The variance matrix of $(\varepsilon, u_1, \ldots, u_{m-1})$ is $Q \Lambda Q'$. Compute the lower triangular matrix C such that $CC' = Q \Lambda Q'$ by the Cholesky decomposition. Given the observed sample and values of parameters,

   (i)   compute $\xi_1 = (y - x\beta)/C_{11}$;

   (ii) generate a truncated $N(0, 1)$ variable $\xi_2^{(s)}$ with a support on $[-(z_1\gamma + C_{21}\xi_1)/C_{22}, \; \infty)$ as $\xi_2^{(s)} = -\Phi^{-1}[e_1^{(s)}\Phi((z_1\gamma + C_{21}\xi_1)/C_{22})]$; compute the probability $P(U_1 > 0 \mid \varepsilon)$ as $\Phi((z_1\gamma + C_{21}\xi_1)/C_{22})$;

   (iii) with $\xi_2^{(s)}, \cdots, \xi_l^{(s)}$ generated, compute $P(U_1 > U_l \mid \varepsilon_1, \bar{U}_{l-1})$ as $\Phi([(z_1 - z_l)\gamma + C_{21}\xi_1 + C_{22}\xi_2^{(s)} - C_{l+1,1}\xi_1 - \cdots - C_{l+1,l}\xi_l^{(s)}]/C_{l+1,l+1})$; and generate a truncated normal variable $\xi_{l+1}^{(s)} = \Phi^{-1}[e_l^{(s)}\Phi([(z_1 - z_l)\gamma + C_{21}\xi_1 + C_{22}\xi_2^{(s)} - C_{l+1,1}\xi_1 - \cdots - C_{l+1,l}\xi_l^{(s)}]/C_{l+1,l+1})]$, for $l = 2, \ldots, m - 1$.

Steps (ii) and (iii) can be repeated S times to obtain S simulation runs.

(2) For the $I_j = 1$ likelihood component, where $2 \le j \le m - 1$, let P_j be a permutation matrix that permutes $(u_1, \ldots, u_{m-1})$ to $(u_j, u_1, \ldots, u_{j-1}, u_{j+1}, \ldots, u_{m-1})$ by a permutation matrix P_j. The variance matrix of $(u_j, u_1, \ldots, u_{j-1}, u_{j+1}, \ldots, u_{m-1})$ is $P_j B_1 B_1' P_j'$. Compute the lower triangular matrix B_j such that $B_j B_j' = P_j B_1 B_1' P_j'$. Permute the $Z\gamma$ into $Z^{(j)}\gamma$, i.e., $Z^{(j)}\gamma = P_j Z\gamma$.

   (i)   Compute the probability $P(U_j > 0)$ as $\Phi(z_1^{(j)}\gamma/B_{j,1,1})$; generate a truncated $N(0, 1)$ variable $\xi_1^{(s)}$ on $[-z_1^{(j)}\gamma/B_{j,1,1}, \; \infty)$ as $\xi_1^{(s)} = -\Phi^{-1}[e_1^{(s)}\Phi(z_1^{(j)}\gamma/B_{j,1,1})]$;

   (ii) with $\xi_1^{(s)}, \ldots, \xi_{l-1}^{(s)}$ generated, compute $P(U_1 > U_l \mid \bar{U}_{l-1})$ as $\Phi([(z_1^{(j)} - z_l^{(j)})\gamma + B_{j,1,1}\xi_1^{(s)} - B_{j,l,1}\xi_1^{(s)} - \cdots - B_{j,l,l-1}\xi_{l-1}^{(s)}]/B_{j,l,l})$, and generate a truncated normal variable $\xi_l^{(s)} = \Phi^{-1}[e_l^{(s)}\Phi([(z_1^{(j)} - z_l^{(j)})\gamma + B_{j,1,1}\xi_1^{(s)} - B_{j,l,1}\xi_1^{(s)} - \cdots - B_{j,l,l-1}\xi_{l-1}^{(s)}]/B_{j,l,l})]$, for $l = 2, \cdots, m - 1$.

(3) For the $I_m = 1$ likelihood,
  (i) compute the probability $P(0 > U_1)$ as $\Phi(-z_1\gamma/B_{1,1,1})$; generate a truncated $N(0, 1)$ variable $\xi_1^{(s)}$ as $\xi_1^{(s)} = \Phi^{-1}[e_1^{(s)}\Phi(-z_1\gamma/B_{1,1,1})]$;
  (ii) with $\xi_1^{(s)}, \ldots, \xi_{l-1}^{(s)}$ generated, compute $P(0 > U_l \mid \bar{U}_{l-1})$ as

$$\Phi\left(-\frac{z_l\gamma + B_{1,l,1}\xi_1^{(s)} + \cdots + B_{1,l,l-1}\xi_{l-1}^{(s)}}{B_{1,l,l}}\right),$$

and generate a truncated normal variable $\xi_l^{(s)} = \Phi^{-1}[e_l^{(s)}\Phi(-(z_l\gamma + B_{1,l,1}\xi_1^{(s)} + \cdots + B_{1,l,l-1}\xi_{l-1}^{(s)})/B_{1,l,l})]$ for $l = 2, \ldots, m - 1$.

Appendix B: Likelihood simulation, ideal importance sampling, and approximation

A likelihood function may be simulated in various ways. For the sample selection models, (3.4.3) and (3.4.5) provide different likelihood simulators. In the Monte Carlo study, simulation variance of the likelihood based on (3.4.5) turns out to be more accurate than that of the simulation of (3.4.3). In this appendix, we will provide some intuitive explanations in terms of importance samplers.

Importance sampling is a stochastic method for numerical approximation of a definite integral. Let $c = \int_S k(u)\,du$ where k is a nonnegative Lebesgue-integrable function and S is a measurable set in a finite-dimensional Euclidean space. It is important to have a density function g with a support containing the region on which k does not vanish (Geweke 1989). With such a density, c can be rewritten as $c = \int_S [k(u)/g(u)]g(u)\,du$. It is practical to have a g such that random variables can be easily drawn and the kernel function $k(u)/g(u)$ can be evaluated. The average of $k(u)/g(u)$ over a set of random draws provides a simulator. The accuracy of the simulator depends directly on the variance of $k(u)/g(u)$ as a random function of u with density g. If g can be chosen to be similar in shape to k, then $k(u)/g(u)$ will not vary much and it may have a small variance. An ideal importance density is a density proportional to $k(u)$. The resulting simulator with an ideal importance density has zero simulation error. This is so because, with proportionality that $g(u) = \alpha k(u)$ for some α, $\int_S g(u)\,du = 1$ and $\int_S k(u)\,du = c$ jointly imply that $c = 1/\alpha$. While this is often difficult to accomplish, it suggests the selection of g to roughly approximate $k(u)$.

In an importance-sampling approach for likelihood simulation, a particular way of constructing a simulated likelihood function amounts to the selection of an importance-sampling density. In likelihood simulation for econometric models with latent dependent variables, the ideal importance density is simply the conditional density of latent dependent variables conditional on observed dependent variables. To see this in its generality, let y be a vector of sample observations, and let U be the corresponding underlying vector of latent variables. Let $L(y)$ be the likelihood function (with unknown parameter suppressed). Suppose $f(y, U)$ is the joint density function of the y's and U. It follows that $L(y) = \int_{-\infty}^{\infty} f(y, U)\, dU$. Let $g(U \mid y)$ denote the density of U conditional on y. By the factorization of a joint density into a product of conditional and marginal densities, $f(y, U) = g(U \mid y)L(y)$. This indicates that the ideal importance-sampling density is $g(U \mid y)$. The resulting simulator with the kernel function $f(y, U)/g(U \mid y)$ evaluated at random variables drawn from $g(U \mid y)$ has zero variance. For the sample selection model, $g(U \mid y)$ is not readily available.

The corresponding likelihood simulators in both (3.4.3) and (3.4.5) are GHK simulators. Each of the GHK simulators can be regarded as an approximation to the ideal importance-sampling simulator. Without loss of generality, consider the choice probability that $I_1 = 1$. Define a set of dichotomous indicators I_{jk} such that $I_{jk} = 1$ if $U_j > U_k$, 0 otherwise, for $k = 1, \ldots, j - 1, j + 1, \ldots, m - 1$. Define $I_{jj} = 1$ if $U_j > U_m (= 0)$, 0 otherwise. Since $I_1 = 1$ is equivalent to the joint events $I_{11} = 1, \ldots, I_{1,m-1} = 1$,

$$g(\bar{U}_{m-1} \mid I_1 = 1) = \prod_{j=1}^{m-1} g(U_j \mid \bar{U}_{j-1}, I_1 = 1), \qquad (3.B.1)$$

with

$$g(U_j \mid \bar{U}_{j-1}, I_1 = 1) = g(U_j \mid \bar{U}_{j-1}, I_{11} = 1, \ldots, I_{1,m-1} = 1)$$
$$= g(U_j \mid \bar{U}_{j-1}, I_{1j} = 1, \ldots, I_{1,m-1} = 1) \qquad (3.B.2)$$

and $\bar{U}_0$ is an empty vector as a convention. Except for $j = m - 1$, the densities in (3.B.2) are multivariate truncated densities which may not be easy to work with. A feasible and computationally simpler density to approximate $g(U_j \mid \bar{U}_{j-1}, I_{1j} = 1, \ldots, I_{1,m-1} = 1)$ may be the $g(U_j \mid \bar{U}_{j-1}, I_{1j} = 1)$ which simply ignores information contained in $I_{1k} = 1$ for $k = j + 1, \ldots, m - 1$. This approximated density is a univariate truncated density function. The ideal importance density in (3.B.1) can thus be approximated by $\prod_{j=1}^{m-1} g(U_j \mid \bar{U}_{j-1}, I_{1j} = 1)$ and the corresponding kernel function is $\prod_{j=1}^{m-1} P(I_{1j} = 1 \mid \bar{U}_{j-1})$ for the choice probability of alternative 1. If continuous outcome y_1 is observed when alternative 1 is chosen, the corresponding likelihood component will be $\int f(\varepsilon_1, \bar{U}_{m-1}, I_1 = 1)\, d\bar{U}_{m-1}$, where $\varepsilon_1 = y_1 - x_1\beta_1$. The corresponding ideal importance density is $g(\bar{U}_{m-1} \mid \varepsilon_1, I_1)$. Similar to the above analysis, a desirable approximation to this ideal importance density will be $\prod_{j=1}^{m-1} g(U_j \mid \varepsilon_1, \bar{U}_{j-1}, I_{1j} = 1)$ and the corresponding kernel function is $\prod_{j=1}^{m-1} P(I_{1j} = 1 \mid \varepsilon_1, \bar{U}_{j-1})$. This suggests the likelihood simulator (3.4.5). The difference of the two simulated likelihoods in (3.4.3) and (3.4.5) is on the likelihood components involving observable continuous outcomes. The simulated likelihood (3.4.3) uses the density decomposition $f(\varepsilon_1, \bar{U}_{m-1}, I_1 = 1) = f(\varepsilon_1 \mid \bar{U}_{m-1})g(\bar{U}_{m-1} \mid I_1 = 1)$, and its importance-sampling density used to approximate $g(\bar{U}_{m-1} \mid I_1 = 1)$ ignores the sample observation ε in its approximation. One may expect intuitively that the approximation in (3.4.5) may be better than that of (3.4.3), as it utilizes the sample information of ε_1.

REFERENCES

Albert, J. and Chib, S. (1993), "Bayesian Analysis of Binary and Polychotomous Data," *Journal of the American Statistical Association*, **88**, 669–679.

Amemiya, T. (1974), "Multivariate Regression and Simultaneous Equation Models When the Dependent Variables are Truncated Normal," *Econometrica*, **42**, 999–1012.

(1978), "The Estimation of a Simultaneous Equation Generalized Probit Model," *Econometrica*, **46**, 1193–1205.

(1984), "Tobit Models: A Survey," *Journal of Econometrics*, **24**, 3–61.

Borsch-Supan, A. and Hajivassiliou, V. A. (1993), "Smooth Unbiased Multivariate Probability Simulators for Maximum Likelihood Estimation of Limited Dependent Variable Models," *Journal of Econometrics*, **58**, 347–368.

Chambers, J. M., Cleveland, W. S., Kleiner, B., and Tukey, P. A. (1983), *Graphical Methods for Data Analysis* (Pacific Grove, CA: Wadsworth and Brooks/Cole).

Chen, X. and Shen, X. (1998), "Sieve Extremum Estimates for Weakly Dependent Data," *Econometrica*, **66**, 289–314.

Danielsson, J. and Richard, J. F. (1993), "Accelerated Gaussian Importance Sampler with Application to Dynamic Latent Variable Models," *Journal of Applied Econometrics*, **8**, S153–S173.

Duan, N., Manning, W. G. Jr., Morris, C. N., and Newhouse, J. P. (1984), "Choosing Between the Sample Selection Model and the Multi-Part Model," *Journal of Business and Economic Statistics*, **2**, 283–289.

Dubin, J. and McFadden, D. (1984), "An Econometric Analysis of Residential Electric Appliance Holdings and Consumption," *Econometrica*, **52**, 345–362.

Fenton, V. M. and Gallant, A. R. (1996), "Convergence Rates of SNP Density Estimators," *Econometrica*, **64**, 719–727.

Gallant, A. R. and Nychka, D. (1987), "Semi-Nonparametric Maximum Likelihood Estimation," *Econometrica*, **55**, 363–390.

Geman, S. and Geman, D. (1984), "Stochastic Relaxation, Gibbs Distribution and the Bayesian Restoration of Images," *IEEE Transactions on Pattern Analysis and Machine Intelligence*, **6**, 721–741.

Geweke, J. (1989), "Bayesian Inference in Econometric Models Using Monte Carlo Integration," *Econometrica*, **24**, 1317–1339.

(1991), "Efficient Simulation from the Multivariate Normal and Student-*t* Distributions Subject to Linear Constraints," in: Computer science and statistics: *Proceedings of the twenty-third symposium on the interface* (American Statistical Association, Alexandria, VA), 571–578.

Geweke, J., Keane, M., and Runkle, D. (1994), "Alternative Computational Approaches to Inference in the Multinomial Probit Model," *The Review of Economics and Statistics*, **76**, 609–632.

——— (1997), "Statistical Inference in the Multinomial Multiperiod Probit Model," *Journal of Econometrics*, **80**, 125–165.

Gourieroux, C. and Monfort, A. (1993), "Simulation-Based Inference: A Survey with Special Reference to Panel Data Models," *Journal of Econometrics*, **59**, 5–33.

Hajivassiliou, V. (1993), "Simulation Estimation Methods for Limited Dependent Variable Models," in: G. S. Maddala, C. R. Rao, and H. D. Vinod, eds., *Handbook of Statistics*, Vol. 11 (Amsterdam: North Holland), 519–543.

Hajivassiliou, V. and McFadden, D. (1998), "The Method of Simulated Scores for the Estimation of LDV Models," *Econometrica*, **66**, 863–896.

Hajivassiliou, V. and Ruud, P. (1994), "Classical Estimation Methods for LDV Models Using Simulation," Chapter 40 in: R. F. Engle and D. L. McFadden, eds., *Handbook of Econometrics*, Vol. 4 (Amsterdam: North Holland), 2383–2441.

D. McFadden and Ruud, P. (1996), "Simulation of Multivariate Normal Orthant Probabilities: Theoretical and Computational Results," *Journal of Econometrics*, **72**, 85–134.

Hausman, J. A. and Wise, D. A. (1978), "A Conditional Probit Model for Qualitative Choice: Discrete Decisions Recognizing Interdependence and Heterogeneous Preferences," *Econometrica*, **46**, 403–426.

Hay, J. and Olsen, R. J. (1984), "Let Them Eat Cake: A Note on Comparing Alternative Models of the Demand for Medical Care," *Journal of Business and Economic Statistics*, **2**, 279–282.

Heckman, J. J. (1990), "Varieties of Selection Bias," *American Economic Association Papers and Proceedings*, **80**, 313–318.

Hendry, D. F. and Richard, J. F. (1992), "Likelihood Evaluation for Dynamic Latent Variables Models," in: H. M. Amman, D. A. Belsley, and L. F. Pau, eds., *Computational Economics and Econometrics* (Amsterdam: Kluwer).

Keane, M. P. (1993), "Simulation Estimation Methods for Panel Data Limited Dependent Variable Models," in: G. S. Maddala, C. R. Rao, and H. D. Vinod, eds., *Handbook of Statistics*, Vol. 11 (Amsterdam: North-Holland).

——— (1994), "A Computationally Practical Simulation Estimator for Panel Data," *Econometrica*, **62**, 95–116.

Lee, L. F. (1982), "Some Approaches to the Correction of Selectivity Bias," *Review of Economic Studies*, **49**, 355–372.

——— (1983), "Generalized Econometrics Models with Selectivity," *Econometrica*, **51**, 507–512.

——— (1992), "On Efficiency of Methods of Simulated Moments and Maximum Simulated Likelihood Estimation of Discrete Response Models," *Econometric Theory*, **8**, 518–552.

——— (1995a), "The Computation of Opportunity Costs in Polychotomous Choice Models with Selectivity," *The Review of Economics and Statistics*, **77**, 423–435.

——— (1995b), "Asymptotic Bias in Maximum Simulated Likelihood Estimation of Discrete Choice Models," *Econometric Theory*, **11**, 437–483.

Maddala, G. S. (1983), *Limited-Dependent and Qualitative Variables in Econometrics* (Cambridge: Cambridge University Press).

McCulloch, R. and P. E. Rossi (1994), "An Exact Likelihood Analysis of the Multinomial Probit Model," *Journal of Econometrics*, **64**, 207–240.

McFadden, D. (1989), "A Method of Simulated Moments for Estimation of Discrete Choice Models Without Numerical Integration," *Econometrica*, **57**, 995–1026.

118   References

McFadden, D. and Ruud, P. A. (1994), "Estimation by Simulation," *The Review of Economics and Statistics*, **76**, 591–608.

Newey, W., Powell, J. J., and Walker, J. R. (1990), "Semiparametric Estimation of Selection Models: Some Empirical Results," *American Economic Review Papers and Proceedings*, **80**, 324–328.

Pakes, A. and Pollard, D. (1989), "Simulation and the Asymptotics of Optimization Estimators," *Econometrica*, **54**, 755–785.

Schmertmann, C. P. (1994), "Selectivity Bias Correction Methods in Polychotomous Sample Selection Models," *Journal of Econometrics*, **60**, 101–132.

Shen, X. (1997), "On Methods of Sieves and Penalization," *The Annals of Statistics*, **25**, 2555–2591.

Tanner, M. A. and Wong, W. H. (1987), "The Calculation of Posterior Distribution by Data Augmentation," *Journal of the American Statistical Association*, **82**, 528–550.

CHAPTER 4

A new approach to the attrition problem in longitudinal studies

Keunkwan Ryu

1   Introduction

This chapter proposes a new approach to tackling attrition problems in panel studies. Panel data are obtained by observing cross-sectional units such as individuals or households more than once over an extended period of time. Panel data sets are typically unbalanced due to attrition. In the first year of a panel survey, researchers pay full attention to making the sample as representative as possible. Therefore, the first year observations can be regarded as forming a random sample, able to represent the underlying population. However, over time, initial cross-sectional units are dissipated, possibly in a nonrandom fashion. Attrition may negate the initial randomization. If the variable of interest is stochastically related to the factors governing attrition process, then the attrition is nonrandom and potentially causes bias. In this sense, attrition bias can be regarded as a sample selection bias. A major difference between the attrition bias and the typical sample selection bias is that the attrition occurs through a multistage process.

Fuller and Battese (1974), Biørn (1981), Baltagi (1985), and Wansbeek and Kapteyn (1989) have discussed incomplete panel data models, with data unbalanced due to attrition. However, they all assumed that the attrition process is exogenous, and thus assumed away the possible attrition bias.

Attrition bias in panel studies was first considered by Hausman and Wise (1979) using a random effects model for the individual response. The existence of attrition bias was postulated as due to nonrandomness of the remaining cross-sectional units after the initial survey years. In other words, attrition bias is simply a sample selection bias. It is an application of Heckman's (1976, 1979) sample selection model to the unbalanced panel data setting. However, the generalization of their model to the multiperiod attrition is rather complicated.

I wish to thank three anonymous referees and C. Hsiao for useful comments. Any remaining errors are mine. Support from the Seoul National University Development Fund is gratefully acknowledged.

119

Van den Berg, Lindeboom, and Ridder (1994) consider the attrition problem, jointly with the left-censoring problem, in studying dynamic labor market behavior. They are interested in studying those duration variables related to a worker's dynamic labor market behavior, such as job duration and unemployment duration. They suggest several ways of modeling the labor market duration variable, jointly with attrition and left censoring. Their basic idea is to introduce unmeasured heterogeneity terms through which labor market dynamics and attrition process might be correlated. Left censoring arises from using a sample of employed in the study of job duration, and using a sample of unemployed in the study of unemployment spell.

Ridder (1992) considers several models for nonrandom attrition in panel data. In particular, he extends Hausman and Wise (1979) to a multiperiod setting. However, his extension is rather limited in the sense that the variable of interest and the variables driving the attrition process are only allowed to be contemporaneously correlated, thus reducing the multistage selection process as a sequence of single-stage sample selections. Being so, his model is simply a replication of the single-stage sample selection model. Wooldridge's (1995) model faces the same problem as in Ridder (1992), though it is more general in that it additionally considers a time-constant individual heterogeneity in the equation of interest. If one reasonably assumes that an individual's latent type affects the attrition process as well as the variable of interest, then the attrition variables and the variable of interest should be correlated at all time periods if an individual's type has a time-persistent component, obviously violating Ridder's and Wooldridge's models. This chapter will relax this restrictive assumption, while still keeping tractability of the model.

Assuming that the attrition process is irreversible, we can conveniently model it using grouped duration techniques. To capture a nonrandom attrition process, we introduce unmeasured heterogeneity among cross-sectional units. For example, an individual who disappears in the second wave of a panel is regarded as different in latent type from an individual who stays throughout. This chapter, adopting group duration techniques with unmeasured heterogeneity, proposes a natural and easy-to-use method for taking account of the attrition problem in unbalanced panel studies. This chapter can be viewed as an extension of Hausman and Wise (1979), Ridder (1992), and Wooldridge (1995).

We model the unmeasured heterogeneity by introducing an i.i.d. (across individuals) random variable, say v_i, which follows a certain population distribution at the beginning due to the initial random sampling. This v_i is assumed to affect the attrition process together with other observed attributes through the hazard rate of leaving the sample. Then, by fitting a group duration model with unmeasured heterogeneity to the attrition data, discretely observed, one can estimate the population distribution of v_i. Also, by using the Bayes updating formula, one can update the distribution of v_i using information on attrition. Once one identifies the nature of the attrition, there are several ways of taking account of the attrition problem, and thus obtaining consistent parameter estimates. We propose two sequential estimation procedures together with a joint maximum likelihood estimation.

The rest of the chapter is organized as follows. Section 2 introduces the model together with basic issues. Joint maximum likelihood estimation of the behavioral equation and attrition process is discussed in Section 3. Section 4 proposes two different methods of estimating the behavioral equation of interest, once the attrition process is estimated in the first step. Section 5 operationalizes the model by suggesting two heterogeneity distributions, gamma heterogeneity and discrete heterogeneity. Section 6 concludes the chapter.

2   The model

Panel data are obtained by interviewing the same individuals at regular intervals over time. At the first interview, information is collected on a certain number of individuals. However, not all individuals from the first interview are available for the second interview. Some are simply not reachable, and others refuse to cooperate. As a result, the second interview ends up with successful interviews of a subset of the original members. The shrinkage of sample size over panel waves is called sample attrition. The attrition process continues as the panel waves proceed.

Let r be the maximum number of panel waves available now. That is, if an individual had not experienced panel attrition, he or she should have been interviewed r times in total. Let T_i^* be a continuous duration variable representing the latent time till attrition for individual i. Let T_i be a discrete version of T_i^* such that $T_i = t_i$ if T_i^* falls between the t_ith and the $(t_i + 1)$st interviews, $t_i = 1, \ldots, r - 1$. If the ith individual is still in sample at the last (rth) interview, we say that it is right-censored. For those right-censored observations, let us define T_i as $T_i = r$. Taking the first interview time as the absolute time origin and the interval between two consecutive interviews as the unit time, the fact that T_i^* falls in between the t_ith and the $(t_i + 1)$st interviews can be represented as $t_i - 1 \le T_i^* < t_i \Longleftrightarrow T_i = t_i$ for $t_i = 1, \ldots, r - 1$. For the right-censored observations, $T_i^* \ge r - 1 \Longleftrightarrow T_i = r$. We observe T_i, but not T_i^*. Let y_{it} be a variable of interest for individual i at the tth interview. For those individuals with $T_i = t_i$, we observe $y_{i1}, \ldots, y_{it_i}$, but not $y_{it_i+1}, \ldots, y_{ir}$.

For generality, covariates are assumed time-varying, though in fact they are at best recorded up to intervals. Let x_{it} be a collection of exogenous variables which affect either the variable of interest y_{it} or the hazard rate of T_i^* in the tth interval, $t - 1 \le u < t$. Let $X_i = \{x_{it}, 0 \le t < \infty\}$ denote its entire process, and $X_{it} = \{x_{iu}, 0 \le u < t\}$ only the history up to the tth interval.

Assumption 1 (modeling T_i^* conditional on (X_i, v_i)): Let us model T_i^* through the following mixed proportional hazard model. For $t - 1 \leq u < t$, the hazard rate of T_i^* conditional on x_{it} and v_i is

$$h(u \mid x_{it}, v_i) = h_0(u) \exp(x_{it}'\beta) v_i, \qquad v_i \sim \text{i.i.d.} \ g(v), \qquad v > 0, \qquad (4.1)$$

where $h_0(u)$ is the baseline hazard rate at time u, $\exp(x_{it}'\beta)$ is a proportionality factor, x_{it} and β are $k \times 1$ vectors of covariates and parameters, and v_i captures unmeasured heterogeneity having population density $g(v)$. Let v_i be independent of X_i.

Assumption 2 (modeling y_{it} conditional on (x_{it}, v_i)): Now, let us model y_{it} through the following regression model with individual random effects:

$$y_{it} = x_{it}'\delta + dv_i + \varepsilon_{it}, \qquad (4.2)$$

where v_i is the same individual effect as appeared in $h(u \mid x_{it}, v_i)$, and the ε_{it}'s are i.i.d. idiosyncratic error terms. Let v_i and ε_{it} be independent.

Lancaster and Intrator (1998) use a similar formulation to study medical expenditure (y), considering nonrandom attrition due to death (T^*).

We use the same notation x_{it} to denote the explanatory variables in both the hazard and the regression. They do not have to be the same in general, which case can be covered by restricting certain elements of β and δ to be equal to zero.

The sign of d will tell which type of individuals are more likely to experience attrition: if $d > (<) 0$, then the individuals who are more likely to disappear are those whose y's are high (low, respectively). Ignoring the attrition problem can be understood as omitting the dv_i term in the above specification; thus attrition bias can be viewed as a misspecification bias. By testing $H_0: d = 0$, one can test the existence of the attrition bias.

We have n individuals to start with; that is, for $t = 1$, we have data on $y_{11}, \ldots, y_{n1}$. Attrition causes the set of remaining individuals to shrink over time, resulting in unbalanced panel data. The source of attrition bias can be described as follows. At the time of initial panel design ($t = 1$), randomization is applied and thus v_i follows the population distribution. However, over the panel waves, some individuals drop out of the sample, and the conditional distribution of v_i given attrition information on the individual will be different from the initial population distribution. Without allowing for this selection due to attrition, one cannot obtain consistent parameter estimates.

Equation (4.2) is a conventional random effects model if there is no attrition. With balanced panel data, it is easy to estimate the equation (see Hsiao 1984). In this case, T_i degenerates to a constant integer, and thus does not provide any extra information on the underlying heterogeneity, which justifies ignoring the attrition problem altogether. However, in many longitudinal studies, we have unbalanced panel data due to attrition. Attrition is often nonrandom. In this case, by analyzing T_i using group duration techniques with unmeasured heterogeneity, we can identify the nature of attrition through estimating $g(v)$ and then updating it. By using the updated heterogeneity distribution, we can allow for the attrition when estimating the equation of interest.

One way of allowing for the attrition is to estimate the attrition process and the equation of interest jointly. Another way is (i) to identify the nature of heterogeneity in the first step, and then (ii) to take account of the attrition in the second step estimation of the equation of interest. For the first step, one can apply a grouped duration method with unmeasured heterogeneity to the attrition data. For the second step, one can apply either a likelihood-based estimation or a regression-based estimation.

3   Joint maximum likelihood estimation

Let us consider the ith individual, who drops out of sample after the t_ith but before the $(t_i + 1)$st interview. For this person we know that $T_i = t_i$, and we observe y_{i1} through y_{it_i}. The joint density or probability we would like to assign to this person is as follows[1]:

$$f\left(t_i, y_{i1}, \ldots, y_{it_i}\right) = E_v\left[f(t_i \mid v) \prod_{t=1}^{t_i} f(y_{it} \mid v)\right]$$

$$= \int_0^\infty f(t_i \mid v)\left\{\prod_{t=1}^{t_i} f(y_{it} \mid v)\right\} g(v)\, dv. \qquad (4.3)$$

Here, $f(t_i \mid v)$ can be derived easily from the hazard rate specification in (4.1), $h(t \mid x_{it}, v) = h_0(t) \exp(x_{it}'\beta)v$, as

$$f(t_i \mid v) = P(t_i - 1 \leq T_i^* < t_i \mid v)$$

$$= \exp\left[-\int_0^{t_i-1} h_0(u)e^{x_{iu}'\beta}v\, du\right] - \exp\left[-\int_0^{t_i} h_0(u)e^{x_{iu}'\beta}v\, du\right]$$

$$= \alpha_1(x_{i1}, v) \times \cdots \times \alpha_{t_i-1}\left(x_{it_i-1}, v\right)\left(1 - \alpha_{t_i}\left(x_{it_i}, v\right)\right)$$

$$\text{for} \quad t_i = 1, \ldots, r-1, \qquad (4.4)$$

$$f(r \mid v) = P(T_i^* \geq r - 1 \mid v) = \exp\left[-\int_0^{r-1} h_0(u)e^{x_{iu}'\beta}v\, du\right]$$

$$= \alpha_1(x_{i1}, v) \times \cdots \times \alpha_{r-1}(x_{ir-1}, v), \qquad \text{for} \quad t_i = r,$$

---

[1] Hereafter, integration with respect to v means summation with respect to v when the distribution of v is discrete.

where

$$\alpha_t(x_{it}, v) = \exp\left[-\int_{t-1}^{t} h_0(u)e^{x'_{iu}\beta}v\,du\right].$$

In practice, time-varying covariates are recorded just once within an observed interval. So, for all practical purposes, we assume that $x_{iu} = x_{it}$ for all u in the tth interval, $t - 1 \leq u < t$. By defining

$$c_{it} = \exp(\gamma_t + x'_{it}\beta)$$

with $\gamma_t = \log \int_{t-1}^{t} h_0(u)\,du$, $\alpha_t(x_{it}, v)$ can be written as $\alpha_t(x_{it}, v) = \exp(-c_{it}v)$. Note that $\alpha_t(x_{it}, v)$ is the conditional probability of staying in sample until the $(t + 1)$st interview, conditional on the information that the ith individual characterized by (X_{it}, v) has already survived (not experiencing attrition) until the tth interview.

The joint log likelihood function is obtained as

$$L(\theta) = \sum_{i=1}^{n} \log f\left(t_i, y_{i1}, \ldots, y_{it_i}\right). \tag{4.5}$$

For later reference, let us decompose the parameter vector θ into the attrition parameters θ_1 and the rest θ_2. That is, θ_1 includes all the parameters in (4.1) such as β, parameters characterizing $h_0(t)$, and parameters in $g(v)$, whereas θ_2 includes all the parameters in (4.2) such as δ, d, and parameters appearing in the distribution of ε_{it}.

To complete the model, we need to make distributional assumptions on v_i and ε_{it}, considering computational simplicity and flexibility in modeling. We will make a normality assumption on ε_{it} if necessary. Later, in Section 5, we will propose two distributions for v_i: a gamma distribution and a discrete distribution.

Once the modeling assumptions are completed, the estimation and inference is straightforward from the maximum likelihood estimation theory. Under a set of quite general regularity conditions (see Amemiya 1985, Chapter 4), the maximum likelihood estimator will converge to a normal distribution with mean equal to the true parameters and variance–covariance matrix equal to the inverse of the information matrix.

4   Sequential estimation

To save on computational complexity, one can estimate the model in two steps. In the first step, estimate the attrition process using a grouped duration technique. Then, in the second step, estimate the equation of interest after allowing for the attrition effect identified through the first step. For the second step, one can adopt either a likelihood-based estimation or a regression-based estimation.

4.1   *First step*

In the first step, we fit a grouped duration model with unmeasured heterogeneity to the attrition process. Under the mixed proportional hazard assumption in (4.1), the distribution of the unmeasured heterogeneity is identified under general conditions (see Elbers and Ridder 1982, Heckman and Honore 1989, and Heckman and Singer 1984b).

Panel attrition information is available only up to intervals, not up to exact points. Let $I_t = [t - 1, t)$, $t = 1, \ldots, r - 1$, and $I_r = [r - 1, \infty)$. The discrete duration T_i can be considered as a sequence of binary indicator variables, that is, $T_i \iff (d_{i1}, \ldots, d_{i\,r-1})$, where d_{it} is a binary variable which takes the value one if the ith individual survives I_t and zero otherwise. The effective number of terms in the sequence varies with the interval in which the individual experiences panel attrition. Note that d_{i2}'s are meaningfully defined only for those who have survived I_1.

By constructing a synthetic binary data set treating each combination (individual, interval) as a new unit of indexation, we can reduce a grouped duration analysis to a sequential binary choice analysis (Kiefer 1988, Prentice and Gloeckler 1978, Ryu 1994, Sueyoshi 1991, Thompson 1977). Note that $\alpha_t(x_{it}, v)$ is the probability that T_i survives I_t conditional on the information that it has already survived all previous intervals and that the ith individual has characteristics (x_{it}, v) in the current interval. For each combination (individual, interval), the probability of surviving the tth interval is

$$\alpha_t(x_{it}) = P(T_i^* \geq t \mid T_i^* \geq t - 1, x_{it}) = E_t \alpha_t(x_{it}, v) \qquad (4.6)$$

if his or her covariate is recorded as x_{it}, where E_t denotes expectation over v using the tth stage heterogeneity density, say $g_{ti}(v)$. Since $\alpha_t(x_{it})$ is only defined for those who satisfy $T_i \geq t$, the tth stage density $g_{ti}(v)$ should take this selection into account.

We first characterize two types of conditional heterogeneity distribution, and then discuss the estimation of the attrition process.

4.1.1   *Two types of conditional heterogeneity distribution*

Before looking at the first step estimation of the attrition process, let us define and characterize two types of conditional heterogeneity distribution. These conditional distributions are interesting in themselves and are also used later for estimation. Different types of conditional distributions are used for different purposes.

Given a density specification $v \sim g(v)$ for the heterogeneity, we cannot use this density to integrate out the unobserved heterogeneity in the y_{it} equation when the panel data are unbalanced due to panel attrition. That is because the attrition status of individuals has a relation to their underlying heterogeneity type.

For example, those who are continuing in a graduate program will be different from the entering class in their latent type distribution, that is, unmeasured heterogeneity. Over time, diligent students will finish the program, whereas lazy students will still hang around – the so-called weeding-out effect. Heckman and Singer (1984b) write, "More mobility prone persons are the first to leave the population leaving the less mobile behind." This effect reflects selection over time with respect to unobserved heterogeneity.

Let us define two different types of conditional densities of v. One is conditional on *survival*, and the other is conditional on *exit*. When one has information that an individual is alive at the tth interview time point, one has survival information in the form of $T_i \geq t$. Let $g_{ti}(v) = g(v \mid T_i \geq t)$ be the heterogeneity density conditional on survival, $t = 1, \dots, r$. On the other hand, for those who have left the panel before the last interview, one has exit information in the form of $T_i = t$, $t = 1, \dots, r - 1$. Let $q_{ti}(v) = g(v \mid T_i = t)$ be the heterogeneity density conditional on exit. Note the difference between $g_{ti}(v)$ and $q_{ti}(v)$. The fact that $g_{ti}(v)$'s and $q_{ti}(v)$'s are different for different t's reflects selection over time with respect to unobserved heterogeneity.

Let us first compute the heterogeneity distribution applicable to those who are still in sample at the tth interview. Due to selection over time, the tth stage heterogeneity density $g_{ti}(v)$ will be different from the initial density $g(v)$ except for $t = 1$. Assuming that x is exogenous, this conditional density $g_{ti}(v)$ is given by

$$g_{ti}(v) = g(v \mid T_i \geq t, X_{it}) = \frac{P(T_i^* \geq t - 1 \mid X_{it}, v)g(v)}{\int_0^\infty P(T_i^* \geq t - 1 \mid X_{it}, v)g(v)\, dv}$$

$$= \frac{e^{-(c_{i1} + \dots + c_{it-1})v}g(v)}{M_v(c_{i1} + \dots + c_{it-1})}, \tag{4.7}$$

where $M_v(c) = E_v(e^{-cv})$ is the moment generating function of $g(v)$. Note that $g_{1i}(v) = g(v)$ for all i. Since each c_{it} is positive, $g_{ti}(v)$ is first order stochastically decreasing in t.

Now, for $t = 1, 2, \dots, r - 1$, the heterogeneity distribution applicable to those who left the sample between the tth and the $(t + 1)$st interviews is

$$q_{ti}(v) = g(v \mid t \leq T_i < t + 1, X_{it+1})$$

$$= \frac{P(t - 1 \leq T_i^* < t \mid X_{it+1}, v)g(v)}{\int_0^\infty P(t - 1 \leq T_i^* < t \mid X_{it+1}, v)g(v)\, dv}$$

$$= \frac{e^{-(c_{i1} + \dots + c_{it-1})v}g(v) - e^{-(c_{i1} + \dots + c_{it})v}g(v)}{M_v(c_{i1} + \dots + c_{it-1}) - M_v(c_{i1} + \dots + c_{it})}. \tag{4.8}$$

Again, $q_{ti}(v)$ is first order stochastically decreasing in t.

Now, the two step, sequential estimation proceeds as follows. In the first step, estimate θ_1 by fitting a grouped duration model with unmeasured heterogeneity to the attrition process. Once we estimate θ_1, we can estimate the above two types of conditional distributions, $g_{ti}(v)$ and $q_{ti}(v)$. Using these estimated distributions, say $\hat{g}_{ti}(v)$ and $\hat{q}_{ti}(v)$, one can allow for the attrition problem in the second step estimation of the equation of interest. Let us study these two steps in more detail.

4.1.2 *Estimation of the attrition process*

In grouped duration data, we know for each interval whether an individual survives the current interval or not, conditional on the information that the individual has already survived all previous intervals. Due to this condition, one needs to use $g_{ti}(v)$ to integrate out v from the conditional interval survival probability $\alpha_t(x_{it}, v)$. Recalling that $\alpha_t(x_{it}, v) = \exp(-c_{it}v)$ with $c_{it} = \exp(\gamma_t + x'_{it}\beta)$, $t = 1, \ldots, r - 1$, we have

$$\alpha_t(x_{it}) = E_t\alpha_t(x_{it}, v) = \int_0^\infty \alpha_t(x_{it}, v)g_{ti}(v)\, dv$$

$$= \frac{\int_0^\infty \exp[-(c_{i1} + \cdots + c_{i\,t-1} + c_{it})v]g(v)}{M_v(c_{i1} + \cdots + c_{i\,t-1})}$$

$$= M_v(c_{i1} + \cdots + c_{it})/M_v(c_{i1} + \cdots + c_{i\,t-1}) \quad (4.9)$$

with $\alpha_1(x_{i1}) = M_v(c_{i1})$.

The interval survival probability in (4.9) is represented as a ratio of the moment generating functions of $g(v)$, evaluated at two different points. Therefore, we readily notice that any heterogeneity distribution $g(v)$ will yield an analytical solution for the interval survival probability insofar as $g(v)$ admits an analytical moment generating function. Later, in Section 5, we will study two such heterogeneity distributions, the gamma distribution and the discrete distribution.

Let us look at the first step more closely. Recall that θ_1 denotes the collection of parameters appearing in the attrition process. The log likelihood function of the first step is

$$L_1(\theta_1) = \sum_{i=1}^n \sum_{t=1}^{r-1} s_{it}[d_{it} \log \alpha_{it} + (1 - d_{it})\log(1 - \alpha_{it})], \quad (4.10)$$

where α_{it} is a shorthand notation for $\alpha_t(x_{it})$, and $s_{it} = d_{i1} \times \cdots \times d_{i\,t-1}$ is the cumulative survival indicator, which takes the value one if the ith individual is still in sample at the tth interview, and zero otherwise. Define $s_{i1} = 1$ for all $i = 1, \ldots, n$.

The above representation shows a similarity between grouped duration analyses and sequential binary choice analyses. Passing I_1, one of two outcomes occurs: to survive or not. Conditional on the individual's having survived I_1, again one of the binary outcomes occurs, and so forth. Here, the cumulative survival indicator s_{it} tells whether or not the ith individual is alive at the beginning of the tth interval. It takes value one if alive and zero otherwise.

By maximizing the log likelihood function in (4.10), one obtains the maximum likelihood estimator of θ_1, say $\hat{\theta}_1$. It is straightforward to show that

$$-\frac{1}{n}\frac{\partial^2 L_1}{\partial \theta_1 \partial \theta_1'} = \frac{1}{n}\sum_{i=1}^{n}\sum_{t=1}^{r-1} s_{it} \frac{1}{\alpha_{it}(1-\alpha_{it})} \frac{\partial \alpha_{it}}{\partial \theta_1} \frac{\partial \alpha_{it}}{\partial \theta_1'} + o_p(1). \quad (4.11)$$

The asymptotic variance–covariance matrix of $\sqrt{n}(\hat{\theta}_1 - \theta_1)$ can be consistently estimated as the inverse of the above information matrix, evaluated at $\hat{\theta}_1$, after ignoring the $o_p(1)$ term. By evaluating $g_{ti}(v)$ and $q_{ti}(v)$ at $\hat{\theta}_1$, we derive the estimated, conditional heterogeneity distributions, $\hat{g}_{ti}(v)$ and $\hat{q}_{ti}(v)$, respectively.

4.2   *Second step*

Once two types of conditional heterogeneity distributions are estimated through the first step, one can apply either a likelihood-based procedure or a regression-based procedure to estimate the y_{it} process. Here, these conditional heterogeneity distributions, $\hat{g}_{ti}(v)$ and $\hat{q}_{ti}(v)$, are utilized to take account of the selection effect due to nonrandom attrition.

4.2.1   *Likelihood-based estimation*

The sequential, likelihood-based estimation is a two step breakdown of the aforementioned joint maximum likelihood estimation. To see the relationship, let us write down the joint probability or density in an alternative form. Using the probability multiplication rule, we derive

$$f\left(t_i, y_{i1}, \ldots, y_{it_i}\right) = f(t_i) f\left(y_{i1}, \ldots, y_{it_i} \mid t_i\right), \quad (4.12)$$

where (i) $f(t_i) = \alpha_{i1} \times \cdots \times \alpha_{it_i-1}(1-\alpha_{it_i})$ for $t_i = 1, \ldots, r-1$, (ii) $f(t_i) = \alpha_{i1} \times \cdots \times \alpha_{ir-1}$ for $t_i = r$ (right-censored observations), and (iii) $f(y_{i1}, \ldots, y_{it_i} \mid t_i) = \int_0^\infty [\prod_{t=1}^{t_i} f(y_{it} \mid v)] f(v \mid t_i) dv$. Here, $f(v \mid t_i)$ is the conditional distribution of v given t_i. This conditional distribution will take one of the two forms depending on whether the ith observation is still in sample at the last interview ($g_{ri}(v)$) or not ($q_{t_i i}(v), t_i = 1, \ldots, r-1$).

From (4.12), the joint log likelihood function can be decomposed into two parts:

$$L(\theta_1, \theta_2) = L_1(\theta_1) + L_2(\theta_1, \theta_2), \quad (4.13)$$

where $L_1(\theta_1) = \sum_{i=1}^{n} \log f(t_i)$ and $L_2(\theta_1, \theta_2) = \sum_{i=1}^{n} \log f(y_{i1}, \ldots, y_{it_i} | t_i)$. Note that $L_1(\theta_1)$ here is in fact the same as the one in equation (4.10), the marginal log likelihood contribution of the attrition process alone.

The sequential maximum likelihood estimation proceeds as follows. In the first step, maximize $L_1(\theta_1)$ with respect to θ_1 as explained in Section 4.1.2. Let $\hat{\theta}_1$ be the resulting estimator. In the second step, maximize $L_2(\hat{\theta}_1, \theta_2)$ with respect to θ_2 given $\hat{\theta}_1$. To obtain a consistent variance–covariance matrix for the second step estimator, one has to allow for the randomness in $\hat{\theta}_1$.

Let us consider the ith individual. If he or she drops out of sample after the t_ith but before the $(t_i + 1)$st interview, we have $T_i = t_i$, and we observe y_{i1} through y_{it_i}, $t_i = 1, \ldots, r - 1$. Given $\hat{\theta}_1$, the second step likelihood contribution is

$$f\left(y_{i1}, \ldots, y_{it_i} \mid t_i, \hat{\theta}_1\right) = \int_0^\infty \left[\prod_{t=1}^{t_i} f(y_{it} \mid v)\right] \hat{q}_{t_i i}(v)\, dv, \qquad t_i = 1, \ldots, r-1.$$

(4.14)

On the other hand, if the ith individual is still in sample at the last interview, we observe y_{i1} through y_{ir}. In this case, the second step likelihood contribution becomes

$$f(y_{i1}, \ldots, y_{ir} \mid t_i, \hat{\theta}_1) = \int_0^\infty \left[\prod_{t=1}^{r} f(y_{it} \mid v)\right] \hat{g}_{ri}(v)\, dv, \qquad t_i = r. \quad (4.15)$$

In (4.14) and (4.15), $f(y_{it} \mid v)$ is the conditional density of y_{it} given v. Assume that ε_{it}'s are independent and normally distributed with mean zero and variance σ_ε^2. Then, from (4.2), we obtain $f(y_{it} \mid v) = (1/\sqrt{2\pi}\sigma_\varepsilon) \exp[-(1/2\sigma_\varepsilon^2)(y_{it} - x_{it}'\delta - dv)^2]$.

The second step log likelihood function is

$$L_2(\hat{\theta}_1, \theta_2) = \sum_{i=1}^{n} \log f(y_{i1}, \ldots, y_{it_i} \mid t_i, \hat{\theta}_1), \qquad (4.16)$$

where $f(y_{i1}, \ldots, y_{it_i} | t_i, \hat{\theta}_1)$ takes one of the two forms in (4.14) and (4.15) depending on whether $t_i = 1, \ldots, r - 1$ or $t_i = r$. By maximizing this likelihood function with respect to θ_2 (given $\hat{\theta}_1$), one obtains a consistent estimator of θ_2, say $\hat{\theta}_2$.

By Taylor series expansion of the first order condition, we have

$$0 = \frac{1}{n} \frac{\partial L_2(\hat{\theta}_1, \hat{\theta}_2)}{\partial \theta_2}$$

$$= \frac{1}{n} \frac{\partial L_2(\theta_1, \theta_2)}{\partial \theta_2} + \frac{1}{n} \frac{\partial^2 L_2(\theta_1, \theta_2)}{\partial \theta_2 \, \partial \theta_2'}(\hat{\theta}_2 - \theta_2)$$

$$+ \frac{1}{n} \frac{\partial^2 L_2(\theta_1, \theta_2)}{\partial \theta_2 \, \partial \theta_1'}(\hat{\theta}_1 - \theta_1) + o_p(1/\sqrt{n}).$$

Rearranging terms using

$$\sqrt{n}(\hat{\theta}_1 - \theta_1) = \left[-\frac{1}{n}\frac{\partial^2 L_1(\theta_1)}{\partial\theta_1\,\partial\theta_1'}\right]^{-1}\frac{1}{\sqrt{n}}\sum_{i=1}^{n}\frac{\partial l_{1i}(\theta_1)}{\partial\theta_1} + o_p(1),$$

where l_{1i} is the ith log likelihood function in the first step, we have

$$\sqrt{n}(\hat{\theta}_2 - \theta_2) = \left[-\frac{1}{n}\frac{\partial^2 L_2(\theta_1,\theta_2)}{\partial\theta_2\,\partial\theta_2'}\right]^{-1}$$
$$\times\left[\frac{1}{\sqrt{n}}\frac{\partial L_2(\theta_1,\theta_2)}{\partial\theta_2} + \frac{1}{n}\frac{\partial^2 L_2(\theta_1,\theta_2)}{\partial\theta_2\,\partial\theta_1'}\right.$$
$$\times\left.\left[-\frac{1}{n}\frac{\partial^2 L_1(\theta_1)}{\partial\theta_1\,\partial\theta_1'}\right]^{-1}\frac{1}{\sqrt{n}}\sum_{i=1}^{n}\frac{\partial l_{1i}(\theta_1)}{\partial\theta_1}\right] + o_p(1).$$

(4.17)

By the central limit theorem, the zero expected score property, and the information matrix equality, we derive

$$\sqrt{n}(\hat{\theta}_2 - \theta_2) \sim N\left(0, I_2^{-1}\left[I_2 + M_{21}I_1^{-1}M_{12}\right]I_2^{-1}\right),$$ (4.18)

where I_1 and I_2 are $(1/n$ times) the information matrix from L_1 and L_2, respectively, $M_{21} = \text{plim}\,(1/n)\partial^2 L_2(\theta_1,\theta_2)/\partial\theta_2\,\partial\theta_1'$, and M_{12} is the transpose of M_{21}. Note that the variance of $\hat{\theta}_2$ is larger than I_2^{-1} due to the estimated nature of $\hat{\theta}_1$.

4.2.2   *Regression-based estimation*

To analyze y_{it} without attrition bias, the two-step procedure (i) computes $\hat{E}_{t_i}v_i = \hat{E}(v_i\mid T_i = t_i) = \int_0^\infty v\hat{q}_{t_i i}(v)\,dv$ for $t_i = 1,\ldots,r-1$ or $\hat{E}_r v_i = \hat{E}(v_i\mid T_i = r) = \int_0^\infty v\hat{g}_{ri}(v)\,dv$ for $t_i = r$ using the estimated conditional heterogeneity distributions $\hat{q}_{t_i i}(v)$ or $\hat{g}_{ri}(v)$, and then (ii) runs the following augmented regression equation:

$$y_{it} = x_{it}'\delta + d\hat{E}_{t_i}v_i + \left[d\left(v_i - E_{t_i}v_i\right) + \varepsilon_{it}\right] + d\left(E_{t_i}v_i - \hat{E}_{t_i}v_i\right),$$
$$i = 1,\ldots,n, \quad t = 1,\ldots,t_i, \quad (4.19)$$

where $d(v_i - E_{t_i}v_i) + \varepsilon_{it}$ is the model error and $d(E_{t_i}v_i - \hat{E}_{t_i}v_i)$ is the approximation error.

Since we model δ and d as time-constant parameters, it is more efficient to stack the data across years as well as across the individuals. The number of observed years differs across different individuals due to attrition. Let us look at these two steps in more detail.

First Step: Fit the grouped duration model with unmeasured heterogeneity to the attrition data as explained previously. Using the parameter estimates, compute $\hat{q}_{t_i i}(v) = \hat{g}(v \mid T_i = t_i)$, $\hat{g}_{ri}(v) = \hat{g}(v \mid T_i = r)$, $\hat{E}_{t_i} v_i = \int_0^\infty v\hat{q}_{t_i i}(v)\,dv$ for each i such that $t_i < r$, and $\hat{E}_r v_i = \int_0^\infty v\hat{g}_{ri}(v)\,dv$ for each i such that $t_i = r$.

Second Step: Using all available observations, apply ordinary least squares to

$$y_{it} = x'_{it}\delta + d\hat{E}_{t_i} v_i + e_{it} + \eta_i \qquad \text{for} \quad i = 1, \ldots, n, \quad t = 1, \ldots, t_i, \qquad (4.20)$$

where $e_{it} = d(v_i - E_{t_i} v_i) + \varepsilon_{it}$ is the model error and $\eta_i = d(E_{t_i} v_i - \hat{E}_{t_i} v_i)$ is the approximation error. These two error terms are asymptotically independent, and thus the total variance can be decomposed into the model error variance and the approximation error variance.

The resulting two-step estimator of θ_2 is

$$\hat{\theta}_2 = (\hat{Z}'\hat{Z})^{-1}\hat{Z}'y = \theta_2 + (\hat{Z}'\hat{Z})^{-1}\hat{Z}'(e + \eta), \qquad (4.21)$$

where y is a $\sum_{i=1}^n t_i \times 1$ vector of y_{it} defined as $y_{it} = (y_{11}, \ldots, y_{1t_1} : \ldots : y_{n1}, \ldots, y_{nt_n})'$, $\hat{Z} = (X : \hat{E}_t v)$ is a $\sum_{i=1}^n t_i \times (k+1)$ matrix of regressors with X a $\sum_{i=1}^n t_i \times k$ matrix of x'_{it} and $\hat{E}_t v$ a $\sum_{i=1}^n t_i \times 1$ vector of $\hat{E}_{t_i} v_i$, $\theta_2 = (\delta' : d)'$ is a $(k+1) \times 1$ vector of parameters with $\hat{\theta}_2$ its estimator, e is a $\sum_{i=1}^n t_i \times 1$ vector of e_{it}, and η is a $\sum_{i=1}^n t_i \times 1$ vector of η_i. (Here, X, $\hat{E}_t v$, e, and η are arranged in the same way as the vector y is arranged.)

To compute the variance–covariance matrix of $\hat{\theta}_2$ correctly, one needs to pay attention to the effect of approximation error in addition to the model error (see Greene 1981, Heckman 1979, Lee 1982, McFadden and Newey 1994, Newey 1984, Pagan 1984, Ryu 1996a). We propose a hybrid approach to computing the variance–covariance matrix. It is hybrid in the sense that it combines White's idea of estimating pure variance components with an idea of analytically estimating the rest. This hybrid approach has also been used in Ham and Hsiao (1984), Lee (1982), and Ryu (1996a).

One may wonder why we do not use either White's (1980) or Newey and West's (1987) idea for simplifying the variance–covariance matrix computation. Since the second step regression errors $e_{it} + \eta_i$ are serially correlated as well as heteroscedastic, White's heteroscedasticity-robust variance–covariance matrix estimator cannot be consistent in our case. Further, since serial correlations are not dying out even though errors are getting farther apart, Newey and West's heteroscedasticity and autocorrelation-robust variance–covariance matrix estimator is not applicable either.

Under a set of general conditions (see, for example, Amemiya 1973, Jennrich 1969), one derives the limiting distribution of $\hat{\theta}_2$ as

$$\hat{\theta}_2 = (\hat{Z}'\hat{Z})^{-1}\hat{Z}'y = \theta_2 + (\hat{Z}'\hat{Z})^{-1}\hat{Z}'(e + \eta)$$

$$\sim N(\theta, (Z'Z)^{-1}Z'[\text{Var}(e) + \text{Var}(\eta)]Z(Z'Z)^{-1}), \qquad (4.22)$$

where $\sim$ means that the left hand side is asymptotically distributed according to the right hand side distribution.

Note that η_i is $O_p(1/\sqrt{n})$, while e_{it} is $O_p(1)$. Observing this apparent difference in the stochastic orders, one might jump to the conclusion that η_i is asymptotically negligible relative to e_{it}. But this conclusion is incorrect. Even though η_i is of a smaller order than e_{it} *individually*, the η_i's, being correlated across the $\sum_{i=1}^{n} t_i$ observations, have a *wider* impact than the e_{it}'s, which are independent. As a result, the variance–covariance matrix in (4.22) is composed of two parts sharing the same stochastic order: the model error component $(Z'Z)^{-1}Z'\operatorname{Var}(e)Z(Z'Z)^{-1}$ and the approximation error component $(Z'Z)^{-1}Z'\operatorname{Var}(\eta)Z(Z'Z)^{-1}$. For details on this point, see Ryu (1996a).

Recall that the model error e_{it} is a sum of two independent terms: $d(v_i - E_{t_i}v_i)$, which is the same within each individual across different time points, and ε_{it}, which is i.i.d. across both individuals and time points. Thus, we have

$$\operatorname{Var}(e) = d^2 \begin{pmatrix} \sigma_1^2 l_1 l_1' & 0 & \cdots & 0 \\ 0 & \sigma_2^2 l_2 l_2' & \cdots & 0 \\ \vdots & \vdots & \ddots & \vdots \\ 0 & 0 & \cdots & \sigma_n^2 l_n l_n' \end{pmatrix} + \sigma_\varepsilon^2 I,$$

where σ_i^2 is the conditional variance of v_i given $T_i = t_i$, and l_i is a $t_i \times 1$ column vector of ones.

By distinguishing the diagonal elements from the off-diagonal elements, we can equivalently represent $\operatorname{Var}(e)$ as a sum of two matrices, $\operatorname{Var}(e) = D(e) + O(e)$, where

$$D(e) = \operatorname{diag}\left[(d^2\sigma_1^2 + \sigma_\varepsilon^2)l_1' : \cdots : (d^2\sigma_n^2 + \sigma_\varepsilon^2)l_n' \right]$$

is a diagonal matrix and

$$O(e) = d^2 \begin{pmatrix} \sigma_1^2(l_1 l_1' - I_1) & 0 & \cdots & 0 \\ 0 & \sigma_2^2(l_2 l_2' - I_2) & \cdots & 0 \\ \vdots & \vdots & \ddots & \vdots \\ 0 & 0 & \cdots & \sigma_n^2(l_n l_n' - I_n) \end{pmatrix}$$

is an off-diagonal matrix. In the above, $\operatorname{diag}[x']$ denotes a diagonal matrix composed of the elements in the row vector x', and I_i is a $t_i \times t_i$ identity matrix.

Therefore, the variance–covariance matrix of θ_2 can be decomposed into the following three terms: $(Z'Z)^{-1}Z'D(e)Z(Z'Z)^{-1}$, $(Z'Z)^{-1}Z'O(e)Z(Z'Z)^{-1}$, and $(Z'Z)^{-1}Z'\operatorname{Var}(\eta)Z(Z'Z)^{-1}$. The proposed variance–covariance matrix estimator computes the first component using White's idea, and the last two components analytically.

Lemmas 1–3 explain how to estimate each variance component consistently. Then, Theorem 1 combines them to suggest a consistent variance–covariance matrix estimator for $\hat{\theta}_2$.

Lemma 1: *Let $\hat{e}_{it}$ be the second step regression residuals. Under general conditions, we have*

$$\underset{n}{\text{plim}} \sum_{i=1}^{n} \sum_{t=1}^{t_i} \frac{\hat{e}_{it}^2 \hat{z}_{it} \hat{z}_{it}'}{n} = \underset{n}{\text{plim}} \sum_{i=1}^{n} \sum_{t=1}^{t_i} [\text{Var}(e_{it}) + \text{Var}(\eta_i)] \frac{z_{it} z_{it}'}{n}$$

$$= \underset{n}{\text{plim}} \frac{Z' D(e) Z}{n} + \underset{n}{\text{plim}} O_p(1/n)$$

$$= \underset{n}{\text{plim}} \frac{Z' D(e) Z}{n}, \tag{4.23}$$

where $z_{it} = (x_{it}' : E_{t_i} v_i)'$, $\hat{z}_{it} = (x_{it}' : \hat{E}_{t_i} v_i)'$, the first equality holds by the same argument as in White (1980), and the second equality follows from $\text{Var}(\eta_i) = O(1/n)$.

Note that individual variances of η_i are asymptotically negligible relative to those of e_{it}. Thus, one can ignore the effect of η_i on the pure variance component.

Lemma 2: *Under general conditions, we have*

$$\underset{n}{\text{plim}} \sum_{i=1}^{n} \sum_{t=1}^{t_i} \sum_{s=1}^{t_i} \frac{\hat{d}^2 \hat{\sigma}_i^2 1_{(t \neq s)} \hat{z}_{it} \hat{z}_{is}'}{n} = \underset{n}{\text{plim}} \frac{Z' O(e) Z}{n}, \tag{4.24}$$

where $\hat{d}$ is a consistent estimate of d, $\hat{\sigma}_i^2$ is a consistent estimate of $\text{Var}(v_i \mid T_i = t_i)$, and the equality follows from the same arguments as in Heckman (1979).

Lemma 3: *Under general conditions, we have*

$$\underset{n}{\text{plim}} \sum_{i=1}^{n} \sum_{t=1}^{t_i} \sum_{j=1}^{n} \sum_{s=1}^{t_j} \widehat{\text{Cov}}(\eta_i, \eta_j) \frac{\hat{z}_{it} \hat{z}_{js}'}{n} = \underset{n}{\text{plim}} \frac{Z' \text{Var}(\eta) Z}{n}, \tag{4.25}$$

where $\widehat{\text{Cov}}(\eta_i, \eta_j)$ is a consistent estimate of $\text{Cov}(\eta_i, \eta_j)$, and the equality follows from the same arguments as in Heckman (1979).

To compute $\widehat{\text{Cov}}(\eta_i, \eta_j)$ in Lemma 3, let us expand the approximation error using a Taylor series,

$$\eta_i = d \frac{\partial E_{t_i} v_i}{\partial \theta_1'} (\theta_1 - \hat{\theta}_1) + o_p(1/\sqrt{n}). \tag{4.26}$$

Therefore,

$$\text{Cov}(\eta_i, \eta_j) = d^2 \frac{\partial E_{t_i} v_i}{\partial \theta_1'} \text{Var}(\hat{\theta}_1) \frac{\partial E_{t_j} v_j}{\partial \theta_1} + o(1/n), \tag{4.27}$$

where $\text{Var}(\hat{\theta}_1)$ can be consistently estimated from the first step. Finally, $\text{Cov}(\eta_i, \eta_j)$ is obtained by evaluating (4.27) at the estimated parameter values after ignoring the $o(1/n)$ term.

By combining the above three lemmas, we obtain the following theorem, which offers a consistent variance–covariance matrix estimator for $\hat{\theta}_2$.

Theorem 1: *Under general conditions, the variance of $\sqrt{n}(\hat{\theta}_2 - \theta_2)$ can be consistently estimated by $(\hat{Z}'\hat{Z}/n)^{-1}(\hat{V}_1(e) + \hat{V}_2(e) + \hat{V}_3(\eta))(\hat{Z}'\hat{Z}/n)^{-1}$, where $\hat{V}_1(e) = \sum_{i=1}^{n} \sum_{t=1}^{t_i} \hat{e}_{it}^2 \hat{z}_{it} \hat{z}'_{it}/n$, $\hat{V}_2(e) = \sum_{i=1}^{n} \sum_{t=1}^{t_i} \sum_{s=1}^{t_i} \hat{d}^2 \hat{\sigma}_i^2 1_{(t \neq s)} \hat{z}_{it} \hat{z}'_{is}/n$, and $\hat{V}_3(\eta) = \sum_{i=1}^{n} \sum_{t=1}^{t_i} \sum_{j=1}^{n} \sum_{s=1}^{t_j} \widehat{\text{Cov}}(\eta_i, \eta_j) \hat{z}_{it} \hat{z}'_{js}/n$.*

Procedures are simpler for the case of using only the observations from the most recent panel wave, and are deferred to Appendix A.

In the next section, we consider two heterogeneity distributions, the gamma distribution and the discrete distribution. We will spell out some details of the above estimation procedures using these two examples.

5   Two heterogeneity distributions

To provide concrete models, we would like to specialize the above procedures and formulas for the gamma and discrete heterogeneity distributions.

5.1   *Gamma heterogeneity*

Let us consider gamma heterogeneity first. Assume that v follows a gamma distribution with parameters a and b, denoted gamma(a, b): $v \sim g(v) = b^a v^{a-1} e^{-bv}/\Gamma(a)$, where $\Gamma(a) = \int_0^\infty t^{a-1} e^{-t}\, dt$. It is easy to show that the moment generating function is $M_v(c) = [b/(b+c)]^a$. The mean and variance are $Ev = a/b$ and $\text{Var}(v) = a/b^2$. To fix the level of v, let us assume that $Ev = 1$. This identification condition imposes $a = b$. That is, the heterogeneity is modeled through a gamma distribution with mean one and variance $1/b$. Thus, in the case of gamma heterogeneity, $\theta_1 = (\beta' : b : \gamma_1, \ldots, \gamma_{r-1})'$ is a $(k+r) \times 1$ vector of parameters specifying the attrition process.

From (4.7),

$$
g_{ti}(v) = \frac{e^{-(c_{i1}+\cdots+c_{i\,t-1})v} g(v)}{M_v(c_{i1} + \cdots + c_{i\,t-1})}
$$

$$
= \frac{b^b e^{-(b+c_{i1}+\cdots+c_{i\,t-1})v} v^{b-1}}{\Gamma(b) M_v(c_{i1} + \cdots + c_{i\,t-1})} = \frac{b_{it}^b v^{b-1} e^{-b_{it}v}}{\Gamma(b)}, \tag{4.28}
$$

where $b_{it} = b + c_{i1} + \cdots + c_{i\,t-1}$ with $b_{i1} = b$. Note that $g_{ti}(v)$ is the density corresponding to a gamma distribution with parameters b and b_{it}, denoted gamma(b, b_{it}). Since this distribution has mean b/b_{it} and variance b/b_{it}^2, we observe that $g_{ti}(v)$ exhibits decreasing mean and variance as t increases. For $t = 1, \ldots, r - 1$, we have from (4.9)

$$
\alpha_{it} = \frac{M_v(c_{i1} + \cdots + c_{it})}{M_v(c_{i1} + \cdots + c_{i\,t-1})}
$$

$$
= \left(\frac{b + c_{i1} + \cdots + c_{i\,t-1}}{b + c_{i1} + \cdots + c_{it}} \right)^b = \left(\frac{b_{it}}{b_{i\,t+1}} \right)^b. \tag{4.29}
$$

For $t = 1, \ldots, r - 1$, we have from (4.8)

$$
q_{ti}(v) = \frac{e^{-(c_{i1} + \cdots + c_{i\,t-1})v} g(v) - e^{-(c_{i1} + \cdots + c_{it})v} g(v)}{M_v(c_{i1} + \cdots + c_{i\,t-1}) - M_v(c_{i1} + \cdots + c_{it})}
$$

$$
= \frac{b_{i\,t+1}^b}{b_{i\,t+1}^b - b_{it}^b} \frac{b_{it}^b v^{b-1} e^{-b_{it}v}}{\Gamma(b)} - \frac{b_{it}^b}{b_{i\,t+1}^b - b_{it}^b} \frac{b_{i\,t+1}^b v^{b-1} e^{-b_{i\,t+1}v}}{\Gamma(b)}, \tag{4.30}
$$

which is a linear combination of two densities, gamma(b, b_{it}) and gamma(b, b_{it+1}), with weights $b_{i\,t+1}^b/(b_{i\,t+1}^b - b_{it}^b)$ and $-b_{it}^b/(b_{i\,t+1}^b - b_{it}^b)$, respectively.

To compute the information matrix, we need $\partial \alpha_{it}/\partial \theta_1 = (\partial \alpha_{it}/\partial \beta' : \partial \alpha_{it}/\partial b : \partial \alpha_{it}/\partial \gamma_1, \ldots, \partial \alpha_{it}/\partial \gamma_{r-1})'$. We have

$$
\frac{\partial \alpha_{it}}{\partial \beta} = -bc_{it} \frac{b_{it}^{b-1}}{b_{i\,t+1}^{b+1}} [b_{it} x_{it} - (c_{i1} x_{i1} + \cdots + c_{i\,t-1} x_{i\,t-1})],
$$

$$
\frac{\partial \alpha_{it}}{\partial b} = \frac{\alpha_{it}}{b} \log \alpha_{it} + b[\alpha_{it}]^{(b-1)/b} \frac{c_{it}}{b_{i\,t+1}^2}, \tag{4.31}
$$

$$
\frac{\partial \alpha_{it}}{\partial \gamma_k} = b[\alpha_{it}]^{(b-1)/b} \frac{c_{ik}}{b_{i\,t+1}^2} \left[1_{(t \leq k-1)} c_{it} - 1_{(t=k)} b_{it} \right], \quad k = 1, \ldots, r - 1,
$$

where 1_A is an indicator function which takes value one if A is true and zero otherwise.

To complete the formula, we need to compute $\partial E_t v_i/\partial \theta_1$. Since $E_t v_i = b/(b + c_{i1} + \cdots + c_{i\,t-1})$, we have $\partial E_t v_i/\partial \gamma_k = 0$ for all $k = t, \ldots, r - 1$. Thus, by letting $s = \max(t_i, t_j)$ and $\theta_1^{(s)} = (\beta' : b : \gamma_1, \ldots, \gamma_{s-1})$, (4.27) can be simplified as

$$
\text{Cov}(\eta_i, \eta_j) = d^2 \frac{\partial E_{t_i} v_i}{\partial \theta_1^{(s)'}} \text{Var}(\hat{\theta}_1^{(s)}) \frac{\partial E_{t_j} v_j}{\partial \theta_1^{(s)}} + o(1/n). \tag{4.27'}
$$

Note that

$$
\frac{\partial E_t v_i}{\partial \beta} = \frac{-b(c_{i1}x_{i1} + \cdots + c_{it-1}x_{it-1})}{b_{it}^2},
$$

$$
\frac{\partial E_t v_i}{\partial b} = \frac{c_{i1} + \cdots + c_{it-1}}{b_{it}^2}, \tag{4.32}
$$

$$
\frac{\partial E_t v_i}{\partial \gamma_k} = \frac{-1_{(k \le t-1)} b c_{ik}}{b_{it}^2}, \qquad k = 1, \ldots, r-1.
$$

Using the above results together with numerical optimization routines, one can carry out the joint and sequential estimation procedures.

5.2   *Discrete heterogeneity*

Next, let us consider a discrete heterogeneity distribution following Heckman and Singer (1984a), who show that as the number of mass points increases toward infinity, discrete distributions can approximate any distribution arbitrarily well.

For practical purposes, assume that v takes M finite values, say $v_1, \ldots, v_M$, with probabilities $p_1, \ldots, p_M$. If M is not set in advance, it causes an incidental parameter problem. This distribution describes that there are M unobserved types. For level identification, let us fix $v_M = 1$. For v_m, the following parameterization is convenient:

$$
v_M = 1 \quad \text{(level normalization)}, \qquad v_m = e^{w_m}, \qquad m = 1, \ldots, M-1, \tag{4.33}
$$

where the w_m's are unrestricted, $-\infty < w_m < \infty$. For p_m, the following parameterization is again useful:

$$
p_M = \frac{1}{1 + \sum_{m=1}^{M-1} e^{\pi_m}}, \qquad p_m = \frac{e^{\pi_m}}{1 + \sum_{m=1}^{M-1} e^{\pi_m}}, \qquad m = 1, \ldots, M-1, \tag{4.34}
$$

where the π_m's are unrestricted too, $-\infty < \pi_m < \infty$. The moment generating function of this discrete distribution is $M_v(c) = E_v e^{-cv} = \sum_{m=1}^{M} e^{-cv_m} p_m$. Note that, in the case of discrete heterogeneity, $\theta_1 = (\beta' : w_1, \ldots, w_{M-1}, \pi_1, \ldots, \pi_{M-1} : \gamma_1, \ldots, \gamma_{r-1})'$ is a $(k + 2M + r - 3) \times 1$ vector of parameters specifying the attrition process.

From (4.7) and (4.8), we derive

$$
g_{ti}(v_m) = \frac{e^{-(c_{i1} + \cdots + c_{it-1})v_m} p_m}{\sum_{k=1}^{M} e^{-(c_{i1} + \cdots + c_{it-1})v_k} p_k},
$$

$$
q_{ti}(v_m) = \frac{e^{-(c_{i1} + \cdots + c_{it-1})v_m} p_m - e^{-(c_{i1} + \cdots + c_{it})v_m} p_m}{\sum_{k=1}^{M} e^{-(c_{i1} + \cdots + c_{it-1})v_k} p_k - \sum_{k=1}^{M} e^{-(c_{i1} + \cdots + c_{it})v_k} p_k}. \tag{4.35}
$$

From (4.9), we obtain

$$
\alpha_{it} = \frac{M_v(c_{i1} + \cdots + c_{it})}{M_v(c_{i1} + \cdots + c_{i\,t-1})}
$$

$$
= \frac{\sum_{m=1}^{M} e^{-(c_{i1}+\cdots+c_{it})v_m}\, p_m}{\sum_{m=1}^{M} e^{-(c_{i1}+\cdots+c_{i\,t-1})v_m}\, p_m}, \qquad t = 1, \ldots, r-1. \tag{4.36}
$$

Computing the expected value of v_i using $q_{t_i i}(v)$ (for $t_i = 1, \ldots, r-1$) or $g_{t_i i}(v)$ (for $t_i = r$), we obtain

$$
E_{t_i} v_i = \frac{\sum_{m=1}^{M} v_m p_m \left[e^{-(c_{i1}+\cdots+c_{i\,t_i-1})v_m} - e^{-(c_{i1}+\cdots+c_{it_i})v_m} \right]}{\sum_{k=1}^{M} e^{-(c_{i1}+\cdots+c_{i\,t_i-1})v_k}\, p_k - \sum_{k=1}^{M} e^{-(c_{i1}+\cdots+c_{it_i})v_k}\, p_k},
$$
$$
t_i = 1, \ldots, r-1, \tag{4.37}
$$

$$
E_{t_i} v_i = \frac{\sum_{m=1}^{M} v_m e^{-(c_{i1}+\cdots+c_{i\,t_i-1})v_m}\, p_m}{\sum_{k=1}^{M} e^{-(c_{i1}+\cdots+c_{i\,t_i-1})v_k}\, p_k}, \qquad t_i = r.
$$

From α_{it} and $E_{t_i} v_i$, one can compute $\partial \alpha_{it}/\partial \theta_1$ and $\partial E_{t_i} v_i/\partial \theta_1$. The computations are straightforward, though time consuming. They are omitted here.

6   Concluding remarks

In this chapter, we propose several ways of handling the attrition problem in longitudinal studies. After introducing a random variable to take into account the unobserved heterogeneity, we suggest grouped duration techniques to estimate and update the unobserved heterogeneity distribution.

Once one identifies the population distribution of the unobserved heterogeneity together with its changing pattern over panel waves, there are several ways of taking account of the attrition problem. We propose a joint maximum likelihood estimation of the attrition process and the equation of interest, together with two sequential estimation methods. The two methods differ in the second step estimation procedure, depending whether they use likelihood-based estimation or regression-based estimation. The likelihood-based estimation is a two-step breakdown of the joint maximum likelihood estimation, whereas the regression-based estimation is a conditional mean correction procedure.

The joint maximum likelihood estimation yields more efficient estimator, though more demanding in terms of computation. On the other hand, the sequential estimation yields a less efficient, but easier-to-use, estimator. In particular, the regression-based sequential estimator is very convenient to use and reveals the nature of attrition as a well-known sample selection problem.

By modeling the error terms in the equation of interest more flexibly as $u_i + \varepsilon_{it}$ rather than restrictively as $dv_i + \varepsilon_{it}$, we can generalize the underlying relationship between the attrition mechanism and the main equation of interest. In this generalization, depending on the sign and magnitude of the correlation between v_i and u_i, one can determine the nature and strength of the attrition problem.

In the equation of interest we have specified, individual heterogeneity is modeled as a time-constant random variable. Since this is the only source of attrition bias, one can simply apply within estimation methods to avoid attrition bias. Then, why not? There are three reasons why we have not addressed the attrition problem in this simpler way. First, there is information loss due to the within transformation. Second, we cannot identify the nature of the attrition by using within estimation, whereas our approach allows us to do so. Third, when the individual heterogeneity in the equation of interest is generalized to be time varying, within estimation can no longer get rid of the heterogeneity term and thus can no longer avoid the attrition bias. However, our approach can still tackle the attrition problem so far as the time-varying heterogeneity is conditionally i.i.d. given v_i.

The approach in this chapter also differs from Wooldridge's. His model is more general in that he allows the error term ε_{it} to be correlated with the error terms governing the attrition process. However, his model is seriously restricted by assuming that the equation of interest and the attrition process are only contemporaneously correlated. Our model allows the attrition process and the equation of interest to be correlated at all time points through v_i.

Appendix A: Regression-based two step estimation using one year of data

Oftentimes, researchers use just one year of data. They are interested in estimating the behavioral equation using the most up-to-date panel wave. Let r represent the most recent panel wave, and accordingly let the equation of interest be

$$y_{ir} = x'_{ir}\delta_r + d_r v_i + \varepsilon_{ir}, \qquad i = 1, \ldots, n_r, \qquad (4.A1)$$

where n_r is the number of observations available in the most recent panel wave. Over time, as new waves become available, the equation will be updated subsequently.

If the parameters δ_t and d_t are constant across $t = 1, \ldots, r$, researchers are likely to stack the data across years to improve the efficiency, as done in the text. So, to justify researchers' practices of using the most recent year of data, we should treat δ_t and d_t as time-varying parameters. If the parameters are time constant, such practices are for convenience only. Since, in this appendix, we use just one year of data, let us drop the subscript r from δ_r and d_r for notational simplicity.

Here, to analyze y_{ir} without attrition bias, the two-step procedure (i) computes $\hat{E}_r v_i = \hat{E}(v_i \mid T_i = r) = \int_0^\infty v \hat{g}_{ri}(v)\,dv$ using the estimated conditional heterogeneity distribution $\hat{g}_{ri}(v)$, and then (ii) applies the ordinary least squares to the following augmented regression equation:

$$y_{ir} = x_{ir}'\delta + d\hat{E}_r v_i + [d(v_i - E_r v_i) + \varepsilon_{ir}] + d(E_r v_i - \hat{E}_r v_i),$$

$$i = 1, \ldots, n_r. \quad (4.\text{A}2)$$

The resulting two-step estimator of θ_2 is

$$\hat{\theta}_2 = (\hat{Z}_r'\hat{Z}_r)^{-1}\hat{Z}_r' y_r = \theta_2 + (\hat{Z}_r'\hat{Z}_r)^{-1}\hat{Z}_r'(e_r + \eta_r), \quad (4.\text{A}3)$$

where y_r is an $n_r \times 1$ vector of y_{ir} defined as $y_r = (y_{1r}, \ldots, y_{n_r r})'$; $\hat{Z}_r = (X_r : \hat{E}_r v)$ is an $n_r \times (k+1)$ matrix of regressors with X_r an $n_r \times k$ matrix of x_{ir}', and $\hat{E}_r v$ an $n_r \times 1$ vector of $\hat{E}_r v_i$; $\theta_2 = (\delta' : d)'$ is a $(k+1) \times 1$ vector of parameters with $\hat{\theta}_2$ its estimator; e_r is an $n_r \times 1$ vector of $e_{ir} = d(v_i - E_r v_i) + \varepsilon_{ir}$; and η_r is an $n_r \times 1$ vector of $\eta_i = d(E_r v_i - \hat{E}_r v_i)$. (Here, X_r, $\hat{E}_r v$, e_r, and η_r are arranged in the same way as the vector y_r is arranged.)

The limiting distribution of $\hat{\theta}_2$ is

$$\hat{\theta}_2 \sim N(\theta_2, (Z_r'Z_r)^{-1}Z_r'[\text{Var}(e_r) + \text{Var}(\eta_r)]Z_r(Z_r'Z_r)^{-1}). \quad (4.\text{A}4)$$

Theorem A1 explains how to compute the above variance–covariance matrix consistently.

Theorem A1: *Let $\hat{e}_{ir}$ be the residuals from the second step regression, and let $\text{Cov}(\eta_{ir}, \eta_{jr}) = d^2(\partial E_r v_i / \partial \theta_1') \text{Var}(\hat{\theta}_1) \partial E_r v_j / \partial \theta_1$. Under general conditions, the variance of $\sqrt{n_r}(\hat{\theta}_2 - \theta_2)$ can be consistently estimated by $(\hat{Z}_r'\hat{Z}_r/n_r)^{-1}(\hat{V}_1(e_r) + \hat{V}_3(\eta_r))(\hat{Z}_r'\hat{Z}_r/n_r)^{-1}$, where $\hat{V}_1(e_r) = \sum_{i=1}^{n_r} \hat{e}_{ir}^2 \hat{z}_{ir} \hat{z}_{ir}'/n_r$ and $\hat{V}_3(\eta_r) = \sum_{i=1}^{n_r} \sum_{j=1}^{n_r} \widehat{\text{Cov}(\eta_{ir}, \eta_{jr})} \hat{z}_{ir} \hat{z}_{jr}'/n_r$, with $\text{Cov}(\eta_i, \eta_j)$ being equal to $\text{Cov}(\eta_i, \eta_j)$ evaluated at the estimated parameter values. This estimator is positive definite.*

The rest of the details can be computed easily by referring to relevant results in the text. Just notice that the relevant conditional heterogeneity distribution in this case is always $g_{ri}(v)$.

Appendix B: Two step procedure with gamma heterogeneity

B.1   *Conditional variance of v_i, given $T_i = t_i$*

Given $T_i = r$, the conditional distribution of v_i is $g_{ri}(v)$, a gamma distribution with parameters (b, b_{ri}). By denoting as σ_i^2 the conditional variance of v_i, we have $\sigma_i^2 = b/b_{ri}^2$ for $t_i = r$. For $t_i < r$, the conditional distribution of v_i given $T_i = t_i$ is a weighted average of two gamma distributions, one with parameters (b, b_{it_i}) and the other with parameters $(b, b_{i\,t_i+1})$, with weights $w_{i1} = b_{i\,t_i+1}^b/(b_{i\,t_i+1}^b - b_{it_i}^b)$ and $w_{i2} = -b_{it_i}^b/(b_{i\,t_i+1}^b - b_{it_i}^b)$, respectively. Therefore, $\sigma_i^2 = w_{i1}b(b+1)/b_{it_i}^2 + w_{i2}b(b+1)/b_{i\,t_i+1}^2 - (w_{i1}b/b_{it_i} + w_{i2}b/b_{i\,t_i+1})^2$ for $t_i < r$.

B.2   *Conditional covariance of η_i and η_j, given $T_i = t_i$ and $T_j = t_j$*

Let σ_{ij} denote the conditional covariance of η_i and η_j given $T_i = t_i$ and $T_j = t_j$. From (4.27), we have $\sigma_{ij} = d^2(\partial E_{t_i} v_i/\partial \theta_1')\,\mathrm{Var}(\hat{\theta}_1)\,\partial E_{t_j} v_j/\partial \theta_1 + o(1/n)$, where $\theta_1 = (\beta' : b : \gamma_1, \ldots, \gamma_{r-1})'$ is a vector of the first step parameters. Since $\mathrm{Var}(\hat{\theta}_1)$ is available from the first step duration analysis, it suffices to derive the form of $\partial E_{t_i} v_i/\partial \beta$, $\partial E_{t_i} v_i/\partial b$, and $\partial E_{t_i} v_i/\partial \gamma_k$ $(k = 1, \ldots, r-1)$ for each of $t_i = r$ and $t_i < r$.

For $t_i = r$: Using $E_r v_i = b/b_{ir}$ and $b_{ir} = b + c_{i1} + \cdots + c_{i\,r-1}$, we derive

$$\frac{\partial E_r v_i}{\partial \beta} = \frac{-b(c_{i1}x_{i1} + \cdots + c_{i\,r-1}x_{i\,r-1})}{b_{ir}^2},$$

$$\frac{\partial E_r v_i}{\partial b} = \frac{c_{i1} + \cdots + c_{i\,r-1}}{b_{ir}^2}, \tag{4.B1}$$

$$\frac{\partial E_r v_i}{\partial \gamma_k} = \frac{-bc_{ik}}{b_{ir}^2}.$$

For $t_i < r$: Using $E_{t_i} v_i = w_{i1}b/b_{it_i} + w_{i2}b/b_{i\,t_i+1}$, we derive

$$\frac{\partial E_{t_i} v_i}{\partial \beta} = -w_{i1}\frac{b(c_{i1}x_{i1} + \cdots + c_{i\,t_i-1}x_{i\,t_i-1})}{b_{it_i}^2}$$

$$- w_{i2}\frac{b(c_{i1}x_{i1} + \cdots + c_{it_i}x_{it_i})}{b_{i\,t_i+1}^2}$$

$$+ \left(\frac{b}{b_{it_i}}\right)\frac{\partial w_{i1}}{\partial \beta} + \left(\frac{b}{b_{i\,t_i+1}}\right)\frac{\partial w_{i2}}{\partial \beta},$$

$$\frac{\partial E_{t_i} v_i}{\partial b} = w_{i1}\frac{c_{i1} + \cdots + c_{i\,t_i-1}}{b_{it_i}^2} + w_{i2}\frac{c_{i1} + \cdots + c_{it_i}}{b_{i\,t_i+1}^2} \tag{4.B2}$$

$$+ \left(\frac{b}{b_{it_i}}\right)\frac{\partial w_{i1}}{\partial b} + \left(\frac{b}{b_{i\,t_i+1}}\right)\frac{\partial w_{i2}}{\partial b},$$

$$\frac{\partial E_{t_i} v_i}{\partial \gamma_k} = -w_{i1}\frac{1_{(k \leq t_i-1)}bc_{ik}}{b_{it_i}^2} - w_{i2}\frac{1_{(k \leq t_i)}bc_{ik}}{b_{i\,t_i+1}^2}$$

$$+ \left(\frac{b}{b_{it_i}}\right)\frac{\partial w_{i1}}{\partial \gamma_k} + \left(\frac{b}{b_{i\,t_i+1}}\right)\frac{\partial w_{i2}}{\partial \gamma_k},$$

where

$$\frac{\partial w_{i1}}{\partial \beta} = \frac{1}{D_i^2}\left[bb_{i\,t_i+1}^{b-1}\left(c_{i1}x_{i1} + \cdots + c_{it_i}x_{it_i}\right)D_i\right]$$
$$-\frac{1}{D_i^2}b_{i\,t_i+1}^{b}\left[bb_{i\,t_i+1}^{b-1}\left(c_{i1}x_{i1} + \cdots + c_{it_i}x_{it_i}\right)\right.$$
$$\left. - bb_{it_i}^{b-1}\left(c_{i1}x_{i1} + \cdots + c_{i\,t_i-1}x_{i\,t_i-1}\right)\right],$$

$$\frac{\partial w_{i1}}{\partial b} = \frac{1}{D_i^2}\left[bb_{i\,t_i+1}^{b-1} + b_{i\,t_i+1}^{b}\log b_{i\,t_i+1}\right]D_i$$
$$-\frac{1}{D_i^2}b_{i\,t_i+1}^{b}\left[bb_{i\,t_i+1}^{b-1} + b_{i\,t_i+1}^{b}\log b_{i\,t_i+1}\right]$$
$$+\frac{1}{D_i^2}b_{i\,t_i+1}^{b}\left[bb_{it_i}^{b-1} + b_{it_i}^{b}\log b_{it_i}\right],$$

$$\frac{\partial w_{i1}}{\partial \gamma_k} = \frac{1}{D_i^2}bb_{i\,t_i+1}^{b-1}c_{ik}1_{(k\le t_i)}D_i$$
$$-\frac{1}{D_i^2}bb_{i\,t_i+1}^{b}\left[b_{i\,t_i+1}^{b-1}c_{ik}1_{(k\le t_i)} - b_{it_i}^{b-1}c_{ik}1_{(k\le t_i-1)}\right],$$

with D_i being defined as $D_i = b_{i\,t_i+1}^{b} - b_{it_i}^{b}$. Similarly for partial derivatives of w_{i2} with respect to β, b, and γ_k.

REFERENCES

Amemiya, T. (1973), "Regression Analysis When the Dependent Variable is Truncated Normal," *Econometrica*, **41**, 997–1017.

——— (1985), *Advanced Econometrics* (Boston, MA: Harvard University Press).

Baltagi, B. (1985), "Pooling Cross-Sections with Unequal Time-Series Lengths," *Economics Letters*, **18**, 133–136.

Berndt, E. K., Hall, B. H., Hall, R. E., and Hausman, J. A. (1974), "Estimation and Inference in Nonlinear Structural Models," *Annals of Economic and Social Measurement*, **3**, 653–665.

Biørn, E. (1981), "Estimating Economic Relations from Incomplete Cross-Section/ Time-Series Data," *Journal of Econometrics*, **16**, 221–236.

Cox, D. R. (1972), "Regression Models and Life-Tables," *Journal of the Royal Statistical Society B*, **34**, 187–220.

——— (1975), "Partial Likelihood," *Biometrika*, **62**, 269–279.

Cox, D. R. and Oakes, D. (1984), *Analysis of Survival Data* (London: Chapman & Hall).

Elbers, C. and Ridder, G. (1982), "True and Spurious Duration Dependence: The Identifiability of the Proportional Hazard Model," *Review of Economic Studies*, **49**, 403–409.

Fuller, W. and G. Battese (1974), "Estimation of Linear Functions with Crossed-Error Structure," *Journal of Econometrics*, **2**, 67–78.

Greene, W. (1981), "Sample Selection Bias as a Specification Error: Comment," *Econometrica*, **49**, 795–798.

Ham, J. and Hsiao, C. (1984), "Two-Stage Estimation of Structural Labor Supply Parameters Using Interval Data from the 1971 Canadian Census," *Journal of Econometrics*, **24**, 133–158.

Han, A. K. and Hausman, J. A. (1990), "Flexible Parametric Estimation of Duration and Competing Risk Models," *Journal of Applied Econometrics*, **5**, 1–28.

Hausman, J. A. (1978), "Specification Tests in Econometrics," *Econometrica*, **46**, 1251–1272.

Hausman, J. A. and Wise, D. (1979), "Attrition Bias in Experimental and Panel Data," *Econometrica*, **47**, 455–473.

Heckman, J. (1976), "The Common Structure of Statistical Models of Truncation, Sample Selection and Limited Dependent Variables and a Simple Estimator for Such Models," *The Annals of Economic and Social Measurement*, **5**, 475–492.

(1979), "Sample Selection Bias as a Specification Error," *Econometrica*, **47**, 153–161.

Heckman, J. and Honore, B. (1989), "The Identifiability of the Competing Risks Model," *Biometrika*, **76**, 325–330.

Heckman, J. and Singer, B. (1984a), "A Method for Minimizing the Impact of Distributional Assumptions in Econometric Models for Duration Data," *Econometrica*, **52**, 271–320.

(1984b), "Econometric Duration Analysis," *Journal of Econometrics*, **24**, 63–132.

Hsiao, C. (1984), *Panel Data Analysis*, Econometric Society Monograph.

Jennrich, R. (1969), "Asymptotic Properties of Non-linear Least Squares Estimators," *The Annals of Mathematical Statistics*, **40**, 633–643.

Kalbfleisch, J. D. and Prentice, R. L. (1980), *The Statistical Analysis of Failure Time Data* (New York: John Wiley & Sons).

Kiefer, N. M. (1988), "Analysis of Grouped Duration Data," *Contemporary Mathematics*, **80**, 107–137.

Lancaster, T. and Intrator, O. (1998), "Panel Data with Survival: Hospitalization of HIV-Positive Patients," *Journal of the American Statistical Association*, **93**, 46–53.

Lee, L. F. (1982), "Some Approaches to the Correction of Selectivity Bias," *Review of Economic Studies*, **49**, 355–372.

Lin, D. Y. (1991), "Goodness-of-Fit Analysis for the Cox Regression Model Based on a Class of Parameter Estimators," *Journal of the American Statistical Association*, **86**, 725–728.

McFadden, D. and W. Newey (1994), "Large Sample Estimation and Hypothesis Testing," in R. F. Engle and D. McFadden, eds., *Handbook of Econometrics*, IV, 2111–2245.

Moffitt, R. (1985), "Unemployment Insurance and the Distribution of Unemployment Spells," *Journal of Econometrics*, **28**, 85–101.

Newey, W. (1984), "A Method of Moments Interpretation of Sequential Estimators," *Economics Letters*, **14**, 201–206.

Newey, W. and K. West (1987), "A Simple Positive Semi-Definite, Heteroscedasticity and Auto-Correlation Consistent Covariance Matrix," *Econometrica*, **55**, 703–708.

Nickell, S. (1979), "Estimating the Probability of Leaving Unemployment," *Econometrica*, **47**, 1249–1266.

Pagan, A. (1984), "Econometric Issues in the Analysis of Regressions with Generated Regressors," *International Economic Review*, **25**, 221–247.

(1986), "Two Stage and Related Estimators and Their Applications," *Review of Economic Studies*, **53**, 517–538.

Prentice, R. and Gloeckler, L. (1978), "Regression Analysis of Grouped Survival Data with Application to Breast Cancer Data," *Biometrics*, **34**, 57–67.

Ridder, Geert (1992), "An Empirical Evaluation of Some Models for Non-Random Attrition in Panel Data," *Structural Change and Economic Dynamics*, **3**, 337–355.

Ryu, Keunkwan (1993), "Monotonicity of the Fisher Information and the Kullback–Leibler Divergence Measure," *Economics Letters*, **42**, 121–128.

(1994), "Group Duration Analysis of the Proportional Hazard Model: Minimum Chi-Square Estimators and Specification Tests," *Journal of the American Statistical Association*, **89**, 1386–1397.

(1996a), "Consistent, Positive-Definite Covariance Matrix Estimation of Heckman's Two-step Estimators," *Journal of Economic Theory and Econometrics*, **2**, 65–76.

(1996b), "Maximum Likelihood Estimation and Specification Test of the Proportional Hazard Model Using Grouped Durations," mimeo, Seoul National University.

Sueyoshi, G. T. (1991), "Evaluating Simple Alternatives to the Proportional Hazard Model: Unemployment Insurance Receipt and the Duration of Unemployment," mimeo, San Diego, CA: University of California.

Thompson, W. A. (1977), "On the Treatment of Grouped Observations in Life Studies," *Biometrics*, **33**, 463–470.

Van den Berg, G., Lindeboom, M., and Ridder, G. (1994), "Attrition in Longitudinal Panel Data and the Empirical Analysis of Dynamic Labor Market Behavior," *Journal of Applied Econometrics*, **9**, 421–435.

Wansbeek, T. and Kapteyn, A. (1989), "Estimation of the Error-Components Model with Incomplete Panels," *Journal of Econometrics*, **41**, 341–361.

White, H. (1980), "A Heteroscedasticity-Consistent Covariance Matrix Estimator and a Direct Test for Heteroscedasticity," *Econometrica*, **48**, 817–838.

Wooldridge, J. (1995), "Selection Corrections for Panel Data Models under Conditional Mean Independence Assumptions," *Journal of Econometrics*, **68**, 115–132.

CHAPTER 5

Semiparametric estimation for left-censored duration models

Fumihiro Goto

1   Introduction

The problem of left censoring was discussed by Professor Amemiya in his book *Advanced Econometrics* in 1985 (see Amemiya 1985, pp. 447–448). Consider the estimation of unemployment duration when the statistician samples individuals from the pool of unemployed persons and later interviews them and asks how long have they been unemployed. This incurs the problem of left censoring; ignoring it leads to overestimating the mean duration, since longer spells tend to be observed more frequently than shorter spells. This effect is called selectivity bias and needs a special treatment.

Some other authors have noticed and studied the problem (see, e.g., Lancaster 1979, Chesher and Lancaster 1983, Ridder 1984, and Heckman and Singer 1984). To the best of our knowledge, however, Amemiya (1991) is the first paper to give a complete, unified treatment of this problem, including asymptotic properties. According to it, three types of left censoring arise. We assume that spells in progress at the time of the first observation are either completely or partially observed. Suppose such a spell started at x, continued to 0 (the time of the first observation), and ended at s. The statistician may observe both s and x (by asking how long the spell lasted), only s, or only x. Amemiya (1991) calls those cases types 1, 2, and 3, respectively.

In each possible case we have to consider how the selectivity bias is eliminated. If the model is fully specified, including the distribution of the starting time x, this is accomplished by the method of maximum likelihood estimation, which is fully efficient and comprehensively discussed by Amemiya (1991). However, without any knowledge of the starting time distribution, a less efficient but more robust method may be desirable. For instance, Lancaster (1979) used a conditional maximum likelihood estimator (MLE) that does not require the knowledge of the starting time distribution in the type 1 model. In this chapter we employ a semiparametric approach to treat this problem comprehensively, which assumes the functional form of the starting time distribution to be unknown. We also evaluate Lancaster's model from this point of view with emphasis on asymptotic efficiency.

To give an asymptotic efficiency criterion to estimation methods, we use semiparametric efficiency bounds. Among various methods of calculating semiparametric efficiency bounds (see Newey 1990 and Bickel et al. 1993 for a survey), those developed by Beran (1977) and Begun et al. (1983) are especially useful for the left-censored duration models. We use their approaches with some necessary modifications.

In Section 2, we provide the basic theory of semiparametric efficiency bounds following Begun et al. (1983), but in a more concise manner, by applying the standard inverse formula for partitioned operators. Section 3 is the main part of this chapter, where we obtain the semiparametric MLE of the type 1 model, of which the parametric component turns out to be the conditional MLE adopted by Lancaster (1979). We show that the semiparametric MLE achieves the efficiency bounds for both parametric and nonparametric components by directly comparing its asymptotic efficiency with the semiparametric efficiency bounds. Finally, Section 4 briefly discusses the models of types 2 and 3, and the hybrid models of various types of left censoring.

2   Theory of semiparametric efficiency bounds

First we establish the notation and quote some results from Begun et al. (1983) with some modifications suitable for our present purposes. Consider the sequence of i.i.d. $\mathcal{Y}$-valued random variables $\{Y_1, \ldots, Y_n\}$ with density function $g = g(y \mid \theta, h)$ with respect to a σ-finite measure μ on the measurable space $(\mathcal{Y}, \mathcal{C})$, where $\mathcal{Y} \subset R^k$. Here θ is the parametric component and assumed to be one-dimensional (i.e., $\theta \in \Theta \subset R^1$) for notational simplicity, while h, the nonparametric component, belongs to $\mathcal{H}$, the collection of all densities with respect to a σ-finite measure ν on the measurable space $(\mathcal{X}, \mathcal{D})$, where $\mathcal{X} \subset R^1$. In the present chapter we assume that $\mathcal{X} = [a, 0]$ for some $a < 0$. Let $L^2(\mu) = L^2(\mathcal{Y}, \mu)$ and $L^2(\nu) = L^2(\mathcal{X}, \nu)$ denote the usual L^2 spaces of square-integrable functions, and let $\langle \cdot, \cdot \rangle_\mu$ ($\|\cdot\|_\mu$) and $\langle \cdot, \cdot \rangle_\nu$ ($\|\cdot\|_\nu$) denote the usual inner products (and norms) in $L^2(\mu)$ and $L^2(\nu)$, respectively. Thus $g^{1/2} \in L^2(\mu)$, $h^{1/2} \in L^2(\nu)$, and $\|g^{1/2}\|_\mu = 1 = \|h^{1/2}\|_\nu$. Convergence of sequences $\{g_n\}$ and $\{h_n\}$ is with respect to the L^2 norms $\|\cdot\|_\mu$ and $\|\cdot\|_\nu$, while convergence of sequences $\{\theta_n\}$ is with respect to the ordinary Euclidean norm $|\cdot|$ for R^1.

Now let $\Theta(\theta, \lambda)$ denote the collection of all sequences $\{\theta_n\}$ such that $|n^{1/2}(\theta_n - \theta) - \lambda| \to 0$ as $n \to \infty$, where $\lambda \in R^1$, and let $\Theta(\theta) = \cup \{\Theta(\theta, \lambda): \lambda \in R^1\}$. Similarly, let $\mathcal{H}(h, \beta)$ denote the collection of all sequences $\{h_n\}$ such that $\|n^{1/2}(h_n^{1/2} - h^{1/2}) - \beta\|_\nu \to 0$ as $n \to \infty$, where $\beta \in L^2(\nu)$, let $\mathcal{B}_h$ be the set of all such limit functions for a given h, and let $\mathcal{H}(h) = \cup\{\mathcal{H}(h, \beta): \beta \in \mathcal{B}_h\}$.

It can be shown that $\mathcal{B}_h$ corresponds to the closed subspace $\{\beta \in L^2(\nu):$ $\langle \beta, h^{1/2} \rangle_\nu = 0\}$ of $L^2(\nu)$.

We assume the Hellinger differentiability of $g^{1/2}$: For given (θ, h), there exists a function $\rho_\theta \in L^2(\mu)$ and a bounded linear operator $A: \mathcal{B}_h \to L^2(\mu)$ such that for any sequence $\{(\theta_n, h_n)\} \in \Theta(\theta, \lambda) \times \mathcal{H}(h, \beta)$,

$$\left\| n^{1/2}\left(g_n^{1/2} - g^{1/2}\right) - \lambda\rho_\theta - A\beta \right\|_\mu \to 0$$

as $n \to \infty$, where $g_n = g(\cdot \mid \theta_n, h_n)$ and $g = g(\cdot \mid \theta, h)$. Let $\alpha = \lambda\rho_\theta + A\beta$; then $\mathcal{A}_g = \{\alpha \in L^2(\mu): \alpha = \lambda\rho_\theta + A\beta$ for some $\lambda \in R^1, \beta \in \mathcal{B}\}$ is a closed subspace of $L^2(\mu)$ and orthogonal to $g^{1/2}$. Let H denote the distribution function corresponding to $h \in \mathcal{H}$. Then a regular estimator of (θ, H) can be defined as follows: Let $\{(\theta_n, h_n)\} \in \Theta(\theta) \times \mathcal{H}(h)$, and let $g_n = g(\cdot \mid \theta_n, h_n)$. The estimator $(\hat{\theta}_n, \hat{H}_n)$ of (θ, H) at $g = g(\cdot \mid \theta, h)$ is regular if the process $(n^{1/2}(\hat{\theta}_n - \theta_n), n^{1/2}(\hat{H}_n - H_n))$ under g_n converges to a limit process $(S, \mathbb{S})$ which depends on g but not on the particular sequence $\{g_n\}$.

The following lemma plays an essential role in proving the main theorem.

Lemma 2.1 (Local asymptotic normality). *Let $\{g_n\}$ be a sequence of densities such that*

$$\left\| n^{1/2}\left(g_n^{1/2} - g^{1/2}\right) - \alpha \right\|_\mu \to 0 \qquad as \quad n \to \infty$$

for some $\alpha \in L^2(\mu)$. Then for every $\varepsilon > 0$, the following holds:

$$P_g\left\{ \left| L_n - 2n^{-1/2}\sum_{i=1}^n \alpha(Y_i)g^{-1/2}(Y_i) + 2\|\alpha\|_\mu^2 \right| > \varepsilon \right\} \to 0 \qquad as \quad n \to \infty,$$

where $L_n = 2\log\{\prod_{i=1}^n[g_n^{1/2}(Y_i)/g^{1/2}(Y_i)]\}$. Thus, under P_g,

$$L_n \to_d N\left(-2\|\alpha\|_\mu^2, 4\|\alpha\|_\mu^2 \right) \qquad as \quad n \to \infty,$$

and the sequence $\{\prod_{i=1}^n g_n(y_i)\}$ is contiguous to $\{\prod_{i=1}^n g(y_i)\}$.

Proof: This is a consequence of arguments of Le Cam (1969). See also Bickel et al. (1993, pp. 498–513). $\qquad\qquad\qquad\qquad\qquad\qquad\qquad\qquad\qquad\qquad\quad\square$

Before proceeding to the main theorem, we need to define some Hilbert space operators. Let $A^*: L^2(\mu) \to L^2(\nu)$ denote the adjoint of the linear operator A (see, e.g., Luenberger 1969, p. 150). The product space $R^1 \times L^2(\nu)$ is a Hilbert space with the inner product defined as $\langle (\lambda_1, \beta_1), (\lambda_2, \beta_2) \rangle = \lambda_1\lambda_2 + \langle \beta_1, \beta_2 \rangle_\nu$. Let $I: R^1 \times L^2(\nu) \to R^1 \times L^2(\nu)$ denote the operator such that

$$\langle (\lambda_1, \beta_1), I(\lambda_2, \beta_2) \rangle = 4\langle \lambda_1\rho_\theta + A\beta_1, \lambda_2\rho_\theta + A\beta_2 \rangle_\mu,$$

whose explicit form is

$$I(\lambda, \beta) = 4\big(\lambda\|\rho_\theta\|_\mu^2 + \langle A^*\rho_\theta, \beta\rangle_v, \lambda A^*\rho_\theta + A^*A\beta\big). \tag{5.2.1}$$

We call I the information operator analogous to the Fisher information matrix for parametric models. Now let $v \in BV$ be any function of bounded variation on $[a, 0]$ with $v(0) = 0$. The operator $\tau_0 : \mathcal{B}_h \to B_0 \equiv \{w \in C[a, 0] : w(a) = w(0) = 0\}$ is defined by

$$\tau_0\beta(r) = 2\langle\beta, H_r\rangle_v \qquad \text{for} \quad a \leq r \leq 0,$$

where $H_r = (1_{[a,r]} - H(r))h^{1/2}$. Let $\langle\tau_0\beta, v\rangle = \int_a^0 \tau_0\beta \, dv$. Then the adjoint τ_0^* : $BV = B_0^* \to \mathcal{B}_h$ is calculated as $\tau_0^* v = 2\langle H_r, v\rangle$. Finally, define $\tau : R^1 \times \mathcal{B}_h \to R^1 \times B_0$ as $\tau(\lambda, \beta) = (\lambda, \tau_0\beta)$. Let $\langle(\lambda, \tau_0\beta), (u, v)\rangle = \lambda u + \langle\tau_0\beta, v\rangle$, and the adjoint $\tau^* : R^1 \times BV \to R^1 \times \mathcal{B}_h$ be defined by $\tau^*(u, v) = (u, \tau_0^* v)$ as well.

Now we state the main theorem and give the proof, which is more concise than that of Begun et al. (1983), especially for the nonparametric component.

Theorem 2.1. *Suppose that $(\hat\theta_n, \hat H_n)$ is a regular estimator of (θ, H) in the model $g = g(\cdot \,|\, \theta, h)$, and that the root density $g^{1/2}$ is Hellinger-differentiable at (θ, h). Moreover the information operator I is assumed to be invertible. Then the process $(n^{1/2}(\hat\theta_n - \theta), n^{1/2}(\hat H_n - H))$ converges weakly to a limit process $(S, \mathbb{S}) = (Z, \mathbb{Z}) + (W, \mathbb{W})$, where $(Z, \mathbb{Z})$ and $(W, \mathbb{W})$ are independent and $(Z, \mathbb{Z})$ is a zero-mean Gaussian process with the covariance*

$$\mathrm{Cov}\left(u_1 Z + \int \mathbb{Z}\, dv_1, u_2 Z + \int \mathbb{Z}\, dv_2\right) = \langle\tau I^{-1}\tau^*(u_1, v_1), (u_2, v_2)\rangle, \tag{5.2.2}$$

where $u_1, u_2 \in R^1$ and $v_1, v_2 \in BV$.

Proof: Let $\{(\theta_n, h_n)\} \in \Theta(\theta, \lambda) \times \mathcal{H}(h, \beta)$ and $\alpha = \lambda\rho_\theta + A\beta$. The characteristic functional of $(n^{1/2}(\hat\theta_n - \theta), n^{1/2}(\hat H_n - H))$ under g_n is

$$E_{g_n} \exp\left[iun^{1/2}(\hat\theta_n - \theta_n) + i\int_a^0 n^{1/2}(\hat H_n - H_n)\, dv\right]$$

$$= E_{g_n} \exp\left[iun^{1/2}(\hat\theta_n - \theta) + i\int_a^0 n^{1/2}(\hat H_n - H)\, dv\right.$$

$$\left. - i\langle\tau^*(u, v), (\lambda, \beta)\rangle\right] + o(1) \tag{a}$$

$$= E_g \exp\left[iun^{1/2}(\hat\theta_n - \theta) + i\int_a^0 n^{1/2}(\hat H_n - H)\, dv\right.$$

$$\left. + L_n - i\langle\tau^*(u, v), (\lambda, \beta)\rangle\right] + o(1). \tag{b}$$

This holds for all $\alpha \in \mathcal{A}_g$. We choose $\alpha = \lambda' \rho_\theta + A\beta'$, where $(\lambda', \beta') = kI^{-1}\tau^*(u, v)$, $k \in R^1$; then $4\|\alpha\|_\mu^2 = k^2 \langle \tau I^{-1}\tau^*(u, v), (u, v) \rangle$. Hence, under g, $(n^{1/2}(\hat{\theta}_n - \theta), n^{1/2}(\hat{H}_n - H), L_n)$ converge coordinatewise to $(S, \mathbb{S}, kZ_* - k^2 \langle \tau I^{-1}\tau^*(u, v), (u, v) \rangle /2)$ with $Z_* \sim N(0, \langle \tau I^{-1}\tau^*(u, v), (u, v) \rangle)$ by Lemma 2.1; and by considering only a subsequence if necessary, they converge jointly as well. We obtain the following equation:

$$E \exp\left(iuS + i \int_a^0 \mathbb{S} \, dv \right) = E \exp\left(iuS + i \int_a^0 \mathbb{S} \, dv + kZ_* \right)$$

$$\times \exp[-ik\langle \tau I^{-1}\tau^*(u, v), (u, v) \rangle$$
$$- k^2 \langle \tau I^{-1}\tau^*(u, v), (u, v) \rangle /2], \qquad \text{(c)}$$

because by regularity of $(\hat{\theta}_n, \hat{H}_n)$ the characteristic functional (a) converges to the left hand side of (c), while (b) converges, by contiguity and uniform integrability arguments on L_n, to the right hand side of (c). Both sides of (c) are functions of k analytic on the complex plane. Therefore identity holds for $k = -i$ as well. Then (c) becomes

$$E \exp\left(iuS + i \int_a^0 \mathbb{S} \, dv \right) = E \exp\left(iuS + i \int_a^0 \mathbb{S} \, dv - iZ_* \right)$$

$$\times \exp[-\langle \tau I^{-1}\tau^*(u, v), (u, v) \rangle /2].$$

This factorization into the characteristic functions of $(W, \mathbb{W}) = (S, \mathbb{S}) - (Z, \mathbb{Z})$ and $(Z, \mathbb{Z})$ completes the proof. $\qquad\square$

The efficiency bound for the parameter (θ, H) is described in terms of the covariance functional (5.2.2). The efficiency bound for each component is obtained by applying the standard inverse formula for partitioned operators to (5.2.1) and (5.2.2) on the assumption that $\|\rho_\theta\|_\mu^2 > 0$ and A^*A is invertible. For the parametric component θ, the efficiency bound is given in terms of the variance $I^{-1}(\theta)$ of Z:

$$I^{-1}(\theta) = 1/I_*, \qquad (5.2.3)$$

where $I_* = 4\|\rho_\theta - A(A^*A)^{-1}A^*\rho_\theta\|_\mu^2$ and is called the asymptotic information. For the nonparametric component, the efficiency bound is in terms of the variance $I^{-1}(H, v)$ of $\int \mathbb{Z} \, dv$:

$$I^{-1}(H, v) = \frac{\langle \tau_0^* v, (A^*A)^{-1}\tau_0^* v \rangle_v}{4} + \frac{\langle \tau_0^* v, (A^*A)^{-1}A^*\rho_\theta \rangle_v^2}{I_*}, \qquad (5.2.4)$$

whose covariance function $K(r, s)$ on $[a, 0] \times [a, 0]$ is

$$K(r, s) = \langle H_r, (A^*A)^{-1}H_s \rangle_v$$
$$+ 4\langle H_r, (A^*A)^{-1}A^*\rho_\theta \rangle_v I_*^{-1} \langle (A^*A)^{-1}A^*\rho_\theta, H_s \rangle_v. \qquad (5.2.5)$$

Note that the information operator I is invertible if and only if $I_* > 0$, assuming that $\|\rho_\theta\|_\mu^2 > 0$ and A^*A is invertible.

3   The type 1 model

In this section we introduce two approaches to obtain the efficient estimator of the type 1 model. The first approach calculates the semiparametric MLE of the parameter of interest and nuisance parameter jointly. The second approach calculates the conditional MLE. Although the latter is easier to handle, it obtains the estimator for the parameter of interest only.

Throughout the chapter we consider a single state model with a homogeneous population. We briefly discuss the extension of the results to models with explanatory variables or a heterogeneous population at the end of this section. In this model the duration data are generated according to the following scheme. A duration starts in an interval $[a, 0] \subset R^1$, and the starting time variable X is distributed according to distribution function $H(x)$ and density $h(x)$ with respect to a σ-finite measure ν on the measurable space $([a, 0], \mathcal{D})$. The duration variable T is distributed according to the distribution function $F(t)$ and density $f(t)$ with respect to a σ-finite measure ω on the measurable space $([0, \infty], \mathcal{C})$. The measures ν and ω are usually Lebesgue measures. We assume the independence between X and T. The density of the duration $f(t)$ is parametrically specified as $f(t \mid \theta)$, where we assume that θ belongs to R^1 for simplicity. (It is not difficult to extend the whole argument to a vector parameter case.) Further, let $f(t \mid \theta)$ be differentiable with respect to θ. On the other hand, the starting time distribution $H(x)$ is parametrically unspecified and allowed to be any distribution with support $[a, 0]$. $\mathcal{H}$ denotes the set of $H(x)$. We call our method semiparametric estimation because it is a mixture of parametric and nonparametric parts.

In the type 1 model, the statistician observes only those spells which end at or after 0, of which he observes both the starting time x and the duration t. Then the vector random variable (T, X) is distributed according to the density

$$g(t, x \mid \theta, h) = \frac{f(t \mid \theta)h(x)}{\int_a^0 \bar{F}(-x \mid \theta)\, dH(x)} 1_{[t+x \geq 0]}$$

with respect to the product measure $\mu = \omega \times \nu$ on $([0, \infty) \times [a, 0], \mathcal{C} \times \mathcal{D})$, where $\bar{F}(-x \mid \theta)$ denotes the survival function $1 - F(-x \mid \theta)$.

Consider the sequence of i.i.d. vector random variables $\{(T_1, X_1), \ldots, (T_n, X_n)\}$ with density function $g = g(t, x \mid \theta, h)$. To apply the method of semiparametric maximum likelihood, let us define a likelihood function for the parameter (θ, H):

$$L = \prod_{i=1}^n \frac{f(T_i \mid \theta)h(X_i)}{\int_a^0 \bar{F}(-x \mid \theta)\, dH(x)}. \tag{5.3.1}$$

Here, $h(X_i)$ denotes the point mass on each observed point X_i instead of the probability density. We want to obtain the parameter value $(\hat{\theta}, \hat{H})$ to maximize (5.3.1). Let us fix θ first and get the optimal $H(x)$. In view of maximization, we may restrict $\hat{H}(x)$ to a discrete distribution on the set $\{X_i\}$. The reason is as follows. Suppose not. Then there exists another $\hat{H}(x)$ with more weight put on $\{X_i\}$ and less on elsewhere in $[a, 0]$, leading to an increase in L.

The optimization problem is reduced to

$$\max_{\{h_i\}} L = \prod_{i=1}^{n} \frac{h_i f(T_i \mid \theta)}{\sum_{j=1}^{n} h_j \bar{F}(-X_j \mid \theta)} \qquad \text{subject to} \quad \sum_{i=1}^{n} h_i = 1, \quad (5.3.2)$$

where h_i denotes $h(X_i)$. By forming a Lagrangean and using the first order conditions, we get the unique interior solution:

$$\hat{h}(X_i) \equiv \hat{h}_i = \frac{1}{\bar{F}(-X_i \mid \theta) \sum_{j=1}^{n} \frac{1}{\bar{F}(-X_j \mid \theta)}}. \qquad (5.3.3)$$

Instead of checking the second order conditions, we show directly that this $\{h_i\}$ attains the global maximum of L. Let $\mathbf{h} = (h_i) \in R^n$. Then L is a real-valued continuous function of $\mathbf{h}$ defined on $D^{n-1} \equiv \{\mathbf{h} : 0 \le h_i \le 1, \sum_{i=1}^{n} h_i = 1\}$. Since D^{n-1} is compact, L achieves a global maximum on D^{n-1} by the Weierstrass theorem. If $\mathbf{h}$ is on the boundary of D^{n-1}, then $L = 0$, since at least one $h_i = 0$. Therefore L cannot attain a maximum on the boundary, which implies that the maximum is achieved at an interior point. But since an interior maximum satisfies the first order conditions and $\mathbf{h}$ of (5.3.3) is its unique solution, it must be the unique global maximization solution as well.

Substitute (5.3.3) into (5.3.2) to obtain the concentrated likelihood function of θ:

$$L^*(\theta) = n^{-n} \prod_{i=1}^{n} \frac{f(T_i \mid \theta)}{\bar{F}(-X_i \mid \theta)}. \qquad (5.3.4)$$

Apart from the constant term, this is the conditional likelihood function (with a homogeneous population) used in Lancaster (1979), which yields a consistent estimator without using a starting time distribution. Therefore the parametric part of the semiparametric MLE is the same as the conditional MLE in Lancaster's.

As for the nonparametric part, the estimated distribution can be written as

$$\hat{H}(x \mid \hat{\theta}) = \frac{n^{-1} \sum_{i=1}^{n} \frac{1_{[a,x]}(X_i)}{\bar{F}(-X_i \mid \hat{\theta})}}{n^{-1} \sum_{i=1}^{n} \frac{1}{\bar{F}(-X_i \mid \hat{\theta})}}, \qquad (5.3.5)$$

where $\hat{\theta}$ is the MLE of (5.3.4). It is not difficult to show the consistency of $\hat{\theta}$ and $\hat{H}(x \mid \hat{\theta})$ provided that $f(t \mid \theta)$ satisfies certain general conditions.

3.1   *Efficiency bounds*

Next we compare the asymptotic efficiency of the semiparametric MLE with the efficiency bounds in the sense of Begun et al. (1983). In the present model, the asymptotic information $I_* = 4\|\rho_\theta - A(A^*A)^{-1}A^*\rho_\theta\|_\mu^2$ defined in (5.2.3) is obtained as follows. We use the same notation as in Section 2 unless stated otherwise. First, the Hellinger differentiability of $g^{1/2}$ holds and

$$\rho_\theta = \frac{1}{2}\left(\frac{f_\theta}{f} - \frac{P_\theta}{P}\right)g^{1/2},$$

where f_θ and P_θ denote $\partial f/\partial\theta$ and $\partial P/\partial\theta$, respectively, and $P = \int_a^0 \bar{F}h\,dv$. Note that $\bar{F}$ always denotes $\bar{F}(-x\,|\,\theta)$. For notational simplicity we sometimes omit θ and h in $f(\cdot\,|\,\theta)$, $\bar{F}(\cdot\,|\,\theta)$, and $g(\cdot\,|\,\theta, h)$ when they are the true parameter values. The operator $A : L^2(v) \to L^2(\mu)$ is

$$A\beta(t, x) = g^{1/2}(t, x)\left[\beta(x)h^{-1/2}(x) - \frac{1}{P}\int_a^0 \bar{F}\beta h^{1/2}\,dv\right]. \qquad (5.3.6)$$

The adjoint $A^* : L^2(\mu) \to L^2(v)$ of A is obtained so that $\langle A^*\gamma, \beta\rangle_v = \langle\gamma, A\beta\rangle_\mu$ holds for all $\gamma \in L^2(\mu)$ and $\beta \in \mathcal{B}_h$:

$$A^*\gamma(x) = h^{-1/2}(x)\int_0^\infty \gamma(t, x)g^{1/2}(t, x)\,d\omega(t)$$

$$- \frac{\bar{F}(-x)h^{1/2}(x)}{P}\int_Q \gamma g^{1/2}\,d\mu, \qquad (5.3.7)$$

where Q denotes $[0, \infty] \times [a, 0]$. See, e.g., Luenberger (1969, pp. 152–154) for calculation of the adjoint operator A^*. Combining (5.3.6) and (5.3.7) yields

$$A^*A\beta(x) = \frac{\bar{F}(-x)\beta(x)}{P} - \frac{\bar{F}(-x)h^{1/2}(x)}{P^2}\int_a^0 \bar{F}\beta h^{1/2}\,dv,$$

which intuitively leads us to

$$(A^*A)^{-1}\beta(x) = \frac{P\beta(x)}{\bar{F}(-x)} - Ph^{1/2}(x)\int_a^0 \frac{\beta h^{1/2}}{\bar{F}}\,dv.$$

Note that no simple formula exists for calculating the inverse operator $(A^*A)^{-1}$ in general. The above equation follows from some guesswork. Finally, we have

$$(A^*A)^{-1}A^*\rho_\theta(x) = \frac{1}{2}h^{1/2}(x)\left[\frac{\bar{F}_\theta(-x)}{\bar{F}(-x)} - \int_a^0 \frac{\bar{F}_\theta}{\bar{F}}h\,dv\right], \qquad (5.3.8)$$

where $\bar{F}_\theta$ denotes $\partial \bar{F}/\partial\theta$. Hence, combining the above equalities, the asymptotic information I_* is computed as

$$I_* = E_g \left[\frac{\partial}{\partial\theta} \log \frac{f(T)}{\bar{F}(-X)} \right]^2, \tag{5.3.9}$$

and the efficiency bound $I^{-1}(\theta)$ for the parametric component θ is

$$I^{-1}(\theta) = \left\{ E_g \left[\frac{\partial}{\partial\theta} \log \frac{f(T)}{\bar{F}(-X)} \right]^2 \right\}^{-1}. \tag{5.3.10}$$

To compute the efficiency bound for the nonparametric component h defined in (5.2.5), we have

$$(A^*A)^{-1} H_r(x) = Ph^{1/2}(x) \left[\frac{1_{[a,r]}(x) - H(r)}{\bar{F}(-x)} - \int_a^0 \frac{1_{[a,r]} - H(r)}{\bar{F}} h \, dv \right]$$

and

$$\langle H_r, (A^*A)^{-1} H_s \rangle_v = P \int_a^0 \frac{\left[1_{[a,r]} - H(r) \right] \left[1_{[a,s]} - H(s) \right]}{\bar{F}} h \, dv. \tag{5.3.11}$$

Further, by (5.3.8) and (5.3.9), we get

$$4 \langle H_r, (A^*A)^{-1} A^* \rho_\theta \rangle_v I_*^{-1} \langle (A^*A)^{-1} A^* \rho_\theta, H_s \rangle_v$$

$$= \left\{ E_g \left[\frac{\partial}{\partial\theta} \log \frac{f(T)}{\bar{F}(-X)} \right]^2 \right\}^{-1} \int_a^0 \frac{\partial \log \bar{F}}{\partial\theta} \left[1_{[a,r]} - H(r) \right] h \, dv$$

$$\times \int_a^0 \frac{\partial \log \bar{F}}{\partial\theta} \left[1_{[a,s]} - H(s) \right] h \, dv. \tag{5.3.12}$$

Finally, combining (5.3.11) and (5.3.12), we obtain the covariance function by

$$K(r, s) = P \int_a^0 \frac{\left[1_{[a,r]} - H(r) \right] \left[1_{[a,s]} - H(s) \right]}{\bar{F}} h \, dv$$

$$+ \left\{ E_g \left[\frac{\partial}{\partial\theta} \log \frac{f(T)}{\bar{F}(-X)} \right]^2 \right\}^{-1} \int_a^0 \frac{\partial \log \bar{F}}{\partial\theta} \left[1_{[a,r]} - H(r) \right] h \, dv$$

$$\times \int_a^0 \frac{\partial \log \bar{F}}{\partial\theta} \left[1_{[a,s]} - H(s) \right] h \, dv. \tag{5.3.13}$$

3.2   *Comparison*

Next we compute the asymptotic efficiency of the semiparametric MLE in the type 1 model directly from (5.3.4) and (5.3.5) to compare with the efficiency bound obtained above. Since the parametric component $\hat{\theta}$ of the semiparametric MLE is the conditional MLE by (5.3.4), the asymptotic variance of $n^{1/2}(\hat{\theta} - \theta)$ is easily computed and shown to be the same as (5.3.10).

As for the nonparametric component $\hat{H}(x \mid \hat{\theta})$, we obtain the limit process of $n^{1/2}[\hat{H}(x \mid \hat{\theta}) - H(x)]$ from (5.3.5):

$$n^{1/2}[\hat{H}(x \mid \hat{\theta}) - H(x)] = \frac{n^{-1/2}\sum_{i=1}^{n}\frac{1_{[a,x]}(X_i)-H(x)}{\bar{F}(-X_i \mid \hat{\theta})}}{n^{-1}\sum_{i=1}^{n}\frac{1}{\bar{F}(-X_i \mid \hat{\theta})}}. \tag{5.3.14}$$

Let $\phi(\hat{\theta})$ denote the numerator of (5.3.14) and apply a Taylor expansion

$$\phi(\hat{\theta}) = \phi(\theta) + \frac{\partial\phi(\theta^*)}{\partial\theta}(\hat{\theta} - \theta),$$

where θ^* lies between $\hat{\theta}$ and θ. Then

$$\text{numerator} = n^{-1/2}\sum_{i=1}^{n}\frac{1_{[a,x]}(X_i) - H(x)}{\bar{F}(-X_i \mid \theta)} + n^{1/2}(\hat{\theta} - \theta)\hat{G}(\theta^*), \tag{5.3.15}$$

where

$$\hat{G}(\theta^*) = -n^{-1}\sum_{i=1}^{n}\frac{\bar{F}_\theta(-X_i \mid \theta^*)}{[\bar{F}(-X_i \mid \theta^*)]^2}\left[1_{[a,x]}(X_i) - H(x)\right].$$

But since $\hat{\theta} = \arg\max_\theta \sum \log[f(T_i \mid \theta)/\bar{F}(-X_i \mid \theta)]$, another Taylor expansion gives

$$n^{1/2}(\hat{\theta} - \theta) = n^{-1/2}[\hat{I}_*(\theta^{**})]^{-1}\sum_{i=1}^{n}\frac{\partial}{\partial\theta}\log\frac{f(T_i \mid \theta)}{\bar{F}(-X_i \mid \theta)},$$

where

$$\hat{I}_*(\theta^{**}) = -n^{-1}\sum_{i=1}^{n}\frac{\partial^2}{\partial\theta^2}\log\frac{f(T_i \mid \theta^{**})}{\bar{F}(-X_i \mid \theta^{**})},$$

and θ^{**} lies between $\hat{\theta}$ and θ. Therefore (5.3.15) is reduced to

$$\text{numerator} = n^{-1/2}\sum_{i=1}^{n}\left[\frac{1_{[a,x]}(X_i) - H(x)}{\bar{F}(-X_i \mid \theta)} + M(x)\frac{\partial}{\partial\theta}\log\frac{f(T_i \mid \theta)}{\bar{F}(-X_i \mid \theta)}\right]$$

$$+ \left[\frac{\hat{G}(\theta^*)}{\hat{I}_*(\theta^{**})} - M(x)\right]\left[n^{-1/2}\sum_{i=1}^{n}\frac{\partial}{\partial\theta}\log\frac{f(T_i \mid \theta)}{\bar{F}(-X_i \mid \theta)}\right], \tag{5.3.16}$$

where

$$M(x) = \left\{ E_g\left[\frac{\partial^2}{\partial \theta^2} \log \frac{f(T)}{\bar{F}(-X)} \right] \right\}^{-1} E_g \frac{\bar{F}_\theta(-X)}{[\bar{F}(-X)]^2} \left[1_{[a,x]}(X) - H(x) \right]$$

$$= -\left\{ E_g\left[\frac{\partial}{\partial \theta} \log \frac{f(T)}{\bar{F}(-X)} \right]^2 \right\}^{-1} \times P^{-1} \int_a^0 \frac{\partial \log \bar{F}}{\partial \theta} \left[1_{[a,x]} - H(x) \right] h \, dv.$$

Under the general conditions, the second term in the right hand side of (5.3.16) converges in distribution to 0 as $n \to \infty$, from the fact that $\hat{G}(\theta^*)/\hat{I}_*(\theta^{**}) \to_d M(x)$. As for the first term, the multivariate central limit theorem ensures that it converges in distribution to a Gaussian process $\mathbb{Z}^n(x)$, the covariance function $K^n(r, s)$ of which is

$$K^n(r, s) = E_g\left[\frac{1_{[a,r]}(X) - H(r)}{\bar{F}(-X)} + M(r)\frac{\partial}{\partial \theta} \log \frac{f(T)}{\bar{F}(-X)} \right]$$

$$\times \left[\frac{1_{[a,s]}(X) - H(s)}{\bar{F}(-X)} + M(s)\frac{\partial}{\partial \theta} \log \frac{f(T)}{\bar{F}(-X)} \right]$$

$$= E_g\left[\frac{1_{[a,r]}(X) - H(r)}{\bar{F}(-X)} \right]\left[\frac{1_{[a,s]}(X) - H(s)}{\bar{F}(-X)} \right]$$

$$+ M(r)M(s)E_g\left[\frac{\partial}{\partial \theta} \log \frac{f(T)}{\bar{F}(-X)} \right]^2$$

$$= P^{-1} \int_a^0 \frac{\left[1_{[a,r]} - H(r) \right]\left[1_{[a,s]} - H(s) \right]}{\bar{F}} h \, dv$$

$$+ \left\{ P^2 E_g\left[\frac{\partial}{\partial \theta} \log \frac{f(T)}{\bar{F}(-X)} \right]^2 \right\}^{-1} \int_a^0 \frac{\partial \log \bar{F}}{\partial \theta} \left[1_{[a,r]} - H(r) \right] h \, dv$$

$$\times \int_a^0 \frac{\partial \log \bar{F}}{\partial \theta} \left[1_{[a,s]} - H(s) \right] h \, dv.$$

Thus, as the denominator of (5.3.14) converges in probability to P^{-1}, the covariance function of the limit process of $n^{1/2}[\hat{H}(x \mid \hat{\theta}) - H(x)]$ coincides with $K(r, s)$ of (5.3.13).

Hence, we have proved the following proposition:

Proposition 3.1. *The semiparametric MLE in the type 1 left-censored duration model achieves the semiparametric efficiency bounds for both parametric and nonparametric components.*

3.3   *A simple condition for achieving efficiency bounds*

As for the parametric component, Goto (1996) gave a simple sufficient condition for achieving efficiency bounds in general semiparametric models.

Theorem 3.1. *Consider the sequence of i.i.d. vector random variables $\{(T_i, Y_i)\}$ with a joint density $g(t, y \mid \theta, \mathbf{h})$, where θ is a vector (the parametric component) and $\mathbf{h}$ is a vector of functions (the nonparametric component). Suppose that the likelihood function of $\{(T_i, Y_i)\}$ is decomposed into conditional and marginal likelihood functions such that the conditional likelihood function does not contain the nonparametric component $\mathbf{h}$:*

$$L = \prod_{i=1}^{n} g(T_i, Y_i \mid \theta, \mathbf{h}) = \prod_{i=1}^{n} g(T_i \mid Y_i, \theta) g(Y_i \mid \theta, \mathbf{h}).$$

In addition, suppose that θ is not identifiable from $\mathbf{h}$ in the marginal likelihood function, i.e., for any $\theta^{(1)}$, $\mathbf{h}^{(1)}$, and $\theta^{(2)}$ there exists some $\mathbf{h}^{(2)}$ such that $g(y \mid \theta^{(1)}, \mathbf{h}^{(1)}) = g(y \mid \theta^{(2)}, \mathbf{h}^{(2)})$. Then the following holds: (i) the semiparametric MLE is equal to the conditional MLE, and (ii) the semiparametric MLE achieves the efficiency bound.

A conditional–marginal decomposition of the likelihood function (5.3.1) for the type 1 model yields the following conditional and marginal likelihood functions:

$$L_c = \prod_{i=1}^{n} \frac{f(T_i \mid \theta)}{\bar{F}(-X_i \mid \theta)}$$

and

$$L_m = \prod_{i=1}^{n} \frac{\bar{F}(-X_i \mid \theta) h(X_i)}{\int_a^0 \bar{F}(-x \mid \theta) \, dH(x)}.$$

It has been shown that this satisfies the conditions of Theorem 3.1. See Goto (1996) for details. Hence, we get another proof of Proposition 3.1 for the parametric component. Besides, it directly shows that the conditional MLE adopted by Lancaster (1979) coincides with the semiparametric MLE and achieves the efficiency bound.

3.4   *Efficiency gains in parametric models*

A referee has asked whether efficiency gains could be obtained from (hypothetically) knowing either H or the parameter θ as well as whether the efficiency could be improved if one knew H except for a finite number of parameters.

The answer is yes, and it can be shown for general parametric and semi-parametric models. Goto (1999) discusses the issue for both parametric and nonparametric components. This chapter only demonstrates it in terms of the parametric component of the type 1 model.

Consider these three kinds of the type 1 model:

$$g_1(t, x \mid \theta, h) = \frac{f(t \mid \theta)h(x)}{\int_a^0 \bar{F}(-x \mid \theta)\, dH(x)} 1_{[t+x \geq 0]}$$

with the true parameter value (θ_0, h_0),

$$g_2(t, x \mid \theta, \tau) = \frac{f(t \mid \theta)h(x \mid \tau)}{\int_a^0 \bar{F}(-x \mid \theta)\, dH(x \mid \tau)} 1_{[t+x \geq 0]}$$

with the true parameter value (θ_0, τ_0), and

$$g_3(t, x \mid \theta) = \frac{f(t \mid \theta)h_0(x)}{\int_a^0 \bar{F}(-x \mid \theta)\, dH_0(x)} 1_{[t+x \geq 0]}$$

with the true parameter value θ_0, where we assume that τ is one-dimensional for simplicity and that $h(x \mid \tau_0) \equiv h_0(x)$. Note that g_1 is a semiparametric model and both g_2 and g_3 are parametric models with the common true distribution $g_1(t, x \mid \theta_0, h_0) \equiv g_2(t, x \mid \theta_0, \tau_0) \equiv g_3(t, x \mid \theta_0)$. According to (5.3.9) the asymptotic information I_1 for θ of g_1 is expressed as

$$I_1 = E_0 \left[\frac{\partial}{\partial \theta} \log \frac{f(T \mid \theta_0)}{\bar{F}(-X \mid \theta_0)} \right]^2,$$

where the expectation is taken under the true distribution. As for the asymptotic information I_2 for θ of g_2, straightforward calculations show that

$$I_2 = E_0 \left[\frac{\partial}{\partial \theta} \log \frac{f(T \mid \theta_0)}{\bar{F}(-X \mid \theta_0)} \right]^2 + \inf_{\lambda} E_0 \left[\frac{\partial}{\partial \theta} \log \frac{\bar{F}(-X \mid \theta_0)}{\int_a^0 \bar{F}(-x \mid \theta_0)\, dH(x \mid \tau_0)} \right.$$

$$\left. - \lambda \frac{\partial}{\partial \tau} \log \frac{h(X \mid \tau_0)}{\int_a^0 \bar{F}(-x \mid \theta_0)\, dH(x \mid \tau_0)} \right]^2,$$

where $\lambda \in R^1$. Lastly the asymptotic information I_3 for θ of g_3 is given by

$$I_3 = E_0 \left[\frac{\partial}{\partial \theta} \log \frac{f(T \mid \theta_0)}{\bar{F}(-X \mid \theta_0)} \right]^2 + E_0 \left[\frac{\partial}{\partial \theta} \log \frac{\bar{F}(-X \mid \theta_0)}{\int_a^0 \bar{F}(-x \mid \theta_0)\, dH_0(x)} \right]^2.$$

The inequalities $I_1 \leq I_2 \leq I_3$ follow from the above equations.

3.5   *Models with explanatory variables*

Many applications in economics have explanatory variables. The results of the chapter can in principle apply to that case as well. We briefly demonstrate this statement here. Consider the type 1 model with time-invariant explanatory variables $Z \in R^k$. Then the vector random variable (T, X, Z) is distributed according to the density

$$g(t, x, z \mid \theta, h, m) = \frac{f(t \mid z, \theta)h(x \mid z)m(z)}{\int_a^0 \bar{F}(-x \mid z, \theta) \, dH(x \mid z)} 1_{[t+x \geq 0]},$$

where $m(z)$ denotes the unknown distribution of the observed Z. It is shown that under some regularity conditions the semiparametric MLE achieves the efficiency bounds for both parametric and nonparametric components. See Goto (1998) for details.

As a referee pointed out, however, if the explanatory variables are time varying, the problem becomes much more complicated in general. See, e.g., Cox and Oakes (1984) for time-varying explanatory variables or covariates. Consider, for instance, the proportional hazards model in which the hazard is

$$\lambda(t \mid z) = \lambda(t) \exp(\beta' z),$$

where $\lambda(t)$ denotes the common underlying hazard. If $\lambda(t)$ is known up to a fixed number of parameters, the problem is reduced to that of the ordinary left-censored model. However, if $\lambda(t)$ is unknown, it is yet to be solved.

4   **Other types of left censoring**

In this section we consider other types of left censoring: types 2 and 3, and hybrids of various types. We only give brief and heuristic arguments here. Rigorous treatments are given in Goto (1998).

4.1   *Type 2*

In the type 2 model, the spell that was going on at time 0 is observed only after 0. The setting is otherwise the same as in the type 1 model. Let s denote the observed duration. Then the random variable S is distributed according to the density

$$g_2(s \mid \theta, h) = \frac{\int_a^0 f(s - x \mid \theta) \, dH(x)}{\int_a^0 \bar{F}(-x \mid \theta) \, dH(x)} \tag{5.4.1}$$

with respect to a σ-finite measure ω on the measurable space $([0, \infty), C)$. Here, symbols like f and h are the same as in the type 1 model.

Consider the sequence of i.i.d. random variables $\{S_1, \ldots, S_n\}$ with density function $g_2 = g_2(s \mid \theta, h)$. The likelihood function is

$$L_2 = \prod_{i=1}^{n} \frac{\int_a^0 f(S_i - x \mid \theta) \, dH(x)}{\int_a^0 \bar{F}(-x \mid \theta) \, dH(x)}. \tag{5.4.2}$$

These expressions of the type 2 model are not easy to handle. But by the reparametrization

$$dK(x) = \frac{\bar{F}(-x \mid \theta) \, dH(x)}{\int_a^0 \bar{F}(-x \mid \theta) \, dH(x)} \tag{5.4.3}$$

we can simplify (5.4.1) and (5.4.2) to

$$g_2(s \mid \theta, k) = \int_a^0 \frac{f(s - x \mid \theta)}{\bar{F}(-x \mid \theta)} \, dK(x) \tag{5.4.4}$$

and

$$L_2 = \prod_{i=1}^{n} \int_a^0 \frac{f(S_i - x \mid \theta)}{\bar{F}(-x \mid \theta)} \, dK(x), \tag{5.4.5}$$

where k denotes the density of K with respect to ν on the measurable space $([a, 0], \mathcal{D})$. Since the map $\phi(\theta, H) = (\theta, K)$ is one-to-one and onto, it can be shown that if $(\hat{\theta}, \hat{K})$ is the semiparametric MLE of (5.4.5), then $(\hat{\theta}, \hat{H})$ becomes the semiparametric MLE of (5.4.2), too. It is also shown that if $(\hat{\theta}, \hat{K})$ is efficient, so is $(\hat{\theta}, \hat{H})$. Therefore we can concentrate on the model described by (5.4.4) and (5.4.5) in what follows.

This is a typical mixture model, and by the arguments based on van der Vaart's work (see, e.g., van der Vaart 1996), the semiparametric MLE $(\hat{\theta}, \hat{K})$ is shown to be efficient under identifiability and some regularity conditions. Here, identifiability is a delicate problem and not always satisfied in the type 2 model. A sufficient condition for nonidentifiability for the mixture model (5.4.4) is when the conditional density function

$$\phi(s \mid x, \theta) = \frac{f(s - x \mid \theta)}{\bar{F}(-x \mid \theta)}$$

is complete with respect to K. That is, given θ and a function $\psi(s)$,

$$E_\phi[\psi(S)] = 0 \qquad \text{a.e. } K$$

implies

$$\psi(s) = 0 \quad \text{a.e. } \phi(s \mid x, \theta) \qquad \text{for all} \quad x \in [a, 0].$$

See, e.g., Lehmann (1986, pp. 140–145) for the definition of completeness.

To obtain the semiparametric MLE in the type 2 model (5.4.5), Lindsay's method is useful. We assume that we have n distinct observations $\{S_i\}$. Lindsay (1983) shows that given θ in the mixture model

$$L_2 = \prod_{i=1}^{n} \int_a^0 \phi(S_i \mid x, \theta)\, dK(x), \tag{5.4.6}$$

the nonparametric MLE $\tilde{K}$ for the nonparametric component K is expressed as a discrete distribution with at most n points of support.

Note that since his method only aims at obtaining the nonparametric MLE for K on the assumption that θ is known, to apply it to our particular problem we need an iterative procedure that starts from an initial estimator for θ and eventually reaches the semiparametric MLE $(\hat{\theta}, \hat{K})$. It is desirable that the initial estimator be consistent, but it is usually not easy to find a consistent one.

4.2   Type 3

In the type 3 model, the spell that was going on at time 0 is observed only up to 0. The setting is otherwise the same as in the type 1 model. Describing the starting time as x, the observed duration becomes $-x$. Then the random variable X is distributed according to the density

$$g_3(x \mid \theta, h) = \frac{\bar{F}(-x \mid \theta)h(x)}{\int_a^0 \bar{F}(-x \mid \theta)\, dH(x)}$$

with respect to a σ-finite measure ν on the measurable space $([a, 0], \mathcal{D})$.

Consider the sequence of i.i.d. random variables $\{X_1, \ldots, X_n\}$ with density function $g_3 = g_3(x \mid \theta, h)$. The likelihood function is

$$L_3 = \prod_{i=1}^{n} \frac{\bar{F}(-X_i \mid \theta)h(X_i)}{\int_a^0 \bar{F}(-x \mid \theta)\, dH(x)}.$$

The type 3 model does not satisfy the identifiability condition. Therefore no consistent estimator for (θ, h) exists. To see this, given (θ, h) and θ^*, define

$$h^*(x) = \frac{\bar{F}(-x \mid \theta)h(x)}{\bar{F}(-x \mid \theta^*)} \left[\int_a^0 \frac{\bar{F}(-x \mid \theta)\, dH(x)}{\bar{F}(-x \mid \theta^*)} \right]^{-1}.$$

Then $g_3(x \mid \theta, h) = g_3(x \mid \theta^*, h^*)$ a.e. ν, which means that the two structures are observationally equivalent and the model is unidentified. See, e.g., Hsiao (1983) for the concept of observationally equivalent structures. In this case no consistent estimator for (θ, h) exists. One might think that the reason the parameters of the duration distribution are not identified given only the starting times is pretty obvious. But that is not correct. The information contained in the type 3 model is not about uncensored starting times, but about those of the spells that reach the sampling point, thereby including some information about the duration itself. The true reason identification fails is that h is completely unknown.

4.3   Hybrid left censoring

The statistician might observe spells with various types of left censoring from a common population. This is a kind of missing data problem. Consider independent i.i.d. samples $S_1, \ldots, S_m$ and $X_1, \ldots, X_n$ from the type 2 density

$$g_2(s \mid \theta, h) = \frac{\int_a^0 f(s - x \mid \theta) \, dH(x)}{\int_a^0 \bar{F}(-x \mid \theta) \, dH(x)}$$

and the type 3 density

$$g_3(x \mid \theta, h) = \frac{\bar{F}(-x \mid \theta) \, h(x)}{\int_a^0 \bar{F}(-x \mid \theta) \, dH(x)},$$

respectively. This is what we call the hybrid model of types 2 and 3. It can be shown that the semiparametric MLE $(\hat{\theta}, \hat{H})$ which maximizes the likelihood

$$L_{23} = \prod_{i=1}^m \frac{\int_a^0 f(S_i - x \mid \theta) \, dH(x)}{\int_a^0 \bar{F}(-x \mid \theta) \, dH(x)} \prod_{i=1}^n \frac{\bar{F}(-X_i \mid \theta) \, h(X_i)}{\int_a^0 \bar{F}(-x \mid \theta) \, dH(x)} \qquad (5.4.7)$$

exists and is asymptotically efficient. See Goto (1998) for details. This is a remarkable feature of the hybrid model, because the type 2 model is sometimes unidentifiable and the type 3 model is always unidentifiable, neither of those "pure models" being useful by itself for estimation.

Another advantage of the hybrid model is with respect to the computation of the semiparametric MLE. To see this, we transform (5.4.7) into

$$L_{23} = \prod_{i=1}^m \int_a^0 \frac{f(S_i - x \mid \theta)}{\bar{F}(-x \mid \theta)} \, dK(x) \prod_{i=1}^n k(X_i) \qquad (5.4.8)$$

by reparametrization in (5.4.3) with efficiency maintained. We want the semiparametric MLE that maximizes (5.4.8). Lindsay's method is useful here, as in the type 2 model. As we have already seen, however, since his method only aims at obtaining the nonparametric MLE for K on the assumption that θ is known, we need an iterative procedure that starts from an initial estimator for θ.

Unlike the pure model of type 2, we can easily find an initial estimator here. First, construct the empirical distribution $\tilde{K}$ from

$$L_3 = \prod_{i=1}^{n} k(X_i),$$

and then substitute it into (5.4.8) to obtain the concentrated likelihood function

$$L(\theta) = \prod_{i=1}^{m} \int_{a}^{0} \frac{f(S_i - x \mid \theta)}{\bar{F}(-x \mid \theta)} \, d\tilde{K}(x). \tag{5.4.9}$$

The MLE $\tilde{\theta}$ of θ in (5.4.9) is not usually efficient, because $\tilde{\theta}$ and $\tilde{K}$ are not jointly estimated. But it is consistent and becomes an initial estimator of the kind we want.

REFERENCES

Amemiya, T. (1985), *Advanced Econometrics* (Cambridge, MA: Harvard University Press).

Amemiya, T. (1991), "A Note on Left Censoring," CEPR Technical Paper No. 235, Stanford University.

Begun, J. M., Hall, W., Huang, W. M., and Wellner, J. A. (1983), "Information and Asymptotic Efficiency in Parametric–Nonparametric Models," *Annals of Statistics*, **11**, 432–452.

Beran, R. (1977), "Estimating a Distribution Function," *Annals of Statistics*, **6**, 400–404.

Bickel, P. J., Klaassen, C. A. J., Ritov, Y., and Wellner, J. A. (1993), *Efficient and Adaptive Estimation for Semi-parametric Models* (Baltimore: Johns Hopkins University Press).

Chesher, A. and Lancaster, T. (1983), "The Estimation of Models of Labor Market Behaviour," *Review of Economic Studies*, **50**, 609–624.

Cox, D. R. and Oakes, D. (1984), *Analysis of Survival Data* (London: Chapman & Hall).

Goto, F. (1996), "Achieving Semiparametric Efficiency Bounds in Left-Censored Duration Models," *Econometrica*, **64**, 439–442.

(1998), "Efficient Semiparametric Estimation for Hybrid Left-Censoring," manuscript.

(1999), "Information in Semiparametric Models," manuscript.

Heckman, J. J. and Singer, B. (1984), "Econometric Duration Analysis," *Journal of Econometrics*, **24**, 63–132.

Hsiao, C. (1983), "Identification," in *Handbook of Econometrics, Volume I*, Z. Griliches and M. D. Intriligator, eds. (Amsterdam: North-Holland).

Lancaster, T. (1979), "Economic Methods for the Duration of Unemployment," *Econometrica*, **47**, 939–956.

Le Cam, L. (1969), *Théorie Asymptotique de la Decision Statistique* (Montreal: Les Presses de l'Universite de Montreal).

Lehmann, E. L. (1986), *Testing Statistical Hypotheses*, 2nd ed. (reprint, 1994). (New York: Chapman & Hall).

Lindsay, B. G. (1983), "The Geometry of Mixture Likelihoods: A General Theory," *Annals of Statistics*, **11**, 86–94.

Luenberger, D. G. (1969), *Optimization by Vector Space Methods* (New York: John Wiley & Sons).

Newey, W. K. (1990), "Semiparametric Efficiency Bounds," *Journal of Applied Econometrics*, **5**, 99–135.

Ridder, G. (1984), "The Distribution of Single Spell Duration Data," in *Studies in Labor Market Dynamics*, G. R. Neumann and N. C. Westergaard-Nielsen, eds. (Berlin: Springer-Verlag).

van der Vaart, A. W. (1996), "On a Model of Hasminskii and Ibragimov," in *Probability Theory and Mathematical Statistics*, I. A. Ibragimov and A. Y. Zaitsev, eds. (Amsterdam: Gordon & Breach), pp. 297–308.

CHAPTER 6

Semiparametric estimation of censored selection models

James L. Powell

1 Introduction

The object of this chapter is the investigation of a particular approach to estimation of the parameters of bivariate (and multivariate) latent dependent variable models under weak assumptions on the distributions of the unobservable error terms. The class of latent variable models considered includes a number of microeconometric applications, including the censored *sample selection* models of Gronau (1973) and Heckman (1974), the disequilibrium regression model with observed regimes proposed by Fair and Jaffee (1972), and other *simultaneous Tobit* models. A survey of such models can be found in Chapter 10 of Amemiya (1985).

A common feature of these models is the noninvertibility of the transformation from the unobserved error terms to the observed dependent variables; since the error terms therefore cannot be written as a known function of observable random variables and the unknown parameters, zero mean and other moment restrictions on the errors are inadequate to identify the parameters of interest. Another feature common to these models, which distinguishes them from multinomial and other discrete response models, is the continuous distribution of the dependent variable in one (or more) equation of interest on some subset of its support. Unlike discrete response models, where some normalization of the parameter vector is typically required, the units of the regression coefficients relating the dependent variable to the regressors are well defined, and the scale of the parameter vector should (in principle) be identified.

Because of the inadequacy of conditional moment restrictions for identification of the parameters of these models, estimation of these models has

This research was supported by the National Science Foundation and the Alfred P. Sloan Foundation. I am grateful to Ricardo Barros, Gary Chamberlain, Edwin Charlier, Arthur Goldberger, Lars Hansen, James Heckman, Keith Heyen, Bo Honoré, Charles Manski, Whitney Newey, Ariel Pakes, and anonymous reviewers for their helpful comments.

165

heretofore been based upon an assumed parametric form of the likelihood function of the error terms. As is by now well known (and fairly well documented – see, for example, Goldberger 1983 and Arabmazar and Schmidt 1981, 1982), maximum likelihood estimation and other likelihood-based estimation methods yield inconsistent estimators of the parameters of interest if either the parametric form of the error distribution is misspecified or conditional heteroskedasticity of the errors given the exogenous variables is not correctly modeled. Since parametric restrictions on the shape of the error distribution or the functional form of heteroskedasticity cannot generally be obtained from economic theory, much recent attention has been devoted in recent theoretical econometrics to the possibility of *semiparametric* estimation, i.e., identification and consistent estimation of the parameters of interest for these models without restricting the conditional distribution of the error terms to a finite-dimensional parametric family.

Early econometric work on semiparametric estimation problems focused on univariate latent variable models – in particular, the binary response model and the censored regression model. Because these models involve only one error term, semiparametric estimation of their parameters can be based upon certain weak restrictions on the error distribution, such as conditional quantile restrictions (Manski 1975, 1985; Powell 1984, 1986a) or conditional symmetry (Powell 1986b), which apparently do not suffice to identify the parameters in multivariate settings. One class of restrictions on the error distributions which does appear to carry over to multivariate latent variable models is that of *single-index* restrictions, in which certain characteristics of the error distribution are assumed to depend on the conditioning variables only through a single (unknown) linear combination of those variables. These restrictions have been applied to a variety of econometric latent variable models, by Ruud (1983), Chung and Goldberger (1984), Stoker (1986), Ruud (1986), Ichimura (1986), and Powell, Stock, and Stoker (1989), among others. While the first three of these studies impose strong restrictions on the stochastic behavior of the conditioning variables (e.g., a known parametric distribution function or linearity of the conditional expectations of the conditioning variable given the single index), the remaining studies depend only on weaker smoothness restrictions on the distributions of the errors and exogenous variables. The single-index restriction is also slightly more general than an assumption of independence of the errors and exogenous variables (as imposed by Cosslett 1983, Horowitz 1984, and Han 1987), in that conditional heteroskedasticity of the error terms is allowed for, although only in a restrictive form (namely, depending only on the single index).

Prior to the original draft of this chapter, the econometric literature on semiparametric estimation of the class of bivariate models considered here consisted of three papers, by Cosslett (1991), Robinson (1988a), and Chamberlain

(1986b). The approach considered here is similar to these studies in several respects, but differs in at least two important ways. Unlike Cosslett's results (but like the results of the latter two studies), the object of the present approach is not just consistent estimation, but rather estimation which can be shown to be root-n-consistent (where n denotes the number of observations in the sample) and asymptotically normal; this permits inference on the parameters of interest to be carried out using the usual normal theory in large samples, and also ensures that the estimation approach is not infinitely inefficient relative to parametric methods when the latter are correctly specified. On the other hand, as in Cosslett's study (but not Robinson's and Chamberlain's), the bivariate structure of the latent variable models and the single-index restriction on the conditional distribution of the error terms are exploited.

This chapter, a revision of Powell (1987), investigates identification of the parameters of interest in censored selection models, demonstrates the feasibility of root-n-consistent estimation for such models, and gives the groundwork for more recent extensions of this particular semiparametric estimation approach. While some parts of the discussion below have appeared in a follow-up paper, Ahn and Powell (1993), that paper cites some of the results of the present chapter and omits much of the discussion of parameter identification and interpretation of the estimation strategy. And, though the recent literature suggests a number of extensions to this chapter, they are not pursued here, so that this chapter will more accurately reflect the unpublished results of Powell (1987), and will serve as a useful companion to Ahn and Powell (1993).

The following section describes the generic form of the equation of interest which arises in many bivariate limited dependent variable models, and discusses conditions under which the parameters of that model fail to be identified under the weak conditions imposed. Section 3 shows how two econometric models, the censored sample selection and disequilibrium regression models, can be written in the generic form of Section 2. The estimator itself is defined and motivated in Section 4, and regularity conditions to ensure its root-n consistency are given in Section 5. The final sections of the chapter construct consistent estimators of the asymptotic covariance matrix for the estimator and consider more recent extensions and related approaches of the estimation strategy proposed in this chapter. Proofs of the main results are given in a technical appendix.

2   The generic econometric model

The object of the statistical analysis is taken to be the estimation of the regression coefficients in a generic *equation of interest*, which can be written in the form

$$Y_i = X_i'\beta_0 + V_i, \qquad i = 1, \ldots, n, \tag{6.2.1}$$

where n is the sample size, Y_i is an observable dependent variable for each observation i, X_i is a p-dimensional vector of explanatory variables, and V_i is an unobservable (scalar) error term. Two characteristics of the stochastic behavior of V_i differentiate this model from the standard linear regression model. First, restrictions are not imposed on the conditional distribution of V_i given X_i, but rather on the conditional distribution of V_i given W_i, where W_i is a k-dimensional vector of exogenous variables; as will be seen in the following section, bivariate latent variable models can often be written in the form (6.2.1) only by allowing for *simultaneity* of the explanatory variables and error terms. A more fundamental departure from the standard linear model concerns the centering of the conditional distribution of V_i given W_i; unlike the usual assumption, in which the conditional mean (or median, or other location measure) of V_i is assumed to be zero, the conditional mean of V_i given W_i is assumed to be an unknown function of a particular linear combination of W_i. That is,

$$E(V_i \mid W_i) = \lambda(W_i' \delta_0), \tag{6.2.2}$$

where $\lambda(\cdot)$ is an unknown (but sufficiently smooth) function and δ_0 is an unknown k-dimensional coefficient vector. Thus the model can be rewritten as

$$Y_i \equiv X_i' \beta_0 + \lambda(W_i' \delta_0) + U_i, \tag{6.2.3}$$

where by construction $E(U_i \mid W_i) = 0$.

The dependence of the conditional mean of the errors on a single linear combination $W_i' \delta_0$ (referred to hereafter as the *single index*) arises from a relationship between the error term V_i and another dependent variable D_i embodying a *sample selection* effect which depends on W_i. The stochastic behavior of D_i is assumed to be characterized by the relationship

$$E(D_i \mid W_i) = \gamma(W_i' \delta_0), \tag{6.2.4}$$

where $\gamma(\cdot)$ is another unknown (but smooth) function of the single index $W_i' \delta_0$. The dependence of the error term V_i in the equation of interest on the single index is thus induced by its dependence on the selection variable D_i.

It is apparent that identification of the parameter vectors β_0 and δ_0 in (6.2.1) and (6.2.3) will require additional restrictions on the parameters and regressors. For example, neither X_i nor W_i can contain a constant term, since constant terms can be absorbed into the unknown function $\lambda(\cdot)$ without affecting its smoothness. Similarly, the parameter vector δ_0 can only be determined up to an unknown scaling factor, so some normalization must be imposed upon it.

A more disturbing result is the lack of identification of β_0 when the components of W_i are a subset of X_i. More generally, even if δ_0 is known, identification of β_0 will fail if some nontrivial linear combination of X_i has conditional expectation (given W_i) that only depends upon the index $W_i' \delta_0$, i.e., for some $\alpha \neq 0$,

$$E(X_i'\alpha \mid W_i) = a(W_i'\delta_0), \tag{6.2.5}$$

where the function $a(\cdot)$ satisfies similar smoothness restrictions to those imposed on $\lambda(\cdot)$. If (6.2.5) holds, then for any scalar c, (6.2.1) can be rewritten as

$$Y_i = X_i'[\beta_0 + c\alpha] + [V_i - cX_i'\alpha] \equiv X_i'\beta^* + V_i^*, \tag{6.2.6}$$

where

$$E[V_i^* \mid W_i] = \lambda(W_i'\delta_0) + c \cdot a(W_i'\delta_0) \equiv \lambda^*(W_i'\delta_0). \tag{6.2.7}$$

Thus, under condition (6.2.5), both (6.2.1) and (6.2.6) satisfy the stochastic restriction (6.2.2), so restriction (6.2.2) is insufficient to distinguish β_0 from β^*. Conversely, identification of β_0 requires that (6.2.5) hold only for $\alpha = 0$; thus, identification under these restrictions implies that some component of the selection regressors W_i must be excluded from the set of regressors X_i for the equation of interest, a restriction noted and imposed by Cosslett (1991).

The need for this latter exclusion restriction is a consequence of the linearity of the underlying regression functions in the selection and outcome equations, and might be avoided if either function were nonlinear. For example, if (6.2.3) were replaced by

$$Y_i \equiv X_i'\beta_0 + \lambda(g(W_i, \delta_0)) + U_i \tag{6.2.3'}$$

and the parameter δ_0 were identified, then the argument for lack of identification in (6.2.6) and (6.2.7) would require an alternative to condition (6.2.5),

$$E(X_i'\alpha \mid W_i) = a(g(W_i, \delta_0)) \qquad \text{for some} \quad \alpha \neq 0. \tag{6.2.5'}$$

Unlike (6.2.5), this condition would not necessarily hold even if W_i were a subset of X_i, provided the function $g(\cdot)$ is nonlinear in W_i. In a sense, any difference between the the index function $g(\cdot)$ and its best linear approximation might be considered an *excluded regressor* in the outcome equation, which could be used in identification of β_0.

In the linear index framework of this chapter, though, identification of β_0 requires that one or more exclusion restrictions be imposed on the model, so that condition (6.2.5) is ruled out. In the following section, conditions under which (6.2.5) either does or does not hold are derived in the context of two models which can be written in the form (6.2.1).

3   Two econometric applications

Given below are two econometric models of bivariate latent variables – the censored sample selection model and the disequilibrium regression model with observed regime – that can be expressed in the form of the generic model of the preceeding section. These examples are by no means exhaustive; they are, however, fairly representative of the models used in empirical applications.

3.1   *The censored sample selection model*

This model, termed the "type 2 Tobit model" by Amemiya (1985), was applied by Gronau (1973) to a model of female labor supply. It consists of two equations: a binary response *selection* equation which determines the observability of a continuously distributed dependent variable, and a *supply* equation determining the relationship of the latter dependent variable to observable explanatory variables when the dependent variable is observed. The selection equation can be written algebraically as

$$d_i = 1(w_i'\delta_0 + \varepsilon_i > 0), \qquad i = 1, \ldots, n, \tag{6.3.1}$$

while the supply, or *wage*, equation takes the form

$$y_i = d_i \cdot (x_i'\beta_0 + u_i), \qquad i = 1, \ldots, n, \tag{6.3.2}$$

where $1(A)$ denotes an indicator function of the statement A, w_i and x_i are vectors of explanatory variables (which may have components in common), d_i and y_i are observable dependent variables, and ε_i and u_i are unobserved disturbances.

There are two ways to represent this model in terms of the notation given in the previous section. In either case, $d_i = D_i$ and $w_i = W_i$; here the nuisance function $\gamma(\cdot)$ of (6.2.4) represents the conditional c.d.f. of $-\varepsilon_i$ given w_i, evaluated at the index $w_i'\delta_0$. One representation of the supply equation uses all n observations on y_i, with the correspondences $y_i = Y_i$, $d_i \cdot x_i = X_i$, and $d_i \cdot u_i = V_i$ (in this representation, the potential "endogeneity" of X_i arises from its dependence on the selection variable D_i, and need not involve any true endogeneity of the regression vector x_i). Alternatively, as noted by Heckman (1976), the observations with $y_i = 0$ can be ignored, and analysis can proceed conditionally on $d_i = 1$; in this form the sample size n is interpreted as the number of nonzero observations on y_i, where $y_i = Y_i$, $x_i = X_i$, and $u_i = V_i$ [the dependence of $E(V_i \mid W_i'\delta_0)$ on $W_i'\delta_0$ results from conditioning on $d_i = 1$ and dependence between ε_i and u_i].

Standard parametric approaches to estimation of the parameters of this model assume the error terms ε_i and u_i are jointly normally distributed, independently of w_i and x_i, with zero mean and unknown covariance matrix. With this assumption, the parameters can be estimated by maximum likelihood or the more convenient two-step estimator of Heckman (1976); this latter method is the parametric precursor to the approach described below, with the nuisance function $\gamma(\cdot)$ of (6.2.4) parametrized as a standard normal cumulative and the function $\lambda(\cdot)$ of (6.2.2) having a known parametric form (but depending on the unknown components of the covariance matrix of ε_i and u_i). While restricting the distribution of the errors to a known parametric form (independent of the explanatory variables) suffices to establish (6.2.2) and (6.2.4) above, such a restriction is by no means necessary; in fact, it is not necessary to assume that any conditional location measure of the errors (e.g., conditional mean or median) is zero. For (6.2.2) and (6.2.4) to hold, it suffices that the conditional expection of the outcome error u_i given the selection equation regressors depend only on w_i through the single index $w_i'\delta_0$; this permits asymmetry and conditional heteroskedasticity of the errors, as long as they are of single index form.

However, the lack of necessity of a conditional location restriction on the error terms implies that any intercept term in the equation will not be identified, since it can be absorbed in the selection correction term. Furthermore, as noted in the previous section, some component of the selection regressors w_i must be excluded from the regressors x_i in the outcome equation. And, if the errors ε_i and u_i are indeed assumed to be independent of w_i, or even just dependent upon w_i through the index $w_i'\delta_0$, then other restrictions besides the conditional mean restriction (2.2) can be derived which could aid identification of β_0. For example, if the joint conditional distribution of the errors ε_i and u_i depends on w_i only through $w_i'\delta_0$, then *all* moments of $d_i(y_i - x_i'\beta_0)$, not just its mean, will depend only upon $w_i'\delta_0$, yielding extra moment restrictions on β_0. This chapter only considers imposition of the weaker restrictions

$$E(d_i \mid w_i) = \gamma(w_i'\delta_0), \qquad E(u_i \mid d_i = 1, w_i) = \lambda(w_i'\delta_0), \qquad (6.3.3)$$

which can still suffice to identify β_0, but stronger restrictions on the underlying error terms in this model could clearly make identification easier.

An extreme version of this model, the (Type I) censored regression model, has $x_i'\beta_0 + u_i$ identical to the latent variable $w_i'\delta_0 + \varepsilon_i$ determining the selection variable d_i; that is, equation (6.2.2) takes the form

$$y_i = \max\{0, w_i'\delta_0 + \varepsilon_i\}, \qquad i = 1, \dots, n. \qquad (6.3.4)$$

For this special case, the coefficient vector $\beta_0 = \delta_0$ is not identified under (6.3.3); since $X_i = D_i W_i$ in this case, $E[X_i'\delta_0 \mid W_i] = \gamma(W_i'\delta_0) \cdot W_i'\delta_0$, so condition (6.2.5) holds with $\alpha = \delta_0$. Hence the single-index restrictions of (6.2.1) through (6.2.4) are not sufficient to identify the scale of the coefficient vector β_0, though it can be estimated up to scale using either $D_i = d_i$ or $D_i = y_i$ and relation (6.2.2). Semiparametric estimation of $\beta_0 = \delta_0$ for this model must be based upon some other stochastic restrictions on $u_i = \varepsilon_i$, such as those imposed by Powell (1984, 1986b) or Horowitz (1984).

3.2   *The disequilibrium regression model with observable regime*

This model, a special case of Amemiya's (1985) "type 5 Tobit models," was proposed by Fair and Jaffee (1972), and specifies the dependent variable of interest as the minimum of two latent variables generated by linear regression models. Also, for each observation, the *regime* (i.e., the regression equation from which the observed dependent variable was generated) is assumed known. Thus, the information on the regime for each observation can be represented as an indicator variable of the form

$$d_i = 1(x_{1i}'\beta_1 + \varepsilon_i < x_{2i}'\beta_2 + u_i), \qquad i = 1, \ldots, n, \tag{6.3.5}$$

while the observed dependent variable is generated as

$$y_i = d_i \cdot (x_{1i}'\beta_1 + \varepsilon_i) + (1 - d_i) \cdot (x_{2i}'\beta_2 + u_i), \qquad i = 1, \ldots, n. \tag{6.3.6}$$

As above, x_{1i} and x_{2i} are vectors of exogenous variables, and ε_i and u_i are unobserved error terms; the objects of estimation are the coefficient vectors β_1 and β_2. And, as above, there are two ways to represent this model in the notation of the preceeding section. In either representation, $d_i = D_i$, and W_i is the vector made up of the distinct components of x_{1i} and x_{2i} (with δ_0 the corresponding linear combination of the parameter vectors β_1 and β_2). Then, with the representation $y_i = Y_i$, the explanatory variables and parameters can be written $X_i = (d_i x_{1i}', (1 - d_i)x_{2i}')'$ and $\beta_0 = (\beta_1', \beta_2')'$. With this notation, the counterpart to assumption (6.3.3) above is

$$E(d_i \mid w_i) = \gamma(w_i'\delta_0), \qquad E(\varepsilon_i \mid d_i = 1, w_i) = \lambda_\varepsilon(w_i'\delta_0),$$

$$\text{and} \quad E(u_i \mid d_i = 0, w_i) = \lambda_u(w_i'\delta_0), \tag{6.3.7}$$

which, for example, would permit a common measurement error, independent of d_i with conditional mean zero given w_i, to be included in equation (6.3.6) for the outcome variable y_i. Identification under condition (6.3.7) will require that both x_{1i} and x_{2i} have components that are excluded from the other vector of regressors, a restriction similar to the usual "zero restrictions" imposed in simultaneous equations estimation. Alternatively, the sample may be partitioned into the subsamples with $d_i = 0$ and $d_i = 1$; then Y_i can be taken to be the value of y_i in either subsample, and X_i and β_0 to be the vectors of regressors and parameters corresponding to that regime. Thus, the parameters of a particular regime may be identifiable even if the parameters of the other regime are not.

Another common latent variable model, the Type II censored regression model (also known as the linear model with random right censoring), is a special case of this model, with $x_{2i} = 0$ $(=\beta_2)$. As for the Type I censored regression model of the previous section, this special case does not satisfy the conditions for identification of $\beta_0 \equiv \beta_1$ under (6.2.7) alone; because X_i is proportional to

$x_{1i} = W_i$ in either representation, condition (6.2.5) will hold with $\alpha = \delta_0$, as above. Again, semiparametric estimation of the coefficients in this special case must be based upon some other set of restrictions on the behavior of the error terms.

4 Derivation and motivation of the proposed estimator

It is assumed that a random sample of observations on Y_i, X_i, W_i, and D_i is available, so that, in principle, (6.2.3) and (6.2.4) could be used jointly to estimate the unknown parameters β_0 and δ_0. However, a two-step approach to estimation is proposed here; estimation of δ_0 is assumed to be based solely on equation (6.2.4), and the corresponding *preliminary estimator* $\hat{\delta}$ is used in the estimation of β_0 in the second step. While this two-step approach would undoubtedly be inefficient in general, it does simplify the analysis considerably, particularly since $\sqrt{n}$-consistent and asymptotically normal estimators of δ_0 under model (6.2.1) have already been proposed (e.g., Ichimura 1986 and Powell, Stock, and Stoker 1989). It is also worth noting that the convenient assumption of random sampling is not essential; the approach can be extended to permit nonidentical or serially dependent distributions of the data, provided the relationships in (6.2.1) through (6.2.4) remain valid.

The proposed approach to estimation of the parameters of interest in the second stage is based on a comparison of pairs of observations for which the estimated indices $W_i'\hat{\delta}$ and $W_j'\hat{\delta}$ are "close." To motivate the approach, consider an ideal situation in which two observations are known to have identical indices; that is, $W_i'\delta_0 = W_j'\delta_0$. In this case, by equation (6.2.1) the difference in the corresponding dependent variables Y_i and Y_j satisfies

$$Y_i - Y_j = (X_i - X_j)'\beta_0 + V_i - V_j = (X_i - X_j)'\beta_0 + U_i - U_j, \qquad (6.4.1)$$

where the latter equality follows from $\lambda(W_i'\delta_0) = \lambda(W_j'\delta_0)$. Since

$$E(U_i - U_j \mid W_i, W_j) = 0 \qquad (6.4.2)$$

by construction, this moment condition could be used to estimate the unknown parameters β_0 in the usual way. In particular, the exogenous variables W_i can be used to construct a p-dimensional vector Z_i of *instrumental variables* for X_i, i.e.,

$$Z_i = z(W_i) \qquad \text{for some function} \quad z : R^k \to R^p. \qquad (6.4.3)$$

Then the parameter vector β_0 could be estimated using a subsample of observations with $W_i'\delta_0 = W_j'\delta_0$ by regressing the differences $Y_i - Y_j$ of dependent variables on the differences $X_i - X_j$ of explanatory variables using the corresponding differences $Z_i - Z_j$ of instrumental variables, provided the covariance matrix of the instruments with the explanatory variables is of full rank. Note that, although the difference in the indices $W_i'\delta_0 - W_j'\delta_0$ is zero, the distribution of the corresponding difference $Z_i - Z_j$ of instrumental variables can still be constructed to have a full-dimensional distribution. Also note that the derivation of large-sample properties for such an estimator would have to allow for the fact that the instrumental variables fit would use $\binom{n}{2}$ pairs of observations, and the resulting estimator would be composed of second-order U-statistics rather than simple sample averages.

Of course, this estimation scheme cannot be directly implemented. In the first place, the parameter vector δ_0 is unknown, so even if pairs of observations with identical single index values existed in the sample, it would not be possible to precisely determine which pairs they were. Moreover, in order to obtain a preliminary $\sqrt{n}$-consistent estimator $\hat{\delta}$ of δ_0 under the weak restriction (6.2.2), it appears necessary to require that the index $W_i'\delta_0$ be continuously distributed, so that no two observations in a random sample would have identical indices, with probability one. Nevertheless, if the conditional mean $\lambda(W_i'\delta_0)$ of V_i is a continuous function of $W_i'\delta_0$ and $\hat{\delta}$ is a consistent estimator of δ_0, observations for which the difference $W_i'\hat{\delta} - W_j'\hat{\delta}$ is near zero should also have $E(V_i - V_j \mid W_i, W_j) \cong 0$ so the preceeding argument would hold approximately for such pairs.

As a practical matter, it is necessary to specify how close an estimated difference $W_i'\hat{\delta} - W_j'\hat{\delta}$ of indices is to zero for the approximation to be satisfactory. In this approach, each of the $\binom{n}{2}$ distinct pairs of observations is assigned a weight w_{ijn} which declines to zero as the magnitude of the difference $W_i'\hat{\delta} - W_j'\hat{\delta}$ increases; the weights depend on the sample size n as well, with larger values of n corresponding to lower weight on pairs with a given value of $|W_i'\hat{\delta} - W_j'\hat{\delta}|$. A convenient algebraic form for such a weight function is a *kernel* weight; that is, given any known, symmetric function $K(u)$ which integrates to one, and sequence of *bandwidths* h_n which tends to zero as the sample size increases, the weight w_{ijn} for each pair of observations is defined here to be

$$\hat{w}_{ijn} \equiv \frac{1}{h_n} K\left(\frac{(W_i - W_j)'\hat{\delta}}{h_n}\right) \equiv w_{ijn}(\hat{\delta}), \qquad (6.4.4)$$

where

$$K(u) = K(-u), \qquad \int K(u)\, du = 1.$$

Since the kernel function $K(\cdot)$ necessarily declines to zero as its argument tends to infinity in magnitude, any pair of observations with $W_i'\delta_0 \neq W_j'\delta_0$ should receive declining weight as the sample size grows (and the bandwidth shrinks to zero).

Given the form of the weights w_{ijn}, an estimator $\hat{\beta}$ of the parameters of interest can be defined as a weighted instrumental variables estimator which regresses the $\binom{n}{2}$ distinct differences $Y_i - Y_j$ in dependent variables on the corresponding differences $X_i - X_j$ in regressors, using $Z_i - Z_j$ as instrumental variables and w_{ijn} as weights. Algebraically,

$$
\hat{\beta} \equiv \left(\binom{n}{2}^{-1} \sum_{i=1}^{n-1} \sum_{j=i+1}^{n} \hat{w}_{ijn} \cdot (Z_i - Z_j)(X_i - X_j)' \right)^{-1}
$$
$$
\times \binom{n}{2}^{-1} \sum_{i=1}^{n-1} \sum_{j=i+1}^{n} \hat{w}_{ijn} \cdot (Z_i - Z_j)(Y_i - Y_j). \tag{6.4.5}
$$

In the next section, conditions are given under which $\hat{\beta}$ is $\sqrt{n}$-consistent and asymptotically normal, provided the preliminary estimator $\hat{\delta}$ is also $\sqrt{n}$-consistent and asymptotically normal and the kernel $K(u)$ and bandwidth h_n are chosen appropriately.

The estimator $\hat{\beta}$ has an alternative derivation, which is more in the spirit of Robinson's (1988a) estimation strategy. This derivation is based upon the following relation, obtained from (6.2.1) and (6.2.2):

$$
Y_i - E(Y_i \mid W_i'\delta_0) = (X_i - E(X_i \mid W_i'\delta_0))'\beta_0 + V_i - E(V_i \mid W_i'\delta_0)
$$
$$
\equiv X_i - E(X_i \mid W_i'\delta_0))'\beta_0 + U_i. \tag{6.4.6}
$$

If the conditional means $E(Y_i \mid W_i'\delta_0)$ and $E(X_i \mid W_i'\delta_0)$ were known for each observation, a consistent estimator of β_0 could be obtained by an instrumental variables fit of equation (4.6). Furthermore, consistent estimates of these conditional means can be obtained for each observation by nonparametric regression; specifically, an estimated value $\hat{Y}_i$ of the conditional mean $E(Y_i \mid W_i'\delta_0)$ can be constructed by fitting a kernel regression of Y_j on $W_j'\hat{\delta}$ using the remaining observations ($j \neq i$), and then evaluating this estimated regression function at the estimated index $W_i'\hat{\delta}$. Using the same kernel $K(u)$ as in (6.2.8) above, the estimated conditional means Y_i for each observation are of the form

$$
\hat{Y}_i \equiv \left(\sum_{j=1}^{n} 1(j \neq i) \cdot \hat{w}_{ijn} Y_j \right) \cdot \left(\sum_{j=1}^{n} 1(i \neq j) \cdot \hat{w}_{ijn} \right)^{-1}, \tag{6.4.7}
$$

where $1(\cdot)$ is an indicator function and the $\hat{w}_{ijn}$ are as defined earlier [corresponding estimates $\hat{X}_i$ of $E(X_i \mid W_i'\delta_0)$ are defined analogously, replacing Y with X in (4.7)]. Now, an instrumental variables regression of the differences $Y_i - \hat{Y}_i$ on $X_i - \hat{X}_i$ should (heuristically) yield a consistent estimator of β_0. To avoid technical difficulties associated with the random denominators of Y_i and X_i (which need not be bounded away from zero), a convenient choice of instrumental variables is the product of the original instruments Z_i with the sum in the denominators of $\hat{Y}_i$ and $\hat{X}_i$; that is, the new instruments $\hat{Z}_i$ are defined as

$$\hat{Z}_i \equiv Z_i \cdot \left(\sum_{j=1}^{n} 1(i \neq j) \cdot \hat{w}_{ijn} \right). \tag{6.4.8}$$

(Note that, apart from the preliminary estimate $\hat{\delta}$, the variables $\hat{Z}_i$ are functions only of the $\{W_i\}$, so they will be asymptotically valid instruments.) With these definitions, the coefficients of an instrumental variables regression of $Y_i - \hat{Y}_i$ on $X_i - \hat{X}_i$ using the instrumental variables $\hat{Z}_i$ can be shown to be algebraically equivalent to $\hat{\beta}$, defined in (6.4.5) above. A variant of this approach, which would reduce to Robinson's (1988a) estimator when $Z_i = X_i$ and $\delta_0 \equiv \hat{\delta} \equiv 1$, would replace (6.4.8) by

$$\hat{Z} \equiv Z_i \cdot 1\left(n^{-1} \sum_{j=1}^{n} 1(i \neq j) \cdot \hat{w}_{ijn} > b_n \right) = Z_i \cdot 1(\hat{f}_w(W_i'\hat{\delta}_0) > b_n), \tag{6.4.8'}$$

where $\hat{f}_w(W_i)$ is a kernel estimator for the density of $W'\delta_0$ at $W'\delta_0 = W_i'\hat{\delta}$ and b_n is a sequence of *trimming* constants assumed to tend to zero at a particular rate. The use of either the density weighting approach here [in (6.4.8')] or the trimming approach (6.4.8) serves a similar purpose, namely, to downweight (or eliminate) observations in the tails of the distribution of $W_i'\delta_0$, where kernel estimation methods would be necessarily imprecise. Density weighting is adopted here for mathematical convenience, since it avoids the need to impose conditions upon an additional trimming sequence b_n and yields an estimator which is approximately a simpler (matrix) ratio of second-order U-statistics.

This estimation approach is also similar in spirit to that taken by Powell, Stock, and Stoker (1989), which proposed a $\sqrt{n}$-consistent and asymptotically normal estimator of δ_0 under the restriction (6.2.4). The ℓth component of the estimator $\hat{\delta}$ proposed in that chapter could be written in the form

$$\hat{\delta}_\ell \equiv \binom{n}{2}^{-1} \sum_{i=1}^{n-1} \sum_{j=i+1}^{n} w_{ijn\ell} \cdot \left(\frac{D_i - D_j}{w_{i\ell} - w_{j\ell}} \right); \tag{6.4.9}$$

that is, as a weighted average of the $\binom{n}{2}$ distinct pairwise slopes relating the differences $D_i - D_j$ to the ℓth component of the corresponding difference $W_i - W_j$ in the conditioning variables. The derivation of this estimator was based upon the proportionality of δ_0 to $\partial E(D_i \mid W_i)/\partial W_i$; the weights $w_{ijn\ell}$, which vary across components ℓ as well as the sample size n, are kernel weights which downweight pairs of observations with relatively large values of $\|W_i - W_j\|$. The rationale for this approach – namely, that $E(D_i - D_j \mid W_i, W_j)/(W_{i\ell} - W_{j\ell}) \cong$

$\partial E(D_i \mid W_i)/\partial W_{i\ell} \propto \delta_0$ when $\| W_i - W_j \| \cong 0$ – is analogous to the reasoning given above that $E(V_i - V_j \mid W_i, W_j) \cong 0$ when $|W_i'\hat{\delta} - W_j'\hat{\delta}| \cong 0$. The estimator defined in (6.4.9) imposes a particular scaling, but, when used as a first-step estimator of δ_0 in this problem, it could be normalized in a different manner (e.g., $\hat{\delta}$ could be replaced by $\hat{\delta}/\|\hat{\delta}\|$ in the construction of the estimated selection index $W_i'\hat{\delta}$).

Because of the similarity of the two estimation approaches, much of the technical apparatus used to derive the large-sample properties of the estimator in Powell, Stock, and Stoker (1989) will be applicable to the present problem. Like $\hat{\delta}$ defined by (6.4.9), $\hat{\beta}$ of (4.5) is given in a closed form rather than as a solution to an extremum problem; thus, its asymptotic behavior can be derived directly from analysis of the two averages which define it. And, apart from the preliminary estimate $\hat{\delta}$ which appears in the weights $\hat{w}_{ijn}$, both components of definition (6.4.5) are of the second-order U-statistic form analyzed in that earlier chapter. Thus, Lemma 3.1 of Powell, Stock, and Stoker (1989) can be applied, after some manipulation, to characterize the large-sample behavior of the two components on the right hand side of (6.4.5).

A final analogy for this estimation approach is to the standard *fixed effect* estimator for linear panel data models. In a panel data model of the form

$$y_{it} = \alpha_i + x_{it}'\beta_0 + u_{it}, \qquad t = 1, \ldots, T_i, \quad i = 1, \ldots, n, \quad (6.4.10)$$

where the unknown individual-specific intercepts α_i have an unspecified relation to the time-varying regressors x_{it}, one approach to estimation of β_0 would use time differences of observations for each individual, since the differences

$$y_{it} - y_{is} = (x_{it} - x_{is})'\beta_0 + (u_{it} - u_{is}) \qquad (6.4.11)$$

no longer involve the fixed effect α_i. The estimation approach for censored selection models proposed here is based upon a similar differencing of pairs of observations with the same estimated selection index $W_i'\hat{\delta}$, with the unknown selection correction term $\lambda(W_i'\delta_0)$ being analogous to the fixed effect term α_i. By way of comparison, Robinson's (1988a) approach is analogous to estimation of panel data models using deviations from individual ("cell") means,

$$y_{it} - y_{i\cdot} = (x_{it} - x_{i\cdot})'\beta_0 + (u_{it} - u_{i\cdot}), \qquad (6.4.12)$$

where

$$y_{i\cdot} = T_i^{-1} \sum_{t=1}^{T_i} y_{it}, \qquad \text{etc.} \qquad (6.4.13)$$

In a *balanced panel*, with $T_i = T$ (which would correspond to a constant density function of the index $W_i'\delta_0$), the two approaches would coincide, but in general they will differ, and their relative efficiency will depend upon the distribution of the selection index and the conditional variance of the outcome equation errors given W_i.

5   Large-sample properties of the estimator

An asymptotic characterization of $\hat{\beta}$ can be obtained under the following regularity conditions (which are discussed in more detail below).

Assumption 5.1 (Random sampling and bounded moments). The vectors $(Y_i, W_i', X_i', Z_i')'$ satisfying (6.2.1), (6.2.2), (6.2.3), and (6.4.3) are independently and identically distributed across i, with finite sixth-order moments for each component.

Assumption 5.2 (Consistent preliminary estimator). The preliminary estimator $\hat{\delta}$ of δ_0 is $\sqrt{n}$-consistent, i.e., $\sqrt{n}(\hat{\delta} - \delta_0) = O_p(1)$.

Assumption 5.3 (Continuous index). The index function $W_i'\delta_0$ is absolutely continuously distributed, with density function $f(\cdot)$ that is continuous and bounded above.

Assumption 5.4 (Identification). The matrix

$$\Sigma_{ZX} \equiv 2E(f(W_i'\delta_0) \cdot (Z_i - E(Z_i \mid W_i'\delta_0)) \cdot (X_i' - E(X_i' \mid W_i'\delta_0)))$$

is nonsingular.

Assumption 5.5 (Kernel regularity). The kernel function $K(\cdot)$ used to define the weights $w_{ijn}(\hat{\delta})$ in (6.4.4) satisfies $\int K(u)\, du = 1$, $K(u) = K(-u)$ (as imposed above), and

(i) $K(u)$ is twice differentiable, with $|K''(u)| < L_0$ for some $L_0 > 0$;
(ii) $K(u) = 0$ if $|u| > \ell_0$ for some $\ell_0 > 0$; and
(iii) $\int u^\ell K(u)\, du = 0$ for $\ell = 1, 2, 3$.

Assumption 5.6 (Bandwidth rates). The bandwidth sequence h_n used to define the weights $w_{ijn}(\hat{\delta})$ in (6.4.4) has $h_n \to 0$, $n(h_n)^6 \to \infty$, and $n(h_n)^8 \to 0$ as $n \to \infty$.

Assumption 5.7 (Smoothness). Define

$$g_W(u) \equiv E[W_i \mid W_i'\delta_0 = u],$$

with analogous definitions of $g_X(u)$, $g_Z(u)$, $g_{ZX}(u) \equiv E[Z_i X_i' \mid W_i'\delta_0 = u]$, and $g_{ZW}(u)$. Then the density function $f(u)$ and the components of the conditional expectation functions $g_W(u)$, $g_X(u)$, $g_Z(u)$, $g_{ZX}(u)$, $g_{ZW}(u)$, $\lambda(u) \equiv E[V_i \mid W_i'\delta_0 = u] \equiv g_V(u)$, and its derivative $\lambda'(u)$ all satisfy the following smoothness condition [stated in terms of $\lambda(\cdot)$, for convenience]: for all v in some fixed open interval about zero, $\lambda(\cdot)$ admits the third-order Taylor series expansion

$$\lambda(u + v) - \lambda(u) = \sum_{\ell=1}^{3} \left(\frac{d^\ell \lambda(u)}{du^\ell}\right)\frac{v^\ell}{\ell!} + r(u, v),$$

where the derivative functions evaluated at the single index, $d\lambda(W_i'\delta_0)/du^\ell$, have finite fourth-order moments for $\ell = 1, 2, 3$, and where the remainder term $r(u, v)$ has $|r(u, v)| \le m(u) \cdot v^4$ for some function $m(u)$ satisfying $E[m(W_i'\delta_0)^4] < \infty$.

Of these regularity conditions, Assumptions 5.1 and 5.2 are the most straightforward; since the asymptotic analysis relies heavily on mean and variance calculations, sixth moments of the data are required so that terms which arise involving multiplication of three components – e.g., $(V_i - V_j)(Z_i - Z_j)(W_i' - W_j')$ – will have bounded second moments. And, though δ_0 need only be identified up to an arbitrary scale parameter, Assumption 5.2 is assumed to hold for some particular choice of scaling of δ_0 and the preliminary estimator $\hat{\delta}$.

As noted by Chamberlain (1986a), semiparametric identification of β_0 is quite difficult to establish without continuity of the distribution of the single index, as imposed in Assumption 5.3. If, for example, all of the components of W_i are discrete, then $W_i'\delta_0$ and $E[X_i \mid W_i'\delta_0]$ will also be discrete. In this situation, knowledge of $W_i'\delta_0$ will often be sufficient to uniquely determine the corresponding component of W_i, so condition (6.2.5) above will hold for some nonzero α. Assumption 5.4 implies that condition (6.2.5) holds only for $\alpha = 0$, so that the necessary condition for identification is satisfied; otherwise, post-multiplication of Σ_{ZX} by the $\alpha \ne 0$ satisfying (6.2.5) would yield a zero vector. The nonsingularity of Σ_{ZX} implies that the matrix inverse in the definition of $\hat{\beta}$ [the first term of (6.4.5) above] is well defined in large samples, as the following lemma implies (proofs of this lemma and the following theorem are given in the appendix).

Lemma 5.1. *Under Assumptions 5.1 through 5.7 above, as $n \to \infty$,*

$$\hat{\Sigma}_{ZX} \equiv \binom{n}{2}^{-1} \sum_{i=1}^{n-1} \sum_{j=i+1}^{n} \hat{w}_{ijn} \cdot (Z_i - Z_j)(X_i - X_j)' \xrightarrow{p} \Sigma_{ZX},$$

where Σ_{ZX} is defined in Assumption 5.4.

Of the restrictions imposed on the kernel function in Assumption 5.5, the least intuitive is condition (iii), which implies that $K(\cdot)$ is of a *higher-order bias-reducing* form (such a restriction was also imposed by Robinson 1988a and by Powell, Stock, and Stoker 1989). While this condition for $\ell = 1$ and 3 follows from the symmetry of $K(\cdot)$ and boundedness of its higher-order moments, satisfaction of the condition for $\ell = 2$ requires negativity of $K(\cdot)$ on part of its domain. As Robinson (1988a) notes, though, it is straightforward to construct kernel functions satisfying (6.2.17); for example, if $k(\cdot)$ denotes any symmetric, nonnegative density function satisfying parts (i) and (ii) of Assumption 5.5, then part (iii) will be satisfied if $K(\cdot)$ is chosen to be

$$K(u) = \frac{\tau^2}{\tau^2 - 1}[k(u) - \tau \cdot k(u/\tau)] \tag{6.5.1}$$

for any positive $\tau \neq 1$.

The smoothness conditions in Assumption 5.7, along with the conditions on the kernel and bandwidth in Assumptions 5.5 and 5.6, ensure that the asymptotic bias of the estimator $\hat{\beta}$ tends to zero at a rate faster than $\sqrt{n}$. This asymptotic bias term will be of the form $\int B(h_n u)K(u)\,du$, and Assumption 5.7 ensures that the function $B(\cdot)$ has a fourth-order Taylor series expansion in its argument. Thus Assumption 5.5(iii) implies that the asymptotic bias is $O(h_n^4)$, which in turn is $o(1/\sqrt{n})$ under the rate conditions of Assumption 5.6.

Under these conditions, the following result can be established:

Theorem 5.1. *Under Assumptions 5.1 through 5.7 above, the estimator $\hat{\beta}$ defined in (4.5) is $\sqrt{n}$-consistent, i.e., $\sqrt{n}(\hat{\beta} - \beta_0) = O_p(1)$, and satisfies the asymptotic linearity condition*

$$\hat{\beta} = \beta_0 + \Sigma_{ZX}^{-1} \cdot \frac{2}{n} \sum_{i=1}^{n} f(W_i'\delta_0) \cdot \{Z_i - E[Z_i \mid W_i'\delta_0]\} \cdot U_i$$

$$+ \Sigma_{ZX}^{-1}\Omega_{ZW} \cdot (\hat{\delta} - \delta_0) + o_p(1/\sqrt{n}),$$

where Σ_{ZX} is defined in Assumption 5.4 above and

$$\Omega_{ZW} \equiv 2E(\lambda'(W_i'\delta_0) \cdot f(W_i'\delta_0) \cdot (Z_i - E(Z_i \mid W_i'\delta_0)) \cdot (W_i' - E(W_i' \mid W_i'\delta_0)))$$

for $\lambda'(u)$ denoting the first derivative of $\lambda(u)$.

The form of the expression for $\hat{\beta}$ in Theorem 5.1 is the same as would be obtained if instrumental variables estimation were applied to (6.4.6) above, assuming all conditional expectation functions of the data given the index $W_i'\delta_0$ were known but the index coefficients δ_0 were unknown and replaced by $\hat{\delta}$.

Using the approximation

$$\lambda(W_i'\hat{\delta}) \cong \lambda(W_i'\delta_0) + \lambda'(W_i'\delta_0) \cdot W_i'(\hat{\delta} - \delta_0), \tag{6.5.2}$$

the following analog to equation (6.4.6) can be derived:

$$Y_i - g_Y(W_i'\hat{\delta}) \cong [X_i - g_X(W_i'\hat{\delta})]'\beta_0 + U_i$$
$$+ \lambda'(W_i'\hat{\delta}) \cdot [W_i - g_W(W_i'\hat{\delta})] \cdot (\hat{\delta} - \delta_0), \tag{6.5.3}$$

where $g_Y(u) \equiv E[Y_i \mid W_i'\delta_0 = u]$, etc. Instrumental variables estimation of β_0 in (6.5.3), using $f(W_i'\hat{\delta}) \cdot [\hat{Z}_i - g_Z(W_i'\hat{\delta})]$ as instruments, would yield the same asymptotic linearity relationship as in Theorem 5.1. Thus, while the estimation of δ_0 affects the asymptotic distribution of the estimator $\hat{\beta}$, the estimation of the nuisance functions $g_X(\cdot)$, $g_Y(\cdot)$, $g_Z(\cdot)$, $\lambda(\cdot)$, and $f(\cdot)$ do not, at least under the regularity conditions imposed above.

If the preliminary estimator $\hat{\delta}$ satisfies an asymptotic linearity condition similar to that given in Theorem 5.1, the asymptotic normality of $\hat{\beta}$ can be obtained.

Corollary 5.1. *Define*

$$\zeta_i \equiv 2f(W_i'\delta_0) \cdot [Z_i - E[Z_i \mid W_i'\delta_0]] \cdot U_i,$$

and suppose the preliminary estimator $\hat{\delta}$ has an asymptotically linear representation of the form

$$\hat{\delta} = \delta_0 + \frac{1}{n}\sum_{i=1}^{n}\psi(D_i, W_i, \delta_0) + o_p(n^{-1/2})$$

for some function $\psi(D_i, W_i, \delta_0) \equiv \psi_i$ with $E[\psi_i] = 0$ and $E[\|\psi_i\|^2] < \infty$. Then

$$\sqrt{n}(\hat{\beta} - \beta_0) \xrightarrow{d} N(0, V_0),$$

where

$$V_0 \equiv \Sigma_{ZX}^{-1} \cdot [C_{\zeta\zeta} + \Omega_{ZW}C_{\psi\zeta} + C_{\zeta\psi}\Omega_{ZW}' + \Omega_{ZW}C_{\psi\psi}\Omega_{ZW}'] \cdot [\Sigma_{ZX}^{-1}]'$$

for $C_{\zeta\zeta} \equiv E[\zeta_i\zeta_i']$, $C_{\psi\psi} \equiv E[\psi_i\psi_i']$, and $C_{\psi\zeta} \equiv E[\psi_i\zeta_i'] \equiv C_{\zeta\psi}'$.

The result of Corollary 5.1 gives the asymptotic variance V_0 of the second-step estimator $\hat{\beta}$ as the covariance matrix of the i.i.d. variable $\Sigma_{ZX}^{-1}(\zeta_i - \Omega_{ZW}\psi_i)$. The asymptotic covariance matrix between the first-step estimator $\hat{\delta}$ and the second-step estimator $\hat{\beta}$ would have a similar formula, computed as the covariance between the influence function ψ_i for $\hat{\delta}$ and the corresponding variable $\Sigma_{ZX}^{-1}(\zeta_i - \Omega_{ZW}\psi_i)$ for $\hat{\beta}$.

The explicit expression for the asymptotic covariance matrix of $\hat{\beta}$, which depends upon the instrumental variable $Z_i = z(W_i)$, raises the question of the optimal choice of the function $z(\cdot)$, which might be viewed in terms of minimization of the functional $V_0 = V_0(z(\cdot))$. This question, and the more general question of best attainable efficiency of estimation of the parameters of semiparametric selection models, has been addressed in a more recent article by Chamberlain (1992), which derives semiparametric efficiency bounds for estimators of β_0 (and δ_0). These efficiency bounds, and the related lower bounds for instrumental variables estimators of the form proposed here, depend upon the exact form of the restrictions on the error terms in the selection models considered here (and, in particular, their conditional variances), as well as the distribution of the conditioning variables W_i.

6   Estimation of the asymptotic covariance matrix

In order for large-sample inference on β_0 to be carried out using the estimator $\hat{\beta}$, a consistent estimator of the asymptotic covariance matrix of $\hat{\beta}$ must be constructed. As Corollary 5.1 shows, this requires consistent estimators of the matrices Σ_{ZX} and Ω_{ZW}, as well as estimators of the covariance matrices $C_{\zeta\zeta}$, $C_{\psi\zeta}$, and $C_{\psi\psi}$. Lemma 5.1 establishes that $\hat{\Sigma}_{ZX}$ is a consistent estimator for Σ_{ZX}; an analogous estimator for Ω_{ZW} is

$$
\hat{\Omega}_{ZW} \equiv \hat{\Omega}_{ZW}(\hat{\delta})
$$

$$
\equiv \binom{n}{2}^{-1} \sum_{i=1}^{n-1} \sum_{j=i+1}^{n} \hat{v}_{ijn} \cdot (\hat{V}_i - \hat{V}_j)(Z_i - Z_j)(W_i - W_j)', \quad (6.6.1)
$$

where

$$
\hat{v}_{ijn} \equiv \frac{1}{h^2} K'\left(\frac{(W_i - W_j)'\hat{\delta}}{h}\right), \qquad \hat{V}_i \equiv Y_i - X_i'\hat{\beta}, \quad (6.6.2)
$$

and where $K'(u)$ denotes the first derivative of the kernel function $K(u)$. The consistency of $\hat{\Omega}_{ZW}$ is established in the same way as for $\hat{\Sigma}_{ZW}$ in Lemma 5.1.

Lemma 6.1. *Under Assumptions 5.1 through 5.7 above, $\hat{\Omega}_{ZW} \xrightarrow{p} \Omega_{ZW}$, where Ω_{ZW} is defined in the statement of Theorem 5.1.*

Consistent estimation of the matrices $C_{\zeta\psi}$ and $C_{\psi\psi}$ requires suitable estimators of the influence function terms $\{\psi_i\}$ for the preliminary estimator $\hat{\delta}$ given in the assumption of Corollary 5.1. Specifically, it is useful to assume that, along with the first-step estimator $\hat{\delta}$, a sequence $\{\hat{\psi}_i\}$ is available which satisfies

$$\frac{1}{n}\sum_{i=1}^{n}\|\hat{\psi}_i - \psi_i\|^2 = o_p(1). \tag{6.6.3}$$

This sequence will, of course, depend upon the particular first-step estimator of δ_0; typically, the asymptotic variance matrix of the preliminary estimator $\hat{\delta}$ will be the sample second-moment matrix of the $\{\hat{\psi}_i\}$. An example of an appropriate sequence $\{\hat{\psi}_i\}$ for a particular preliminary estimator $\hat{\delta}$ is given by Powell, Stock, and Stoker (1989).

In addition to the sequence $\{\hat{\psi}_i\}$, an analogous sequence $\{\zeta_i\}$ of estimators of the terms $\{\zeta_i\}$ (defined in the statement of Corollary 5.1) is also needed; in this case, such a sequence can be constructed using

$$\hat{\zeta}_i \equiv \frac{2}{n-1}\sum_{\substack{j\neq i \\ j=1}}^{n}\frac{1}{h}K\left(\frac{(W_i - W_j)'\hat{\delta}}{h}\right)\cdot(Z_i - Z_j)(\hat{V}_i - \hat{V}_j), \tag{6.6.4}$$

where $\hat{V}_i$ is defined as in (6.6.2). The following lemma shows that the sequence $\{\hat{\zeta}_i\}$ satisfies a similar property to that imposed on the sequence $\{\hat{\psi}_i\}$ in (6.6.3).

Lemma 6.2. *Under Assumptions 5.1 through 5.7 above,*

$$\frac{1}{n}\sum_{i=1}^{n}\|\hat{\zeta}_i - \zeta_i\|^2 = o(1). \tag{6.6.5}$$

With the sequences $\{\hat{\psi}_i\}$ and $\{\hat{\zeta}_i\}$, the remaining components of the asymptotic covariance matrix of $\hat{\beta}$ can be consistently estimated.

Theorem 6.1. *Define*

$$\hat{C}_{\zeta\psi} \equiv \frac{1}{n}\sum_{i=1}^{n}\hat{\zeta}_i\hat{\psi}_i',$$

with analogous definitions of $\hat{C}_{\zeta\zeta}$ and $\hat{C}_{\psi\psi}$. Then if $\{\hat{\psi}_i\}$ satisfies condition (6.3) and Assumptions 5.1 through 5.7 hold, $\hat{C}_{\zeta\psi}$, $\hat{C}_{\zeta\zeta}$, and $\hat{C}_{\psi\psi}$ are (weakly) consistent for $C_{\zeta\psi}$, $C_{\zeta\zeta}$, and $C_{\psi\psi}$, respectively.

7 Estimation with a stochastic bandwidth

In a practical application of the estimation method proposed above, a stochastic bandwidth sequence $\hat{h}_n$, depending upon the realized values $\{W_i'\hat{\delta}\}$, will typically be substituted for the nonstochastic sequence h_n characterized in Assumption 5.6. A reasonable criterion for the bandwidth $\hat{h}_n$ is that it must be equivariant with respect to scale changes in $W_i'\hat{\delta}$; for example, $\hat{h}_n$ may be of the form

$$\hat{h}_n = K_0\hat{\sigma}n^{-\alpha}, \qquad \alpha \in \left(\tfrac{1}{8}, \tfrac{1}{6}\right), \tag{6.7.1}$$

where $\hat{\sigma}$ is an estimate of a scale parameter for the density $f(\cdot)$ of $W_i'\delta_0$ based upon the observed $\{W_i'\hat{\delta}\}$ (for example, the sample standard deviation or interquartile range), and K_0 is some constant term. Such a formulation is common for nonparametric density and regression estimation problems (see, e.g., Silverman 1986, Section 3.4.2).

Provided the random bandwidth sequence $\hat{h}_n$ is suitably close (in probability) to some deterministic sequence h_n satisfying the conditions of Assumption 5.6, the results of the previous sections hold if $\hat{h}_n$ is substituted for h_n in the definition of $\hat{\beta}$ and the components of its covariance matrix estimator. Specifically, suppose that

$$\sqrt{n}\left(\frac{\hat{h}_n}{h_n} - 1\right) = O_p(1) \tag{6.7.2}$$

for some sequence h_n satisfying Assumption 5.6; then, given a preliminary estimator $\tilde{\delta}$ of δ_0 with $\sqrt{n}(\tilde{\delta} - \delta_0) = O_p(1)$, a new estimator δ^* can be defined as $\delta^* \equiv \tilde{\delta}(\hat{h}_n/h_n)$, and the estimators using the first-step estimator $\tilde{\delta}$ and the random bandwidth $\hat{h}_n$ are identical to estimators using the first-step estimator δ^* and the deterministic bandwidth h_n. The rescaled estimator δ^* satisfies Assumption 5.1, since

$$\sqrt{n}(\hat{\delta} - \delta_0) = \frac{\hat{h}_n}{h_n}\sqrt{n}(\tilde{\delta} - \delta_0) + \sqrt{n}\left(\frac{\hat{h}_n}{h_n} - 1\right)\delta_0 = O_p(1); \tag{6.7.3}$$

thus, all of the conclusions of the previous sections hold when the corresponding estimators use $\hat{h}_n$ and $\tilde{\delta}$. Moreover, since $\Omega_{ZW}\delta_0 = 0$ (where Ω_{ZW} is defined in the result of Theorem 5.1), the asymptotic distribution of $\hat{\beta}$ depends only upon the asymptotic distribution of the ratios of components of the preliminary estimator $\tilde{\delta}$ (or δ^*), and not upon the asymptotic distribution of the ratio $\hat{h}_n/h_n$. (This is a consequence of the fact that δ_0 needs be identified only up to scale for the feasibility of the two-step estimation approach.) In fact, the $\sqrt{n}$-consistency imposed in (7.2) is stronger than needed; with minor modifications to the proofs, all of the results in Sections 5 and 6 can be shown to hold if h_n is replaced by $\hat{h}_n$ in all of the estimators, provided

$$n^{1/4}\left(\frac{\hat{h}_n}{h_n} - 1\right) = o_p(1) \tag{6.7.4}$$

for some nonstochastic sequence h_n satisfying Assumption 5.6.

Of course, these results do not address the more challenging problem of the optimal choice of bandwidth h_n, or construction of a feasible estimator $\hat{h}_n$ of it, even within the restricted context of (6.7.1), where the problem reduces to the best choice of the constant term K_0. This question has been addressed in Powell and Stoker (1996), which investigates the relationship of the optimal bandwidth for the smoothed U-statistics which are the components of $\hat{\beta}$ to the problem of bandwidth choice for the related pointwise nonparametric estimation problems.

8   Some recent extensions

The results of the preceding sections show that $\sqrt{n}$-consistent estimation of β_0 is possible under the weak conditions imposed, and that, with a suitable choice of the first-step estimator $\hat{\delta}$ for the equation of interest, confidence regions and hypothesis tests can be constructed which will be asymptotically valid. Since the original drafts (Powell 1987, 1989) of this chapter, a large literature on efficient estimation of the parameters of semiparametric models of selectivity bias has developed. Though some of the more recent contributions to this literature (Chamberlain 1992, Powell and Stoker 1996) have been mentioned previously, it is beyond the scope of the present chapter to summarize the results of that literature, which is reviewed in surveys by Robinson (1988b), Stoker (1992), and Powell (1994), among others. However, three more recent collaborations – Newey, Powell, and Walker (1990), Ahn and Powell (1993), and Honoré and Powell (1997) – make extensive use of the approach and derivations of this chapter, and are singled out for comment here.

Newey, Powell, and Walker (1990) apply the estimator proposed in this chapter, and an alternative estimator for the semiparametric selection model proposed by Newey (1988), to an empirical model of married women's labor force participation, hours of work, and wages, using a data set originally collected and analyzed by Mroz (1987). Relative to the parametric results presented in Mroz's study, the coefficient estimates based upon the semiparametric approaches were comparable in magnitude, and not significantly different from, estimates using Heckman's (1976) parametric two-step estimator which assumes the error terms are jointly normal. The semiparametric coefficient estimates, like their parametric counterparts, were generally smaller in magnitude and significantly different from estimates obtained without correcting for selectivity bias.

Ahn and Powell's (1993) paper extends the present approach by consideration of a nonparametric formulation for the index function for the selection variable. Specifically, it is assumed that the outcome equation of interest has the form

$$Y_i = X_i'\beta_0 + \theta(g(W_i)) + U_i, \tag{6.8.1}$$

where now

$$g(W_i) \equiv E[D_i \mid W_i] \tag{6.8.2}$$

and the functions $\theta(\cdot)$ and $g(\cdot)$ are unknown; that is, the selection bias term is assumed to depend upon the (nonparametrically specified) conditional mean of the selection variable D_i. This formulation is based upon the idea, pointed out earlier by Heckman and Robb (1986), that equations (6.8.1) and (6.2.3) are equivalent if the function $\gamma(\cdot)$ in (6.2.4) above is invertible, with $\theta(\cdot) \equiv \lambda(\gamma^{-1}(\cdot))$. This extension allows the linear selection index $W_i'\delta_0$ to be replaced by a nonparametric version $\tau(W_i)$ in the selection models considered in Section 3 above; when D_i is binary, the function $\tau(W_i)$ is the selection probability, or "propensity score," of Rosenbaum and Rubin (1983), who proposed similar matching methods to control for selection bias in selection-on-observables models (Rosenbaum and Rubin 1984, 1985). Ahn and Powell (1993) give conditions under which replacement of the estimated linear index $W_i'\hat{\delta}$ by a nonparametric counterpart $\hat{g}(W_i)$ still yields root-n consistency of the estimator $\hat{\beta}$ defined above; the article also applies the proposed estimator to the Mroz (1987) data set, with similar results to those obtained in Newey, Powell, and Walker (1990).

Honoré and Powell (1997) extend the approach of this chapter in a different manner, by replacing the implicit squared-error-loss criterion of the present chapter with a more general, nonquadratic criterion. That is, for the special case that $Z_i \equiv X_i$, the estimator $\hat{\beta}$ defined in (6.4.5) above can be defined as a minimizer of the function

$$Q_n(\beta) \equiv \binom{n}{2}^{-1} \sum_{i=1}^{n} \sum_{j=i+1}^{n} \hat{w}_{ijn} \cdot ((Y_i - Y_j) - (X_i - X_j)'\beta)^2 \tag{6.8.3}$$

over β; Honoré and Powell (1997) investigate the properties of the minimizer of the more general criterion

$$S_n(\beta) \equiv \binom{n}{2}^{-1} \sum_{i=1}^{n} \sum_{j=i+1}^{n} \hat{w}_{ijn} s(Y_i, Y_j, X_i, X_j, \beta), \tag{6.8.4}$$

for some function $s(\cdot)$ which is assumed invariant to interchange of the subscripts i and j. For example, the quadratic loss function in (6.8.3) might be replaced by an absolute value loss criterion, in the interest of obtaining a more robust estimator of the parameter β_0. Unlike $Q_n(\beta)$ of (6.8.3), the minimizer of $S_n(\beta)$ in (6.8.4) cannot generally be written in closed form, which complicates the derivation of its asymptotic sampling behavior. The advantage of the more general formulation is that it permits the differencing approach of this chapter to be applied to certain nonlinear outcome equations of interest, e.g., a semilinear version (as in Robinson 1988a) of the logistic regression model. Similar results are given by Bhattacharya and Zhao (1997), who propose estimators of β_0 which solve estimating equations of the form

$$0 = \binom{n}{2}^{-1} \sum_{i=1}^{n} \sum_{j=i+1}^{n} \hat{w}_{ijn} \psi(Y_i - Y_j - (X_i - X_j)'\hat{\beta}) \cdot (X_i - X_j), \qquad (6.8.5)$$

with $\psi(\cdot)$ nondecreasing and W_i scalar in model (6.2.3) (so that $\delta_0 \equiv 1$ in the current setting). Because there is no problem of preliminary estimation of δ_0 in the model they consider, their regularity conditions permit the bandwidth h_n to converge to zero at a rate faster than $\sqrt{n}$, and do not require $K(\cdot)$ to be a higher-order kernel; however, these weaker conditions apparently cannot cannot be extended when W_i is multivariate and δ_0 must be estimated.

Appendix

Except for the presence of the preliminary estimator $\hat{\delta}$ in place of the unknown vector δ_0, the components of the estimators proposed above are in the general form of a *second-order U*-statistic; that is, they are of the form

$$U_n \equiv \binom{n}{2}^{-1} \sum_{i=1}^{n-1} \sum_{j=i+1}^{n} p_n(\xi_i, \xi_j),$$

where $\{\xi_i, i = 1, \ldots, n\}$ is an i.i.d. sample of random vectors and $p_n(\cdot)$ is a symmetric kernel, i.e., $p_n(\xi_i, \xi_j) = p_n(\xi_j, \xi_i)$. Define

$$r_n(\xi_i) = E[p_n(\xi_i, \xi_j) \mid \xi_i],$$
$$\tau_n = E[r_n(\xi_i)] = E[p_n(\xi_i, \xi_j)],$$

as well as the *projection* of the statistic U_n,

$$\hat{U}_n = \tau_n + \frac{2}{n} \sum_{i=1}^{n} [r_n(\xi_i) - \tau_n]$$

(see, e.g., Serfling 1980, Chapter 5). The following result is useful in establishing the large-sample behavior of the statistic U_n:

Lemma A.1 (Lemma 3.1 of Powell, Stock, and Stoker 1989). *If* $E[\|p_n(z_i, z_j)\|^2] = o(n)$, *then*

(i) $U_n = \tau_n + o_p(1)$, *and*
(ii) $\sqrt{n}(\hat{U}_n - U_n) = o_p(1)$.

Proof of Lemma 5.1: The first step is to demonstrate that $\hat{\delta}$ can be replaced by δ_0 in the definition of $\hat{\Sigma}_{ZX}$ without affecting its probability limit. Writing $\hat{\Sigma}_{ZX}$ explicitly in terms of $\hat{\delta}$,

$$\hat{\Sigma}_{ZX}(\hat{\delta}) \equiv \binom{n}{2}^{-1} \sum_{i=1}^{n-1} \sum_{j=i+1}^{n} w_{ijn}(\hat{\delta}) \cdot (Z_i - Z_j)(X_i - X_j)', \quad (6.A.1)$$

and defining the matrix norm $\|A\|^2 \equiv \mathrm{tr}(A'A)$, it is straightforward to show that

$$\|\hat{\Sigma}_{ZX}(\hat{\delta}) - \hat{\Sigma}_{ZX}(\delta_0)\|$$

$$\leq \binom{n}{2}^{-1} \sum_{i=1}^{n-1} \sum_{j=i+1}^{n} |w_{ijn}(\hat{\delta}) - w_{ijn}(\delta_0)| \cdot \|Z_i - Z_j\| \cdot \|X_i - X_j\|$$

$$\leq \left(\binom{n}{2}^{-1} \sum_{i=1}^{n-1} \sum_{j=i+1}^{n} \|Z_i - Z_j\| \cdot \|X_i - X_j\| \cdot \|W_i - W_j\| \right)$$

$$\times \frac{K_1}{\sqrt{n}h^2} \sqrt{n}\|\hat{\delta} - \delta_0\|, \quad (6.A.2)$$

where K_1 is an upper bound for $|dK(u)/du|$ (Assumption 5.5). Since the first term on the last line of (6.A.2) is a U-statistic whose kernel has finite expectation, it converges to that expectation almost surely by the SLLN for U-statistics (see Serfling 1980, Theorem A, p. 190). Furthermore, since $\sqrt{n}\|\hat{\delta} - \delta_0\| = O_p(1)$ and $\sqrt{n}h^2 \to \infty$ by Assumptions 5.2 and 5.6,

$$\|\hat{\Sigma}_{ZX}(\hat{\delta}) - \hat{\Sigma}_{ZX}(\delta_0)\| = o_p(1).$$

Next, $\hat{\Sigma}_{ZX}(\delta_0)$ is shown to satisfy the result of part (i) of Lemma A.1. Note that $\hat{\Sigma}_{ZX}(\delta_0)$ can be written as a second-order U-statistic with kernel function of the form

$$p_n(\xi_i, \xi_j) \equiv \frac{1}{h} K\left(\frac{(W_i - W_j)'\delta_0}{h} \right) \cdot (Z_i - Z_j)(X_i - X_j)', \quad (6.A.3)$$

with $\xi_i \equiv (W_i', X_i', Z_i')'$. Since, in this case,

$$\|p_n(\xi_i, \xi_j)\| \leq \frac{K_0}{h} \|Z_i - Z_j\| \cdot \|X_i - X_j\|, \quad (6.A.4)$$

where K_0 is an upper bound for $|K(u)|$,

$$E\|p_n(\xi_i, \xi_j)\|^2 = O(1/h^2) = O(n/nh^2) = o(n), \quad (6.A.5)$$

since $nh^2 \to \infty$ by Assumption 5.6. Part (i) of Lemma A.1 thus yields

$$\hat{\Sigma}_{ZX}(\delta_0) = \tau_n + o_p(1) = E[r_n(\xi_i)] + o(1), \quad (6.A.6)$$

with

$$r_n(\xi_i) \equiv E\left(\frac{1}{h} K\left(\frac{(W_i - W_j)'\delta_0}{h}\right) \cdot (Z_i - Z_j)(X_i - X_j)' \mid Z_i, W_i, X_i\right)$$

$$= \int [Z_i - g_Z(W_i'\delta_0 - hu)] \cdot [X_i - g_X(W_i'\delta_0 - hu)]'$$

$$\times f(W_i\delta_0 - hu) \cdot K(u)\, du$$

$$+ \int [g_{ZX}(W_i'\delta_0 - hu) - g_Z(W_i'\delta_0 - hu) \cdot [g_X(W_i'\delta_0 - hu)]']$$

$$\times f(W_i\delta_0 - hu) \cdot K(u)\, du, \qquad (6.A.7)$$

and $\tau_n \equiv E[r_n(\xi_i)] = E[p_n(\xi_i, \xi_j)]$.

Now, defining

$$r(\xi_i) \equiv [Z_i - g_Z(W_i'\delta_0)] \cdot [X_i - g_X(W_i'\delta_0)]' \cdot f(W_i'\delta_0)$$

$$+ [g_{ZX}(W_i'\delta_0) - g_Z(W_i'\delta_0) \cdot g_{X'}(W_i'\delta_0)] \cdot f(W_i'\delta_0), \qquad (6.A.8)$$

it can be shown, with some tedious algebra, that Assumptions 5.5 and 5.7 imply

$$\|r_n(\xi_i) - r(\xi_i)\| \le \sum_{j=1}^{12} h^j \|\rho_j(\xi_i)\| \cdot \left|\int u^j \cdot K(u)\, du\right| \qquad (6.A.9)$$

when h is sufficiently close to zero, where the matrices $\rho_j(\xi_i)$ are products of the Taylor series coefficients specified in Assumption 5.7, and have $E[\|\rho_j(\xi_i)\|] < \infty$. For example,

$$\rho_1(\xi_i) \equiv f(W_i'\delta_0) \cdot \left(g_Z^{(1)}(W_i'\delta_0) \cdot [X_i - g_X(W_i'\delta_0)]'\right.$$

$$+ [Z_i - g_Z(W_i'\delta_0)] \cdot [g_X^{(1)}(W_i'\delta_0)]' + g_{ZX}^{(1)}(W_i'\delta_0)$$

$$- g_Z^{(1)}(W_i'\delta_0) \cdot [g_X(W_i'\delta_0)]' - g_Z(W_i'\delta_0) \cdot [g_X^{(1)}(W_i'\delta_0)]'\big)$$

$$+ f^{(1)}(W_i'\delta_0) \cdot ([Z_i - g_Z(W_i'\delta_0)] \cdot [X_i - g_X(W_i'\delta_0)]'$$

$$+ g_{ZX}(W_i'\delta_0) - g_Z(W_i'\delta_0) \cdot [g_X(W_i'\delta_0)]'), \qquad (6.A.10)$$

where the superscript (1) denotes the first derivative of each component with respect to the scalar argument $W_i'\delta_0$. [Existence of the integrals in (6.A.9) is ensured by the compact support of the kernel function, Assumption 5.5(iii).] Thus, by part (iv) of Assumption 5.5, the first three terms of the series on the right hand side of (6.A.9) vanish, so that

$$E[\|r_n(\xi_i) - r(\xi_i)\|] = O(h^4). \qquad (6.A.11)$$

This implies that

$$\tau_n \equiv E[r_n(\xi_i)] = E[r(\xi_i)] + o(1) = \Sigma_{ZX} + o(1), \qquad (6.A.12)$$

and that

$$\frac{1}{n} \sum_{i=1}^{n} r_n(\xi_i) = \frac{1}{n} \sum_{i=1}^{n} r(\xi_i) + o_p(1), \qquad (6.A.13)$$

since $E[\|n^{-1} \sum_i \{r_n(\xi_i) - r(\xi_i)\}\|] \le E[\|r_n(\xi_i) - r(\xi_i)\|]$. Substituting these results into (6.A.6) and applying the weak law of large numbers yields

$$\|\hat{\Sigma}_{ZX}(\hat{\delta}) - \Sigma_{ZX}\| = \|\hat{\Sigma}_{ZX}(\delta_0) - \Sigma_{ZX}\| + o_p(1) = o_p(1), \quad (6.A.14)$$

as asserted. $\square$

Proof of Theorem 5.1: Defining $\hat{\Sigma}_{ZV}(\hat{\delta})$ analogously to $\hat{\Sigma}_{ZX}(\hat{\delta})$ of (6.A.1) above, the normalized difference $\sqrt{n}(\hat{\beta} - \beta_0)$ can be rewritten in the usual way as

$$\sqrt{n}(\hat{\beta} - \beta_0) = [\hat{\Sigma}_{ZX}(\hat{\delta})]^{-1} \sqrt{n}[\hat{\Sigma}_{ZV}(\hat{\delta})] = \Sigma_{ZX}^{-1} \sqrt{n}[\hat{\Sigma}_{ZV}(\hat{\delta})] + o_p(1),$$
$$(6.A.15)$$

provided $\sqrt{n}[\hat{\Sigma}_{ZV}(\hat{\delta})] = O_p(1)$ is shown.

As in the preceding proof, a Taylor series expansion of $\sqrt{n}[\hat{\Sigma}_{ZV}(\hat{\delta})]$ about $\hat{\delta} = \delta_0$ yields

$$\sqrt{n}[\hat{\Sigma}_{ZV}(\hat{\delta})] = \sqrt{n}[\hat{\Sigma}_{ZV}(\delta_0)] + \tilde{\Omega}_{ZW} \sqrt{n}(\hat{\delta} - \delta_0)$$
$$+ \sqrt{n} \cdot \binom{n}{2}^{-1} \sum_{i=1}^{n-1} \sum_{j=i+1}^{n} w_{ijn}^{(2)}(V_i - V_j)(Z_i - Z_j)$$
$$\times [(W_i - W_j)'(\hat{\delta} - \delta_0)]^2, \qquad (6.A.16)$$

where

$$\tilde{\Omega}_{ZW} \equiv \binom{n}{2}^{-1} \sum_{i=1}^{n-1} \sum_{j=i+1}^{n} w_{ijn}^{(1)}(V_i - V_j)(Z_i - Z_j)(W_i - W_j)',$$

$$(6.A.17)$$
$$w_{ijn}^{(1)} \equiv \frac{1}{h^2} K'\left(\frac{(W_i - W_j)'\delta_0}{h}\right), \qquad w_{ijn}^{(2)} \equiv \frac{1}{h^3} K''\left(\frac{\kappa_{ij}^*}{h}\right),$$

$K'(\cdot)$ and $K''(\cdot)$ denote the first and second derivatives of $K(\cdot)$, and κ_{ij}^* is some intermediate value between $(W_i - W_j)'\hat{\delta}$ and $(W_i - W_j)'\delta_0$. Thus

$$\|\sqrt{n}[\hat{\Sigma}_{ZV}(\hat{\delta})] - \sqrt{n}[\hat{\Sigma}_{ZV}(\delta_0)] - \tilde{\Omega}_{ZW} \sqrt{n}(\hat{\delta} - \delta_0)\|$$
$$\le \left(\binom{n}{2}^{-1} \sum_{i=1}^{n-1} \sum_{j=i+1}^{n} \|V_i - V_j\| \cdot \|Z_i - Z_j\| \cdot \|W_i - W_j\|^2\right)$$
$$\times \frac{K_2}{\sqrt{n}h^3} n\|\hat{\delta} - \delta_0\|^2, \qquad (6.A.18)$$

where K_2 is an upper bound for $K''(\cdot)$. Since the first term in the last line of (6.A.18) converges to its expectation (by the SLLN for U-statistics), and since $n\|\hat{\delta} - \delta_0\|^2 = O_p(1)$ and $\sqrt{n}h^3 \to \infty$,

$$\sqrt{n}[\hat{\Sigma}_{ZV}(\hat{\delta})] = \sqrt{n}[\hat{\Sigma}_{ZV}(\delta_0)] + \tilde{\Omega}_{ZW}\sqrt{n}(\hat{\delta} - \delta_0) + o_p(1). \quad (6.A.19)$$

Furthermore, the proof of Lemma 6.1 below yields

$$\tilde{\Omega}_{ZW} = \Omega_{ZW} + o_p(1), \quad (6.A.20)$$

where Ω_{ZW} is defined in the statement of Theorem 5.1.

Finally, $\sqrt{n}[\hat{\Sigma}_{ZV}(\delta_0)]$ can be written as a normalized U-statistic, with kernel

$$p_n(\xi_i, \xi_j) \equiv \frac{1}{h}K\left(\frac{(W_i - W_j)'\delta_0}{h}\right) \cdot (Z_i - Z_j)(V_i - V_j). \quad (6.A.21)$$

Since $E\|p_n(\xi_i, \xi_j)\|^2 = O(1/h^2) = o(n)$, Lemma A.1 yields

$$\sqrt{n}(\hat{\Sigma}_{ZV}(\delta_0) - \tau_n) = \frac{2}{\sqrt{n}}\sum_{i=1}^{n}r_n(\xi_i) + o_p(1), \quad (6.A.22)$$

where

$$r_n(\xi_i) \equiv E\left(\frac{1}{h}K\left(\frac{(W_i - W_j)'\delta_0}{h}\right) \cdot (Z_i - Z_j)(V_i - V_j) \mid Z_i, W_i, X_i\right)$$

$$= \int [Z_i - g_Z(W_i'\delta_0 - hu)] \cdot [V_i - \lambda(W_i'\delta_0 - hu)]'$$

$$\times f(W_i'\delta_0 - hu) \cdot K(u)\, du. \quad (6.A.23)$$

Again defining

$$r(\xi_i) \equiv f(W_i'\delta_0) \cdot [Z_i - g_Z(W_i'\delta_0)] \cdot U_i, \quad (6.A.24)$$

the smoothness conditions of Assumptions 5.5 and 5.7 imply that $\|r_n(\xi_i) - r(\xi_i)\|$ has a series expansion of the form (6.A.9) above, where now $E[\|\rho_j(\xi_i)\|^2] < \infty$. Here, for example,

$$\rho_1(\xi_i) \equiv \lambda'(W_i'\delta_0) \cdot [Z_i - g_Z(W_i'\delta_0)] \cdot f(W_i'\delta_0)$$

$$+ \left(g_Z^{(1)}(W_i'\delta_0) \cdot f(W_i'\delta_0) + [Z_i - g_Z(W_i'\delta_0)]f^{(1)}(W_i'\delta_0)\right) \cdot U_i, \quad (6.A.25)$$

which has bounded second moment by Assumption 5.7. Writing

$$\frac{2}{\sqrt{n}}\sum_{i=1}^{n}[r_n(\xi_i) - \tau_n] = \frac{2}{\sqrt{n}}\sum_{i=1}^{n}r(\xi_i) + R_n, \quad (6.A.26)$$

with

$$R_n \equiv \frac{2}{\sqrt{n}} \sum_{i=1}^{n} (r_n(\xi_i) - r(\xi_i) - E[r_n(\xi_i) - r(\xi_i)]), \qquad (6.A.27)$$

a straightforward calculation yields

$$E[\|R_n\|^2] \le E[4\|r_n(\xi) - r(\xi)\|^2] = O(h^8) = o(1), \qquad (6.A.28)$$

so

$$\frac{2}{\sqrt{n}} \sum_{i=1}^{n} [r_n(\xi_i) - \tau_n] = \frac{2}{\sqrt{n}} \sum_{i=1}^{n} r(\xi_i) + o_p(1). \qquad (6.A.29)$$

With

$$\sqrt{n}\|\tau_n\| = \sqrt{n}\|E[r_n(\xi_i) - r(\xi_i)]\|$$

$$\le \sqrt{n} \left\{ \sum_{j=1}^{12} h^j E\|\rho_j(\xi_i)\| \cdot \left| \int u^j K(u)\, du \right| \right\}$$

$$= O(\sqrt{n} h^4) = o(1) \qquad (6.A.30)$$

by Assumptions 5.5 and 5.6, results (6.A.15), (6.A.19), (6.A.20), (6.A.22), (6.A.29), and (6.A.30) yield the result stated in Theorem 5.1. $\square$

Proof of Lemma 6.1: This proof is analogous to the proof of Lemma 5.1. Distinguishing between $\hat{\Omega}_{ZW} \equiv \hat{\Omega}_{ZW}(\hat{\delta}, \hat{\beta})$ and $\tilde{\Omega}_{ZW}$ of (6.A.17) (which substitutes the true values δ_0 and β_0 for $\hat{\delta}$ and $\hat{\beta}$), their difference satisfies

$$\|\hat{\Omega}_{ZW} - \tilde{\Omega}_{ZW}\|$$

$$\le \left(\binom{n}{2}^{-1} \sum_{i=1}^{n-1} \sum_{j=i+1}^{n} \|Z_i - Z_j\| \cdot \|W_i - W_j\| \cdot \|X_i - X_j\| \right)$$

$$\times \frac{K_1}{\sqrt{n} h^2} \sqrt{n} \|\hat{\beta} - \beta_0\|$$

$$+ \left(\binom{n}{2}^{-1} \sum_{i=1}^{n-1} \sum_{j=i+1}^{n} \|V_i - V_j\| \cdot \|Z_i - Z_j\| \cdot \|W_i - W_j\|^2 \right)$$

$$\times \frac{K_2}{\sqrt{n} h^3} \sqrt{n} \|\hat{\delta} - \delta_0\|, \qquad (6.A.31)$$

where K_1 and K_2 are upper bounds for $K'(\cdot)$ and $K''(\cdot)$, so it follows that

$$\hat{\Omega}_{ZW} = \tilde{\Omega}_{ZW} + o_p(1)$$

by the $\sqrt{n}$-consistency of $\hat{\delta}$ and $\hat{\beta}$, along with Assumption 5.6. Then, writing

$$p_n(\xi_i, \xi_j) \equiv \frac{1}{h^2} K' \left(\frac{(W_i - W_j)' \delta_0}{h} \right) \cdot (V_i - V_j)(Z_i - Z_j)(W_i - W_j)',$$

(6.A.32)

the second moment of this kernel satisfies $E[\| p_n(\xi_i, \xi_j) \|^2] = O(h^{-4}) = o(n)$, so the preliminary lemma on U-statistics is applicable. Using integration by parts to calculate the conditional mean of this kernel, the same argument used to derive (6.A.28) above can be employed to show

$$E[\| E[p_n(\xi_i, \xi_j) | \xi_i] - r(\xi_i) \|^2] = o(h^8) = o(1)$$

(6.A.33)

for this kernel function, where now

$$r(\xi_i) \equiv \lambda'(W_i' \delta_0) \cdot [Z_i - g_Z(W_i' \delta_0)] \cdot [W_i - g_W(W_i' \delta_0)]' \cdot f(W_i' \delta_0)$$
$$+ \lambda'(W_i' \delta_0) \cdot (g_{ZW}(W_i' \delta_0) - g_Z(W_i' \delta_0) \cdot [g_W(W_i' \delta_0)]') \cdot f(W_i' \delta_0).$$

(6.A.34)

Since $E[r(\xi_i)] = \Omega_{ZW}$, consistency of $\hat{\Omega}_{ZW}$ follows in the same way as for Σ_{ZX} above. $\qquad\square$

Proof of Lemma 6.2: Defining

$$\tilde{\zeta}_i \equiv \frac{2}{n-1} \sum_{\substack{j \neq i \\ j=1}}^{n} \frac{1}{h} K \left(\frac{(W_i - W_j)' \delta_0}{h} \right) \cdot (Z_i - Z_j)(V_i - V_j), \quad (6.A.35)$$

the same Taylor series argument as follows (6.A.31) yields

$$\frac{1}{n} \sum_{i=1}^{n} \| \hat{\zeta}_i - \tilde{\zeta}_i \|^2 = o_p(1).$$

(6.A.36)

Now

$$\tilde{\zeta} \equiv \frac{2}{n-1} \sum_{\substack{j \neq i \\ j=1}}^{n} p_n(\xi_i, \xi_j)$$

(6.A.37)

for the kernel function $p_n(\cdot)$ given in (6.A.21), with conditional expectation $r_n(\xi_i)$ given in (6.A.23). Following the proof of Theorem 3.4 of Powell, Stock, and Stoker (1989), the difference between $\tilde{\zeta}_i$ and its conditional expectation satisfies

$$E[\| \tilde{\zeta}_i - 2r_n(\xi_i) \|^2] \leq \frac{4}{n-1} E[\| p_n(\xi_i, \xi_j) \|^2] = O(1/nh^2) = o(1),$$

(6.A.38)

and by (6.A.28) above, $E[\|r_n(\xi_i) - r(\xi_i)\|^2] = o(1)$, where $r(\xi_i) \equiv \zeta_i/2$ is given in (6.A.24). Thus

$$E[\|\tilde{\xi}_i - \zeta_i\|^2] = o(1), \tag{6.A.39}$$

which, with the strong law of large numbers, gives

$$\frac{1}{n} \sum_{i=1}^{n} \|\tilde{\xi}_i - \zeta_i\|^2 = o_p(1). \tag{6.A.40}$$

The desired result follows from (6.A.36) and (6.A.40). $\square$

Proof of Theorem 6.1: The result follows immediately from condition (6.6.3), Lemma 6.2, and the strong law of large numbers. $\square$

REFERENCES

Ahn, H. and Powell, J. L. (1993), "Semiparametric Estimation of Censored Selection Models with a Nonparametric Selection Mechanism," *Journal of Econometrics*, **58**, 3–29.

Amemiya, T. (1985), *Advanced Econometrics* (Cambridge, MA: Harvard University Press).

Arabmazar, A. and Schmidt, P. (1981), "Further Evidence on the Robustness of the Tobit Estimator to Heteroscedasticity," *Journal of Econometrics*, **17**, 253–258.

(1982), "An Investigation of the Robustness of the Tobit Estimator to Non-normality," *Econometrica*, **50**, 1055–1063.

Bhattacharya, P. K. and Zhao, P.-L. (1997), "Semiparametric Inference in a Partial Linear Model," *Annals of Statistics*, **25**, 244–262.

Bierens, H. J. (1987), "Kernel Estimators of Regression Functions," in T. F. Bewley, ed., *Advances in Econometrics, Fifth World Congress*, Volume 1 (Cambridge: Cambridge University Press).

Chamberlain, G. (1986a), "Asymptotic Efficiency in Semiparametric Models with Censoring," *Journal of Econometrics*, **32**, 189–218.

(1986b), "Notes on Semiparametric Regression," manuscript, Department of Economics, University of Wisconsin – Madison.

(1992), "Efficiency Bounds for Semiparametric Regression," *Econometrica*, **60**, 567–596.

Chung, C.-F. and Goldberger, A. S. (1984), "Proportional Projections in Limited Dependent Variable Models," *Econometrica*, **52**, 531–534.

Cosslett, S. R. (1983), "Distribution-Free Maximum Likelihood Estimator of the Binary Choice Model," *Econometrica*, **51**, 765–782.

(1991), "Semiparametric Estimation of a Regression Model with Sample Selectivity," in W. A. Barnett et al., eds., *Nonparametric and Semiparametric Estimation Methods in Econometrics and Statistics* (Cambridge: Cambridge University Press).

Fair, R. C. and Jaffe, D. M. (1972), "Methods of Estimation for Markets in Disequilibrium," *Econometrica*, **40**, 497–514.

Goldberger, A. S. (1983), "Abnormal Selection Bias," in S. Karlin et al., eds., *Studies in Econometrics, Time Series, and Multivariate Statistics* (New York: Academic Press).

Gronau, R. (1973), "The Effects of Children on the Housewife's Value of Time," *Journal of Political Economy*, **81**, S168–S199.

Han, A. K. (1987), "Non-parametric Analysis of a Generalized Regression Model: The Maximum Rank Correlation Estimator," *Journal of Econometrics*, **35**, 303–316.

Heckman, J. J. (1974), "Shadow Prices, Market Wages, and Labor Supply," *Econometrica*, **42**, 679–693.

(1976), "The Common Structure of Statistical Models of Truncation, Sample Selection and Limited Dependent Variables and a Simple Estimator for Such Models," *Annals of Economic and Social Measurement*, **5**, 475–492.

Heckman, J. J. and Robb, R. (1986), "Alternative Methods for Solving the Problem of Selection Bias in Evaluating the Impact of Treatments on Outcomes," in H. Wainer, ed., *Drawing Inferences from Self-selected Samples* (New York: Springer-Verlag).

Honoré, B. E. and Powell, J. L. (1997), "Pairwise Difference Estimation of Nonlinear Models," manuscript, Department of Economics, Princeton University.

Horowitz, J. L. (1984), "A Distribution-Free Least Squares Estimator for Censored Linear Regression Models," *Journal of Econometrics*, **32**, 59–84.

Ichimura, H. (1986), "Consistent Estimation of Index Model Coefficients," manuscript, Department of Economics, M.I.T.

Manski, C. F. (1975), "Maximum Score Estimation of the Stochastic Utility Model of Choice," *Journal of Econometrics*, **3**, 205–228.

(1985), "Semiparametric Analysis of Discrete Response: Asymptotic Properties of the Maximum Score Estimator," *Journal of Econometrics*, **27**, 313–333.

Mroz, T. A. (1987), "The Sensitivity of an Empirical Model of Married Women's Hours of Work to Economic and Statistical Assumptions," *Econometrica*, **55**, 765–799.

Newey, W. K. (1988), "Two Step Series Estimation of Sample Selection Models," manuscript, Department of Economics, Princeton University.

Newey, W. K., Powell, J. L., and Walker, J. R. (1990), "Semiparametric Estimation of Selection Models: Some Empirical Results," *American Economic Review*, **80**, 324–238.

Powell, J. L. (1984), "Least Absolute Deviations Estimation for the Censored Regression Model," *Journal of Econometrics*, **25**, 303–325.

(1986a), "Censored Regression Quantiles," *Journal of Econometrics*, **32**, 143–155.

(1986b), "Symmetrically Trimmed Least Squares Estimation of Tobit Models," *Econometrica*, **54**, 1435–1460.

(1987), "Semiparametric Estimation of Bivariate Latent Variable Models," Working Paper No. 8704, Social Systems Research Institute, University of Wisconsin – Madison.

(1989), "Semiparametric Estimation of Censored Selection Models," manuscript, Department of Economics, University of Wisconsin-Madison.

(1994), "Estimation of Semiparametric Models," in R.F. Engle, and D.L. McFadden, eds., *Handbook of Econometrics*, Volume IV (Amsterdam: Elsevier Science B.V.).

Powell, J. L., Stock, J. H., and Stoker, T. M. (1989), "Semiparametric Estimation of Index Coefficients," *Econometrica*, **57**, 1403–1430.

Powell, J. L. and Stoker, T. M. (1996), "Optimal Bandwidth Choice for Density-Weighted Averages," *Journal of Econometrics*, **75**, 291–316.

Robinson, P. M. (1988a), "Root-n-Consistent Semiparametric Regression," *Econometrica*, **56**, 931–954.

   (1988b), "Semiparametric Econometrics, a Survey," *Journal of Applied Econometrics*, **3**, 35–51.

Rosenbaum, P. R. and Rubin, D. B. (1983), "The Central Role of the Propensity Score in Observational Studies for Causal Effects," *Biometrika*, **70**, 41–55.

   (1984), "Reducing Bias in Observational Studies Using Subclassification on the Propensity Score," *Journal of the American Statistical Association*, **79**, 516–524.

   (1985), "Constructing a Control Group Using Multivariate Matching Methods that Include the Propensity Score," *American Statistician*, **39**, 33–38.

Ruud, P. (1983), "Sufficient Conditions for Consistency of Maximum Likelihood Estimation Despite Misspecification of Distribution," *Econometrica*, **51**, 225–228.

   (1986), "Consistent Estimation of Limited Dependent Variable Models Despite Misspecification of Distribution, *Journal of Econometrics*, **32**, 157–187.

Serfling, R. J. (1980), *Approximation Theorems of Mathematical Statistics* (New York: John Wiley & Sons).

Silverman, B. W. (1986), *Density Estimation for Statistics and Data Analysis* (London: Chapman and Hall).

Stoker, T. M. (1986), "Consistent Estimation of Scaled Coefficients," *Econometrica*, **54**, 1461–1481.

   (1992), *Lectures on Semiparametric Econometrics*. Louvan-La-Nueve, Belgium: CORE Lecture Series.

CHAPTER 7

Studentization in Edgeworth expansions for estimates of semiparametric index models

Y. Nishiyama and P. M. Robinson

1   Introduction

During the 1970s, Takeshi Amemiya considerably advanced the asymptotic theory of estimation of parametric econometric models for cross-sectional data. Previously, most work had concerned closed form estimates, such as generalized least squares and instrumental variable estimates of linear regressions, or two- or three-stage least squares estimates of linear (in equations and parameters) simultaneous equation systems. Prompted by Jennrich's (1969) work on strong consistency and asymptotic normality of nonlinear least squares, Amemiya developed asymptotic theory for implicitly defined extremum estimates of a variety of econometric models.

Let Y_i, X_i, $i = 1, 2, \ldots$, be sequences of, respectively, scalar and $d \times 1$ vector observables, and define

$$Y_i = (\beta^\tau X_i + \epsilon_i) \, 1(\beta^\tau X_i + \epsilon_i > 0), \qquad i = 1, 2, \ldots, \qquad (7.1.1)$$

where ϵ_i, $i = 1, 2, \ldots$, is a sequence of unobservable zero-mean random variables, β is a $d \times 1$ unknown vector, τ denotes transposition, and $1(\cdot)$ is the indicator function. (7.1.1) is called a Tobit model. Least squares regression of Y_i on X_i, using either all observations or all observations such that $Y_i > 0$, inconsistently estimates β. Assuming the ϵ_i are independent and identically distributed (iid) normal variates, maximum likelihood (ML) estimates based on (7.1.1) can be consistent. These, however, are only implicitly defined. Amemiya (1973) established their strong consistency and asymptotic normality, later extending these results (Amemiya 1974a) to a multivariate version of (7.1.1).

Another model of econometric interest is

$$\frac{Y_i^\lambda - 1}{\lambda} 1(\lambda > 0) + (\log Y_i) 1(\lambda = 0) = \beta^\tau X_i + \epsilon_i, \qquad (7.1.2)$$

Research supported by ESRC Grant R000235892. The second author's research was also supported by a Leverhulme Trust Personal Professorship.

where the scalar λ is unknown. This is called a Box–Cox transformation model. If λ is specified incorrectly, least squares regression inconsistently estimates β. Thus, methods have been proposed for estimating β and λ simultaneously. One such purports to be ML, based on normal ϵ_i, but unless $\lambda = 0$ or $1/\lambda$ is odd, the left hand side of (7.1.2) cannot possibly be conditionally normal. Alternative, logically consistent distributions have been proposed, e.g., Amemiya and Powell (1981), but if the distribution is misspecified, inconsistent estimates again result. Amemiya and Powell (1981) also applied nonlinear two-stage least squares estimation, which applies to a general class of models including (7.1.2), and whose asymptotic theory was earlier developed by Amemiya (1974b). This estimate, which again is only implicitly defined, is consistent over a wide class of ϵ_i. Amemiya (1977) also developed asymptotic theory for nonlinear three-stage least squares and ML estimates of nonlinear simultaneous equations, to provide an extension to vector dependent variables.

Both models (7.1.1) and (7.1.2) are of the single linear index type

$$E(Y_i \mid X_i) = G(\beta^\tau X_i), \qquad i = 1, 2, \ldots, \tag{7.1.3}$$

almost surely (a.s.), for a function $G : R \to R$. Let F be the distribution function of ϵ_i. In (7.1.1),

$$G(u) = u \int_{-u}^{\infty} dF(v) - \int_{-\infty}^{-u} v \, dF(v).$$

If F is an unknown, nonparametric function, then so is G. Then β can be identified only up to scale. But if we can estimate β up to scale in (7.1.3), with unknown G, we have a form of robustness with respect to F. In (7.1.2),

$$G(u) = \int \{1 + \lambda(u + v)\}^{1/\lambda} \, dF(v) \, 1(\lambda > 0) + e^u \int e^v \, dF(v) \, 1(\lambda = 0),$$

so the same considerations arise. As already noted, we can robustly estimate β (and also λ) in (7.1.2) using nonlinear two-stage least squares. However, the general index form (7.1.3) indicates that we may be able to estimate β up to scale whether or not the transformation of Y_i is of Box–Cox type. Note that β can be identifiable on the basis of objective functions used in other semiparametric methods such as LAD (Powell 1984), symmetrically trimmed least squares (Powell 1986), semiparametric M-estimation (Horowitz 1988), and semiparametric least squares (Horowitz 1986, Lee 1992).

We can estimate β up to scale by the density-weighted averaged derivative statistic

$$U = \binom{n}{2}^{-1} \sum_{i=1}^{n-1} \sum_{j=i+1}^{n} U_{ij},$$

where

$$U_{ij} = h^{-d-1} K' \left(\frac{X_i - X_j}{h} \right) (Y_i - Y_j),$$

such that $K'(u) = (\partial/\partial u)K(u)$, where $K : R^d \to R$ is a differentiable (kernel) function such that $\int_{R^d} K(u)\, du = 1$, and $h = h_n$ is a positive (bandwidth or smoothing) sequence which tends to zero slowly as $n \to \infty$. For an unknown scalar c, $n^{1/2}(U - c\beta)$ was shown to be asymptotically normal when the Y_i, X_i are iid (Powell, Stock, and Stoker 1989) and when they are weakly dependent (Robinson 1989), and to be possibly asymptotically nonnormal in case of an element of long-range dependence (Cheng and Robinson 1994).

Thus, in case of the Tobit model (7.1.1), for example, U achieves the same rate of convergence as that of the ML estimate established by Amemiya (1973) where the ϵ_i are normal, and by Robinson (1982) where the ϵ_i are normal but actually weakly dependent. (Robinson (1982) also established consistency when the ϵ_i are long-range dependent normal.) On the other hand, the smoothing entailed in U might be expected to produce inferior higher-order asymptotic properties, since these more closely approximate the finite-sample situation. We know of no explicit treatment of higher-order properties of the Tobit MLE (or of the Box–Cox estimates we have mentioned), but general results of Pfanzagl (1971, 1973), Bhattacharya and Ghosh (1978), and Linton (1996) suggest that, under suitable conditions, they are likely to have an $O(n^{-1/2})$ Berry–Esseen bound (uniform rate of convergence to normality) and valid Edgeworth expansion in powers of $n^{-1/2}$, and Robinson (1991) established a Berry–Esseen bound for an optimal version of Amemiya's (1977) nonlinear three-stage least squares estimate. Robinson (1995) showed that while in general U has a Berry–Esseen bound of order greater than $n^{-1/2}$, it can be implemented (using suitable h and K) to have an $O(n^{-1/2})$ bound. Correspondingly, Nishiyama and Robinson (2000) (hereafter NR) established that the leading Edgeworth expansion term is $O(n^{-1/2})$ or larger.

Theorems 1 and 2 of NR established valid theoretical and empirical Edgeworth expansions of $Z = n^{-1/2} \sigma_v^{-1} v^\tau (U - c\beta)$ for any $d \times 1$ vector v, where $\sigma_v^2 = v^\tau \Sigma v$ and Σ is the asymptotic variance matrix of $n^{1/2}(U - c\beta)$. Of course Σ is unknown, so that these Edgeworth expansions fall short of being operational. For a consistent estimate, $\hat{\Sigma}$, of Σ, we are led to consideration of $\hat{Z} = n^{1/2} \hat{\sigma}_v^{-1} v^\tau (U - c\beta)$, where $\hat{\sigma}_v^2 = v^\tau \hat{\Sigma} v$. NR in fact proposed such a (jackknife) estimate $\hat{\Sigma}$, and reported valid theoretical and empirical Edgeworth expansions for $\hat{Z}$ in their Theorems 3 and 4. NR also derived a choice of h that is optimal in the sense of minimizing the maximal deviation of Edgeworth correction terms from the normal approximation, and proposed also a consistent estimate of the scale factor of this, leading to a feasible approximately optimal h. NR also reported a Monte Carlo examination of their Edgeworth expansions, and of their bandwidth choice proposal. However, NR did not include the proofs of their Theorems 3 and 4, which entail additional regularity conditions and a considerable and lengthy development beyond that of their Theorems 1 and 2. By marked contrast with the routine application of Slutsky's lemma, which is all that is needed to deduce asymptotic normality of $\hat{Z}$ from that of Z, the Edgeworth expansions for $\hat{Z}$ involve considerable extra work and actually differ from those for Z. The present chapter fills this gap, by providing the proofs of NR's Theorems 3 and 4, while taking for granted the proofs of their Theorems 1 and 2. Callaert and Veraverbeke (1981) and Helmers (1985, 1991) have established higher-order asymptotics for studentized versions of standard U-statistics. Though we follow their broad approach, our U is a U-statistic with an n-dependent "kernel" (through h) which significantly complicates matters, whence we must also make substantial use of lemmas established by Robinson (1995) and NR.

The following section presents regularity conditions and theorem statements. Section 3 contains the main details of the proofs, with some detailed technical material left to appendices.

2   Theoretical and empirical Edgeworth expansions

Our conditions below imply that X has a probability density, $f(x)$, and the existence of the conditional moments $g = E(Y \mid X), q = E(Y^2 \mid X), r = E(Y^3 \mid X)$, where, for a function $h : R^d \to R$, we write $h = h(X)$. For such a function, suitably smooth, we define $h' = (\partial/\partial X)h(X)$, $h'' = (\partial/\partial X^\tau)h'(X)$, and $h''' = (\partial/\partial X^\tau) \text{vec}(h'')$. Write $e = fg$, $\mu = \mu(X, Y) = Yf' - e'$, $a = g'f - E(g'f)$, $\mu \cdot = E(\mu) = -E(g'f)$, and $\Sigma = 4\,\text{Var}(\mu)$. We introduce the following assumptions.

(i) $E(Y^6) < \infty$.

(ii) Σ is finite and positive definite.

(iii)   The underlying measure of (X^τ, Y) can be written as $\mu_X \times \mu_Y$, where μ_X and μ_Y are Lebesgue measure on R^d and R respectively, and (X_i^τ, Y_i) are iid observations on (X^τ, Y).

(iv) f is $L + 1$ times differentiable, and f and its first $L + 1$ derivatives are bounded, for $2L > d + 2$.

(v) g is $L + 1$ times differentiable, and e and its first $L + 1$ derivatives are bounded, for $L \geq 1$.

(vi) q is twice differentiable, and $q', q'', g', g'', g''', E(|Y|^3 \mid X)f$, and qf' are bounded.

(vii) $f, gf, g'f$, and qf vanish on the boundaries of their convex (possibly infinite) supports.

(viii) $K(u)$ is even and differentiable,

$$\int_{R^d} \{(1 + \|u\|^L)|K(u)| + \|K'(u)\|\}\, du + \sup_{u \in R^d} \|K'(u)\| < \infty,$$

and for the same L as in (iv),

$$\int_{R^d} u_1^{l_1} \cdots u_d^{l_d} K(u)\, du \begin{cases} = 1 & \text{if } l_1 + \cdots + l_d = 0, \\ = 0 & \text{if } 0 < l_1 + \cdots + l_d < L, \\ \neq 0 & \text{if } l_1 + \cdots + l_d = L. \end{cases}$$

(ix) $(\log n)^9 / nh^{d+2} + nh^{2L} \to 0$ as $n \to \infty$.
(x) $\sup_{v^\tau v = 1} \lim\sup_{|t| \to \infty} |E \exp\{it\sigma_v^{-1} v^\tau (\mu - \mu.)\}| < 1$.

These assumptions are the same as those of Theorem 1 of NR except that (i) strengthens their third-moment assumption to sixth moments, our treatment of studentization requiring finite third moments of certain squared terms.

In our studentized statistic $\hat{Z}$ we take

$$\hat{\Sigma} = \frac{4}{(n-1)(n-2)^2} \sum_{i=1}^n \left\{ \sum_{j \neq i}^n (U_{ij} - U) \right\} \left\{ \sum_{k \neq i}^n (U_{ik} - U)^\tau \right\}, \tag{7.2.1}$$

a jackknife estimate of Σ. We are concerned with approximating

$$\hat{F}(z) = P(\hat{Z} \leq z)$$

by the Edgeworth expansion

$$F^+(z) = \Phi(z) - \phi(z)$$
$$\times \left[n^{1/2} h^L \kappa_1 - \frac{\kappa_2}{nh^{d+2}} z - \frac{4}{3n^{1/2}} \{(2z^2 + 1)\kappa_3 + 3(z^2 + 1)\kappa_4\} \right],$$

where $\Phi(z)$ and $\phi(z)$ are respectively the distribution function and density function of the standard normal, and, with

$$\Delta^{(l_1, \ldots, l_d)} = \frac{\partial^{l_1 + \cdots + l_d}}{\partial x_1^{l_1} \cdots \partial x_d^{l_d}},$$

$$\kappa_1 = \frac{2(-1)^L \sigma_v^{-1}}{L!} \sum_{\substack{0 \leq l_1, \ldots, l_d \leq L \\ l_1 + \cdots + l_d = L}} \cdots \sum \left\{ \int \prod_{i=1}^d u_i^{l_i} K(u)\, du \right\} E\left[(\Delta^{(l_1, \ldots, l_d)} v^\tau f') g \right],$$

$$\kappa_2 = 2\sigma_v^{-2} \int \{v^\tau K'(u)\}^2\, du\, E\{(q - g^2)f\},$$

$$\kappa_3 = \sigma_v^{-3} E[\{r - 3(q - g^2)g - g^3\}(v^\tau f')^3 - 3(q - g^2)(v^\tau f')^2(v^\tau a) - (v^\tau a)^3],$$

$$\kappa_4 = -\sigma_v^{-3} E[f(q - g^2)(v^\tau f')(v^\tau a'v) - f(v^\tau f')\{v^\tau(q' - 2gg')\}(v^\tau a)$$
$$- f(q - g^2)(v^\tau a)(v^\tau f''v) + f(v^\tau g')(v^\tau a)^2].$$

Theorem A. *Under assumptions* (i)–(x), *as* $n \to \infty$,

$$\sup_{v:v^\tau v=1} \sup_z |\hat{F}(z) - F^+(z)| = o(n^{-1/2} + n^{-1}h^{-d-2} + n^{1/2}h^L).$$

The correction terms in $F^+(z)$ are of the same orders as those in the un-studentized case (see. Theorem 1 of NR), though their coefficients are mostly different.

The κ_i are unknown, but a feasible, empirical Edgeworth expansion is

$$\hat{F}^+(z) = \Phi(z) - \phi(z)\left[n^{1/2}h^L \tilde{\kappa}_1 - \frac{\tilde{\kappa}_2}{nh^{d+2}}z - \frac{4}{3n^{1/2}}\{(2z^2+1)\tilde{\kappa}_3 + 3(z^2+1)\tilde{\kappa}_4\}\right],$$

where

$$\tilde{\kappa}_1 = \frac{2(-1)^L \hat{\sigma}_v^{-1}}{L!} \sum_{\substack{0 \le l_1,\ldots,l_d \le L \\ l_1+\cdots+l_d=L}} \cdots \sum \left\{\int \prod_{i=1}^d u_i^{l_i} K(u)\, du\right\}$$

$$\times \frac{1}{n}\sum_{i=1}^n \{\Delta^{(l_1,\ldots,l_d)} v^\tau \tilde{f}'(X_i)\} Y_i,$$

$$\tilde{\kappa}_2 = \hat{\sigma}_v^{-2} \binom{n}{2}^{-1} \sum_{i=1}^{n-1}\sum_{j=i+1}^n h^{d+2}\bar{W}_{ij}^2, \qquad \hat{\kappa}_3 = \frac{\hat{\sigma}_v^{-3}}{n}\sum_{i=1}^n \bar{V}_i^3,$$

$$\hat{\kappa}_4 = \frac{\hat{\sigma}_v^{-3}}{n(n-1)}\sum_{i=1}^n\sum_{j\ne i}^n v^\tau U_{ij}\bar{V}_i\bar{V}_j,$$

where for positive b and a function $H: R^d \to R$

$$\tilde{f}(X_i) = \frac{1}{(n-1)b^d}\sum_{j\ne i}^n H\left(\frac{X_i - X_j}{b}\right),$$

and

$$\bar{U}_i = \frac{1}{n-1}\sum_{j\ne i}^n U_{ij}, \quad \bar{V}_i = v^\tau(\bar{U}_i - U), \quad \bar{W}_{ij} = v^\tau(U_{ij} - \bar{U}_i - \bar{U}_j + U).$$

$$(7.2.2)$$

We impose the following additional assumptions, which are identical to those of Theorem 2 of NR:

(iv′) f is $L + 2$ times differentiable, and f and its first $L + 2$ derivatives are bounded, where $2L > d + 2$.

(v′) g is $L + 2$ times differentiable, and e and its first $L + 2$ derivatives are bounded.

(ix') $(\log n)^9/nh^{d+3} + nh^{2L} \to 0$ as $n \to \infty$.

(xi') $H(u)$ is even and $L+1$ times differentiable, and

$$\int_{R^d} H(u)\, du = 1,$$

$$\int_{R^d} \left\| \Delta^{(l_1,\dots,l_d)} H'(u) \right\| du + \sup_{u\in R^d} \left\| \Delta^{(l_1,\dots,l_d)} H'(u) \right\| < \infty$$

for any integers $l_1, \dots, l_d$ satisfying $0 \le l_1 + \cdots + l_d \le L$ and $0 \le l_i \le L, i = 1, \dots, d$.

(xii) $b \to 0$ and $(\log n)^2/nb^{d+2+2L} = O(1)$ as $n \to \infty$.

Theorem B. *Under assumptions* (i)–(iii), (iv'), (v'), (vi)–(viii), (ix'), *and* (x)–(xii),

$$\sup_{v\,:\,v^\tau v=1}\ \sup_z |\hat{F}(z) - \hat{F}^+(z)| = o(n^{-1/2} + n^{-1}h^{-d-2} + n^{1/2}h^L) \qquad a.s.$$

3 Proof of Theorems A and B

Proof of Theorem A: In the sequel, C denotes a generic, finite, positive constant and the qualification "for sufficiently large n" may be omitted.

As is standard in U-statistic theory, we write

$$n^{1/2}\sigma_v^{-1}v^\tau(U - \mu.)$$

$$= \frac{2}{\sqrt{n}} \sum_{i=1}^n V_i + n^{1/2}\binom{n}{2}^{-1} \sum_{i=1}^{n-1}\sum_{j=i+1}^n W_{ij} + n^{1/2}\sigma_v^{-1}v^\tau(EU-\mu.)$$

$$= \quad \bar{V} \qquad\quad + \qquad\quad \bar{W} \qquad\quad + \quad \Delta. \qquad (7.3.1)$$

where $U_i = E(U_{ij}\,|\,i)$, $V_i = \sigma_v^{-1}v^\tau(U_i - EU)$, and $W_{ij} = \sigma_v^{-1}v^\tau(U_{ij} - EU) - V_i - V_j$, such that $E(\cdot\,|\,i_1,\dots,i_r) = E(\cdot\,|\,(X_{i_j}, Y_{i_j}), j = 1, \dots, r)$. Writing $S = 4\,\mathrm{Var}(U_i)$, $s^2 = \sigma_v^{-2}v^\tau S v$, Taylor's theorem gives

$$\sigma_v\hat{\sigma}_v^{-1} = s^{-1} - \frac{s^{-3}}{2}\left(\hat{\sigma}_v^{-2}\hat{\sigma}_v^2 - s^2\right) + \frac{3}{8}\left\{s^2 + \theta\left(\hat{\sigma}_v^{-2}\hat{\sigma}_v^2 - s^2\right)\right\}^{-5/2}\left(\hat{\sigma}_v^{-2}\hat{\sigma}_v^2 - s^2\right)^2$$

$$= s^{-1} + \qquad \tilde{R} \qquad + \qquad\qquad \tilde{\tilde{R}} \qquad\qquad (7.3.2)$$

for some $\theta\in[0,\,1]$. Similarly to Callaert and Veraverbeke (1981), we expand $\tilde{R}$ as follows. With $\tilde{V}_i = E(V_j W_{ij}\,|\,i)$, $\tilde{W}_{jk} = E(W_{ij} W_{ik}\,|\,j, k)$, we have

$$\tilde{R} = T + Q + R, \qquad T = T_1 + T_2 + T_3, \qquad Q = Q_1 + Q_2,$$

$$R = R_1 + R_2 + R_3 + R_4 + R_5$$

where

$$T_1 = \frac{4\delta n}{(n-2)^2} E\left(W_{12}^2\right), \qquad T_2 = \frac{\delta}{n} \sum_{i=1}^{n} \left\{ (4V_i^2 - S^2) + 8\tilde{V}_i \right\},$$

$$T_3 = 4\delta \binom{n-1}{2}^{-1} \sum_{i<j}^{n} \tilde{W}_{ij},$$

$$Q_1 = 4\delta \binom{n}{2}^{-1} \sum_{i<j} \{(V_i + V_j)W_{ij} - \tilde{V}_i - \tilde{V}_j\},$$

$$Q_2 = -\frac{8\delta}{n} \binom{n-1}{2}^{-1} \sum_{i=1}^{n} \sum_{k<m}^{n} {}^{(i)} V_i W_{km},$$

$$R_1 = -4\delta \binom{n}{2}^{-1} \sum_{i<j} V_i V_j,$$

$$R_2 = \frac{4\delta}{n-2} \binom{n-1}{2}^{-1} \sum_{i=1}^{n} \sum_{k<m}^{n} {}^{(i)} (W_{ik}W_{im} - \tilde{W}_{km}),$$

$$R_3 = \frac{4\delta n}{(n-2)^2} \binom{n}{2}^{-1} \sum_{i<j} \left\{ W_{ij}^2 - \tilde{W}_{ii} - \tilde{W}_{jj} + E\left(W_{12}^2\right) \right\},$$

$$R_4 = \frac{8\delta}{(n-2)^2} \sum_{i=1}^{n} \left\{ \tilde{W}_{ii} - E\left(W_{12}^2\right) \right\},$$

$$R_5 = -\frac{4\delta n(n-1)}{(n-2)^2} \left\{ \binom{n-1}{2}^{-1} \sum_{i<j} W_{ij} \right\}^2,$$

where $\delta = -s^{-3}/2$, and

$$\sum_{k<m}^{n} {}^{(i)}$$

denotes summation with respect to k and m for $1 \le k < m \le n$ excluding $k = i$ and $m = i$. Because

$$\hat{Z} = (s^{-1} + \tilde{R} + \tilde{\tilde{R}})(\bar{V} + \bar{W} + \Delta),$$

by a standard inequality

$$\sup_z |\hat{F}(z) - F^+(z)| \le \sup_z |P((s^{-1} + T + Q)(\bar{V} + \bar{W}) + s^{-1}\Delta \le z) - F^+(z)|$$

$$+ P(|(R + \tilde{\tilde{R}})(\bar{V} + \bar{W} + \Delta) + (T + Q)\Delta| \ge a_n) + O(a_n)$$

$$(7.3.3)$$

for $a_n > 0$; here and subsequently we drop reference to $\sup_{\nu : \nu^\tau \nu = 1}$. Taking

$a_n = (1/\log n) \max(n^{-1/2}, n^{-1}h^{-d-2}, n^{1/2}h^L)$, we bound the second term on the right of (7.3.3) by

$$P\left(|(R+\tilde{\tilde{R}})(\bar{V}+\bar{W}+\Delta)| \geq \frac{a_n}{2}\right) + P\left(|(T+Q)\Delta| \geq \frac{n^{1/2}h^L}{2\log n}\right)$$

$$\leq P\left(|R+\tilde{\tilde{R}}| \geq \frac{a_n}{2\log n}\right) + P(|\bar{V}+\bar{W}+\Delta| \geq \log n)$$

$$+ P\left(|(T+Q)\Delta| \geq \frac{n^{1/2}h^L}{2\log n}\right). \tag{7.3.4}$$

The first term in (7.3.4) is, by an elementary inequality, bounded by

$$P\left(|R| \geq \frac{a_n}{4\log n}\right) + P\left(\frac{|\tilde{\tilde{R}}|}{\tilde{R}^2} \geq C_0\right) + P\left(\tilde{R}^2 \geq \frac{a_n}{4C_0\log n}\right) \tag{7.3.5}$$

for a constant C_0 determined later. The third term of (7.3.5) is bounded by

$$P\left(T_2^2 \geq \frac{a_n}{12C_0\log n}\right) + P\left(|T_1+T_3|^2 \geq \frac{a_n}{12C_0\log n}\right) + P\left(|Q+R|^2 \geq \frac{a_n}{12C_0\log n}\right)$$

$$= \quad (a) \quad + \quad (b) \quad + \quad (c).$$

Lemmas 10–19 and Markov's inequality give, for $\zeta > 0$,

$$(a) \leq \frac{E|T_2|^{2(1+\zeta)}}{\left(\frac{a_n}{12C_0\log n}\right)^{1+\zeta}} \leq \frac{Cn^{-(1+\zeta)}(\log n)^{2(1+\zeta)}}{n^{-\frac{1}{2}(1+\zeta)}} = o(n^{-1/2}),$$

$$(b) \leq \frac{E|T_1+T_3|^{2(1+\zeta)}}{\left(\frac{a_n}{12C_0\log n}\right)^{1+\zeta}} \leq \frac{C(n^{-1}h^{-d-2})^{2(1+\zeta)}(\log n)^{2(1+\zeta)}}{(n^{-1}h^{-d-2})^{1+\zeta}}$$

$$= o(n^{-1}h^{-d-2}),$$

$$(c) \leq \frac{E|R+Q|^2}{\frac{a_n}{12C_0\log n}} \leq \frac{Cn^{-2}h^{-d-2}(\log n)^2}{n^{-1/2}} = o(n^{-1}h^{-d-2}),$$

where $\zeta = \frac{2}{7}$ suffices in (b), and ζ arbitrarily small suffices in (a).

The first term of (7.3.5) is, using Markov's inequality, (ix), and Lemmas 15–19, bounded by

$$\frac{16E(R^2)(\log n)^2}{a_n^2} \leq C(n^{-1}+n^{-2}h^{-2d-4})(\log n)^4$$

$$= o(n^{-1/2}+n^{-1}h^{-d-2}).$$

Now, in view of (7.3.2), $\tilde{\tilde{R}} = \frac{3}{2}s(1-2\theta s\tilde{R})^{-5/2}\tilde{R}^2$ so that because $\tilde{\tilde{R}} \geq 0$ and

$0 \le \theta \le 1$,

$$P\left(\frac{\tilde{\tilde{R}}}{\tilde{R}^2} \ge C_0\right) = P\left(\frac{3}{2}s(1 - 2\theta s\tilde{R})^{-5/2} \ge C_0\right)$$

$$\le P\left(|\tilde{R}| \ge \frac{1}{2s}\left\{1 - \left(\frac{3s}{2C_0}\right)^{2/5}\right\}\right). \quad (7.3.6)$$

Taylor's expansion of s^r around $s^2 = 1$ and Lemma 2 of Robinson (1995) give, for integer r,

$$s^r = 1 + O\left(\sigma_v^{-2} v^\tau (S - \Sigma)v\right) = 1 + O(h^L), \quad (7.3.7)$$

so that we can choose C_0 such that $C_0 > \frac{3}{2}s$ for sufficiently large n by (ii). Then by (7.3.7) and Markov's inequality, (7.3.6) is bounded by a constant times $E|T + Q + R|^3 = O(n^{-3/2} + n^{-3}h^{-3d-6})$ from Lemmas 10–19, so that the second term of (7.3.5) is $O(n^{-3/2} + n^{-3}h^{-3d-6})$. Therefore,

$$P\left(|R + \tilde{R}| \ge \frac{a_n}{\log n}\right) = O(n^{-1/2} + n^{-1}h^{-d-2}). \quad (7.3.8)$$

Put $F(z) = P[n^{1/2}\sigma_v^{-1} v^\tau (U - \mu.) \le z]$. Then

$$P(|\bar{V} + \bar{W} + \Delta| \ge \log n) = 1 - F(\log n) + F(-\log n). \quad (7.3.9)$$

NR proved in Theorem 1 that

$$\sup_z |F(z) - \tilde{F}(z)| = o(n^{-1/2} + n^{-1}h^{-d-2} + n^{1/2}h^L),$$

where

$$\tilde{F}(z) = \Phi(z) - \phi(z)\left\{n^{1/2}h^L\kappa_1 + \frac{\kappa_2}{nh^{d+2}}z + \frac{4(\kappa_3 + 3\kappa_4)}{3n^{1/2}}(z^2 - 1)\right\}, \quad (7.3.10)$$

which implies that for any z

$$1 - F(z) + F(-z) = 1 - \tilde{F}(z) + \tilde{F}(-z) + o(n^{-1/2} + n^{-1}h^{-d-2} + n^{1/2}h^L). \quad (7.3.11)$$

Now by (7.3.10),

$$1 - \tilde{F}(z) + \tilde{F}(-z) = 1 - \Phi(z) + \Phi(-z) + \phi(z)\frac{2\kappa_2}{nh^{d+2}}z$$

$$= 2 - 2\Phi(z) + \phi(z)\frac{2\kappa_2}{nh^{d+2}}z. \quad (7.3.12)$$

Substituting (7.3.12) into (7.3.11) and putting $z = \log n$, because $1 - \Phi$ $(\log n) = o(n^{-1/2})$ and $\phi(\log n)\log n = o(n^{-1/2})$, we have

$$1 - F(\log n) + F(-\log n) = o(n^{-1/2} + n^{-1}h^{-d-2} + n^{1/2}h^L). \quad (7.3.13)$$

By (7.3.9) and (7.3.13),

$$P(|\bar{V} + \bar{W} + \Delta| \geq \log n) = o(n^{-1/2} + n^{-1}h^{-d-2} + n^{1/2}h^L). \tag{7.3.14}$$

Finally, Markov's inequality, (ix), Lemma 1 of Robinson (1995), and Lemmas 10–14 bound the last term of (7.3.4) by

$$\frac{\Delta^2 E\,|T + Q|^2 (2\log n)^2}{nh^{2L}} \leq C(n^{-1} + n^{-2}h^{-2d-4})(\log n)^2$$

$$= o(n^{-1/2} + n^{-1}h^{-d-2}). \tag{7.3.15}$$

Substituting (7.3.8), (7.3.14), and (7.3.15) into (7.3.4),

$$P(|(R + \tilde{R})(\bar{V} + \bar{W} + \Delta) + (T + Q)\Delta| \geq a_n)$$

$$= o(n^{-1/2} + n^{-1}h^{-d-2} + n^{1/2}h^L). \tag{7.3.16}$$

To deal with the first term on the right of (7.3.3), write $b_2 = s^{-1}\bar{V}$, $b_3 = s^{-1}\bar{W}$, $\tilde{b}_2 = (T + Q)\bar{V}$, $\tilde{b}_3 = (T + Q)\bar{W}$, $b_1 = b_2 + b_3$, $\tilde{b}_1 = \tilde{b}_2 + \tilde{b}_3$, $B = b_1 + \tilde{b}_1$, and define

$$\chi^+(t) = \int e^{itz}\,dF^+(z)$$

$$= e^{-t^2/2}\left[1 + \left\{n^{1/2}h^L\kappa_1 - \frac{4(\kappa_3 + 2\kappa_4)}{n^{1/2}}\right\}(it)\right.$$

$$\left. - \frac{\kappa_2}{nh^{d+2}}(it)^2 - \frac{4(2\kappa_3 + 3\kappa_4)}{3n^{1/2}}(it)^3\right].$$

Essen's smoothing lemma gives, for $N_0 = \log n \min(\eta n^{1/2}, nh^{d+2})$, $\eta = (E|2s^{-1}V_1|^3)^{-1}$,

$$\sup_z |P((s^{-1} + T + Q)(\bar{V} + \bar{W}) + s^{-1}\Delta \leq z) - F^+(z)|$$

$$\leq \int_{-N_0}^{N_0}\left|\frac{Ee^{it(B+s^{-1}\Delta)} - \chi^+(t)}{t}\right|\,dt + O\left(N_0^{-1}\right),$$

which, for $p = \min(\log n, \varepsilon n^{1/2}, nh^{d+2})$, is bounded by

$$\int_{-p}^{p}\left|\frac{Ee^{it(B+s^{-1}\Delta)} - \chi^+(t)}{t}\right|\,dt + \int_{p\leq|t|\leq N_0}\left|\frac{Ee^{it(B+s^{-1}\Delta)}}{t}\right|\,dt$$

$$+ \int_{|t|\geq p}\left|\frac{\chi^+(t)}{t}\right|\,dt + o(n^{-1/2} + n^{-1}h^{-d-2})$$

$$= \text{(I)} + \text{(II)} + \text{(III)} + o(n^{-1/2} + n^{-1}h^{-d-2}).$$

Here we can set $\varepsilon \in (0, \eta]$ for sufficiently large n as discussed in the proof of the theorem of Robinson (1995), using (7.3.7) also, so that $p \leq N_0$. We first mention an inequality frequently used hereafter:

$$\left| e^{ix} - 1 - ix - \cdots - \frac{(ix)^{k-1}}{(k-1)!} \right| \le \frac{|x|^k}{k!} \tag{7.3.17}$$

for integer k and real x.

Estimation of (I): Since $s^{-1}\Delta$ is nonstochastic,

$$E\{e^{it(B+s^{-1}\Delta)}\} = e^{its^{-1}\Delta} E(e^{itB}), \tag{7.3.18}$$

where (7.3.7) and (7.3.17) yield

$$e^{its^{-1}\Delta} = 1 + it\Delta + O(t^2\Delta^2 + |t|h^L\Delta). \tag{7.3.19}$$

Writing $\tilde{b}_2 = \tilde{b}_2' + \tilde{b}_2''$, where $\tilde{b}_2' = T\bar{V}$ and $\tilde{b}_2'' = Q\bar{V}$, and applying (7.3.17) repeatedly, we have

$$
\begin{aligned}
E(e^{itB}) &= E(e^{itb_1}) + E(e^{itB} - e^{itb_1}) \\
&= E(e^{itb_1}) + \left\{ Ee^{it(b_1+\tilde{b}_2+\tilde{b}_3)} - Ee^{it(b_1+\tilde{b}_2')} \right\} + \left\{ Ee^{it(b_1+\tilde{b}_2)} - E(e^{itb_1}) \right\} \\
&= E(e^{itb_1}) + O(|t|E|\tilde{b}_2'' + \tilde{b}_3|) + \left\{ Ee^{it(b_1+\tilde{b}_2')} - E(e^{itb_1}) \right. \\
&\quad - it\, E(\tilde{b}_2'e^{itb_1}) \} + it\, E(\tilde{b}_2'e^{itb_1} - \tilde{b}_2'e^{itb_2}) + it\, E(\tilde{b}_2'e^{itb_2}) \\
&= E(e^{itb_1}) + it\, E(\tilde{b}_2'e^{itb_2}) + O(|t|E|\tilde{b}_2'' + \tilde{b}_3| + t^2(E|\tilde{b}_2'|^2 + E|\tilde{b}_2'\tilde{b}_3|)).
\end{aligned} \tag{7.3.20}
$$

Write

$$E(e^{itb_1}) = E\left[e^{itb_2} \left\{ 1 + itb_3 + \frac{(it)^2}{2}b_3^2 \right\} \right] + O(|t|^3 E|b_3|^3), \tag{7.3.21}$$

and put $\gamma(t) = E(e^{it(2/\sqrt{ns})V_1})$. As in Appendix A of NR,

$$E(e^{itb_2}) = \{\gamma(t)\}^n, \tag{7.3.22}$$

$$E(b_3 e^{itb_2}) = \{\gamma(t)\}^{n-2} \left[\frac{4(it)^2}{n^{1/2}} E(W_{12}V_1V_2) \right.$$
$$\left. + O\left(\frac{t^2h^L}{n^{1/2}} + \left(\frac{t^4}{n^{3/2}} + \frac{|t|^3}{n} \right)h^{-\frac{2}{3}d-1} \right) \right], \tag{7.3.23}$$

$$E(b_3^2 e^{itb_2}) = \frac{2}{n-1}\{\gamma(t)\}^{n-2}\left[E(W_{12}^2) + O\left(\frac{h^L}{nh^{d+2}}n + |t|n^{-1/2}h^{-\frac{4}{3}d-2} \right) \right]$$
$$+ \{\gamma(t)\}^{n-3} O\left(|t|n^{-3/2}h^{-\frac{4}{3}d-2} \right)$$
$$+ \{\gamma(t)\}^{n-4} O\left(t^4 n^{-1} + t^8 n^{-3}h^{-\frac{4}{3}d-2} + t^6 n^{-2}h^{-\frac{4}{3}d-2} \right). \tag{7.3.24}$$

Since, for $m = 0, 1, 2, 3$,

$$\{\gamma(t)\}^{n-m} = e^{-t^2/2}\left\{1 + \frac{E(2V_1)^3}{6n^{1/2}s^3}(it)^3\right\} + o\left(n^{-1/2}(|t|^3 + t^6)e^{-t^2/4}\right),$$

(7.3.25)

by Lemma 1 of Robinson (1995), (a) in Appendix B, and (7.3.18)–(7.3.25),

$$E\{e^{it(B+s^{-1}\Delta)}\} = \{1 + it\Delta + O(t^2 nh^{2L} + |t|n^{1/2}h^{2L})\}$$

$$\times \left\{\left[e^{-t^2/2}\left\{1 + \frac{4E(2V_1^3)}{3n^{1/2}s^3}(it)^3\right\} + o\left(n^{-1/2}(|t|^3 + t^6)e^{-t^2/4}\right)\right]\right.$$

$$\times \left[1 + \frac{4(it)^3}{n^{1/2}}E(W_{12}V_1V_2) + \frac{(it)^2}{n}E(W_{12}^3) - \frac{2(it)^2}{n}E(W_{12}^2)\right.$$

$$\left. - \frac{(it)^3 + (it)}{n^{1/2}}\{4E(V_1^3) + 8E(W_{12}V_1V_2)\} + O(A_n)\right]$$

$$\left. + (|t|E|\tilde{b}_2''| + \tilde{b}_3| + t^2(E|\tilde{b}_2'|^2 + E|\tilde{b}_2'b_3|))\right\},$$

(7.3.26)

where

$$A_n = \frac{|t|^3 h^L}{n^{1/2}} + \left(\frac{|t|^5}{n^{3/2}} + \frac{t^4}{n}\right)h^{-\frac{2}{3}d-1} + \frac{t^2}{n^2 h^{d+2}} + \frac{t^2 h^L}{n^2 h^{d+2}}$$

$$+ \frac{|t|^3}{n^{3/2}h^{\frac{4}{3}d+2}} + \frac{t^6}{n} + \frac{t^{10}}{n^3 h^{\frac{4}{3}d+2}} + \frac{t^8}{n^2 h^{\frac{4}{3}d+2}} + \frac{|t|^3}{(nh^{d+2})^{3/2}}$$

$$+ \frac{t^2}{n^2 h^{d+2}} + \frac{|t|^3}{n^{3/2}h^{d+2}} + \frac{t^2 h^L}{nh^{d+2}} + \frac{t^2}{n} + \frac{|t|^3 + t^4}{n} + \frac{|t|^3}{n^{3/2}}$$

$$+ \frac{|t|^7}{n^3 h^{d+2}} + \frac{t^6}{n^{5/2}h^{d+2}} + \frac{|t|^5 + t^4}{n^2 h^{d+2}}$$

$$= o\left(\frac{t^2 + t^{10}}{nh^{d+2}} + \frac{t^2 + t^6}{n^{1/2}}\right).$$

Expanding (7.3.26), we have

$$E\{e^{it(B+s^{-1}\Delta)}\} = e^{-t^2/2}\left[1 + \left\{\Delta - \frac{4E(V_1^3) + 8E(W_{12}V_1V_2)}{n^{1/2}}\right\}(it)\right.$$

$$\left. - \frac{E(W_{12}^2)}{n}(it)^2 - \frac{4\{2E(V_1^3) + 3E(W_{12}V_1V_2)\}}{3n^{1/2}}(it)^3\right] + D_n,$$

(7.3.27)

where

$$D_n = O\left(\left\{e^{-t^2/2}\frac{|t|^3}{n^{1/2}} + o\left(n^{-1/2}(t^6 + |t|^3)e^{-t^2/4}\right)\right\}\left\{\frac{t^2}{n^2h^{d+2}} + \frac{|t|^3 + |t|}{n^{1/2}} + A_n\right\}\right.$$

$$+ e^{-t^2/2}(|t|n^{1/2}h^L + t^2h^{2L} + |t|n^{1/2}h^{2L})\left(\frac{t^2}{n^2h^{d+2}} + \frac{|t|^3 + |t|}{n^{1/2}} + A_n\right)$$

$$+ (|t|n^{1/2}h^L + t^2nh^{2L})\left\{e^{-t^2/2}\frac{|t|^3}{n^{1/2}} + o\left(n^{-1/2}(t^6 + |t|^3)e^{-t^2/4}\right)\right\}$$

$$+ (|t|n^{1/2}h^L + t^2nh^{2L})\left\{e^{-t^2/2}\frac{|t|^3}{n^{1/2}} + o\left(n^{-1/2}(t^6 + |t|^3)e^{-t^2/4}\right)\right\}$$

$$\times \left(\frac{t^2}{n^2h^{d+2}} + \frac{|t|^3 + |t|}{n^{1/2}} + A_n\right) + (|t| + t^2n^{1/2}h^L + |t|^3nh^{2L})$$

$$\times \left. E|\tilde{b}_2'' + \tilde{b}_3| + (t^2 + |t|^3n^{1/2}h^L + t^4nh^{2L})(E|\tilde{b}_2'|^2 + E|\tilde{b}_2'b_3|)\right).$$

(7.3.28)

By Hölder's inequality, equation (14) of Robinson (1995), and Lemmas 9–14,

$$E|\tilde{b}_2''| = E|Q\bar{V}| \le (E|Q|^2E|\bar{V}|^2)^{1/2} = O\left(n^{-1}h^{-(d+2)/2}\right), \quad (7.3.29)$$

$$E|\tilde{b}_3| = E|(T + Q)\bar{W}| \le (E|T + Q|^2E|\bar{W}|^2)^{1/2}$$
$$= O((n^{-1/2} + n^{-1}h^{-d-2})(n^{-1}h^{-d-2})^{1/2}). \quad (7.3.30)$$

Writing $E|\tilde{b}_2'|^2 \le C(|T_1|^2E|\bar{V}|^2 + E|T_2\bar{V}|^2 + E|T_3\bar{V}|^2)$, Lemmas 9, 10, and 12 and Hölder's inequality give

$$|T_1|^2E|\bar{V}|^2 + E|T_3\bar{V}|^2 \le |T_1|^2E|\bar{V}|^2 + (E|T_3|^4E|\bar{V}|^4)^{1/2} = O(n^{-2}h^{-2d-4}),$$

and (7.3.7), (i), (iii), Lemma 1(d) of NR, and (7.A.1) give

$$E|T_2\bar{V}|^2 \le \frac{C}{n^3}E\left|\sum_{i=1}^{n}\left(4V_i^2 - s^2 + 8\tilde{V}_i\right)\sum_{j=1}^{n}V_j\right|^2$$

$$= \frac{C}{n^3}\left\{nE\left|\left(4V_1^2 - s^2 + 8\tilde{V}_1\right)V_1\right|^2\right.$$

$$\left. + n(n - 1)E\left|\left(4V_1^2 - s^2 + 8\tilde{V}_1\right)V_2\right|^2\right\}$$

$$= O(n^{-1}).$$

Thus

$$E|\tilde{b}_2'|^2 = E|T\bar{V}|^2 = O(n^{-1} + n^{-2}h^{-2d-4}). \quad (7.3.31)$$

Hölder's inequality, (7.3.31), and equation (14) of Robinson (1995) yield

$$E|\tilde{b}'_2 b_3| = \left(E|\tilde{b}'_2|^2 E|b_3|^2\right)^{1/2} = O((n^{-1/2} + n^{-1}h^{-d-2})(n^{-1}h^{-d-2})^{1/2}).$$
$$(7.3.32)$$

It is straightforward due to (C.1) of NR that $E(V_1^3) = E(v_1^3) + o(1)$ and $E(W_{12}V_1V_2) = E(W_{12}v_1v_2) + o(1)$, where $v_i = \sigma_v^{-1}v^\tau\{\mu(X_i, Y_i) - \mu.\}$. Therefore, using (7.3.27)–(7.3.32) and Lemmas 11–13 of NR,

$$(\mathrm{I}) \le \int_{-\log n}^{\log n} \left| \frac{Ee^{it(B+s^{-1}\Delta)} - \chi^+(t)}{t} \right| dt = o(n^{-1/2} + n^{-1}h^{-d-2} + n^{1/2}h^L).$$

Estimation of (II): Put $\tilde{b}'_3 = T\bar{W}$, $\tilde{b}''_3 = Q\bar{W}$; then, noting that $\tilde{b}_3 = \tilde{b}'_3 + \tilde{b}''_3$ and $B = b_1 + \tilde{b}_2 + (\tilde{b}'_3 + \tilde{b}''_3)$, we have, using (7.3.17),

$$\left|Ee^{itB}\right| \le \left|Ee^{itB} - Ee^{it\,(b_1+\tilde{b}_2+\tilde{b}'_3)} - it\,E\tilde{b}''_3 e^{it(b_1+\tilde{b}_2+\tilde{b}'_3)}\right|$$
$$+ \left|Ee^{it(b_1+\tilde{b}_2+\tilde{b}'_3)}\right| + |t|\left|E\tilde{b}''_3 e^{it(b_1+\tilde{b}_2+\tilde{b}'_3)}\right|$$
$$\le |t|^2 E|\tilde{b}''_3|^2 + \left|Ee^{it(b_1+\tilde{b}_2+\tilde{b}'_3)}\right| + |t|\left|E\tilde{b}''_3 e^{it(b_1+\tilde{b}_2+\tilde{b}'_3)}\right|.$$
$$(7.3.33)$$

Writing $E|b''_3|^2 \le C(E|Q_1\bar{W}|^2 + E|Q_2\bar{W}|^2)$, we have from Hölder's inequality, equation (14) of Robinson (1995), and Lemma 14

$$E|Q_2\bar{W}|^2 \le \left(E|Q_2|^4\right)^{1/2}(E|\bar{W}|^4)^{1/2} = O((n^{-4}h^{-3d-4})^{1/2}n^{-1}h^{-d-2})$$
$$(7.3.34)$$

and

$$E|Q_1\bar{W}|^2 \le \frac{C}{n^7}E\left|\sum_{i<j}\sum\{(V_i + V_j)W_{ij} - \tilde{V}_i - \tilde{V}_j\}\sum_{k<l}\sum W_{kl}\right|^2$$

$$\le \frac{C}{n^7}E\left|\sum_{i<j<k<l}\sum\sum\sum\{(V_i + V_j)W_{ij} - \tilde{V}_i - \tilde{V}_j\}W_{kl}\right|^2$$

$$+ \frac{C}{n^7}E\left|\sum_{i<j<l}\sum\sum\{(V_i + V_j)W_{ij} - \tilde{V}_i - \tilde{V}_j\}W_{il}\right|^2$$

$$+ \frac{C}{n^7}E\left|\sum_{i<j}\sum\{(V_i + V_j)W_{ij} - \tilde{V}_i - \tilde{V}_j\}W_{ij}\right|^2$$

$$\leq \frac{C}{n^7} \sum \sum_{i<j<k<l} \sum \sum E|\{(V_i + V_j)W_{ij} - \tilde{V}_i - \tilde{V}_j\}W_{kl}|^2$$

$$+ \frac{C}{n^7} \sum_{j>l\geq 2} \sum n^2 E|\{(V_1 + V_j)W_{1j} - \tilde{V}_1 - \tilde{V}_j\}W_{1l}|^2$$

$$+ \frac{C}{n^7} n^4 E|\{(V_1 + V_2)W_{12} - \tilde{V}_1 - \tilde{V}_2\}W_{12}|^2$$

$$= O(n^{-3}h^{-3d-4}), \tag{7.3.35}$$

where the third inequality uses the Theorem of Dharmardhikari, Fabian, and Jogdeo (1968; abbreviated to DFJ hereafter), and the equality uses nested conditional expectation, Lemmas 1(d) and 4 of NR, Lemma 4 of Robinson (1995), and Lemma 2. Therefore by (7.3.34) and (7.3.35),

$$E|\tilde{b}_3''|^2 = E|Q\bar{W}|^2 = O(n^{-3}h^{-3d-4}). \tag{7.3.36}$$

To investigate the second term of (7.3.33), let

$$d_i = \left(4V_i^2 - s^2\right) + 8\tilde{V}_i, \quad e_{ij} = 4\left\{(V_i + V_j)W_{ij} - \tilde{V}_i - \tilde{V}_j + \frac{n}{n-2}\tilde{W}_{ij}\right\}; \tag{7.3.37}$$

then

$$\tilde{b}_2 = -\frac{s^{-3}}{2}\left\{\frac{4n}{(n-2)^2}E\left(W_{12}^2\right) + \frac{1}{n}\sum_{i=1}^{n} d_i + \binom{n}{2}^{-1}\sum_{i=1}^{n-1}\sum_{j=i+1}^{n} e_{ij}\right.$$

$$\left. -\frac{4}{n}\binom{n-1}{2}^{-1}\sum_{i=1}^{n}\sum_{k=1}^{n-1}{}^{(i)}\sum_{l=k+1}^{n}{}^{(i)}V_i W_{kl}\right\}\bar{V},$$

$$\tilde{b}_3' = -\frac{s^{-3}}{2}\left\{\frac{4n}{(n-2)^2}E\left(W_{12}^2\right) + \frac{1}{n}\sum_{i=1}^{n} d_i + \binom{n}{2}^{-1}\sum_{j=1}^{n-1}\sum_{k=j+1}^{n} 4\tilde{W}_{jk}\right\}\bar{W}.$$

Define

$$b_{3m} = s^{-1}n^{1/2}\binom{n}{2}^{-1}\sum_{i=1}^{m}\sum_{j=i+1}^{n} W_{ij},$$

$$\tilde{b}_{2m} = -\frac{s^{-3}}{2}\left[\frac{8n^{1/2}}{(n-2)^2}E\left(W_{12}^2\right)\sum_{i=1}^{m} V_i + \frac{2}{n^{3/2}}\left(\sum_{i=1}^{n}\sum_{s=1}^{m} d_i V_s + \sum_{i=1}^{m}\sum_{s=m+1}^{n} d_i V_s\right)\right.$$

$$\left. + \frac{2}{n^{1/2}}\binom{n-1}{2}^{-1}\left(\sum_{i=1}^{n-1}\sum_{j=i+1}^{n}\sum_{s=1}^{m} e_{ij}V_s + \sum_{i=1}^{m}\sum_{j=i+1}^{n}\sum_{s=m+1}^{n} e_{ij}V_s\right)\right.$$

$$-\frac{8}{n^{3/2}}\binom{n-1}{2}^{-1}\left(\sum_{i=1}^{n}\sum_{k<l}^{(i)}\sum_{s=1}^{m}V_i W_{kl}V_s\right.$$

$$+\sum_{i=1}^{n}\sum_{k=1}^{m}{}^{(i)}\sum_{l=k+1}^{n}{}^{(i)}\sum_{s=m+1}^{n}V_i W_{kl}V_s$$

$$+\left.\sum_{i=1}^{m}\sum_{k=m+1}^{n-1}{}^{(i)}\sum_{l=k+1}^{n}{}^{(i)}\sum_{s=m+1}^{n}V_i W_{kl}V_s\right)\Bigg],$$

$$\tilde{b}'_{3m}=-\frac{s^{-3}}{2}\left[\frac{4n^{3/2}}{(n-2)^2}E\left(W_{12}^2\right)\binom{n}{2}^{-1}\sum_{l=1}^{m}\sum_{s=l+1}^{n}W_{ls}\right.$$

$$+\frac{1}{\sqrt{n}}\binom{n}{2}^{-2}\left(\sum_{i=1}^{m}\sum_{l=1}^{n-1}\sum_{s=l+1}^{n}d_i W_{ls}+\sum_{i=m+1}^{n}\sum_{l=1}^{m}\sum_{s=l+1}^{n}d_i W_{ls}\right)$$

$$+n^{1/2}\binom{n}{2}^{-2}\left(\sum_{j=1}^{m}\sum_{k=j+1}^{n}\sum_{l=1}^{n-1}\sum_{s=l+1}^{n}4\tilde{W}_{jk}W_{ls}\right.$$

$$+\left.\left.\sum_{j=m+1}^{n-1}\sum_{k=j+1}^{n}\sum_{l=1}^{m}\sum_{s=l+1}^{n}4\tilde{W}_{jk}W_{ls}\right)\right]$$

for $m=1,\ldots,n-1$. Note that b_1-b_{3m}, $\tilde{b}_2-\tilde{b}_{2m}$, and $\tilde{b}'_3-\tilde{b}'_{3m}$ are independent of $(X_1^\tau,Y_1),\ldots,(X_m^\tau,Y_m)$. Putting $\bar{B}_m=(b_1-b_{3m})+(\tilde{b}_2-\tilde{b}_{2m})+(\tilde{b}'_3-\tilde{b}'_{3m})$, and using (7.3.17) repeatedly, we have

$$\left|Ee^{it(b_1+\tilde{b}_2+\tilde{b}'_3)}\right|\leq\frac{t^2}{2}E|\tilde{b}_{2m}+\tilde{b}'_{3m}|^2+\left|Ee^{it(\bar{B}_m+b_{3m})}\right|$$

$$+|t|\left|Ee^{it(\bar{B}_m+b_{3m})}(\tilde{b}_{2m}+\tilde{b}'_{3m})\right|$$

$$\leq\frac{t^2}{2}E|\tilde{b}_{2m}+\tilde{b}'_{3m}|^2+\left[\frac{|t|^3}{6}E|b_{3m}|^3\right.$$

$$+\left.\left|Ee^{it\bar{B}_m}\left\{1+itb_{3m}+\frac{(it)^2}{2}b_{3m}^2\right\}\right|\right]$$

$$+[t^2 E|b_{3m}||\tilde{b}_{2m}+\tilde{b}'_{3m}|+|t||Ee^{it\bar{B}_m}(\tilde{b}_{2m}+\tilde{b}'_{3m})|]$$

$$=\left[\frac{t^2}{2}E|\tilde{b}_{2m}+\tilde{b}'_{3m}|^2+t^2 E|b_{3m}||\tilde{b}_{2m}+\tilde{b}'_{3m}|\right]$$

$$+\left[\frac{|t|^3}{6}E|b_{3m}|^3+\left|Ee^{it\bar{B}_m}\left\{1+itb_{3m}+\frac{(it)^2}{2}b_{3m}^2\right\}\right|\right]$$

$$+[|t||Ee^{it\bar{B}_m}(\tilde{b}_{2m}+\tilde{b}'_{3m})|]. \tag{7.3.38}$$

By elementary inequalities, (ix), items (d) and (e) in Appendix B, and equation (14) of Robinson (1995), the first bracketed term is bounded by

$$Ct^2\{E|\tilde{b}_{2m}|^2 + E|\tilde{b}'_{3m}|^2 + (E|b_{3m}|^2)^{1/2}(E|\tilde{b}_{2m}|^2 + E|\tilde{b}'_{3m}|^2)^{1/2}\}$$

$$\le Cmt^2\left\{\frac{1}{n^3 h^{2d+4}} + \frac{1}{n^2} + \frac{1}{n^4 h^{3d+6}}\right.$$

$$\left. + \frac{1}{(n^2 h^{d+2})^{1/2}}\left(\frac{1}{(n^3 h^{2d+4})^{1/2}} + \frac{1}{n} + \frac{1}{(n^4 h^{3d+6})^{1/2}}\right)\right\}$$

$$\le Cmt^2\left(\frac{1}{n^2 h^{(d+2)/2}} + \frac{1}{n^{5/2} h^{(3d+6)/2}}\right). \tag{7.3.39}$$

The second bracketed term on the right of (7.3.38) is bounded by

$$C\left[|t|^3\left(\frac{m}{n^2 h^{d+2}}\right)^{3/2} + \left\{1 + \frac{m|t|}{n^{1/2}h} + \frac{m|t|}{n^2 h^{d+2}} + \frac{t^2 m^2}{nh^2}\right\}|\gamma(t)|^{m-4}\right], \tag{7.3.40}$$

which is verified as in equations (13)–(19) of Robinson (1995), because s^{-1} is bounded due to (7.3.7) and $\bar{B}_m$ is the sum of $(2/\sqrt{n}s)\sum_{i=1}^n V_i$ and $(b_3 - b_{3m}) + (\tilde{b}_2 - \tilde{b}_{2m}) + (\tilde{b}'_3 - \tilde{b}'_{3m})$, the latter being independent of $(X_1^\tau, Y_1), \ldots, (X_m^\tau, Y_m)$. Items (b) and (c) in Appendix B bound the last term in (7.3.38) by

$$\frac{Cm|t|}{n^{1/2}h^3}|\gamma(t)|^{m-4}. \tag{7.3.41}$$

Now we investigate the third term on the right of (7.3.33). Using elementary inequalities, (7.3.17), (7.3.36), equation (14) of Robinson (1995), and (d), (e), (f) of Appendix B, we have

$$\left|E\tilde{b}''_3 e^{it(b_1+\tilde{b}_2+\tilde{b}'_3)}\right|$$

$$\le \left|E\tilde{b}''_3 e^{it(b_1+\tilde{b}_2+\tilde{b}'_3)} - E\tilde{b}''_3 e^{it(b_1-b_{3m}+\tilde{b}_2-\tilde{b}_{2m}+\tilde{b}'_3-\tilde{b}'_{3m})}\right| + |E\tilde{b}''_3 e^{it\bar{B}_m}|$$

$$\le |t|E|\tilde{b}''_3||b_{3m} + \tilde{b}_{2m} + \tilde{b}'_{3m}| + |E\tilde{b}''_3 e^{it\bar{B}_m}|$$

$$\le C|t|(E|\tilde{b}''_3|^2)^{1/2}[(E|b_{3m}|^2)^{1/2} + (E|\tilde{b}_{2m}|^2)^{1/2}$$

$$+ (E|\tilde{b}'_{3m}|^2)^{1/2}] + |E\tilde{b}''_3 e^{it\bar{B}_m}|$$

$$\le \frac{C|t|h}{(nh^{d+2})^{3/2}}\left[\left(\frac{m}{n^2 h^{d+2}}\right)^{1/2} + \left(\frac{m}{n^3 h^{2d+4}}\right)^{1/2}\right.$$

$$\left. + \left(\frac{m}{n^2}\right)^{1/2} + \left(\frac{m}{n^4 h^{3d+6}}\right)^{1/2}\right] + \frac{Cn^{1/2}}{h^2}|\gamma(t)|^{m-5}$$

$$\le \frac{C|t|hm^{1/2}}{n^{1/2}(nh^{d+2})^2} + \frac{Cn^{1/2}}{h^2}|\gamma(t)|^{m-5}. \tag{7.3.42}$$

Therefore, by (7.3.33), (7.3.36), (7.3.38)–(7.3.42),

$$|Ee^{itB}| \leq \frac{Ct^2}{n^3h^{3d+4}} + Cmt^2\left(\frac{1}{n^2h^{(d+2)/2}} + \frac{1}{n^{5/2}h^{(3d+6)/2}}\right)$$

$$+ C\left[|t|^3\left(\frac{m}{n^2h^{d+2}}\right)^{3/2} + \left\{1 + \frac{m|t|}{n^{1/2}h} + \frac{m|t|}{n^2h^{d+2}} + \frac{t^2m^2}{nh^2}\right\}|\gamma(t)|^{m-4}\right]$$

$$+ \frac{Cm|t|}{n^{1/2}h^3}|\gamma(t)|^{m-4} + \frac{Chm^{1/2}t^2}{n^{1/2}(nh^{d+2})^2} + \frac{Cn^{1/2}|t|}{h^2}|\gamma(t)|^{m-5}.$$

$$(7.3.43)$$

Now divide (7.3.43) by $|t|$ and integrate over $p \leq |t| \leq N_0$, where we partition the range of integration into two parts, $p \leq |t| \leq N_1$ and $N_1 \leq |t| \leq N_0$, for $N_1 = \min(\eta n^{1/2}, nh^{d+2})$:

(i) $p \leq |t| \leq N_1$. We can choose $m = [(9n \log n)/t^2]$ to satisfy $1 \leq m \leq n - 1$ for large n. For this m, since $E(2V_1/s) = 0$ and $\text{Var}(2V_1/s) = 1$,

$$|\gamma(t)|^{m-4} \leq \exp\left(-\frac{m-4}{3n}t^2\right) \leq C\exp(-3\log n) = \frac{C}{n^3}. \quad (7.3.44)$$

By (7.3.43), (7.3.44), and (ix), we obtain

$$\int_{p\leq|t|\leq N_1}\left|\frac{Ee^{itB}}{t}\right|dt$$

$$\leq \frac{C}{n^3h^{3d+4}}\int_{p\leq|t|\leq nh^{d+2}}|t|\,dt$$

$$+ C\left(\frac{n\log n}{n^2h^{(d+2)/2}} + \frac{n\log n}{n^{5/2}h^{(3d+6)/2}}\right)\int_{p\leq|t|\leq\eta n^{1/2}}\frac{dt}{|t|}$$

$$+ C\left(\frac{n\log n}{n^2h^{d+2}}\right)^{3/2}\int_{p\leq|t|\leq\eta n^{1/2}}\frac{dt}{|t|}$$

$$+ \frac{C}{n^3}\int_{p\leq|t|\leq\eta n^{1/2}}\left\{\frac{1}{|t|} + \frac{n\log n}{n^{1/2}ht^2} + \frac{(n\log n)^2}{nh^2|t|^3}\right\}dt$$

$$+ \frac{Cn\log n}{n^{7/2}h^3}\int_{p\leq|t|\leq\eta n^{1/2}}\frac{dt}{t^2} + \frac{Ch(n\log n)^{1/2}}{n^{1/2}(nh^{d+2})^2}$$

$$\times \int_{p\leq|t|\leq nh^{d+2}}dt + \frac{C}{n^{5/2}h^2}\int_{p\leq|t|\leq\eta n^{1/2}}dt$$

$$= o(n^{-1/2} + n^{-1}h^{-d-2}). \quad (7.3.45)$$

(ii) $N_1 \leq |t| \leq N_0$. For sufficiently large n, there exists $\xi > 0$ such that $|\gamma(t)| < 1 - \xi$ by assumption (x). We may take $m = [-(3\log n)/\log(1-\xi)]$ to satisfy $1 \leq m \leq n - 1$ for sufficiently large n. Since

$$|\gamma(t)|^{m-4} \leq Cn^{-3},$$

$$\int_{N_1 \leq |t| \leq N_0} \left| \frac{E e^{itB}}{t} \right| dt$$

$$\leq \frac{C}{n^3 h^{3d+4}} \int_{N_1 \leq |t| \leq nh^{d+2} \log n} |t| \, dt$$

$$+ C \left(\frac{\log n}{n^2 h^{(d+2)/2}} + \frac{\log n}{n^{5/2} h^{(3d+6)/2}} \right) \int_{N_1 \leq |t| \leq n^{1/2} \log n} |t| \, dt$$

$$+ C \left(\frac{\log n}{n^2 h^{d+2}} \right)^{3/2} \int_{N_1 \leq |t| \leq n^{1/2} \log n} |t|^2 \, dt$$

$$+ \frac{C}{n^3} \int_{N_1 \leq |t| \leq n^{1/2} \log n} \left\{ \frac{1}{|t|} + \frac{\log n}{n^{1/2} h} + \frac{(\log n)^2}{nh^2} |t| \right\} dt$$

$$+ \frac{C \log n}{n^{7/2} h^3} \int_{N_1 \leq |t| \leq n^{1/2} \log n} dt$$

$$+ \frac{Ch (\log n)^{1/2}}{n^{1/2} (nh^{d+2})^2} \int_{N_1 \leq |t| \leq nh^{d+2} \log n} |t| \, dt$$

$$+ \frac{C}{n^{5/2} h^2} \int_{N_1 \leq |t| \leq n^{1/2} \log n} dt$$

$$= o(n^{-1/2} + n^{-1} h^{-d-2}) \tag{7.3.46}$$

by (ix). Therefore, by (7.3.45) and (7.3.46),

$$(\text{II}) = o(n^{-1/2} + n^{-1} h^{-d-2}).$$

Estimation of (III).

$$(\text{III}) \leq C \left[\int_p^\infty \frac{1}{t} e^{-t^2/2} \, dt + n^{1/2} h^L \int_p^\infty e^{-t^2/2} \, dt \right.$$

$$\left. + \frac{1}{nh^{d+2}} \int_p^\infty t e^{-t^2/2} \, dt + \frac{1}{n^{1/2}} \int_p^\infty (t + t^2) e^{-t^2/2} \, dt \right]. \tag{7.3.47}$$

The first integral in (7.3.47) is bounded by

$$\frac{1}{p^2} \int_p^\infty t e^{-t^2/2} \, dt = \frac{1}{p^2} e^{-p^2/2} = o(n^{-1}),$$

because $p = \min(\log n, \epsilon n^{1/2})$. The remaining integrals are clearly $o(1)$ as $p \to \infty$. Therefore,

$$(\text{III}) = o(n^{-1/2} + n^{-1}h^{-d-2} + n^{1/2}h^L).$$

to complete the proof. □

Proof of Theorem B: In view of the proof of Theorem 2 of NR, $\tilde{\kappa}_i \to \kappa_i$, $i = 1, 2, 3, 4$, a.s. Combine this with Theorem A. □

Appendix A

Lemma 1. *Under assumptions* (i), (iii), (iv), (v), (vi), (vii), *and* (viii),

$$E|V_1 W_{12}|^r = E|V_2 W_{12}|^r = O\left(h^{-(r-1)d-r}\right) \qquad \text{for} \quad 1 \le r \le 3.$$

Proof: Using Lemmas 1(d) and 4 of NR,

$$E|V_1 W_{12}|^r \le E\{|V_1|^r E(|W_{12}|^r|1)\}$$
$$\le CE\{(|Y_1|^r + 1)^2\}h^{-(r-1)d-r}$$
$$\le Ch^{-(r-1)d-r} \quad \text{for } 1 \le r \le 3 \qquad \text{by (i).}$$

$E|V_1 W_{12}|^r = E|V_2 W_{12}|^r$ is obvious by the symmetry of W_{12} and (iii). □

Lemma 2. *Under assumptions* (i), (iii), (iv), (v), (vi), (vii), *and* (viii),

$$E|\tilde{V}_1|^r = O(1) \qquad \text{for} \quad 1 \le r \le 6.$$

Proof: As in the proof of Lemma 3 of Robinson (1995),

$$|\tilde{V}_1|^r = |E(V_2 W_{12}|1)|^r \le C(|Y_1|^r + 1) \qquad \text{a.s.,} \tag{7.A.1}$$

so (i) immediately produces the conclusion. □

Lemma 3. *Under assumptions* (i), (iii), (iv), (v), (vi), *and* (viii),

(a) $E|\tilde{W}_{11}|^r = O(h^{-r(d+2)})$ for $1 \le r \le 3$,
(b) $E|\tilde{W}_{12}|^r = O(h^{-r(r-1)d-2r})$ for $1 \le r \le 6$.

Proof: (a): $\tilde{W}_{11} = E(W_{12}^2|1) \le C(|Y_1|^2 + 1)h^{-d-2}$ a.s. by Lemma 4 of NR, so again application of (i) completes the proof.
    (b): Apply Lemma 6 of NR. □

Lemma 4. *Under assumptions* (i), (iii), (iv), (v), (vi), (vii), *and* (viii), *for d_1 given in* (7.3.37),

(a) $E|d_1 V_2|^r = O(1)$ for $1 \leq r \leq 3,$

(b) $E|d_1 V_1|^r = O(1)$ for $1 \leq r \leq 2.$

Proof: (a): By (iii), $E|d_1 V_2|^r = E|d_1|^r E|V_2|^r$, where the second factor is bounded due to Lemma 1(d) of NR. From Lemma 1(d) of NR and (7.A.1),

$$|d_1|^r \leq C\big(|V_1^2|^r + |\tilde{V}_1|^r + 1\big) \leq C(|Y_1|^{2r} + 1); \tag{7.A.2}$$

then apply (i).

(b): By an elementary inequality and (7.3.7), $E|d_1 V_1|^r \leq C(E|V_1^3|^r + E|\tilde{V}_1 V_1|^r + E|V_1|^r)$. By Lemma 1(d) of NR and (7.A.1), $E|V_1^3|^r + E|V_1|^r = O(1)$ *for* $1 \leq r \leq 2$, and

$$E|\tilde{V}_1 V_1|^r \leq C E(|Y_1|^r + 1)^2 = O(1) \tag{7.A.3}$$

for $1 \leq r \leq 3$ by (i).   □

Lemma 5. *Under assumptions* (i), (iii), (iv), (v), (vi), (vii), *and* (viii),

(a) $E|W_{12} V_1 V_3|^r = E|W_{12} V_2 V_3|^r = O(h^{-(r-1)d-r})$ for $1 \leq r \leq 3,$

(b) $E|W_{12} V_1 V_1^2|^r = E|W_{12} V_2^2|^r = O(h^{-(r-1)d-r})$ for $1 \leq r \leq 2.$

Proof: (a): Using (iii), Lemma 1(d) of NR, and Lemma 1, for $1 \leq r \leq 3$,

$$E|W_{12} V_1 V_3|^r = E|W_{12} V_1|^r E|V_3|^r = O\big(h^{-(r-1)d-r}\big).$$

$E|W_{12} V_1 V_3|^r = E|W_{12} V_2 V_3|^r$ is straightforward by (iii) and symmetry of W_{12}.

(b): By Lemmas 1(d) and 4 of NR, the left side is

$$E\{|V_1|^{2r} E(|W_{12}|^r |1)\} \leq E\big\{C(|Y_1|^{3r} + 1)h^{-(r-1)d-r}\big\} = O\big(h^{-(r-1)d-r}\big).$$

$E|W_{12} V_1^2|^r = E|W_{12} V_2^2|^r$ is straightforward by (iii) and symmetry of W_{12}.   □

Lemma 6. *Under assumptions* (i), (iii), (iv), (v), (vi), (vii), *and* (viii), *with e_{12} given in* (7.3.37),

(a) $E|e_{12} V_3|^r = O(h^{-(r-1)d-2r)})$ for $1 \leq r \leq 3,$

(b) $E|e_{12} V_1|^r = E|e_{12} V_2|^r = O(h^{-(r-1)d-2r)})$ for $1 \leq r \leq 2.$

Proof: (a): By (iii) and Lemma 1(d) of NR, write

$$E|e_{12} V_3|^r = E|e_{12}|^r E|V_3|^r \leq C(E|V_1 W_{12}|^r + E|\tilde{V}_1|^r + E|\tilde{W}_{12}|^r).$$

Then apply Lemmas 1, 2, and 3(b).

(b): An elementary inequality gives

$$E|e_{12}V_1|^r \le C\left(E|V_1V_2W_{12}|^r + E\left|V_1^2W_{12}\right|^r + E|\tilde{V}_1V_1|^r\right.$$
$$\left. + E|\tilde{V}_1V_2|^r + E|\tilde{W}_{12}V_1|^r\right). \tag{7.A.4}$$

Writing $E|V_1V_2W_{12}|^r = \{E|V_1|^r E(|V_2W_{12}|^r|1)\}$, the proof of Lemma 4 of NR applies to yield $E(|V_2W_{12}|^r|1) \le C(|Y_1|^r + 1)h^{-(r-1)d-r}$ a.s. Thus, for $1 \le r \le 3$,

$$E|V_1V_2W_{12}|^r = O\left(h^{-(r-1)d-r}\right). \tag{7.A.5}$$

The second term in (7.A.4) has the same order bound as (7.A.5) by Lemma 5(b) for $1 \le r \le 2$. The third term in (7.A.4) is bounded due to (7.A.3), while the fourth term is bounded due to Lemma 1(d) of NR and Lemma 2. We handle the last term in (7.A.4) similarly to Lemma 6 of NR:

$$E|\tilde{W}_{12}V_1|^r = E|E(W_{13}W_{23}|1,2)V_1|^r = O\left(h^{-(r-1)d-2r}\right). \tag{7.A.6}$$

$E|e_{12}V_1|^r = E|e_{12}V_2|^r$ is straightforward by (iii) and symmetry of e_{12}. $\quad\square$

Lemma 7. *Under assumptions* (i), (iii), (iv), (v), (vi), (vii), *and* (viii),

(a) $\quad E|d_1W_{23}|^r = O(h^{-(r-1)d-r}) \qquad\qquad$ for $\quad 1 \le r \le 3$,

(b) $\quad E|d_1W_{12}|^r = E|d_2W_{12}|^r = O(h^{-(r-1)d-r}) \qquad$ for $\quad 1 \le r \le 2$.

Proof: (a): Using (7.A.2) and Lemma 4 of Robinson (1995),

$$E|d_1W_{23}|^r = E|d_1|^r E|W_{23}|^r = O\left(h^{-(r-1)d-r}\right)$$

for $1 \le r \le 3$.

(b): Using (7.A.2) and Lemma 4 of NR, the left side is

$$E\{|d_1|^r E(|W_{12}|^r|1)\} \le E\left\{(|Y_1|^{2r} + 1)C(|Y_1|^r + 1)h^{-(r-1)d-r}\right\}$$
$$\le CE(|Y_1|^{3r} + 1)h^{-(r-1)d-r} = O\left(h^{-(r-1)d-r}\right)$$

for $1 \le r \le 2$ under (i). $E|d_1W_{12}|^r = E|d_2W_{12}|^r$ is straightforward by (iii) and symmetry of W_{12}. $\quad\square$

Lemma 8. *Under assumptions* (i), (iii), (iv), (v), (vi), (vii), *and* (viii),

(a) $\quad E|\tilde{W}_{12}W_{12}|^r = O(h^{-(2r-1)d-3r}) \qquad$ for $\quad 1 \le r \le 3$,

(b) $\quad E|\tilde{W}_{12}W_{13}|^r = O(h^{-2(r-1)d-3r}) \qquad$ for $\quad 1 \le r \le 3$,

(c) $\quad E|\tilde{W}_{12}W_{23}|^r = O(h^{-2(r-1)d-3r}) \qquad$ for $\quad 1 \le r \le 3$,

(d) $\quad E|\tilde{W}_{12}W_{34}|^r = O(h^{-2(r-1)d-3r}) \qquad$ for $\quad 1 \le r \le 6$.

Proof: (a): In view of the proof of Lemma 6 of NR,

$$
\begin{aligned}
E|\tilde{W}_{12}W_{12}|^r &= E|\tilde{W}_{12}|^r W_{12}|^r \\
&\leq h^{-r(d+2)}CE(1 + |Y_1|^r + |Y_2|^r + |Y_1|^r|Y_2|^r)|W_{12}|^r \\
&\leq Ch^{-r(d+2)}(E|W_{12}|^r + E|Y_1 W_{12}|^r \\
&\quad + E|Y_2 W_{12}|^r + E|Y_1 Y_2 W_{12}|^r).
\end{aligned}
$$

The first term in parentheses is $O(h^{-(r-1)d-r})$ by Lemma 4 of Robinson (1995). From inspecting their proofs, Lemma 1 and (7.A.5) still hold with V_1 and V_2 replaced by Y_1 and Y_2 so that the other terms are $O(h^{-(r-1)d-r})$ for $1 \leq r \leq 3$.

(b): Using Lemma 4 of NR, for $1 \leq r \leq 6$,

$$
\begin{aligned}
E|\tilde{W}_{12}W_{13}|^r &= E\{|\tilde{W}_{12}|^r E(|W_{13}|^r | 1, 2)\} \\
&\leq E\{|\tilde{W}_{12}|^r C(|Y_1|^r + 1)h^{-(r-1)d-r}\} \\
&= Ch^{-(r-1)d-r}(E|\tilde{W}_{12}Y_1|^r + E|\tilde{W}_{12}|^r).
\end{aligned}
$$

We may replace V_1 by Y_1 in (7.A.6), so that, using also Lemma 3(b),

$$
E|\tilde{W}_{12}W_{13}|^r = O\left(h^{-2(r-1)d-3r}\right) \qquad \text{for} \quad 1 \leq r \leq 3.
$$

(c): The proof is as in (b).

(d): Writing $E|\tilde{W}_{12}W_{34}|^r = E|\tilde{W}_{12}|^r E|\tilde{W}_{12}|^r$ by (iii), the proof is straightforward by Lemma 4 of Robinson (1995) and Lemma 3(b). □

Lemma 9. *Under assumptions* (i), (iii), (iv), (v), (vi), (vii), *and* (viii),

$$
E|\bar{V}|^r = O(1) \qquad \text{for} \quad 2 \leq r \leq 6.
$$

Proof: Since V_i, $i = 1, \ldots, n$, is an iid sequence, the result follows straightforwardly by DFJ and Lemma 1(d) of NR. □

Lemma 10. *Under assumptions* (i), (v), (vi), (vii), *and* (viii),

$$
|T_1|^r = O\left(n^{-r}h^{-r(d+2)}\right) \qquad \text{for} \quad r > 0.
$$

Proof: Using Lemma 4 of Robinson (1995) and $|\delta| < C$ due to (7.3.7),

$$
|T_1|^r \leq \frac{C}{n^r}\left|E\left(W_{12}^2\right)\right|^r = O\left(n^{-r}h^{-r(d+2)}\right). \qquad \square
$$

Lemma 11. *Under assumptions* (i), (iii), (iv), (v), (vi), (vii), *and* (viii),

$$
E|T_2|^r = O(n^{-r/2}) \qquad \text{for} \quad 2 \leq r \leq 3.
$$

Proof: Using (7.3.7), write

$$E|T_2|^r \leq \frac{C}{n^r} E \left| \sum_{i=1}^{n} (4V_i^2 - s^2) \right|^r + \frac{C}{n^r} E \left| \sum_{i=1}^{n} 8\tilde{V}_i \right|^r.$$

Since $E(4V_i^2) = s^2$ and $E(\tilde{V}_i) = 0$, by (iii) both the $4V_i^2 - s^2$ and $\tilde{V}_i$ are martingale differences, and thus the Theorem of DFJ applies to yield

$$E \left| \sum_{i=1}^{n} (4V_i^2 - s^2) \right|^r \leq Cn^{r/2} E |4V_1^2 - s^2|^r = O(n^{r/2})$$

for $2 \leq r \leq 3$ by (7.3.7) and Lemma 1(d) of NR and

$$E \left| \sum_{i=1}^{n} 8\tilde{V}_i \right|^r \leq Cn^{r/2} E |\tilde{V}_1|^r = O(n^{r/2})$$

by Lemma 2. $\qquad \square$

Lemma 12. *Under assumptions* (i), (iii), (iv), (v), (vi), *and* (viii),

$$E|T_3|^r = O\left(n^{-r} h^{-(r-1)d-2r}\right) \qquad \text{for} \quad 2 \leq r \leq 6.$$

Proof: Using (7.3.7), write

$$E|T_3|^r \leq Cn^{-2r} E \left| \sum_{k=1}^{n-1} Z_k \right|^r, \tag{7.A.7}$$

where $Z_k = \sum_{m=k+1}^{n} \tilde{W}_{km}$ for $k = 1, \dots, n-1$. Since

$$E(\tilde{W}_{12} | 2) - E(\tilde{W}_{12} | 1) = E\{E(W_{13}W_{23} | 1, 2) | 1\} = E(W_{13}W_{23} | 1) = 0 \qquad \text{a.s.},$$

$Z_k, k = n-1, \dots, 1$, is a martingale difference sequence. Thus we apply DFJ to bound (7.A.7) by $Cn^{-2r}(n-1)^{r/2-1} \sum_{k=1}^{n-1} E|Z_k|^r$. Since $E(\tilde{W}_{km} | m) = 0$ a.s. for $m = k+1, \dots, n$, the $\tilde{W}_{km}$ are martingale differences. We use DFJ again and get, by Lemma 3(b),

$$E|Z_k|^r \leq C(n-k)^{r/2-1} \sum_{m=k+1}^{n} E|\tilde{W}_{km}|^r \leq C(n-k)^{r/2-1}(n-k)h^{-(r-1)d-2r}.$$

$\qquad \square$

Lemma 13. *Under assumptions* (i), (iii), (iv), (v), (vi), (vii), *and* (viii),

$$E|Q_1|^r = O\left(n^{-r} h^{-(r-1)d-r}\right) \qquad \text{for} \quad 2 \leq r \leq 3.$$

Proof: Write $P_{ij} = (V_i + V_j)W_{ij} - \tilde{V}_i - \tilde{V}_j$. Then $\sum_{j=i+1}^{n} P_{ij}$ is a martingale difference sequence for $i = n-1, \ldots, 1$. We can proceed by replacing $\tilde{W}_{km}$ in Lemma 12 by P_{ij} due to the property $E(P_{ij} \mid j) = 0$ a.s. for $i \neq j$. Applying DFJ and (7.3.7),

$$E|Q_1|^r \leq C \binom{n}{2}^{-r} E \left| \sum_{i=1}^{n-1} \sum_{j=i+1}^{n} P_{ij} \right|^r \leq C \binom{n}{2}^{-r} n^{r/2-1} \sum_{i=1}^{n-1} E \left| \sum_{j=i+1}^{n} P_{ij} \right|^r.$$

Since P_{ij}, $j = n, \ldots, i+1$ is a martingale difference for fixed i, we can apply the theorem of DJF again and obtain $E|\sum_{j=i+1}^{n} P_{ij}|^r \leq C(n-i)^{r/2-1} \sum_{j=i+1}^{n} E|P_{ij}|^r$. By Lemmas 1 and 2,

$$E|P_{ij}|^r \leq C[E|\tilde{V}_i|^r + E|V_i W_{ij}|^r] = O\left(h^{-(r-1)d-r}\right) \qquad \text{for} \quad 1 \leq r \leq 3. \qquad \square$$

Lemma 14. *Under assumptions* (i), (iii), (iv), (v), (vi), (vii), *and* (viii),

$$E|Q_2|^r = O\left(n^{-r}h^{-(r-1)d-r}\right) \qquad \text{for} \quad 2 \leq r \leq 6.$$

Proof: By an elementary inequality and (7.3.7),

$$E|Q_2|^r \leq \frac{C}{n^r} \binom{n-1}{2}^{-r} E \left| \sum_{i=1}^{n} \sum_{k=1}^{n-1}{}^{(i)} \sum_{m=k+1}^{n}{}^{(i)} V_i W_{km} \right|^r$$

$$= \frac{C}{n^r} \binom{n-1}{2}^{-r} n^{r-1} \sum_{i=1}^{n} E \left| \sum_{k=1}^{n-1}{}^{(i)} \sum_{m=k+1}^{n}{}^{(i)} V_i W_{km} \right|^r.$$

$V_i W_{km}$, $m = k+1, \ldots, n$, is a martingale difference for fixed i, k, $k \neq i$ and $m \neq i$, and $\sum_{m=k+1}^{n(i)} V_i W_{km}$, $k = n-1, \ldots, 1$, is also a martingale difference for fixed i and $k \neq i$, so that we apply DFJ repeatedly as in the proof of the previous lemma and get

$$\sum_{i=1}^{n} E \left| \sum_{k=1}^{n-1}{}^{(i)} \sum_{m=k+1}^{n}{}^{(i)} V_i W_{km} \right|^r$$

$$\leq C \sum_{i=1}^{n} (n-2)^{r/2-1} \sum_{k=1}^{n-1}{}^{(i)} E \left| \sum_{m=k+1}^{n}{}^{(i)} V_i W_{ij} \right|^r$$

$$\leq C(n-1)^{r/2-1} \sum_{i=1}^{n} \sum_{k=1}^{n-1}{}^{(i)} (n-k)^{r/2-1} \sum_{m=k+1}^{n}{}^{(i)} E|V_i W_{km}|^r$$

$$\leq Cn^{r+1}h^{-(r-1)d-r}$$

for $2 \leq r \leq 6$, by (iii), Lemma 1(d) of NR, and Lemma 4 of Robinson (1995).

$$\square$$

Lemma 15. *Under assumptions* (i), (iii), (iv), (v), (vi), (vii), *and* (viii),

$$E|R_1|^r = O(n^{-r}) \qquad \text{for} \quad 2 \le r \le 6.$$

Proof: Writing

$$E|R_1|^r \le C \binom{n}{2}^{-r} E \left| \sum_{i=1}^{n-1} \sum_{j=i+1}^{n} V_i V_j \right|^r$$

due to (7.3.7), as in Lemma 12 or 13, $V_i V_j$, $i = 1, \ldots, j-1$ is a martingale difference sequence for fixed j as well as $\sum_{j=i+1}^{n} V_i V_j$, $i = n-1, \ldots, 1$. We use DFJ repeatedly again and (i), (iii), and Lemma 1(d) of NR to obtain

$$E \left| \sum_{i=1}^{n-1} \sum_{j=i+1}^{n} V_i V_j \right|^r \le C(n-1)^{r/2-1} \sum_{i=1}^{n-1} E \left| \sum_{j=i+1}^{n} V_i V_j \right|^r$$

$$\le C(n-1)^{r/2-1} \sum_{i=1}^{n-1} (n-i)^{r/2-1} \sum_{j=i+1}^{n} E|V_i V_j|^r$$

$$= O(n^r). \qquad \square$$

Lemma 16. *Under assumptions* (i), (iii), (iv), (v), (vi), *and* (viii),

$$E|R_2|^r = O\left(n^{-3(r-1)} h^{-2(r-1)d-2r}\right) \qquad \text{for} \quad 2 \le r \le 3.$$

Proof: Using (7.3.7), write

$$E|R_2|^r = \frac{C}{n^r} \binom{n-1}{2}^{-r} E \left| \sum_{i=1}^{n} \sum_{k=1}^{n-1} {}^{(i)} \sum_{m=k+1}^{n} {}^{(i)} (W_{ik} W_{im} - \tilde{W}_{km}) \right|^r.$$

Since R_2 has the same martingale structure as Q_2, the same method of proof as in Lemma 14 applies. The difference is in the moment bounds of the two summands, i.e.

$$E|V_i W_{km}|^r = O\left(h^{-(r-1)d-r}\right) \qquad \text{for} \quad 1 \le r \le 6$$

and

$$E|W_{ik} W_{im} - \tilde{W}_{km}|^r = O\left(h^{-2(r-1)d-2r}\right), \qquad i \ne k \ne m,$$

by Lemmas 1(d), 4 of NR and Lemma 3(b). $\qquad \square$

Lemma 17. *Under assumptions* (i), (iii), (iv), (v), (vi), *and* (viii),

$$E|R_3|^r = O\left(n^{-2r} h^{-(2r-1)d-2r}\right) \qquad \text{for} \quad 2 \le r \le 3.$$

Proof: Write

$$E|R_3|^r \le \frac{C}{n^r} \binom{n}{2}^{-r} E \left| \sum_{i=1}^{n-1} \sum_{j=i+1}^{n} \{W_{ij}^2 - \tilde{W}_{ii} - \tilde{W}_{jj} + E(W_{12}^2)\} \right|^r$$

using (7.3.7). Since

$$E\{W_{ij}^2 - \tilde{W}_{ii} - \tilde{W}_{jj} + E(W_{12}^2) \,|\, j\} = E\{W_{ij}^2 - \tilde{W}_{ii} - \tilde{W}_{jj} + E(W_{12}^2) \,|\, i\} = 0$$

for $j > i$, R_3 has the same martingale structure as T_3. Therefore, we apply DFJ to obtain

$$E \left| \sum_{i=1}^{n-1} \sum_{j=i+1}^{n} \{W_{ij}^2 - \tilde{W}_{ii} - \tilde{W}_{jj} + E(W_{12}^2)\} \right|^r$$

$$\le C(n-1)^{r/2-1} \sum_{i=1}^{n-1} E \left| \sum_{j=i+1}^{n} \{W_{ij}^2 - \tilde{W}_{ii} - \tilde{W}_{jj} + E(W_{12}^2)\} \right|^r$$

$$\le C(n-1)^{r/2-1} \sum_{i=1}^{n-1} (n-i)^{r/2-1}$$

$$\times \sum_{j=i+1}^{n} E |\{W_{ij}^2 - \tilde{W}_{ii} - \tilde{W}_{jj} + E(W_{12}^2)\}|^r$$

$$= O\left(n^r h^{-(2r-1)d-2r}\right)$$

by Lemma 4 of Robinson (1995) and Lemma 3(a). $\qquad\square$

Lemma 18. *Under assumptions* (i), (iv), (v), (vi), *and* (viii),

$$E|R_4|^r = O\left(n^{-\frac{3}{2}r} h^{-r(d+2)}\right) \qquad \text{for} \quad 1 \le r \le 3.$$

Proof: Write $E|R_4|^r \le (C/n^{2r}) E| \sum_{i=1}^{n} \{\tilde{W}_{ii} - E(W_{12}^2)\}|^r$, using (7.3.7). Since $\tilde{W}_{ii} - E(W_{12}^2)$ is a martingale difference, by (iii), DFJ, and Lemma 3(a),

$$E \left| \sum_{i=1}^{n} \{\tilde{W}_{ii} - E(W_{12}^2)\} \right|^r \le Cn^{r/2-1} \sum_{i=1}^{n} E|\tilde{W}_{ii} - E(W_{12}^2)|^r = O\left(n^{r/2} h^{-r(d+2)}\right).$$

Lemma 19. *Under assumptions* (i), (iii), (iv), (v), (vi), (vii), *and* (viii),

$$E|R_5|^r = O\left(n^{-2r} h^{-r(d+2)}\right) \qquad \text{for} \quad 1 \le r \le 3.$$

Proof: Using (7.3.7), DFJ, and Lemma 6 of Robinson (1995),

$$E|R_5|^r \le \frac{C}{n^{4r}} E \left| \sum_{i=1}^{n-1} \sum_{j=i+1}^{n} W_{ij} \right|^{2r} \le \frac{C}{n^{4r}} (n-1)^{r-1} \sum_{i=1}^{n-1} E \left| \sum_{j=i+1}^{n} W_{ij} \right|^{2r}$$

$$= O\left(n^{-2r} h^{-r(d+2)}\right). \qquad \square$$

Appendix B

Here, we present some of the derivations used in the proof of Theorem A, namely:

(a) $E(\tilde{b}'_2 e^{itb_2})$

$$= -\{\gamma(t)\}^{n-1} \left\{ it \frac{2}{n} E\left(W_{12}^2\right) + O\left(\frac{|t|}{n^2 h^{d+2}} + \frac{t^2}{n^{3/2} h^{d+2}} + \frac{|t| h^L}{n h^{d+2}}\right) \right\}$$

$$- \{\gamma(t)\}^{n-1} \left\{ \frac{4E\left(V_1^3\right) + 8E(W_{12} V_1 V_2)}{n^{1/2}} + O\left(\frac{|t|}{n}\right) \right\}$$

$$- \{\gamma(t)\}^{n-2} \left[\frac{(it)^2}{n^{1/2}} \left\{ 4E\left(V_1^3\right) + 8E(W_{12} V_1 V_2) \right\} \right.$$

$$\left. + O\left(\frac{t^2 + |t|^3}{n} + \frac{t^4}{n^{3/2}}\right) \right] + \{\gamma(t)\}^{n-3}$$

$$\times \left[O\left(\frac{|t|^3 + |t|}{n} + \frac{t^2}{n^{3/2} h^{d+2}} + \frac{t^6}{n^3 h^{d+2}} + \frac{|t|^5}{n^{5/2} h^{d+2}} + \frac{t^4 + |t|^3}{n^2 h^{d+2}}\right) \right],$$

(b) $|E(\tilde{b}_{2m} e^{it\bar{B}_m})| \le \dfrac{Cm}{n^{1/2} h^2} |\gamma(t)|^{m-4},$

(c) $|E(\tilde{b}'_{3m} e^{it\bar{B}_m})| \le \dfrac{Cm}{n^{1/2} h^3} |\gamma(t)|^{m-4},$

(d) $E|\tilde{b}_{2m}|^2 \quad \le Cm\left(\dfrac{1}{n^3 h^{2d+4}} + \dfrac{1}{n^2}\right),$

(e) $E|\tilde{b}'_{3m}|^2 \quad \le \dfrac{Cm}{n^4 h^{3d+6}},$

(f) $|E\tilde{b}''_3 e^{it\bar{B}_m}| \le \dfrac{Cn^{1/2}}{h^2} |\gamma(t)|^{m-5}.$

for $1 \le m \le n-1$.

Proof: (a): Write

$$E(\tilde{b}_2' e^{itb_2}) = E(T\bar{V}e^{itb_2})$$

$$= E\left(T_1 \frac{2}{\sqrt{n}} \sum_{j=1}^{n} V_j e^{itb_2}\right) + E\left(T_2 \frac{2}{\sqrt{n}} \sum_{j=1}^{n} V_j e^{itb_2}\right)$$

$$+ E\left(T_3 \frac{2}{\sqrt{n}} \sum_{j=1}^{n} V_j e^{itb_2}\right)$$

$$= (A) + (B) + (C). \tag{7.B.1}$$

Thus

$$(A) = -\frac{4n^{1/2}}{(n-2)^2 s^3} E\left(W_{12}^2\right) \sum_{j=1}^{n} \left(V_j e^{itb_2}\right). \tag{7.B.2}$$

Due to (iii), (7.3.17), $\gamma(t) = E(e^{it(2/\sqrt{ns})V_1})$, $4E(V_1^2) = s^2$, (7.3.7), and Lemma 1(d) of NR,

$$E(V_j e^{itb_2}) = E\left(V_j e^{it(2/\sqrt{ns})V_j}\right) E\left(e^{it(2/\sqrt{ns})\sum_{k\neq j}^{n} V_k}\right)$$

$$= \left[E\left\{V_j\left(e^{it(2/\sqrt{ns})V_j} - 1 - it\frac{2V_j}{n^{1/2}s}\right)\right\}\right.$$

$$\left.+ (it)E\left(\frac{2V_j^2}{n^{1/2}s}\right)\right]\{\gamma(t)\}^{n-1}$$

$$= \{\gamma(t)\}^{n-1}\left\{\frac{its}{2n^{1/2}} + O\left(\frac{t^2}{n}\right)\right\}$$

$$= \{\gamma(t)\}^{n-1}\left\{\frac{it}{2n^{1/2}} + O\left(\frac{t^2}{n} + \frac{|t|h^L}{n^{1/2}}\right)\right\}. \tag{7.B.3}$$

Substituting (7.B.3) into (7.B.2),

$$(A) = -\{\gamma(t)\}^{n-1} \frac{4n^{3/2}}{(n-2)^2 s^3} E\left(W_{12}^2\right)\left\{\frac{it}{2n^{1/2}} + O\left(\frac{t^2}{n} + \frac{|t|h^L}{n^{1/2}}\right)\right\}$$

$$= -\frac{\{\gamma(t)\}^{n-1}}{s^3}\left\{\frac{2it}{n} E\left(W_{12}^2\right) + O\left(\frac{|t|}{n^2 h^{d+2}} + \frac{t^2}{n^{3/2}h^{d+2}} + \frac{|t|h^L}{nh^{d+2}}\right)\right\}. \tag{7.B.4}$$

Now write $(B) = (B') + (B'')$, where

$$(B') = -\frac{1}{n^{3/2}s^3} \sum_{j=1}^{n} E\left(4V_j^2 - s^2 + 8\tilde{V}_j\right) V_j e^{itb_2}, \tag{7.B.5}$$

$$(B'') = -\frac{1}{n^{3/2}s^3} \sum_{j=1}^{n} \sum_{k\neq j}^{n} E(4V_j - s^2 + 8\tilde{V}_j)V_k e^{itb_2}. \tag{7.B.6}$$

The summand of (B') is, using (7.3.17) and Lemma 1(d) of NR,

$$E\left\{\left(4V_1^2 - s^2 + 8\tilde{V}_1\right) V_i e^{it\, 2V_1/\sqrt{ns}}\right\} E\left(e^{it(2/\sqrt{ns})\sum_{l\neq 1} V_l}\right)$$

$$= \{\gamma(t)\}^{n-1} E\left\{\left(4V_1^2 - s^2 + 8\tilde{V}_1\right) V_1 e^{it\, 2V_1/\sqrt{ns}}\right\}$$

$$= \{\gamma(t)\}^{n-1}\left\{4E\left\{(V_1^3)\right\} + 8E(W_{12}V_1 V_2) + O\left(\frac{|t|}{n^{1/2}}\right)\right\}.$$

$$\text{(7.B.7)}$$

Substituting (7.B.7) into (7.B.5),

$$(\text{B}') = -\frac{1}{n^{1/2}s^3}\{\gamma(t)\}^{n-1}\left\{4E\left(V_1^3\right) + 8E(W_{12}V_1 V_2) + O\left(\frac{|t|}{n^{1/2}}\right)\right\}. \quad \text{(7.B.8)}$$

For $j \neq k$, the summand of (B'') is, due to (iii),

$$E\left\{\left(4V_1^2 - s^2 + 8\tilde{V}_1\right) V_2 e^{it\, 2(V_1+V_2)/\sqrt{ns}}\right\} E\left(e^{it(2/\sqrt{ns})\sum_{l\neq 1,2} V_l}\right)$$

$$= \{\gamma(t)\}^{n-2} E\left\{\left(4V_1^2 - s^2\right) + 8\tilde{V}_1\right) V_2 e^{it\, 2(V_1+V_2)/\sqrt{ns}}\right\}$$

$$= \{\gamma(t)\}^{n-2} E\left\{\left(4V_1^2 - s^2\right) + 8\tilde{V}_1\right) e^{it\, 2V_1/\sqrt{ns}}\right\} E\left(V_2 e^{it\, 2V_2/\sqrt{ns}}\right)$$

$$= \{\gamma(t)\}^{n-2}\left[E\left\{\left(4V_1^2 - s^2 + 8\tilde{V}_1\right)\left(e^{it\, 2V_1/\sqrt{ns}} - 1 - it\frac{V_1}{\sqrt{ns}}\right)\right\}\right.$$

$$+ itE\frac{V_1}{\sqrt{ns}}\left(4V_1^2 - s^2 + 8\tilde{V}_1\right)\right]$$

$$\times\left[E\left\{V_2\left(e^{it\, 2V_2/\sqrt{ns}} - 1 - it\frac{V_2}{\sqrt{ns}}\right)\right\} + it\, E\frac{V_2^2}{\sqrt{ns}}\right]$$

$$= \{\gamma(t)\}^{n-2}\left[itE\frac{V_1}{\sqrt{ns}}\left(4V_1^2 - s^2 + 8\tilde{V}_1\right) + O\left(\frac{|t|^2}{n}\right)\right]$$

$$\times\left[it\frac{E\left(V_2^2\right)}{\sqrt{ns}} + O\left(\frac{|t|^2}{n}\right)\right]$$

$$= \{\gamma(t)\}^{n-2}\left[\frac{it}{\sqrt{ns}}\left\{E\left(4V_1^3\right) + 8E(W_{12}V_1 V_2)\right\}\right.$$

$$\left. + O\left(\frac{|t|^2}{n}\right)\right]\left[\frac{its}{\sqrt{n}} + O\left(\frac{|t|^2}{n}\right)\right]$$

$$= \{\gamma(t)\}^{n-2}\left[\frac{(it)^2}{n}\left\{E\left(4V_1^3\right) + 8E(W_{12}V_1 V_2)\right\}\right.$$

$$\left. + O\left(\frac{|t|^3}{n^{3/2}} + \frac{|t|^4}{n^2}\right)\right] \qquad \text{(7.B.9)}$$

by (7.3.17). Therefore, substituting (7.B.9) into (7.B.6) yields

$$(\text{B}'') = -\frac{n(n-1)}{n^{3/2}s^3}\left[\frac{(it)^2}{n}\left\{4E(V_1^3) + 8E(W_{12}V_1V_2)\right\}\right.$$

$$\left. + O\left(\frac{|t|^3}{n^{3/2}} + \frac{|t|^4}{n^2}\right)\right]\{\gamma(t)\}^{n-2}. \tag{7.B.10}$$

By (7.B.8) and (7.B.10),

$$(\text{B}) = -\frac{\{\gamma(t)\}^{n-1}}{s^3}\left\{\frac{4E(V_1^3) + 8E(W_{12}V_1V_2)}{n^{1/2}} + O\left(\frac{|t|}{n}\right)\right\}$$

$$-\frac{\{\gamma(t)\}^{n-2}}{s^3}\left[\frac{(it)^2}{n^{1/2}}\left\{4E(V_1^3) + 8E(W_{12}V_1V_2)\right\}\right.$$

$$\left. + O\left(\frac{t^2 + |t|^3}{n} + \frac{t^4}{n^{3/2}}\right)\right]. \tag{7.B.11}$$

Now, write

$$(\text{C}) = -\frac{4}{n^{1/2}s^3}E\left\{\binom{n-1}{2}^{-1}\sum_{1\le j<k\le n}\tilde{W}_{jk}\right\}\frac{1}{\sqrt{n}}\sum_{l=1}^{n}V_l e^{itb_2}$$

$$= -\frac{4}{n^{1/2}s^3}\binom{n-1}{2}^{-1}\sum_{l=1}^{n}\sum_{j<k}^{(l)}E(\tilde{W}_{jk}V_l e^{itb_2})$$

$$-\frac{4}{n^{1/2}s^3}\binom{n-1}{2}^{-1}\sum_{j=1}^{n-1}\sum_{k=j+1}^{n}E(\tilde{W}_{jk}V_j e^{itb_2})$$

$$-\frac{4}{n^{1/2}s^3}\binom{n-1}{2}^{-1}\sum_{j=1}^{n-1}\sum_{k=j+1}^{n}E(\tilde{W}_{jk}V_k e^{itb_2})$$

$$= (\text{C}') + (\text{C}'') + (\text{C}''').$$

Using (iii), Lemma 1(d) of NR, $E(V_j) = 0$, and $E(\tilde{W}_{km}) = E(\tilde{W}_{km}\,|\,k) = E(\tilde{W}_{km}\,|\,m) = 0$, the summand of (C') is

$$E\left\{\tilde{W}_{12}V_3 e^{it(2/\sqrt{n}s)(V_1+V_2+V_3)}\right\}E\left(e^{it(2\sqrt{n}s)\sum_{l\ne 1,2,3}^{n}V_l}\right)$$

$$= E\left\{\tilde{W}_{12}V_3 e^{it(2/\sqrt{n}s)(V_1+V_2+V_3)}\right\}\{\gamma(t)\}^{n-3}$$

$$= \left\{E\tilde{W}_{12}\left(e^{it\,2V_1/\sqrt{n}s} - 1 - it\frac{2V_1}{\sqrt{n}s}\right)\left(e^{it\,2V_2/\sqrt{n}s} - 1 - it\frac{2V_2}{\sqrt{n}s}\right)\right.$$

$$+ (it)^2\frac{4}{ns^2}E(\tilde{W}_{12}V_1V_2)$$

$$
+ (it)\frac{2}{\sqrt{ns}} E\left\{ \tilde{W}_{12} V_1 \left(e^{it\, 2V_2/\sqrt{ns}} - 1 - it\frac{2V_2}{\sqrt{ns}} \right) \right\}
$$

$$
+ (it)\frac{2}{\sqrt{ns}} E\left\{ \tilde{W}_{12} V_2 \left(e^{it\, 2V_1/\sqrt{ns}} - 1 - it\frac{2V_1}{\sqrt{ns}} \right) \right\} \Bigg\}
$$

$$
\times \left\{ E\left\{ V_3 \left(e^{it\, 2V_3/\sqrt{ns}} - 1 - it\frac{2V_3}{\sqrt{ns}} \right) \right\} + (it)\frac{2}{\sqrt{ns}} E\left(V_3^2 \right) \right\} \{\gamma(t)\}^{n-3}
$$

$$
= \left\{ (it)^2 \frac{4}{ns^2} E(\tilde{W}_{12} V_1 V_2) + O\left(\frac{t^4}{n^2 h^{d+2}} + \frac{|t|^3}{n^{3/2} h^{d+2}} \right) \right\}
$$

$$
\times \left\{ (it)\frac{2}{\sqrt{ns}} E\left(V_3^2 \right) + O\left(\frac{t^2}{n} \right) \right\} \{\gamma(t)\}^{n-3}.
$$

The last equality uses (7.3.17) and

$$
E\left| \tilde{W}_{12} V_1^2 V_2^2 \right| \le \{E|\tilde{W}_{12}|^3\}^{1/2} (E|V_1 V_2|^3)^{2/3} \le Ch^{-\frac{2}{3}d-2} = O(h^{-d-2})
$$

due to Hölder's inequality, Lemma 3(b), (i), (iii), and Lemma 1(d) of NR. Next,

$$
\text{(C')} = -\frac{\{\gamma(t)\}^{n-3}}{s^3} \frac{8n(n-1)(n-2)}{n^{5/2}}
$$

$$
\times \left\{ \frac{8(it)^3}{n^{3/2} s^3} E(\tilde{W}_{12} V_1 V_2)s^2 + O\left(\frac{t^6}{n^3 h^{d+2}} + \frac{|t|^5}{n^{5/2} h^{d+2}} + \frac{t^4}{n^2 h^{d+2}} \right) \right\}
$$

$$
= \frac{\{\gamma(t)\}^{n-3}}{s^3} O\left(\frac{|t|^3}{n} + \frac{t^6}{n^3 h^{d+2}} + \frac{|t|^5}{n^{5/2} h^{d+2}} + \frac{t^4 + |t|^3}{n^2 h^{d+2}} \right).
$$

$$
(7.B.12)
$$

Here we use, due to (iii) and Lemma 2,

$$
E(\tilde{W}_{12} V_1 V_2) = E(W_{13} W_{23} V_1 V_2) = E[E(W_{13} V_1 \mid 3) E(W_{23} V_2 \mid 3)]
$$

$$
= E\left(\tilde{V}_3^2 \right) = O(1).
$$

$$
(7.B.13)
$$

The summand of (C'') can be expressed as follows using (iii), $E(\tilde{W}_{12} V_1 e^{it(2/\sqrt{ns})V_1}) = 0$, Lemma 3(b), and (7.3.17):

$$
E\left(\tilde{W}_{jk} V_j e^{itb_2} \right) = \{\gamma(t)\}^{n-2} E\left(\tilde{W}_{12} V_1 e^{it(2/\sqrt{ns})(V_1+V_2)} \right)
$$

$$
= \{\gamma(t)\}^{n-2} E\left\{ \tilde{W}_{12} V_1 e^{it\, 2V_1/\sqrt{ns}} \right.
$$

$$
\times \left(e^{it\, 2V_2/\sqrt{ns}} - 1 - it\frac{2V_2}{\sqrt{ns}} \right) + \frac{2it}{\sqrt{ns}} \tilde{W}_{12} V_1 V_2 \Bigg\}
$$

$$
= \{\gamma(t)\}^{n-2} \left\{ \frac{2it}{\sqrt{ns}} E(\tilde{W}_{12} V_1 V_2) + O\left(\frac{|t|^2}{n h^{d+2}} \right) \right\}.
$$

Thus, using (7.3.7) and (7.B.13),

$$
\begin{aligned}
(\mathrm{C}'') &= \frac{\{\gamma(t)\}^{n-2}}{s^3}\left[-\frac{8n(n-1)}{n^{5/2}}\left\{\frac{2it}{\sqrt{ns}}E(\tilde{W}_{12}V_1V_2)+O\left(\frac{t^2}{nh^{d+2}}\right)\right\}\right]\\
&= \frac{\{\gamma(t)\}^{n-2}}{s^3}O\left(\frac{|t|}{n}+\frac{t^2}{n^{3/2}h^{d+2}}\right).
\end{aligned}
\tag{7.B.14}
$$

Similarly,

$$
(\mathrm{C}''') = \frac{\{\gamma(t)\}^{n-2}}{s^3}O\left(\frac{|t|}{n}+\frac{t^2}{n^{3/2}h^{d+2}}\right).
\tag{7.B.15}
$$

By (7.B.12), (7.B.14), and (7.B.15),

$$
\begin{aligned}
(\mathrm{C}) &= (\mathrm{C}')+(\mathrm{C}'')+(\mathrm{C}''')\\
&= \frac{\{\gamma(t)\}^{n-3}}{s^3}\left[O\left(\frac{|t|^3+|t|}{n}+\frac{t^2}{n^{3/2}h^{d+2}}+\frac{t^6}{n^3h^{d+2}}\right.\right.\\
&\quad\left.\left.+\frac{|t|^5}{n^{5/2}h^{d+2}}+\frac{t^4+|t|^3}{n^2h^{d+2}}\right)\right].
\end{aligned}
\tag{7.B.16}
$$

Therefore, by (7.3.7), (7.B.1), (7.B.4), (7.B.11), and (7.B.16),

$$
\begin{aligned}
E(\tilde{b}_2'E^{itb_2}) &= (\mathrm{A})+(\mathrm{B})+(\mathrm{C})\\
&= -\{\gamma(t)\}^{n-1}\left\{it\frac{2}{n}E(W_{12}^2)+O\left(\frac{|t|}{n^2h^{d+2}}+\frac{t^2}{n^{3/2}h^{d+2}}+\frac{|t|h^L}{nh^{d+2}}\right)\right\}\\
&\quad -\{\gamma(t)\}^{n-1}\left\{\frac{4E(V_1^3)+8E(W_{12}V_1V_2)}{n^{1/2}}+O\left(\frac{|t|}{n}\right)\right\}\\
&\quad -\{\gamma(t)\}^{n-2}\left[\frac{(it)^2}{n^{1/2}}\{4E(V_1^3)+8E(W_{12}V_1V_2)\}\right.\\
&\quad\left.+O\left(\frac{t^2+|t|^3}{n}+\frac{t^4}{n^{3/2}}\right)\right]+\{\gamma(t)\}^{n-3}\left[O\left(\frac{|t|^3+|t|}{n}\right.\right.\\
&\quad\left.\left.+\frac{t^2}{n^{3/2}h^{d+2}}+\frac{t^6}{n^3h^{d+2}}+\frac{|t|^5}{n^{5/2}h^{d+2}}+\frac{t^4+|t|^3}{n^2h^{d+2}}\right)\right].
\end{aligned}
$$

(b): Writing, using (7.3.7) and Lemma 4 of Robinson (1995),

$$
\begin{aligned}
|E(\tilde{b}_{2m}e^{it\bar{B}_m})| &\le \frac{C}{n^{3/2}h^{d+2}}\sum_{j=1}^m |E(V_je^{it\bar{B}_m})|\\
&\quad +\frac{C}{n^{3/2}}\left\{\sum_{j=1}^n\sum_{k=1}^m |E(d_jV_ke^{it\bar{B}_m})|+\sum_{j=1}^m\sum_{k=m+1}^n |E(d_jV_ke^{it\bar{B}_m})|\right\}
\end{aligned}
$$

$$+ \frac{C}{n^{5/2}} \left\{ \sum_{j=1}^{n-1} \sum_{k=j+1}^{n} \sum_{s=1}^{m} |E(e_{jk} V_s e^{it\bar{B}_m})| \right.$$

$$\left. + \sum_{j=1}^{m} \sum_{k=j+1}^{n} \sum_{s=m+1}^{n} |E(e_{jk} V_s e^{it\bar{B}_m})| \right\}$$

$$+ \frac{C}{n^{7/2}} \left[\sum_{j=1}^{n} \sum_{k<l}^{n}{}^{(j)} \sum_{s=1}^{m} |E(V_j W_{kl} V_s e^{it\bar{B}_m})| \right.$$

$$+ \sum_{j=1}^{n} \sum_{k=m+1}^{m_{(j)}} \sum_{l=k+1}^{n}{}^{(j)} \sum_{s=m+1}^{n} |E(V_j W_{kl} V_s e^{it\bar{B}_m})|$$

$$\left. + \sum_{j=1}^{m} \sum_{k=m+1}^{n-1}{}^{(j)} \sum_{l=k+1}^{n}{}^{(j)} \sum_{s=m+1}^{n} |E(V_j W_{kl} V_s e^{it\bar{B}_m})| \right], \quad (7.B.17)$$

$$|E(V_j e^{it\bar{B}_m})| = \left| E\left(V_j e^{it(2/\sqrt{n}s)V_j}\right) E\left\{ e^{it((2/\sqrt{n}s)\sum_{k\neq j}^{n} V_k + b_3 - b_{3m} + \tilde{b}_2 - \tilde{b}_{2m} + \tilde{b}_3' - \tilde{b}_{3m}')} \right\} \right|$$

$$\leq E|V_j| |\gamma(t)|^{m-1} \qquad (7.B.18)$$

for $j = 1, \ldots, m$, since $b_3 - b_{3m} + \tilde{b}_2' - b_{2m}' + \tilde{b}_3' - \tilde{b}_{3m}'$ is independent of $V_1, \ldots, V_m$.

For $j \leq m$, $k \leq m$, and $j \neq k$,

$$|E(d_j V_k e^{it\bar{B}_m})|$$

$$= \left| E\left[d_j V_k e^{it\left\{ (2/\sqrt{n}s)\left(V_j + V_k + \sum_{l=m+1}^{n} V_l\right) + b_3 - b_{3m} + \tilde{b}_2 - \tilde{b}_{2m} + \tilde{b}_3' - \tilde{b}_{3m}'\right\}} \right] \right|$$

$$\times \left| E\left\{ e^{it(2/\sqrt{n}s)\sum_{l\neq j,k}^{m} V_l} \right\} \right|$$

$$\leq E|d_j V_k| |\gamma(t)|^{m-2}. \qquad (7.B.19)$$

For $j = k \leq m$,

$$|E(d_j V_j e^{it\bar{B}_m})|$$

$$= \left| E\left[d_j V_j e^{it\left\{ (2/\sqrt{n}s)\left(V_j + \sum_{k=m+1}^{n} V_k\right) + b_3 - b_{3m} + \tilde{b}_2 - \tilde{b}_{2m} + \tilde{b}_3' - \tilde{b}_{3m}'\right\}} \right] \right|$$

$$\times \left| E\left\{ e^{it(2/\sqrt{n}s)\sum_{k\neq j}^{m} V_k} \right\} \right|$$

$$\leq E|d_j V_j| |\gamma(t)|^{m-1} \leq E|d_j V_j| |\gamma(t)|^{m-2}. \qquad (7.B.20)$$

For $j \leq m$ and $k \geq m+1$,

$$|E(d_j V_k e^{it\tilde{B}_m})|$$

$$= \left| E\left[d_j V_k e^{it\left\{ (2/\sqrt{n}s)\left(V_j + \sum_{l=m+1}^n V_l\right) + b_3 - b_{3m} + \tilde{b}_2 - \tilde{b}_{2m} + \tilde{b}'_3 - \tilde{b}'_{3m} \right\}} \right] \right|$$

$$\times \left| E\left\{ e^{it\,(2/\sqrt{n}s)\sum_{l\neq j}^m V_l} \right\} \right|$$

$$\leq E|d_j V_k||\gamma(t)|^{m-1}$$

$$\leq E|d_j V_k||\gamma(t)|^{m-2}. \tag{7.B.21}$$

For $j \geq m+1$ and $k \leq m$, similarly to (7.B.21),

$$|E(d_j V_k e^{it\tilde{B}_m})| \leq E|d_j V_k||\gamma(t)|^{m-2}. \tag{7.B.22}$$

Therefore, by (7.B.19)–(7.B.22) and Lemma 4, for all j, k,

$$|E(d_j V_k e^{it\tilde{B}_m})| \leq E|d_j V_k||\gamma(t)|^{m-2}. \tag{7.B.23}$$

Similarly to the derivation of (7.B.23), for any j, k, l, s,

$$|E(e_{jk} V_s e^{it\tilde{B}_m})| \leq E|e_{jk} V_s||\gamma(t)|^{m-3}, \tag{7.B.24}$$

$$|E(V_j W_{kl} V_s e^{it\tilde{B}_m})| \leq E|V_j W_{kl} V_s||\gamma(t)|^{m-4}. \tag{7.B.25}$$

Substituting (7.B.18), (7.B.23)–(7.B.25) into (7.B.17), using $|\gamma(t)| \leq 1$,

$$|E(\tilde{b}_{2m} e^{it\tilde{B}_m})| \leq C|\gamma(t)|^{m-4}\left[\frac{1}{n^{3/2}h^{d+2}} \sum_{j=1}^m E|V_j| \right.$$

$$+ \frac{1}{n^{3/2}}\left(\sum_{j=1}^n \sum_{k=1}^m E|d_j V_k| + \sum_{j=1}^m \sum_{k=m+1}^n E|d_j V_k| \right)$$

$$+ \frac{1}{n^{5/2}}\left(\sum_{j=1}^{n-1} \sum_{k=j+1}^n \sum_{s=1}^m E|e_{jk} V_s| + \sum_{j=1}^m \sum_{k=j+1}^n \sum_{s=m+1}^n E|e_{jk} V_s| \right)$$

$$+ \frac{1}{n^{7/2}}\left(\sum_{j=1}^n \sum_{k<l}^{(j)} \sum_{s=1}^m E|V_j W_{kl} V_s| \right.$$

$$+ \sum_{j=1}^n \sum_{k=l}^{m} {}^{(j)} \sum_{l=k+1}^n {}^{(j)} \sum_{s=m+1}^n E|V_j W_{kl} V_s|$$

$$+ \left.\left. \sum_{j=1}^m \sum_{k=m+1}^{n-1} {}^{(j)} \sum_{l=k+1}^n {}^{(j)} \sum_{s=m+1}^n E|V_j W_{kl} V_s| \right)\right]. \tag{7.B.26}$$

The summations in the square brackets have the following bounds.

$$\sum_{j=1}^{m} E|V_j| \le C_m \qquad \text{by Lemma 1(d) of NR;} \tag{7.B.27}$$

$$\sum_{j=1}^{n}\sum_{k=1}^{m} E|d_j V_k| = \sum_{j=1}^{m} E|d_j V_j| + \sum_{j=1}^{n}\sum_{k=l}^{m}{}^{(j)} E|d_j V_k|$$
$$\le C(m + mn) \qquad \text{by Lemma 4;} \tag{7.B.28}$$

$$\sum_{j=1}^{m}\sum_{s=m+1}^{n} E|d_j V_s| \le Cmn \qquad \text{by Lemma 4(a);} \tag{7.B.29}$$

$$\sum_{j=1}^{n-1}\sum_{k=j+1}^{n}\sum_{s=1}^{m} E|e_{jk} V_s| = \sum_{j=1}^{n=1}\sum_{k=j+1}^{n}\sum_{s=1}^{m}{}^{(j,k)} E|e_{jk} V_s|$$
$$+ \sum_{j=1}^{m}\sum_{k=j+1}^{n} E|e_{jk} V_j| + \sum_{j=1}^{m-1}\sum_{k=j+1}^{m} E|e_{jk} V_k|$$
$$\le C(mn^2 + mn + m^2)h^{-2} \qquad \text{by Lemma 6,} \tag{7.B.30}$$

$\sum_{s}^{(i_1,i_2,\dots,i_r)}$ denoting summation excluding $s = i_1, i_2, \dots, i_r$;

$$\sum_{j=1}^{m}\sum_{k=j+1}^{n}\sum_{s=m+1}^{n} E|e_{jk} V_s|$$
$$= \sum_{j=1}^{m}\sum_{k=j+1}^{n}\sum_{s=m+1}^{n}{}^{(j)} E|e_{jk} V_s| + \sum_{j=1}^{m}\sum_{k=j+1}^{n} E|e_{jk} V_k|$$
$$\le C(mn^2 + mn)h^{-2} \qquad \text{by Lemma 6;} \tag{7.B.31}$$

$$\sum_{j=1}^{n}\sum_{k<l}^{n}{}^{(j)}\sum_{s=1}^{m} E|V_j W_{kl} V_s|$$
$$= \sum_{j=1}^{n}\sum_{k<l}^{n}{}^{(j)}\sum_{s=1}^{m}{}^{(j,k,l)} E|V_j|E|W_{kl}|E|V_s| + \sum_{j=1}^{m}\sum_{k<l}^{m}{}^{(j)} E|V_j^2 W_{kl}|$$
$$+ \sum_{j=1}^{n}\sum_{k<l}^{m}{}^{(j)} E|V_j W_{kl} V_k| + \sum_{j=1}^{n}\sum_{k<l}^{m}{}^{(j)} E|V_j W_{kl} V_l|$$
$$\le C(mn^3 + mn^2 + m^2 n)h^{-1} \tag{7.B.32}$$

by (iii), Lemma 1(d) of NR, Lemma 4 of Robinson (1995), and Lemma 5;

$$\sum_{j=1}^{n}\sideset{}{^{(j)}}\sum_{k=l}^{m}\sideset{}{^{(j)}}\sum_{l=k+1}^{n}\sum_{s=m+1}^{n} E|V_j W_{kl} V_s|$$

$$= \sum_{j=1}^{n}\sideset{}{^{(j)}}\sum_{k=l}^{m}\sideset{}{^{(j)}}\sum_{l=k+1}^{n}\sideset{}{^{(j,l)}}\sum_{s=m+1}^{n} E|V_j||E|W_{kl}||E|V_s|$$

$$+ \sum_{j=m+1}^{n}\sideset{}{^{(j)}}\sum_{k=l}^{m}\sideset{}{^{(j)}}\sum_{l=k+1}^{n} E|V_j^2 W_{kl}| + \sum_{j=1}^{n}\sideset{}{^{(j)}}\sum_{k=l}^{m}\sideset{}{^{(j)}}\sum_{l=k+1}^{n} E|V_j W_{kl} V_l|$$

$$\leq C(mn^3 + mn^2)h^{-1} \tag{7.B.33}$$

by (iii), Lemma 1(d) of NR, Lemma 4 of Robinson (1995), and Lemma 5; and

$$\sum_{j=1}^{m}\sideset{}{^{(j)}}\sum_{m<k<l}^{n}\sum_{s=m+1}^{n} E|V_j W_{kl} V_s|$$

$$= \sum_{j=1}^{m}\sideset{}{^{(j)}}\sum_{m<k<l}^{n}\sideset{}{^{(k,l)}}\sum_{s=m+1}^{n} E|V_j||E|W_{kl}||E|V_s|$$

$$+ \sum_{j=1}^{m}\sideset{}{^{(j)}}\sum_{m<k<l}^{n} (E|V_j W_{kl} V_k| + E|V_j W_{kl} V_l|)$$

$$\leq C(mn^3 + mn^2)h^{-1} \tag{7.B.34}$$

by (iii), Lemma 1(d) of NR, Lemma 4 of Robinson (1995), and Lemma 5. Therefore, substituting (7.B.27)–(7.B.34) into (7.B.26), using $1 \leq m \leq n - 1$,

$$|E(\tilde{b}'_{2m} e^{it\bar{B}_m})| \leq C|\gamma(t)|^{m-4}\left(\frac{m}{n^{3/2}h^{d+2}} + \frac{mn}{n^{3/2}} + \frac{mn^2}{n^{5/2}h^2} + \frac{mn^3}{n^{7/2}h}\right)$$

$$\leq \frac{Cm}{n^{1/2}h^2}|\gamma(t)|^{m-4}, \tag{7.B.35}$$

the third term in parentheses dominating for sufficiently large n by assumption (ix).

(c): Using (7.3.7) and Lemma 4 of Robinson (1995), we write

$$|E(\tilde{b}'_{3m} e^{it\bar{B}_m})|$$

$$\leq C\left[\frac{1}{n^{5/2}h^{d+2}}\sum_{l=1}^{m}\sum_{s=l+1}^{n} |E(W_{ls} e^{it\bar{B}_m})|\right.$$

$$+ \frac{1}{n^{5/2}}\left(\sum_{j=1}^{m}\sum_{l<s}^{n} |E(d_j W_{ls} e^{it\bar{B}_m})| + \sum_{j=m+1}^{n}\sum_{l=1}^{m}\sum_{s=l+1}^{n} |E(d_j W_{ls} e^{it\bar{B}_m})|\right)$$

$$+ \frac{1}{n^{7/2}} \left(\sum_{j=1}^{m} \sum_{k=j+1}^{n} \sum_{l<s}^{n} |E(\tilde{W}_{jk} W_{ls} e^{it\bar{B}_m})| \right.$$

$$\left. + \sum_{m<j<k}^{n} \sum_{l=1}^{m} \sum_{s=l+1}^{n} |E(\tilde{W}_{jk} W_{ls} e^{it\bar{B}_m})| \right) \right]. \tag{7.B.36}$$

Similarly to (7.B.23)–(7.B.25), for all j, k, l, s,

$$|E(W_{ls} e^{it\bar{B}_m})| \leq E|W_{ls}| |\gamma(t)|^{m-2}, \tag{7.B.37}$$

$$|E(d_j W_{ls} e^{it\bar{B}_m})| \leq E|d_j W_{ls}| |\gamma(t)|^{m-3}, \tag{7.B.38}$$

$$|E(\tilde{W}_{jk} W_{ls} e^{it\bar{B}_m})| \leq E|\tilde{W}_{jk} W_{ls}| |\gamma(t)|^{m-4}. \tag{7.B.39}$$

Substituting (7.B.37)–(7.B.39) into (7.B.36), we have, due to $|\gamma(t)| \leq 1$,

$$|E(\tilde{b}_{3m}' e^{it\bar{B}_m})| \leq C|\gamma(t)|^{m-4} \left[\frac{1}{n^{5/2} h^{d+2}} \sum_{l=1}^{m} \sum_{s=l+1}^{n} E|W_{ls}| \right.$$

$$+ \frac{1}{n^{5/2}} \left(\sum_{j=1}^{m} \sum_{l<s}^{n} E|d_j W_{ls}| + \sum_{j=m+1}^{n} \sum_{l=1}^{m} \sum_{s=l+1}^{n} E|d_j W_{ls}| \right)$$

$$+ \frac{1}{n^{7/2}} \left(\sum_{j=1}^{m} \sum_{k=j+1}^{n} \sum_{l<s}^{n} E|\tilde{W}_{jk} W_{ls}| \right.$$

$$\left. \left. + \sum_{j=m+1}^{n-1} \sum_{k=j+1}^{n} \sum_{l=1}^{m} \sum_{s=l+1}^{n} E|\tilde{W}_{jk} W_{ls}| \right) \right].$$

Applying Lemma 4 of Robinson (1995), Lemmas 7 and 8, and (ix),

$$|E(\tilde{b}_{3m}' e^{it\bar{B}_m})| \leq C|\gamma(t)|^{m-4} \left\{ \frac{mn}{n^{5/2} h^{d+3}} + \frac{mn^2}{n^{5/2} h} + \frac{1}{n^{7/2}} \left(\frac{mn}{h^{d+3}} + \frac{mn^3}{h^3} \right) \right\}$$

$$= Cm|\gamma(t)|^{m-4} \left(\frac{1}{n^{3/2} h^{d+3}} + \frac{1}{n^{1/2} h} + \frac{1}{n^{5/2} h^{d+3}} + \frac{1}{n^{1/2} h^3} \right)$$

$$\leq \frac{Cm}{n^{1/2} h^3} |\gamma(t)|^{m-4}.$$

(d): Write, using (7.3.7) and Lemma 4 of Robinson (1995),

$$E|\tilde{b}_{2m}|^2 \leq C \left[\frac{1}{n^3 h^{2d+4}} E \left| \sum_{i=1}^{m} V_i \right|^2 + \frac{1}{n^3} \left(E \left| \sum_{i=1}^{n} \sum_{s=1}^{m} d_i V_s \right|^2 + E \left| \sum_{i=1}^{m} \sum_{s=m+1}^{n} d_i V_s \right|^2 \right) \right.$$

$$\left. + \frac{1}{n^5} \left(E \left| \sum_{i=1}^{n-1} \sum_{j=i+1}^{n} \sum_{s=1}^{m} e_{ij} V_s \right|^2 + E \left| \sum_{i=1}^{m} \sum_{j=i+1}^{n} \sum_{s=m+1}^{n} e_{ij} V_s \right|^2 \right) \right.$$

$$+ \frac{1}{n^7} \left(E \left| \sum_{i=1}^{n} \sum_{k<l}^{m} \sum_{s=1}^{m(i)} V_i W_{kl} V_s \right|^2 + E \left| \sum_{i=1}^{n} \sum_{k=1}^{m} \sum_{l=k+1}^{(i)} \sum_{s=m+1}^{(i)} \sum_{s=m+1}^{n} V_i W_{kl} V_s \right|^2 \right.$$

$$+ E \left| \sum_{i=1}^{m} \sum_{k=m+1}^{n-1(i)} \sum_{l=k+1}^{n} \sum_{s=m+1}^{n} V_i W_{kl} V_s \right|^2 \right) \Bigg]. \tag{7.B.40}$$

We show bounds only of some typical terms. Since V_i is an iid sequence with zero mean, by Lemma 1(d) of NR we have $E|\sum_{i=1}^{m} V_i|^2 m E|V_1|^2 \le Cm$. Writing

$$E \left| \sum_{i=1}^{n} \sum_{s=1}^{m} d_i V_s \right|^2 \le C \left(E \left| \sum_{i=1}^{m} d_i V_i \right|^2 + E \left| \sum_{i=1}^{m-1} \sum_{s=i+1}^{m} d_i V_s \right|^2 \right.$$

$$+ E \left| \sum_{s=1}^{m} \sum_{i=s+1}^{n} d_i V_s \right|^2 \right), \tag{7.B.41}$$

the first term in parentheses is bounded by

$$m E|d_1 V_1|^2 + m(m - 1) E|d_1 V_1| E|d_2 V_2| \le Cm^2 \tag{7.B.42}$$

due to (iii) and Lemma 4(b). Since d_i and V_s are iid with zero mean,

$$E \left| \sum_{i=1}^{m-1} \sum_{s=i+1}^{m} d_i V_s \right|^2 = \sum_{i=1}^{m-1} E\left(d_i^2\right) \sum_{s=i+1}^{m} E\left(V_s^2\right) \le Cm^2 \tag{7.B.43}$$

by Lemma 1(d) of NR and (7.A.2) under (i). Similarly, using Lemma 4(a),

$$E \left| \sum_{s=1}^{m} \sum_{i=s+1}^{n} d_i V_s \right|^2 \le \sum_{s=1}^{m} \sum_{i=s+1}^{n} E\left(d_i^2\right) E\left(V_s^2\right) \le Cmn. \tag{7.B.44}$$

From (7.B.41)–(7.B.44),

$$E \left| \sum_{i=1}^{n} \sum_{s=1}^{m} d_i V_s \right|^2 \le C(m^2 + mn).$$

Similarly,

$$E \left| \sum_{i=1}^{m} \sum_{j=m+1}^{n} d_i V_s \right|^2 = \sum_{i=1}^{m} E\left(d_i^2\right) \sum_{s=m+1}^{n} E\left(V_s^2\right) \le Cmn.$$

We next consider

$$E\left|\sum_{i=1}^{n-1}\sum_{j=i+1}^{n}\sum_{s=1}^{m} e_{ij} V_s\right|^2 \le C\left\{E\left|\sum_{s=1}^{m-1}\sum_{i=s+1}^{n-1}\sum_{j=i+1}^{n} e_{ij} V_s\right|^2 + E\left|\sum_{i=1}^{m}\sum_{j=i+1}^{n} e_{ij} V_i\right|^2\right.$$

$$+ E\left|\sum_{i=1}^{m-1}\sum_{s=i+1}^{m}\sum_{j=s+1}^{n} e_{ij} V_s\right|^2 + E\left|\sum_{i=1}^{m-1}\sum_{j=i+1}^{m} e_{ij} V_j\right|^2$$

$$\left. + E\left|\sum_{i=1}^{m-2}\sum_{j=i+1}^{m-1}\sum_{s=j+1}^{m} e_{ij} V_s\right|^2\right\}. \tag{7.B.45}$$

Due to (iii), $E(e_{ij} \mid i) = E(e_{ij} \mid j) = 0$, $E(V_s) = 0$, and Lemma 6, the triple summation on the right of (7.B.45) is $O((m^3 + m^2 n + mn^2)h^{-d-4})$. Using Lemma 6 and Hölder's inequality, the second term in (7.B.45) is

$$\sum_{i=1}^{m}\sum_{j=i+1}^{n} E(e_{ij} V_i)^2 + 2\sum_{i=1}^{m-1}\sum_{k=i+1}^{m}\sum_{j=k+1}^{n} E(e_{ij} V_i e_{kj} V_k)$$

$$\le C[mn E(e_{12} V_1)^2 + m^2 n\{E(e_{13} V_1)^2 E(e_{23} V_2)^2\}^{1/2}]$$

$$\le C m^2 n h^{-d-4}. \tag{7.B.46}$$

Similarly, the fourth term of (7.B.45) is $O(m^3 h^{-d-4})$. Using Lemma 5, as above, the terms involving $V_i W_{kl} V_s$ in (7.B.40) are $O((m^4 + m^3 n + m^2 n^2 + mn^3)h^{-d-2})$, so by (ix)

$$E|\tilde{b}_{2m}|^2 \le \frac{C}{nh^{d+2}}\left(\frac{m}{n^2 h^{d+2}}\right) + \frac{C}{n^3}(m^2 + mn) + \frac{C}{n^5}(m^3 + m^2 n + mn^2)h^{-d-4}$$

$$+ \frac{C}{n^7}(m^4 + m^3 n + m^2 n^2 + mn^3)h^{-d-2}$$

$$\le Cm\left(\frac{1}{n^3 h^{2d+4}} + \frac{1}{n^2}\right).$$

(e): The derivation is similar, using Lemma 4 of Robinson (1995) and Lemmas 7 and 8. As in (d), we can show

$$E|\tilde{b}'_{3m}|^2 \le \frac{C}{n^5 h^{2d+4}}mnh^{-d-2} + \frac{C}{n^5}(m^3 + m^2 n + mn^2)h^{-d-2}$$

$$+ \frac{C}{n^7}(m^4 + m^3 n + m^2 n^2 + mn^3)h^{-3d-6}$$

$$\le \frac{Cm}{n^4 h^{3d+6}}.$$

(f): Write

$$|E\tilde{b}_3'' e^{it\bar{B}_m}| = |EQ\bar{W}e^{it\bar{B}_m}| \le |EQ_1\bar{W}e^{it\bar{B}_m}| + |EQ_2\bar{W}e^{it\bar{B}_m}|. \tag{7.B.47}$$

By (7.3.7),

$$|E(Q_1\bar{W}e^{it\bar{B}_m})|$$

$$\le \frac{C}{n^{7/2}}\left|\sum_{j=1}^{n-1}\sum_{k=j+1}^{n}\sum_{l=1}^{n-1}\sum_{s=l+1}^{n} E\{(V_j + V_k)W_{jk} - \tilde{V}_j - \tilde{V}_k\}W_{ls}e^{it\bar{B}_m}\right|$$

$$\le \frac{6C}{n^{7/2}}\sum_{j=1}^{n-3}\sum_{k=j+1}^{n-2}\sum_{l=k+1}^{n-1}\sum_{s=l+1}^{n} E|\{(V_j + V_k)W_{jk} - \tilde{V}_j - \tilde{V}_k\}W_{ls}||\gamma(t)|^{m-4}$$

$$+ \frac{6C}{n^{7/2}}\sum_{j=1}^{n-2}\sum_{k=j+1}^{n-1}\sum_{s=k+1}^{n} E|\{(V_j + V_k)W_{jk} - \tilde{V}_j - \tilde{V}_k\}W_{ks}||\gamma(t)|^{m-3}$$

$$+ \frac{C}{n^{7/2}}\sum_{j=1}^{n-1}\sum_{k=j+1}^{n} E|\{(V_j + V_k)W_{jk} - \tilde{V}_j - \tilde{V}_k\}W_{jk}||\gamma(t)|^{m-2}$$

$$\le Cn^{1/2}E|\{(V_1 + V_2)W_{12} - \tilde{V}_1 - \tilde{V}_2\}W_{34}||\gamma(t)|^{m-4}$$

$$+ \frac{C}{n^{1/2}}E|\{(V_1 + V_2)W_{12} - \tilde{V}_1 - \tilde{V}_2\}W_{13}||\gamma(t)|^{m-3}$$

$$+ \frac{C}{n^{3/2}}E|\{(V_1 + V_2)W_{12} - \tilde{V}_1 - \tilde{V}_2\}W_{12}||\gamma(t)|^{m-3}. \tag{7.B.48}$$

Using (i), (iii), Lemmas 1(d) and 4 of NR, (7.A.1), and Lemma 4 of Robinson (1995), the first expectation of (7.B.48) is bounded by

$$CE\{(|Y_1| + |Y_2| + 1)|W_{12}|\}E|W_{34}| \le Ch^{-2}.$$

Using (i), Lemmas 1(d) and 4 of NR, (7.A.1), and Lemma 4 of Robinson (1995), the second expectation of (7.B.48) is bounded by

$$CE\{(|Y_1| + |Y_2| + 1)|W_{12}||W_{13}|\}$$
$$\le CE\{(|Y_1| + |Y_2| + 1)|W_{12}|E(|W_{13}||1)\}$$
$$\le Ch^{-1}E\{(|Y_1| + |Y_2| + 1)(|Y_1| + 1)|W_{12}|\}.$$

Similarly to Lemma 1 and (7.A.5), $E|Y_1W_{12}| + E|Y_1^2 W_{12}| + E|Y_1 Y_2 W_{12}| = O(h^{-1})$, so that the above quantity is $O(h^{-2})$. The third expectation of (7.B.48) is bounded by

$$CE|V_1 W_{12}^2| + E|\tilde{V}_1 W_{12}| \le C(h^{-d-2} + h^{-1}) = O(h^{-d-2})$$

due to Lemmas 1(d) and 4 of NR, Lemma 4 of Robinson (1995), and Lemma 2. Therefore,

$$|E(Q_1\bar{W}e^{it\bar{B}_m})| \le C\left(\frac{n^{1/2}}{h^2} + \frac{1}{n^{3/2}h^{d+2}}\right)|\gamma(t)|^{m-4} \le \frac{Cn^{1/2}}{h^2}|\gamma(t)|^{m-4}.$$

The second term of (7.B.47) is bounded, using (7.3.7), by

$$
\frac{C}{n^{9/2}} \left| \sum_{r=1}^{n} \sum_{j=1}^{n-1}{}^{(r)} \sum_{k=j+1}^{n}{}^{(r)} \sum_{l=1}^{n-1} \sum_{s=l+1}^{n} E(V_r W_{jk} W_{ls} e^{it\bar{B}_m}) \right|
$$

$$
\leq \frac{C}{n^{9/2}} \sum_{r=1}^{n-4} \sum_{j=r+1}^{n-3} \sum_{k=j+1}^{n-2} \sum_{l=k+1}^{n-1} \sum_{s=l+1}^{n} E|V_r W_{jk} W_{ls}| |\gamma(t)|^{m-5}
$$

$$
+ \frac{C}{n^{9/2}} \sum_{r=1}^{n-3} \sum_{j=r+1}^{n-2} \sum_{k=j+1}^{n-1} \sum_{s=k+1}^{n} E|V_r W_{jk} W_{ks}| |\gamma(t)|^{m-4}
$$

$$
+ \frac{C}{n^{9/2}} \sum_{r=1}^{n-3} \sum_{j=r+1}^{n-2} \sum_{k=j+1}^{n-1} \sum_{s=k+1}^{n} E|V_r W_{jk} W_{rs}| |\gamma(t)|^{m-4}
$$

$$
+ \frac{C}{n^{9/2}} \sum_{r=1}^{n-2} \sum_{j=r+1}^{n-1} \sum_{k=j+1}^{n} E|V_r W_{jk} W_{jk}| |\gamma(t)|^{m-3}
$$

$$
+ \frac{C}{n^{9/2}} \sum_{r=1}^{n-2} \sum_{j=r+1}^{n-1} \sum_{k=j+1}^{n} E|V_r W_{jk} W_{rk}| |\gamma(t)|^{m-3}
$$

$$
\leq C n^{1/2} E|V_1| E|W_{23}| E|W_{45}| |\gamma(t)|^{m-5}
$$

$$
+ \frac{C}{n^{1/2}} (E|V_1| E|W_{23} W_{24}| + E|V_1 W_{14}| E|W_{23}|) |\gamma(t)|^{m-4}
$$

$$
+ \frac{C}{n^{3/2}} (E|V_1| E|W_{23}|^2 + E|V_1 W_{23} W_{13}|) \gamma(t)|^{m-3}
$$

$$
\leq C \left(\frac{n^{1/2}}{h^2} + \frac{1}{n^{1/2} h^2} + \frac{1}{n^{3/2} h^{d+2}} \right) |\gamma(t)|^{m-5}
$$

by (i), (iii), Lemmas 1(d) and 4 of NR, Lemma 4 of Robinson (1995), and Lemma 1. Then apply (ix).

REFERENCES

Amemiya, T. (1973), "Regression Analysis When the Dependent Variable is Truncated Normal," *Econometrica*, **41**, 997–934.

——— (1974a), "Multivariate Regression and Simultaneous Equation Models When the Dependent Variables are Truncated Normal," *Econometrica*, **42**, 999–1012.

——— (1974b), "The Non-Linear Two Stage Least Squares Estimator," *Journal of Econometrics*, **2**, 105–110.

——— (1977), "The Maximum Likelihood and the Nonlinear Three-Stage Least Squares Estimator in the General Nonlinear Simultaneous Equation Model," *Econometrica*, **45**, 955–968.

Amemiya, T. and Powell, J. L. (1981), "A Comparison of the Box–Cox Maximum Likelihood Estimator and the Non-Linear Two-Stage Least Squares Estimator," *Journal of Econometrics*, **17**, 351–381.

Bhattacharya, R. N. and Ghosh, J. K. (1978), "On the Validity of the Formal Edgeworth Expansion," *Annals of Statistics*, **6**, 434–451.

Bhattacharya, R. N. and Rao, R. R. (1976), *Normal Approximation and Asymptotic Expansions* (New York: Wiley).

Callaert, H. and Veraverbeke, N. (1981), "The Order of Normal Approximation to a Studentized U-Statistic," *Annals of Statistics*, **9**, 194–200.

Cheng, B. and Robinson, P. M. (1994), "Semiparametric Estimation for Time Series with Long Range Dependence," *Journal of Econometrics*, **64**, 335–353.

Dharmardhikari, S. W., Fabian, V., and Jogdeo, K. (1968), "Bounds on the Moments of Martingales," *Annals of Mathematical Statistics*, **39**, 1719–1723.

Helmers, R. (1985), "The Berry–Esseen Bound for Studentized U-Statistics," *Canadian Journal of Statistics*, **13**, 1, 79–82.

(1991), "On the Edgeworth Expansion and the Bootstrap Approximation for a Studentized U-Statistic," *Annals of Statistics*, **19**, 1, 470–484.

Horowitz, J. L. (1986), "A Distribution-Free Least Squares Estimator for Censored Linear Regression Models," *Journal of Econometrics*, **32**, 59–84.

(1988), "Semiparametric M-Estimation of Censored Linear Regression Models," *Advances in Econometrics*, **7**, 45–83.

Jennrich, R. I. (1969), "Asymptotic Properties of Non-Linear Least Squares Estimators," *Annals of Mathematical Statistics*, **40**, 633–643.

Lee L.-F. (1992), "Semiparametric Nonlinear Least Squares Estimation of Truncated Regression Models," *Econometric Theory*, **8**, 52–94.

Linton, O. B. (1996), "Edgeworth Approximation for MINPIN Estimators in Semiparametric Regression Models," *Econometric Theory*, **12**, 30–60.

Nishiyama, Y. and Robinson, P. M. (2000), "Edgeworth Expansions for Semiparametric Averaged Derivatives," *Econometrica*, **68**, 931–979.

Pfanzagl, J. (1971), "The Berry–Esseen Bound for Minimum Contrast Estimates," *Metrika*, **17**, 82–91.

(1973), "Asymptotic Expansions Related to Minimum Contrast Estimators," *Annals of Statistics*, **1**, 993–1026.

Powell, J. L. (1984), "Least Absolute Deviations Estimation for the Censored Regression Model," *Journal of Econometrics*, **25**, 303–325.

(1986), "Symmetrically Trimmed Least Squared Estimation for Tobit Models" *Econometrica*, **54**, 1435–1460.

Powell, J. L., Stock, J. H., and Stoker, T. M. (1989), "Semiparametric Estimation of Index Coefficients," *Econometrica*, **57**, 6, 1403–1430.

Robinson, P. M. (1982), "On the Asymptotic Properties of Estimators of Models Containing Limited Dependent Variables," *Econometrica*, **50**, 27–41.

(1989), "Hypothesis Testing in Semiparametric and Non-Parametric Models for Econometric Time Series," *Review of Economic Studies*, **56**, 511–534.

(1991), "Best Nonlinear Three-Stage Least Squares Estimation of Certain Econometric Models," *Econometrica*, **59**, 755–786.

(1995), "The Normal Approximation for Semiparametric Averaged Derivatives," *Econometrica*, **63**, 3, 667–680.

Serfling, R. J. (1980), *Approximation Theorems of Mathematical Statistics* (New York: Wiley).

CHAPTER 8

Nonparametric identification under response-based sampling

Charles F. Manski

1   Introduction

Consider a population each of whose members is described by a vector of covariates z and a binary response y. A common problem of empirical research is to infer the conditional response probabilities $P(y \mid z)$ when the population is divided into response strata and random samples are drawn from one or both strata. This sampling process is known to epidemiologists studying the incidence of disease as *case-control, case-referent,* or *retrospective* sampling, and has been prominent in epidemiological research since the work of Cornfield (1951). The same sampling process in known to economists studying individual behavior as *choice-based* sampling (Manski and Lerman 1977) or as *response-based* sampling (Manski 1986). The final synonym will be used here.

Sampling from the stratum with $y = 1$ reveals the distribution $P(z \mid y = 1)$ of covariates within this stratum. Sampling from the stratum with $y = 0$ reveals $P(z \mid y = 0)$. So response-based sampling raises this basic inferential question: What does knowledge of $P(z \mid y = 1)$ and/or $P(z \mid y = 0)$ reveal about $P(y \mid z)$?

Analysis of response-based sampling has concentrated on situations in which the empirical researcher is able to draw random samples from both response strata, and thus learns both $P(z \mid y = 1)$ and $P(z \mid y = 0)$. The epidemiological and econometrics literatures have emphasized the identifying power of auxiliary information on the distribution of response and covariates. These literatures have, however, differed in important ways.

The epidemiological literature has devoted much attention to *relative risks* and *attributable risks*; that is, to ratios and differences of conditional response probabilities at distinct covariate values. Cornfield (1951) showed that

This paper draws in part on material in Chapter 4 of the author's book *Identification Problems in the Social Sciences* and in part on previously unpublished work by the author. This research was supported by National Science Foundation Grant SBR-9722846. I am grateful to an anonymous reviewer for useful comments.

response-based sampling identifies *odds ratios,* that is, ratios of response to non-response odds at distinct covariate values. He went on to prove that odds ratios reduce to relative risks in the limit as the response probabilities themselves approach zero. That is, relative risks are identified under the *rare-disease assumption.* Attributable risks are also identified under the rare-disease assumption – they are zero.

The econometrics literature has steered clear of the rare-disease assumption, which has little appeal in economic applications. Manski and Lerman (1977) used knowledge of the marginal response distribution $P(y)$ to identify and estimate the response probabilities themselves, and hence both relative and attributable risks. Hsieh, Manski, and McFadden (1985) showed that information about the marginal covariate distribution $P(z)$ can substitute for knowledge of $P(y)$. Manski and McFadden (1981) and Manski (1986) examined the identifying power of parametric and semiparametric models for the response probabilities when neither $P(z)$ nor $P(y)$ is known. Much of the econometric literature on response-based sampling has been concerned not with identification but rather with the asymptotic precision of estimates of identified parametric models for response probabilities (e.g., Cosslett 1981, Amemiya and Vuong 1987, Imbens 1992).

Section 2 of this chapter exposits the main findings on identification using auxiliary distributional information. Recently, in Manski (1995, Chapter 4), I have investigated the identifiability of relative and attributable risks when no auxiliary distributional information is available. It turns out that the relative risk must lie between one and the odds ratio, while the attributable risk must lie between zero and a certain function of the conditional covariate distributions. These bounds on relative and attributable risks are sharp. Section 3 presents the findings and draws implications for empirical practice.

Whereas Sections 2 and 3 mainly describe published work, the analysis in Section 4 is mostly new. Here I drop the hitherto maintained assumption that the empirical researcher can draw samples from both response strata and suppose instead that he is able to sample from only one response stratum. Hsieh, Manski, and McFadden (1985) noted that the conditional response probabilities $P(y \mid z)$ are identified if observations from one response stratum can be combined with auxiliary knowledge of the marginal distributions $P(y)$ and $P(z)$. The new findings reported in this chapter concern two previously unstudied scenarios assuming less extensive auxiliary information. I examine the case in which $P(y)$ is known but not $P(z)$, and that in which $P(z)$ is known but not $P(y)$. In both cases, I prove that the available information implies informative sharp bounds on response probabilities, relative risks, and attributable risks.

I have stressed in Manski (1995) and elsewhere that identification is often not an all-or-nothing proposition: although one may not have information rich enough to identify the exact value of a quantity of interest, one may nevertheless be able to bound the quantity. The findings presented in Sections 3 and 4 exemplify this theme. This chapter limits attention to identification, so the analysis assumes the researcher to know the distributions $P(z \mid y)$ revealed by response-based sampling. In empirical practice, these distributions can be estimated nonparametrically. This done, the estimates of $P(z \mid y)$ can be used to form consistent nonparametric estimates of the bounds. Nonparametric sampling confidence bands can be placed around the bound estimates, much as they have been in recent studies reporting estimates of nonparametric bounds in other settings where the sampling process does not yield point identification. See Manski et al. (1992) and Horowitz and Manski (1998).

The analysis in this chapter is limited to the case of binary response. Epidemiological work on response-based sampling has been concerned almost entirely with binary response, but econometric work has considered more general settings in which the outcome variable y is multinomial and samples are drawn from multiple strata, each composed of a subset of the values of y (see Manski and McFadden 1981). These more general settings are not examined here.

Bayes' theorem plays a large role in the analysis of response-based sampling, so it simplifies the exposition to assume that the covariates z have a discrete distribution. I maintain this assumption throughout the chapter, but the reader should understand that it is not essential. To treat situations in which some components of z have continuous distributions, it suffices in most of the chapter to replace probabilities of z-values by densities in the statement of Bayes' theorem. Replacing probabilities by densities leads to a substantively different analysis only in Section 4.1, where I call attention to this fact.

2   Combining response-based samples with auxiliary distributional information

2.1   *The classical epidemiological approach*

Relative and attributable risk

Let $z = (x, r)$, where x denotes some covariates characterizing a person and r denotes another covariate referred to as a *risk factor* for a specified disease. A longstanding concern of epidemiology is to learn how the value of the risk factor r affects the prevalence of the disease among persons with covariates x. Let $r = j$ and $r = k$ indicate any two values of the risk factor. Let the presence or absence of the disease be indicated by a binary variable y, with $y = 1$ if a person is ill and $y = 0$ if healthy. Let $P(y = 1 \mid x, r = k)$ be the probability of illness for a person with covariates x who has value k of the risk factor, and let $P(y = 1 \mid x, r = j)$ be the probability of illness for a person with covariates x who has value j of the risk factor. The problem is to compare $P(y = 1 \mid x, r = k)$ and $P(y = 1 \mid x, r = j)$.

Epidemiologists compare these conditional disease probabilities through the *relative risk*

$$\text{RR} \equiv \frac{P(y = 1 \mid x, r = k)}{P(y = 1 \mid x, r = j)} \tag{8.1}$$

and the *attributable risk*

$$\text{AR} \equiv P(y = 1 \mid x, r = k) - P(y = 1 \mid x, r = j). \tag{8.2}$$

For example, let y indicate the occurrence of heart disease, let r indicate whether a person smokes cigarettes (yes $= k$, no $= j$), and let x give a person's age, sex, and occupation. For each value of x, RR gives the ratio of the probability of heart disease conditional on smoking to the probability of heart disease conditional on not smoking, while AR gives the difference between these probabilities.

Texts on epidemiology discuss both relative and attributable risk, but empirical research has focused on relative risk. This focus is hard to justify from the perspective of public health. The health impact of altering a risk factor presumably depends on the number of illnesses averted; that is, on the attributable risk times the size of the population. The relative risk statistic is uninformative about this quantity. It seems odd that epidemiological research emphasizes relative risk rather than attributable risk. Indeed, the practice has long been criticized (see Berkson 1958; Fleiss 1981, Section 6.3; and Hsieh, Manski, and McFadden 1985). The rationale, such as it is, seems to rest on the widespread use in epidemiology of response-based sampling.

Response-based sampling and the rare-disease assumption

Random sampling of the population reveals the distribution $P(y, x, r)$, hence the conditional response probabilities $P(y = 1 \mid x, r = k)$ and $P(y = 1 \mid x, r = j)$. Epidemiologists have, however, found that random sampling can be a costly way to gather data. So they have often turned to less expensive stratified sampling designs, especially to response-based designs. One divides the population into ill ($y = 1$) and healthy ($y = 0$) response strata and samples at random within each stratum. Response-based designs are considered to be particularly cost-effective in generating observations of serious diseases, as ill persons are clustered in hospitals and other treatment centers.

Cost-effectiveness in data collection is a virtue only if the sampling process reveals something useful to the researcher. Response-based sampling identifies only the conditional covariate distributions $P(x, r \mid y = 1)$ and $P(x, r \mid y = 0)$, which are not directly of interest to epidemiologists. How then have epidemiologists used response-based samples?

I begin with an important negative fact. Consider any value of (x, r) such that $P(x, r \mid y = 1) > 0$ and $P(x, r \mid y = 0) > 0$. Response-based-sampling data alone reveal nothing about the magnitude of $P(y = 1 \mid x, r)$.

To see this, use Bayes' theorem to write

$$P(y = 1 \mid x, r) = \frac{P(x, r \mid y = 1)P(y = 1)}{P(x, r)}$$

$$= \frac{P(x, r \mid y = 1)P(y = 1)}{P(x, r \mid y = 1)P(y = 1) + P(x, r \mid y = 0)P(y = 0)}. \tag{8.3}$$

Response-based sampling identifies $P(x, r \mid y = 1)$ and $P(x, r \mid y = 0)$, but provides no information about $P(y = 1)$. The fact that $P(y = 1)$ can lie anywhere between zero and one implies that $P(y = 1 \mid x, r)$ can lie anywhere between zero and one.[1]

Facing this situation, epidemiologists have commonly combined response-based-sampling data with the assumption that the disease under study occurs rarely in the population. Formally, analysis under the *rare-disease assumption* is concerned with the limiting behavior of relative and attributable risk as $P(y = 1 \mid x)$ approaches zero.

The rare-disease assumption identifies both relative and attributable risk. To see this, rewrite (8.3) in the equivalent form

$$P(y = 1 \mid x, r) = \frac{P(r \mid x, y = 1)P(y = 1 \mid x)}{P(r \mid x)}$$

$$= \frac{P(r \mid x, y = 1)P(y = 1 \mid x)}{P(r \mid x, y = 1)P(y = 1 \mid x) + P(r \mid x, y = 0)P(y = 0 \mid x)}. \tag{8.4}$$

Inserting the right-side expression into the definitions of relative and attributable risk yields

$$RR = \frac{P(r = k \mid x, y = 1)}{P(r = j \mid x, y = 1)}$$

$$\times \frac{P(r = j \mid x, y = 1)P(y = 1 \mid x) + P(r = j \mid x, y = 0)P(y = 0 \mid x)}{P(r = k \mid x, y = 1)P(y = 1 \mid x) + P(r = k \mid x, y = 0)P(y = 0 \mid x)} \tag{8.5}$$

---

[1] This negative result does not hold if $P(x, r \mid y = 1)$ or $P(x, r \mid y = 0)$ equals zero. If $P(x, r \mid y = 1) > 0$ but $P(x, r \mid y = 0) = 0$, then (8.3) implies that $P(y = 1 \mid x, r) = 1$. If $P(x, r \mid y = 1) = 0$ but $P(x, r \mid y = 0) > 0$, then $P(y = 1 \mid x, r) = 0$. These positive identification findings are degenerate exceptions to the general rule that response-based sampling does not identify response probabilities.

and

$$AR = \frac{P(r = k \mid x, y = 1)P(y = 1 \mid x)}{P(r = k \mid x, y = 1)P(y = 1 \mid x) + P(r = k \mid x, y = 0)P(y = 0 \mid x)}$$
$$- \frac{P(r = j \mid x, y = 1)P(y = 1 \mid x)}{P(r = j \mid x, y = 1)P(y = 1 \mid x) + P(r = j \mid x, y = 0)P(y = 0 \mid x)}.$$

(8.6)

Letting $P(y = 1 \mid x)$ approach zero, we obtain

$$\lim_{P(y=1 \mid x) \to 0} RR = \frac{P(r = k \mid x, y = 1)P(r = j \mid x, y = 0)}{P(r = j \mid x, y = 1)P(r = k \mid x, y = 0)}$$

(8.7)

and

$$\lim_{P(y=1 \mid x) \to 0} AR = 0.$$

(8.8)

Cornfield (1951) showed that (8.7) is the relative risk under the rare-disease assumption. The expression on the right side of (8.7) is called the *odds ratio*, and may also be written as a function of the conditional response probabilities. In particular, it follows from (8.4) that

$$OR \equiv \frac{P(r = k \mid x, y = 1)P(r = j \mid x, y = 0)}{P(r = j \mid x, y = 1)P(r = k \mid x, y = 0)}$$
$$= \frac{P(y = 1 \mid x, r = k)P(y = 0 \mid x, r = j)}{P(y = 0 \mid x, r = k)P(y = 1 \mid x, r = j)}.$$

(8.9)

Cornfield's finding motivates the widespread epidemiological practice of using response-based samples to estimate the odds ratio, and invoking the rare-disease assumption to interpret the odds ratio as relative risk.

2.2   *Use of information on marginal distributions in econometrics*

The problem of inference from response-based samples is that this sampling process does not reveal the marginal response distribution $P(y)$. If $P(y)$ were known, then we would have all the information needed to identify the joint distribution $P(y, x, r)$. Hence the conditional response probabilities $P(y \mid x, r)$ would be identified.

Beginning with Manski and Lerman (1977), the econometric literature on response-based sampling has emphasized that it is often possible to learn $P(y)$ directly from auxiliary data sources. Hsieh, Manski, and McFadden (1985) call attention to the fact that $P(y)$ may be inferred indirectly from information on the marginal distribution of the risk factor or of other covariates. The marginal probability that the risk factor takes value i is

$$P(r = i) = P(r = i \mid y = 1)P(y = 1) + P(r = i \mid y = 0)[1 - P(y = 1)].$$
$$(8.10)$$

Response-based sampling identifies $P(r = i \mid y = 1)$ and $P(r = i \mid y = 0)$. Suppose that $P(r = i)$ is known. Then (8.10) implies that $P(y)$ is identified, provided only that $P(r = i \mid y = 1) \neq P(r = i \mid y = 0)$. For example, in a study of smoking and heart disease, national survey data may reveal the fraction of the population who are smokers. This information may then be combined with response-based-sampling data to learn the fraction of the population with heart disease.

The same reasoning shows that $P(y)$ may be inferred from knowledge of the expected value of some covariate. For example, let the first component of x be a person's age. Suppose that the average age $E(x_1)$ of the population is known. Observe that

$$E(x_1) = E(x_1 \mid y = 1)P(y = 1) + E(x_1 \mid y = 0)[1 - P(y = 1)].$$
$$(8.11)$$

Response-based sampling identifies $E(x_1 \mid y = 1)$ and $E(x_1 \mid y = 0)$, the average ages of ill and healthy people respectively. Hence knowledge of $E(x_1)$ implies knowledge of $P(y)$, provided only that the average age of ill people is not the same as the average age of healthy ones.

3   Response-based sampling with no auxiliary distributional information

In this section I suppose that the empirical researcher is able to draw random samples from both response strata, but has no auxiliary distributional information. Although response-based sampling reveals nothing about the magnitude of the conditional response probabilities $P(y = 1 \mid x, r)$ at fixed values of the covariates (x, r), the researcher can reach conclusions about the way that response probabilities vary with the covariates. We already know that the odds ratio (8.9) is identified. Moreover, inspection of (8.9) shows that knowledge of the odds ratio reveals whether $P(y = 1 \mid x, r = k)$ is larger than $P(y = 1 \mid x, r = j)$. In particular,

$$\text{OR} < 1 \quad \Rightarrow \quad P(y = 1 \mid x, r = k) < P(y = 1 \mid x, r = j), \quad (8.12a)$$
$$\text{OR} = 1 \quad \Rightarrow \quad P(y = 1 \mid x, r = k) = P(y = 1 \mid x, r = j), \quad (8.12b)$$
$$\text{OR} > 1 \quad \Rightarrow \quad P(y = 1 \mid x, r = k) > P(y = 1 \mid x, r = j). \quad (8.12c)$$

Manski (1995, Chapter 4) goes beyond the well-known result (8.12) to prove that response-based sampling implies informative lower and upper bounds on relative and attributable risks. These bounds are developed in Sections 3.1 and 3.2. Some implications of the bounds for empirical practice are drawn in Section 3.3.

I use a numerical example concerning smoking and heart disease to illustrate the findings. Among persons with covariates x, let the actual probabilities of heart disease conditional on smoking ($r = k$) and nonsmoking ($r = j$) be .12 and .08, and let the fraction of persons who smoke be .50. These values imply that the probability of heart disease unconditional on smoking behavior is .10, and that the probabilities of smoking conditional on being ill and healthy are .60 and .49. The implied odds ratio is 1.57, relative risk is 1.50, and attributable risk is .04. Thus the parameters of the example are

$$P(y = 1 \mid x, r = k), \quad P(y = 1 \mid x, r = j), \qquad P(r = k \mid x) = P(r = j \mid x)$$
$$= .12 \qquad\qquad = .08 \qquad\qquad\qquad = .50,$$
$$P(y = 1 \mid x) = .10, \quad P(r = k \mid x, y = 1) = .60, \quad P(r = k \mid x, y = 0) = .49,$$
$$OR = 1.57, \qquad RR = 1.50, \qquad\qquad AR = .04.$$

3.1   Bound on relative risk

Examine the expression for relative risk given in (8.5). All the quantities on the right side of this equation are identified by response-based sampling except for $P(y \mid x)$. All that is known is that $P(y = 1 \mid x)$ and $P(y = 0 \mid x)$ are both nonnegative and sum to one. So we may determine the range of possible values for RR by analyzing how the right side of (8.5) varies across the logically possible values of $P(y \mid x)$.

The result is that the relative risk must lie between the odds ratio and the value 1. That is,

Proposition 1. *Let $P(x, r \mid y = 1)$ and $P(x, r \mid y = 0)$ be known. Then sharp bounds on RR are*

$$OR < 1 \quad \Rightarrow \quad OR \le RR \le 1, \tag{8.13a}$$
$$OR = 1 \quad \Rightarrow \quad RR = 1, \tag{8.13b}$$
$$OR > 1 \quad \Rightarrow \quad 1 \le RR \le OR. \tag{8.13c}$$

Proof: Relative risk is monotone in $P(y = 1 \mid x)$, the direction of change depending on the magnitude of the odds ratio. To see this, let $p \equiv P(y = 1 \mid x)$, and let $P_{im} \equiv P(r = i \mid x, y = m)$ for $i = j, k$ and $m = 0, 1$. Write the relative risk (8.5) explicitly as a function of p. Thus define

$$RR_p = \frac{P_{k1}}{P_{j1}} \cdot \frac{(P_{j1} - P_{j0})p + P_{j0}}{(P_{k1} - P_{k0})p + P_{k0}}.$$

The derivative of RR_p with respect to p is

$$\frac{P_{k1}}{P_{j1}} \cdot \frac{P_{j1}P_{k0} - P_{k1}P_{j0}}{[(P_{k1} - P_{k0})p + P_{k0}]^2}.$$

This derivative is positive if $OR < 1$, zero if $OR = 1$, and negative if $OR > 1$.

The fact that relative risk is monotone in $P(y = 1 \mid x)$ implies that the extreme values occur when $P(y = 1 \mid x)$ equals its extreme values of 0 and 1. Setting $P(y = 1 \mid x) = 0$ makes $RR = OR$, and setting $P(y = 1 \mid x) = 1$ makes $RR = 1$.   □

In the example concerning smoking and heart disease, the odds ratio is 1.57. So we may conclude that the probability of heart disease conditional on smoking is at least as large as but no more than 1.57 times the probability conditional on nonsmoking. Recall that the rare-disease assumption makes relative risk equal the odds ratio. Thus this conventional epidemiological assumption always makes relative risks appear further from one than they actually are. The magnitude of the bias depends on the actual prevalence of the disease under study. In particular, the bias grows as $P(y = 1 \mid x)$ moves away from zero. (This follows from the fact, shown in the proof to Proposition 1, that RR_p is monotone in p.) In the smoking–heart-disease example, the bias is small, as the actual relative risk is 1.50.

3.2   *Bound on attributable risk*

Examine the expression for attributable risk given in (8.6). Again, all the quantities on the right side are identified by response-based sampling except for $P(y \mid x)$. So we may determine the range of possible values for AR by analyzing how the right-hand side of (8.6) varies across the logically possible values of $P(y \mid x)$.

Define

$$\beta \equiv \left(\frac{P(r = j \mid x, y = 1)P(r = j \mid x, y = 0)}{P(r = k \mid x, y = 1)P(r = k \mid x, y = 0)} \right)^{1/2} \tag{8.14}$$

and

$$\pi \equiv \frac{\beta P(r = k \mid x, y = 0) - P(r = j \mid x, y = 0)}{[\beta P(r = k \mid x, y = 0) - P(r = j \mid x, y = 0)] - [\beta P(r = k \mid x, y = 1) - P(r = j \mid x, y = 1)]}. \tag{8.15}$$

Let

$$AR_\pi = \frac{P(r = k \mid x, y = 1)\pi}{P(r = k \mid x, y = 1)\pi + P(r = k \mid x, y = 0)(1 - \pi)}$$
$$- \frac{P(r = j \mid x, y = 1)\pi}{P(r = j \mid x, y = 1)\pi + P(r = j \mid x, y = 0)(1 - \pi)} \tag{8.16}$$

be the value that the attributable risk would take if $P(y = 1 \mid x)$ were to equal π. The result is that AR must lie between AR_π and zero. That is,

Proposition 2. *Let $P(x, r \mid y = 1)$ and $P(x, r \mid y = 0)$ be known. Then sharp bounds on* AR *are*

$$OR < 1 \quad \Rightarrow \quad AR_\pi \leq AR \leq 0, \tag{8.17a}$$

$$OR = 1 \quad \Rightarrow \quad AR = 0, \tag{8.17b}$$

$$OR > 1 \quad \Rightarrow \quad 0 \leq AR \leq AR_\pi. \tag{8.17c}$$

Proof: As $P(y = 1 \mid x)$ increases from 0 to 1, the attributable risk changes parabolically, the orientation of the parabola depending on the magnitude of the odds ratio. To see this, again let $p \equiv P(y = 1 \mid x)$ and let $P_{im} \equiv P(r = i \mid x, y = m)$ for $i = j$, k and $m = 0, 1$. Write the attributable risk (8.6) explicitly as a function of p. Thus define

$$AR_p \equiv \frac{P_{k1} p}{(P_{k1} - P_{k0})p + P_{k0}} - \frac{P_{j1} p}{(P_{j1} - P_{j0})p + P_{j0}}.$$

The derivative of AR_p with respect to p is

$$\frac{P_{k1} P_{k0}}{[(P_{k1} - P_{k0})p + P_{k0}]^2} - \frac{P_{j1} P_{j0}}{[(P_{j1} - P_{j0})p + P_{j0}]^2}.$$

The derivative equals zero at

$$\pi = \frac{\beta P_{k0} - P_{j0}}{(\beta P_{k0} - P_{j0}) - (\beta P_{k1} - P_{j1})}$$

and at

$$\pi^* = \frac{\beta P_{k0} + P_{j0}}{(\beta P_{k0} + P_{j0}) - (\beta P_{k1} + P_{j1})},$$

where $\beta \equiv (P_{j1} P_{j0} / P_{k1} P_{k0})^{1/2}$ was defined in (8.14). Examination of the two roots reveals that π always lies between zero and one, but π^* always lies outside the unit interval; so π is the only relevant root. Thus AR_p varies parabolically as p rises from zero to one.

Observe that $AR_p = 0$ at $p = 0$ and at $p = 1$. Examination of the derivative of AR_p at $p = 0$ and at $p = 1$ shows that the orientation of the parabola depends on the magnitude of the odds ratio. If OR is less than one, then as p rises from zero to one, AR_p falls from zero to its minimum at π and then rises back to zero. If the odds ratio is greater than one, then AR_p rises from zero to its maximum at π and then falls back to zero. In the borderline case where the odds ratio equals one, AR_p does not vary with p. $\qquad \square$

In the heart-disease example, $\beta = .83, \pi = .51$, and $AR_\pi = .11$. Hence, response-based sampling reveals that the attributable risk associated with smoking lies between 0 and .11. This seems a useful finding from a public-health perspective. After all, in the absence of empirical evidence, AR could take any value between -1 and 1.

3.3   *Implications for empirical practice*

The bounds on relative risks and attributable risks derived in Propositions 1 and 2 are easily estimated. The quantities OR and AR_π that form the data-dependent end points of the bounds are smooth functions of the conditional covariate distributions $P(r \mid x, y)$, which are nonparametrically estimable under response-based sampling. Asymptotically valid measures of the precision of estimates of OR and AR_π may be obtained by the δ-method.

Reporting estimates of these bounds would improve on the conventional practice in epidemiology, which has been to report the odds ratio and use the rare-disease assumption to interpret OR as relative risk. Reporting the bound on relative risk allows the reader to decide how OR should be interpreted, as the relative risk or as the end point of the bound on relative risk. Reporting the bound on attributable risk provides the reader with information that is useful from a public-health perspective. In contrast, the rare-disease assumption implies that attributable risk is zero.

Reporting bound estimates would also improve on the conventional practice in econometrics, which has been to base inference entirely on estimates of parametric models for conditional response probabilities. Assertions of particular parametric forms are commonly motivated more by considerations of convenience than by arguments for their realism. Hence the credibility of the inferences based on these models is often suspect. The nonparametric bounds on relative and attributable risk yield inferences that are weaker but more credible than those obtained through parametric modeling. Hence reporting the bounds offers a logical starting point for the empirical analysis of response-based sampling data.[2]

4   **Sampling from one response stratum**

The literature on response-based sampling has concentrated on situations in which one samples at random from both response strata, and so learns both $P(x, r \mid y = 1)$ and $P(x, r \mid y = 0)$. Often, however, one is able to sample from only one response stratum, say from the subpopulation with $y = 1$, and so learns

---

[2] Researchers who wish to base inference on parametric models can use the bounds to perform nonparametric tests of model specification. The general idea is that the estimates of relative and attributable risks implied by a correctly specified parametric model should lie within, or at least not too far outside, the estimates of the bounds.

only $P(x, r \mid y = 1)$. An epidemiologist studying the prevalence of a disease, for example, may use hospital records to learn the distribution of covariates among persons who are ill ($y = 1$), but have no comparable data on persons who are healthy ($y = 0$). A social-policy analyst studying participation in welfare programs may use the administrative records of the welfare system to learn the backgrounds of welfare recipients ($y = 1$), but has no comparable information on nonrecipients ($y = 0$).

Sampling from one response stratum obviously reveals nothing about the magnitude of response probabilities. Nor does it reveal anything about relative and attributable risks. Inference becomes possible, however, if auxiliary distributional information is available. Hsieh, Manski, and McFadden (1985) have pointed out that conditional response probabilities are identified if auxiliary data sources reveal the marginal response distribution $P(y)$ and the marginal covariate distribution $P(x, r)$. The result also holds if auxiliary data sources reveal the conditional distributions $P(y \mid x)$ and $P(r \mid x)$.

To see this, recall (8.3) and (8.4), where Bayes' theorem was used to write the response probabilities in the equivalent forms

$$P(y = 1 \mid x, r) = \frac{P(x, r \mid y = 1)P(y = 1)}{P(x, r)} = \frac{P(r \mid x, y = 1)P(y = 1 \mid x)}{P(r \mid x)}.$$

Sampling from the response stratum with $y = 1$ reveals $P(x, r \mid y = 1)$. Hence auxiliary knowledge of $P(y)$ and $P(x, r)$ reveals $P(y = 1 \mid x, r)$. Alternatively, auxiliary knowledge of $P(y \mid x)$ and $P(r \mid x)$ suffices.

In this section, I analyze two previously unstudied settings in which less extensive auxiliary data are available. Section 4.1 supposes that auxiliary data reveal only the distribution of responses. Section 4.2 supposes that auxiliary data reveal only the distribution of covariates. In each case, the results are informative sharp bounds on response probabilities, relative risks, and attributable risks. The two sets of bounds are quite different, though. Auxiliary data on the distribution of responses do not suffice for the researcher to determine whether the response probability is increasing or decreasing in the risk factor. Auxiliary data on the distribution of covariates do suffice for this purpose. In fact, auxiliary data on the distribution of covariates identify the relative risk.

Given the appropriate data, the bounds derived in Propositions 3 and 4 are easily estimated in the manner described in Section 3.3. The findings reported here also have implications for sample design. These are brought out in Section 4.3, which concludes the chapter.

4.1   *Inference when the distribution of responses is known*

Suppose that response-based sampling data from one stratum can be combined with auxiliary data revealing the distribution $P(y \mid x)$ of responses conditional on covariates x. Alternatively, suppose that response-based sampling data from one stratum can be combined with auxiliary data revealing the marginal response distribution $P(y)$. Both situations imply bounds on response probabilities, relative risks, and attributable risks. The bounds on response probabilities are informative only from below. The bounds on relative and attributable risks are informative both above and below, but do not reveal whether $P(y = 1 \mid x, r = k)$ is greater or less than $P(y = 1 \mid x, r = j)$. These results are proved in Proposition 3.

Proposition 3.

(A) *Let $P(r \mid x, y = 1)$ and $P(y = 1 \mid x)$ be known. Then sharp bounds on $P(y = 1 \mid x, r)$, RR, and AR are*

$$\frac{P(r \mid x, y = 1)P(y = 1 \mid x)}{P(r \mid x, y = 1)P(y = 1 \mid x) + P(y = 0 \mid x)} \leq P(y = 1 \mid x, r) \leq 1, \tag{8.18}$$

$$\frac{P(r = k \mid x, y = 1)P(y = 1 \mid x)}{P(r = k \mid x, y = 1)P(y = 1 \mid x) + P(y = 0 \mid x)} \leq \text{RR}$$

$$\leq \frac{P(r = j \mid x, y = 1)P(y = 1 \mid x) + P(y = 0 \mid x)}{P(r = j \mid x, y = 1)P(y = 1 \mid x)}, \tag{8.19}$$

and

$$-\frac{P(y = 0 \mid x)}{P(r = k \mid x, y = 1)P(y = 1 \mid x) + P(y = 0 \mid x)} \leq \text{AR}$$

$$\leq \frac{P(y = 0 \mid x)}{P(r = j \mid x, y = 1)P(y = 1 \mid x) + P(y = 0 \mid x)}. \tag{8.20}$$

(B) *Let $P(x, r \mid y = 1)$ and $P(y = 1)$ be known. Then sharp bounds on $P(y = 1 \mid x, r)$, RR, and AR are*

$$\frac{P(x, r \mid y = 1)P(y = 1)}{P(x, r \mid y = 1)P(y = 1) + P(y = 0)} \leq P(y = 1 \mid x, r) \leq 1, \tag{8.21}$$

$$\frac{P(x, r = k \mid y = 1)P(y = 1)}{P(x, r = k \mid y = 1)P(y = 1) + P(y = 0)} \leq \text{RR}$$

$$\leq \frac{P(x, r = j \mid y = 1)P(y = 1) + P(y = 0)}{P(x, r = j \mid y = 1)P(y = 1)}, \tag{8.22}$$

and

$$-\frac{P(y = 0)}{P(x, r = k \mid y = 1)P(y = 1) + P(y = 0)} \leq \text{AR}$$

$$\leq \frac{P(y = 0)}{P(x, r = j \mid y = 1)P(y = 1) + P(y = 0)}. \tag{8.23}$$

Proof: (A): Inspect the right side of (8.4). The only unknown quantity is $P(r \mid x, y = 0)$, which may lie anywhere between zero and one. Letting $P(r \mid x, y = 0)$ equal one yields the sharp lower bound on $P(y = 1 \mid x, r)$, and letting $P(r \mid x, y = 0)$ equal zero yields the sharp upper bound.

Sharp lower bounds on relative and attributable risks are obtained by letting $P(r = j \mid x, y = 0)$ equal zero and $P(r = k \mid x, y = 0)$ equal one in (8.5) and (8.6). Sharp upper bounds are obtained by letting $P(r = j \mid x, y = 0)$ equal one and $P(r = k \mid x, y = 0)$ equal zero.

(B): Use the version of Bayes' theorem given in (8.3) to express response probabilities, relative risk, and attributable risk. Then apply the same reasoning as in part (A).   □

Proposition 3, like the findings reported earlier in the paper, assumes the covariates (x, r) to have a discrete distribution. Suppose that r is continuous conditional on $(x, y = 1)$, and consider part (A). Then $P(r = j \mid x, y = 1) = P(r = k \mid x, y = 1) = 0$. So bounds (8.18) through (8.20) are uninformative. The same negative result holds in part (B) if either x or r has continuous components conditional on $y = 1$.[3]

The smoking-and-heart-disease example of Section 3 gives a sense of these bounds. The bounds on conditional response probabilities are $.06 \le P(y = 1 \mid x, r = k) \le 1$ and $.04 \le P(y = 1 \mid x, r = j) \le 1$. The bound on relative risk is $.06 \le RR \le 23.5$, and that on attributable risk is $-.94 \le AR \le .96$. Thus, knowing the probability of heart disease among people with covariates x reveals little in this example.

4.2   *Inference when the distribution of covariates is known*

Suppose that response-based sampling data from one stratum can be combined with auxiliary data revealing the distribution $P(r \mid x)$ of risk factors conditional on other covariates x. Alternatively, suppose that response-based sampling data from one stratum can be combined with auxiliary data revealing the joint distribution $P(x, r)$ of risk factors and other covariates. Both situations imply that relative risks are identified, and both imply bounds on response probabilities

---

[3] An alternative way to show these negative results is to replace probabilities with densities in the statement of Bayes' theorem and then reconsider the proof of Proposition 3. Consider part (A), the reasoning being the same in part (B). The key fact in the proof was that the unknown probabilities $P(r = j \mid x, y = 0)$ and $P(r = k \mid x, y = 0)$ must lie between zero and one. Let r be absolutely continuous with respect to Lebesgue measure conditional on $x, y = 1$, and let the probabilities $P(r \mid x, y = 1)$ be replaced by Lebesgue densities ϕ in the statement of (8.4). The density values $\phi(r = j \mid x, y = 0)$ and $\phi(r = k \mid x, y = 0)$ must lie between zero and infinity, not between zero and one. So (8.18) through (8.20) become the uninformative bounds $0 \le P(y = 1 \mid x, r) \le 1$, $0 \le RR \le \infty$, and $-1 \le AR \le 1$. Thus, knowing $P(y \mid x)$ has no identifying power when r is absolutely continuous.

and attributable risks. The bounds on response probabilities are informative at most from above, but the bounds on attributable risks are informative both above and below. These results are proved in Proposition 4.

Proposition 4.

(A)   *Let* $P(r \mid x, y = 1)$ *and* $P(r \mid x)$ *be known. Then*

$$\text{RR} = \frac{P(r = k \mid x, y = 1)P(r = j \mid x)}{P(r = j \mid x, y = 1)P(r = k \mid x)} \tag{8.24}$$

is identified. Sharp bounds on $P(y = 1 \mid x, r)$ *are*

$$0 \le P(y = 1 \mid x, r) \le c\frac{P(r \mid x, y = 1)}{P(r \mid x)}, \tag{8.25}$$

where $c \equiv \min_{i \in R} P(r = i \mid x)/P(r = i \mid x, y = 1)$ *and where R is the domain of r. Sharp bounds on* AR *are*

$$d < 0 \quad \Rightarrow \quad cd \le \text{AR} \le 0 \tag{8.26a}$$
$$d = 0 \quad \Rightarrow \quad \text{AR} = 0 \tag{8.26b}$$
$$d > 0 \quad \Rightarrow \quad 0 \le \text{AR} \le cd, \tag{8.26c}$$

where $d \equiv P(r = k \mid x, y = 1)/P(r = k \mid x) - P(r = j \mid x, y = 1)/P(r = j \mid x)$.

(B)   *Let* $P(x, r \mid y = 1)$ *and* $P(x, r)$ *be known. Then* RR *is given by* (8.24). *Sharp bounds on* $P(y = 1 \mid x, r)$ *are*

$$0 \le P(y = 1 \mid x, r) \le C\frac{P(x, r \mid y = 1)}{P(x, r)}, \tag{8.27}$$

where $C \equiv \min_{h \in X, i \in R}[P(x = h, r = i)/P(x = h, r = i \mid y = 1)]$ *and X is the domain of x. Sharp bounds on* AR *are*

$$D < 0 \quad \Rightarrow \quad CD \le \text{AR} \le 0, \tag{8.28a}$$
$$D = 0 \quad \Rightarrow \quad \text{AR} = 0, \tag{8.28b}$$
$$D > 0 \quad \Rightarrow \quad 0 \le \text{AR} \le CD, \tag{8.28c}$$

where $D \equiv P(x, r = k \mid y = 1)/P(x, r = k) - P(x, r = j \mid y = 1)/P(x, r = j)$.

Proof: (A): The proof analyzes the form of the response probabilities given in the middle expression of (8.4), namely

$$P(y = 1 \mid x, r) = \frac{P(r \mid x, y = 1)P(y = 1 \mid x)}{P(r \mid x)}.$$

Equation (8.24) uses this form of the response probabilities to state the relative risk. All of the quantities on the right side of (8.24) are known, so relative risk is identified.

Consider the response probabilities themselves. The quantities $P(r \mid x, y = 1)$ and $P(r \mid x)$ are known, but $P(y = 1 \mid x)$ is not. The available information does, however, imply an upper bound on $P(y = 1 \mid x)$. To see this, let $i \in R$ and write $P(r = i \mid x)$ as

$$P(r = i \mid x) = P(r = i \mid x, y = 1)P(y = 1 \mid x)$$
$$+ P(r = i \mid x, y = 0)[1 - P(y = 1 \mid x)].$$

Solve for $P(r = i \mid x, y = 0)$, yielding

$$P(r = i \mid x, y = 0) = \frac{P(r = i \mid x) - P(r = i \mid x, y = 1)P(y = 1 \mid x)}{1 - P(y = 1 \mid x)}.$$

The probabilities $P(r = i \mid x, y = 0)$, $i \in R$, are not known. They must, however, satisfy the adding-up condition, namely $\sum_{i \in R} P(r = i \mid x, y = 0) = 1$, and the inequality conditions $0 \leq P(r = i \mid x, y = 0)$, all $i \in R$.[4] A value of $P(y = 1 \mid x)$ is feasible if and only if it implies that $P(r = i \mid x, y = 0)$, $i \in R$, satisfy these conditions.

The adding-up condition holds for all values of $P(y = 1 \mid x)$, but the inequality conditions imply restrictions on $P(y = 1 \mid x)$. Consider the inequalities

$$0 \leq \frac{P(r = i \mid x) - P(r = i \mid x, y = 1)P(y = 1 \mid x)}{1 - P(y = 1 \mid x)}, \qquad i \in R.$$

These inequalities hold if $P(y = 1 \mid x) \leq P(r = i \mid x)/P(r = i \mid x, y = 1)$, $i \in R$. Hence $P(y = 1 \mid x) \leq c$, implying that the response probabilities satisfy (8.25).

Now consider the attributable risk. Use the form of the response probabilities given in the middle expression of (8.4) to write

$$AR = P(y = 1 \mid x)d.$$

The quantity d is identified, and we have found that $P(y = 1 \mid x) \leq c$. Hence the attributable risk must satisfy (8.26).

(B): Begin from the version of the response probabilities given in the middle expression of (8.3), and apply the same reasoning as in part (A).   □

The smoking-and-heart-disease example gives a sense of these bounds. The parameters of the example imply that $c = .83$. Hence the bounds on conditional response probabilities are $0 \leq P(y = 1 \mid x, r = k) \leq 1$ and

---

[4] There also are inequality conditions $P(r = i \mid x, y = 0) \leq 1$, all $i \in R$, but the adding-up condition makes these redundant.

$0 \leq P(y = 1 \mid x, r = j) \leq .67$. The quantity $d = .4$, so the bound on attributable risk is $0 \leq \text{AR} \leq .33$. Thus, knowing the prevalence of smoking among people with covariates x reveals little about the magnitudes of the response probabilities but reveals a fair bit about attributable risk.

4.3   *Implications for sample design*

I indicated at the beginning of Section 4 that there are situations in which an empirical researcher can sample covariates from one response stratum. For example, the epidemiologist may use hospital records to sample ill persons, and the social-policy analyst may use administrative records to sample welfare recipients. A researcher having covariate data from one response stratum must somehow augment these data if he is to make useful inferences. Thus the researcher faces a problem of sample design.

Propositions 1 through 4 of this chapter show what the researcher may achieve with three different data augmentation strategies. These are

(i)   sampling of covariates from the other response stratum (Propositions 1 and 2),

(ii)   sampling of responses from the full population, or from the subpopulation with covariates x (Proposition 3),

(iii)   sampling of covariates from the full population, or sampling risk factors from the subpopulation with covariates x (Proposition 4).

The three strategies yield nonnested information. Hence we cannot say that one strategy dominates another in the inferences they enable. Whereas strategy (i) reveals nothing about the magnitudes of the conditional response probabilities, strategies (ii) and (iii) place distinct bounds on these quantities. Whereas strategy (ii) does not enable the researcher to determine whether the conditional response probabilities are increasing or decreasing in the value of the risk factor, strategies (i) and (iii) do reveal this information. Whereas strategies (i) and (ii) only bound the relative risk, strategy (iii) identifies the value of this quantity. All three strategies yield bounds on attributable risk, but the bounds differ. In the smoking-and-heart-disease example, strategies (i), (ii), and (iii) yield the bounds $[0, .11]$, $[-.94, .96]$, and $[0, .33]$ on attributable risk (see Sections 3.2, 4.1, and 4.2).

If sampling cost is not a concern, it is better to combine two of the three strategies than to choose just one. As shown in Hsieh, Manski, and McFadden (1985), any combination of two strategies yields point identification of the conditional response probabilities (see Section 2.2 and the introduction to Section 4). Sampling cost is, however, exactly the practical concern that has motivated interest in response-based sampling. Hence the findings reported in Propositions 1 through 4 should be useful to empirical researchers.

REFERENCES

Amemiya, T. and Vuong, Q. (1987), "A Comparison of Two Consistent Estimators in the Choice Based Sampling Qualitative Response Model," *Econometrica*, **55**, 699–702.

Berkson, J. (1958), "Smoking and Lung Cancer: Some Observations on Two Recent Reports," *Journal of the American Statistical Association*, **53**, 28–38.

Cornfield, J. (1951), "A Method of Estimating Comparative Rates From Clinical Data. Applications to Cancer of the Lung, Breast, and Cervix," *Journal of the National Cancer Institute*, **11**, 1269–1275.

Cosslett, S. (1981), "Efficient Estimation of Discrete Choice Models," in C. Manski and D. McFadden, eds., *Structural Analysis of Discrete Data with Econometric Applications* (Cambridge, MA: MIT Press).

Fleiss, J. (1981), *Statistical Methods for Rates and Proportions* (New York: Wiley).

Horowitz, J. and Manski, C. (1998), "Censoring of Outcomes and Regressors due to Survey Nonresponse: Identification and Estimation Using Weights and Imputations," *Journal of Econometrics*, **84**, 37–58.

Hsieh, D., Manski, C., and McFadden, D. (1985), "Estimation of Response Probabilities from Augmented Retrospective Observations," *Journal of the American Statistical Association*, **80**, 651–662.

Imbens, G. (1992), "An Efficient Method of Moments Estimator for Discrete Choice Models with Choice-Based Sampling," *Econometrica*, **60**, 1187–1214.

Manski, C. (1986), "Semiparametric Analysis of Binary Response from Response-Based Samples," *Journal of Econometrics*, **31**, 31–40.

(1995), *Identification Problems in the Social Sciences* (Cambridge, MA: Harvard University Press).

Manski, C. and Lerman, S. (1977), "The Estimation of Choice Probabilities from Choice-Based Samples," *Econometrica*, **45**, 1977–1988.

Manski, C. and McFadden, D. (1981), "Alternative Estimators and Sample Designs for Discrete Choice Analysis," in C. Manski and D. McFadden, eds., *Structural Analysis of Discrete Data with Econometric Applications* (Cambridge, MA: MIT Press).

Manski, C., Sandefur, G., McLanahan, S., and Powers, D. (1992), "Alternative Estimates of the Effect of Family Structure during Adolescence on High School Graduation," *Journal of the American Statistical Association*, **87**, 25–37.

CHAPTER 9

On selecting regression variables
to maximize their significance

Daniel McFadden

1   Introduction

Often in applied linear regression analysis one must select an explanatory variable from a set of candidates. For example, in estimating production functions one must select among alternative measures of capital stock constructed using different depreciation assumptions. Or, in hedonic analysis of housing prices, one may use indicator or ramp variables that measure distance from spatial features such as parks or industrial plants, with cutoffs at distances that are determined as parameters. In the second example, the problem can be cast as one of nonlinear regression. However, when there are many linear parameters in the regression, direct nonlinear regression can be computationally inefficient, with convergence problematic. It is often more practical to approach this as a linear regression problem with variable selection.

This chapter shows that selecting variables in a linear regression to maximize their conventional significance is equivalent to direct application of nonlinear least squares. Thus, this method provides a practical computational shortcut that shares the statistical properties of the nonlinear least-squares solution. However, standard errors and test statistics produced by least squares are biased by variable selection, and are often inconsistent. This chapter gives practical consistent estimators for covariances and test statistics, and shows in examples that kernel-smoothing or bootstrap methods appear to give adequate approximations in samples of moderate size.

The problem is to estimate the parameters of the linear regression

$$y = X\alpha + Z(\gamma)\beta + u, \qquad \gamma \in \Gamma, \tag{9.1}$$

This research was supported by the E. Morris Cox Endowment. I thank David Freedman, Tom Rothenberg, and James Powell for useful discussions, and two anonymous referees for helpful comments.

where y is $n \times 1$, X is an $n \times p$ array of observations on prespecified explanatory variables, $Z = Z(\gamma)$ is an $n \times q$ array of observations on selected explanatory variables, where γ indexes candidates from a set of alternatives Γ, and u is an $n \times 1$ vector of disturbances with a scalar covariance matrix. Let $k = p + q$, and assume $\Gamma \subseteq \mathbb{R}^h$. The set Γ is finite in the traditional problem of variable selection, but will be a continuum for parametric data transformations. Assume the data in (9.1) are generated by independent random sampling from a model $y = x\alpha_0 + z(\gamma_0, w)\beta_0 + u$, where $(y, x, w) \in \mathbb{R} \times \mathbb{R}^p \times \mathbb{R}^m$ is an observed data vector, $z : \Gamma \times \mathbb{R}^m \to \mathbb{R}^q$ is a well-behaved parametric transformation of the data w, $(\alpha_0, \beta_0, \gamma_0)$ denote the true parameter values, and the distribution of u, conditioned on x and w, has mean zero and variance σ_0^2. There may be overlapping variables in w and x. Examples of common parametric data transformations are (a) a Box–Cox transformation $z(\gamma, w) = w^{\gamma-1}/(\gamma - 1)$ for $\gamma \neq 0$ and $z(0, w) = \log w$; (b) a ramp (or linear spline) function $z(\gamma, w) = \max(\gamma - w, 0)$ with a knot at γ; (c) a structural break $z(\gamma, w) = 1(w < \gamma)$ with a break at γ; and (d) an exponential decay $z(\gamma, w) = e^{-\gamma w}$.

One criterion for variable selection is to pick a $\hat{\gamma} \in \Gamma$ that maximizes the conventional least-squares test statistic for the significance of the $Z(\gamma)$ variables, using enumeration, a grid search, or Gauss–Newton iteration, and then obtain least-squares estimates $(\hat{\alpha}, \hat{\beta}, \hat{\sigma}^2)$ for the selected $Z(\hat{\gamma})$. For short, term this the *prescreened least squares* (PLS) criterion for estimating (9.1). I show that PLS is equivalent to selecting $Z(\gamma)$ to maximize R^2, and is also equivalent to estimating $(\alpha, \beta, \gamma, \sigma^2)$ in (9.1) jointly by nonlinear least squares. Hence, PLS shares the large-sample statistical properties of nonlinear least squares. However, standard errors and test statistics for $\hat{\alpha}$ and $\hat{\beta}$ that are provided by least squares at the selected $Z(\hat{\gamma})$ fail to allow for the influence of variable selection, and will usually be biased downward. When Γ is a continuum, a Gauss–Newton auxiliary regression associated with the nonlinear least-squares formulation of the problem can be used in many cases to obtain consistent estimates of standard errors and test statistics. When Γ is finite, the effects of variable selection will be asymptotically negligible, but least-squares estimates of standard errors will be biased downward in finite samples.

Let $M = I - X(X'X)^{-1}X'$, and rewrite the model (9.1) in the form

$$y = X[\alpha + (X'X)^{-1}X'Z(\gamma)\beta] + MZ(\gamma)\beta + u. \tag{9.2}$$

The explanatory variables X and $MZ(\gamma)$ in (9.2) are orthogonal by construction, so that the sum of squared residuals satisfies

$$\text{SSR}(\gamma) = y'My - y'MZ(\gamma)[Z(\gamma)'MZ(\gamma)]^{-1}Z(\gamma)'My. \tag{9.3}$$

Then, the estimate $\hat{\gamma}$ that minimizes SSR(γ) for $\gamma \in \Gamma$ also maximizes the expression

$$S(\gamma) \equiv \frac{1}{n} y' M Z(\gamma)[Z(\gamma)' M Z(\gamma)]^{-1} Z(\gamma)' M y. \tag{9.4}$$

Nonlinear least-squares estimators for α, β, and σ^2 can be obtained by least-squares estimation of (9.1) using $Z = Z(\hat{\gamma})$; in particular, the estimator of σ^2 is $\hat{\sigma}^2 = \text{SSR}(\hat{\gamma})/(n-k)$, and the estimator of β is $\hat{\beta} = [Z(\hat{\gamma})' M Z(\hat{\gamma})]^{-1} Z(\hat{\gamma})' M y$. Since R^2 is monotone decreasing in SSR(γ), and therefore monotone increasing in $S(\gamma)$, the estimator $\hat{\gamma}$ also maximizes R^2. Least-squares estimation of (9.1) also yields an estimator $\hat{V}(\hat{\beta}) = \hat{\sigma}^2 [Z(\hat{\gamma})' M Z(\hat{\gamma})]^{-1}$ of the covariance matrix of the estimator $\hat{\beta}$; however, this estimator does not take account of the influence of estimation of the embedded parameter γ on the distribution of the least-squares estimates. The conventional least-squares F-statistic for the null hypothesis that the β-coefficients in (9.1) are zero, treating Z as if were predetermined rather than a function of the embedded parameter $\hat{\gamma}$, is

$$F = \frac{\hat{\beta}' \hat{V}(\hat{\beta})^{-1} \hat{\beta}}{q} = \frac{y' M Z(\hat{\gamma})[Z(\hat{\gamma})' M Z(\hat{\gamma})]^{-1} Z(\hat{\gamma})' M y}{\hat{\sigma}^2 q}$$

$$= \frac{(n-k) \cdot S(\hat{\gamma})}{q \cdot (y' M y/n - S(\hat{\gamma}))}. \tag{9.5}$$

But the nonlinear least-squares estimator selects $\gamma \in \Gamma$ to maximize $S(\gamma)$, and (9.5) is an increasing function of $S(\gamma)$. Then *estimation of $(\alpha, \beta, \gamma, \sigma^2)$ in (9.1) by nonlinear least squares, with $\gamma \in \Gamma$, is equivalent to estimation of this equation by least squares with $\hat{\gamma} \in \Gamma$ selected to maximize the F-statistic (9.5) for a least-squares test of significance for the hypothesis that $\beta = 0$.* When there is a single variable that depends on the embedded parameter γ, the F-statistic equals the square of the T-statistic for the significance of the coefficient β, and the PLS procedure is equivalent to selecting $\hat{\gamma}$ to maximize the significance of the T-statistic.

I have not found this result stated explicitly in the literature, but it is an easy special case of selection of regressors in nonlinear least squares using unconditional mean square prediction error, which in this application (where all candidate vectors are of the same dimension) coincides with the Mallows criterion and the Akaike information criterion; see Amemiya (1980). Many studies have noted the effects of variable selection or embedded parameters on covariance matrix estimates and have given examples showing that least-squares estimates that ignore these effects can be substantially biased; see Amemiya (1978), Freedman (1983), Freedman, Navidi, and Peters (1988), Lovell (1983), Newey and McFadden (1994), and Peters and Freedman (1984).

2   Consistency and asymptotic normality

Estimation of (9.1) by the PLS procedure will be consistent and asymptotically normal if nonlinear least squares applied to this equation is consistent and asymptotically normal. The large-sample statistical properties of nonlinear least squares have been treated in detail by Jenrich (1969), Amemiya (1985, Theorems 4.3.1 and 4.3.2), Tauchen (1985), Gallant (1987), Davidson and MacKinnon (1993), and Newey and McFadden (1994, Theorems 2.6, 3.4). I give a variant that exploits the semilinear structure of (9.1) to limit the required regularity conditions: I avoid requiring a compactness assumption on the linear parameters, and impose only the usual least-squares conditions on moments of x and $z(\gamma_0, w)$. For consistency, I require an almost sure continuity condition on $z(\gamma, w)$ that is sufficiently mild to cover ramp and structural break functions. For asymptotic normality, I require almost sure smoothness conditions on $z(\gamma, w)$ that are sufficiently mild to cover ramp functions. These conditions are chosen so that they will cover many applications and are easy to check.

Several definitions will be needed. A function $g : \Gamma \times \mathbb{R}^m \to \mathbb{R}^q$ will be termed *well behaved* if

(i) $g(\gamma, w)$ is *measurable* in w for each $\gamma \in \Gamma$,

(ii) $g(\gamma, w)$ is *separable*, i.e., Γ contains a countable dense subset Γ_0, and the graph of $g : \Gamma \times \mathbb{R}^m \to \mathbb{R}^q$ is contained in the closure of the graph of $g : \Gamma_0 \times \mathbb{R}^m \to \mathbb{R}^q$, and

(iii) $g(\gamma, w)$ is *pointwise almost surely continuous* in γ, i.e., for each $\gamma' \in \Gamma$, the set of w for which $\lim_{\gamma \to \gamma'} g(\gamma, w) = g(\gamma', w)$ has probability one.

Condition (iii) allows the exceptional set to vary with γ', so that a function can be pointwise almost surely continuous without requiring that it be continuous on Γ for any w. For example, the structural break function $1(\gamma < w)$ has a discontinuity for every w, but is nevertheless separable and pointwise almost surely continuous when Γ is compact and the distribution of w has no point mass. A function $g : \Gamma \times \mathbb{R}^m \to \mathbb{R}^q$ is said to be *dominated* by a function $r : \mathbb{R}^m \to \mathbb{R}$ if $|g(\gamma, w)| \le r(w)$ for all $\gamma \in \Gamma$.

The main result on large-sample properties of PLS draws from the following assumptions:

Assumption 1: The data in (9.1) are generated by an independent random sample of size n, with data (y, x, w), from a model $y = x\alpha_0 + z(\gamma_0, w)\beta_0 + u$, with $\gamma_0 \in \Gamma$ and $\beta_0 \ne 0$. The u are independently identically distributed, independent of x and w, and have mean zero and variance σ_0^2. The vector x has a finite second moment, and the function $z(\gamma, w)$ is dominated by a function $r(w)$ that is square-integrable. For each $\gamma \in \Gamma$, the array $H(\gamma) = \mathbf{E}(x, z(\gamma, w))'(x, z(\gamma, w))$ is positive definite.

Assumption 2: Let $\sigma^2(\gamma) = \min_{\alpha,\beta} \mathbf{E}(y - x\alpha - z(\gamma, w)\beta)^2$. When minimands exist, denote them by $\alpha(\gamma)$ and $\beta(\gamma)$. Then $\alpha(\gamma_0) = \alpha_0$, $\beta(\gamma_0) = \beta_0$, and $\min_{\gamma \in \Gamma} \sigma^2(\gamma) = \sigma^2(\gamma_0) = \sigma_0^2$. For each $\delta > 0$, assume the identification condition

$$\inf_{\substack{\gamma \in \Gamma \\ |\gamma - \gamma_0| \geq \delta}} \frac{\sigma^2(\gamma)}{\sigma_0^2} > 1.$$

Assumption 3: The set Γ is compact, and the function $z(\gamma, w)$ is well behaved.

Assumption 4: The random disturbance u has a proper moment generating function. There exist an open set Γ_0 with $\gamma_0 \in \Gamma_0 \subseteq \Gamma$ and a bounded function $r(w)$ such that $z(\gamma, w)$ satisfies a Lipschitz property $|z(\gamma, w) - z(\gamma', w)| \leq r(w) \cdot |\gamma - \gamma'|$ for all $\gamma, \gamma' \in \Gamma_0$. The derivative $d(\gamma, \beta, w) = \beta' \nabla_\gamma z(\gamma, w)$ exists almost surely for $\gamma \in \Gamma_0$ and is well behaved, implying that $\mathbf{E}d(\gamma, \beta, w) = \beta' \nabla_\gamma \mathbf{E}z(\gamma, w)$ and $J(\gamma, \beta) = \mathbf{E}(x, z(\gamma, w), d(\gamma, \beta, w))'$ $(x, z(\gamma, w), d(\gamma, \beta, w))$ exist and are continuous for $\gamma \in \Gamma_0$. The matrix $J(\gamma_0, \beta_0)$ is positive definite.

Assumption 1 guarantees that the regression (9.1) is almost surely of full rank and satisfies Gauss–Markov conditions. The independence assumption on u is stronger than necessary for large-sample results, but nonlinear dependence of $z(\gamma, w)$ on w implies more is needed than just an assumption that u is uncorrelated with x and w. The independence assumption also rules out conditional heteroscedasticity and (spatial or temporal) serial correlation in the disturbances, which may be important in some applications. This is not fundamental, and establishing large-sample results with weaker assumptions on u merely requires substituting appropriate statistical limit theorems in the proof of Theorem 1 below, with the additional regularity conditions that they require. Weakening the independence assumption on u may require more substantial modification of the bootstrap estimator of variances in Section 3.

Assumption 2 is a mild identification condition that requires that asymptotically the nonlinear least-squares problem have a unique solution at γ_0. One must have $\beta_0 \neq 0$ for Assumption 2 to hold. Assumption 3 holds trivially if Γ is finite, and when Γ is not finite it is needed to guarantee consistency of the nonlinear least-squares estimator of (9.1). It can be relaxed, at a considerable cost in complexity, to a condition that the family of functions $z(\gamma, w)$ for $\gamma \in \Gamma$ can be approximated to specified accuracy by finite subfamilies that are not too numerous; see Pollard (1984, VII.4.15). Pakes and Pollard (1989) characterize some families of functions that satisfy such conditions.

Assumption 4 is used when Γ is a continuum to guarantee that the nonlinear least-squares estimator is asymptotically normal. It will also imply that a Gauss–Newton auxiliary regression can be used to iterate to a solution of the nonlinear least-squares problem, and to obtain consistent estimates of standard errors and test statistics for $\hat{\alpha}$ and $\hat{\beta}$. I have chosen this assumption to cover applications like ramp functions where $z(\gamma, w)$ is not continuously differentiable. The price for generality in this dimension is that I require a strong assumption on the tails of the distribution of the disturbance u (the moment-generating-function condition) and a strong form of continuity (the uniform Lipschitz condition). The first of these conditions is palatable for most applications, and the second is easy to check. Again, both can be relaxed, using empirical process methods, at the cost of introducing conditions that are more difficult to check. The requirement that $J(\gamma_0, \beta_0)$ be nonsingular is a local identification condition. The proof of the following result is given in an appendix.

Theorem 1. *Suppose Assumptions 1–3. Then PLS is strongly consistent. In particular, the functions $(\alpha(\gamma), \beta(\gamma), \sigma^2(\gamma))$ are continuous on Γ; least-squares estimators $(\hat{\alpha}(\gamma), \hat{\beta}(\gamma), \hat{\sigma}^2(\gamma))$ from (9.1) satisfy $\sup_{\gamma \in \Gamma} |(\hat{\alpha}(\gamma) - \alpha(\gamma), \hat{\beta}(\gamma) - \beta(\gamma), \sigma^2(\gamma) - \sigma^2(\gamma))| \overset{a.s.}{\to} 0$; and $\hat{\gamma} \overset{a.s.}{\to} \gamma_0$. Equivalently, nonlinear least squares applied to (9.1) is strongly consistent for the parameters $(\alpha_0, \beta_0, \gamma_0, \sigma_0^2)$.*

If γ_0 is an isolated point of Γ, then $\sqrt{n}(\hat{\gamma} - \gamma_0) \overset{p}{\to} 0$ and

$$\sqrt{n} \begin{bmatrix} \hat{\alpha} - \alpha_0 \\ \hat{\beta} - \beta_0 \end{bmatrix} \overset{d}{\to} N(0, \sigma_0^2 H(\gamma_0)^{-1}). \tag{9.6}$$

Alternatively, if Assumtption 4 holds, then

$$\sqrt{n} \begin{bmatrix} \hat{\alpha} - \alpha_0 \\ \hat{\beta} - \beta_0 \\ \hat{\gamma} - \gamma_0 \end{bmatrix} \overset{d}{\to} N(0, \sigma_0^2 J(\gamma_0, \beta_0)^{-1}). \tag{9.7}$$

This theorem establishes consistency and asymptotic normality in the case of the classical variable selection problem where Γ is finite, and in the parametric transformation problem where the derivative of the transformation with respect to the index parameters is well behaved. This covers most applications, including linear spline functions with parametric knots. However, it is possible that γ_0 is not isolated and $z(\gamma, w)$ fails to have a well-behaved derivative, so that Assumption 4 fails. The structural break function $z(\gamma, w) = 1(\gamma < w)$ is an example that fails to satisfy the Lipschitz condition. The asymptotic distribution of $\hat{\gamma}$ and the properties of various covariance matrix estimators must be resolved on an individual basis for such cases.

3   Gauss–Newton auxiliary regression and bootstrap covariance estimates

When Assumptions 1–4 hold, so that γ_0 is in the interior of Γ and $z(\gamma, w)$ is almost surely continuously differentiable, Theorem 1 establishes that nonlinear least squares applied to (9.1) is strongly consistent and asymptotically normal. Consider a least-squares regression,

$$y = Xa + Z(\gamma^j)b + D(\gamma^j, \beta^j)c + v, \tag{9.8}$$

where $(\alpha^j, \beta^j, \gamma^j)$ are preliminary estimates of the model parameters and $D(\gamma^j, \beta^j)$ is the $n \times h$ array with rows $d(\gamma^j, \beta^j, w) = \beta^{j'}\nabla_\gamma z(\gamma^j, w)$. The rule for updating parameter estimates is $\alpha^{j+1} = \hat{a}$, $\beta^{j+1} = \hat{b}$, and $\gamma^{j+1} = \gamma^j + \hat{c}$, The regression (9.8) is called the Gauss–Newton auxiliary regression for model (9.1), and the updating procedure is called Gauss–Newton iteration; see Davidson and MacKinnon (1993). Comparing the least-squares formulas for $(\hat{a}, \hat{b}, \hat{c})$ with the first-order conditions for nonlinear least squares applied to (9.1), one sees that $(\hat{\alpha}, \hat{\beta}, \hat{\gamma})$ is a fixed point of Gauss–Newton iteration: If one starts from $(\hat{\alpha}, \hat{\beta}, \hat{\gamma})$ as preliminary estimates, one obtains $\hat{c} = 0$, and the linear regressions (9.1) and (9.8) will yield identical estimates $\hat{a} = \hat{\alpha}$ and $\hat{b} = \hat{\beta}$ for the regression coefficients. Comparing the least-squares estimate from (9.8) of the covariance matrix of the estimates $(\hat{a}, \hat{b}, \hat{c})$ with the covariance matrix of the nonlinear least-squares estimates $(\hat{\alpha}, \hat{\beta}, \hat{\gamma})$, one sees that these estimates are asymptotically equivalent. Summarizing, we have the following results:

(a)   The nonlinear least-squares estimates $(\hat{\alpha}, \hat{\beta}, \hat{\gamma})$ of (9.1) are a fixed point of the Gauss–Newton auxiliary regression (9.8), and the estimated covariance matrix of the regression coefficients from this auxiliary regression at this fixed point is a strongly consistent estimate of the covariance matrix of $(\hat{\alpha}, \hat{\beta}, \hat{\gamma})$.

(b)   For an initial value γ^1, the initial values (α^1, β^1) should be obtained from the regression (9.1) using $Z(\gamma^1)$. For γ^1 in some neighborhood of γ_0, Gauss–Newton iteration will converge to the fixed point $(\hat{\alpha}, \hat{\beta}, \hat{\gamma})$. Gauss–Newton iteration from a sufficiently dense grid of initial values for γ^1 will determine all fixed points of the process, and the fixed point at which $S(\gamma)$ is largest is $(\hat{\alpha}, \hat{\beta}, \hat{\gamma})$.

The reason for considering a grid of starting values γ^1 is that Gauss–Newton iteration may fail to converge outside some neighborhood of $\hat{\gamma}$, or if the fixed point is not unique may converge to a fixed point where $S(\gamma)$ is at a secondary maximum. The requirements in Assumption 4 that γ_0 be an interior point of Γ and that $z(\gamma, w)$ be Lipschitz and its derivative $\nabla_\gamma z(\gamma, w)$ well behaved are essential in general for use of the Gauss–Newton auxiliary regression to obtain covariance estimates. For example, the structural break function $1(w > \gamma)$ fails to satisfy the Lipschitz condition, and (9.8) fails to give a consistent estimate of the covariance matrix.[1] However, even in cases where direct application of the Gauss–Newton auxiliary regression fails, it may be possible to use approximate Gauss–Newton auxiliary regression or a bootstrap procedure to obtain covariance estimates that are reasonably accurate for samples of moderate size.

The idea behind an approximation Gauss–Newton auxiliary regression in a model $y = x\alpha + z(\gamma, w) + u$ satisfying Assumptions 1–3, but not Assumption 4, is that one can replace a poorly behaved $z(\gamma, w)$ by a kernel smoother $z^*(\gamma, w) = \int z(\gamma', w)k((\gamma - \gamma')/\lambda)\,d\gamma'\lambda$, where $k(\cdot)$ is a continuously differentiable probability density that has mean zero and variance one, and λ is a small positive bandwidth. For fixed λ, $z^*(\gamma, w)$ satisfies the continuous differentiability condition in Assumption 4. Let $(\alpha_*, \beta_*, \gamma_*)$ be the minimand of $E(y - x\alpha - z^*(\gamma, w)\beta)^2$. Theorem 1 can be adapted to show that PLS applied to $y = x\alpha + z^*(\gamma, w)\beta + u$ is strongly consistent for $(\alpha_*, \beta_*, \gamma_*)$ and asymptotically normal, and that the auxiliary regression $y = xa + z^*(\gamma, w)b + \hat{\beta}'\nabla_\gamma z^*(\gamma, w)c + u^*$ provides a consistent estimate of the correct covariance matrix for PLS in the smoothed model. The bias in $(\alpha_*, \beta_*, \gamma_*)$ goes to zero as $\lambda \to 0$. Then, decreasing λ until the coefficients $(\alpha_*, \beta_*, \gamma_*)$ stabilize, and using the Gauss–Newton auxiliary regression at this λ to estimate the covariance matrix, can provide a reasonable approximation when the underlying model is consistent and asymptotically normal.

To illustrate the kernel smoothing approximation, consider the simple structural break model $y = 1(w \leq \gamma_0)\beta_0 + u$, where Assumptions 1–3 are satisfied and w has a CDF $F(w)$ with bounded support and a density $f(w)$ that is positive in a neighborhood of γ_0. The asymptotics of structural break problems have been characterized for discrete time series by Andrews (1993) and Stock (1994). The structural break example here is simpler in that w is continuously distributed and the disturbances are i.i.d. The features of this example often appear in spatial models where the span of proximity effects must be estimated. The kernel approximation to $1(w \leq \gamma)$ is $K((\gamma - w)/\lambda)$, where K is the kernel CDF. The asymptotic covariance matrix obtained from the kernel approximation is J^{-1},

---

[1] When the distribution of w has no point mass, the example of a linear spline function $z(\gamma, w)$ satisfies Assumption 4 at all γ interior to the support of w, and the example of a Box–Cox transformation when w is contained in a closed subset of the positive real line satisfies Assumption 4 when $\gamma \neq 1$, but fails to be almost surely continuously differentiable at $\gamma = 1$. In the last case, the Gauss–Newton iteration will be erratic in a neighborhood of $\gamma = 1$, and will fail to provide consistent covariance-matrix estimates when $\gamma_0 = 1$.

Table 9.1. *Monte carlo estimates of a structural break PLS model*

Statistic	Sample size n			
	100	400	1600	6400
Mean c ($\gamma_0 = 0.5$)	0.495	0.496	0.500	0.500
Mean b ($\beta_0 = 1$)	1.023	1.005	1.001	1.000
Mean s^2 ($\sigma_0^2 = 1$)	1.004	1.001	1.001	1.000
$\mathrm{Var}(n^{1/2}(c - \gamma_0))$	0.293	0.093	0.027	0.006
$\mathrm{Var}(n^{1/2}(b - \beta_0))$	2.823	2.135	2.024	1.956
$\mathrm{Cov}(n^{1/2}(c - \gamma_0), n^{1/2}(b - \beta_0))$	-0.469	-0.083	-0.023	-0.007
$\mathrm{Prob}(F > n/2)$	0.317	0.433	0.470	0.682
$1 - F(n/2, 1, n-1, \delta)$	0.281	0.415	0.464	0.680
Noncentrality parameter δ	41	193	794	3259

where

$$
J = \begin{bmatrix} \int K((\gamma - w)/\lambda)^2 f(w)\, dw & \int k(q)K(q)f(\gamma - \lambda q)\, dq \\ \int k(q)K(q)f(\gamma - \lambda q)\, dq & \int k(q)^2 f(\gamma - \lambda q)\, dq/\lambda \end{bmatrix}
$$

$$
\rightarrow \begin{bmatrix} F(\gamma) & f(\gamma)\int k(q)K(q)\, dq \\ f(\gamma)\int k(q)K(q)\, dq & +\infty \end{bmatrix}
$$

as $\lambda \to 0$. This implies that $\hat{\gamma}$ converges to γ_0 at a greater than $\sqrt{n}$ rate, and that the asymptotic covariance matrix of $\hat{\beta}$ is given by the least-squares formula with γ_0 known. A Monte Carlo experiment completes the illustration. Let $y = 1(w \le \gamma_0)\beta_0 + u$ with w uniformly distributed on $[0,1]$, u standard normal, $\gamma_0 = 0.5$, and $\beta_0 = 1$. The calculation of PLS estimates is staightforward. The probability of ties is zero, so the observations can be ordered almost surely with $w_1 < \cdots < w_n$. Let $\bar{y}_k = \sum_{i=1}^{k} y_i / k$. The sum of squares explained, $S(\gamma)$ from (9.4), is piecewise constant and right-continuous with jumps at w_i, and $S(w_i) = i\bar{y}_i^2$. Then $\hat{\gamma}$ equals the value w_k that maximizes $k\bar{y}_k^2$, and $\hat{\beta} = \bar{y}_k$. Table 9.1 gives exact finite-sample moments, calculated using 10,000 Monte Carlo trials for u, conditioned on one sample of w_i's. Finite-sample bias is small and disappears rapidly as the sample size grows. The variance of $\sqrt{n}(\gamma - \gamma_0)$ is substantial at $n = 100$, but drops rapidly with increasing n. Correspondingly, the variance of $\sqrt{n}(\hat{\beta} - \beta_0)$ at $n = 100$ is substantially above its asymptotic value of 1.90, but drops rapidly toward this limit as n increases.[2] The probability that the conventional PLS F-statistic exceeds $n/2$ is given next. If γ_0 were known and fixed, then this probability would equal the upper tail probability from the noncentral F-distribution $F(n/2, 1, n - 1, \delta)$, with $\delta = \sum 1(w_i \le 0.5)$ the

---

[2] The unconditional variance, formed by taking the expectation of the conditional variance with respect to the distribution of w, is 2.

noncentrality parameter. This probability and δ are given in the last two rows. The actual finite-sample distribution of the F-statistic has a larger upper tail than the corresponding noncentral F-distribution, with the difference disappearing with growing sample size.

A kernel-smoothed approximation to the covariance matrix for $n \geq 100$ is accurate to two significant digits for a normal kernel and $\lambda = 15/n$; I omit the detailed results. A disadvantage of kernel smoothing is the lack of a cross-validation method for determining values of λ that give a good empirical approximation.

A possible alternative to the use of a Gauss–Newton auxiliary regression to estimate covariances is a bootstrap procedure. The following procedure for estimating the covariances of PLS estimates is called the *conditional bootstrap*; see Peters and Freedman (1984), Brown and Newey (1995), and Veal (1992):

(a) Given PLS estimates $(\hat{\alpha}, \hat{\beta}, \hat{\gamma})$ from (9.1), form residuals $\hat{u} = y - X\hat{\alpha} - Z(\hat{\gamma})\hat{\beta}$.

(b) Let $\hat{u}^r$ be an $n \times 1$ vector drawn randomly, with replacement, from elements of $\hat{u}$ for bootstrap trials $r = 1, \dots, R$, calculate $y^r = X\hat{\alpha} + Z(\hat{\gamma})\hat{\beta} + \hat{u}^r$, and apply PLS to model (9.1) with dependent variable y^r to obtain estimates $(\hat{\alpha}^r, \hat{\beta}^r, \hat{\gamma}^r)$. Form bootstrap means $(\bar{\alpha}^R, \bar{\beta}^R, \bar{\gamma}^R) = \frac{1}{n} \sum_{r=1}^{R} (\hat{\alpha}^r, \hat{\beta}^r, \hat{\gamma}^r)$ and the bootstrap covariance matrix

$$V^R = \frac{1}{n} \sum_{r=1}^{R} \left(\hat{\alpha}^r - \bar{\alpha}^R, \hat{\beta}^r - \bar{\beta}^R, \hat{\gamma}^r - \bar{\gamma}^R\right)'$$
$$\times \left(\hat{\alpha}^r - \bar{\alpha}^R, \hat{\beta}^r - \bar{\beta}^R, \hat{\gamma}^r - \bar{\gamma}^R\right).$$

(c) The vector $(\hat{\alpha}^*, \hat{\beta}^*, \hat{\gamma}^*) = 2(\hat{\alpha}, \hat{\beta}, \hat{\gamma}) - (\bar{\alpha}^R, \bar{\beta}^R, \bar{\gamma}^R)$ is a bias-corrected bootstrap estimate of the parameters of (9.1), and V^R is a bootstrap estimate of the covariance matrix of $(\hat{\alpha}^*, \hat{\beta}^*, \hat{\gamma}^*)$.

An alternative that can handle conditional heteroscedasticity is the *conditional wild bootstrap*, where $\hat{u}^r = \hat{u}\zeta^r$, with ζ^r a vector of independent identically distributed draws from a distribution that has $E\zeta_i = 0$, $E\zeta_i^2 = 1$, and $E\zeta_i^3 = 1$. A typical construction is $\zeta_i = \eta_i/\sqrt{2} + (\eta_i^2 - 1)/2$ with η_i standard normal; see Liu (1988) and Davidson and Flachaire (1996).

Suppose Assumptions 1–3 hold, then PLS is strongly consistent by Theorem 1. Suppose in addition that $\sqrt{n}[(\hat{\alpha}, \hat{\beta}, \hat{\gamma}) - (\alpha_0, \beta_0, \gamma_0)]$ is asymptotically normal, either because Assumption 4 holds or because $\sqrt{n}(\hat{\gamma} - \gamma_0) \overset{P}{\to} 0$. Then, the bootstrap procedure with $R \to +\infty$ will give consistent estimates of its covariance matrix. The simple bootstrap procedure just described will not guarantee a higher-order approximation to the finite-sample covariance matrix than

Table 9.2. *Conditional bootstrap for the structural break PCL model*

Statistic	Sample size n			
	100	400	1600	6400
Exact mean c	0.495	0.496	0.500	0.500
Bootstrap mean c	0.499	0.493	0.500	0.500
Exact mean b	1.023	1.005	1.001	1.000
Bootstrap mean b	1.062	1.007	0.999	1.000
Exact $\text{Var}(n^{1/2}(c - \gamma_0))$	0.293	0.093	0.027	0.006
Bootstrap $\text{Var}(n^{1/2}(c - \gamma_0))$	0.385	0.090	0.029	0.006
Exact $\text{Var}(n^{1/2}(b - \beta_0))$	2.823	2.135	2.024	1.956
Bootstrap $\text{Var}(n^{1/2}(b - \beta_0))$	2.893	2.070	2.014	1.926

conventional first-order asymptotics, although in practice it may capture some sources of variation that appear in finite samples.[3]

Consider the structural break example $y = 1(w \leq \gamma_0)\beta_0 + u$ with w uniformly distributed on $[0,1]$, u standard normal, $\gamma_0 = 0.5$, and $\beta_0 = 1$. As indicated by the kernel-smoothing analysis, this is a case where asymptotic normality holds because $\sqrt{n}(\hat{\gamma} - \gamma_0) \overset{p}{\to} 0$. For a single sample of w's, we draw 100 samples from the true model, and then apply the conditional bootstrap with $R = 100$ repetitions to each sample. Table 9.2 gives exact sample and bootstrap estimates of the means and variances of the estimators of γ_0 and β_0. As in Table 9.1, the bias in the estimated coefficients is small, and attenuates rapidly; a bootstrap bias correction has a negligible effect. The bootstrap variance estimates are relatively accurate for the sample sizes larger than 100, and do appear to capture some of the finite-sample effects that disappear asymptotically.

Summarizing, the conditional bootstrap appears in one example where an explanatory variable is poorly behaved to provide acceptable covariance estimates. It appears to be at least as accurate in samples of moderate size as Gauss–Newton regression using a kernel-smoothing asymptotic approximation, and in addition avoids having to choose a smoothing parameter.

4   The effects of selection from a finite set of candidates

When Γ is finite, so that γ_0 is isolated, Theorem 1 establishes that the effects of variable selection are asymptotically negligible, and one can treat $\hat{\gamma}$ as if it were known and fixed in forming least-squares estimates of asymptotic standard errors or test statistics for α and β. However, in finite samples, variable selection will have a nonnegligible effect on standard errors and test statistics,

---

[3] Various iterated bootstrap schemes are available to get higher-order corrections; see Beran (1988) and Martin (1990).

and the least-squares estimates will generally be biased downward. This problem and several closely related ones have been investigated in the statistics and econometrics literature. Amemiya (1980) and Breiman and Freedman (1983) deal with the question of how many variables to enter in a regression. Freedman (1983) and Freedman, Navidi, and Peters (1988) show that variable selection leads least-squares standard errors to be biased downward. There is a related literature on pretest estimators; see Judge and Bock (1978). Also closely related is the econometrics literature on the problem of testing for a structural break at an unknown date; see Andrews (1993) and Stock (1994).

Suppose the disturbances in (9.1) are normal. If γ_0 were known and $Z(\gamma_0)$ always selected, then the test statistic (9.5) for the significance of Z would be distributed noncentral $F(q, n - k, \delta)$, with noncentrality parameter $\delta = \beta_0'(Z(\gamma_0)'MZ(\gamma_0))\beta_0/\sigma^2$. When γ_0 is unknown and $\hat{\gamma}$ is selected to maximize (9.5), then this statistic will always be at least as large as the F-statistic when $Z(\gamma_0)$ is always selected. This implies that the probability in the upper tail of the distribution of (9.5) exceeds the probability in the corresponding upper tail of the $F(q, n - k, \delta)$ distribution.

An example provides an idea of the magnitude of the bias in the PLS test statistic. Suppose univariate candidate variables z_0 and z_1 have the distribution

$$(z_0, z_1) = \begin{cases} (1, 1) & \text{w.p } (1 + \rho)/4, \\ (-1, -1) & \text{w.p } (1 + \rho)/4, \\ (1, -1) & \text{w.p } (1 - \rho)/4, \\ (-1, 1) & \text{w.p } (1 - \rho)/4. \end{cases}$$

Suppose $y = z_0\beta_0 + u$, with u normal with mean 0 and variance σ_0^2, so that z_0 is the correct variable. In a random sample of size n, conditioned on the covariates, the alternative estimates of β_0 when z_0 or z_1 are selected, respectively, are jointly distributed

$$\begin{bmatrix} \hat{\beta}_0 \\ \hat{\beta}_1 \end{bmatrix} \sim N\left(\begin{bmatrix} \beta_0 \\ \beta_0\rho_n \end{bmatrix}, \frac{\sigma_0^2}{n} \begin{bmatrix} 1 & \rho_n \\ \rho_n & 1 \end{bmatrix} \right),$$

where $\rho_n = \sum z_0 z_1/n$. Independently, the residuals from these respective regressions are jointly distributed

$$\begin{bmatrix} W_0 \\ W_1 \end{bmatrix} \sim N\left(\begin{bmatrix} 0 \\ Q_1 Z_0\beta_0 \end{bmatrix}, \sigma_0^2 \begin{bmatrix} Q_0 & Q_0 Q_1 \\ Q_1 Q_0 & Q_1 \end{bmatrix} \right),$$

where Z_k is the $n \times 1$ vector of z_0's for $k = 0$ and of z_1's for $k = 1$; $Q_k = I - Z_k Z_k'/n$; and $s_k^2 = W_k'W_k/(n - 1)$. The T-statistics are $T_k = \sqrt{n}\hat{\beta}_k/s_k$, and Z_0 is selected if T_0 is larger in magnitude than T_1. The statistic T_0 has unconditionally a T-distribution with $n - 1$ degrees of freedom, and conditioned on W_0 and W_1, $T_0 \sim N(\beta_0\sqrt{n}/s_0, \sigma_0^2/s_0^2)$. The distribution of T_1, given W_0, W_1, and $T_0 = t$, is $N[ts_0\rho_n/s_1, (\sigma_0^2/s_1^2)(1 - \rho_n^2)]$. Let c be the critical level for a

Table 9.3. *Exact power of PLS test for selected variable significance*

			ρ		
β_0	n	π_0	0.00	0.45	0.90
0.0	100	0.050	0.097	0.093	0.070
0.0	1000	0.050	0.097	0.093	0.070
0.01	100	0.051	0.093	0.093	0.072
0.01	1000	0.062	0.107	0.104	0.084
0.1	100	0.168	0.208	0.208	0.200
0.1	1000	0.885	0.890	0.893	0.899
0.2	100	0.508	0.532	0.539	0.546
0.2	1000	0.999	0.999	0.999	0.999

conventional T-test of significance level α, and let π_0 denote the conventional power of this test; i.e., $\pi_0 = \text{Prob}(F(1, n-1, \delta) > c)$, with $\delta = \beta_0^2 n / s_0^2$. Then, the probability that PLS yields a test statistic of magnitude larger than c is

$$\text{Prob}(\max\{|T_0|, |T_1|\} > c)$$

$$= \pi_0 + \mathbf{E}_{W_0, W_1} \int_{-c}^{c} \text{Prob}(|T_1| > c \mid T_0 = t) \cdot \phi\left(\frac{s_0 t - \beta_0 \sqrt{n}}{\sigma_0}\right) \cdot \frac{s_0}{\sigma_0} \, dt$$

$$= \pi_0 + \mathbf{E}_{W_0, W_1} \int_{-c}^{c} \left[\Phi\left[\frac{-s_1 c - t s_0 \rho_n}{\sigma_0 \sqrt{1 - \rho_n^2}}\right] + \Phi\left(\frac{-s_1 c + t s_0 \rho_n}{\sigma_0 \sqrt{1 - \rho_n^2}}\right) \right]$$

$$\cdot \phi\left(\frac{s_0 t - \beta_0 \sqrt{n}}{\sigma_0}\right) \cdot \frac{s_0}{\sigma_0} \, dt.$$

Table 9.3 gives this probability, denoted π, as well as the probability π_0, for $\alpha = 0.05$, $\sigma_0 = 1$, and selected values of ρ, β_0, and n. When $\beta_0 = 0$, the identification condition (Assumption 2) fails, and the probability of reject-ing the null hypothesis using either z_0 or z_1 alone equals the nominal signifi-cance level, 0.05. When z_0 and z_1 are uncorrelated, $\pi = 1 - (0.95)^2 = 0.0975$; the bias is reduced when z_0 and z_1 are correlated. This effect continues to domi-nate for n and β_0 where π_0 is low. When π_0 is large, the bias is smaller in relative terms, and increases when z_0 and z_1 are correlated. Adding more candidates would increase the biases.

In the previous section, we found that the bootstrap estimates of standard errors were relatively accurate for an example where convergence of $\hat{\gamma}$ to γ_0 occurs at a better than $\sqrt{n}$ rate, so that $\sqrt{n}(\hat{\gamma} - \gamma_0)$ is asymptotically degenerate normal. The problem of isolated γ_0 is similar, so that bootstrap estimates of covariances and asymptotic tests utilizing these bootstrap covariances may also be reasonably accurate in samples of moderate size.

5   Conclusions

This chapter demonstrates that prescreened least squares, where explanatory variables are selected to maximize their conventional least-squares significance level, or to maximize R^2, are statistically consistent and equivalent to nonlinear least squares under general regularity conditions. However, standard errors and test statistics provided by least-squares software are biased. When explanatory variables are smooth in the parameters that index the selection alternatives, a Gauss–Newton auxiliary regression provides a convenient procedure for getting consistent covariance-matrix estimates, and asymptotic tests from nonlinear least squares employing these covariance estimates are consistent. In situations where regularity conditions for Gauss–Newton auxiliary regression are not met, such as explanatory variables that are not smooth in the index parameters, or an isolated value for the true index parameter, bootstrap estimates of the covariance matrix appear from examples to be reasonably accurate in samples of moderate size.

Appendix: Proof of Theorem 1

I will employ a uniform stong law of large numbers established by Tauchen (1985):

Lemma 1. *If w_i are independently and identically distributed for $i = 1, \ldots, n$, Γ is compact, and $g : \Gamma \times \mathbb{R}^m \to \mathbb{R}^q$ is well behaved and dominated by an integrable function r, then $\mathbf{E}_w g(\gamma, w)$ exists and is continuous on Γ, and a uniform strong law of large numbers holds; i.e.,*

$$\sup_{\gamma \in \Gamma} \left| \frac{1}{n} \sum_{i=1}^{n} g(\gamma, w_i) - \mathbf{E}_w g(\gamma, w) \right| \overset{\text{a.s.}}{\to} 0.$$

Let δ_n be a sequence of numbers. A random variable R_n is said to be of order $O_p(\delta_n)$, or $R_n = O_p(\delta_n)$, if for each $\varepsilon > 0$ there exists $M > 0$ such that $P(|R_n| > M\delta_n) < \varepsilon$ for all n sufficiently large. Then convergence in probability, $R_n \overset{\text{p}}{\to} 0$, is equivalent to $R_n = O_p(\delta_n)$ for a sequence $\delta_n \to 0$. For $\sqrt{n}$-consistency under the conditions in Assumption 4, I use a result on uniform stochastic boundedness which may be of independent interest.

Lemma 2. *Suppose $y(\theta, w)$ is measurable in a random vector w for each θ in an open set $\Theta \subseteq \mathbb{R}^k$ that contains 0, with $y(0, w) \equiv 0$ and $\mathbf{E}y(\theta, w) = 0$. Suppose $y(\theta, w)$ satisfies a Lipschitz condition $|y(\theta', w) - y(\theta, w)| \leq r(w)|\theta' - \theta|$ for θ and θ' in Θ, where $r(w)$ is a random variable that has a proper moment* *generating function (MGF). Suppose $y(\theta, w_i)$ are independent draws. Then*

$$\sup_{|\theta| < \delta} \left| \frac{1}{\sqrt{n}} \sum_{i=1}^{n} y(\theta, w_i) \right| = O_p(\delta).$$

In further detail, there exist positive constants τ and A determined by $r(w)$ such that for $M^2 \geq 256kA$ and $n > (M/8A\tau)^2$,

$$P\left(\sup_{|\theta| < \delta} \left| \frac{1}{\sqrt{n}} \sum_{i=1}^{n} y(\theta, w_i) \right| > M\delta \right) \leq 2e^{-M^2/256A}.$$

Corollary. *Suppose the assumptions of Lemma 2, and suppose that $y(\theta, w)$ satisfies the Lipschitz condition $|y(\theta', w) - y(\theta, w)| \leq s(\delta, w)r(w)|\theta' - \theta|$ for θ and θ' in Θ and $|\theta| < \delta$, with $s(\delta, w)$ a well-behaved function satisfying $0 \leq s(\delta, w) \leq 1$ and $\mathbf{E}s(\delta, w) \to 0$ when $\delta \to 0$. Then*

$$\sup_{|\theta| < \delta} \left| \frac{1}{\sqrt{n}} \sum_{i=1}^{n} y(\theta, w_i) \right| = o_p(\delta).$$

Proof of Lemma 2: There exists $\tau > 0$ such that $\mathbf{E}e^{\tau r(w)} < +\infty$ on an open interval that contains $[0, \tau]$; an implication of this is $A = \mathbf{E}r(w)^2 e^{\tau r(w)} < +\infty$. Since $|y(\theta, w)| \leq r(w) \cdot |\theta|$, the MGF of $y(\theta, w_i)$ exists for $|t\theta| \leq \tau$ and has a Taylor expansion

$$\mu(t) = \mathbf{E}e^{ty(\theta, w)} = 1 + \frac{t^2}{2} \mathbf{E}y(\theta, w)^2 e^{\lambda t y(\theta, w)}$$

for some $\lambda \in (0, 1)$, implying $\mu(t) \leq 1 + (t^2/2)|\theta|^2 \cdot \mathbf{E}r(w)^2 \cdot e^{|t\theta|r(w)} \leq 1 + A|\theta|^2 t^2/2$. The MGF of $\sum_{i=1}^{n} y(\theta, w_i)/\sqrt{n}$ is then bounded by $[1 + A|\theta|^2 t^2/2n]^n \leq \exp(A|\theta|^2 t^2/2)$ for $|t\theta|/\sqrt{n} \leq \tau$.

Any random variable X satisfies the bound $P(|X| > m) \leq \int_{x > m} e^{-tm} e^{tx} F(dx) + \int_{x < -m} e^{-tm} e^{-tx} F(dx) \leq e^{-tm}[\mathbf{E}e^{tX} + \mathbf{E}e^{-tX}]$ for $t > 0$. Apply this inequality to obtain

$$\sup_{|\theta| < \omega} P\left(\frac{1}{\sqrt{n}} \left| \sum_{i=1}^{n} y(\theta, w_i) \right| > m \right) \leq 2 \exp\left(-tm + \frac{A\omega^2 t^2}{2} \right) \quad (9.A1)$$

for $|t\theta|\sqrt{n} \leq \tau$.

I use this exponential inequality and a chaining argument to complete the proof. The δ-neighborhood of 0 is contained in the cube $[-\delta/2, \delta/2]^k$. Recursively partition this cube into 2^{kj} cubes with sides of length $\delta \times 2^{-j}$. Let Θ_j denote the set of centroids of these cubes for partition j, and let $\theta_j(\theta)$ denote the point in Θ_j closest to θ. Note that $|\theta_j(\theta) - \theta_{j-1}(\theta)| \leq \delta \times 2^{-j}$, and that

$$\frac{1}{\sqrt{n}} \sum_{i=1}^{n} y(\theta, w_i) = \sum_{j=1}^{\infty} \frac{1}{\sqrt{n}} \sum_{i=1}^{n} [y(\theta_j(\theta), w_i) - y(\theta_{j-1}(\theta), w_i)].$$

Therefore, for $M^2 \geq 256kA$ and $n > (M/8A\tau)^2$,

$$P\left(\sup_{|\theta|<\delta} \frac{1}{\sqrt{n}} \left| \sum_{i=1}^{n} y(\theta, w_i) \right| > M\delta \right)$$

$$\leq \sum_{j=1}^{\infty} P\left(\sup_{|\theta|<\delta} \frac{1}{\sqrt{n}} \left| \sum_{i=1}^{n} [y(\theta_j(\theta), w_i) - y(\theta_{j-1}(\theta), w_i)] \right| > j \times 2^{-j-3} M\delta \right)$$

$$\leq \sum_{j=1}^{\infty} 2^{jk} \max_{\Theta_j} P\left(\frac{1}{\sqrt{n}} \left| \sum_{i=1}^{n} [y(\theta_j, w_i) - y(\theta_{j-1}, w_i)] \right| > j \times 2^{-j-3} M\delta \right)$$

$$\leq \sum_{j=1}^{\infty} 2^{jk} \times 2 \exp\left(-j \times 2^{-j-3} M\delta \cdot t_j + \frac{A\delta^2 \times 2^{-2j} t_j^2}{2} \right)$$

$$\text{for} \quad t_j \delta \times 2^{-j} \leq \tau \sqrt{n}$$

$$\leq \sum_{j=1}^{\infty} 2^{jk} \times 2 \exp\left(-\frac{(j - 1/2) \times 2^{-6} M^2}{A} \right) \quad \text{for} \quad t_j = \frac{2^{j-3} M}{A\delta}$$

$$\text{and} \quad n > \left(\frac{M}{8A\tau} \right)^2$$

$$\leq \frac{e^{-M^2/256A}}{1 - e^{-M^2/256A}} \leq 2e^{-M^2/256A} \quad \text{for} \quad M^2 \geq 256kA. \tag{9.A2}$$

The first inequality in (9.A2) holds because the event on the left is contained in the union of the events on the right. The second inequality holds because the event on the left at partition level j is contained in one of the 2^{jk} events on the right for the partition centroids. The third inequality is obtained by applying the exponential inequality (9.A1) to the difference $y(\theta_j, w_i) - y(\theta_{j-1}, w_i)$, with m replaced by $Mj \times 2^{-j-3}$ and ω replaced by $\delta \times 2^{-j}$. The next inequality is obtained by substituting the specified t_j arguments, and the final inequality is obtained by using the lower bound imposed on M and summing over j. $\square$

To prove the corollary, note that the MGF of $y(\theta, w_i)$ now satisfies $\mu(t) \leq 1 + A|\theta|^2 t^2/2$ for $|t\theta| \leq \tau/2$, with $A = Es(w)^2 r(w)^2 e^{\tau r(w)} \leq \{[Es(w)^4][Er(w)^4 e^{2\tau r(w)}]\}^{1/2}$ by the Cauchy–Schwartz inequality. The remainder of the proof of the lemma holds for this A, and $\mathbf{E}s(w)^4 \leq \mathbf{E}s(w) \to 0$ implies $A \to 0$ as $\delta \to 0$, giving the result.

Let θ be a finite-dimensional parameter varying in a set Θ. Suppose θ_0 minimizes a function $q(\theta)$ defined on Θ. Suppose further that a sample analog $Q_n(\theta)$ is minimized at a point $\hat{\theta}_n$ that converges in probability to θ_0. Define $Q_n(\theta) - q(\theta)$ to be uniformly convergent at rate $O_p(\varepsilon_n)$ on $O_p(\delta_n)$ neighborhoods of θ_0 if for each sequence of random variables R_n of order $O_p(\delta_n)$ there exists a sequence of random variables S_n of order $O_p(\varepsilon_n)$ such that $\sup_{|\theta - \theta_0| \leq R_n} |Q_n(\theta) - q(\theta)| \leq S_n$. I will employ conditions for $\sqrt{n}$-consistency established by Sherman (1993):

Lemma 3. *Suppose $\hat{\theta}$ minimizes $Q_n(\theta)$ and θ_0 minimizes $q(\theta)$ on Θ. If*

(i) *$|\hat{\theta}_n - \theta_0)| = O_p(\delta_n)$ for a sequence of numbers $\delta_n \to 0$,*
(ii) *for some neighborhood Θ_0 of θ_0 and constant $\kappa > 0$, $q(\theta) - q(\theta_0) \geq \kappa |\theta - \theta_0|^2$,*
(iii) *uniformly over $O_p(\delta_n)$ neighborhoods of θ_0,*

$$Q_n(\theta) - q(\theta) - Q_n(\theta_0) + q(\theta_0)$$
$$= O_p\left(\frac{|\theta - \theta_0|}{\sqrt{n}}\right) + o_p(|\theta - \theta_0|^2) + O_p(1/n),$$

then $|\hat{\theta}_n - \theta_0| = O_p(1/\sqrt{n})$. Suppose, in addition, that uniformly over $O_p(1/\sqrt{n})$ neighborhoods of θ_0,

$$Q_n(\theta) - Q_n(\theta_0) = (\theta - \theta_0)' R_n/\sqrt{n} + \tfrac{1}{2}(\theta - \theta_0) J(\theta - \theta_0) + o_p(1/n),$$

where R_n is asymptotically normal with mean 0 and covariance matrix K. Then

$$\sqrt{n}(\hat{\theta}_n - \theta_0) \xrightarrow{d} N(0, \mathbf{J}^{-1}\mathbf{K}\mathbf{J}^{-1}).$$

Proof of Theorem 1: We can absorb x into $z(\gamma, w)$, so that the model is simply $y = z(\gamma, w)\beta + u$. Assumptions 1 and 3 imply that $z(\gamma, w)'z(\gamma, w)$ is well behaved and dominated by integrable $r(w)^2$, and $z(\gamma, w)'y$ is well behaved and dominated by $r(w)y$ which satisfies $\mathbf{E}|r(w)y| \leq \mathbf{E}r(w)^2|\beta_0|$. Then, by Lemma 1, $H(\gamma) = \mathbf{E}z(\gamma, w)'z(\gamma, w)$ and $\psi(\gamma) = \mathbf{E}z(\gamma, w)'y$ are continuous in γ, and

$$\sup_{\gamma \in \Gamma} \left| \frac{1}{n} \sum_{i=1}^{n} z(\gamma, w)'z(\gamma, w) - H(\gamma) \right| \xrightarrow{a.s.} 0 \quad \text{and}$$

$$\sup_{\gamma \in \Gamma} \left| \frac{1}{n} \sum_{i=1}^{n} z(\gamma, w)'y - \psi(\gamma) \right| \xrightarrow{a.s.} 0.$$

From Assumption 1, $H(\gamma)$ is positive definite. Therefore, $\beta(\gamma) = H(\gamma)^{-1}\psi(\gamma)$ and $s(\gamma) \equiv \beta(\gamma)'H(\gamma)\beta(\gamma)$ are continuous on Γ, $\sup_{\gamma \in \Gamma}|S(\gamma) - s(\gamma)| \overset{\text{a.s.}}{\to} 0$, and $\sigma^2(\gamma) + s(\gamma) = \mathbf{E}y^2$. Given $\varepsilon, \delta > 0$, let

$$
\inf_{\substack{\gamma \in \Gamma \\ |\gamma - \gamma_0| \geq \delta}} \frac{\sigma^2(\gamma)}{\sigma_0^2} > 1 = \lambda > 1
$$

from Assumption 2. Note that $\sigma^2(\gamma) \geq \lambda\sigma_0^2$ implies $s(\gamma_0) \geq s(\gamma) + (\lambda - 1)\sigma_0^2$. Choose n such that Prob $(\sup_{n' \geq n} \sup_{\gamma \in \Gamma}|S(\gamma) - s(\gamma)| > (\lambda - 1)\sigma_0^2/3) < \varepsilon$. For $n' \geq n$ and $|\gamma - \gamma_0| \geq \delta$, one then has with probability $1 - \varepsilon$ or higher the inequality $S(\gamma_0) \geq S(\gamma) + (\lambda - 1)\sigma_0^2/3$. Then with at least this probability, the maximand $\hat{\gamma}$ of $S(\gamma)$ is contained within a δ-neighborhood of γ_0 for all $n' \geq n$. Therefore $\hat{\gamma} \overset{\text{a.s.}}{\to} \gamma_0$. Uniform a.s. convergence then implies $\hat{\sigma}^2 = \text{SSR}(\hat{\gamma})/(n - k) \overset{\text{a.s.}}{\to} \sigma_0^2$. Let

$$
\hat{\beta}(\gamma) = \left[\frac{1}{n}\sum_{i=1}^{n} z(\gamma, w)'z(\gamma, w)\right]^{-1} \frac{1}{n}\sum_{i=1}^{n} z(\gamma, w)'y.
$$

The preceding results establish that $\sup_{\gamma \in \Gamma}|\hat{\beta}(\gamma) - \beta(\gamma)| \overset{\text{a.s.}}{\to} 0$, and hence that $\hat{\beta}(\hat{\gamma}) \overset{\text{a.s.}}{\to} \beta_0$. This establishes strong consistency.

Suppose γ_0 is an isolated point of Γ. Then an implication of $\hat{\gamma} \overset{\text{a.s.}}{\to} \gamma_0$ is that Prob$(\hat{\gamma} \neq \gamma_0$ for $n' \geq n) \to 0$, and hence Prob$(\sqrt{n}(\hat{\gamma} - \gamma_0) \neq 0) \to 0$. Hence for $\varepsilon, \delta > 0$, there exists n_0 such that Prob$(\sqrt{n}|\beta(\hat{\gamma}) - \beta(\gamma_0)| > \delta) \leq$ Prob$(\sqrt{n}(\hat{\gamma} - \gamma_0) \neq 0) < \varepsilon$ for $n \geq n_0$. But $\sqrt{n}(\hat{\beta}(\gamma_0) - \beta_0) \overset{\text{d}}{\to} N(0, \sigma_0^2 H(\gamma_0)^{-1})$ by application of the Lindeberg–Levy central limit theorem to $(1/\sqrt{n})\sum_{i=1}^{n}[z(\gamma_0, w_i)'y_i - H(\gamma_0)\beta_0]$. Combining these results establishes that $\sqrt{n}(\hat{\beta}(\hat{\gamma}) - \beta_0) \overset{\text{d}}{\to} N(0, \sigma_0^2 H(\gamma_0)^{-1})$. This establishes asymptotic normality in the case of isolated γ_0.

Suppose Assumption 4 holds. Then $d(\gamma, \beta, w) = \nabla_\gamma z(\gamma, w)\beta$ exists a.s. and is well behaved, implying that it is piecewise a.s. continuous in γ. Then given $\varepsilon > 0$, there a.s. exists $\delta(\varepsilon, \gamma, w) > 0$ such that $|\gamma' - \gamma| < \delta(\varepsilon, \gamma, w)$ implies $|d(\gamma', \beta, w) - d(\gamma, \beta, w)| < \varepsilon|\beta|$ and, by the theorem of the mean, $(z(\gamma', w) - z(\gamma, w))\beta = d(\tilde{\gamma}, \beta, w)(\gamma' - \gamma)$ for $\tilde{\gamma} \in (\gamma, \gamma')$. Let $W(\varepsilon, \gamma, \nu)$ be the set of w for which $\delta(\varepsilon, \gamma, w) < \nu$. The a.s. continuity of $d(\gamma, \beta, w)$ implies the (outer) probability of $W(\varepsilon, \gamma, \nu)$ approaches zero as $\nu \to 0$. Choose ν such that the probability of $W(\varepsilon, \gamma, \nu)$ is less than ε and $\mathbf{E}r(w) \cdot 1(w \in W(\varepsilon, \gamma, \nu)) < \varepsilon$. Then $\lambda(\gamma, \gamma', \beta, w) \equiv (z(\gamma', w) - z(\gamma, w))\beta - d(\gamma, \beta, w)(\gamma' - \gamma)$ satisfies the bounds $|\lambda(\gamma, \gamma'\beta, w)| \leq \varepsilon|\beta| \cdot |\gamma' - \gamma|$ for $w \notin W(\varepsilon, \gamma, \nu)$ and $|(\lambda(\gamma, \gamma'\beta, w)| \leq 3r(w)|\beta| \cdot |\gamma' - \gamma|$ a.s. Since ε is arbitrary, this establishes that $\lambda(\gamma, \gamma', \beta, w) = o_p(|\beta| \cdot |\gamma' - \gamma|)$ and $\mathbf{E}_\gamma(\gamma, \gamma', \beta, w) = o(|\beta| \cdot |\gamma' - \gamma|)$.

The same argument establishes the approximations

$$\mathbf{E}z(\gamma, w)'(z(\gamma, w) - z(\gamma_0, w))\beta$$
$$= \mathbf{E}z(\gamma, w)'d(\gamma_0, \beta, w)(\gamma - \gamma_0) + o(|\gamma - \gamma_0|) \qquad (9.A3)$$

and

$$\beta'\mathbf{E}(z(\gamma, w) - z(\gamma_0, w))'(z(\gamma, w) - z(\gamma_0, w))\beta$$
$$= (\gamma - \gamma_0)'\mathbf{E}d(\gamma_0, \beta, w)'d(\gamma_0, \beta, w)(\gamma - \gamma_0) + o(|\gamma - \gamma_0|^2). \qquad (9.A4)$$

Define $\theta = (\gamma, \beta)$ and $Q_n(\theta) = (1/n)\sum_{i=1}^n (y_i - z(\gamma, w_i)\beta)^2$. Then $q(\theta_0) = \sigma_0^2$ and

$$q(\theta) = \mathbf{E}(y - z(\gamma, w)\beta)^2 \equiv \sigma_0^2 + \mathbf{E}(z(\gamma_0, w)\beta_0 - z(\gamma, w)\beta)^2.$$

Write $(z(\gamma, w)\beta - z(\gamma_0, w))\beta_0 = z(\gamma_0, w)(\beta - \beta_0) + (z(\gamma, w) - z(\gamma_0, w))\beta = z(\gamma_0, w)(\beta - \beta_0) + d(\gamma_0, \beta, w)(\gamma - \gamma_0) + \lambda(\gamma_0, \gamma, \beta, w)$. Then

$$q(\theta) - q(\theta_0)$$
$$= (\beta - \beta_0)'\mathbf{E}z(\gamma_0, w)'z(\gamma_0, w)(\beta - \beta_0)$$
$$+ 2(\beta - \beta_0)'\mathbf{E}z(\gamma_0, w)'(z(\gamma, w) - z(\gamma_0, w))\beta$$
$$+ \beta_0'\mathbf{E}(z(\gamma, w) - z(\gamma_0, w))'(z(\gamma, w) - z(\gamma_0, w))\beta_0$$
$$= \begin{bmatrix} \beta - \beta_0 \\ \gamma - \gamma_0 \end{bmatrix}' \begin{bmatrix} \mathbf{E}z(\gamma, w)'z(\gamma, w) & \mathbf{E}z(\gamma, w)'d(\gamma_0, \beta, w) \\ \mathbf{E}d(\gamma_0, \beta, w)'z(\gamma, w) & \mathbf{E}d(\gamma_0, \beta_0, w)'d(\gamma_0, \beta, w) \end{bmatrix}$$
$$\times \begin{bmatrix} \beta - \beta_0 \\ \gamma - \gamma_0 \end{bmatrix} + 2\mathbf{E}\lambda(\gamma, \beta, w)[d(\gamma_0, \beta, w)(\gamma - \gamma_0)$$
$$+ z(\gamma_0, w)(\beta - \beta_0)] + \mathbf{E}\lambda(\gamma, \beta, w)^2. \qquad (9.A5)$$

The final terms in this expression are $o(|\theta - \theta_0|^2)$, and the conditions from Assumption 4 that $J(\gamma, \beta)$ is continuous and $J(\gamma_0, \beta_0)$ is positive definite imply that $q(\theta) - q(\theta_0) = (\theta - \theta_0)'J(\gamma_0, \beta_0)(\theta - \theta_0) + o(|\theta - \theta_0|^2) \geq \kappa|\theta - \theta_0|^2$ for some $\kappa > 0$ on a neighborhood of θ_0

Consider the expression

$$Q_n(\theta) - q(\theta) - Q_n(\theta_0) + q(\theta_0)$$
$$= \frac{1}{n}\sum_{i=1}^n u_i(z(\gamma, w_i)\beta - z(\gamma_0, w_i)\beta_0)$$
$$+ \frac{1}{n}\sum_{i=1}^n \{(z(\gamma, w_i)\beta - z(\gamma_0, w_i)\beta_0)^2$$
$$- \mathbf{E}(z(\gamma, w)\beta - z(\gamma_0, w)\beta_0)^2\}. \qquad (9.A6)$$

The first term on the right-hand side of this expression can be written

$$\frac{1}{n}\sum_{i=1}^{n}u_i(z(\gamma, w_i)\beta - z(\gamma_0, w_i)\beta_0)$$

$$= \frac{1}{n}\sum_{i=1}^{n}u_i[z(\gamma_0, w_i) \quad d(\gamma_0, \beta, w_i)]\begin{bmatrix}\beta - \beta_0 \\ \gamma - \gamma_0\end{bmatrix}$$

$$+ \frac{1}{n}\sum_{i=1}^{n}u_i\lambda(\gamma_0, \gamma, \beta, w_i). \tag{9.A7}$$

A central limit theorem implies

$$R_n \equiv \frac{1}{\sqrt{n}}\sum_{i=1}^{n}u_i[z(\gamma_0, w_i) \quad d(\gamma_0, \beta, w_i)] \xrightarrow{d} N\left(0, \sigma_0^2 J(\gamma_0, \beta)\right); \tag{9.A8}$$

hence

$$\frac{1}{n}\sum_{i=1}^{n}u_i[z(\gamma_0, w_i) \quad d(\gamma_0, \beta, w_i)]\begin{bmatrix}\beta - \beta_0 \\ \gamma - \gamma_0\end{bmatrix} = O_p\left(\frac{|\theta - \theta_0|}{\sqrt{n}}\right).$$

The provisions in Assumption 4 that u has a proper MGF and $r(w)$ is bounded imply that $u\lambda(\gamma_0, \gamma, \beta, w)$ has a proper MGF. An application of the Corollary to Lemma 2, utilizing the condition that $\lambda(\gamma, \gamma', \beta, w) = o_p(|\beta| \cdot |\gamma' - \gamma|)$, implies that uniformly $(1/n)\sum_{i=1}^{n}u_i\lambda(\gamma_0, \gamma, \beta, w) = o_p(|\beta| \cdot |\gamma - \gamma_0|/\sqrt{n})$. Finally, write

$$\frac{1}{n}\sum_{i=1}^{n}\{(z(\gamma, w_i)\beta - z(\gamma_0, w_i)\beta_0)^2 - \mathbf{E}(z(\gamma, w)\beta - z(\gamma_0, w)\beta_0)^2\}$$

$$= \frac{1}{n}\sum_{i=1}^{n}\{d(\gamma_0, \beta, w_i)(\gamma - \gamma_0) + z(\gamma_0, w_i)(\beta - \beta_0)$$

$$+ \lambda(\gamma_0, \gamma, \beta, w_i)\}^2 - \mathbf{E}\{d(\gamma_0, \beta, w)(\gamma - \gamma_0)$$

$$+ z(\gamma_0, w)(\beta - \beta_0) + \lambda(\gamma_0, \gamma, \beta, w)\}^2. \tag{9.A9}$$

The squares and cross-products that do not involve $\lambda(\gamma_0, \gamma, \beta, w)$ will be $O_p(|\theta - \theta_0|^2/\sqrt{n})$ by a central limit theorem. The terms that involve $\lambda(\gamma_0, \gamma, \beta, w)$ or its square will be uniformly $o_p(|\theta - \theta_0|^2/\sqrt{n})$ by the Corollary to Lemma 2.

Conditions (i) to (iii) of Lemma 3 are now established, implying the nonlinear least-squares estimates satisfy $\hat{\theta} - \theta_0 = O_p(1/\sqrt{n})$. Next, observe from (9.A5) to (9.A8) that

$$Q_n(\theta) - Q_n(\theta_0)$$

$$= \frac{2}{n} \sum_{i=1}^{n} u_i [z(\gamma_0, w) \quad d(\gamma_0, \beta, w)] \begin{bmatrix} \beta - \beta_0 \\ \gamma - \gamma_0 \end{bmatrix}$$

$$+ o_p \left(\frac{|\beta| \cdot |\gamma - \gamma_0|}{\sqrt{n}} \right) + \begin{bmatrix} \beta - \beta_0 \\ \gamma - \gamma_0 \end{bmatrix}'$$

$$\times \begin{bmatrix} \mathbf{E}z(\gamma, w)'z(\gamma, w) & \mathbf{E}z(\gamma, w)'d(\gamma_0, \beta, w) \\ \mathbf{E}d(\gamma_0, \beta, w)'z(\gamma, w) & \mathbf{E}d(\gamma_0, \beta_0, w)'d(\gamma_0, \beta, w) \end{bmatrix}$$

$$\times \begin{bmatrix} \beta - \beta_0 \\ \gamma - \gamma_0 \end{bmatrix} + o(|\theta - \theta_0|^2)$$

$$= \frac{2}{\sqrt{n}} R_n \begin{bmatrix} \beta - \beta_0 \\ \gamma - \gamma_0 \end{bmatrix} + \begin{bmatrix} \beta - \beta_0 \\ \gamma - \gamma_0 \end{bmatrix}' J(\theta_0) \begin{bmatrix} \beta - \beta_0 \\ \gamma - \gamma_0 \end{bmatrix}$$

$$+ o_p \left(\frac{|\beta| \cdot |\gamma - \gamma_0|}{\sqrt{n}} \right) + o(|\theta - \theta_0|^2).$$

Then the final condition of Lemma 3 is satisfied, and the nonlinear least-squares estimator is asymptotically normal with covariance matrix $\sigma_0^2 J(\theta_0)^{-1}$.

REFERENCES

Amemiya, T. (1978), "On a Two-Step Estimation of a Multinomial Logit Model," *Journal of Econometrics*, **8**, 13–21.

(1980), "Selection of Regressors," *International Economic Review*, **21**, 331–354.

(1985), *Advanced Econometrics* (Cambridge, MA: Harvard University Press).

Andrews, D. (1993), "Tests for Parameter Instability and Structural Change with Unknown Change Point," *Econometrica*, **61**, 821–856.

Beran, R. (1988), "Prepivoting Test Statistics: A Bootstrap View of Asymptotic Refinements," *Journal of the American Statistical Association*, **83**, 687–697.

Breiman, L. and Freedman, D. (1983), "How Many Variables Should Enter a Regression Equation," *Journal of the American Statistical Association*, **78**, 131–136.

Brown, B. and Newey, W. (1995), "Bootstrapping for GMM," MIT Working Paper.

Brownstone, D. (1990), "Bootstrapping Improved Estimators for Linear Regression Models," *Journal of Econometrics*, **44**, 171–188.

(1992) "Bootstrapping Admissible Model Selection Procedures," in R. LePage and L. Billard, eds., *Exploring the Limits of Bootstrap* (New York: Wiley), 327–344.

Davidson, R. and Flachaire, E. (1996), "Monte Carlo Evidence on the Behavior of the Wild Bootstrap in the Presence of Leverage Points," NSF Symposium on the Bootstrap, University of California, Berkeley.

Davidson, R. and MacKinnon, J. (1993), *Estimation and Inference in Econometrics* (New York: Oxford).

Freedman, D. (1983), "A Note on Screening Regression Equations," *The American Statistician*, **37**, 152–155.

Freedman, D., Navidi, W., and Peters, S. (1988), "On the Impact of Variable Selection in Fitting Regression Equations," in T. Dijkstra, ed., *On Model Uncertainty and its Statistical Implications* (Berlin: Springer).

Gallant, R. (1987), *Nonlinear Statistical Models* (New York: Wiley).

Jenrich, R. (1969), "Asymptotic Properties of Nonlinear Least Squares Estimators," *The Annals of Mathematical Statistics*, **40**, 633–643.

Judge, G. and Bock, M. (1978), *The Statistical Implications of Pre-test and Stein-Rule Estimators in Econometrics* (Amsterdam: North Holland).

Liu, R. (1988), "Bootstrap Procedure under Some Non-I.I.D. Models," *Annals of Statistics*, **16**, 1696–1708.

Lovell, M. (1983), "Data Mining," *Review of Economics and Statistics*, **65**, 1–12.

Martin, M. (1990), "On Bootstrap Iteration for Coverage Correction in Confidence Intervals," *Journal of the American Statistical Association*, **85**, 1105–1118.

Newey, W. and McFadden, D. (1994), "Large Sample Estimation and Hypothesis Testing," in R. Engle and D. McFadden, eds., *Handbook of Econometrics*, **4**, 2111–2245.

Pakes, A. and Pollard, D. (1989), "Simulation and the Asymptotics of Optimization Estimation," *Econometrica*, **57**, 1027–1057.

Peters, S. and Freedman, D. (1984), "Some Notes on the Bootstrap in Regression Problems," *Journal of Business and Economic Statistics*, **2**, 406–409.

Pollard, D. (1984), *Convergence of Stochastic Processes* (Berlin: Springer-Verlag).

Sherman, R. (1993), "The Limiting Distribution of the Maximum Rank Correlation Estimator," *Econometrica*, **61**, 123–137.

Stock, J. (1994), "Unit Roots, Structural Breaks, and Trends," in R. Engle and D. McFadden, eds., *Handbook of Econometrics*, **4**, 2739–2841.

Tauchen, G. (1985), "Diagnostic Testing and Evaluation of Maximum Likelihood Models," *Journal of Econometrics*, **30**, 415–433.

Veal, M. (1992), "Bootstrapping the Process of Model Selection: An Econometric Example," *Journal of Applied Econometrics*, **7**, 93–99.

CHAPTER 10

Using information on the moments of disturbances to increase the efficiency of estimation

Thomas E. MaCurdy

1   Foreword

This chapter was originally written in 1981, with a draft distributed as a National Bureau of Economic Research Working paper (No. 2, May 1982). Although this study was never publicly disseminated in another form, several articles published in the 1980s and 1990s cited and built upon its findings. No paper of mine better reflects just how much Takeshi has influenced my education and research. It is a sentimental favorite of mine for this reason and, thus, is an especially fitting offering for my contribution to Takeshi's Festschrift. The chapter that follows – a modest revision of the NBER Working paper completed in June 1982 – is the version I have sent upon receiving requests for the paper. To preserve its authenticity, the following text incorporates nothing more than editorial changes.

Subsequent work has, of course, expanded and refined many of the results presented in this 1982 paper. The Afterword at the end of this chapter summarizes these developments, attempting to place the 1982 findings presented here into the context of the current literature.

Finally, an appendix follows the Afterword summarizing the results of a small Monte Carlo analysis that investigates the practical applicability of the estimation approach proposed in this chapter. The absence of such evidence made the results of the original work of theoretical interest, but of little functional use. Contrary to many researchers' suspicions, these Monte Carlo findings suggest that substantial efficiency gains may be attainable by implementing these estimation procedures.

A major part of this chapter was originally distributed as an NBER Working Paper in 1982. This research was supported by NSF grant no. SES-8023043. I owe a great deal to Takeshi Amemiya for many valuable discussions about the topics in this chapter. In the updated parts of this chapter and the newly done appendix, I am grateful for many useful comments and expert research assistance from Frank McIntyre and James Pearce.

2   Introduction

This study develops new estimators for regression and simultaneous equations that are in general strictly efficient relative to the conventional least squares and two-stage least squares estimators. The analysis encompasses both linear and nonlinear estimation in situations where random variables are distributed independently across observations. The discussion deals with many alternative assumptions concerning the specific distributional properties of the disturbances associated with the equation under consideration, ranging from a situation in which the variance of disturbances varies across observations in an unknown and arbitrary fashion, to one in which errors are identically distributed over the sample. For each of these distributional assumptions, the discussion formulates estimation procedures that yield a gain in large-sample efficiency over the familiar ordinary, weighted, and two-stage least squares procedures, except when these latter procedures correspond directly to the application of maximum likelihood methods. Thus, unless the exact distribution of random variables is known, making maximum likelihood an option, one can typically improve the asymptotic efficiency of estimation using the procedures described here.

The properties of the second and higher-order moments of the disturbances constitute the source of information used to improve the efficiency of estimation in this analysis. Estimators are formulated by jointly estimating the regression or simultaneous equation under consideration with various transformations of this equation which are obtained by weighting schemes and/or by raising both sides of the equation to a power (e.g., squaring or cubing both sides). The particular transformations included in the joint estimation procedure are chosen in a way to exploit the distributional properties of the disturbances for the sample under investigation. As a by-product of this work, general methods are developed for testing the hypotheses that any particular moment or combination of moments of the disturbances are constant across observations for both the cases of regression and simultaneous equations. This analysis also provides a natural framework for discussing recent important contributions by Chamberlain (1982) and Cragg (1983), related work by Amemiya (1983), and results reported in White (1982).

Section 3 presents notation and results used throughout the chapter. Section 4 discusses estimating the parameters of a linear multiple regression model, and Section 5 considers the general problem of estimating the parameters of a nonlinear simultaneous equation.

3   Combining information to compute estimators

This section reviews a familiar procedure for computing parameter estimates that optimally combines information and constraints from various sources. The purpose of this discussion is to establish the notation and derive formulas used in the subsequent analysis.

3.1   General estimation approach

Suppose one is interested in obtaining a consistent estimate of the true value of a $p \times 1$ parameter vector θ that is an unknown determinant of the distribution generating a random vector Y. Denote this true value as θ_0; it is assumed to be an interior point in a convex compact set Θ. Let Y_i and Z_i, $i = 1, \ldots, N$, denote N observations on Y and on a vector of measured characteristics Z. The Y_i's are assumed to be independently distributed across observations after conditioning on the Z_i's, or when these characteristics are treated as known constants.

The most widely used method for computing a consistent estimate for θ_0 is to solve a system of equations that implicitly defines a value for θ and is known to be satisfied when $\theta = \theta_0$ as the sample size goes to infinity. In particular, let $\ell_i(\theta) \equiv \ell(\theta, Y_i, Z_i)$, $i = 1, \ldots, N$, represent an $r \times 1$ vector of known functions with $r \geq p$, and consider the system of equations

$$L_N(\theta) \equiv \frac{1}{N} \sum_{i=1}^{N} \ell_i(\theta) = 0. \tag{10.1}$$

Assuming each ℓ_i possesses a sufficiently well-behaved distribution and is chosen so that $E(\ell_i(\theta_0)) = 0$, one can show that setting $\theta = \theta_0$ solves (10.1) in the sense that $L_N(\theta_0)$ converges in probability to zero as the sample size goes to infinity. For most estimation procedures the ℓ_i's are gradient vectors associated with the optimization of a particular function of the data defined over the parameter space Θ. By introducing additional assumptions which guarantee the satisfaction of a set of regularity conditions, one may further demonstrate that computing a solution to (10.1) yields a strongly consistent estimate for θ_0 that is asymptotically normally distributed.

Some notation and assumptions are needed for the following discussion. The matrices of first partials $\partial \ell_i / \partial \theta'$, $i = 1, \ldots, N$, are assumed to exist with each element uniformly continuous in θ. Denote the average of these partials by $S_N(\theta) \equiv (1/N) \sum_{i=1}^{N} \partial \ell_i / \partial \theta'$, assumed to possess full column rank. Define the matrix $V_N(\theta) \equiv (1/N) \sum_{i=1}^{N} \ell_i(\theta) \ell_i'(\theta)$ as an average of outer products; and further define $L(\theta) \equiv \lim E(L_N(\theta))$, $S(\theta) \equiv \lim E(S_N(\theta))$, and $V(\theta) \equiv \lim E(V_N(\theta))$ with limits computed as $N \to \infty$. To derive the asymptotic results cited below, the distributions associated with the ℓ_i's and the matrices of first partials cannot have too much weight in the tails.[1] Given

---

[1] Letting ℓ_{ji} and s_{jki} denote the j and (j, k) elements of ℓ_i and $\partial \ell_i / \partial \theta'$, respectively, sufficient conditions restricting the tails of distributions are: $E|\ell_{ji}|^{2+\delta_2} \leq C_1 < \infty$ and $E|s_{jki}|^{1+\delta_1} \leq C_2 \leq \infty$ for some $\delta_1, \delta_2 > 0$ and all $\theta \in \Theta$.

such distributional assumptions and the independence of the ℓ_i's, one may show the following strong convergence results: $L_N(\theta) \overset{p}{\to} L(\theta)$, $S_N(\theta) \overset{p}{\to} S(\theta)$, and $V_N(\theta) \overset{p}{\to} V(\theta)$, where $\overset{p}{\to}$ designates convergence in probability and with results holding for each $\theta \in \Theta$. Thus, if $E(\ell_i(\theta_0)) = 0$, it follows that $L_N(\theta_0) \overset{p}{\to} 0$, implying θ_0 solves (10.1) as the sample size goes to infinity. Furthermore, one may show that $\sqrt{N} L_N(\theta_0) \overset{d}{\to} N(0, V(\theta_0))$, where $\overset{d}{\to}$ denotes convergence in distribution, and $N(\cdot, \cdot)$ signifies a normal probability law. In many applications one cannot rule out the possibility that values of θ other than θ_0 may also satisfy (10.1) in the limit. One can, however, easily resolve this issue for the estimation problems considered below, and for simplicity this analysis assumes the solution to (10.1) is unique. To prove consistency and asymptotic normality of this solution, the convergence of L_N, S_N, and V_N to their respective limits must be uniform in θ, and this assumption is maintained throughout the discussion.

When the number of equations in (10.1) used to compute estimates exceeds the number of parameters, one requires a weighting scheme for comparing the errors obtained in solving the various equations; one cannot typically find a value for θ that solves all equations exactly in finite samples. This is, of course, a familiar problem in statistics. The theory of ordinary least squares derives an estimate for θ by minimizing the sum of squared errors associated with the r equations appearing in (10.1), which implies minimization of the quantity $L_N'(\theta)L_N(\theta)$. It is well known, however, that applying generalized least squares yields a more efficient parameter estimate. According to this procedure, one solves equation (10.1) by choosing θ to minimize the quantity $L_N'(\theta)[E(V_N(\theta_0))]^{-1}L_N(\theta)$, where this expression uses the relation $E(L_N(\theta_0)L_N'(\theta_0)) = (1/N)E(V_N(\theta_0))$ following from the independence of observations. The matrix $E(V_N(\theta_0))$ is unknown, but, as with many generalized least squares analyses, a consistent estimate for this matrix is easily constructed and the asymptotic properties of estimators are unaffected if one substitutes this consistent estimate for the true value of the matrix. Accordingly, when computing an estimate for θ_0, one sacrifices no estimation asymptotic efficiency by instead minimizing the quadratic form

$$L_N'(\theta)\hat{V}_N^{-1}L_N(\theta), \tag{10.2}$$

where $\hat{V}_N \equiv V_N(\hat{\theta})$ with $\hat{\theta}$ representing any strongly consistent estimate for θ_0 implying $\hat{V}_N \overset{p}{\to} V(\theta_0)$. Essentially any solution to (10.1) or to any subset of this system of equations may serve as $\hat{\theta}$. Let $\tilde{\theta}$ denote that value of θ minimizing (10.2).

Identifying the asymptotic properties of the estimator $\tilde{\theta}$ is a straightforward task once one recognizes that (10.2) is in the form of the quantities minimized to compute conventional nonlinear two- and three-stage least squares estimators. Following the work of Amemiya (1974, 1977), who initiated the study of this class of estimators, one can readily verify that $\tilde{\theta} \xrightarrow{s} \theta_0$ and

$$\sqrt{N}(\tilde{\theta} - \theta_0) \xrightarrow{d} N(0, [S'(\theta_0)V^{-1}(\theta_0)S(\theta_0)]^{-1}). \tag{10.3}$$

Thus, the approximate distribution for $\tilde{\theta}$ in large samples is

$$\tilde{\theta} \stackrel{\sim}{\sim} N\left(\theta_0, \frac{1}{N}[\tilde{S}'_N \hat{V}_N^{-1} \tilde{S}_N]^{-1}\right),$$

where $\tilde{S}_N \equiv S_N(\tilde{\theta})$. Recent work by Hansen (1982) also examines this method for computing estimators and derives (10.3) using a general set of assumptions.

3.2   Conditions implying efficiency gains when adding information

The interesting problem in estimation concerns the choice of the equations included in system (10.1). When the distributions of random variables are known, setting L_N equal to the gradient associated with the log of the likelihood function is well known to produce an estimator that is asymptotically efficient. In this instance, adding more equations to (10.1) obviously provides no gain in estimation efficiency, and changing any one of the equations leads, in general, to a loss in efficiency. Without knowledge of distributions, however, the choice of equations used to compute estimators is an open question. The subsequent analysis examines the strategy of adding equations to those typically used in the conventional application of least squares or instrumental variable estimation methods as a way of deriving more efficient estimators.

To determine the gain in efficiency as one introduces more information or equations to compute estimators, suppose one has two sets of equations available for estimating a parameter vector α: one system of equations associated with the ith observation consists of the vector of functions $g_i(\alpha, \mu)$, which also depends on unknown parameters μ; and a second system consists of the vector of functions $h_i(\alpha, \psi)$ depending on a third set of parameters ψ. The expectations of both g_i and h_i are assumed to vanish at the true parameter values for each i, making it possible to use the averages of either vector to compute a consistent estimate for α_0. Combining these equations to obtain a single estimate for α_0, one sets $\theta' = (\alpha', \mu', \psi')$ and $\ell'_i = (g'_i, h'_i)$, and minimizes (10.2) with respect to θ. According to (10.3), the covariance matrix associated with the resulting estimate is $[S'V^{-1}S]^{-1}$, where the argument θ_0 indicating the point of evaluation is dropped for notational convenience. Consider the following partitions of the matrices S and V:

$$S \equiv \lim E \left[\frac{1}{N} \sum_{i=1}^{N} \frac{\partial \ell_i}{\partial \theta'} \Big|_{\theta_0} \right]$$

$$= \lim E \begin{bmatrix} \frac{1}{N} \sum_{i=1}^{N} \frac{\partial g_i}{\partial \alpha'} \big|_{\theta_0} & \frac{1}{N} \sum_{i=1}^{N} \frac{\partial g_i}{\partial \mu'} \big|_{\theta_0} & \frac{1}{N} \sum_{i=1}^{N} \frac{\partial g_i}{\partial \psi'} \big|_{\theta_0} \\ \frac{1}{N} \sum_{i=1}^{N} \frac{\partial h_i}{\partial \alpha'} \big|_{\theta_0} & \frac{1}{N} \sum_{i=1}^{N} \frac{\partial h_i}{\partial \mu'} \big|_{\theta_0} & \frac{1}{N} \sum_{i=1}^{N} \frac{\partial h_i}{\partial \psi'} \big|_{\theta_0} \end{bmatrix}$$

$$\equiv \begin{bmatrix} S_{11} & S_{12} & 0 \\ S_{21} & 0 & S_{23} \end{bmatrix}$$

and

$$V \equiv \lim E \left[\frac{1}{N} \sum_{i=1}^{N} \ell_i(\theta_0)\ell_i'(\theta_0) \right]$$

$$= \lim E \begin{bmatrix} \frac{1}{N} \sum_{i=1}^{N} g_i(\theta_0)g_i'(\theta_0) & \frac{1}{N} \sum_{i=1}^{N} g_i(\theta_0)h_i'(\theta_0) \\ \frac{1}{N} \sum_{i=1}^{N} h_i(\theta_0)g_i'(\theta_0) & \frac{1}{N} \sum_{i=1}^{N} h_i(\theta_0)h_i'(\theta_0) \end{bmatrix}$$

$$= \begin{bmatrix} V_{11} & V_{12} \\ V_{21} & V_{22} \end{bmatrix}.$$

The matrix V is assumed to be nonsingular, which in essence requires each of the functions added to the analysis contained in h_i to constitute a unique piece of information. Defining the matrices $V_{22 \cdot 1} \equiv V_{22} - V_{21} V_{11}^{-1} V_{12}$ and $F \equiv (S_{21}\ 0) - V_{21} V_{11}^{-1}(S_{11}\ S_{12}) \equiv (G\ F_2)$ with $G \equiv S_{21} - V_{21} V_{11}^{-1} S_{11}$ and $F_2 \equiv -V_{21} V_{11}^{-1} S_{12}$, use of the partition inverse formula for V^{-1} yields

$$[S'V^{-1}S]^{-1} = \left[\begin{pmatrix} S_{11}' & S_{21}' \\ S_{12}' & 0 \\ 0 & S_{23}' \end{pmatrix} \begin{pmatrix} I & -V_{11}^{-1}V_{12} \\ 0 & I \end{pmatrix} \begin{pmatrix} V_{11}^{-1} & 0 \\ 0 & V_{22 \cdot 1}^{-1} \end{pmatrix} \right.$$

$$\left. \times \begin{pmatrix} I & 0 \\ -V_{21}V_{11}^{-1} & I \end{pmatrix} \begin{pmatrix} S_{11} & S_{12} & 0 \\ S_{21} & 0 & S_{23} \end{pmatrix} \right]^{-1}$$

$$= \left[\begin{matrix} \begin{pmatrix} S_{11}' \\ S_{12}' \end{pmatrix} V_{11}^{-1}(S_{11}\ S_{12}) + F'V_{22 \cdot 1}^{-1}F & F'V_{22 \cdot 1}^{-1}S_{23} \\ S_{23}' V_{22 \cdot 1}^{-1}F & S_{23}' V_{22 \cdot 1}^{-1}S_{23} \end{matrix} \right]^{-1}$$

Given this partition, the implied precision matrix (i.e., the inverse of the variance–covariance matrix) associated with estimates for α and μ is

$$\begin{pmatrix} S_{11}' \\ S_{12}' \end{pmatrix} V_{11}^{-1}(S_{11}\ S_{12}) + \begin{pmatrix} G' \\ F_2' \end{pmatrix} A(G\ F_2)$$

with $A \equiv V_{22\cdot1}^{-1} - V_{22\cdot1}^{-1} S_{23}(S_{23}' V_{22\cdot1}^{-1} S_{23})^{-1} S_{23}' V_{22\cdot1}^{-1}$.[2] Since the first matrix in this expression is the precision matrix obtained if one uses only the vector of functions g_i to estimate the parameters α and μ, the second matrix shows the gain in precision achieved in estimating α and μ by also using the equations h_i in the computation of estimates. In particular, the matrix determining the efficiency gain in estimating the parameters of interest α is $G'AG$. Not surprisingly, introducing more information to compute estimates never results in a loss of efficiency, since $G'AG$ is a positive semidefinite matrix.

Appealing to familiar results from least squares theory provides the conditions implying rank$(G'AG) > 0$, which is needed to attain an improvement in asymptotic efficiency. The elements of the matrix $G'AG$ correspond directly to sums of squares of least squares residuals associated with regressing the columns of $V_{22\cdot1}^{-1/2} G$ on the columns of $V_{22\cdot1}^{-1/2} S_{23}$. Consequently, for $G'AG \neq 0$, the column rank of the matrix $V_{22\cdot1}^{-1/2}[G \vdots S_{23}]$ must exceed the column rank of the matrix $V_{22\cdot1}^{-1/2} S_{23}$. Since $V_{22\cdot1}^{-1/2}$ is nonsingular, this observation indicates that using the additional information conveyed in the h_i's to estimate α_0 leads to increased efficiency if

$$\text{rank}[G \vdots S_{23}] > \text{rank}[S_{23}]. \tag{10.4}$$

Clearly, this condition requires

$$G \equiv S_{21} - V_{21} V_{11}^{-1} S_{11} \neq 0. \tag{10.5}$$

In a situation where the h_i's do not depend on a new set of parameters ψ, one can readily verify that the above formulas indicating efficiency gains are applicable if one simply sets $A = V_{22\cdot1}^{-1}$. In this special case, condition (10.5) alone determines whether there is an increase in the precision of estimation.

4 Least squares estimation

Suppose observations on the random variable Y are generated by the multiple regression model

$$Y_i = X_i'\beta_0 + \varepsilon_i, \qquad i = 1, \ldots, N, \tag{10.6}$$

where X_i is a column vector of explanatory variables selected from a set of measured characteristics Z_i associated with the ith observation, β_0 is an unknown parameter vector, and the ε_i's are independently distributed errors with $E(\varepsilon_i) = 0$, where expectations here implicitly condition on the Z_i's. The following analysis primarily considers two distinct assumptions relating to the distributional properties of the disturbances: first, the ε_i's are not identically distributed,

---

[2] This formulation merely represents the $(1,1)$ block of the partitioned inverse of the variance–covariance matrix.

with variances $\sigma_i^2 \equiv E(\varepsilon_i^2)$ differing across observations; and, second, the variance and higher order moments of the errors are constant across observations.

4.1   *Using exclusion restrictions to gain efficiency*

In the presence of heteroscedasticity, Chamberlain (1982) and Cragg (1983) develop the first estimators of which I am aware that are asymptotically efficient relative to the least squares estimator and whose computation does not rely on specific knowledge or modeling of the form taken by the heteroscedasticity. A discussion of this estimator offers a convenient opportunity for emphasizing several features of the estimation framework outlined in the previous section before proceeding to the alternative estimators proposed below. Amemiya (1983) offers a more straightforward interpretation and derivation of Chamberlain's estimator, and it is Amemiya's simpler formulation of this estimator that is presented here.

Instead of directly estimating equation (10.6), one may interpret the estimation approaches proposed by Chamberlain and Cragg as adding variables to this equation and forming a constrained estimator using a particular variant of the procedure oulined in Section 3. In particular, letting Q_i denote a vector of measured variables linearly independent of X_i, consider the expanded model

$$Y_i = X_i'\beta_0 + Q_i'\gamma_0 + \varepsilon_i, \qquad i = 1, \ldots, N, \tag{10.7}$$

where $\gamma_0 = 0$ according to (10.6). In terms of the notation of the previous section, with $Z_i' = (X_i', Q_i')$, one can view constrained least squares estimation of (10.7) with the restriction $\gamma = 0$ as choosing an estimate for β_0 by minimizing a quadratic form like (10.2) with $\ell_i(\beta) = Z_i(Y_i - X_i'\beta)$ and with the matrix $\hat{V}_N$ in (10.2) replaced by $M_N \equiv (1/N)\sum_{i=1}^{N} Z_i Z_i'$. Chamberlain in effect uses the same expressions for the $\ell_i(\beta)$'s, but derives his estimator by directly minimizing (10.2) with no substitution for $\hat{V}_N$. For this problem,

$$\hat{V}_N = \frac{1}{N}\sum_{i=1}^{N} \ell_i(\hat{\beta})\ell_i'(\hat{\beta}) = \frac{1}{N}\sum_{i=1}^{N} Z_i Z_i' \hat{\varepsilon}_i^2,$$

where $\hat{\varepsilon}_i$ represents a residual consistent for $Y_i - X_i'\beta_0$. For the class of estimators defined by minimizing a quadratic form in the vector L_N, the use of (10.2) and the matrix $\hat{V}_N$ produces the most efficient estimate for β_0 when constraints make it impossible to solve the equations $L_N = 0$ exactly. A standard application of asymptotic theory implies $\hat{V}_N \xrightarrow{s} \lim[(1/N)\sum_{i=1}^{N} Z_i Z_i'\sigma_i^2]$. When the variances of disturbances vary across observations, it is evident that the matrices $\hat{V}_N$ and M_N do not have asymptotic limits that are proportional to one another; and, as a consequence, the use of constrained least squares implies an efficiency loss. Since unconstrained least squares estimation of (10.6) and constrained least squares estimation of (10.7) produce the same estimate of β_0, it follows that Chamberlain's estimator generally achieves greater efficiency than the conventional least squares estimator when heteroscadasticity exists.

Identifying the exact gain in efficiency is easily accomplished using the results of the previous section. Unconstrained least squares applied to equation (10.6) in effect computes an estimate for β_0 by minimizing the quadratic form given by (10.2) with the vector of functions $g_i(\beta) = X_i(Y_i - X_i'\beta)$ used in place of the ℓ_i's. One may, then, view Chamberlain's and Cragg's procedure as combining these g_i's with the information contained in the relations $h_i(\beta) = Q_i(Y_i - X_i'\beta)$ and minimizing (10.2) with $\ell_i' = (g_i', h_i')$. According to the previous section, the matrix $G'AG$ shows the gain in precision achieved by including the h_i's in the computation of an estimate for β_0. For this problem, G is the asymptotic limit of the matrix

$$\left[-\frac{1}{N}\sum_{i=1}^{N}Q_iX_i'\right] - \left[\frac{1}{N}\sum_{i=1}^{N}Q_iX_i'\sigma_i^2\right]\left[\frac{1}{N}\sum_{i=1}^{N}X_iX_i'\sigma_i^2\right]^{-1}\left[-\frac{1}{N}\sum_{i=1}^{N}X_iX_i'\right],$$

and A is the asymptotic limit of

$$\left[\left[\frac{1}{N}\sum_{i=1}^{N}Q_iQ_i'\sigma_i^2\right] - \left[\frac{1}{N}\sum_{i=1}^{N}Q_iX_i'\sigma_i^2\right]\left[\frac{1}{N}\sum_{i=1}^{N}X_iX_i'\sigma_i^2\right]^{-1}\left[\frac{1}{N}\sum_{i=1}^{N}X_iQ_i'\sigma_i^2\right]\right]^{-1}.$$

Obviously, when the σ_i's are constant across observations (i.e., σ_i's do not vary as a function of X_i), then $G = 0$, and there is no gain in precision, as expected.

A major deficiency with this approach concerns the absence of a strategy for choosing the variables to be included in Q; it is unclear how to go about choosing an optimal Q. For this reason, the following estimation procedure offers an attractive alternative to the above approach.

4.2   Weighted regressions

With heteroscedasticity present, the most familiar method for improving the efficiency of estimating β_0 is to consider a weighted version of equation (10.6) and apply least squares to this new equation. Let the variables ω_i, $i = 1, \ldots, N$, denote measured quantities depending on the characteristics Z and on a set of known or estimated coefficients. Using the ω_i's to weight (10.6) yields the equation

$$\omega_iY_i = \omega_iX_i'\beta_0 + \omega_i\varepsilon_i, \qquad i = 1, \ldots, N. \tag{10.8}$$

Obviously, if one knows how the σ_i's vary across observations and chooses the ω_i's to adjust for this variation, then least squares estimation of equation (10.8) rather than (10.6) generates a more efficient estimate for β_0. Without this knowledge, however, or given an arbitrary choice for the ω_i's, there is no a priori reason for preferring either the weighted or the ordinary least squares estimate on efficiency grounds.

Combining the information used to compute these distinct estimates offers an alternative procedure for constructing an estimate for β_0. In terms of the framework outlined in Section 3, unconstrained least squares estimation of equation (10.6) computes an estimate for β_0 using the vector of functions $g_i(\beta) \equiv X_i(Y_i - X_i'\beta)$; and weighted least squares uses the vectors $h_i(\beta) \equiv \omega_i^2 X_i(Y_i - X_i'\beta)$.[3] To compute a single estimate for β_0 that combines these different relations, one sets $\ell_i' = (g_i', h_i')$ and minimizes (10.2). Satisfaction of condition (10.5) determines whether adding the h_i's leads to a more efficient estimator. For this problem, the matrix G appearing in this condition is the asymptotic limit of

$$
\left[-\frac{1}{N} \sum_{i=1}^{N} X_i X_i' \omega_i^2 \right] - \left[\frac{1}{N} \sum_{i=1}^{N} X_i X_i' \omega_i^2 \sigma_i^2 \right]
$$

$$
\times \left[\frac{1}{N} \sum_{i=1}^{N} X_i X_i' \sigma_i^2 \right]^{-1} \left[-\frac{1}{N} \sum_{i=1}^{N} X_i X_i' \right],
$$

which does not in general equal the zero matrix unless $\sigma_i^2 = \sigma_0^2$ for all i. In the presence of heteroscedasticity, then, the new estimator produced by jointly estimating equations (10.6) and (10.8) is strictly more efficient than the ordinary least squares estimator. Furthermore, it can be shown that this new estimator also possesses greater efficiency than the familiar weighted least squares estimator unless the weights are optimally chosen (i.e., $\omega_i = 1/\sigma_i$).

In contrast to the previous approach based on the use of exclusion restrictions, this procedure for computing an estimator offers a natural strategy for choosing the weights and the additional relations to be combined with those used in conventional least squares estimation. While an optimal choice for the weights is assumed not to be an option in this analysis, one intuitively wants to choose each ω_i so that it approximates $1/\sigma_i$ as closely as possible. One procedure for obtaining such weights involves a simple regression analysis. In particular, letting

---

[3] If the ω_i's depend on estimated coefficients, it is, of course, not in general true that $E(h_i(\beta_0)) = 0$. All the consistency and asymptotic normality results of Section 3, however, remain valid in this case as long as each $|\omega_i - \bar{\omega}_i| \xrightarrow{P} 0$ uniformly in i or in some other suitable metric, with $\bar{\omega}_i$ nonstochastic, and as long as the vectors $\bar{h}_i = \bar{\omega}_i^2 X_i(Y_i - X_i'\beta)$ satisfy the properties of the ℓ_i's outlined in the previous section.

$b_i \equiv b(Z_i, \lambda)$ denote a function designed to capture the suspected variability of the σ_i's across observations, a regression of the squared least squares residuals $\hat{\varepsilon}_i^2$ on $b(\cdot)$ estimates the unknown parameters λ and provides for the construction of a fitted value b_i and a weight $\omega_i = 1/\sqrt{b_i}$.

To the extent that this choice for the weights fails to adjust for the variability of the σ_i's, one may construct an estimator for β_0 with improved efficiency by introducing yet another weighted variant of the regression equation. Joint least squares estimation of this new equation along with (10.6) and (10.8), using the above procedure to combine the relations defining the individual least squares estimates for each equation, provides the framework for computing this new estimator. A natural choice for this new equation is to consider a weighted version of (10.8) with the new weights chosen to reduce the variation in the variances $\omega_i^2 \sigma_i^2$ associated with the disturbances of this equation.

4.3   *Using information on second moments*

When disturbances are homoscedastic, there are other equations one may jointly estimate along with the regression equation to obtain an estimator more efficient than the one produced by ordinary least squares. This analysis works directly with equation (10.6), presuming that weights are not needed to induce homoscedasticity. If this presumption is false, then one must interpret equation (10.6) in this discussion as the appropriately weighted variant of the original regression equation. Squaring both sides of equation (10.6) yields

$$Y_i^2 = \sigma_0^2 + (X_i'\beta_0)^2 + \upsilon_i, \qquad i = 1, \ldots, N, \tag{10.9}$$

where σ_0^2 is an intercept term, and $\upsilon_i \equiv 2(X_i'\beta_0)\varepsilon_i + \varepsilon_i^2 - \sigma_0^2$ is a disturbance with mean zero. Assuming the orthogonality conditions $\lim E((1/N)\sum_{i=1}^{N} X_i X_i'(\varepsilon_i^2 - \sigma_0^2)) = 0$, which obviously follows if $\sigma_i^2 = \sigma_0^2$ for all i, nonlinear constrained least squares applied to (10.9) offers an alternative method for computing a consistent estimate of β_0. Indeed, except for a sign convention, the components of β are in general identified using the information of equation (10.9) alone, assuming X_i includes more than an intercept; fixing the sign of one nonzero component of β solves the sign convention problem. While least squares estimation of (10.9) yields a less efficient estimate for β_0 than the one obtained by least squares applied to (10.6), combining the relations used to compute these distinct estimates provides for the formulation of a new estimator that is in general efficient relative to either of the estimators computed using a single equation alone.

Jointly estimating equations (10.6) and (10.9) without restricting the β-coefficients to be equal for the two equations provides sufficient information to test (i) whether the second moments of disturbances satisfy the orthogonality conditions needed to justify an equality restriction for the estimates of β across equations, and (ii) whether the variances of disturbances are constant over the sample. Least squares applied to equation (10.6) uses the vector of functions $g_i(\beta_1) = X_i(Y_i - X_i'\beta_1)$ to compute an estimate for β_0; and, with $v_i^* \equiv Y_i^2 - \sigma^2 - (X_i'\beta_2)^2$, nonlinear least squares applied to (10.9) calculates estimates for β_0 and σ_0^2 using the relations

$$h_i(\beta_2, \sigma^2) = -\frac{1}{2}\frac{\partial v_i^{*2}}{\partial \binom{\beta}{\sigma^2}} = \binom{2X_i(X_i'\beta_2)}{1}(Y_i^2 - \sigma^2 - (X_i'\beta_2)^2).$$

Joint least squares estimation of these equations means in this analysis that one sets $\ell_i'(\beta_1, \beta_2, \sigma^2) = (g_i', h_i')$ and minimizes (10.2) with respect to β_1, β_2, and σ^2. Using the implied joint asymptotic distribution for the estimates $\tilde{\beta}_1$ and $\tilde{\beta}_2$ given by (10.3), one may use a standard Wald statistic to test the null hypothesis that the probability limit of $\tilde{\beta}_1 - \tilde{\beta}_2$ is zero. Acceptance of this hypothesis indicates that the moments $E(\varepsilon_i^2)$ satisfy the orthogonality conditions needed for $\tilde{\beta}_2 \xrightarrow{s} \beta_0$. However, more is required to test the assumption of homoscedasticity, because the restriction $\beta_1 = \beta_2$ does not rule out the possibility that the variances σ_i^2 may depend on a set of measured variables that are orthogonal to $X_i X_i'$. Including these other variables in equation (10.9) permits one to estimate their relationship to the σ_i^2's. A test for homoscedasticity, then, involves a null hypothesis with two parts: (i) the quantity $\tilde{\beta}_1 - \tilde{\beta}_2$ converges in probability to zero; and (ii) other variables assumed to determine the σ_i^2's have zero coefficients when entered into equation (10.9).[4]

Rejection of the restriction $\beta_1 = \beta_2$ means that one cannot use information from equation (10.9) to attain an efficiency gain for the estimate of β_0. At the same time, however, rejection of this hypothesis ensures that the joint estimation scheme described above – combining the regression equation and its weighted variants – yields an improvement in efficiency over conventional least squares estimation.

---

[4] For the current problem, there is a simpler procedure for testing the hypotheses concerning the orthogonality conditions and/or the homoscedasticity assumption that avoids the need for jointly estimating equations (10.6) and (10.9). Following the work of White (1980), one may carry out these tests using a multiple regression framework with squares of residuals treated as dependent variables and with the unique components of $X_i X_i'$ and possibly other explanatory variables serving as regressors. Performing a conventional F-test of the hypothesis that coefficients other than the intercept are zero yields an asymptotically valid test for either of the hypotheses cited above, assuming the constancy of the fourth moments of disturbances. One cannot, however, use this simpler testing framework for any of the similar situations considered below, including those concerned with testing for the constancy of third or higher-order moments in the regression case or for the constancy of any moments in the simultaneous equation case. In contrast to White's case, one cannot in these latter situations ignore the fact that residuals are estimated quantities when forming large-sample test statistics.

Acceptance of the restriction $\beta_1 = \beta_2$ indicates that one can carry out joint estimation of equations (10.6) and (10.9) imposing this equality constraint. In particular, one sets $\ell_i'(\beta, \sigma^2) = (g_i'(\beta), h_i'(\beta, \sigma^2))$ using the specifications of g_i and h_i cited directly above and minimizes quadratic form (10.2) with respect to β and σ^2. Since ordinary least squares only uses the g_i relations to compute an estimate for β_0, checking condition (10.4) for the relevant specifications of g_i and h_i determines whether this joint estimation procedure leads to an efficiency gain over the usual least squares procedure.

Concerning the implied specifications of the matrices G and S_{23} appearing in condition (10.4), the matrix G is the asymptotic limit of

$$
\left[-\frac{1}{N} \sum_{i=1}^{N} \binom{4(X_i'\beta_0)^2 X_i X_i'}{2(X_i'\beta_0)X_i'} \right] - \left[\frac{1}{N} \sum_{i=1}^{N} \binom{2(X_i'\beta_0)X_i X_i'}{X_i'} E(\varepsilon_i \upsilon_i) \right]
$$
$$
\times \left[\frac{1}{N} \sum_{i=1}^{N} X_i X_i' E\left(\varepsilon_i^2\right) \right]^{-1} \left[-\frac{1}{N} \sum_{i=1}^{N} X_i X_i' \right].
$$

Given the definition of υ_i, $E(\varepsilon_i \upsilon_i) = 2(X_i'\beta_0)E(\varepsilon_i^2) + E(\varepsilon_i^3)$. In the presence of homoscedasticity, with $E(\varepsilon_i^2) = \sigma_0^2$ for all i, the matrix G reduces to

$$
-\frac{1}{\sigma_0^2 N} \left[\sum_{i=1}^{N} \binom{2(X_i'\beta_0)X_i X_i'}{X_i'} E\left(\varepsilon_i^3\right) \right].
$$

If the third moments of disturbances are nonzero, then $G \neq 0$, since $E(\varepsilon_i^3) \neq 0$.[5] The implied specification for the matrix S_{23} is the asymptotic limit of

$$
-\frac{1}{N} \left[\sum_{i=1}^{N} \binom{2(X_i'\beta_0)X_i}{1} \right].
$$

It is evident that there are columns of G which are in general linearly independent of the single column of S_{23}, and consequently condition (10.4) is typically satisfied. Thus, this joint estimation procedure can be expected to lead to an efficiency gain over the usual least squares procedure if the distribution of errors is nonsymmetric.

Accounting for the heteroscedasticity associated with the disturbances of the equations used in this joint estimation procedure provides for the formulation of an even more efficient estimator of β_0. The covariance matrix associated

---

[5] In those situations where the disturbances ε_i are heteroscedastic and still satisfy the orthogonality conditions needed to estimate β_0 consistently using equation (10.9), we have $G \neq 0$ even if $E(\varepsilon_i^3) = 0$, generally implying that joint estimation in these instances can still lead to a gain in efficiency over conventional least squares.

with the errors of equations (10.6) and (10.9) for the ith observation is

$$\Phi_i \equiv E\left[\begin{pmatrix}\varepsilon_i \\ v_i\end{pmatrix}(\varepsilon_i \quad v_i)\right]$$

$$= \begin{bmatrix} E(\varepsilon_i^2) & 2(X_i'\beta_0)E(\varepsilon_i^2) + E(\varepsilon_i^3) \\ 2(X_i'\beta_0)E(\varepsilon_i^2) + E(\varepsilon_i^3) & 4(X_i'\beta_0)^2 E(\varepsilon_i^2) + 4(X_i'\beta_0)E(\varepsilon_i^3) + E(\varepsilon_i^4) - \sigma_0^4 \end{bmatrix}.$$

The disturbances of the squared regression equation have nonconstant variances by construction. In addition, there exists several other potential sources of heteroscedasticity: the moments $E(\varepsilon_i^3)$ and $E(\varepsilon_i^4)$ may vary across observations; and, as noted above, the ability to use the information from equation (10.9) in computing an estimate for β_0 does not rule out the possibility that the second moments $E(\varepsilon_i^2)$ are nonconstant. One method of improving the efficiency of estimation by introducing adjustments for heteroscedasticity involves the implementation of an approach like the one followed above; that is, in addition to equations (10.6) and (10.9), one may also use information from weighted variants of these equations in the computation of an estimate for β_0.

4.4   Using information on third and higher-order moments

If one is willing to assume that the disturbances ε_i have constant moments up to fourth order, then there exists a more efficient method of accounting for the remaining heteroscedasticity in estimation. Treating equations (10.6) and (10.9) as a seemingly unrelated regression model, one can estimate the parameters of these equations by joint generalized least squares. Using least squares residuals and fitted values, one can easily form consistent estimates for the parameters $E(\varepsilon^2)$, $E(\varepsilon^3)$, and $E(\varepsilon^4)$, and for the quantities $X_i'\beta_0$. With these estimates, it is possible to construct a consistent estimate for each covariance matrix Φ_i, denoted by $\hat{\Phi}_i$. Defining $\varepsilon_i^* \equiv Y_i - X_i'\beta$ and $v_i^* \equiv Y_i^2 - \sigma^2 - (X_i'\beta)^2$, joint generalized least squares in effect sets

$$\ell_i(\beta, \sigma^2) = -\frac{\partial(\varepsilon_i^* \quad v_i^*)}{\partial\begin{pmatrix}\beta \\ \sigma^2\end{pmatrix}}\hat{\Phi}_i^{-1}\begin{pmatrix}\varepsilon_i^* \\ v_i^*\end{pmatrix}$$

$$= \begin{pmatrix} X_i & 2X_i(X_i'\beta) \\ 0 & 1 \end{pmatrix}\hat{\Phi}_i^{-1}\begin{pmatrix}(Y_i - X_i'\beta) \\ (Y_i^2 - \sigma^2 - (X_i'\beta)^2)\end{pmatrix}$$

and computes an estimate for β_0 and σ_0^2 by minimizing (10.2). While this procedure yields a more efficient estimator for β_0 than the one based on the joint least squares estimation of (10.6) and (10.9), it is still necessary for third moments to be nonzero before an efficiency gain is attained over the conventional least squares estimator.

As soon as one assumes that moments of the ε_i's above second order are constant across observations, there are even more sources of information available for improving estimation efficiency. The constancy of third moments suggests consideration of a cubic version of the regression equation. Cubing both sides of (10.6) yields

$$Y_i^3 = \tau_0 + 3(X_i'\beta_0)\sigma_0^2 + (X_i'\beta_0)^3 + \eta_i, \qquad i = 1, \ldots, N, \qquad (10.10)$$

where τ_0 and σ_0^2 are unknown parameters, and

$$\eta_i \equiv 3(X_i'\beta_0)^2\varepsilon_i + 3(X_i'\beta_0)\left(\varepsilon_i^2 - \sigma_0^2\right) + \left(\varepsilon_i^3 - \tau_0\right)$$

is a disturbance with zero mean. Nonlinear least squares applied to (10.10) yields consistent estimates for β_0, σ_0^2, and τ_0 assuming satisfaction of the orthogonality conditions $\lim E[(1/N)\sum_{i=1}^{N} X_i X_i'(X_i'\beta_0)(\varepsilon_i^2 - \sigma_0^2)] = 0$ and $\lim E[(1/N)\sum_{i=1}^{N} X_i X_i'(X_i'\beta_0)(\varepsilon_i^3 - \tau_0)] = 0$. These orthogonality conditions obviously follow if $E(\varepsilon_i^2)$ and $E(\varepsilon_i^3)$ do not vary with i. It is also interesting to note that these conditions necessarily follow in those situations where the combined estimation of (10.6) and (10.9) produces a consistent estimate for β_0, but yields no efficiency gain.

Joint least squares estimation of equations (10.6), (10.9), and (10.10) then, imposing all the constraints implied across equations, offers yet another procedure for constructing an estimator for β_0. Before constraining the estimates of β_0 obtained from these three equations to be equal, it is a straightforward matter to test the orthogonality conditions required for imposing this constraint using a direct analog of the testing procedure described above. In particular, with the ℓ_i relations made up of the gradient vectors associated with least squares estimation of equations (10.6), (10.9), and (10.10), and with the coefficients representing β_0 and σ_0^2 made distinct across equations, one can test the orthogonality conditions by checking for equality of the probability limits for the different estimates of β and σ^2 using a Wald statistic and the asymptotic distribution implied by (10.3). The above discussion also indicates what is required to test the hypothesis that third moments are constant across observations. In addition to testing the restriction that the estimates of β and σ^2 obtained from equations (10.6), (10.9), and (10.10) are the same, a test for the constancy of third moments also implies that any other measured variables entered into equation (10.10) have zero coefficients.

As in the previous case dealing with the joint estimation of only equations (10.6) and (10.9), several options are available for simultaneously estimating the regression equation and its squared and cubic variants. Assuming the ε_i's have constant moments across the sample up to sixth order, joint generalized least squares offers the most efficient estimation procedure. Treating equations (10.6), (10.9), and (10.10) as a seemingly unrelated regression model, let

$e'_i = (\varepsilon_i, \upsilon_i, \eta_i)$ denote the vector of disturbances associated with this model for the ith observation; define $\Psi_i \equiv E(e_i e'_i)$ as the implied covariance matrix; let $\hat{\Psi}_i$ represent a consistent estimate for Ψ_i; and define $e^{*\prime}_i = (\varepsilon^*_i, \upsilon^*_i, \eta^*_i)$, where $\eta^*_i \equiv Y^3_i - \tau - 3(X'_i\beta)\sigma^2 - (X'_i\beta)^3$. Joint generalized least squares applied to this system of equations in effect computes estimates for β_0, σ^2_0, and τ_0 by minimizing quadratic form (10.2) with

$$h_i(\beta, \sigma^2, \tau) = C_i \hat{\Psi}^{-1}_i e^*_i, \qquad i = 1, \ldots, N,$$

where

$$C_i \equiv -\frac{\partial e^{*\prime}_i}{\partial \begin{pmatrix} \beta \\ \sigma^2 \\ \tau \end{pmatrix}} \equiv \begin{pmatrix} X_i & 2X_i(X'_i\beta) & 3X_i(\sigma^2 + (X'_i\beta)^2) \\ 0 & 1 & 3(X'_i\beta) \\ 0 & 0 & 1 \end{pmatrix}.$$

To discover when this procedure yields improved efficiency for the estimate of β_0 over ordinary least squares, consider the implied specification of the matrices G and S_{23} needed to evaluate condition (10.4). Least squares applied to (10.6) computes estimates using the relations $g_i(\beta) = X_i(Y_i - X'_i\beta)$; and joint generalized least squares applied to (10.6), (10.9), and (10.10) uses the relations $h_i(\beta, \sigma^2, \tau) = C_i \hat{\Psi}^{-1}_i e^*_i$ to calculate estimates. Partition the matrix C_i as $C'_i = [C'_{1i} \ C'_{2i}]$ with $C_{1i} = [X_i \vdots 2X_i(X'_i\beta) \vdots 3X_i(\sigma^2 + (X'_i\beta)^2)]$, and let 0 superscript on these matrices indicate evaluation at the true parameter values. With constant second and third moments, it is possible to show that the matrix G associated with this problem is the asymptotic limit of

$$-\left[\frac{1}{N}\sum_{i=1}^N C^0_i \Psi^{-1}_i K_i\right], \quad \text{where} \quad K_i \equiv \frac{1}{\sigma^2_0}\begin{pmatrix} 0 \\ \tau_0 X'_i \\ (3\tau_0(X'_i\beta_0) + E(\varepsilon^4_i) - 3\sigma^4_0)X'_i \end{pmatrix}.$$

The implied specification for the matrix S_{23} is the asymptotic limit of

$$-\frac{1}{N}\sum_{i=1}^N C^0_i \Psi^{-1}_i C^{0\prime}_{2i}.$$

The matrix G involves both the third and the fourth moments of the ε_i's, and it does not in general vanish even when the distribution of ε is symmetric. Hence, condition (10.5) is typically satisfied. In one special case, it is possible to show that $G = 0$ and any potential gain in efficiency is unattainable. Since least squares corresponds to the application of maximum likelihood when disturbances are normally distributed, it is not surprising to find that this case arises when $E(\varepsilon^3_i) = 0$, $E(\varepsilon^4_i) = 3\sigma^4_0$, and $K_i = 0$ as a consequence. When either $E(\varepsilon^3_i) \neq 0$ or $E(\varepsilon^4_i) \neq 3E(\varepsilon^2_i)^2$, inspection of the specifications of G and S_{23} reveals that the rank condition given by (10.4) is satisfied in general. Accordingly, joint estimation of the regression equation and its squared and cubed variants yields an estimator for β_0 that is strictly efficient relative to the conventional least squares estimator in those instances where the distribution of errors have moments of lower than fifth order which differ from those associated with normality.

One can, of course, continue and consider a quartic variant and higher powers of the regression equation. Joint least squares estimation of these new equations along with those introduced above without constraints across equations offers a framework for testing (i) whether one can justify imposing an equality restriction for the estimates of β obtained from the different equations, and (ii) whether one can accept the stronger hypotheses that fourth and possibly higher order moments of the disturbances are constant across observations. If the estimates of β computed using the different equations are all consistent for β_0, then joint estimation of these equations constraining all the estimates of β to be equal will almost certainly lead to a more efficient estimator for β_0 than the one computed using fewer equations and, consequently, less information on the moments of disturbances. Knowing the ε_i's have constant moments across the sample offers yet another source of information to attain further gains in efficiency. Such information makes it possible to estimate at least a subset of the equations under consideration by generalized rather than least squares procedures.

4.5   *Extending results to nonlinear regression*

All the procedures outlined in this section for improving on the least squares estimate may be applied in the nonlinear regression case as well. In particular, instead of (10.6), suppose observations on Y are generated by the equation

$$Y_i = \pi(X_i, \beta_0) + \varepsilon_i, \qquad i = 1, \ldots, N, \tag{10.11}$$

where $\pi(\cdot)$ is a known function. One may readily verify that the results and the relations derived above remain valid after making the following modifications: replace $X_i'\beta$ and $X_i'\beta_0$ by $\pi(X_i, \beta)$ and $\pi(X_i, \beta_0)$, respectively, and substitute $(\partial\pi_i/\partial\beta)|_{\hat{\beta}}$ for X_i where the point of evaluation $\hat{\beta}$ is consistent for β_0.[6] Thus, when the ε_i's are heteroscedastic, joint nonlinear least squares estimation of (10.11) and weighted versions of these equations yields a more efficient estimator for β_0 than conventional nonlinear least squares. If, on the other hand, the ε_i's have moments above first order that satisfy the orthogonality conditions associated with the nonlinear model or that are constant across observations, then joint least squares or generalized least squares estimation of (10.11) and its squared and cubed variants creates an estimator for β_0 whose efficiency in general dominates that obtained from a standard application of nonlinear least

---

[6] Alternatively, one may substitute the vector $\partial\pi_i/\partial\beta$ viewed as a function of β for X_i when forming the ℓ_i's, and replace X_i by $(\partial\pi_i/\partial\beta)|_{\beta_0}$ in those expressions for the matrices G and A.

squares. Because the demonstration of these results for nonlinear regression involves no new concepts and follows directly from the previous analysis, the discussion instead considers the applications of the above estimation procedures to a more general representation of a nonlinear equation of the sort encountered in simultaneous equation analysis which includes (10.11) as a special case.

5   Instrumental variable estimation

Suppose observations on a random vector Y obey the equation

$$f(Y_i, X_i, \gamma_0) = \varepsilon_i, \qquad i = 1, \ldots, N, \tag{10.12}$$

where $f(\cdot)$ is a known function, and γ_0 is an unknown parameter vector. As in the previous analysis, the ε_i's are assumed to be distributed independently across observations with $E(\varepsilon_i) = 0$ and $E(\varepsilon_i^2) \equiv \sigma_i^2$, where expectations are calculated given a measured set of characteristics Z.

5.1   *Basics on nonlinear two- and three-stage least squares*

Given a vector of instruments q_i for each observation, nonlinear two-stage least squares estimation of (10.12) uses the orthogonality conditions $E(q_i f(Y_i, X_i, \gamma_0)) = 0$ to compute an estimate for γ_0. Formally, the elements of q_i may depend on estimated coefficients that are asymptotically nonstochastic, as well as on the measured characteristics Z. A standard application of nonlinear two-stage least squares sets $\ell_i(\gamma) = q_i f_i$ with $f_i \equiv f(Y_i, X_i, \gamma)$ and calculates an estimate by minimizing a quadratic form like (10.2) with the matrix $B_N = (1/N) \sum_{i=1}^{N} q_i q_i'$ replacing the matrix $\hat{V}_N$. Observing that the implied specification for $\hat{V}_N$ is $(1/N) \sum_{i=1}^{N} q_i q_i' \hat{\varepsilon}_i^2$, where $\hat{\varepsilon}_i$ is a residual consistent for $f(Y_i, X_i, \gamma_0)$, it is not surprising to find that direct minimization of (10.2) in general yields a more efficient estimator for γ_0. Referring to the discussion of Chamberlain's approach for improving on least squares estimation, it is evident that conventional instrumental variable techniques construct estimators in a way analogous to constrained least squares procedures and thus suffer from the same deficiencies. In particular, one can demonstrate that conventional two-stage least squares yields a less efficient estimator for γ_0 than the one obtained by directly minimizing (10.2) when disturbances are heteroscedastic and there are exclusion or overidentifying restrictions. Chamberlain (1982), White (1982), and Amemiya (1983) each propose estimators for linear simultaneous equations that exploit exactly this observation. Clearly, one can exploit this same source of efficiency gain when constructing estimators for nonlinear simultaneous equations as well.

The optimal choice for the vectors of instruments varies according to whether disturbances are homoscedastic or heteroscedastic. For the class of estimators defined by minimizing (10.2) with $\ell_i = q_i f_i$, Amemiya (1975) shows that setting q_i equal to $E[(\partial f_i/\partial\gamma)|_{\gamma_0}]$ or to a consistent estimate of this quantity yields the most efficient estimator for γ_0 when errors are homoscedastic. An estimator with approximately the same efficiency is obtained if one instead sets q_i equal to any vector of explanatory variables W_i where a regression of the elements $(\partial f_i/\partial\gamma)|_{\gamma_0}$ on W would in principle produce fitted values that closely approximate $E[(\partial f_i/\partial\gamma)|_{\gamma_0}]$.[7] While these alternative choices for the vector of instruments are essentially equivalent in the homoscedastic case, choosing $q_i = W_i$ will in general yield the more efficient parameter estimate in the heteroscedastic case. Using $q_i = E[(\partial f_i/\partial\gamma)|_{\gamma_0}]$ creates a just-identified model (i.e., the dimensions of q and γ are equal), and minimizing (10.2) for such a model yields the same estimator for γ_0 regardless of whether or not errors are heteroscedastic. The use of W_i as instruments, on the other hand, typically involves some degree of overidentification, and as noted above the minimization of (10.2) exploits overidentifying restrictions in the presence of heteroscedasticity to develop an estimator with greater efficiency than one that ignores such restrictions. While one can argue that W_i dominates $E[(\partial f_i/\partial\gamma)|_{\gamma_0}]$ as an instrument set in the heteroscedastic case, there is, unfortunately, no clear strategy for choosing the optimal W_i in this case if one views the problem purely as introducing overidentifying restrictions.

The following analysis applies the strategies proposed in the previous section to formulate estimators for γ_0 that possess greater efficiency than those obtained from the application of conventional two-stage least squares. In this analysis, the optimal choice for instruments is the same as in the homoscedastic case. Thus, it is assumed throughout this discussion that one sets the vector of instruments equal either to the expected value of the gradient vector associated with the nonlinear equation under consideration or to a vector W_i designed to predict this gradient vector accurately.

5.2   Nonconstant moments

To construct an estimator for γ_0 with improved efficiency when the disturbances of equation (10.12) are heteroscedastic, one may jointly estimate (10.12) and a weighted variant of this equation. Letting the weights ω_i represent

---

[7] According to formula (10.3), the use of $q_i = E[(\partial f_i/\partial\gamma)|_{\gamma_0}]$ to compute an estimate for γ_0 implies a covariance matrix equal to the limit of $\sigma_0^2[(1/N)\sum_{i=1}^{N} E[(\partial f_i/\partial\gamma)|_{\gamma_0}]E[(\partial f_i/\partial\gamma')|_{\gamma_0}]]^{-1}$; and setting $q_i = W_i$ yields a covariance matrix that may be written as the asymptotic limit of the matrix $\sigma_0^2[(1/N)\sum_{i=1}^{N} P_i P_i']^{-1}$, where $P_i = [\sum_{j=1}^{N}(\partial f_j/\partial\gamma)|_{\gamma_0} W_j'][\sum_{k=1}^{N} W_k W_k']^{-1} W_i$ represents the vector of fitted values obtained from regressing each of the elements of $(\partial f_i/\partial\gamma)|_{\gamma_0}$ on W_i. Thus, as stated in the text, if $P_i = E[(\partial f_i/\partial\gamma)|_{\gamma_0}]$, these two covariance matrices are approximately equal.

asymptotically nonstochastic variables designed to eliminate the variation in the transformed variances $\omega_i^2 \varepsilon_i^2$ across observations, weighting (10.12) yields

$$\omega_i f(Y_i, X_i, \gamma_0) = \omega_i \varepsilon_i, \qquad i = 1, \ldots, N. \tag{10.13}$$

Nonlinear two-stage least squares applied to (10.12) uses the vector of functions $g_i(\gamma) = q_i f_i$ to compute an estimate for γ_0; and applying this procedure to estimate (10.13) uses the vector of functions $h_i(\gamma) = \omega_i^2 q_i f_i$. Joint two-stage least squares estimation of equations (10.12) and (10.13) in this analysis means that one sets $\ell_i' = (g_i', h_i')$ and minimizes (10.2) with respect to γ.

The resulting estimator is strictly efficient relative to the conventional two-stage least squares estimator in the presence of heteroscedasticity; and it also dominates the weighted two-stage least squares estimator unless the weights are optimally chosen (i.e., $\omega_i = 1/\sigma_i$), in which case the efficiencies of these two estimators are the same. As in the analysis of Section 4, one only needs to consider the form of the matrix G to verify these propositions concerning efficiency. The matrix G for this problem is the asymptotic limit of

$$\left[\frac{1}{N} \sum_{i=1}^{N} \omega_i^2 q_i E\left(\left.\frac{\partial f_i}{\partial \gamma'}\right|_{\gamma_0} \right) \right] - \left[\frac{1}{N} \sum_{i=1}^{N} \omega_i^2 q_i q_i' \sigma_i^2 \right] \left[\frac{1}{N} \sum_{i=1}^{N} q_i q_i' \sigma_i^2 \right]^{-1}$$
$$\times \left[\frac{1}{N} \sum_{i=1}^{N} q_i E\left(\left.\frac{\partial f_i}{\partial \gamma'}\right|_{\gamma_0} \right) \right].$$

As expected, given an optimal choice for the vector of instruments $q_i = E[(\partial f_i/\partial \gamma)|_{\gamma_0}]$, $G = 0$ when variances are constant across observations, implying no efficiency gain. In general, however, $G \neq 0$ and the joint estimation of equations (10.12) and (10.13) leads to an improvement in efficiency over the estimation of equation (10.12) alone.

As noted previously, regressing the squared residuals $\hat{\varepsilon}_i^2$ on a function of explanatory variables and treating the resulting fitted values as a measure of $1/\omega_i^2$ offers a simple and natural procedure for forming the weights used in (10.13). If this choice for the weights fails to adjust for the variability of the σ_i's, one may introduce a weighted version of equation (10.13) and jointly estimate this new equation along with the others to obtain a further improvement in efficiency.

5.3   *Incorporating infomation on constant second moments*

Given the knowledge that the disturbances of the equation under consideration are homoscedastic, the analysis of the previous section suggests that jointly estimating this equation along with its squared variant will typically produce an increase in efficiency in estimating the parameters of interest. Squaring both sides of equation (10.12) and introducing an intercept yields

$$f^2(Y_i, X_i, \gamma_0) - \sigma_0^2 = u_i, \qquad i = 1, \ldots, N, \tag{10.14}$$

where $u_i \equiv \varepsilon_i^2 - \sigma_0^2$. If the variances of the ε_i's are constant across observations and equal to σ_0^2, then $E(u_i) = 0$ and (10.14) is in the form of a nonlinear structural equation. One must exercise caution, however, in applying a nonlinear two-stage least squares routine to estimate the parameters of this equation. Such a routine uses the vector of functions $\ell_i(\gamma, \sigma^2) = q_i^s(f_i^2 - \sigma^2)$ to compute estimates for γ_0 and σ_0^2 with q_i^s representing a vector of instruments. A problem encountered with implementing this routine relates to the properties of the matrix of the averaged partial derivatives associated with vectors of functions $\ell_i(\gamma, \sigma^2)$. As noted in the discussion of this general class of estimation schemes in Section 3, application of these schemes requires the matrix $S_N \equiv (1/N) \sum_{i=1}^N \partial \ell_i / \partial \theta'$ to possess full column rank over the relevant portion of the parameter space. For the estimation problem considered here, the form of this matrix evaluated at the true parameter values is $S_N^0 \equiv S_N(\gamma_0, \sigma_0^2) = (1/N) \sum_{i=1}^N q_i^s r_i'$, where $r_i' = (r_{1i}' \ \ r_{2i})$ denotes a row vector with $r_{1i} = 2\varepsilon_i(\partial f_i / \partial \gamma)|_{\gamma_0}$ and $r_{2i} = -1$. It is easy to find cases for which S_N^0 possesses less than full column rank in the limit. Such situations arise, for example, whenever equation (10.14) refers to a regression relation [e.g., $f(Y_i, X_i, \gamma_0) = Y_i - X_i'\gamma_0$ or $= Y_i - \varphi(X_i, \gamma_0)$], in which case $E(r_{1i}) = 0$, implying $S_N^0 \xrightarrow{s} [0 \ \vdots \ -q^{-s}]$ where $q^{-s} \equiv \lim(1/N) \sum_{i=1}^N q_i^s$.

While difficulties may arise with regard to the direct estimation of equation (10.14), forming a linear combination of equations (10.12) and (10.14) creates an estimable specification that depends on the squared representation of the structural equation and incorporates second moment information. Instead of (10.14), then, consider the linear combination

$$f^2(Y_i, X_i, \gamma_0) - \sigma^2 + a_i f(Y_i, X_i, \gamma_0) = u_i + a_i \varepsilon_i, \qquad i = 1, \ldots, N, \tag{10.15}$$

where the a_i's denote asymptotically nonstochastic variables. Nonlinear two-stage least squares applied to (10.15) uses the vectors of functions $\ell_i(\gamma, \sigma^2) = q_i^a(f_i^2 - \sigma^2 + a_i f_i)$ to calculate estimates for γ_0 and σ_0^2 with q_i^a representing a vector of instruments. Assuming the original structural equation given by (10.12) is estimable and the a_i's are nonzero, one may readily verify that the matrix of averaged partials S_N associated with this estimation problem possesses full column rank. Equation (10.15), then, may be directly estimated using nonlinear two-stage least squares, and this routine produces consistent estimates for γ_0 and σ_0^2 if the ε_i's are homoscedastic. If one sets the a_i's equal to the constant $\bar{a}$, the optimal choice for instruments is

$$q_i^a = E\left(\left.\frac{\partial\left(f_i^2 - \sigma^2 + \bar{a} f_i\right)}{\partial \binom{\gamma}{\sigma^2}}\right|_{\gamma_0, \sigma_0}\right) = \left(\begin{array}{c} 2E\left(\varepsilon_i \left.\frac{\partial f_i}{\partial \gamma}\right|_{\gamma_0}\right) + \bar{a} E\left(\left.\frac{\partial f_i}{\partial \gamma}\right|_{\gamma_0}\right) \\ -1 \end{array}\right).$$

Notice that the squared variant of the linear regression equation considered in the previous section given by (10.9) is in the form of (10.15) with $f_i = Y_i - X_i'\beta_0$ and $a_i = 2X_i'\beta_0$.

Jointly estimating equations (10.12) and (10.15) without constraints across equations provides a framework for testing both (i) the orthogonality conditions needed for the estimate of γ computed using equation (10.15) alone to be consistent for γ_0, and (ii) whether the disturbances of the original structural equation have constant variances across observations. Joint nonlinear two-stage least squares estimation of these equations means that one sets $\ell_i'(\gamma_1, \gamma_2, \sigma^2) = (g_i', h_i')$ with $g_i(\gamma_1) = q_i f_i$ and $h_i(\gamma_2, \sigma^2) = q_i^a(f_i^2 - \sigma^2 + a_i f_i)$, where γ_1 and γ_2 represent distinct coefficient vectors, and minimizes (10.2) with respect to γ_1, γ_2, and σ^2. The orthogonality conditions imply that the estimates $\tilde{\gamma}_1$ and $\tilde{\gamma}_2$ have the same probability limits, and one may test this hypothesis by computing a Wald statistic using the asymptotic distribution of estimates implied by (10.3). In addition to this equality restriction, a homoscedasticity assumption also implies that no other function of the explanatory variables enters equation (10.15). If one considers only relationships between the σ_i^2's and the explanatory variables that may be described by functions linear in parameters, then checking for homoscedasticity amounts to performing tests of hypotheses consisting of the constraint $\gamma_1 = \gamma_2$ and zero restrictions for all parameters other than γ_1, γ_2, and σ^2. Once again, then, standard Wald statistics offer a simple method for testing the homoscedasticity assumption in the case of simultaneous equations.

Given acceptance of the equality restriction for the γ-coefficients across equations, joint nonlinear two-stage least squares estimation of equations (10.12) and (10.15) imposing the constraint $\gamma_1 = \gamma_2$ generates an estimator for γ_0 that is typically more efficient than the conventional two-stage least squares estimator. Inspecting the matrix G and S_{23} for the choice of g and h used by this estimation procedure reveals the exact conditions needed to achieve this efficiency gain. Assuming $a_i = 1$ for all i, G is the asymptotic limit of

$$\left[\frac{1}{N} \sum_{i=1}^{N} q_i^a E\left((2\varepsilon_i + 1) \frac{\partial f_i}{\partial \gamma'}\bigg|_{\gamma_0} \right) \right] - \left[\frac{1}{N} \sum_{i=1}^{N} q_i^a q_i' E\left(\varepsilon_i^3 + \varepsilon_i^2 \right) \right]$$

$$\times \left[\frac{1}{N} \sum_{i=1}^{N} q_i q_i' E\left(\varepsilon_i^2 \right) \right]^{-1} \left[\frac{1}{N} \sum_{i=1}^{N} q_i E\left(\frac{\partial f_i}{\partial \gamma'}\bigg|_{\gamma_0} \right) \right].$$

Evaluating this expression assuming $E(\varepsilon_i^2) = \sigma_0^2$ and for the optimal choice of instruments (i.e., $q_i = E[(\partial f_i/\partial \gamma)|_{\gamma_0}]$ and $q_i^{a'} = (q_{1i}^{a'} \ q_{2i}^a)$ with $q_{1i}^a = 2E(\varepsilon_i(\partial f_i/\partial \gamma)|_{\gamma_0}) + q_i$ and $q_{2i}^a = -1$), it is evident that $G \neq 0$ if at least one of the following conditions are satisfied: (i) $E(\varepsilon_i^3) \neq 0$ or (ii) $E(\varepsilon_i(\partial f_i/\partial \gamma)|_{\gamma_0}) \neq 0$. The specification for the matrix S_{23} is the asymptotic limit of $-N^{-1} \sum_{i=1}^{N} q_i^a$, which in general does not span the columns of G, implying satisfaction of condition (10.4). In contrast, then, to the above findings on least squares estimation, jointly estimating a structural equation and its squared variants in the presence of homoscedasticity can yield a more efficient estimator for the parameters of interest even if the third moments of the ε_i's are zero for all observations; a nonzero correlation between ε_i and the gradient vector $(\partial f_i / \partial \gamma)|_{\gamma_0}$ also implies that joint estimation yields an efficiency gain.

5.4   *Incorporating information on constant higher order moments*

Extending the analysis to consider cubic and higher order powers of the structural relation involves no concepts not already discussed above. Joint nonlinear two-stage least squares estimation of these new equations along with (10.12) and (10.15) without equality constraints across equations offers a framework for testing the appropriateness of imposing such constraints. Given that one can justify these equality restrictions, joint estimation imposing these constraints will yield further efficiency gains for the resulting estimator of γ_0. One may also test hypotheses concerning the constancy of third and higher order moments of the disturbances using this joint estimation framework. As outlined above, hypotheses of this nature translate into equality constraints across equations and into zero restrictions for the effects of any other explanatory variables one might choose to include in these equations. Information of this nature determines whether it is possible to attain additional improvements in efficiency by applying three-stage rather than two-stage least squares procedures. Knowing, for example, that moments of the ε_i's up to fourth order are constant permits one to estimate equations (10.12) and (10.15) using nonlinear three-stage least squares, which makes the choice for the a_i's irrelevant and provides for an optimal combination of these equations in the calculation of estimates.

To illustrate the use of nonlinear three-stage least squares procedures in this analysis, consider the joint estimation of the original specification of the structural equation given by (10.12), its squared representation given by (10.14), and its cubic variant given by

$$f^3(Y_i, X_i, \gamma_0) - \tau_0 = v_i, \qquad i = 1, \ldots, N, \tag{10.16}$$

where $v_i \equiv \varepsilon_i^3 - \tau_0$. Stacking equations (10.12), (10.14), and (10.16) creates a model with $(\varepsilon_i \ u_i \ v_i)$ representing the disturbance vector for the ith observation. This disturbance vector is homoscedastic, assuming the moments $E(\varepsilon_i^k)$ for $k \leq 6$ are constant across the sample. Letting Ω_0 denote the covariance matrix associated with this disturbance vector, and $\hat{\Omega}$ denote a consistent estimate for Ω_0, nonlinear three-stage least squares applied to this three-equation model computes estimates for the parameters γ_0, σ_0^2, and τ_0 by minimizing quadratic form (10.2) with

$$\ell_i(\gamma, \sigma^2, \tau) = R_i \hat{\Omega}^{-1} \begin{pmatrix} f_i \\ f_i^2 - \sigma^2 \\ f_i^3 - \tau \end{pmatrix}$$

and

$$R_i = \begin{bmatrix} q_i & q_{1i}^s & q_{1i}^c \\ 0 & q_{2i}^s & 0 \\ 0 & 0 & q_{2i}^c \end{bmatrix},$$

where q_i, q_{1i}^s, and q_{1i}^c are vectors of instruments with the same dimension as γ, and q_{2i}^s and q_{2i}^c are scalar instruments. According to the results of Amemiya (1977), the optimal choice for these instruments is

$$q_i = E\left(\frac{\partial f_i}{\partial \gamma}\bigg|_{\gamma_0}\right), \qquad q_{1i}^s = 2E\left(\varepsilon_i \frac{\partial f_i}{\partial \gamma}\bigg|_{\gamma_0}\right)$$

$$q_{1i}^c = 3E\left(\varepsilon_i^2 \frac{\partial f_i}{\partial \gamma}\bigg|_{\gamma_0}\right), \quad \text{and} \quad q_{2i}^s = q_{2i}^c = -1.$$

To identify the conditions under which this three-stage procedure yields an efficiency gain over conventional two-stage least squares estimation of equation (10.12), one may set $g_i = q_i f_i$ [used in the estimation of (10.12)], set h_i to the specification for ℓ_i listed directly above, and determine the form for the matrix G. When evaluated at the optimal choice for instruments, this matrix is the asymptotic limit of

$$\frac{1}{N}\sum_{i=1}^{N} R_i \Omega_0^{-1} \begin{pmatrix} q_i & q_{1i}^s & q_{1i}^c \end{pmatrix}' - \frac{1}{\sigma_0^2 N}\sum_{i=1}^{N} R_i (q_i \quad 0 \quad 0)'.$$

The implied specification for the matrix S_{23} is the asymptotic limit of

$$\frac{1}{N}\sum_{i=1}^{N} R_i \Omega_0^{-1} J_i, \qquad \text{where} \quad J_i = \begin{pmatrix} 0 & 0 \\ q_{2i}^s & 0 \\ 0 & q_{2i}^c \end{pmatrix}.$$

In general, rank condition (10.4) holds; consequently, using information on the higher order moments of disturbances can be expected in most instances to produce an improvement in the efficiency of estimation.

6   Conclusion

The overall estimation strategy suggested by this analysis may be summarized as follows. Starting with a form of the regression (or simultaneous) equation whose disturbances are believed to be homoscedastic, one introduces a new equation obtained by squaring both sides of this equation. Joint unconstrained estimation of the regression equation and its squared variant offers a framework for testing (i) whether the second moments of disturbances satisfy the orthogonality conditions needed to justify the imposition of equality constraints across equations, and (ii) whether one can accept the stronger hypothesis that disturbances have constant variances across observations.

Given rejection of the equality restrictions relating the parameters of the regression equation and its squared variant implied by hypothesis (i), one eliminates the equation relating the squares of variables from the analysis and implements the procedure that jointly estimates the regression equation and weighted variants of this equation. More than one weighted regression equation may be included in this joint estimation procedure. While one in principle wants to choose weights in a way to induce homoscedasticity, it is unnecessary to know the form of heteroscedasticity to implement this procedure, and almost any choice for weights will yield an improvement in the efficiency of estimation.

Given acceptance of the equality restrictions implied by hypothesis (i), one acquires further information by considering cubic and possibly higher order powers of the regression relation. Jointly estimating these new equations along with the regression equation and its squared variant initially without constraints across equations allows one to test (iii) whether third and higher-order moments of disturbances satisfy the orthogonality conditions required to restrict the estimates associated with the different equations, and (iv) whether disturbances have constant third and higher-order moments over the sample. Assuming tests of (iii) support the imposition of equality restrictions across equations, carrying out joint estimation imposing these constraints will almost always lead to a more efficient estimator for the parameters of interest than one computed using fewer equations and, consequently, less information on the moments of disturbances. If one finds that moments vary over the sample but still satisfy conditions (i) and (iii), then one can achieve further increases in the efficiency of estimation by also including weighted variants of equations with heteroscedastic errors in the joint estimation procedure as well. If, on the other hand, tests also support property (iv) and the disturbances have constant moments over the sample, one can exploit this information to improve estimation efficiency by using generalized or three-stage least squares methods when jointly estimating equations.

Following this estimation strategy, one can literally proceed indefinitely in finding another equation, which, when jointly estimated along with the equations currently considered, leads generally to a further gain in the asymptotic efficiency of estimation. Essentially, whenever it can be argued that including an equation of one type does not yield an efficiency gain, this fact itself suggests a new source of information that may be exploited by introducing an equation of another type. This study offers no rule indicating where one should stop adding equations to the joint estimation scheme. While specific distributional assumptions provide the basis for formulating these rules, knowledge of such assumptions often means that it is possible to use maximum likelihood techniques to estimate parameters; in which case, on efficiency grounds, there is no reason to consider the estimation procedures proposed in this chapter.

Numerous options exist for expanding the estimation framework considered here. Instead of adding equations based on conventional moments of disturbances (i.e., the second, third, fourth, and higher moments), one can incorporate equations reflecting the constancy of the conditional expectations of any set of functions of the errors, be they reciprocals, square roots, exponentials, or whatever. The conditions reported in Section 3 determine whether the addition of such information on moments enhances the asymptotic efficiency of estimation. Moreover, in the implementation of instrumental-variable procedures, the results presented here suggest approaches for developing new formulations of instruments based on functions of fitted disturbances. Construction of these instruments would exploit and/or replicate the information implied by satisfaction of particular moment properties. For example, knowing that an error distribution obeys a symmetry property means that its third moments are zero. Conceptually, one can incorporate this information in an instrumental-variable procedure by adding an instrument consisting of the squared residual, for this instrument multipied by the quantity representing the equation has a zero expectation as is required for consistency. A multitude of other options are available for constructing instruments when other moment conditions hold. As in the case of adding equations, one can in principle continue to add instruments until the IV estimator achieves an efficiency equivalent to that attained by maximum likelihood. The exploration of these augmented estimation frameworks no doubt offers promising candidates for future research.

7   Afterword

Many of the econometric findings developed in the above 1982 paper have been significantly expanded or independently discovered in other studies published during the past 15 years. Documenting all the studies contributing to this subject constitutes a challenge well beyond the scope of this discussion, but three papers stand out in terms of their relevance to the topics covered in the above chapter.

To provide a context for summarizing the contributions of these studies, reconsider the following structural equation:

$$f(Y_i, X_i, \gamma_0) = \varepsilon_i. \tag{10.12}$$

Recall $f(\cdot)$ represents a known function, γ_0 designates unknown parameters, Y

incorporates all endogenous variables of the model, X includes all exogenous variables, and the randomly distributed variables ε_i possess zero means.

Chamberlain (1987) explores efficient estimation of (10.12) when one only assumes

$$E(\varepsilon_i \mid X_i) = 0. \tag{10.17}$$

He presumes no availability of information about the second or higher order moments of the ε_i, implying that one cannot use knowledge of these moments in estimation. Chamberlain demonstrates that the asymptotic variance–covariance matrix of any estimator exploiting only condition (10.17) must equal or exceed the lower bound

$$\Lambda = \left[E\left(D_i \left[\sigma_i^2 \right]^{-1} D_i' \right) \right]^{-1}, \tag{10.18}$$

where

$$D_i \equiv D(X_i) = E\left(\left. \frac{\partial f_i}{\partial \gamma} \right|_{\gamma_0} \middle| X_i \right) \tag{10.19}$$

and

$$\sigma_i^2 \equiv \sigma^2(X_i) = E(f_i f_i \mid X_i). \tag{10.20}$$

Whereas the expectation in (10.18) averages over the X_i's, the expectations in (10.19) and (10.20) condition on X_i.

Nonliner two-stage least squares (N2SLS) applied to structural equation (10.12) using instrumental variables q_i, with the elements of q_i being any functions of the X_i, represents an important class of estimators relying on condition (10.17) to achieve consistency. Thus, Chamberlain's result dictates that any choice of q_i produces an estimator possessing a variance–covariance matrix that is at least as large as (10.18). In his study of N2SLS estimation, Amemiya (1977) proves the optimal selection of q_i – i.e., the specification achieving the minimum variance–covariance matrix for the N2SLS estimator – takes the form

$$q_i = \frac{1}{\sigma_i^2} D_i. \tag{10.21}$$

Amemiya names this estimator "best" N2SLS. This optimal selection of q_i achieves Chamberlain's lower bound (10.18). It is generally not feasible to take advantage of this formulation, because q_i depends on unknown parameters and/or functions. To construct q_i one must be able to estimate σ_i^2 and D_i consistently – or an appropriate combination of these quantities.

For the estimation schemes discussed in the above chapter, Chamberlain's findings dictate that those procedures exploiting information on heteroscedasticity can at best achieve his lower bound (10.18) as their measures of asymptotic efficiency. Those estimators incorporating properties of the higher order moments of ε_i can in principle improve upon this bound, but such quantities fall outside the class considered by Chamberlain, for they rely on more information than just condition (10.17).

Newey (1988) explores efficiency improvements building on the constant-moments case analyzed in this chapter. He considers properties of generalized method of moments (GMM) estimators – amounting to nonlinear three-stage least squares (N3SLS) estimators in the instances considered here – as one expands equations to capture information conveyed by a variety of different moments. A prominent example consists of starting with a regression specification of equation (10.12) with iid errors and adding not only equations (10.14) and (10.16) reflecting constancy of the second and third moments, but also equations stipulating the constancy of the fourth, fifth, sixth, and higher moments of the ε_i's. When these moments characterize the distribution of ε, he demonstrates that expanding the number of admitted moment conditions at an appropriate rate with sample size produces a GMM estimator that reaches full asymptotic efficiency. More precisely, this GMM estimator attains the same large-sample efficiency as maximum likelihood.

Newey (1988) considers a variety of other moment conditions enabling increased efficiency of estimation. In particular, with $f(\cdot)$ in (10.12) specified as a linear regression model, he investigates adding equations

$$m_j(\varepsilon_i)(Y_i - X_i'\gamma) - \mu_j = \xi_{ij}, \tag{10.22}$$

where

$$E(\xi_{ji}|X_i) = 0,$$

with j indexing different specifications. The quantities m_j represent differentiable functions with bounded fourth moments. Suppose the functions of $m_0(\varepsilon)$ characterize the distribution of ε, and let $m_j = m_0^j$. Allowing the number and variety of these moment conditions to grow at the appropriate rate with sample size, Newey shows this resulting GMM estimator also converges to the same large-sample distribution as maximum likelihood. Selecting the m_j's to be bounded functions potentially offers options for improving efficiency when errors follow thick-tailed distributions.

Newey (1988) also considers situations wherein distributions of ε merely obey a symmetry property. In such instances, selecting the functions m_j in ways to capture odd-order moments produces a set of moment conditions satisfying the properties of (10.22). This is true even when conditional heteroscedasticity exists. Combining equations containing these formulations of m_j with estimation of the original equation offers gains in efficiency over traditional schemes.

Turning to another topic covered in the above chapter, Breusch et al. (1999) independently derive conditions analogous to those developed in Section 3.

These conditions determine whether adding moment conditions to a GMM procedure leads to improved efficiency of an estimator. Breusch et al. (1999) refer to incremental conditions that do not increase efficiency as "redundant." Their analysis rediscovers matrix relations (10.4) and (10.5) as establishing redundancy. They further specify a variety of equivalent representations of these matrix relations that may prove convenient in a number of applications.

No doubt I have missed other studies making contributions fundamentally related to the results presented in the above chapter. After all, the broad area of research incorporating these results has grown from infancy in the mid-1970s to a highly advanced set of findings today. Many of these advancements, like the contents of the above chapter, owe much to the impressive body of work that Takeshi has produced over his career.

Appendix: A Monte Carlo analysis

How well do the estimators presented in this chapter work in practical situations? Most researchers surmise "not very well," for in my discussions with them they conjecture that the asymptotic efficiency gains identified for these estimators will not be attained in modest-sized samples. Moreover, they suspect there may even be an efficiency loss in small samples due to the reliance on higher-order moments which are known to be less precisely estimated. This appendix summarizes the findings of a limited Monte Carlo simulation designed to explore whether the estimation methods discussed here have any practical use. This analysis does not examine the heteroscedastic case, but instead focuses on the small-sample efficiency of adding higher-order moment restrictions to a single linear equation when errors have constant moments. Two reasons motivate this focus: first, it is the constant-moments case that raises the most serious doubts about whether asymptotic efficiency gains are indeed attainable; and, second, it is this estimation approach that constitutes the most innovative method proposed in the original paper at the time it was written – approaches for improving efficiency in the heteroscedastic case had already been developed by others.

A.1   *Specifying the true model*

Selecting the models used in a Monte Carlo exercise is always somewhat controversial, for it typically seems an artificial choice. This is especially true in the selection of explanatory variables, for they seldom represent a critical element of the theoretical econometric results. In recognition of such concerns, this exercise selects exogenous variables from real data from the Current Population Survey (CPS). In particular, it draws data from the 1997 CPS on prime age men to estimate a conventional wage equation of the form

$$\ln(\text{Wage}_i) = \beta_0 + \beta_1 \text{ Edu}_i + \beta_2 \text{ Age}_i + \beta_3 \text{ Agesq}_i + \varepsilon_i, \qquad (10.\text{A}1)$$

where Wage is worker i's hourly wage, Edu is his number of years of education, Age is his age, and Agesq $= \text{Age}^2$. The analysis assumes the true values of the β-coefficients are those obtained by least squares estimation of (10.A1) using the CPS men's sample.

The subsequent discussion investigates models based on four distinct distributions for the ε_i's in (10.A1), assuming these errors iid across the observations i. These Monte Carlo models draw observations from the CPS for the variables Edu, Age, and Agesq, generate ε_i's using a random number generator for an assumed distribution, and produce the values of ln(Wage) using equation (10.A1) and the "true" values of β. These models then serve as the samples used to compare how well various estimators perform.

The sample drawn from the March 1997 CPS consists of 23,681 observations on men aged 25–54. Table 10.1 presents summary statistics for the variables included in this sample. The last column reports values of the OLS estimates of equation (10.A1) using these data, which the simulation treats as the true values of β.

The simulation considers four distributions for the errors terms: normal; Student's t (with degrees of freedom parameter set equal to 5); double exponential, or Laplace (with its parameter set to $\lambda = 1$); and gamma (with parameters set to $\alpha = \frac{9}{16}$ and $\beta = \frac{3}{16}$). These distributions were each normalized to have mean

Table 10.1. *Summary statistics for CPS data*

Variables	Sample size	Mean	Standard deviation	Min	Max	Estimated regression coefficient (s.e.)
Education	23681	13.33	3.01	0	20	0.087 (0.0015)
Age	23681	38.73	8.19	25	54	0.073 (0.0055)
Age squared	23681	1567.2	643.5	625	2916	−0.00074 (0.00007)
Constant	23681					−0.199 (0.107)
ln(Wage)	23681	2.627	0.754	−8.046	7.34	

Notes: Data drawn from the 1997 CPS for men aged 25–54. The estimated coefficients reported in the last column are computed by OLS estimation of equation (10.A1) using the CPS data, with the natural log of wage as the dependent variable. OLS standard errors associated with these coefficients are shown in parentheses.

Table 10.2. *Moments of error distribution used in Monte Carlo analysis*

Error distribution	Mean	Standard deviation	Skewness	Kurtosis
Normal	0.001	0.500	−0.010	−0.016
Student's *t*	−0.001	0.503	−0.095	5.500
Double exponential	0.000	0.507	−0.019	3.168
Gamma	0.000	0.500	2.679	10.785

Note: Statistics are computed from 150,000 draws from random number generator used in Monte Carlo analysis.

0 and standard deviation $\frac{1}{2}$. This value of the standard deviation implies an R^2 closely approximating the value obtained by OLS estimation of equation (10.A1) using the real CPS data.

Table 10.2 reports the first four moments of these distributions using standard measures on skewness and kurtosis. The Student's *t* and double exponential (Laplace) exhibit higher kurtosis than the normal. The gamma primarily offers a skewed distribution relative to the normal, although its kurtosis also deviates significantly from the normal case. The estimation procedures exploiting information on second and third moments should yield no efficiency gains with normally distributed errors, but these procedures should create opportunities for efficiency gains for the three nonnormal distributions.

A.2   *Four alternative estimation methods*

Equation (10.A1) can, of course, be estimated consistently by ordinary least squares. The theory presented in this chapter suggests that, if the error terms are iid and not normally distributed, one can increase asymptotic efficiency by adding equations based on higher-order moments and jointly estimating these equations with (10.A1).[8]

Specifying the wage equation as

$$\ln(\text{Wage}_i) - [\beta_0 + \beta_1 \text{ Edu}_i + \beta_2 \text{ Age}_i + \beta_3 \text{ Agesq}_i] = Y_i - X_i'\beta$$
$$\equiv f(Y_i, X_i, \beta),$$
$$(10.A2)$$

the system of equations corresponding to equations (10.12), (10.14), and (10.16) introduced in the chapter, including those representing higher order moments,

---

[8] Error terms in wage equations are known to exhibit heteroscedasticity in real data – such as the CPS. In this Monte Carlo analysis, however, disturbances are homoscedastic by construction.

takes the form

$$f(Y_i, X_i, \beta) = \varepsilon_i, \tag{10.A3}$$

$$f^2(Y_i, X_i, \beta) - \sigma^2 = u_i, \tag{10.A4}$$

$$f^3(Y_i, X_i, \beta) - \tau = v_i. \tag{10.A5}$$

These equations form a conventional nonlinear simultaneous equation model which one can efficiently estimate by nonlinear three-stage least squares (N3SLS) methods. Exploiting results attributable to Amemiya (1983), the optimal choice of instrumental variables for estimating this model takes the form[9]

$$Z_{ji} = E\left(\frac{\partial m_{ji}}{\partial \theta} \,\Big|\, X_i\right), \tag{10.A6}$$

with the functions m_{ji}, for $j = 1, 2, 3$, given by

$$m_{1i}(\theta) \equiv f(Y_i, X_i, \beta),$$

$$m_{2i}(\theta) \equiv f^2(Y_i, X_i, \beta) - \sigma^2,$$

$$m_{3i}(\theta) \equiv f^3(Y_i, X_i, \beta) - \tau.$$

The vector θ includes all parameters of the model (i.e., the elements of β, σ, and τ). The calculation of the expectation in (10.A6) conditions on the exogenous variables X_i, which includes Edu, Age, and Agesq plus a constant. One can readily verify that selecting

$$Z_{ji} = X_i, \qquad j = 1, 2, 3 \tag{10.A7}$$

spans the optimal choices (10.A6). Thus, applying standard N3SLS to equations (10.A3), (10.A4), and (10.A5) with X_i specified as instrumental variables and with parameter restrictions imposed across equations produces efficient estimates.

This Monte Carlo analysis examines the properties of estimators for four versions of the wage model: (1) a basic linear regression of equation (10.A3) alone; (2) joint estimation of equations (10.A3) and (10.A4), termed the *linear–quadratic* specification; (3) joint estimation of equations (10.A3) and (10.A5), called the *linear–cubic* specification; and (4) joint estimation of all three equations, referred to as the *all* specification below. These specifications cover the theoretical ground explored in Section 3 of the chapter.

A.3   *Summary of findings*

This study presents two sets of statistics for comparing the properties of estimators. All statistics first subtract the true values from estimates, so they are

---

[9] This choice of instrumental variables is optimal, assuming one restricts selection to functions of exogenous variables.

centered around zero asymptotically. Further, reported results multiply all values by 1000 to facilitate comparisons. The first set of statistics includes the *mean* and *standard deviation*. The mean shows how much an estimator deviates from zero (i.e., from the true value), and the standard deviation summarizes the prediction error of the estimator. The second set of statistics gives the percentiles of an estimator's distribution, including its minimum and maximum values, and its 10th, 25th, 50th, 75th, and 90th percentiles. Comparisons of these percentiles give a richer sense of how distributions compare.

Tables 10.3, 10.4, and 10.5 present results for estimates of the education coefficient for sample sizes of 500, 2000, and 5000, respectively. The columns of these tables report the two sets of summary statistics calculated from 300 replications conducted to approximate the sample distributions of the estimators. The rows specify the error distribution under consideration, along with the

Table 10.3. *Distributions of estimated education coefficients using information on different moments for sample size 500*

Distribution of errors and estimation method	Statistics summarizing deviations from true values (multiplied by 1000)								
	Moments		Percentiles						
	Mean	Standard deviation	Min	10%	25%	50%	75%	90%	Max
Normal errors									
Linear	−0.24	170.08	−25.80	−13.75	−6.55	−0.53	7.45	11.95	25.13
Linear–quadratic	−0.39	173.83	−26.33	−14.21	−6.81	−0.87	7.02	12.43	27.00
Linear–cubic	−0.09	169.62	−23.94	−13.14	−7.35	−0.28	7.60	12.41	28.06
All	−0.26	174.56	−24.56	−13.88	−6.97	−0.96	7.06	12.65	27.14
Student's *t* errors									
Linear	−0.46	171.49	−28.72	−14.59	−6.41	0.53	5.66	11.35	26.56
Linear–quadratic	−0.36	174.75	−29.35	−14.10	−6.99	0.65	6.34	11.35	27.48
Linear–cubic	−0.50	158.85	−27.36	−13.59	−6.50	0.60	5.45	10.43	22.95
All	−0.58	161.04	−27.19	−13.84	−6.48	0.61	5.64	10.64	23.62
Double exponential errors									
Linear	0.28	170.77	−26.40	−12.16	−6.42	0.20	5.73	12.78	31.21
Linear–quadratic	0.16	171.54	−26.82	−12.22	−6.60	−0.31	5.87	13.08	30.17
Linear–cubic	0.26	156.62	−27.40	−10.89	−6.17	−0.03	5.50	12.21	27.23
All	0.22	157.57	−26.42	−11.08	−6.32	0.31	5.73	12.04	27.67
Gamma errors									
Linear	−0.80	164.60	−34.70	−13.02	−7.08	−1.11	5.61	10.55	26.02
Linear–quadratic	−0.36	110.68	−19.73	−8.86	−3.96	−0.29	3.57	7.92	21.53
Linear–cubic	−0.42	149.13	−25.65	−12.07	−5.87	−0.38	4.97	9.73	29.62
All	−0.45	79.36	−15.90	−5.63	−3.38	−0.16	2.46	5.21	12.37

Notes: Each row summarizes the finite-sample distribution of the designated estimator assuming the specified error distribution. All statistics are computed by subtracting "true" value of education coefficient from Monte Carlo estimates. All values are multiplied by 1000 to facilitate comparisons. Data on explanatory variables drawn from the 1997 CPS data on men. Moments of the error terms are given in Table 10.2.

Table 10.4. *Distributions of estimated education coefficients using information on different moments for sample size 2000*

Distribution of errors and estimation method	Statistics summarizing deviations from true values (multiplied by 1000)								
	Moments		Percentiles						
	Mean	Standard deviation	Min	10%	25%	50%	75%	90%	Max
Normal errors									
Linear	−0.01	71.61	−11.05	−5.42	−2.68	−0.11	2.78	5.30	10.87
Linear–quadratic	0.00	72.29	−11.05	−5.78	−2.65	−0.01	2.76	5.39	11.53
Linear–cubic	0.01	72.32	−10.88	−5.83	−2.60	−0.03	2.61	5.46	11.31
All	0.02	73.10	−10.87	−5.78	−2.57	−0.12	2.68	5.59	11.94
Student's *t* errors									
Linear	0.06	70.12	−11.02	−5.49	−2.66	−0.33	3.07	4.98	13.72
Linear–quadratic	0.09	69.88	−11.12	−5.49	−2.60	−0.06	3.07	4.91	13.33
Linear–cubic	0.03	64.82	−10.48	−5.27	−2.46	−0.23	2.58	4.74	11.25
All	0.04	65.25	−10.52	−5.28	−2.39	−0.15	2.67	4.74	12.03
Double exponential errors									
Linear	0.04	67.96	−12.39	−4.66	−2.70	0.29	2.37	5.08	11.79
Linear–quadratic	0.07	68.72	−11.63	−4.60	−2.75	0.16	2.44	4.98	12.44
Linear–cubic	−0.02	62.06	−11.21	−4.37	−2.39	−0.04	2.44	4.40	9.86
All	−0.01	62.51	−11.14	−4.47	−2.41	0.00	2.45	4.43	10.20
Gamma errors									
Linear	−0.03	66.45	−13.38	−5.08	−2.60	−0.06	2.50	5.31	9.80
Linear–quadratic	0.13	45.56	− 9.43	−3.10	−1.56	0.38	1.60	3.26	9.60
Linear–cubic	0.11	58.87	−13.30	−4.52	−2.00	0.16	2.29	3.95	10.36
All	0.02	32.91	−4.96	−2.49	−1.21	−0.02	1.17	2.43	6.05

Notes: Each row summarizes the finite-sample distribution of the designated estimator assuming the specified error distribution. All statistics are computed by subtracting "true" value of education coefficient from Monte Carlo estimates. All values are multiplied by 1000 to facilitate comparisons. Data on explanatory variables drawn from the 1997 CPS data on men. Moments of the error terms are given in Table 10.2.

estimation procedure. The uppermost group of rows gives results for the normal distribution; the next group presents findings assuming Student's *t*-distribution; the following set reports results for the double exponential (or Laplace) distribution; and, finally, the bottom group lists values assuming errors come from a gamma distribution. Within each group of rows, results appear for each of the estimation methods. The top row in each group shows the statistics for the estimator obtained by estimating equation (10.A3) alone (i.e., the conventional OLS estimator); the second row reports findings for the estimator calculated jointly estimating equations (10.A3) and (10.A4); the third row presents results for the estimator obtained by jointly estimating equations (10.A3) and (10.A5); and, finally, the fourth row gives statistics for the estimator computed by applying NL3SLS to equations (10.A3), (10.A4), and (10.A5).

Table 10.5. *Distributions of estimated education coefficients using information on different moments for sample size 5000*

Distribution of errors and estimation method	Statistics summarizing deviations from true values (multiplied by 1000)								
	Moments		Percentiles						
	Mean	Standard deviation	Min	10%	25%	50%	75%	90%	Max
Normal errors									
Linear	−0.14	43.74	−6.97	−3.38	−1.80	−0.07	1.54	2.70	8.30
Linear–quadratic	−0.14	43.70	−7.07	−3.38	−1.81	0.05	1.56	2.69	8.33
Linear–cubic	−0.14	43.80	−6.89	−3.32	−1.77	0.01	1.54	2.65	8.61
All	−0.14	43.77	−6.99	−3.22	−1.82	0.06	1.52	2.61	8.65
Student's *t* errors									
Linear	−0.05	42.72	−7.28	−3.33	−1.65	0.03	1.55	3.00	7.57
Linear–quadratic	−0.04	42.18	−7.14	−3.39	−1.60	0.01	1.58	2.98	7.58
Linear–cubic	−0.10	40.71	−6.65	−3.18	−1.59	−0.10	1.43	2.69	7.09
All	−0.10	40.92	−6.75	−3.17	−1.64	−0.15	1.44	2.73	7.25
Double exponential errors									
Linear	0.18	44.63	−7.95	−3.41	−1.62	0.07	2.04	3.28	6.82
Linear–quadratic	0.17	44.84	−7.93	−3.33	−1.64	0.02	1.98	3.38	6.71
Linear–cubic	0.20	41.06	−7.47	−2.86	−1.54	0.19	1.83	3.21	6.26
All	0.20	41.14	−7.49	−2.88	−1.61	0.13	1.91	3.20	6.41
Gamma errors									
Linear	−0.08	44.87	−7.13	−3.40	−1.85	−0.14	1.59	3.08	6.53
Linear–quadratic	−0.10	28.58	−4.24	−2.33	−1.24	−0.11	0.89	2.01	5.93
Linear–cubic	−0.12	39.50	−6.51	−3.19	−1.57	−0.10	1.45	2.74	7.17
All	−0.05	20.13	−3.28	−1.62	−0.84	−0.08	0.65	1.45	3.51

Notes: Each row summarizes the finite-sample distribution of the designated estimator assuming the specified error distribution. All statistics are computed by subtracting "true" value of education coefficient from Monte Carlo estimates. All values are multiplied by 1000 to facilitate comparisons. Data on explanatory variables drawn from the 1997 CPS data on men. Moments of the error terms are given in Table 10.2.

Starting with Table 10.3, inspection of the uppermost group of rows reveals that the different estimators possess quite similar distributions when errors follow a normal distribution. The prediction errors hover around 0.17 for all four estimators. A slight efficiency gain is perhaps realized by restricting estimation to the linear model. The above discussion predicts this result, since the normal distribution is efficiently estimated with linear least squares. The added equations are repetitive information at best. The good news is that no significant efficiency losses result from the inclusion of the higher-moment restrictions with the linear equation. Not only are the standard deviations all almost identical, the percentiles are also very similar. The linear specification possesses an interquartile range of $(−0.0066, 0.0075)$, while the three-equation joint specification of $(10.A3)–(10.A5)$ exhibits an almost identical range of

($-0.0070, 0.0071$). Thus, use of the more complicated estimation method does not lead to small-sample loss of efficiency as many researchers seem to expect.

Further inspection of Table 10.3 reveals some improvement in the double exponential and t distributions when using the third-order moment equation. These distributions are symmetric but have a kurtosis differing from the normal – both have fatter tails. As expected, the addition of the second-order moment restriction alone doesn't increase efficiency, since efficiency gains require a nonzero third moment. The cubic equation, on the other hand, helps to capture the kurtosis of the double exponential and t distributions. Thus, we see a small gain in the prediction error and efficiency in Table 10.3. The prediction error drops in the double exponential distribution from 0.171 to 0.157. For the t-distribution it drops about the same amount, falling from 0.171 to 0.159 for the linear–cubic specification, and to 0.161 for jointly estimating all three equations. The interquartile ranges are very close to one another. The extremes of the linear model seem to be slightly worse than specifications including (10.A5). Therefore, it appears that gains in prediction error arise from slightly better performance in the tails of the estimator distributions.

Substantial gains arise when errors are distributed gamma – even with just the addition of equation (10.A4). This accords with the results of this chapter, since the theory predicts that a nonzero third moment is a requirement for efficiency gains to arise from the inclusion of the second-moment equation. In Table 10.3, the linear model has a standard deviation of 0.165. Prediction error drops with the linear–quadratic specification to 0.111. It falls even further when (10.A3)–(10.A5) are all used, declining to 0.079. The two additional equations help capture both the skewness of the distribution and the fat tails from the high kurtosis. The prediction error of the linear model is two times the error when all three equations are used. The linear–cubic specification shows some gains over the linear equation alone, at 0.149, but the quadratic equation appears more important for reducing prediction error.

Note that not only does prediction error fall, but the addition of second- and third-order moment information in the gamma case strictly dominates the linear model over all ranges. This can be seen by looking at the quartile information. The interquartile range of the linear model in Table 10.3 is ($-0.0071, 0.0056$), but, when equations (10.A3) to (10.A5) are jointly estimated, this range tightens significantly to ($-0.0034, 0.0025$). The estimator from this joint specification continues to dominate out to the extreme minimum and maximum values. The estimator shows marked improvement over linear least squares when the distribution of errors exhibits skewness with fat tails.

Tables 10.4 and 10.5 repeat the same story as Table 10.3 for larger sample sizes. Standard deviations are systematically lower, since better estimates are achieved with larger sample sizes. The qualitative relationships described above all remain.

To check whether results are special to the education coefficient examined in the previous tables, Table 10.6 summarizes results for the estimator distributions of the coefficient on Agesq for sample size 500. The results for this new coefficient are the same as those found for the Edu coefficient. No gain occurs by adding additional information on higher order moments in the case of the normal distribution. The distributions with nonnormal fourth moments improve slightly with the addition of the third-moment restriction. The skewed distribution benefits most from the second-order equation (10.A4), although efficiency gains are also realized by adding the cubic equation.

A.4   *Concluding remarks*

These findings clearly suggest that the addition of higher-order moment information in estimation can yield efficiency gains even in small samples. They fall directly in line with the theoretical predictions of the chapter that distributions deviating substantially from the normal benefit from the addition of higher-order moment restrictions in estimation. One can attain efficiency gains when errors follow either skewed distributions or distributions with fatter tails than the normal. Greater gains appear to arise for distributions exhibiting both skewness and high kurtosis. All estimators produced by these procedures have distributions centered around the true values; and, remarkably, evidence indicates that no efficiency loss occurs by adding extra equations capturing higher-order moment information. Thus, the estimators fulfill the desirable property to "do no harm." Of course, a main consideration associated with adding equations and jointly estimating them concerns the cost of greater complexity; for large models the gains in efficiency may not be worth the increased computing resources and programming complexity. More important, to attain this efficiency improvement one must be confident that errors follow distributions with constant moments.

This appendix represents only the most basic of explorations into the properties of this type of estimator. Specifically, only one example of efficiency gain is examined. Naturally, one requires a more careful analysis to ascertain a more complete picture of the properties of these estimators in small samples. A more comprehensive analysis would involve consideration of richer mixtures of kurtosis and skewness, as well as different sample sizes. No attempt has been made to establish a sample size lower bound where estimators of this kind begin to exhibit beneficial properties. One could further investigate the merits of adding more equations in estimation, capturing information beyond third and fourth moments. Nonlinear regression and simultaneous equations constitute another category of exploration. Moreover, a comprehensive simulation should consider methods for improving estimation with heteroscedastic errors. All of these are possible areas of further study.

Table 10.6. *Distributions of estimated age-squared coefficients using information on different moments for sample size 500*

Distribution of errors and estimation method	Statistics summarizing deviations from true values (multiplied by 1000)								
	Moments		Percentiles						
	Mean	Standard deviation	Min	10%	25%	50%	75%	90%	Max
Normal errors									
Linear	0.002	5.683	−0.827	−0.460	−0.202	−0.001	0.212	0.438	0.901
Linear-quadratic	0.002	5.766	−0.834	−0.457	−0.220	0.001	0.233	0.447	0.889
Linear-cubic	0.001	5.866	−1.011	−0.469	−0.220	0.002	0.223	0.461	0.888
All	0.000	5.97	−1.017	−0.458	−0.233	−0.001	0.233	0.456	0.890
Student's *t* errors									
Linear	0.016	0.169	−1.169	−0.443	−0.201	0.005	0.245	0.480	1.068
Linear-quadratic	0.018	6.055	−1.042	−0.437	−0.221	0.008	0.226	0.465	1.050
Linear-cubic	0.018	5.765	−0.993	−0.408	−0.220	−0.017	0.235	0.449	0.963
All	0.026	5.788	−1.003	−0.418	−0.207	0.022	0.225	0.449	0.994
Double exponential errors									
Linear	−0.019	6.331	−0.841	−0.550	−0.273	0.002	0.241	0.437	1.016
Linear-quadratic	−0.020	6.350	−0.917	−0.527	−0.282	0.016	0.249	0.413	1.015
Linear-cubic	−0.017	5.705	−0.724	−0.501	−0.240	−0.004	0.217	0.405	0.871
All	−0.016	5.771	0.864	0.415	0.278	−0.022	−0.246	−0.501	−0.672
Gamma errors									
Linear	−0.008	6.482	−1.168	−0.506	−0.272	0.014	0.248	0.456	0.956
Linear-quadratic	0.011	4.019	−0.736	−0.229	−0.149	−0.012	0.173	0.304	0.731
Linear-cubic	0.018	5.361	−0.888	−0.395	−0.188	−0.030	0.239	0.431	0.743
All	0.021	3.115	−0.378	−0.202	−0.101	−0.023	0.124	0.258	0.685

Notes: Each row summarizes the finite-sample distribution of the designated estimator assuming the specified error distribution. All statistics are computed by subtracting "true" value of age-squared coefficient from Monte Carlo estimates. All values are multiplied by 1000 to facilitate comparisons. Data on explanatory variables drawn from the 1997 CPS data on men. Moments of the error terms are given in Table 10.2.

REFERENCES

Amemiya, T. (1974), "The Nonlinear Two-Stage Least-Squares Estimator," *Journal of Econometrics*, **2**, 105–110.

(1975), "The Nonlinear Limited-Information Maximum-Likelihood Estimator and the Modified Nonlinear Two-Stage Least-Squares Estimator," *Journal of Econometrics*, **3**, 375–386.

(1977), "The Maximum Likelihood and the Nonlinear Three-Stage Least Squares Estimator in the General Nonlinear Simultaneous Equation Model," *Econometrica*, **45**, 955–968.

(1983), "Partially Generalized Least Squares and Two-Stage Least Squares Estimators," *Journal of Econometrics*, **23**, 275–283.

Breusch, T., Qian, H., Schmidt, P., and Wyhowski, D. (1999), "Redundancy of Moment Conditions," *Journal of Econometrics*, **91**, 89–111.

Chamberlain, G. (1982), "Multivariate Regression Models for Panel Data," *Journal of Econometrics*, **18**, 5–46.

(1987), "Asymptotic Efficiency in Estimation with Conditional Moment Restrictions," *Journal of Econometrics*, **34**, 305–334.

Cragg, J. C. (1983), "More Efficient Estimation in the Presence of Heteroscedasticity of Unknown Form," *Econometrica*, **45**, 955–968.

Hansen, L. P. (1982), "Large Sample Properties of Generalized Methods of Moments Estimators," *Econometrica*, **50**, 1029–1054.

Newey, W. (1988), "Adaptive Estimation of Regression Models via Moments Restrictions," *Journal of Econometrics*, **38**, 301–342.

(1993), "Efficient Estimation of Models with Conditional Moments Restrictions," G. S. Maddalla, C. R. Rao, and H. Vinod, eds., *Handbook of Statistics, Vol. 11, Econometrics* (Amsterdam: Elsevier), 419–454.

Qian, H. and Schmidt, P. (1999), "Improved Instrumental Variables and Generalized Method of Moments Estimators," *Journal of Econometrics*, **91**, 145–169.

Rao, C. R. (1973), *Linear Statistical Inference and Its Applications*, 2nd ed. (New York: John Wiley & Sons).

White, H. (1980), "A Heteroskedasticity-Consistent Covariance Matrix and a Direct Test for Heteroskedasticity," *Econometrica*, **48**, 721–746.

(1982), "Instrumental Variable Regression with Independent Observations," *Econometrica*, **50**, 483–500.

CHAPTER 11

Minimal conditions for weak convergence of the sample standardized spectral distribution function

T. W. Anderson and Linfeng You

Let $\{y_t\}$ be a stationary stochastic process with $\mathcal{E}y_t = 0$, $\mathcal{E}y_t y_{t+h} = \sigma(h)$, and $\rho_h = \sigma(h)/\sigma(0)$, $h = 0, 1, \ldots$. The standardized spectral distribution

$$F(\lambda) = \frac{1}{\pi}\left[\lambda + 2\sum_{h=1}^{\infty}\frac{\sin \lambda h}{h}\frac{\sigma(h)}{\sigma(0)}\right]$$

$$= \frac{1}{\pi}\left[\lambda + 2\sum_{h=1}^{\infty}\frac{\sin \lambda h}{h}\rho_h\right], \qquad 0 \le \lambda \le \pi, \tag{11.1}$$

is useful for specifying patterns of dependence (Anderson 1993). Let $y_1, \ldots, y_T$ be a sample from the process $\{y_t\}$, and define $c_h = \sum_{t=1}^{T-h} y_t y_{t+h}/T$ and $r_h = c_h/c_0$, $h = 0, 1, \ldots, T - 1$. The sample standardized spectral distribution is

$$F_T(\lambda) = \frac{1}{\pi}\left[\lambda + 2\sum_{h=1}^{T-1}\frac{\sin \lambda h}{h}\frac{c_h}{c_0}\right]$$

$$= \frac{1}{\pi}\left[\lambda + 2\sum_{h=1}^{T-1}\frac{\sin \lambda h}{h}r_h\right], \qquad 0 \le \lambda \le \pi. \tag{11.2}$$

The purpose of this chapter is to prove that when the y_t's are independently identically distributed (iid) with $\mathcal{E}y_t^2 < \infty$, $\sqrt{T}[F_T(\lambda) - F(\lambda)]$ converges weakly to a Gaussian stochastic process (Theorem 1).

Theorem 1. *If $\mathcal{E}y_t^2 < \infty$ and the y_t's are iid,*

$$\sqrt{T}[F_T(\lambda) - F(\lambda)] = \frac{2}{\pi c_0}\sqrt{T}\sum_{h=1}^{T-1}\frac{\sin \lambda h}{h}c_h \xrightarrow{w} Z(\lambda), \qquad 0 \le \lambda \le \pi, \tag{11.3}$$

where $Z(\lambda)$ is a Gaussian process with $\mathcal{E}Z(\lambda) = 0$ and

$$\mathcal{E}Z(\lambda)Z(\nu) = 2\left[\frac{\min(\lambda, \nu)}{\pi} - \frac{\lambda\nu}{\pi^2}\right], \qquad 0 \le \lambda, \nu \le \pi. \qquad (11.4)$$

Essentially this result was found independently by Klüppelberg and Mikosch (1996, Proposition 3.3) and Anderson and You (1995, Theorem 2). Grenander and Rosenblatt (1952, 1957) used the condition $\mathcal{E}y_t^8 < \infty$ to prove the tightness condition for weak convergence; this eighth-order moment condition has been quoted frequently in subsequent papers. Since Klüppelberg and Mikosch did not give a proof of Theorem 1, we thought such a proof would be of some interest. The basic innovation of this chapter is Lemma 1.

Lemma 1. *If the y_t's are iid with $\mathcal{E}y_t = 0$ and $\mathcal{E}y_t^2 < \infty$, then for any $\varepsilon > 0$ and $\eta > 0$ there exists a k_0 such that for $k > k_0$*

$$\Pr\left\{\sup_{0 \le \lambda \le \pi} \sqrt{T}\left|\frac{2}{\pi}\sum_{h=2^k}^{T-1}\frac{\sin \lambda h}{h}c_h\right| > \varepsilon\right\} < \eta \qquad (11.5)$$

for all $T > 2^k$.

Proof: Consider

$$\psi_m(\lambda) = \sqrt{T}\sum_{h=m+1}^{2m}\frac{\sin \lambda h}{h}c_h \qquad (11.6)$$

for arbitrary m. (We define $c_h = 0$ for $h \ge T$.) Then

$$|\psi_m(\lambda)|^2 \le \left|\sqrt{T}\sum_{h=m+1}^{2m}\frac{e^{i\lambda h}}{h}c_h\right|^2 = T\sum_{g,h=m+1}^{2m}\frac{e^{i\lambda(g-h)}}{gh}c_g c_h$$

$$= T\sum_{h=m+1}^{2m}\frac{c_h^2}{h^2} + 2T\mathcal{R}\left[\sum_{g>h=m+1}^{2m}\frac{e^{i\lambda(g-h)}}{gh}c_g c_h\right]$$

$$= T\sum_{h=m+1}^{2m}\frac{c_h^2}{h^2} + 2T\mathcal{R}\left[\sum_{j=1}^{m-1}e^{i\lambda j}\sum_{h=m+1}^{2m-j}\frac{c_h c_{h+j}}{h(h+j)}\right]$$

$$\le \frac{T}{m^2}\sum_{h=m+1}^{2m}c_h^2 + 2T\sum_{j=1}^{m-1}\left|\sum_{h=m+1}^{2m-j}\frac{c_h c_{h+j}}{h(h+j)}\right| = \Psi_m^2, \qquad (11.7)$$

say. Note that Ψ_m^2 is independent of λ. Let

$$T\sum_{h=m+1}^{2m-j}\frac{c_h c_{h+j}}{h(h+j)}=\frac{1}{T}\sum_{h=m+1}^{2m-j}\sum_{t=1}^{T-h}\sum_{s=1}^{T-(h+j)}\frac{y_t y_{t+h} y_s y_{s+h+j}}{h(h+j)}$$

$$= X_{1j}+X_{2j}+X_{3j}+X_{4j}+Y_j, \qquad (11.8)$$

$$X_{1j}=\frac{1}{T}\sum_{h=m+1}^{2m-j}\frac{1}{h(h+j)}\sum_{t=1}^{T-(h+j)}y_t^2 y_{t+h}y_{t+h+j}, \qquad (11.9)$$

$$X_{2j}=\frac{1}{T}\sum_{h=m+1}^{2m-j}\frac{1}{h(h+j)}\sum_{t=h+j+1}^{T-h}y_t^2 y_{t+h}y_{t-(h+j)}, \qquad (11.10)$$

$$X_{3j}=\frac{1}{T}\sum_{h=m+1}^{2m-j}\frac{1}{h(h+j)}\sum_{t=1}^{T-(2h+j)}y_t y_{t+h}^2 y_{t+2h+j}, \qquad (11.11)$$

$$X_{4j}=\frac{1}{T}\sum_{h=m+1}^{2m-j}\frac{1}{h(h+j)}\sum_{t=j+1}^{T-h}y_t y_{t+h}^2 y_{t-j}, \qquad (11.12)$$

$$Y_j=\frac{1}{T}\sum_{h=m+1}^{2m-j}\sum_{(t,s)\in S(h,j)}\frac{y_t y_{t+h} y_s y_{s+h+j}}{h(h+j)}, \qquad (11.13)$$

where $S(h,j)$ is the set of (t,s) such that $1\leq t\leq T-h$, $1\leq s\leq T-(h+j)$, $t\neq s, s+h+j, s-h, s+j$. Since each term in Y_j has mean zero and is uncorrelated with the other terms, the variance of Y_j is the sum of the variances of the individual terms. We have

$$\mathcal{E}Y_j^2=\frac{1}{T^2}\sum_{h=m+1}^{2m-j}\sum_{(t,s)\in S(h,j)}\frac{1}{h^2(h+j)^2}\sigma^8$$

$$<\frac{1}{T^2}\sum_{h=m+1}^{2m-j}\sum_{t=1}^{T-h}\sum_{s=1}^{T-(h+j)}\frac{1}{h^2(h+j)^2}\sigma^8$$

$$<\sum_{h=m+1}^{2m-j}\frac{1}{h^2(h+j)^2}\sigma^8$$

$$<\frac{\sigma^8}{m^3}, \qquad (11.14)$$

since $h>m$ and $h+j>m$. Then

$$\mathcal{E}|Y_j|\leq\left(\mathcal{E}Y_j^2\right)^{1/2}<\frac{\sigma^4}{m^{3/2}}. \qquad (11.15)$$

Note that the highest moment of the y_t's that is involved is the second, since the four indices of the y_t's in each summand of Y_j are distinct.

To treat X_{kj} we use the inequality

$$\mathcal{E}|U| \le [\mathcal{E}U^2 + \mathcal{E}V^2]^{1/2}, \tag{11.16}$$

which follows from $\mathcal{E}|U| \le (\mathcal{E}U^2)^{1/2}$.

Exchanging the summations in (11.9) allows us to write

$$X_{1j} = \frac{1}{T} \sum_{t=1}^{T-j-(m+1)} y_t^2 Z_{1t}, \tag{11.17}$$

where

$$Z_{1t} = \sum_{h \in S_{1t}} \frac{y_{t+h} y_{t+h+j}}{h(h+j)} \tag{11.18}$$

and S_{1t} is a set of integers contained in $\{m+1, m+2, \ldots, 2m-j\}$. Consider Z_{1t} and $\sum_{h=m+1}^{2m-j} y_{t+h} y_{t+h+j}/[h(h+j)]$ as U and $U+V$, respectively, in (11.16); then we obtain

$$\mathcal{E}|Z_{1t}| \le \left[\mathcal{E}\left(\sum_{h=m+1}^{2m-j} \frac{y_{t+h} y_{t+h+j}}{h(h+j)} \right)^2 \right]^{1/2} = \left[\sum_{h=m+1}^{2m-j} \frac{1}{h^2(h+j)^2} \right]^{1/2} \sigma^4. \tag{11.19}$$

Since y_t and Z_{1t} in (11.17) are independent and $T - j - (m+1) < T$,

$$\mathcal{E}|X_{1j}| \le \frac{\sigma^4}{m^{3/2}}. \tag{11.20}$$

To prove the same property for X_{2j}, X_{3j}, and X_{4j}, we follow the procedure used for X_{1j}. We can define Z_{kt} of X_{kj}, $k = 2, 3$, and 4, similar to that for $k = 1$. Since for any fixed t, Z_{kt} consists of at most $2m - j - (m+1) + 1$ uncorrelated random variables with coefficients $1/[h^2(h+j)^2]$, $m+1 \le h \le 2m - j$, we obtain

$$\mathcal{E}|Z_{kj}| < \frac{\sigma^4}{m^{3/2}}, \qquad k = 1, 2, 3, 4. \tag{11.21}$$

Furthermore, the number of possible Z_{kt} terms in each X_{kj}, $k = 1, 2, 3, 4$, is less than T; so

$$\mathcal{E}|X_{kj}| < \frac{\sigma^4}{m^{3/2}}, \qquad k = 1, 2, 3, 4. \tag{11.22}$$

Therefore, for $m \le T$,

$$\sum_{j=1}^{m-1} \sum_{k=1}^{4} \mathcal{E}|X_{kj}| < 4\frac{\sigma^4}{m^{1/2}}. \tag{11.23}$$

Then

$$\mathcal{E}\Psi_m^2 \leq \frac{1}{m^2}T\sum_{h=m+1}^{2m}\mathcal{E}c_h^2 + 2\sum_{j=1}^{m-1}\left[\mathcal{E}|Y_j| + \sum_{i=1}^{4}\mathcal{E}|X_{ij}|\right]$$

$$\leq \frac{\sigma^4}{m} + 10\sum_{j=1}^{m-1}\frac{\sigma^4}{m^{3/2}}$$

$$< 11\frac{\sigma^4}{m^{1/2}}. \tag{11.24}$$

Note that the last inequality does not depend on T.

From (11.24) Grenander and Rosenblatt (1957) show that with arbitrarily high probability $\sum_{n=k}^{\log T+1}\Psi_{2^n}^2$ is arbitrarily small for k sufficiently large. Lemma 1 follows from this fact. $\qquad\square$

Proof of Theorem 1: Because the y_t's are iid with $\mathcal{E}y_t^2 = \sigma^2$, $c_0\overset{p}{\to}\sigma^2$, Lemma 1 then implies that $\sqrt{T}[F_T(\lambda_1) - F(\lambda_1)], \ldots, \sqrt{T}[F_T(\lambda_n) - F(\lambda_n)]$ have a limiting multivariate normal distribution, since $\sqrt{T}c_1, \ldots, \sqrt{T}c_H$ for any H have a limiting multivariate normal distribution. The covariance function follows from $T\mathcal{E}c_h^2 = (T-h)\sigma^4/T$ and $T\mathcal{E}c_hc_g = 0$, $h \neq g$, and the fact that $(4\sum_{h=1}^{\infty}\sin\lambda h\sin\nu h)/(\pi^2h^2)$ is (11.4). See Gradshteyn and Ryzhik (1965, p. 39), for example.

For the tightness condition for the weak convergence of $U_T(\lambda) = \sqrt{T}[F_T(\lambda) - F(\lambda)]$ we want to show that for any $\varepsilon > 0$ and $\eta > 0$ there exists a $\delta > 0$ and a $T_0 > 0$ such that $\Pr\{\sup_{|\lambda-\nu|<\delta}|U_T(\lambda) - U_T(\nu)| > \varepsilon\} < \eta$ for all $T > T_0$. We can write

$$U_T(\lambda) - U_T(\nu) = \sqrt{T}\ [F_T(\lambda) - F_T(\nu)]$$

$$= \frac{2\sqrt{T}}{\pi}\sum_{h=1}^{2^k-1}\frac{\sin\lambda h - \sin\nu h}{h}\frac{c_h}{c_0}$$

$$+ \frac{2\sqrt{T}}{\pi}\sum_{h=2^k}^{T-1}\frac{\sin\lambda h - \sin\nu h}{h}\frac{c_h}{c_0}. \tag{11.25}$$

By Lemma 1 and $c_0\overset{p}{\to}\sigma^2$ the absolute value of the second term on the right-hand side of (11.25) can be made small in probability. The first term has $2^k - 1$ terms (k fixed); the coefficients $(\sin\lambda h - \sin\nu h)/h$, $h = 1, \ldots, 2^k - 1$, are uniformly bounded if $|\lambda - \nu|$ is sufficiently small. Moreover c_h, $h = 1, \ldots, 2^k - 1$, have a limiting normal distribution. Hence the first term in (11.25) can also be made small in probability. $\qquad\square$

Theorem 1 can be extended to a general time-series model. Let a time series be $x_t = \sum_{v=-\infty}^{\infty}a_vy_{t-v}$, where the y_t's are iid with $\mathcal{E}y_t = 0$ and $\mathcal{E}y_t^2 = \sigma^2$.

Theorem 2 of Chapter 6 of Grenander and Rosenblatt (1957) states that for

$$|a_\nu| = O(\nu^{-\beta}), \qquad \beta > \frac{3}{2}, \tag{11.26}$$

the stochastic process $U_T(\lambda)$ still converges to a Gaussian process. In fact, their Theorem 2 is based on their Theorem 1, which was modified by the Theorem 1 in this chapter. The modification reduces the moment condition from eighth to second. Therefore, the convergence will still hold for the general case under the condition (11.26). In general, ARMA processes satisfy this condition.

Since the proof of Lemma 1 only depends on the variance of y_t, the lemma holds under the weaker condition $\sup_t \mathcal{E} y_t^2 < \infty$. We have assumed $\mathcal{E} y_t = 0$ for convenience. If this assumption is not appropriate, we can define

$$c_h = \frac{1}{T} \sum_{t=1}^{T-h} (y_t - \bar{y})(y_{t+h} - \bar{y}), \qquad h = 0, 1, \ldots, T-1, \tag{11.27}$$

where $\bar{y} = \sum_{t=1}^{T} y_t / T$. Then Lemma 1 and Theorem 1 hold for y_t iid with $\mathcal{E} y_t^2 < \infty$.

REFERENCES

Anderson, T. W. (1993), "Goodness of Fit Tests for Spectral Distributions," *Annals of Statistics*, **21**, 830–847.

Anderson, T. W. and Linfeng You (1995), "Minimal Conditions for Weak Convergence of the Sample Spectral Distribution Function," Technical Report No. 312, NSF Grant DMS 93-01366, Department of Statistics, Stanford University.

Gradshteyn, I. S. and Ryzhik, I. M. (1965), *Table of Integrals, Series and Products* (New York: Academic Press).

Grenander, U. and Rosenblatt, M. (1952), "On Spectral Analysis of Stationary Time Series," *Proceedings of the National Academy of Sciences*, **38**, 519–521.

——— (1957), *Statistical Analysis of Stationary Time Series* (Stockholm: Almqvist and Wiksell).

Klüppelberg, C. and Mikosch, T. (1996), "Gaussian Limit Fields for the Integrated Periodogram," *Annals of Applied Probability*, **6**, 969–991.

CHAPTER 12

Unit root tests for time series with a structural break when the break point is known

Helmut Lütkepohl, Christian Müller, and Pentti Saikkonen

1 Introduction

A number of studies consider testing for unit roots in univariate time series which have a level shift. Examples are Perron (1989, 1990), Perron and Vogelsang (1992), Banerjee, Lumsdaine, and Stock (1992), Zivot and Andrews (1992), Amsler and Lee (1995), Leybourne, Newbold, and Vougas (1998), Montañés and Reyes (1998), and Saikkonen and Lütkepohl (1999). These tests are important because the trending properties of a set of time series determine to some extent which model and statistical procedures are suitable for analyzing their relationship. In the aforementioned studies different models and assumptions for the structural shift are considered. In some of the studies the timing of the break point is assumed to be known, whereas in others a shift in an unknown period is considered. There seems to be general consensus, however, that if the break point is known, this is useful information which should be taken into account in the subsequent analysis and in particular in testing for unit roots. Therefore we will focus on the latter case in the following. In practice, a known break point is quite common. For instance, many German macroeconomic time series are known to have a shift in 1990 where the German reunification took place.

For the case of a known break point we will propose a framework which generalizes previously considered models. In this framework the shift is modeled as part of the intercept term of the stationary part of the data generation process (DGP) which is clearly separated from the unit root part. Our model has the convenient feature that even simple shift functions result in a smooth transition from one state to another, both under the null of a unit root and under

We thank an anonymous referee for helpful comments. The Deutsche Forschungsgemeinschaft, SFB 373, and the European Commission under the Training and Mobility of Researchers Programme (contract No. ERBFMRXCT980213) provided financial support. Part of this research was done while the third author was visiting the Institute of Statistics and Econometrics at the Humboldt University in Berlin.

the alternative hypothesis of stationarity. Such behaviour is often more realistic than an abrupt one-time shift. For instance, in some German macroeconomic time series such as GNP there is a clear shift in 1990 where the German reunification has occurred. However, the eastern part of the country was in a quite different economic situation than West Germany at that time and entered into a long-lasting adjustment process. Hence, a gradual adjustment after an initial shift may be a more realistic model in this case.

We will compare our new model with previously proposed models in an empirical comparison of different frameworks. A major advantage of the present approach relative to other approaches is that estimation of the nuisance parameters reduces to a fairly simple nonlinear least squares (LS) problem (see Amemiya 1983 for a review of nonlinear regression). In special cases estimation can even be done by linear LS, although the shift from one regime to another is nonlinear.

The structure of this study is as follows. In the next section the general setup is presented, and in Section 3 the tests are considered. Empirical examples are discussed in Section 4, and conclusions are given in Section 5. The proof of a theorem regarding the asymptotic properties of the test statistic is provided in the appendix.

The following notation is used. The lag and differencing operators are denoted by L and Δ, respectively, so that for a time series variable y_t, $Ly_t = y_{t-1}$ and $\Delta y_t = y_t - y_{t-1}$. Convergence in probability and in distribution are denoted by $\xrightarrow{p}$ and $\xrightarrow{d}$, respectively. Independently, identically distributed will be abbreviated as iid$(\cdot, \cdot)$, where the first and second moments are indicated in parentheses. Furthermore, $O(\cdot)$, $o(\cdot)$, $O_p(\cdot)$, and $o_p(\cdot)$ are the usual symbols for the order of convergence and convergence in probability, respectively, of a sequence. The symbol $\lambda_{\min}(A)$ is reserved to denote the minimal eigenvalue of a matrix A. Moreover, $\| \cdot \|$ denotes the Euclidean norm. The abbreviations sup and inf are used as usual for supremum and infimum, respectively. The n-dimensional Euclidean space is signified as $\mathbf{R}^n$.

2   Models for time series with level shifts

Saikkonen and Lütkepohl (1999) (henceforth S&L) consider the following general model for a time series with a unit root and a level shift:

$$y_t = \mu_0 + \mu_1 t + f_t(\theta)'\gamma + x_t, \qquad t = 1, 2, \ldots, \qquad (12.2.1)$$

where the scalars μ_0 and μ_1, the $m \times 1$ vector θ, and the $k \times 1$ vector γ are unknown parameters, and $f_t(\theta)$ is a $k \times 1$ vector of deterministic sequences depending on the parameters θ. The quantity x_t represents an unobservable stochastic error term, which is assumed to have a finite-order autoregressive

(AR) representation,

$$a(L)x_t = \varepsilon_t, \tag{12.2.2}$$

where $a(L) = 1 - a_1 L - \cdots - a_{p+1} L^{p+1}$ is a polynomial in the lag operator and $\varepsilon_t \sim \text{iid}(0, \sigma^2)$. For simplicity, we assume that a suitable number of pre-sample values of the observed series y_t are available. Obviously, if the DGP of x_t has a unit root, then the same is true for y_t. Therefore, S&L derive a test for a unit root in $a(L)$.

A simple version of a function $f_t(\theta)$ that has been considered in the literature is one which represents a single shift in the mean,

$$f_t(\theta) = d_{1t} := \begin{cases} 0, & t < T_1, \\ 1, & t \geq T_1, \end{cases} \tag{12.2.3}$$

that is, d_{1t} is a shift dummy variable which does not depend on any unknown parameters. In other words, the parameter vector θ does not appear in this case. The dummy d_{1t} represents a shift in the mean of the series in period T_1 which is assumed to be known. Smooth transitions from one level to another can also be accommodated in the above model by an appropriate definition of $f_t(\theta)$. An alternative way to generate smooth level shifts over a longer period of time is possible in a model of the form

$$b(L)y_t = \mu_0 + \mu_1 t + \gamma d_{1t} + v_t, \qquad t = 1, 2, \ldots, \tag{12.2.4}$$

where the operator $b(L) = 1 - b_1 L - \cdots - b_p L^p$ is assumed to have all its zeros outside the unit circle, and the error term v_t is assumed to be an AR process of order 1,

$$v_t = \rho v_{t-1} + \varepsilon_t, \tag{12.2.5}$$

where again $\varepsilon_t \sim \text{iid}(0, \sigma^2)$ and $-1 < \rho \leq 1$ with $\rho = 1$ implying a unit root in y_t. In the model (12.2.4) the shift dummy variable generates a smooth transition to a new level via $\gamma b(L)^{-1} d_{1t}$. Defining $b(L)^{-1} = 1 + \sum_{i=1}^{\infty} \alpha_i L^i$, we get for $t > T_1$,

$$b(L)^{-1} d_{1t} = 1 + \sum_{i=1}^{t-T_1} \alpha_i.$$

Thus, in this model a smooth transition of the level of y_t is generated, although just a shift dummy variable appears in the deterministic term. More flexibility of this kind of model can be obtained by replacing d_{1t} by a more general sequence $f_t(\theta)$ as in (12.2.1).

In this study we will consider models of the general type

$$b(L)y_t = \mu_0 + \mu_1 t + f_t(\theta)'\gamma + v_t, \qquad t = 1, 2, \ldots, \tag{12.2.6}$$

where all symbols are as defined in (12.2.1), (12.2.4), and (12.2.5). The parameters μ_0, μ_1, and γ in the model (12.2.6) are supposed to be unrestricted. Conditions required for the parameters θ and the sequence $f_t(\theta)$ are collected in the following set of assumptions from S&L.

Assumption 1:
  (a)   The parameter space of θ, denoted by Θ, is a compact subset of $\mathbf{R}^m$.
  (b)   For each $t = 1, 2, \ldots$, the term $f_t(\theta)$ is a continuous function of θ, and

$$\sup_T \sum_{t=1}^{T} \sup_{\theta \in \Theta} \|\Delta f_t(\theta)\| < \infty,$$

  where $f_0(\theta) = 0$.
  (c)   Defining $g_t(\theta) = [1 : f_t(\theta)']'$ for $t = 1, 2, \ldots$, and $\Delta g_1(\theta) = [1 : f_1(\theta)']'$, there exists a real number $\varepsilon > 0$ and an integer T_* such that, for all $T \geq T_*$,

$$\inf_{\theta \in \Theta} \lambda_{\min} \left\{ \sum_{t=1}^{T} \Delta g_t(\theta) \, \Delta g_t(\theta)' \right\} \geq \varepsilon.$$

The assumption of a compact parameter space Θ and the continuity requirement in Assumption 1(b) are standard in nonlinear estimation and testing problems. If the parameter space Θ is defined in a suitable way, the summability condition in Assumption 1(b) holds in the applications we have in mind and is therefore not restrictive for our purposes. The conditions in Assumption 1(b) and (c) are formulated for differences of the sequences $f_t(\theta)$ and $g_t(\theta)$ because our intention is to study unit root testing. Hence, estimation of the parameters μ, θ, and γ is considered under the null hypothesis that the error process in (12.2.6) contains a unit root. Efficient estimation then requires that the variables in (12.2.6) are differenced. Therefore differences appear in Assumption 1.

To understand Assumption 1(c), assume first that the value of the parameter θ is known and that the parameters μ and γ are estimated by applying LS to the differenced model. Then Assumption 1(c) guarantees linear independence of the regressors $\Delta g_t(\theta)$ for T large enough. When θ is known, there is of course no need to include the infimum in the condition of Assumption 1(c). It is needed, however, when the value of θ is unknown and has to be estimated. Since consistent estimation of θ is not possible, we have to impose an assumption which guarantees that the above-mentioned linear independence of regressors holds whatever the value of θ. This is achieved by Assumption 1(c).

Consistent estimation of θ and γ is not possible because, by Assumption 1(b), the variation of (the differenced) regressors does not increase as $T \to \infty$. The present formulation of Assumption 1(b) is convenient because it also applies when the sequence $f_t(\theta)$ and hence $g_t(\theta)$ depends on T. We have not made this feature explicit, because it is not needed in the present application of Assumption 1. This dependence on T is obtained, for instance, if asymptotic results are derived under the assumption that T_1/T or $T - T_1$ is constant.

Using the terminology in Condition B of Elliott, Rothenberg, and Stock (1996), Assumption 1 implies that, for each value of θ, the sequence $g_t(\theta)$ defines a slowly evolving trend. Note, however, that our conditions are stronger than those of Elliott et al. We will not attempt to weaken Assumption 1, because it is convenient for our purposes and applies to the models of interest in the following. Overall the model (12.2.6) together with Assumption 1 provides a general framework for testing for a unit root in the context of slowly evolving trends. Further discussion of Assumption 1 may be found in S&L.

We will present unit root tests within our model framework. More precisely, we will present a test of the pair of hypotheses

$$H_0 : \rho = 1 \quad \text{vs.} \quad H_1 : |\rho| < 1$$

in the next section.

It is not clear a priori which one of the two general models (12.2.1) or (12.2.6) is best suited for testing for unit roots in time series with level shifts. In fact, this is an empirical question, and therefore we will use both model types in Section 4 to analyze the unit root properties of a number of time series with a level shift at a known point in time. We will compare the resulting tests for some real life macroeconomic time series.

For completeness we mention that seasonal dummies may be added to both models (12.2.1) and (12.2.6) without changing the theoretical analysis in any substantive way. For instance, in that case model (12.2.6) becomes

$$b(L)y_t = \mu_0 + \mu_1 t + \sum_{i=1}^{q} v_i D_{it} + f_t(\theta)'\gamma + v_t, \qquad t = 1, 2, \ldots,$$

where the v_i are scalar parameters and the $D_{it}(i = 1, \ldots, q)$ represent seasonal dummy variables. For example, for quarterly data, D_{it} assumes the value 1 if t is associated with the ith quarter and zero otherwise. For quarterly data $q = 3$ is used, because an intercept term is included in the model. This modification does not affect the asymptotic properties of the subsequently considered test. Therefore, to avoid notational complications, we do not include seasonal dummies at this stage. They will be used in the empirical analysis in Section 4.

3   A unit root test

The basic idea underlying our test procedure is to estimate the nuisance parameters in (12.2.6) first and then apply a Dickey–Fuller test to the residuals $\tilde{v}_t$. Our approach for estimating the nuisance parameters $\mu_0, \mu_1, \theta, \gamma$, and $b_1, \ldots, b_p$ is similar to that in Elliott, Rothenberg, and Stock (1996) and Hwang and Schmidt (1996). These authors use a generalized LS procedure which does not necessarily assume validity of the null hypothesis but is based on appropriate local alternatives to be specified by the analyst. Thus, suppose that the error process v_t specified in (12.2.5) is near integrated, so that

$$\rho = \rho_T = 1 + \frac{c}{T}, \tag{12.3.1}$$

where $c \leq 0$ is a fixed real number. Then the generating process of v_t can be written as

$$v_t = \rho_T v_{t-1} + \varepsilon_t, \qquad t = 1, 2, \ldots. \tag{12.3.2}$$

For simplicity we make the initial value assumption $v_0 = 0$, although our asymptotic results also hold under more general conditions (see Elliott, Rothenberg, and Stock 1996 for a discussion of the implications of initial value assumptions). It follows from the stated assumptions that

$$T^{-1/2} v_{[sT]} \xrightarrow{d} \sigma B_c(s), \tag{12.3.3}$$

where $B_c(s) = \int_0^s \exp\{c(s-u)\}\, dB_0(u)$ with $B_0(u)$ a standard Brownian motion (cf. Elliott, Rothenberg, and Stock 1996).

Our estimation procedure employs an empirical counterpart of the parameter c. This means that we shall replace c by a chosen value $\bar{c}$ and pretend that $\bar{c} = c$, although we do not assume that this presumption is actually true. The choice of $\bar{c}$ will be discussed later. Now, if $\bar{\rho}_T = 1 + \bar{c}/T$, the idea is to first transform the variables in (12.2.6) by the filter $1 - \bar{\rho}_T L$. For convenience we will use matrix notation and define

$$Y = [y_1 : (y_2 - \bar{\rho}_T y_1) : \cdots : (y_T - \bar{\rho}_T y_{T-1})]',$$
$$Z_1 = [1 : (2 - \bar{\rho}_T) : \cdots : (T - \bar{\rho}_T(T-1))]',$$

and

$$Z_2(\theta) = \begin{bmatrix} 1 & 1 - \bar{\rho}_T & \cdots & 1 - \bar{\rho}_T \\ f_1(\theta) & f_2(\theta) - \bar{\rho}_T f_1(\theta) & \cdots & f_T(\theta) - \bar{\rho}_T f_{T-1}(\theta) \end{bmatrix}'.$$

Here, for simplicity, the notation ignores the dependence of the quantities on the chosen value $\bar{c}$. Using this notation, the transformed form of (12.2.6) can be written as

$$Y = W(\theta)\beta + \mathcal{E}, \tag{12.3.4}$$

where $W(\theta) = [V : Z(\theta)]$ with $Z(\theta) = [Z_1 : Z_2(\theta)]$, and V is the $T \times p$ matrix containing lagged values of the y_t transformed in the same way as the other variables. Furthermore, $\beta = [b' : \mu_1 : \mu_0 : \gamma']'$, and $\mathcal{E} = [e_1 : \cdots : e_T]'$ is an error term such that $e_t = v_t - \bar{\rho}_T v_{t-1}$. It follows from the definitions that

$$e_t = \varepsilon_t + T^{-1}(c - \bar{c})v_{t-1}. \tag{12.3.5}$$

We shall consider a nonlinear LS estimation of (12.3.4) by proceeding in the same way as in the case $c = 0$ (that is, $e_t = \varepsilon_t$) or under the null hypothesis. The reason why we still do not assume $\bar{c} = 0$ is that choosing $\bar{c} < 0$ yields tests with better local power (see Elliott, Rothenberg, and Stock 1996). Our estimators are thus obtained by minimizing the sum of squares function

$$S_T(\theta, \beta) = (Y - W(\theta)\beta)'(Y - W(\theta)\beta). \tag{12.3.6}$$

Assuming that the matrix $W(\theta)$ is of full column rank for all values of $\theta \in \Theta$, one can repeat the argument used by S&L for model (12.2.1), and conclude that a minimizer of $S_T(\theta, \beta)$, denoted by $[\tilde{\theta}' : \tilde{\beta}']'$, exists when Assumption 1 holds. It is seen in the appendix that this is the case for all T large enough.

The estimator of β can be written as

$$\tilde{\beta} = (W(\tilde{\theta})'W(\tilde{\theta}))^{-1}W(\tilde{\theta})'Y. \tag{12.3.7}$$

Of course, the computation of $\tilde{\beta}$ requires iterative methods if a parameter θ actually appears in the model. However, if preliminary estimators of θ are available, they can be used on the r.h.s. of (12.3.7) in place of $\tilde{\theta}$ to yield an LS estimator of β conditional on the given θ. If computationally simple alternatives to a full minimization of $S_T(\theta, \beta)$ are desired, conventional two-step estimators may be considered. The asymptotic properties of our test procedures are the same even if these estimators are employed. However, in finite samples it may be worthwhile to use proper (nonlinear) LS estimation, which is still very simple. Obviously, if $W(\theta)$ is independent of θ, as in (12.2.4), the above estimation procedure reduces to linear regression. When $W(\theta)$ is not independent of θ, a grid search over the values of θ may provide a convenient estimation procedure if θ is scalar or possibly even if it is two dimensional but takes values in a reasonably small set. Alternatively, one of the available nonlinear estimation algorithms may be applied (see, e.g., Amemiya 1983, 1985, Section 4.4; Judge et al. 1985, Appendix B; or Seber and Wild 1989, Chapters 13, 14). Asymptotic properties of the nonlinear LS estimators are given in the appendix.

Once the nuisance parameters in (12.2.6) have been estimated, the residual series $\tilde{v}_t = \tilde{b}(L)y_t - \tilde{\mu}_0 - \tilde{\mu}_1 t - f_t(\tilde{\theta})'\tilde{\gamma}$ may be used to obtain unit root tests. There are several possible choices. One possibility is to use Dickey–Fuller (DF) tests like, for instance, Elliott, Rothenberg, and Stock (1996). In the following we shall also consider these tests.

Consider the auxiliary regression model

$$\tilde{v}_t = \rho\tilde{v}_{t-1} + e_t^*, \qquad t = 1, \ldots, T, \tag{12.3.8}$$

where $\tilde{v}_0 = 0$. If $\tilde{v}_t$ is replaced by v_t the error term in (12.3.8) becomes ε_t, so that we can use simple LS to obtain a test statistic. Specifically, define the LS estimator

$$\tilde{\rho} = \left(\sum_{t=1}^{T} \tilde{v}_{t-1}^2 \right)^{-1} \sum_{t=1}^{T} \tilde{v}_{t-1} \tilde{v}_t, \tag{12.3.9}$$

with associated error variance estimator

$$\tilde{\sigma}^2 = T^{-1} \sum_{t=1}^{T} (\tilde{v}_t - \tilde{\rho}\tilde{v}_{t-1})^2, \tag{12.3.10}$$

and introduce the test statistic

$$\tau_{\text{alt}} = \left(\sum_{t=1}^{T} \tilde{v}_{t-1}^2 \right)^{1/2} \frac{\tilde{\rho} - 1}{\tilde{\sigma}}. \tag{12.3.11}$$

The notation τ_{alt} is used here to distinguish the statistic from the one given in S&L and to indicate that it is based on an alternative model. The statistic τ of S&L will be denoted by $\tau_{\text{S\&L}}$ in the following. The limiting distribution of the test statistic τ_{alt} is given in the next theorem.

Theorem 1. *Suppose that Assumption 1 holds and that the matrix $W(\theta)$ is of full column rank for all $T \geq k + p + 2$ and all $\theta \in \Theta$. Then*

$$\tau_{\text{alt}} \xrightarrow{d} \frac{1}{2} \left(\int_0^1 G_c(s; \bar{c})^2 \, ds \right)^{-1/2} (G_c(1; \bar{c})^2 - 1),$$

where

$$G_c(s; \bar{c}) = B_c(s) - s \left(\lambda B_c(1) + 3(1 - \lambda) \int_0^1 s B_c(s) \, ds \right)$$

and $\lambda = (1 - \bar{c})/(1 - \bar{c} + \bar{c}^2/3)$.   □

We have included the condition for the rank of the matrix $W(\theta)$ in the theorem because it is plausible and simplifies the exposition. It is seen in the proof given in the appendix that, as a consequence of Assumption 1(c), this condition always holds for T large enough. The limiting distribution in Theorem 1 is the same as that obtained by S&L for their test statistic $\tau_{\text{S\&L}}$ and also the one Elliott, Rothenberg, and Stock (1996) obtained for their t-statistic in a model whose deterministic part only contained a mean and linear trend term. The limiting null distribution, obtained by setting $c = 0$, is free of unknown nuisance parameters but depends on the quantity $\bar{c}$. Elliott, Rothenberg, and Stock (1996) suggest using $\bar{c} = -13.5$ and give some critical values for this choice. They show that with this choice of $\bar{c}$ the asymptotic local power of their t-test is nearly optimal for all values of c. From their results and Theorem 1 we can conclude that this is also the case for our test. Since our alternative is a stationary process v_t (i.e., $|\rho| < 1$), small values of τ_{alt} are critical. It is shown in the appendix that the limiting distribution of τ_{alt} is unaffected by including seasonal dummies in the model.

In the same way as in Elliott, Rothenberg, and Stock (1996), we could derive point optimal tests. These tests would be based on the statistics $\bar{\sigma}^2(1)$ and $\bar{\sigma}^2(\bar{\rho}_T)$ defined by replacing $\bar{\rho}$ in (12.3.10) by unity and $\bar{\rho}_T$, respectively. According to the simulation results of Elliott, Rothenberg, and Stock (1996), the overall properties of their DF t-statistic appeared somewhat better than those of the point optimal tests. Therefore we use the DF test version τ_{alt} in the following. Finally, note that if we have the a priori restriction that there is no linear trend term so that $\mu_1 = 0$, the above test remains essentially the same except for the limiting distribution, which is then the same as in a model without any deterministic terms. Furthermore Elliott, Rothenberg, and Stock (1996) recommend $\bar{c} = -7$ in this case.

4   Empirical comparison of tests

As mentioned earlier, which model to use for a time series with a shift in mean is primarily an empirical question, because it is usually not clear a priori what kind of adjustment is required to capture the level shift in an adequate way. Therefore we have applied the different tests to some economic time series. In particular, we use a set of German macroeconomic series which was also used by S&L, consisting of quarterly, seasonally unadjusted log GNP [1975(1)–1996(4)] and money stock M1 [1960(1)–1997(1)] and M3 [1972(1)–1996(4)]. In addition we use Polish log industrial production (IP) [1982(1)–1995(4)].[1] S&L used the $\tau_{S\&L}$ test based on the following three shift functions:

$$f_t^{(1)}(\theta) = d_{1t},$$

$$f_t^{(2)}(\theta) = \begin{cases} 0, & t < T_1, \\ 1 - \exp\{-\theta(t - T_1 + 1)\}, & t \geq T_1, \end{cases}$$

---

[1] The data sources are: For GNP, quarterly, seasonally unadjusted data, 1975(1)–1990(2) West Germany, 1990(3)–1996(4) all of Germany; Deutsches Institut für Wirtschaftsforschung, Volkswirtschaftliche Gesamtrechnung. For M1, quarterly, seasonally unadjusted data, 1960(1)–1990(1) West Germany, 1990(2)–1997(1) all of Germany; OECD. For M3, quarterly, seasonally unadjusted data, 1972(1)–1990(2) West Germany, 1990(3)–1996(4) all of Germany; Monatsbericht der Deutschen Bundesbank. For IP, quarterly, seasonally unadjusted data, 1982(1)–1995(4) Poland; International Monetary Fund.

and

$$f_t^{(3)}(\theta) = \left[\frac{d_{1,t}}{1 - \theta L} : \frac{d_{1,t-1}}{1 - \theta L} \right]'.$$

The first of these shift functions in conjunction with model (12.2.1) corresponds to an abrupt shift, whereas $f_t^{(2)}(\theta)$ and $f_t^{(3)}(\theta)$ allow for a smooth transition to a new level. All three functions result in a nonlinear optimization problem in computing the $\tau_{S\&L}$ statistic. In contrast, even $f_t^{(1)}(\theta)$ can generate a smooth adjustment to a new level if the framework of the τ_{alt} statistic is used. Moreover, in computing τ_{alt} for $f_t^{(1)}(\theta)$, linear regression is needed only. Since $f_t^{(2)}(\theta)$ and $f_t^{(3)}(\theta)$ involve just a single parameter θ, the nonlinear LS estimators for these functions are conveniently obtained by a grid search.

In Figures 12.1–12.4 the series and the estimated shift functions $\hat{b}(L)^{-1} f_t^{(i)}(\hat{\theta})'\hat{\gamma}$ ($i = 1, 2, 3$) are plotted. All four series have obvious shifts. In the three German series it occurs in 1990 and is due to the German unification. Before the unification the series refer to West Germany only, and after the unification they are defined for all of Germany. Hence, the shift is due to a change in the definition of the series. In Poland the introduction of a market economy in the first quarter of 1989 had a substantial and quite visible impact on the IP series. Whereas the change in the definition of the German series resulted in a quite abrupt shift, the shift in Polish IP is spread out over a number of periods. Thus, one would expect that the model in (12.2.1) may be better suited for capturing the shift in the German series, whereas it may be necessary to allow for a gradual adjustment in the Polish series, and hence the model (12.2.6) may be advantageous for this series.

The expectation with respect to the German series is supported by the abrupt shifts found by S&L in these series by fitting model (12.2.1) with the three shift functions mentioned earlier. They were in fact quite similar to the shifts depicted in Figures 12.1–12.3 for these series. It turns out that the estimated parameters in $b(L)$ are all very close to zero and hence $\hat{b}(L)^{-1} f_t^{(i)}(\hat{\theta})'\hat{\gamma}$ is very similar to $f_t^{(i)}(\hat{\theta})'\hat{\gamma}$ ($i = 1, 2, 3$). It may be worth noting that there remains some autocorrelation in the residuals of the estimated model (12.2.6), although quite large orders of $b(L)$ are considered and using the same orders for $a(L)$ in (12.2.1) largely removes the residual autocorrelation. This observation indicates that the steep shift dominates the series to such an extent that even the parameter estimates in $\hat{b}(L)$ from (12.2.6) are distorted. They are shrunk towards zero to enforce an abrupt shift in the model and consequently they cannot take care of the residual autocorrelation. In contrast, the estimated shift in the Polish series in Figure 12.4 is more gradual, and hence for this series the model in (12.2.6) may be more suitable.

In Table 12.1 the results for unit root tests for all four series are given. In addition to the $\tau_{S\&L}$ and τ_{alt} tests, we also show the results of ordinary ADF

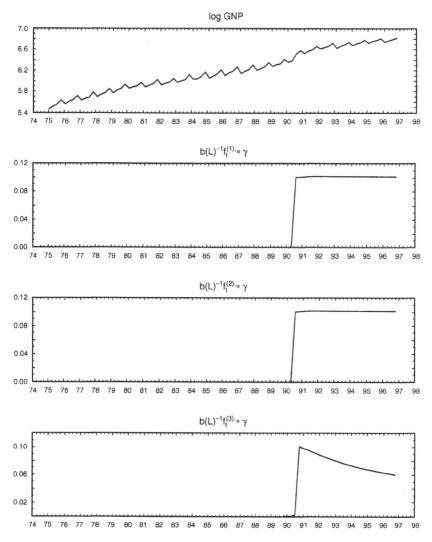

Figure 12.1. Plots of German log GNP and shift functions (based on AR order 4).

tests which allow for a deterministic trend and do not include a shift term. For all series the results for AR order $p = 4$ are given, which is a reasonable order for quarterly data. However, S&L also use different orders in their study, which eliminates residual autocorrelation in the model (12.2.1). These orders are also used in the table for the German series. Similarly, $p = 2$ is sufficient in model

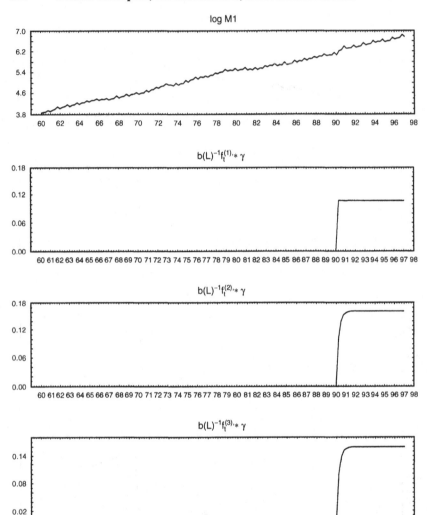

Figure 12.2. Plots of German log M1 and shift functions (based on AR order 4).

(12.2.1) for log IP to remove the residual autocorrelation, and therefore results for that order are also given in Table 12.1 for the Polish series.

S&L found clear support for a unit root in log GNP and log M3, and weak evidence against a unit root in log M1. In Table 12.1 it can be seen that similar results are obtained based on τ_{alt}, although the evidence against a unit root in

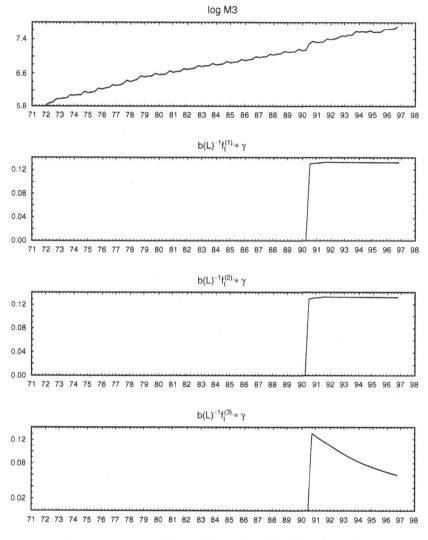

Figure 12.3. Plots of German log M3 and shift functions (based on AR order 4).

log GNP is somewhat stronger when the latter test is used. Still, for log GNP none of the statistics is significant at the 5% level.

A different picture emerges for log IP. Again the ADF test, which does not allow for a shift, is not significant at any reasonable level. Hence, an uncritical application of this test leads to the conclusion that there is a unit root in log IP.

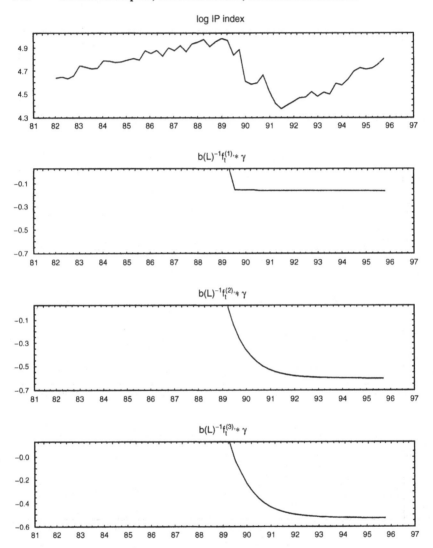

Figure 12.4. Plots of Polish log industrial production and shift functions (based on AR order 4).

Taking the shift into account by applying $\tau_{S\&L}$ or τ_{alt} tests based on the shift functions $f_t^{(i)}(\hat{\theta})$ ($i = 2, 3$), the unit root null hypothesis is clearly rejected at the 10% level and in most cases also at the 5% level if a model with order $p = 2$ is used. The fact that $\tau_{S\&L}$ is not significant for $p = 4$ may be a reflection of the potential power loss due to overfitting the model. Also it may indicate that the model (12.2.1) is not as adequate as the model (12.2.6) for this series. Moreover,

Table 12.1. *Unit root tests*

Variable	AR order	ADF test[a]	$\tau_{\text{S\&L}}$ test[b]			τ_{alt} test[b]		
			$f_t^{(1)}(\theta)$	$f_t^{(2)}(\theta)$	$f_t^{(3)}(\theta)$	$f_t^{(1)}(\theta)$	$f_t^{(2)}(\theta)$	$f_t^{(3)}(\theta)$
log GNP	4	−2.28	−1.59	−1.59	−1.79	−2.33	−2.33	−2.51
	5	−2.52	−1.80	−1.80	−2.19	−2.44	−2.44	−2.60
log M1	4	−3.19	−2.37	−2.25	−2.27	−2.36	−2.22	−2.22
	6	−1.82	−2.61	−2.36	−2.43	−2.37	−2.24	−2.24
log M3	4	−2.40	−0.80	−0.80	−1.15	−1.17	−1.17	−1.38
	6	−2.18	−0.80	−0.80	−1.15	−1.23	−1.23	−1.35
log IP	2	−1.68	−2.02	−3.08	−2.88	−1.68	−3.41	−3.41
	4	−1.80	−2.07	−2.26	−2.07	−1.60	−3.12	−3.10

[a] Critical values: −3.96 (1%), −3.41 (5%), −3.12 (10%) (see Fuller 1976, Table 8.5.2, $\hat{\tau}_\tau$, $n = \infty$).
[b] Critical values: −3.48 (1%), −2.89 (5%), −2.57 (10%) (see Elliott, Rothenberg, and Stock 1996, Table I.C, $T = \infty$).

the insignificant test values based on $f_t^{(1)}$ suggest that this shift function may be too rigid for the presently considered series. The overall conclusion from these examples is that both model types may be valuable tools for unit root analysis when series have level shifts.

5   Conclusions

Many economic time series exhibit level shifts in some known time period due to a special event. It is important to take such shifts into account in unit root tests because the standard tests for unit roots are distorted and may have low power if such shifts are ignored. A quite general class of tests has been proposed in this chapter for taking care of deterministic level shifts. They have the convenient feature that they allow for smooth transitions from one level to some other level over an extended period of time. Such a smooth transition to a new state is often more realistic than assuming an abrupt shift to a new level. Although there are other unit root tests which can accommodate smooth shifts in the level of a time series, the tests proposed here have the advantage that the corresponding test statistics are very easy to compute for quite general shift functions. Moreover, their asymptotic null distribution is known from the unit root literature, and tables with critical values exist. The tests have been applied to economic time series to illustrate how they work in practice.

In empirical work it is quite common that the timing of the level shift is known, as in the examples considered in the foregoing. However, there are also occasions where the exact time of the shift is unknown. We intend to investigate extensions of the tests to this case in future research.

Appendix: Proofs

We will first present some asymptotic properties of the estimators of the nuisance parameters and then prove Theorem 1.

A.1   *Properties of estimators*

Some properties of the nonlinear LS estimators obtained via (12.3.4) are given in the following lemma. The lemma assumes local alternatives as specified by (12.3.1) so that the null hypothesis is obtained by setting $c = 0$.

Lemma A.1. *Suppose that the assumptions of Theorem 1 hold. Then*

$$\tilde{b} \xrightarrow{p} b, \tag{12.A.1}$$

$$\tilde{\theta} = \theta + O_p(1), \tag{12.A.2}$$

$$\tilde{\gamma} = \gamma + O_p(1), \tag{12.A.3}$$

$$\tilde{\mu}_0 = \mu_0 + O_p(1), \tag{12.A.4}$$

and

$$T^{1/2}\left(\tilde{\mu}_1 - \frac{\tilde{b}(1)\mu_1}{b(1)}\right) \xrightarrow{d} \sigma\left(\lambda B_c(1) + 3(1-\lambda)\int_0^1 s B_c(s)\, ds\right), \tag{12.A.5}$$

where $\lambda = (1 - \bar{c})/(1 - \bar{c} + \bar{c}^2/3)$.

Lemma A.1 shows that the estimators $\tilde{b}$ and $\tilde{\mu}_1$ are consistent whereas $\tilde{\mu}_0$, $\tilde{\theta}$, and $\tilde{\gamma}$ are generally not. These latter estimators are only bounded in probability in general. For $\tilde{\theta}$ boundedness is, of course, trivial because the parameter space of θ is compact by assumption. However, for $\tilde{\mu}_0$ and $\tilde{\gamma}$ the situation is different because the parameter space of μ_0 and γ is unrestricted. The situation is similar to Lemma 1 of S&L except that the result for $\tilde{\mu}_1$ now involves the quantities $\tilde{b}(1)$ and $b(1)$. However, this result is precisely the one we need in the proof of Theorem 1. It is also possible to obtain the limiting distribution of $\tilde{\mu}_1$. That distribution is not needed in subsequent derivations, however, and it is therefore omitted. Since Assumption 1(b) implies that $f_t(\theta) - \bar{\rho}_T f_{t-1}(\theta) \approx \Delta f_t(\theta) \to 0$ as $t \to \infty$, the inconsistency of the estimators $\tilde{\gamma}$ and $\tilde{\theta}$ is expected, and a similar argument can be given for $\tilde{\mu}_0$.

The proof uses the same techniques as the proof of Lemma 1 in S&L. The following results from that proof are used here as well:

$$T^{-1}Z_1'Z_1 = h(\bar{c}) + O(T^{-1}), \tag{12.A.6}$$

where $h(\bar{c}) = 1 - \bar{c} + \bar{c}^2/3$,

$$T^{-1/2}Z_1'Z_2(\theta) = O(T^{-1/2}), \tag{12.A.7}$$

$$Z_2(\theta)'Z_2(\theta) = \sum_{t=1}^{T} \Delta g_t(\theta)\,\Delta g_t(\theta)' + O(T^{-1}) \tag{12.A.8}$$

uniformly in θ, where $g_t(\theta) = [1 : f_t(\theta)']'$ and $g_0(\theta) = 0$. Furthermore, defining $D_{1T} = \text{diag}[T^{1/2} : I_k]$ and $M_T(\theta) = \text{diag}[h(\bar{c}) : \sum_{t=1}^{T} \Delta g_t(\theta)\,\Delta g_t(\theta)']$,

$$D_{1T}^{-1}Z(\theta)'Z(\theta)D_{1T}^{-1} = M_T(\theta) + O(T^{-1/2}) \tag{12.A.9}$$

uniformly in θ. We note in passing that (12.A.9) implies that the matrix $Z(\theta)$ is of full column rank for all θ and all T large enough, because, by Assumption 1(c), the matrix $M_T(\theta)$ is positive definite for all θ and all T large enough.

Next we shall obtain an expression for the observed series by solving the difference equation defined by (12.2.6). This yields

$$y_t = s_{1t} + b(1)^{-1}\mu_0 + b(L)^{-1}t\mu_1 + b(L)^{-1}f_t(\theta)'\gamma + x_t, \qquad t = 1, 2, \ldots,$$

where $x_t = b(L)^{-1}v_t$ with $v_t = 0$ for $t \leq 0$, the trend term and the sequence $f_t(\theta)$ are defined as zero for $t \leq 0$, and the sequence s_{1t} contains transient effects due to the presample values of y_t. As is well known, s_{1t} converges to zero exponentially as $t \to \infty$. Using the decomposition $b(L)^{-1} = b(1)^{-1} + b^*(L)\Delta$, we can write $b(L)^{-1}t\mu_1 = b(1)^{-1}\mu_1 t + s_{2t}$, where s_{2t} contains transient effects similar to those in s_{1t} except that now these effects do not converge to zero but are bounded. Thus, we have

$$y_t = \mu_* t + k_t + x_t, \qquad t = 1, 2, \ldots, \tag{12.A.10}$$

where $\mu_* = b(1)^{-1}\mu_1$ and $k_t = s_{1t} + s_{2t} + b(1)^{-1}\mu_0 + b(L)^{-1}f_t(\theta)'\gamma$. Notice that here the parameters indicate true values and that the properties of the sequence k_t are similar to those of $\mu_0 + f_t(\theta)'\gamma$. In particular, when Assumption 1(b) holds, the sequence Δk_t is absolutely summable. Transforming (12.A.10) by the filter $1 - \bar{\rho}_T L$ yields

$$y_t - \bar{\rho}_T y_{t-1} = Z_{1t}\mu_* + k_t - \bar{\rho}_T k_{t-1} + u_t, \qquad t = 1, 2, \ldots, \tag{12.A.11}$$

where $k_0 = 0$ and

$$\begin{aligned}
u_t &= x_t - \bar{\rho}_T x_{t-1} = x_t - \rho_T x_{t-1} + (\rho_T - \bar{\rho}_T)x_{t-1} \\
&= b(L)^{-1}(v_t - \rho_T v_{t-1}) + T^{-1}(c - \bar{c})x_{t-1} \\
&= b(L)^{-1}\varepsilon_t + T^{-1}(c - \bar{c})x_{t-1} \\
&\stackrel{\text{def}}{=} u_t^{(0)} + T^{-1}(c - \bar{c})x_{t-1}.
\end{aligned} \tag{12.A.12}$$

Note that the above remark made for the sequence Δk_t implies that the second sample moments between Z_{1t} and $k_t - \bar{\rho}_T k_{t-1}$ as well as between u_t and $k_t - \bar{\rho}_T k_{t-1}$ converge to zero in probability [for the latter, see the justification of (A.13) of S&L].

We shall demonstrate next that, uniformly in θ,

$$D_T^{-1} W(\theta)' W(\theta) D_T^{-1} = \text{diag}\left[R_{11} : \sum_{t=1}^{T} \Delta g_t(\theta)\, \Delta g_t(\theta)' \right] + o_p(1)$$

$$\stackrel{\text{def}}{=} R_T(\theta) + o_p(1), \qquad (12.\text{A}.13)$$

where $D_T = \text{diag}[T^{1/2} I_{p+1} : I_{k+1}]$ and

$$R_{11} = \begin{bmatrix} \sigma^2 \Sigma(b) + \mu_*^2 h(\bar{c}) \mathbf{1}_p \mathbf{1}_p' & \mu_* h(\bar{c}) \mathbf{1}_p \\ \mu_* h(\bar{c}) \mathbf{1}_p' & h(\bar{c}) \end{bmatrix}.$$

Here $\Sigma(b) = \sigma^{-2} \text{Cov}(u_1^{(0)}, \ldots, u_p^{(0)})$, $\mathbf{1}_p = [1 : \cdots : 1]'$ ($p \times 1$), and the other notation is as before. To justify (12.A.13), recall that $W(\theta) = [V : Z(\theta)]$ where the ith column of the matrix V consists of $y_{t-i} - \bar{\rho}_T y_{t-i-1}$ ($i = 1, \ldots, p$, $t = 1, \ldots, T$). Thus, a typical element of the matrix $T^{-1} V' V$ is

$$T^{-1} \sum_{t=1}^{T} [y_{t-i} - \bar{\rho}_T y_{t-i-1}][y_{t-j} - \bar{\rho} y_{t-j-1}]$$

$$= T^{-1} \sum_{t=1}^{T} [Z_{1,t-i} \mu_* + u_{t-i}][Z_{1,t-j} \mu_* + u_{t-j}] + o_p(1)$$

$$= \mu_*^2 T^{-1} Z_1' Z_1 + T^{-1} \sum_{t=1}^{T} u_{t-i} u_{t-j} + o_p(1)$$

$$= \mu_*^2 T^{-1} Z_1' Z_1 + T^{-1} \sum_{t=1}^{T} u_{t-i}^{(0)} u_{t-j}^{(0)} + o_p(1)$$

$$\stackrel{p}{\rightarrow} \mu_*^2 h(\bar{c}) + \text{Cov}\left(u_{t-i}^{(0)}, u_{t-j}^{(0)}\right). \qquad (12.\text{A}.14)$$

The first equality in (12.A.14) follows from (12.A.11) and the remark made after it. The second equality is based on the fact that the sample mean of u_t is of order $o_p(1)$. This can be established by using (12.A.12) and well-known properties of stationary and near-integrated processes, which also imply the third equality. Finally, the stated convergence in probability is justified by (12.A.6) and a weak law of large numbers.

Next recall the definition $Z(\theta) = [Z_1 : Z_2(\theta)]$, and notice that a typical component of the vector $T^{-1}V'Z_1$ is

$$
T^{-1}\sum_{t=1}^{T} Z_{1t}[y_{t-i} - \bar{\rho}_T y_{t-i-1}] = T^{-1}\sum_{t=1}^{T} Z_{1t}[Z_{1,t-i}\mu_* + u_{t-i-1}] + o_p(1)
$$

$$
= T^{-1}Z_1'Z_1\mu_* + o_p(1)
$$

$$
\xrightarrow{p} \mu_* h(\bar{c}). \tag{12.A.15}
$$

Here the stated conclusions can be justified in the same way as in (12.A.14). Now, from (12.A.14), (12.A.15) and (12.A.6) we can conclude that, as far as the $(p+1) \times (p+1)$ upper left hand corner is concerned, the result stated in (12.A.13) holds. It follows from (12.A.8) that the same is true for the $(k+1) \times (k+1)$ lower right hand corner of the matrix in (12.A.13). Thus, it remains to show that $T^{-1/2}Z_2(\theta)'V = o_p(1)$. A typical column of this matrix is

$$
T^{-1/2}\sum_{t=1}^{T} Z_{2t}(\theta)[y_{t-i} - \bar{\rho}_T y_{t-i-1}]
$$

$$
= T^{-1/2}\sum_{t=1}^{T}\left[\Delta g_t(\theta) - \frac{\bar{c}}{T}g_{t-1}(\theta)\right][y_{t-i} - \bar{\rho}_T y_{t-i-1}]
$$

$$
= o_p(1)
$$

uniformly in θ. Here, the first equality follows from the definition of $Z_2(\theta)$ (see S&L). The second one is based on (12.A.11) and remarks made regarding the properties of the sequences therein. Thus, we have established (12.A.13).

Next note that from (12.3.7) and (12.3.4) it follows that

$$
D_T(\hat{\beta} - \beta) = \left(D_T^{-1}W(\tilde{\theta})'W(\tilde{\theta})D_T^{-1}\right)^{-1}D_T^{-1}W(\tilde{\theta})'\mathcal{E}
$$

$$
+ \left(D_T^{-1}W(\tilde{\theta})'W(\tilde{\theta})D_T^{-1}\right)^{-1}D_T^{-1}W(\tilde{\theta})'\zeta, \tag{12.A.16}
$$

where $\zeta = (Z_2(\theta) - Z_2(\tilde{\theta}))[\mu_0 : \gamma']'$. In the second term on the r.h.s. of (12.A.16) we have

$$
D_T^{-1}W(\tilde{\theta})'\zeta = \begin{bmatrix} T^{-1/2}V'\zeta \\ T^{-1/2}Z_1'\zeta \\ Z_2(\tilde{\theta})'\zeta \end{bmatrix} = \begin{bmatrix} o_p(1) \\ o_p(1) \\ O_p(1) \end{bmatrix}. \tag{12.A.17}
$$

Here the last two results can be established in exactly the same way as (12.A.10) of S&L. As to the first one, note that the components of ζ define an absolutely summable sequence (see the discussion leading to (A.10) of S&L). Then the desired result is obtained by using (12.A.11) and the remarks made below it. It is straightforward to check that the matrix R_{11} in (12.A.13) is positive definite. From this property and Assumption 1(c) it further follows that the matrix $R_T(\theta)$ is positive definite for all θ and all T large enough. Thus, (12.A.13) and Lemma A2 of Saikkonen & Lütkepohl (1996) yield

$$\left(D_T^{-1} W(\tilde{\theta})' W(\tilde{\theta}) D_T^{-1} \right)^{-1} = R_T^{-1}(\tilde{\theta}) + o_p(1). \tag{12.A.18}$$

Using (12.A.11) and (12.3.5), it is straightforward to check that $T^{-1/2} V' \mathcal{E} = O_p(1)$, while $T^{-1/2} Z_1' \mathcal{E} = O_p(1)$ and $Z_2(\tilde{\theta})' \mathcal{E} = O_p(1)$ can be established in the same way as (A.12) and (A.13) of S&L. Thus, combining (12.A.18) with (12.A.16) and (12.A.17) shows that

$$\begin{bmatrix} T^{1/2}(\tilde{b} - b) \\ T^{1/2}(\tilde{\mu}_1 - \mu_1) \end{bmatrix} = R_{11}^{-1} \begin{bmatrix} T^{-1/2} V' \mathcal{E} \\ T^{-1/2} Z_1' \mathcal{E} \end{bmatrix} + o_p(1). \tag{12.A.19}$$

The definition of the matrix R_{11} shows that a premultiplication of (12.A.19) by $[\mu_* \mathbf{1}_p' : 1]$ gives

$$T^{1/2}(\mu_* \mathbf{1}_p'(\tilde{b} - b) + \tilde{\mu}_1 - \mu_1) = h(\bar{c})^{-1} T^{-1/2} Z_1' \mathcal{E} + o_p(1). \tag{12.A.20}$$

On the l.h.s. we have

$$\mu_* \mathbf{1}_p'(\tilde{b} - b) = b(1)^{-1} \mu_1 \left(\sum_{j=1}^p \tilde{b}_i - \sum_{j=1}^p b_j \right)$$
$$= -b(1)^{-1} \mu_1 (\tilde{b}(1) - b(1))$$
$$= -\tilde{b}(1) b(1)^{-1} \mu_1 + \mu_1.$$

Thus, the l.h.s. of (12.A.20) equals the l.h.s. of (12.A.5). Moreover, the r.h.s. of (12.A.20) converges in distribution to the r.h.s. of (12.A.5) by arguments given in Elliott, Rothenberg, and Stock (1996) and in the proof of Lemma 1 of S&L. Thus, we have proved (12.A.5), while (12.A.1) is a straightforward consequence of (12.A.19). Finally, (12.A.2) is trivial, while (12.A.3) and (12.A.4) are obtained from (12.A.16)–(12.A.18) and the fact that the smallest eigenvalue of $R_T(\tilde{\theta})$ is bounded away from zero by (12.A.13) and Assumption 1(c). This completes the proof of Lemma A.1.

If seasonal dummies are included in the model, the matrix $W(\theta)$ is defined as $W(\theta) = [V : Z_1 : Z_3 : Z_2(\theta)]$, where Z_3 is the matrix containing the values of the seasonal dummies corresponding to $y_1, \ldots, y_T$ transformed by the filter $1 - \bar{\rho}_T L$. Redefining the dimension of the identity matrix in the definition of

D_T, we still have (12.A.13) except that R_{11} is changed to

$$
R_{11} = \begin{bmatrix} \sigma^2 \Sigma(b) + \mu_*^2 \mathbf{1}_p \mathbf{1}_p' & \mu_* h(\bar{c}) \mathbf{1}_p & A \\ \mu_* h(\bar{c}) \mathbf{1}_p' & h(\bar{c}) & 0 \\ A' & 0 & B \end{bmatrix},
$$

where $A = \text{plim } T^{-1} V' Z_3$, $B = \text{plim } T^{-1} Z_3' Z_3$, and the zero matrix results because $\text{plim } T^{-1} Z_1' Z_3 = 0$, as shown in S&L. It is not difficult to check that $R_{11} > 0$. Since it is also straightforward to verify that $T^{-1/2} Z_3' \mathcal{E} = O_p(1)$ and $T^{-1/2} Z_3' \zeta = o_p(1)$, we have an analog of (12.A.19) with the two vectors in the brackets augmented to allow for the estimation of the coefficients of the seasonal dummies. Premultiplying this new version of (12.A.19) by the vector $[\mu_* \mathbf{1}_p' : 1 : 0]$ shows that we still have (12.A.20), so that (12.A.5) holds even when seasonal dummies are included in the model. According to what was said above, it is clear that (12.A.1)–(12.A.4) also hold and that the coefficient estimators related to the seasonal dummies are consistent.

A.2   *Proof of Theorem 1*

By the definition of $\tilde{v}_t$ and (12.A.10) one obtains

$$
\begin{aligned}
\tilde{v}_t &= \tilde{b}(L) \mu_* t + \tilde{b}(L) k_t + \tilde{b}(L) x_t - \tilde{\mu}_0 - \tilde{\mu}_1 t - f_t(\tilde{\theta})' \tilde{\gamma} \\
&= v_t + \tilde{b}(L) \mu_* t + \tilde{b}(L) k_t + (\tilde{b}(L) - b(L)) x_t - \tilde{\mu}_0 - \tilde{\mu}_1 t - f_t(\tilde{\theta})' \tilde{\gamma},
\end{aligned}
$$

where $\tilde{b}(L)$ is defined in an obvious way and the latter equality is based on the identity $b(L) x_t = v_t$. Now recall that $\mu_* = b(1)^{-1} \mu_1$ and use the representation $b(L) = b(1) + b_*(L) \Delta$ to obtain from the above

$$
\begin{aligned}
\tilde{v}_t &= v_t - (\tilde{\mu}_1 - \tilde{b}(1) b(1)^{-1} \mu_1) t + \tilde{b}_*(1) \mu_* + \tilde{b}(L) k_t \\
&\quad + (\tilde{b}(1) - b(1)) x_t + (\tilde{b}_*(L) - b_*(L)) \Delta x_t - \tilde{\mu}_0 - f_t(\tilde{\theta})' \tilde{\gamma}.
\end{aligned}
$$

From (12.3.3) we have $T^{-1/2} v_{[Ts]} \xrightarrow{d} \sigma B_c(s)$. Thus, from the above equality, Lemma A.1, and arguments similar to those used in the proof of Theorem 1 in S&L it follows that

$$
\begin{aligned}
T^{-1/2} \tilde{v}_{[Ts]} &= T^{-1/2} v_{[Ts]} - T^{1/2} (\tilde{\mu}_1 - \tilde{b}(1) b(1)^{-1} \mu_1) \frac{[Ts]}{T} + o_p(1) \\
&\xrightarrow{d} \sigma G_c(s; \bar{c}).
\end{aligned}
$$

Proceeding in the same way as in the proof of Theorem 1 of S&L, it is straightforward to use the above result to obtain the limiting distribution of the test statistic τ_{alt}. Details are omitted.

Now suppose that seasonal dummies are included in the model. Then, according to what was said above about parameter estimation in this context, it is clear that the counterpart of the residual series $\tilde{v}_t$ obtained in this case satisfies $T^{-1/2}\tilde{v}_{[Ts]} \xrightarrow{d} \sigma G_c(s; \bar{c})$, so that the resulting test statistic has the same limiting distribution as in the model where no seasonal dummies are included.

REFERENCES

Amemiya, T. (1983), "Non-Linear Regression Models," in Z. Griliches and M. D. Intriligator, eds., *Handbook of Econometrics, Volume I* (Amsterdam: North-Holland), pp. 333–389.

(1985), *Advanced Econometrics* (Cambridge, MA: Harvard University Press).

Amsler, C. and Lee, J. (1995), "An LM Test for a Unit Root in the Presence of a Structural Change," *Econometric Theory*, **11**, 359–368.

Banerjee, A., Lumsdaine, R. L., and Stock, J. H. (1992), "Recursive and Sequential Tests of the Unit-Root and Trend-Break Hypotheses: Theory and International Evidence," *Journal of Business & Economic Statistics*, **10**, 271–287.

Elliott, G., Rothenberg, T. J., and Stock, J. H. (1996), "Efficient Tests for an Autoregressive Unit Root," *Econometrica*, 64, 813–836.

Fuller, W. A. (1976), *Introduction to Statistical Time Series* (New York: John Wiley).

Hwang, J. and Schmidt, P. (1996), "Alternative Methods of Detrending and the Power of Unit Root Tests," *Journal of Econometrics*, **71**, 227–248.

Judge, G. G., Griffiths, W. E., Hill, R. C., Lütkepohl, H., and Lee, T. C. (1985), *The Theory and Practice of Econometrics*, 2nd ed. (New York: John Wiley).

Leybourne, S., Newbold, P., and Vougas, D. (1998), "Unit Roots and Smooth Transitions," *Journal of Time Series Analysis*, **19**, 83–97.

Montañés, A. and Reyes, M. (1998), "Effect of a Shift in the Trend Function on Dickey–Fuller Unit Root Tests," *Econometric Theory*, **14**, 355–363.

Perron, P. (1989), "The Great Crash, the Oil Price Shock and the Unit Root Hypothesis," *Econometrica*, **57**, 1361–1401.

(1990), "Testing for a Unit Root in a Time Series with a Changing Mean," *Journal of Business & Economic Statistics*, **8**, 153–162.

Perron, P. and Vogelsang, T. J. (1992), "Nonstationarity and Level Shifts with an Application to Purchasing Power Parity," *Journal of Business & Economic Statistics*, **10**, 301–320.

Saikkonen, P. and Lütkepohl, H. (1996), "Infinite-Order Cointegrated Vector Autoregressive Processes: Estimation and Inference," *Econometric Theory*, **12**, 814–844.

(1999), "Testing for Unit Roots in Time Series with Level Shifts," Discussion Paper, SFB 373, Humboldt-Universität zu Berlin.

Seber, G. A. F. and Wild, C. J. (1989), *Nonlinear Regression* (New York: John Wiley).

Zivot, E. and Andrews, D. W. K. (1992), "Further Evidence on the Great Crash, the Oil-Price Shock, and the Unit-Root Hypothesis," *Journal of Business & Economic Statistics*, **10**, 251–270.

CHAPTER 13

Power comparisons of the discontinuous trend unit root tests

Kimio Morimune and Mitsuru Nakagawa

1   Introduction

Perron (1989) developed unit root tests which allow for a break in the deterministic trend. The Perron test is asymptotically similar. Related tests have also been suggested by Schmidt and Phillips (1992), Oya and Toda (1998), Bhargava (1986, 1996), and Kiviet and Phillips (1992). In this chapter, we extend the Perron unit root tests to allow for multiple breaks in the trend and investigate both their asymptotic and finite sample properties.

Zivot and Andrews (1992) have studied the unit root test when the location of a break point is unknown. They used the t ratio associated with the lagged dependent variable to find the break point. However, the null distribution requires no break in the trend function. Vogelsang and Perron (1998) used the t ratio of the discontinuous trend variable to find the break point. Hatanaka and Yamada (1997) used the residual variance to find the break point, and extended the Zivot–Andrews test so that the null hypothesis allows a discontinuous trend. Break points resulting from these tests may conflict with common knowledge, since researchers have rough ideas on when the break actually happened. The Perron test may be applied by setting a wide break interval that possibly covers a break point through the use of shock dummy variables.

In Section 2 we propose a unified framework for the unit root tests that allow for multiple breaks in both the intercepts and trend coefficients as in the Perron C model, for multiple breaks in intercepts only as in the Perron A model, and for joined trend lines as in the Perron B model. Both t test and F test statistics are suggested. Section 3 considers other asymptotically similar tests. Asymptotic power comparison of these tests is discussed in Section 4. Finite sample simulation results are also summarized in this section. Conclusions are in Section 5. Proofs are sketched in the Appendix.

The authors thank Mico Loretan, Cheng Hsiao, Yukinobu Kitamura, and Hidetaka Ohara at the Bank of Japan seminar and anonymous referees for their useful comments.

2   Unit root tests allowing for multiple breaks

There are several examples of time series data that may encounter multiple breaks in the trend term. For instance, it is commonly argued that the postwar Japanese macro series have two breaks caused by the oil price shock and by the bubble economy. Kunitomo and Sato (1995) and Ohara (1996) have studied the theoretical and empirical aspects of the test allowing for two or more break points, using the likelihood ratio statistic. We shall begin by considering a generalization of Perron's C formulation that allows changes in both the intercept and trend coefficients. We then indicate how this formulation can be modified to cover Perron's A case in which the trend coefficient stays the same and the intercepts vary, and the B case in which consecutive trends are joined at the break points.

Suppose that the time series observations $1, 2, \ldots, T$ can be broken into K intervals to allow for $K - 1$ breaks in the deterministic trend. Let the number of observations at the end of K intervals be T_i, $i = 1, \ldots, K$, and assume that each break is given as the first observation after the end of an interval. Step dummy variables, denoted by DU_{it}, are 1 for $t = T_{i-1} + 1, \ldots, T_i$ and zero otherwise for $i = 1, \ldots, K$, and $T_0 = 0$. The sample size is T, which is equal to T_k under the assumption of $K - 1$ breaks in the deterministic trend, and $\sum_{i=1}^{K} DU_{it} = 1$ for all t. Shock dummy variables, denoted D_{it}, are 1 when $t = T_{i-1} + 1$ and zero otherwise, $i = 2, \ldots, K$. Then there are $K - 1$ shock dummy variables, that is, one less than the number of intervals.

Let the regression equation of the test be[1]

$$y_t = m(t) + u_t, \qquad u_t = (1 + \phi)u_{t-1} + \varepsilon_t, \qquad u_1 = 0, \qquad (13.1)$$

where $m(t) = \sum_{i=1}^{K}(\alpha_i^* + \beta_i^* t)DU_{it}$. The initial value $y_1 = m(1) = \alpha_1^* + \beta_1^*$, which is nonstochastic. If $m(t)$ is a linear function $(\alpha + \beta t)$, or K is 1, the test proposed below will be identical to the original Dickey–Fuller test.

Following Dickey and Fuller (1981), we rewrite (13.1) as

$$\{1 - (1 + \phi)L\}u_t = \{1 - (1 + \phi)L\}\{y_t - m(t)\} = \varepsilon_t, \qquad t = 2, \ldots, T, \quad (13.2)$$

under the alternative hypothesis. The equation (13.2) is expanded as

$$\Delta y_t = \phi y_{t-1} + \sum_{i=1}^{K}\{\beta_i^* + \phi(\beta_i^* - \alpha_i^*)\}DU_{it} - \sum_{i=1}^{K}\beta_i^* \phi t\, DU_{it}$$

$$+ \sum_{i=2}^{K}(1 + \phi)\{\alpha_i^* - \alpha_{i-1}^* + (\beta_i^* - \beta_{i-1}^*)T_{i-1}\}D_{it} + \varepsilon_t, \quad (13.3)$$

and the error term is independently distributed with mean zero and variance σ^2.

---

[1] We owe this simplification of formulae to a referee.

This equation is recast as

$$\Delta y_t = \phi y_{t-1} + \sum_{i=1}^{K} \alpha_i DU_{it} + \sum_{i=1}^{K} \beta_i t DU_{it} + \sum_{i=2}^{K} \gamma_i D_{it} + \varepsilon_t, \qquad t = 2, \ldots, T,$$

(13.4)

where the coefficients bear nonlinear restrictions, as can be seen by comparing (13.3) and (13.4). The equation (13.4) is an auxiliary regression from which t and F ratio test statistics follow.

The null hypothesis of the unit root test is $H_0 : \phi = 0$ in (13.2) or (13.3). The null regression, or data generating process (abbreviated as DGP hereafter), is

$$\Delta y_t = m(t) - m(t-1) + \varepsilon_t$$
$$= \sum_{i=1}^{k} \beta_i^* DU_{it} + \sum_{i=2}^{k} \{\alpha_i^* - \alpha_{i-1}^* + (\beta_i^* - \beta_{i-1}^*)T_{i-1}\}D_{it} + \varepsilon_t,$$

(13.5)

which is linear in the coefficients, and all coefficients are identified using all observations, including the initial value. The t ratio on the coefficient ϕ in the auxiliary regression (13.4) is the Dickey–Fuller test statistic

$$\hat{t}_{CM} = \frac{\sum_{i=1}^{K} \sum_{t=1}^{T} y_{t-1}^+ \Delta y_t (DU_{it} - D_{it})}{\sqrt{\hat{\sigma}^2 \sum_{i=1}^{K} \sum_{t=1}^{T} y_{t-1}^{+2}(DU_{it} - D_{it})}},$$

(13.6)

where y_{t-1}^+ is the residual of regressing y_{t-1} on all other explanatory variables in (13.4) and is used in the Appendix, and $\hat{\sigma}^2$ is the sum of the squared residuals in the alternative regression (denoted as RSS$_A$) divided by T. The t ratio converges to τ_{CM}, which is defined by (13.A4) in the Appendix. The t test diverges to infinity if the D_{it} terms in (13.4) are neglected, as we can see in many empirical studies. Intuitively, Δy_t in (13.6) must come from one interval and should not have footings in two consecutive intervals. For example, a term in the summation such as Δy_{T_1+1} is $O_p(T)$, since $(y_{T_1+1} - y_{T_1})/T \approx (\beta_2 - \beta_1)T_1/T$, and plim$_T$ $y_{T_1}^+ \Delta_{T_1+1}^y/(T\sqrt{T})$ is proportional to $\tilde{B}_1(1)(\beta_2 - \beta_1)$ where $\tilde{B}_1(1)$ is defined in the Appendix, and is a $n(0, 1/3)$ random variable. This happens only at the break points. It causes an explosion in the asymptotic formula (see Appendix). The factor $DU_{it} - D_{it}$ serves to skip such terms as Δy_{T_1+1} at break points.

The F ratio test statistic associated with the coefficients $\phi, \beta_1, \ldots, \beta_K$ in (13.4) is

$$\Psi_{CM} = \frac{1}{(K+1)\hat{\sigma}^2}(\text{RSS}_0 - \text{RSS}_A)$$

(13.7)

where RSS_0 is the sum of squared residuals under H_0. Here Ψ_{CM} is identical with

$$\Psi_{CM} = \frac{1}{K+1}\left\{(\hat{\tau}_{CM})^2 + \sum_{i=1}^{K}\frac{\{\sum \Delta y_t(t-\bar{t}_i^+)(DU_{it}-D_{it})\}^2}{\hat{\sigma}^2\sum[(t-\bar{t}_i^+)(DU_{it}-D_{it})]^2}\right\}, \qquad (13.8)$$

and $\bar{t}_i^+$ is the mean of the trend in an interval. (This notation is used in the Appendix.) Under the null hypothesis $H_0:\phi = 0$, the F ratio asymptotically converges to

$$\Psi_{CM} \Rightarrow \frac{1}{K+1}\{(\tau_{CM})^2 + \chi^2(K)\} \qquad (13.9)$$

where the two terms in the right hand side are independently distributed. The DGP (13.5) includes the shock and step dummy variables, which do not affect this limit.

It is straightforward to generalize tests (13.6) and (13.7) into the model of higher-order autoregressive processes. The nonparametric approach by Phillips (1987) and Phillips and Perron (1988) can be adapted easily. The tests can be generalized to cover Perron's A and B models. The A test follows by setting all the trend coefficients in $m(t)$ equal, and $m(t) = \alpha + \sum_{i=2}^{k}\alpha_i DU_{it} + \beta t$. In the B test, $m(t) = \alpha + \sum_{i=1}^{K}\beta_i(t-T_{i-1})\sum_{j=i}^{K}DU_{jt}$, which guarantees continuous trend functions under both hypotheses.

3   Nonlinear regression test

Here we give nonlinear regression tests for $H_0:\phi = 0$. Firstly, we estimate coefficients $\theta^* = (\phi, \beta_1^*, \ldots, \beta_k^*, \alpha_1^*, \ldots, \alpha_K^*)$ in the nonlinear equation (13.3) by a nonlinear least squares method, and calculate the sum of squared residuals denoted RSS_A. Secondly, we estimate the null coefficients $\theta_0^* = (0, \beta_1^*, \ldots, \beta_K^*, \alpha_1^*, \ldots, \alpha_K^*)$ in (13.3), and calculate RSS_0. The F ratio is used as a test statistic, that is,

$$F_{CM} = \frac{1}{\hat{\sigma}^2}(RSS_0 - RSS_A), \qquad (13.10)$$

where $\hat{\sigma}^2 = RSS_A/(T-2K-1)$. Under the null hypothesis, the F ratio converges to

$$F_{CM} \Rightarrow (\tau_{CM})^2, \qquad (13.11)$$

which is proved in the Appendix. The difference between Ψ_{CM} and F_{CM} is obvious.

Other tests using the common factor expression (13.1) are derived by Perron (1989), Schmidt and Phillips (1992), and Oya and Toda (1998). In Perron, ϕ is consistently estimated by the OLS estimator of ϕ in the regression equation

$$\Delta \hat{u}_t = \phi \hat{u}_{t-1} + \sum_{i=2}^{K} \gamma_i D_{it} + \text{error}, \tag{13.12}$$

where $\hat{u}_t$ is the OLS residual calculated from $y_t = m(t) + u_t$. It is also noted that the first round least squares estimator can be spurious under the unit root hypothesis. The shock dummy variables such as D_{it} are used to omit observations at the break points in estimation. The t ratio of ϕ for the C model is

$$\hat{\tau}_{CM}^* = \frac{\sum_{t=1}^{T} \hat{u}_{t-1} \, \Delta \hat{u}_t (DU_{it} - D_{it})}{\hat{\sigma} \sqrt{\sum_{i=1}^{T} \hat{u}_{t-1}^2 (DU_{it} - D_{it})}}, \tag{13.13}$$

which converges to τ_{CM} under the null hypothesis $H_0 : \phi = 0$. Note that this test also requires the shock dummy variables. Intuitively, $\Delta \hat{u}_t$ in (13.10) must come from one interval and should not have footings on the two consecutive intervals. For example, $\Delta \hat{u}_{T_1+1} / \sqrt{T}$ is $O_p(\sqrt{T})$, and $\hat{u}_{T_1} \Delta \hat{u}_{T_1+1} / T$ is $O_p(1)$. This causes additional terms in the asymptotic formula. (See Appendix.)

The difference between the two test statistics (13.6) and (13.13) is small once shock dummy variables are incorporated, and (13.6) is interpreted as an auxiliary regression test statistic which replaces (13.13) in testing $H_0 : \phi = 0$ in (13.10).

It is appealing to use the OLS estimator of ϕ in the test, since it is the first-order autocorrelation of the residual, and since the autocorrelation of a random walk process is known to be close to unity and does not fade out. The difference between (13.6) and (13.13) comes mostly from the difference between Δy_t and $\Delta \hat{u}_t$ in the numerator, which is $O_p(1/\sqrt{T})$. See (13.A5) and (13.A6) in the Appendix. The values of y_t^+ and $\hat{u}_t$ are very close.

If the error term has a higher-order autoregression, a regression such as

$$\Delta \hat{u}_t = \phi \hat{u}_{t-1} + b_1 \, \Delta \hat{u}_{t-1} + \cdots + b_{P-1} \, \Delta \hat{u}_{t-P+1} + \sum_{i=2}^{K} \gamma_i D_{it} + \text{error} \tag{13.14}$$

must be estimated. The t ratio of the coefficient ϕ is the test statistic. The limit of the t ratio is τ_{CM}, as is proved in the Appendix.

It is natural to extend the test to the Dickey–Fuller framework without a discontinuous trend. When a time series has an intercept and a trend term, the residuals from $y_t = \alpha + \beta t + u_t$ should be calculated before calculating the t ratio for ϕ, and the τ_τ table must be used. This is Theorem 1 in Oya and Toda (1998). It is also noted that the first round least squares estimator of β is consistent but that of α is spurious under the unit root hypothesis.

4   Power comparison

The four unit root test statistics in a regression with a discontinuous trend are listed as follows:

$$\hat{\tau}_{CM} \text{ of (13.6)} \quad \text{for testing } H_0 : \phi = 0 \text{ in (13.1)}, \qquad (13.15a)$$

$$\Psi_{CM} \text{ of (13.7)} \quad \text{for testing } H_0 : \phi = 0 \text{ in (13.1)}, \qquad (13.15b)$$

$$F_{CM} \text{ of (13.10) for testing } H_0 : \phi = 0 \text{ in (13.3)}, \qquad (13.15c)$$

$$\hat{\tau}_{CM}^* \text{ of (13.13) for testing } H_0 : \phi = 0 \text{ in (13.1)}. \qquad (13.15d)$$

It should be noted that the DGP process is always calculated from (13.1) with $\phi = 0$. (13.15c) is interesting, but its asymptotic power is the same as that of (13.5d), as is proved in the Appendix. Because of its nonlinearity, (13.15c) is replaced by (13.15d), which may be again approximated by (13.6). [In the stationary analyses, the nonlinear estimator required in (13.10) is more efficient than the two-step OLS estimator required in (13.13). However, this difference is of smaller order of magnitude in the unit root analyses.]

The asymptotic powers of (13.13) and (13.6) are the same, as proved in the Appendix. Since the difference between these two formulae is small, the small-sample powers are compared by the simulation technique.

The powers of the t ratio tests are calculated by simulations and tabulated in this section. The upper half of Table 13.1 gives the powers of (13.6) for small ϕ values. The lower half tabulates the difference in the powers of (13.6) and (13.13). The powers of (13.6) and (13.13) are calculated using own critical values, which are tabulated in the bottom part of the Table 13.1, since it is unfair to use critical values of another test. Even though the asymptotic powers are the same for the local alternative hypothesis $\exp(\nu/T)$, (13.6) has greater power than (13.13) in almost all cases. It seems reasonable to recommend the Dickey–Fuller t test in practice, since it is easy to use and has at least as much power as the Perron test. (The initial values are chosen randomly in the simulation results shown in Table 13.1, but we obtained very similar results in simulations with fixed initial values.)

5   Conclusion

The Perron formulation and the Dickey–Fuller formulation are very close, and the asymptotic power of the two tests is the same. Through simulations, the small-sample power of the Dickey–Fuller t test is found to be greater than that of the Perron test. Similar results hold for the coefficient test.

Although other tests studied by Schmidt and Phillips (1992) and Oya and Toda (1998) seem straightforward to derive, the t test is convenient to use. When the break point is unknown, the t ratio (13.6) easily fits in the Zivot–Andrews framework.

Table 13.1. *Power comparison of tests (13.6) and (13.13) using random initial values*

T	$1 + \phi$	Power of (13.6)								
		0.1	0.2	0.3	0.4	0.5	0.6	0.7	0.8	0.9
100	CV(6)	−3.71	−3.98	−4.15	−4.24	−4.27	−4.25	−4.15	−3.98	−3.69
	0.99	5.6	9.8	13.5	15.6	16.5	15.9	13.2	9.5	5.3
	0.95	8.3	13.7	17.7	19.7	20.7	19.7	16.9	13.1	8.0
	0.90	17.5	24.6	28.8	31.2	32.0	31.5	28.6	23.9	17.1
200	CV(6)	−3.70	−3.96	−4.14	−4.20	−4.22	−4.17	−4.09	−3.92	−3.68
	0.99	5.6	9.9	13.5	16.4	17.0	15.6	13.0	9.2	5.6
	0.95	17.4	23.5	27.9	30.7	31.0	30.4	28.0	23.5	17.3
	0.90	56.5	63.3	66.3	68.1	68.0	68.0	66.0	63.6	56.3
500	CV(6)	−3.70	−3.95	−4.09	−4.18	−4.19	−4.20	−4.08	−3.93	−3.73
	0.99	7.5	11.9	15.6	18.0	18.3	17.1	14.5	11.8	7.4
	0.95	73.6	78.0	79.4	80.7	80.7	79.9	79.8	77.8	73.8
	0.90	100.0	100.0	100.0	100.0	100.0	100.0	100.0	100.0	100.0
1000	CV(6)	−3.72	−3.94	−4.09	−4.17	−4.19	−4.19	−4.09	−3.96	−3.73
	0.99	16.3	22.3	25.9	28.4	28.8	27.9	25.9	21.6	15.9
	0.95	100.0	100.0	100.0	100.0	100.0	100.0	100.0	100.0	100.0
	0.90	100.0	100.0	100.0	100.0	100.0	100.0	100.0	100.0	100.0
		Power of (13.13)-Power of (13.6)								
100	CV(13)	−3.74	−4.06	−4.27	−4.37	−4.43	−4.41	−4.35	−4.22	−3.95
	0.99	−2.4	−3.0	−3.0	−2.6	−2.4	−1.9	−1.1	−0.4	−0.1
	0.95	−2.6	−3.6	−3.4	−3.0	−2.7	−2.0	−0.9	−0.5	−0.2
	0.90	−4.8	−4.6	−4.2	−3.6	−3.0	−3.1	−2.0	−1.2	−0.6
200	CV(13)	−3.65	−3.95	−4.18	−4.28	−4.30	−4.29	−4.24	−4.12	−3.91
	0.99	−2.4	−3.4	−3.4	−3.4	−3.2	−2.6	−1.3	−0.4	−0.1
	0.95	−5.6	−5.0	−4.8	−4.7	−4.1	−3.9	−3.3	−2.2	−1.7
	0.90	−9.6	−7.3	−6.0	−5.5	−4.4	−4.7	−4.2	−4.1	−3.2
500	CV(13)	−3.66	−3.94	−4.11	−4.21	−4.27	−4.30	−4.21	−4.09	−3.90
	0.99	−2.8	−3.1	−3.5	−3.1	−2.6	−1.9	−0.7	−1.0	−0.2
	0.95	−7.3	−5.0	−3.7	−3.2	−2.3	−2.4	−3.0	−3.6	−2.6
	0.90	0.0	0.0	0.0	0.0	0.0	0.0	0.0	0.0	0.0
1000	CV(13)	−3.64	−3.93	−4.12	−4.21	−4.26	−4.25	−4.21	−4.08	−3.90
	0.99	−4.9	−4.6	−4.1	−4.3	−3.5	−3.1	−2.6	−1.6	−1.0
	0.95	0.0	0.0	0.0	0.0	0.0	0.0	0.0	0.0	0.0
	0.90	0.0	0.0	0.0	0.0	0.0	0.0	0.0	0.0	0.0

Notes: Critical values are abbreviated as CV. Own critical values are used in calculating powers. The number of iteration is 10,000.

Appendix

A.1   *Limit of* $\hat{\tau}_{CM}$

It is convenient in the derivation below to orthogonalize the regressors in the right hand side of (13.4) but keep the definition of the coefficient ϕ unchanged. Applying the orthogonal transformations, (13.4) is

$$\Delta y_t = \sum_{i=1}^{K} \{\phi y_{t-1}^+ + \alpha_i^+ + \beta_i^+(t - \bar{t}_i^+)\}(DU_{it} - D_{it}) + \sum_{i=2}^{K} \gamma_i^+ D_{it} + \varepsilon_t, \quad (13.A1)$$

where the parameters in (13.4) are $\beta_i = \beta_i^+ - \phi\hat{\beta}_i^0$, $\alpha_i = \alpha_i^+ - \phi\bar{y}_i^+ - \beta_i\bar{t}_i^+$, and $\gamma_i = \phi y_{T_i-1}^+ + \alpha_i^+ + \beta_i^+(T_{i-1} + 1 - \bar{t}_i^+) + \gamma_i^+$; the shock dummy variables are used only to skip observations at break points; $y_{t-1}^+ = \sum_{i=1}^{K}\{y_{t-1} - \bar{y}_i^+ - \hat{\beta}_i^0(t - \bar{t}_i^+)\}(DU_{it} - D_{it})$, which is zero when D_{it} is one; $\bar{y}_i^+ = \sum_{t-1}^{T} y_{t-1}(DU_{it} - D_{it})/(T_i - T_{i\ 1} - 1)$; $\bar{t}_i^+ = (T_i + T_{i-1} + 2)/2$; and $\hat{\beta}_i^0 = \sum_{i=1}^{T}\{(t - \bar{t}_i^+)(DU_{it} - D_{it})y_{t-1}\}/\sum_{i=1}^{T}[(t - \bar{t}_i^+)(DU_{it} - D_{it})]^2$. Denoting the partial sum of the error term up to t as η_t, we have $u_t = \eta_t$, and the DGP under the null hypothesis $H_0 : \phi = 0$ is

$$y_t = \eta_t + m(t). \quad (13.A2)$$

This is consistent with (13.5). Then

$$\hat{\beta}_i^0 - \beta_i^+ \Rightarrow \frac{12\sigma}{\left(\lambda_i^2 + \lambda_i\lambda_{i-1} + \lambda_{i-1}^2\right)\sqrt{T_i - T_{i-1}}}$$

$$\times \int_0^1 \left(r - \frac{1}{2}\right) B_i(r)\, dr \equiv \frac{12\sigma}{\sqrt{T_i - T_{i-1}}}\tilde{\beta}_i, \quad (13.A3)$$

where $B(r)$ is the standard Brownian motion. Then $\hat{\beta}_i^0 - \beta_i^+$ is $O_p(1/\sqrt{T})$. After finding the limit of y_{t-1}^+, and defining $\tilde{B}_i(r) = B_i(r) - \bar{B}_i(1) - 12(r - 1/2)\tilde{\beta}_i$ and $\bar{B}_i(1) = \int_0^1 B_i(r)\, dr$, the t test statistic (13.6) converges to

$$\hat{\tau}_{CM} \Rightarrow \frac{\sum_{i=1}^{K} \lambda_i \int_0^1 \tilde{B}_i(r)\, dB_i(r)}{\sqrt{\sum_{i=1}^{K} \lambda_i^2 \int_0^1 \tilde{B}_i(r)^2\, dr}} \equiv \tau_{CM}. \quad (13.A4)$$

A similar result holds in the A test, where $\tilde{\beta}_i$ is replaced by a common $\tilde{\beta}$.

A.2   *Explosion when the shock dummy variable is omitted*

If D_t is not in (13.4), the numerator of the test statistic has an additional term $\sum_{i=2}^{K} \sum_{t=1}^{T} y_{t-1}^+ \Delta y_t D_{it}$ at $K - 1$ break points. Using (13.5), this term is equal to

$$\sum_{i=2}^{K} y_{T_{i-1}}^{+}\, \Delta y_{T_{i-1}+1} = \sum_{i=2}^{K} y_{T_{i-1}}^{+}\{\varepsilon_{T_{i-1}+1} + (\alpha_i - \alpha_{i-1}) + \beta_i(T_{i-1}+1) - \beta_{i-1}T_{i-1})\},$$

where the term in parentheses is $O_p(T)$. Dividing by $T\sqrt{T}$,

$$\operatorname*{plim}_{T} \frac{1}{T\sqrt{T}} \sum_{i=2}^{K} y_{T_{i-1}}^{+}\, \Delta y_{T_{i-1}+1} = \operatorname*{plim}_{T} \sum_{i=2}^{K} \left(\frac{1}{\sqrt{T}} y_{T_{i-1}}^{+} \right)(\beta_i - \beta_{i-1}) \left(\frac{T_{i-1}}{T} \right)$$

$$\propto \sum_{i=2}^{K} \tilde{B}_{i-1}(1)(\beta_i - \beta_{i-1}).$$

Thus the numerator of (13.A4) diverges.

A.3   Limit of $\hat{\tau}_{CM}^{*}$

Defining $\bar{y}_i = \sum_{t=1}^{T} y_t DU_{it}/(T_i - T_{i-1})$, $\bar{t}_i = (T_i + T_{i-1} + 1)/2$, and $\hat{\beta}_i = \sum_{t=1}^{T} \{(t - \bar{t}_i)DU_{it}y_t\}/\sum_{t=1}^{T}\{(t - \bar{t}_i)DU_{it}\}^2$, we have $\hat{u}_t = \sum_{i=1}^{K}\{y_t - \bar{y}_i - \hat{\beta}_i(t - \bar{t}_i)\}DU_{it}$. The quantities $\hat{u}_{t-1}$ here and y_{t-1}^{+} in (13.A1) are defined in the same subinterval, but the latter does not use the last observation in the interval in calculating the means of y and t and the trend coefficient. Thus, $\operatorname{plim}\sqrt{T}(\hat{u}_{t-1} - y_{t-1}^{+}) = 0$. The first difference in the residual is

$$\Delta\hat{u}_t = \sum_{i=1}^{K}(\Delta y_t - \hat{\beta}_i)(DU_{it} - D_{it}) + \sum_{i=2}^{K}\{\Delta y_t - (\bar{y}_i - \bar{y}_{i-1})$$

$$- \hat{\beta}_i(t - \bar{t}_i) + \hat{\beta}_{i-1}(t - 1 - \bar{t}_{i-1})\}D_{it}. \tag{13.A5}$$

By definition (13.13),

$$\sum_{t=2}^{T} \hat{u}_{t-1}\, \Delta\hat{u}_t \sum_{i=1}^{K}(DU_{it} - D_{it})$$

$$= \sum_{i=1}^{K}\sum_{t=2}^{T} \hat{u}_{t-1}\, \Delta y_t\, (DU_{it} - D_{it}) - \sum_{i=1}^{K}\hat{\beta}_i \sum_{t=2}^{T} \hat{u}_{t-1}(DU_{it} - D_{it}),$$

$$\tag{13.A6}$$

where the first term is the same as the numerator of (13.6) except for the difference between $\hat{u}_{t-1}$ and y_{t-1}^{+}. The second term is simplified to $\sum_{i=1}^{K}\hat{\beta}_i\hat{u}_{T_i}$, since the sum of residuals in each interval is zero. For instance, $(\hat{\beta}_2\hat{u}_{T_1}/\sqrt{T}) \propto \beta_2\tilde{B}_1(1)$ is $O_p(1)$. The RSS of (13.12) divided by T is $\hat{\sigma}^2$, which is a consistent estimator of σ^2. Then the limit of $\hat{\tau}_{CM}^{*}$ is the same as that of τ_{CM}.

A.4   *Bias when the shock dummy variable is omitted*

The second term in (13.A5) comes only from the $K - 1$ break points. Since

$$\frac{1}{\sqrt{T}} \sum_{i=2}^{K} \{[y_t - \bar{y}_i - \hat{\beta}_i(t - \bar{t}_i)] - [y_{t-1} - \bar{y}_{i-1} - \hat{\beta}_{i-1}(t - 1 - \bar{t}_{i-1})]\} D_{it}$$

$$\approx \frac{1}{\sqrt{T}} \sum_{i=2}^{K} \{\varepsilon_t - (\hat{\beta}_i - \beta_i)(t - \bar{t}_i) + (\hat{\beta}_{i-1} - \beta_{i-1})(t - 1 - \bar{t}_{i-1})\} D_{it}$$

$$= \sum_{i=2}^{K} \left\{ \frac{1}{\sqrt{T}} \varepsilon_t - \sqrt{T}(\hat{\beta}_i - \beta_i)\frac{1}{T}(t - \bar{t}_i) \right.$$

$$\left. + \sqrt{T}(\hat{\beta}_{i-1} - \beta_{i-1})\frac{1}{T}(t - 1 - \bar{t}_{i-1}) \right\} D_{it},$$

and since $\sqrt{T}(\hat{\beta}_i - \beta_i)$ is $O_p(1)$ by (13.A3), the second term in (13.A5) is $O_p(\sqrt{T})$. The additional terms in the numerator divided by T are

$$\sum_{i=2}^{K} \frac{1}{T}\hat{u}_{T_{i-1}}\Delta\hat{u}_{T_{i-1}+1} \approx \sum_{i=2}^{K} \frac{1}{\sqrt{T}}\hat{u}_{T_{i-1}} \left\{ \sqrt{T}(\hat{\beta}_i - \beta_i)\frac{1}{T}(T_{i-1} + 1 - \bar{t}_i) \right.$$

$$\left. + \sqrt{T}(\hat{\beta}_{i-1} - \beta_{i-1})\frac{1}{T}(T_{i-1} - \bar{t}_{i-1}) \right\}.$$

Since $\hat{u}_{T_i}/\sqrt{T_i}$ converges to $\hat{B}_i(1)$, additional terms stay in the numerator. Thus it is necessary to get rid of the second term in (13.A5).

A.5   *Higher-order autoregression*

In the general autoregressive process, the error term is $\psi(L)w_t = \varepsilon_t$, where $w_t = (1 - (1 + \phi)L)u_t$. Then η_t is replaced by $\eta_{wt} \equiv \sum_{i=1}^{t} w_i$ in (13.A2). The integral and $\bar{\beta}_i$ in (13.A3) is multiplied by Λ, which is the long-run variance of η_{wt}. The rest of the analysis similar.

A.6   *Nonlinear least squares estimator and the F ratio*

Using the transformation (13.A1), the residual is defined as

$$\varepsilon(\theta^+)_t = \Delta y_t - \sum_{i=1}^{K}\{[\phi y_{t-1}^+ + \alpha_i^+ + \beta_i^+(t - \bar{t}_i^+)](DU_{it} - D_{it}) + \gamma_i^+ D_{it}\},$$

$$\tag{13.A7}$$

where $D_{1t} = 0$, and $\theta^+ = (\phi, \beta_1^+, \ldots, \beta_K^+, \alpha_1^+, \ldots, \alpha_K^+)'$. The residuals at break points are nonzero in the nonlinear estimation of (13.3). The coefficients in

(13.A7) are related to those in (13.4); the relations between them are detailed below (13.A1). They are further related to the original coefficients in (13.3). Define $\theta^* = (\phi, \beta_1^*, \ldots, \beta_K^*, \alpha_1^*, \ldots, \alpha_K^*)'$. The nonlinear least squares estimator $\hat{\theta}^*$ determines the estimator of θ^+. The coefficients under the null hypothesis are $\theta_0^* = (0, \beta_1^*, \ldots, \beta_K^*, \alpha_1^*, \ldots, \alpha_K^*)'$. The limit of the test statistics is derived following the technique due to Amemiya (1985, pp. 142–144). Under the first-order condition of the estimator and using a diagonal normalizing matrix N, i.e., $\mathrm{diag}(T, T\sqrt{T}, \ldots, T\sqrt{T}, \sqrt{T}, \ldots, \sqrt{T})$, the difference in the sum of the squared residuals is

$$\frac{1}{2}\{\mathrm{RSS}(\hat{\theta}^*) - \mathrm{RSS}(\theta^*)\} \approx (\hat{\theta}^* - \theta^*)' N \left(\sum_{t=1}^{T} N^{-1} \frac{\partial \varepsilon_t}{\partial \theta^*} \frac{\partial \varepsilon_t}{\partial \theta^{*'}} N^{-1} \right)_{\theta^*} N(\hat{\theta}^* - \theta^*).$$

(13.A8)

The middle matrix is evaluated at a vector which is between θ^* and $\hat{\theta}^*$, but the latter converges to θ^*. Similarly, using the first-order condition

$$\left(\sum_{t=1}^{T} \frac{\partial \varepsilon_t}{\partial \theta^*} \varepsilon_t \right)_{\hat{\theta}^*} = 0 \approx \left(\sum_{t=1}^{T} \frac{\partial \varepsilon_t}{\partial \theta^*} \varepsilon_t \right)_{\theta^*} + \sum_{t=1}^{T} \left(\frac{\partial \varepsilon_t}{\partial \theta^*} \frac{\partial \varepsilon_t}{\partial \theta^{*'}} \right)_{\theta^*} (\hat{\theta}^* - \theta^*),$$

(13.A9)

then

$$N(\hat{\theta}^* - \theta^*) \approx - \left[N^{-1} \sum_{t=1}^{T} \left(\frac{\partial \varepsilon_t}{\partial \theta^*} \frac{\partial \varepsilon_t}{\partial \theta^{*'}} \right)_{\theta^*} N^{-1} \right]^{-1} \left(N^{-1} \sum_{t-1}^{T} \frac{\partial \varepsilon_t}{\partial \theta^*} \varepsilon_t \right)_{\theta^*} ;$$

(13.A10)

thus (13.A8) can be written as $\varepsilon' U (U'U)^{-1} U' \varepsilon$. For simplicity, the tth row of the matrix U is expressed as

$$\left[\sum_{i=1}^{2} y_{t-1}^{+}(DU_{it} - D_{it}), (t - \bar{t}_1^{+})(DU_{1t} - D_{1t}), \right.$$

$$\left. (t - \bar{t}_2^{+})(DU_{2t} - D_{2t}), (DU_{1t} - D_{1t}), (DU_{2t} - D_{2t}), D_{it} \right] Q$$

in the $K = 2$ case, and $Q \equiv d\theta^*/d\theta^{+'}$ is a 6×6 nonsingular Jacobian matrix from θ^* to θ^+. Then $U = VQ$, where V consists of six orthogonal columns and $\varepsilon' U (U'U)^{-1} U' \varepsilon = \varepsilon' V (V'V)^{-1} V' \varepsilon$. Similar results follow from the restricted parameter estimation. Since columns in V are orthogonal, the F ratio is approximated as

$$\frac{1}{\hat{\sigma}^2}\{\mathrm{RSS}(\hat{\theta}_0) - \mathrm{RSS}(\hat{\theta}^*)\} \approx \frac{1}{\sigma^2} \varepsilon' v (v'v)^{-1} v' \varepsilon = \tau_{CM}^2.$$

(13.A11)

A.7   *The local power of $\hat{t}_{CM}$, $\hat{t}_{CM}^*$, and F tests*

The local alternative hypothesis is $H_a : \phi = \exp(v/T)$. Using an *Ornstein–Uhelenbeck* process

$$K_i(v, r) = B_i(r) + v \int_0^r \exp[v(r - s)] \, B_i(s) \, ds$$

as in Phillips (1987), the common limit of the estimators of the coefficient ϕ in (13.4) and (13.12) is

$$T\hat{\phi} \Rightarrow v + \left\{ \sum_{i=1}^k \left[\frac{1}{2}(\tilde{K}_i(v, 1)^2 - 1) - \frac{v}{\sigma^2} \int_0^1 \tilde{K}_i(v, r)^2 \, dr \right] \right\}$$

$$\times \left\{ \sum_{i=1}^k \lambda_i \int_0^1 \tilde{K}_i(v, r)^2 \, dr \right\}^{-1} \tag{13.A12}$$

where $\tilde{K}_i(v, 1)$ is demeaned and detrended. Then the two test statistics $\hat{t}_{CM}$ and $\hat{t}_{CM}^*$ have the same asymptotic local power. In the F ratio statistic of the nonlinear estimation, (13.A11) can be used again, and $\varepsilon'v(v'v)^{-1}/\sigma$ has the same limit as (13.A12). Thus the local power is the same.

REFERENCES

Amemiya, T. (1985), *Advanced Econometrics* (Cambridge, MA: Harvard University Press).

Bhargava, A. (1986), "On the Theory of Testing for Unit Roots in Observed Time Series," *Review of Economic Studies*, **53**, 369–384.

(1996) "Some Properties of Exact Tests for Unit Roots," *Biometrica*, **83**, 944–949.

Dickey, D. A. and Fuller, W. A. (1981), "Likelihood Ratio Statistics for Autoregressive Time Series with a Unit Root," *Econometrica*, **49**, 1057–72.

Hatanaka, M. and Yamada, M. (1997), "Characteristics of Japanese Macro-Economic Data in Relation to Unit Root Tests," mimeo.

Kiviet, J. and Phillips, G. D. A. (1992), "Exact Similar Tests for Unit Roots and Co-integration," *Oxford Bulletin of Economics and Statistics*, **54**, 349–367.

Kunitomo, N. and Sato, S. (1995), "Tables of Limiting Distribution Useful for Testing Unit Roots and Co-integration with Multiple Structural Breaks," DP 95-F-35, Faculty of Economics, University of Tokyo.

Ohara, H. (1996), "Unit Root Test Against a Trend Stationary Alternative with Multiple Trend Breaks," DP 96-F-57, Institute of Social Science, University of Tokyo.

Oya, K. and Toda, H. (1998), "DF, LM, and Combined Tests for a Unit Root in Autoregressive Time Series," *Journal of Time Series Analysis*, **19**, 325–348.

Perron, P. (1989), "The Great Crash, the Oil Price Shock, and the Unit Root Hypothesis," *Econometrica*, **57**, 1361–1401.

Perron, P. and Vogelsang, J. (1993), "Erratum: The Great Crash, the Oil Price Shock, and the Unit Root Hypothesis," *Econometrica*, **61**, 248–249.

Phillips, P. C. B. (1987), "Towards a Unified Asymptotic Theory of Autoregression," *Biometrica*, **74**, 535–548.

Phillips, P. C. B. and Perron, P. (1988), "Testing for a Unit Root in Time Series Regression," *Biometrica,* **75**, 335–346.

Schmidt, P. and Phillips, P. C. B. (1992), "LM Tests for a Unit Root in the Presence of Deterministic Trend," *Oxford Bulletin of Economics and Statistics,* **54**, 257–287.

Vogelsang, T. J. and Perron, P. (1998), "Additional Tests for a Unit Root Allowing for a Break in the Trend Function at an Unknown Time," *International Economic Review*, **39**, 1073–1100.

Zivot, E. and Andrews, D. W. K. (1992), "Further Evidence on the Great Crash, the Oil-Price Shock, and the Unit Root Hypothesis," *Journal of Business and Economic Statistics,* **10**, 251–270.

CHAPTER 14

On the simultaneous switching
autoregressive model

Naoto Kunitomo and Seisho Sato

1   Introduction

In the past two decades, several nonlinear time series models have been proposed
and investigated in the statistical time series analysis. The general class of
nonlinear time series models is written as

$$y_t = f(y_{t-1}, v_t), \tag{14.1.1}$$

where $f(\cdot)$ is a measurable function, $\{y_t;\ 1 \le t \le T\}$ are a sequence of $m \times 1$
vectors of observable time series, and $\{v_t;\ 1 \le t \le T\}$ are a sequence of $n \times 1$
vectors of independently and identically distributed (i.i.d.) random variables.
The initial value y_0 is either a fixed vector or a random vector in general. This
class is called the Markovian time series model, and many existing time series
models have Markovian representations as (14.1.1). More often, in statistical
time series analysis, a subclass of the Markovian models in the form (14.1.1)
has been used. If we assume the additivity of the past information of time series
and the current disturbance term, the general form can be written as

$$y_t = f^*(y_{t-1}) + v_t, \tag{14.1.2}$$

where we take $m = n$ and $f^*(\cdot)$ is a measurable function. Two important examples of this type are the exponential autoregressive models and the threshold
autoregressive models in the nonlinear time series analysis, which have been
systematically discussed by Tong (1990).

On the other hand, Kunitomo and Sato (1996a) have introduced a simple
stationary simultaneous switching autoregressive (SSAR) time series model.
A *structural form* of the simplest SSAR model for a scalar time series $\{y_t\}$ is

This chapter is dedicated to Professor Takeshi Amemiya of Stanford University. We thank Professor
T. W. Anderson, Professor Cheng Hsiao, and the referees for their comments on the previous
versions.

given by

$$y_t = \begin{cases} a_1 y_{t-1} + \sigma_1 v_t & \text{if} \quad y_t \geq y_{t-1}, \\ b_1 y_{t-1} + \sigma_2 v_t & \text{if} \quad y_t < y_{t-1}, \end{cases} \tag{14.1.3}$$

where a_1, b_1, σ_i ($\sigma_i > 0$; $i = 1, 2$) are unknown parameters, and $\{v_t\}$ are a sequence of i.i.d. random variables with $E(v_t) = 0$ and $E(v_t^2) = 1$. The initial value y_0 is either a fixed number or a random variable, but the latter is used for the stationary time series model. Because the phase conditions in the representation of (14.1.3) depend on the current time series y_t itself, it is not in the form of (14.1.1), and also it does not necessarily define a stochastic process as the probability model.

By imposing the condition

$$\frac{1 - a_1}{\sigma_1} = \frac{1 - b_1}{\sigma_2} = r, \tag{14.1.4}$$

it can be rewritten in a more meaningful way as

$$y_t = \begin{cases} a_1 y_{t-1} + \sigma_1 v_t & \text{if} \quad v_t \geq r y_{t-1}, \\ b_1 y_{t-1} + \sigma_2 v_t & \text{if} \quad v_t < r y_{t-1}, \end{cases} \tag{14.1.5}$$

which is the *reduced form* of the SSAR model. In this Markovian representation for (14.1.3), two phases at t are defined in the space of (v_t, y_{t-1}) such that the sample space for v_t given y_{t-1} is divided into two exhaustive sets. The reduced form of the SSAR model given by (14.1.5) with (14.1.4) and the initial condition on y_0 defines a stochastic process for $\{y_t\}$ as the probability model. This time series model can be written in a compact form as

$$y_t = y_{t-1} + [\sigma_1 I(v_t \geq r y_{t-1}) + \sigma_2 I(v_t < r y_{t-1})][-r y_{t-1} + v_t], \tag{14.1.6}$$

where $I(\cdot)$ is the indicator function. When $\sigma_1 = \sigma_2 = \sigma$, then the SSAR model becomes the standard AR(1) model on reparametrizing $a_1 = b_1 = 1 - \sigma r$. From the Markovian representation we immediately know that the SSAR model given by (14.1.5) with the condition (14.1.4) is well defined in the form of (14.1.1), but not in the form of (14.1.2). Also it is clear that given the past information $\{y_s; s \leq t - 1\}$, there is an uncertainty whether the next phase is $I(v_t \geq r y_{t-1})$ or $I(v_t < r y_{t-1})$.

As we have shown (Kunitomo and Sato 1996a), even this simplest univariate SSAR model defined by (14.1.5) with (14.1.4) [which is called SSAR(1)] gives us some explanations and descriptions of an important aspect of the asymmetrical movement of time series in two different (upward and downward) phases. For an illustration, we give some sample paths of the stationary SSAR(1) process in Figure 14.1. Also some stationary distributions satisfying the SSAR(1) model are shown in Figure 14.2. These figures suggest

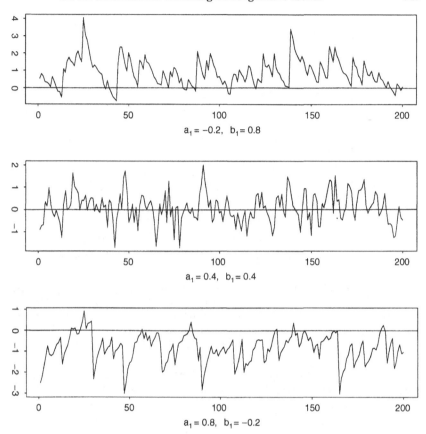

Figure 14.1. Some of sample paths generated by the ergodic SSAR(1) processes without constant terms. When $a_1 = b_1$, the SSAR(1) model is the standard AR(1) model. When $a_1 \neq b_1$, the sample paths in the upward phase are significantly different from those in the downward phase. We set $r = 1$ in all simulations.

that we can produce asymmetrical patterns of sample paths and skewed stationary distributions with flexible moment properties even if the underlying disturbances follow the Gaussian distribution.

The simple SSAR model has been introduced from an econometric application, and there are some intuitive reasons why the SSAR models are useful for econometric applications, as we shall mention in Section 2.2 and Section 5. Also it should be noted that the SSAR time series models are different from the threshold autoregressive (TAR) models, which have been extensively discussed

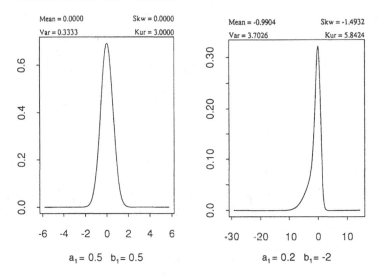

Figure 14.2. Some of the stationary distributions for the SSAR(1) processes. For each distribution the first four moments (Mean, Var, Skw, Kur) are calculated numerically under normal disturbances, where Skw is the skewness and Kur is $3 + \kappa_4$ (where κ_4 is kurtosis). When $a_1 \neq b_1$, we have the stationary distributions, which are quite different from the normal distribution.

in nonlinear time series analysis. Although there are many variants of the TAR models, the simplest form [often denoted as TAR(1)] without constant terms can be written as

$$y_t = \begin{cases} a_1 y_{t-1} + \sigma v_t & \text{if } y_{t-1} \geq r, \\ b_1 y_{t-1} + \sigma v_t & \text{if } y_{t-1} < r, \end{cases} \tag{14.1.7}$$

where r, a_1, b_1, σ are unknown parameters and $\{v_t\}$ are a sequence of i.i.d. random variables with $E(v_t) = 0$ and $E(v_t^2) = 1$. We notice that the TAR model given by (14.1.7) is well defined in the form of (14.1.2). Although there are two phases in the TAR(1) model, given the past information $\{y_s; s \leq t - 1\}$ there is no uncertainty on the next phase of y_t, because it is a function of the realized time series in the past.

In this chapter we shall discuss some statistical properties of the SSAR models and their estimation methods. The distinction between the structural form and the reduced form of the SSAR models will be emphasized. In Section 2, we introduce the SSAR models in the general form and discuss the relation between them and some disequilibrium econometric models. Then we give some statistical properties of the SSAR models in Section 3. In Section 4, two estimation methods for the SSAR models will be discussed. Some concluding remarks will be given in Section 5.

2   The SSAR Models

2.1   *A class of SSAR models*

Let y_t be an $m \times 1$ vector time series. By generalizing (14.1.3), the *structural form* of the SSAR model for y_t $[= (y_{i,t})]$ is given by

$$y_t = \begin{cases} \mu_1 + Ay_{t-1} + D_1v_t & \text{if } e_1'y_t \geq e_1'y_{t-1}, \\ \mu_2 + By_{t-1} + D_2v_t & \text{if } e_1'y_t < e_1'y_{t-1}, \end{cases} \tag{14.2.1}$$

where $e_1' = (1, 0, \ldots, 0)$ and μ_i' $(i = 1, 2)$ are $1 \times m$ vectors of constants, and A, B, and D_i $(i = 1, 2)$ are $m \times m$ matrices. The initial value y_0 $[= (y_{i,0})]$ is either a fixed vector or a random vector, but the latter should be used for the stationary SSAR models. The structural form of the SSAR model given by (14.2.1) is denoted by $\text{SSAR}_m(1)$.

As we mentioned after (14.1.3), the structural form given in (14.2.1) does not necessarily define a stochastic process for $\{y_t\}$ as the probability model. We need some conditions on the underlying parameters which we shall discuss shortly. The condition $e_1'y_t \geq e_1'y_{t-1}$ in (14.2.1) has been used instead of the condition $e_m'y_t \geq e_m'y_{t-1}$ with $e_m' = (0, 0, \ldots, 1)$ in Kunitomo and Sato (1996a), for instance. This change in our formulation does not harm any essential argument below.

The disturbance terms in (14.2.1) satisfy $E(v_t) = 0$ and the variance–covariance matrix of D_iv_t is denoted by Ω_i $[= D_iD_i'; i = 1, 2]$. We assume either

(i) $\{v_t\}$ are a sequence of i.i.d. random variables with the density function $g(v)$, which is continuous and everywhere positive in R^m, or

(ii) $D_iv_t = \sigma_ie_1v_t$ and $\{v_t\}$ are a sequence of i.i.d. scalar random variables with the density function $g(v)$, which is continuous and everywhere positive in R.

In the first case the disturbance terms $\{v_t\}$ are distributed with $E(v_tv_t') = I_m$ and we assume that Ω_i $(i = 1, 2)$ are positive definite matrices. In the second case the disturbance terms $\{v_t\}$ are distributed with $E(v_t) = 0$ and $E(v_t^2) = 1$. The second case corresponds to the *structural form* of the univariate SSAR model given by

$$y_t = \begin{cases} a_0 + \sum_{j=1}^{p} a_jy_{t-j} + \sigma_1v_t & \text{if } y_t \geq y_{t-1}, \\ b_0 + \sum_{j=1}^{p} b_jy_{t-j} + \sigma_2v_t & \text{if } y_t < y_{t-1}, \end{cases} \tag{14.2.2}$$

where $\{a_j; \ j = 0, \ldots, p\}$, $\{b_j; \ j = 0, \ldots, p\}$, and $\{\sigma_i; \ i = 1, 2\}$ are unknown parameters with the condition $\sigma_i > 0$ $(i = 1, 2)$. The initial conditions $y_{-p+1}, y_{-p+2}, \ldots, y_0$ are fixed numbers or random variables, but the latter should be used for the stationary SSAR models. The structural form of the univariate SSAR model represented by (14.2.2) is denoted by SSAR(p).

If we define $p \times 1$ vectors y_t and μ_i $(i = 1, 2)$ by

$$
y_t = \begin{pmatrix} y_t \\ y_{t-1} \\ \vdots \\ y_{t-p+1} \end{pmatrix}, \quad
\mu_1 = \begin{pmatrix} a_0 \\ 0 \\ \vdots \\ 0 \end{pmatrix}, \quad
\mu_2 = \begin{pmatrix} b_0 \\ 0 \\ \vdots \\ 0 \end{pmatrix},
$$

and $p \times p$ matrices

$$
A = \begin{pmatrix} a_1 & \cdots & \cdots & a_p \\ 1 & & \mathbf{0} & \vdots \\ & \ddots & & \vdots \\ \mathbf{0} & & 1 & 0 \end{pmatrix}, \quad
B = \begin{pmatrix} b_1 & \cdots & \cdots & b_p \\ 1 & & \mathbf{0} & \\ & \ddots & & \\ \mathbf{0} & & 1 & 0 \end{pmatrix},
$$

then (14.2.2) can be rewritten as (14.2.1) and the resulting model can be regarded as a special case of (14.2.1) if we set $D_i v_t = \sigma_i e_1 v_t$ and $m = p$. The structural form of the SSAR model in (14.1.3) is a special case of (14.2.2) when $a_0 = b_0 = 0$ and $p = 1$.

We note that in (14.2.1) there are two phases (or regimes) at time t given $\mathcal{F}_{t-1}$, the σ-field generated by $\{y_s; \ s \le t - 1\}$. Because the structural form of (14.2.1) or (14.2.2) does not necessarily define a stochastic process as the probability model, we need some restrictions on the underlying parameters in the structural form, as we have illustrated in Section 1. This problem is the same as the coherency problem discussed in some econometric literature, and the conditions for the restrictions on the underlying parameters have been called the coherency condition in the context of the disequilibrium econometric models (see Quandt 1988, for instance). We shall illustrate this problem further by using an econometric example in Section 2.2.

The conditions $e_1' y_t \ge e_1' y_{t-1}$ and $e_1' y_t < e_1' y_{t-1}$ can be rewritten as

$$
e_1' D_1 v_t \ge e_1' (I_m - A) y_{t-1} - e_1' \mu_1, \tag{14.2.3}
$$

and

$$
e_1' D_2 v_t < e_1' (I_m - B) y_{t-1} - e_1' \mu_2, \tag{14.2.4}
$$

respectively. A set of the coherency conditions for (14.2.1) can be summarized by a $1 \times (m + 1)$ vector of unknown parameters

$$\frac{1}{\sigma_1}[e_1'(I_m - A), -e_1'\mu_1] = \frac{1}{\sigma_2}[e_1'(I_m - B), -e_1'\mu_2]$$

$$= [r', r_0], \qquad (14.2.5)$$

where $r' = (r_1, r_2, \ldots, r_m)$ is a $1 \times m$ vector, r_0 is a scalar, and the (positive) scale parameters σ_j ($j = 1, 2$) satisfy $\sigma_j^2 = e_1'\Omega_j e_1 = e_1'D_jD_j'e_1$. In addition to (14.2.5), we also use a $1 \times m$ vector

$$\frac{1}{\sigma_1}e_1'D_1 = \frac{1}{\sigma_2}e_1'D_2 = d', \qquad (14.2.6)$$

where we have $d'd = 1$ as the normalization factor. The conditions of (14.2.5) and (14.2.6) are sufficient for the two phases at t being properly defined for v_t given $\mathcal{F}_{t-1}$.

Under these conditions, we can define the reduced forms of (14.2.1) and (14.2.2) by using the Markovian representations of the SSAR models in the form of (14.1.1). The *reduced form* of the vector SSAR model [SSAR$_m$(1)] in (14.2.1) can be given by

$$y_t = \begin{cases} \mu_1 + Ay_{t-1} + D_1v_t & \text{if } d'v_t \geq r_0 + r'y_{t-1}, \\ \mu_2 + By_{t-1} + D_2v_t & \text{if } d'v_t < r_0 + r'y_{t-1} \end{cases} \qquad (14.2.7)$$

with the restrictions imposed by (14.2.5) and (14.2.6). In particular, the *reduced form* of the SSAR(p) model in (14.2.2) can be also given by

$$y_t = \begin{cases} a_0 + \sum_{j=1}^{p} a_j y_{t-j} + \sigma_1 v_t & \text{if } v_t \geq r_0 + \sum_{j=1}^{p} r_j y_{t-j}, \\ b_0 + \sum_{j=1}^{p} b_j y_{t-j} + \sigma_2 v_t & \text{if } v_t < r_0 + \sum_{j=1}^{p} r_j y_{t-j}. \end{cases} \qquad (14.2.8)$$

It is apparent from our formulation that the condition given by (14.2.6) is automatically satisfied for the pth order univariate SSAR model.

The most important common feature of the SSAR models is in the fact that the time series variables $\{y_t\}$ at each period may take quite different values in two different phases or regimes, but we do not know in advance which phase in the next period will occur. This type of statistical time series model could be regarded as a *threshold model* in the nonlinear time series literature. However, we should note that there is no simultaneity in the standard threshold models in the nonlinear time series analysis, as we have illustrated in (14.1.7). Since in the reduced forms of the SSAR models given by (14.2.7) or (14.2.8) the time series variables and two phases at time t are determined simultaneously in a particular way, we have called it a *simultaneous switching time series model.* This simultaneity has not only an important economic interpretation, but also a new aspect in nonlinear time series modeling.

In the next subsection we shall discuss the relationship between the SSAR models and one type of disequilibrium econometric model for an illustration. Other types of arguments can also lead to SSAR models, as we have already discussed in Kunitomo and Sato (1999).

2.2   The SSAR models and a disequilibrium econometric model

In order to explain the motivation of introducing the SSAR models, we shall give a simple econometric example, which is a modified version of the disequilibrium econometric model originally investigated by Laffont and Garcia (1977). The disequilibrium econometric model of our concern here was first developed by Fair and Jaffee (1972); since then a number of different econometric models have been proposed.

The standard econometric model consists of the demand and supply functions in a small market. Let D_t and S_t be the demand and supply of a commodity at time t. By assuming that they are linear, these two equations are written as

$$D_t = \beta_1 p_t + \gamma_1' z_{1t} + u_{1t},$$
$$S_t = \beta_2 p_t + \gamma_2' z_{2t} + u_{2t}, \tag{14.2.9}$$

where p_t is the price level, and z_{1t} and z_{2t} are the predetermined variables appearing in the demand and supply equations, respectively. The demand shocks and the supply shocks are described by the disturbance terms u_{1t} and u_{2t}, respectively.

We assume that 1×2 vectors $u_t' = (u_{1t}, u_{2t})$ are a sequence of i.i.d. random variables with $E(u_{1t}) = E(u_{2t}) = 0$, the (positive definite) variance–covariance matrix $E(u_t u_t') = \Sigma \, (>0)$, and the density function is continuous and positive everywhere in R^2. The coefficients β_i and γ_i $(i = 1, 2)$ are unknown parameters with the usual condition $\beta_1 < 0 < \beta_2$. For expository simplicity, we take the number of predetermined variables as 2, γ_1, γ_2 being scalars, and we take $z_{1t} = p_{t-1}$ and $z_{2t} = p_{t-2}$ as an example.

The equilibrium condition explained by economics is given by $q_t = D_t = S_t$, where q_t is the quantity of the commodity traded in the market at time t. Instead of the equilibrium condition, however, Fair and Jaffee (1972) introduced the short-side condition

$$q_t = \min(D_t, S_t). \tag{14.2.10}$$

We note that when we substitute (14.2.10) for the equilibrium condition, the econometric model consisting of (14.2.9) and (14.2.10) is not complete in the proper statistical sense. The quantity variable q_t is determined by (14.2.9) and (14.2.10) once the price variable p_t is given. There should be some dynamic process for the price level (or the quantity traded), and there have been several formulations to make the disequilibrium econometric model complete. In this section we shall adopt one simple formulation by Laffont and Garcia (1977). If $D_t > S_t$ at t in the market, there is excess demand, which raises the price variable p_t. On the other hand, if $S_t > D_t$ at t in the market, there is excess supply, causing p_t to go down. This consideration leads to the linearized price adjustment process[1]

$$\Delta p_t = \begin{cases} \delta_1(D_t - S_t) & \text{if} \quad D_t \geq S_t, \\ \delta_2(D_t - S_t) & \text{if} \quad D_t < S_t, \end{cases} \tag{14.2.11}$$

where $\Delta p_t = p_t - p_{t-1}$. Since the coefficients δ_1 and δ_2 represent the adjustment speeds in the upward phase (or regime) and in the downward phase (or regime), we assume that $\delta_i > 0$ $(i = 1, 2)$ and they do not necessarily take the same value. Possibly there could be some economic justifications for these differences, including the market behaviors of economic agents and the market microstructures.

We now consider the disequilibrium econometric model consisting of (14.2.9), (14.2.10), and (14.2.11). Our investigation aims to shed some new light on the time series aspects of this type of disequilibrium model, as this is an area that has largely been ignored in the econometric literature.

Let the 1×2 vector of endogenous variables $y_t' = (p_t, q_t)$ and the 1×2 vector of predetermined variables $z_t' = (p_{t-1}, p_{t-2})$. If the price variable p_t is in the upward phase, then we have the condition that $\Delta p_t \geq 0$, $q_t = S_t$, and

$$D_t = q_t + (D_t - S_t) = q_t + \frac{1}{\delta_1} \Delta p_t,$$

provided that $\delta_1 > 0$. Hence the system of the demand and supply functions can be rewritten as

$$\begin{pmatrix} -\beta_1 + \delta_1^{-1} & 1 \\ -\beta_2 & 1 \end{pmatrix} y_t = \begin{pmatrix} \delta_1^{-1} & 0 \\ 0 & 0 \end{pmatrix} y_{t-1} + \begin{pmatrix} \gamma_1 & 0 \\ 0 & \gamma_2 \end{pmatrix} z_t + u_t, \tag{14.2.12}$$

where u_t' is a 1×2 vector of the disturbance terms, and γ_i $(i = 1, 2)$ are scalar coefficients in this example. If we assume $\delta_1 > 0$, we can solve (14.2.12) for y_t in the first phase and it becomes

$$y_t = \frac{1}{d_1} \begin{pmatrix} -\delta_1^{-1} & 0 \\ -\beta_2 \delta_1^{-1} & 0 \end{pmatrix} y_{t-1} + \frac{1}{d_1} \begin{pmatrix} -\gamma_1 & \gamma_2 \\ -\beta_2 \gamma_1 & (\beta_1 - \delta_1^{-1})\gamma_2 \end{pmatrix} z_t + v_t^{(1)}, \tag{14.2.13}$$

---

[1] Alternatively, we can use the condition for Δp_{t+1} instead of (14.2.11), as discussed in Kunitomo and Sato (1996a). Then we have a slightly different SSAR model as the result.

where the resulting disturbance vector in this phase is given by

$$v_t^{(1)} = \frac{1}{d_1} \begin{pmatrix} -1 & 1 \\ -\beta_2 & \beta_1 - \delta_1^{-1} \end{pmatrix} u_t, \qquad (14.2.14)$$

and $d_1 = \beta_1 - \beta_2 - \delta_1^{-1}$ (<0). In this phase the first component of y_t, the price level p_t at t, follows

$$p_t = \frac{-1 - \gamma_1 \delta_1}{d_1 \delta_1} p_{t-1} + \frac{\gamma_2}{d_1} p_{t-2} + \sigma_1 v_t^{(p)}, \qquad (14.2.15)$$

where we take $\sigma_1^2 = (1/d_1^2)(-1, 1)\Sigma(-1, 1)'$ and $v_t^{(p)} = [-u_{1t} + u_{2t}]/[d_1 \sigma_1]$. We note that by multiplying $d_1 \delta_1$ by (14.2.15) and using (14.2.9) we can recover the equation $\Delta p_t = \delta_1(D_t - S_t)$.

Similarly, if the price variable p_t is in the downward phase, we have the condition that $\Delta p_t < 0$, $q_t = D_t$, and

$$S_t = q_t - \frac{1}{\delta_2} \Delta p_t,$$

provided that $\delta_2 > 0$. Hence the system of the demand and supply functions in this phase can be written as

$$\begin{pmatrix} -\beta_1 & 1 \\ -\beta_2 - \delta_2^{-1} & 1 \end{pmatrix} y_t = \begin{pmatrix} 0 & 0 \\ -\delta_2^{-1} & 0 \end{pmatrix} y_{t-1} + \begin{pmatrix} \gamma_1 & 0 \\ 0 & \gamma_2 \end{pmatrix} z_t + u_t. \qquad (14.2.16)$$

By using the same arguments to (14.2.12) and (14.2.13), we can solve (14.2.16) in the second phase and it becomes

$$y_t = \frac{1}{d_2} \begin{pmatrix} -\delta_2^{-1} & 0 \\ -\beta_1 \delta_2^{-1} & 0 \end{pmatrix} y_{t-1} + \frac{1}{d_2} \begin{pmatrix} -\gamma_1 & \gamma_2 \\ -(\beta_2 + \delta_2^{-1})\gamma_1 & \beta_1 \gamma_2 \end{pmatrix} z_t + v_t^{(2)}, \qquad (14.2.17)$$

where the resulting disturbance vector in this phase is given by

$$v_t^{(2)} = \frac{1}{d_2} \begin{pmatrix} -1 & 1 \\ -(\beta_2 + \delta_2^{-1}) & \beta_1 \end{pmatrix} u_t, \qquad (14.2.18)$$

and $d_2 = \beta_1 - \beta_2 - \delta_2^{-1}$ (<0). In the second phase the price level p_t at t follows

$$p_t = \frac{-1 - \delta_2 \gamma_1}{d_2 \delta_2} p_{t-1} + \frac{\gamma_2}{d_2} p_{t-2} + \sigma_2 v_t^{(p)}, \qquad (14.2.19)$$

where we take $\sigma_2^2 = (1/d_2^2)(-1, 1)\Sigma(-1, 1)'$. We also note that by multiplying (14.2.19) by $d_2 \delta_2$ and using (14.2.9) we can recover the equation $\Delta p_t = \delta_2(D_t - S_t)$.

In our formulation of parameters we have the relation $d_1\sigma_1 = d_2\sigma_2$ and the i.i.d. random variables $v_t^{(p)}$ are defined properly. The sufficient conditions given by (14.2.5) and (14.2.6) are satisfied in this econometric example because there are two phases and the structural (demand–supply) equations in each phase are well defined. This can be confirmed by cheking the phase conditions in this example as follows.

By taking the 1×2 vector $e_1' = (1, 0)$, the condition that the market is in the excess demand ($\Delta p_t \geq 0$) is equivalent to

$$e_1' y_t \geq e_1' y_{t-1}. \tag{14.2.20}$$

By substituting (14.2.15) into the condition $\Delta p_t \geq 0$, the phase condition in (14.2.20) can be also rewritten[2] as

$$v_t^{(p)} \geq \frac{\beta}{c} p_{t-1} + \frac{1}{c}(\gamma_1 z_{1t} - \gamma_2 z_{2t}), \tag{14.2.21}$$

where we use the notation $\beta = \beta_1 - \beta_2$ and $c = d_1\sigma_1 = d_2\sigma_2$. When the market is in the excess supply, we have an inequality

$$v_t^{(p)} < \frac{\beta}{c} p_{t-1} + \frac{1}{c}(\gamma_1 z_{1t} - \gamma_2 z_{2t}). \tag{14.2.22}$$

The above expressions in (14.2.21) and (14.2.22) are meaningful provided that the explanatory variables $z_t = (z_{1t}', z_{2t}')'$ are predetermined at t. In fact, by noting that in the present example

$$z_t = e_1 e_1' y_{t-1} + e_2 e_1' y_{t-2},$$

we have the two-dimensional second order SSAR model [denoted as SSAR$_2$(2)] without constant terms as the solution of the disequilibrium econometric model given by (14.2.9), (14.2.10), and (14.2.11). The reduced form has also a Markovian representation as the SSAR$_4$(1) model without constant terms in the form of (14.2.7) on defining a 4×1 state vector $Y_t = (y_t', y_{t-1}')'$ and using the corresponding matrices

$$A = \frac{1}{d_1} \begin{pmatrix} -\delta_1^{-1} - \gamma_1 & 0 & \gamma_2 & 0 \\ -\beta_2\delta_1^{-1} - \beta_2\gamma_1 & 0 & (\beta_1 - \delta_1^{-1})\gamma_2 & 0 \\ 1 & 0 & 0 & 0 \\ 0 & 1 & 0 & 0 \end{pmatrix}$$

---

[2] One referee has pointed out that (14.2.21) is better than (14.2.20). In fact, (14.2.21) clearly shows that the space of $v_t^{(p)}$ given $\mathcal{F}_{t-1}$ is partitioned into two disjoint sets.

and

$$\boldsymbol{B} = \frac{1}{d_2} \begin{pmatrix} -\delta_2^{-1} - \gamma_1 & 0 & \gamma_2 & 0 \\ -\beta_1\delta_2^{-1} - (\beta_2 + \delta_2^{-1})\gamma_1 & 0 & \beta_1\gamma_2 & 0 \\ 1 & 0 & 0 & 0 \\ 0 & 1 & 0 & 0 \end{pmatrix}.$$

The price level p_t follows the univariate SSAR(2) model without constant terms in this case, as we have seen from (14.2.15), (14.2.19), (14.2.21), and (14.2.22).

After some simple algebra and using the notation $c = d_1\sigma_1 = d_2\sigma_2$, the conditions in (14.2.5) and (14.2.6) in the Markovian representation become

$$r' = \frac{1}{c}(\beta_1 - \beta_2 + \gamma_1, 0, -\gamma_2, 0), \qquad (14.2.23)$$

and

$$d' = \frac{1}{c}[(-1, 1)\Sigma^{1/2}, 0, 0], \qquad (14.2.24)$$

respectively. We have used a decomposition of the positive definite matrix Σ such that $\Sigma = \Sigma^{1/2}\Sigma^{1/2}$. In the Markovian representation we also have $r_0 = 0$ and $v_t^{(p)} = d'v_t = (1/c)(-1, 1)u_t$.

We further note that when $\delta = \delta_1 = \delta_2$, the vector y_t follows the SSAR$_2$(2) model while the price level p_t follows the standard AR(2) model. It is evident that if there were more exogenous variables in (14.2.9), such as constant terms, time trends, and lagged endogenous variables, for instance, the resulting reduced form would have been in the form of a more complicated SSAR model.

We notice that if we let $\delta_i \to +\infty$ $(i = 1, 2)$ in (14.2.13) and (14.2.17) formally, then $d_i \to \beta = \beta_1 - \beta_2$ $(i = 1, 2)$ and we have the standard vector AR(1) process for the 4×1 state vector $Y_t = (y_t', y_{t-1}')'$ as the solution of (14.2.9), (14.2.10), and (14.2.11). In this situation we always have the equilibrium condition $D_t = S_t$ for all t, which is usually regarded as the standard situation in economics. Thus our formulation allows us to treat this as a special case in the general setting.

3   Some statistical properties

3.1   *The SSAR models and ergodicity*

The first important property of a statistical time series model is whether it is ergodic or not. For the Markovian time series models, geometrical ergodicity and related concepts have been developed in nonlinear time series analysis. For the sake of completeness, we mention its definition and the drift criterion. For more precise definitions of related concepts including irreducibility, aperiodicity, small set, and ergodicity of Markov chains with a general state space, see Tong (1990) or Nummelin (1984). Lemma 1 was taken from Appendix 14.1.3 of Tong (1990).

Definition 1.

(i) $\{y_t\}$ is geometrically ergodic if there exists a probability measure π on $(R^m, \mathcal{B}(R^m))$, a positive constant $\rho < 1$, and a π-integrable nonnegative measurable function $h(\cdot)$ such that

$$\|P^n(x, \cdot) - \pi(\cdot)\|_\tau \leq \rho^n h(x), \tag{14.3.1}$$

where $\| \cdot \|_\tau$ denotes the total variation norm, $x = (x_i)$ is an $m \times 1$ vector, and $P(x, \cdot)$ is the transition probability.

(ii) $\{y_t\}$ is ϕ-irreducible if for any $x \in R^m$ and $A \in \mathcal{B}(R^m)$ with $\phi(A) > 0$ [$\phi(\cdot)$ is a σ-finite measure],

$$\sum_{n=1}^{\infty} P^n(x, A) > 0. \tag{14.3.2}$$

Lemma 14.1. *Let $\{y_t\}$ be ϕ-irreducible and aperiodic Markov chain. Suppose that there exists a small set C, a nonnegative measurable function $G(\cdot)$, and constants $r > 1$, $\gamma > 0$, and $K > 0$ such that for $y \in R^m$*

$$E[rG(y_t) \mid y_{t-1} = y] < G(y) - \gamma \qquad (y \notin C), \tag{14.3.3}$$

and

$$E[G(y_t) \mid y_{t-1} = y] < K \qquad (y \in C). \tag{14.3.4}$$

Then $\{y_t\}$ is geometrically ergodic.

A probability measure $\pi(\cdot)$ in (14.3.1) satisfies the stationarity condition

$$\pi(A) = \int_x P(x, A)\pi(dx) \tag{14.3.5}$$

for any $A \in \mathcal{B}(R^m)$. Then if we take the initial distribution as the same as $\pi(\cdot)$, the process $\{y_t\}$ is strictly stationary.

Now we consider the structural form of the $SSAR_m(1)$ model given by (14.2.1). When $m = 1$, we have the necessary and sufficient condition for the geometric ergodicity of the SSAR model. It is also a sufficient condition for the existence of moments if we assume the existence of moments for the disturbance terms. For the sake of completeness and an illustration, we state this result and its proof in a formal way.

Proposition 1. *In the structural form of the SSAR model given by* (14.2.1) *when* $m = 1$, *assume* (i) *the coherency conditions given by*

$$
r_0 = -\frac{\mu_1}{\sigma_1} = -\frac{\mu_2}{\sigma_2},
$$

$$
r_1 = \frac{1 - A}{\sigma_1} = \frac{1 - B}{\sigma_2},
$$

(14.3.6)

where $D_i = \sigma_i$ $(i = 1, 2)$. *Then necessary and sufficient conditions for geometric ergodicity are given by*

$$
A < 1, \qquad B < 1, \qquad AB < 1.
$$

(14.3.7)

(ii) *In addition to the above conditions, assume that* $E[|v_t|^k] < +\infty$ *for any positive integer* $k \geq 1$ *and* $E[|y_0|^k] < +\infty$ *for any positive integer* $k \geq 1$. *Then*

$$
E[|y_t|^k] < +\infty.
$$

(14.3.8)

Proof: (ii): We first prove the second part. When $m = 1$, we can take the criterion function

$$
G(x) = \begin{cases} k_1^k x^k + c_1, & x > 0, \\ k_2^k |x|^k + c_1, & x \leq 0, \end{cases}
$$

(14.3.9)

where k is any positive integer, c_1 is a positive constant, and positive constants k_1, k_2 are defined shortly. We first consider the case when $y_{t-1} = x > M > 0$. Then

$$
E[G(y_t) \mid y_{t-1} = x] \leq \left[\sum_{i=0}^{k-1} c_i^* x^i \right] + k_1^k A^k x^k P\{v_t \geq r_0 + r_1 x\}
$$

$$
+ k_1^k B^k x^k P\left\{ r_0 + \left(r_1 - \frac{1}{\sigma_2} \right) x < v_t < r_0 + r_1 x \right\}
$$

$$
+ k_2^k B^k x^k P\left\{ v_t \leq r_0 + \left(r_1 - \frac{1}{\sigma_2} \right) x \right\},
$$

(14.3.10)

where c_i^* $(i = 0, \ldots, k - 1)$ are positive constants. Because $A < 1$, $B < 1$, and $AB < 1$, we can take $k_1 > 0$ and $k_2 > 0$ such that $1 > A > -k_2/k_1$ and $1 > B > -k_1/k_2$, and then $k_2^k > (-A)^k k_1^k$ for $A \leq 0$ and $k_1^k > (-B)^k k_2^k$ for $B \leq 0$ for $k \geq 1$. We note that the conditions $B < 0$ and $0 \leq B < 1$ correspond to the cases when $1/\sigma_2 < r_1 < 1/\sigma_2 + 1/\sigma_1$ and $0 < r_1 \leq 1/\sigma_2$, respectively. When $0 < r_1 \leq 1/\sigma_2$ $(0 \leq B < 1)$, the coefficients of second and fourth terms on the right-hand side of (14.3.10) can be small. Then by taking a sufficiently large M, we have

$$
E[G(y_t) \mid y_{t-1} = x] \leq c_2(M) + \delta_1 k_1^k x^k,
$$

(14.3.11)

where $0 < \delta_1 < 1$ and $c_2(M)$ is a positive constant depending on M. When $1/\sigma_2 < r_1 \leq 1/\sigma_2 + 1/\sigma_1$ $(B < 0)$, the coefficients of the second and third terms on the right-hand side of (14.3.10) can be small. Because $k_2^k|B|^k < k_1^k$ in this case, we can take a sufficiently large M and we also have

$$E[G(y_t) \mid y_{t-1} = x] \leq c_3(M) + \delta_2 k_1^k x^k,$$

where $0 < \delta_2 < 1$, and $c_3(M)$ depending on M is a positive constant. By taking $\max\{\delta_1, \delta_2\} < \delta_3 < 1$, we have

$$E[G(y_t) \mid y_{t-1} = x] \leq c_4(M) + \delta_3 G(x),$$

where $c_4(M)$ is a positive constant. We can use similar arguments for the case when $y_{t-1} = x < -M < 0$. Then we can take positive constants $0 < \delta < 1$ and $c_5(M)$ depending on M for any $y_{t-1} = x$ such that

$$E[G(y_t) \mid y_{t-1} = x] \leq c_5(M) + \delta G(x). \tag{14.3.12}$$

Because

$$
\begin{aligned}
E[G(y_t) \mid y_0 = x] &= E\{E[G(y_t) \mid y_{t-1}] \mid y_0\} \\
&\leq c_5(M)[1 + \delta + \cdots + \delta^{t-1}] + \delta^t G(y_0) \tag{14.3.13}
\end{aligned}
$$

is bounded, we have the desired result for any positive integer k.

(i) Sufficiency: Next we consider assertion (i) on the geometrical ergodicity. When $m = 1$, we immediately know that $\{y_t\}$ is an ϕ-irreducible and aperiodic Markov chain. As in the proof of (ii), we take $k = 1$, M^* $(>M > 0)$, and a compact set $C = [-M^*, M^*]$, where M has been taken to satisfy (14.3.12). Then by taking a sufficiently large M^* and using Lemma 1, we obtain that $\{y_t\}$ is geometrically ergodic under the conditions given by (14.3.7).

Necessity: The necessity for the geometrical ergodic conditions (14.3.7) is based on arguments which are similar to the proof of Theorem 14.2.1 of Chan et al. (1985). However, there is one important difference. Because of the coherency conditions given by (14.3.6), we can easily obtain contradictions to the geometrical ergodicity when we have the boundary conditions $A = 1$, $B = 1$, or $AB = 1$. They are straightforward, but quite tedious, and we omit the details. □

We give some sufficient conditions for the existence of higher moments and their boundedness when $m \geq 1$. All of them are sufficient, but they are often too strong and we do not necessarily need them. (See the conditions in Proposition 1.) The proofs of the following two propositions are straightforward and so brief.

Proposition 2. *In the structural form of the SSAR model given by* (14.2.1) *when* $m \geq 1$, *assume* (i) *the coherency conditions given by* (14.2.5) *and* (14.2.6), (ii) *a* *sufficient condition for the geometric ergodicity* $0 < \rho_1 < 1$, *where*

$$\rho_1 = \max\{\lambda_{max}(A'A), \lambda_{max}(B'B)\},$$

and $\lambda_{max}(C)$ *is the maximum characteristic root of a symmetric matrix* C *in its absolute value,* (iii) $E[\|v_t\|^k] < +\infty$ *for any positive integer* $k \geq 1$, *and* (iv) $E[\|y_0\|^k] < +\infty$ *for any positive integer* $k \geq 1$. *Then*

$$E[\|y_t\|^k] < +\infty. \tag{14.3.14}$$

Proof: When $m \geq 1$, we can take the criterion function

$$G(x) = \|x\|^k, \tag{14.3.15}$$

where $x = (x_i)$. We only show (14.3.14) for $k = 1$. When $k = 1$, we have

$$E[G(y_t) \mid y_{t-1} = x] \leq c_6 + E[\|A(t)\|]\|x\| + E[\|D(t)u_t\|]$$
$$\leq c_7 + \sqrt{\rho_1}G(x), \tag{14.3.16}$$

where $A(t) = AI_t^{(1)} + BI_t^{(2)}$ $(I_t^{(1)} = I(e_1'y\mid_t \geq e_1'y\mid_{t-1}), I_t^{(2)} = 1 - I_t^{(1)})$ and c_i $(i = 6, 7)$ are positive constants. The rest of arguments and those for $k \geq 2$ are essentially the same as the proof of Proposition 1. $\qquad\square$

Proposition 3. *In the structural form of the SSAR model given by* (14.2.1) *when* $m \geq 1$, *assume* (i) *the coherency conditions given by* (14.2.5) *and* (14.2.6), (ii) *a sufficient condition for the geometric ergodicity* $0 < \rho_2 < 1$ *or* $0 < \rho_3 < 1$, *where*

$$\rho_2 = \max_{1 \leq j \leq m} \left\{ \sum_{i=1}^m |a_{ij}|, \sum_{i=1}^m |b_{ij}| \right\}$$

and

$$\rho_3 = \max_{1 \leq i \leq m} \left\{ \sum_{j=1}^m |a_{ij}|, \sum_{j=1}^m |b_{ij}| \right\}$$

for $A = (a_{ij})$, $B = (b_{ij})$, (iii) $E[\|v_t\|^k] < +\infty$ *for any positive integer* $k \geq 1$, *and* (iv) $E[\|y_0\|^k] < +\infty$ *for any positive integer* $k \geq 1$. *Then*

$$E[\|y_t\|^k] < +\infty. \tag{14.3.17}$$

Proof: For $x = (x_i)$, we take the criterion function

$$G(x) = \left(\sum_{i=1}^m |x_i| \right)^k \tag{14.3.18}$$

for the first condition in (ii) and

$$G(x) = \left(\max_{i=1,\ldots,m} |x_i| \right)^k \tag{14.3.19}$$

for the second condition in (ii). Then we use the same arguments as the proofs of Proposition 1 and Proposition 2. □

We briefly mention that the results in Propositions 1 and 2 have some applications. For the disequilibrium econometric model consisting of (14.2.9), (14.2.10), and (14.2.11), we can derive a set of sufficient conditions for the geometrical ergodicity of the underlying processes. In particular, when the explanatory variables z_t $[= (z_{1t}', z_{2t}')']$ are a sequence of i.i.d. random variables, it is straightforward to obtain sufficient conditions for geometrical ergodicity.

3.2   The univariate SSAR(p) model

We give some sufficient conditions for the geometric ergodicity and existence of higher order moments for the pth order univariate SSAR model. We need some special consideration because the disturbance term in the Markovian representation is degenerate in a sense. From the Markovian representation for (14.2.8), we know that $\rho_2 = 1$ and $\rho_3 \geq 1$ for the univariate SSAR(p) models when $p \geq 2$. Hence Proposition 3 is useless for these SSAR models. The following conditions we shall give are sufficient, but often too strong, and we do not necessarily need those conditions.[3] The proof of Proposition 4 is based on the method used in Chan and Tong (1985) for threshold autoregressive models with minor modifications.

Proposition 4. *In the structural form of the pth order SSAR model given by* (14.2.2), *assume*

(i)   *the coherency conditions given by*

$$r_0 = -\frac{a_0}{\sigma_1} = -\frac{b_0}{\sigma_2},$$

$$r_1 = \frac{1 - a_1}{\sigma_1} = \frac{1 - b_1}{\sigma_2}, \tag{14.3.20}$$

$$r_j = -\frac{a_j}{\sigma_1} = -\frac{b_j}{\sigma_2} \quad (j = 2, \ldots, p),$$

(ii)   *a sufficient condition* $0 < \rho_4 < 1$, *where*

$$\rho_4 = \max \left\{ \sum_{j=1}^{p} |a_j|, \sum_{j=1}^{p} |b_j| \right\},$$

---

[3] Kunitomo (1999) has investigated the ergodic regions for the TAR(2) models and the SSAR(2) model, which are quite complex even in some special cases.

(iii) *that $\{v_t\}$ has an absolutely continuous distribution with respect to the Lebesgue measure on $\mathbf{R}$, and its density function $g(v)$ is continuous and strictly positive almost everywhere, and*

(iv) $E[|v_t|] < +\infty.$

Then $\{y_t\}$ is geometrically ergodic.

Proof:

(i) Because of the assumption $\sum_{j=1}^p |a_j| < 1$, we can take $\xi_j^{(1)}$ $(j = 1, \ldots, m = p)$ such that

$$1 < \frac{\xi_1^{(1)}}{\xi_2^{(1)}} < \frac{\xi_1^{(1)}}{\xi_3^{(1)}} < \cdots < \frac{\xi_1^{(1)}}{\xi_p^{(1)}} \tag{14.3.21}$$

and

$$1 > \sum_{j=1}^p |a_j| \frac{\xi_1^{(1)}}{\xi_j^{(1)}}. \tag{14.3.22}$$

Then we have $1 > \xi_{j+1}^{(1)}/\xi_j^{(1)}$ $(j = 1, \ldots, p - 1)$. By the same token, for the condition $\sum_{j=1}^p |b_j| < 1$, we can also take $\xi_j^{(2)}$ $(j = 1, \ldots, p)$ such that $1 > \xi_{j+1}^{(2)}/\xi_j^{(2)}$ $(j = 1, \ldots, p - 1)$ and

$$1 > \sum_{j=1}^p |b_j| \frac{\xi_1^{(2)}}{\xi_j^{(2)}}. \tag{14.3.23}$$

By rearranging $v_j = \min\{\xi_1^{(1)}/\xi_j^{(1)}, \xi_1^{(2)}/\xi_j^{(2)}\}$ $(j = 1, \ldots, p)$, under the assumptions $(0 < \rho_4 < 1)$ we can take ξ_j $(j = 1, \ldots, p)$ and θ such that $1 > \theta > \xi_{j+1}/\xi_j$ $(j = 1, \ldots, p - 1)$,

$$1 < \frac{\xi_1}{\xi_2} < \frac{\xi_1}{\xi_3} < \cdots < \frac{\xi_1}{\xi_p}, \tag{14.3.24}$$

and

$$1 > \theta > \max\left\{ \sum_{j=1}^p |a_j| \frac{\xi_1}{\xi_j}, \sum_{j=1}^p |b_j| \frac{\xi_1}{\xi_j} \right\}. \tag{14.3.25}$$

We take the criterion function

$$G(x) = 1 + \max_{1 \le j \le p} |x_j| \xi_j. \tag{14.3.26}$$

Let a vector process $y_t' = (y_t, y_{t-1}, \ldots, y_{t-p+1})$ and consider a

Markovian representation for $\{y_t\}$. Then it is straightforward to show

$$E[G(y_t) \mid y_{t-1} = x]$$

$$\leq c_8 + E\left[\max\left\{\sum_{j=1}^{p} |A_j(t)| \, |y_{t-j}|\xi_1, |x_1|\xi_2, \ldots, \right.\right.$$

$$\left.\left. |x_{p-1}|\xi_p\right\} \middle| y_{t-1} = x\right]$$

$$\leq c_9 + E\left[\max\left\{\sum_{j=1}^{p} |A_j(t)| \, |y_{t-j}|\xi_1, \theta|x_1|\xi_1, \ldots, \right.\right.$$

$$\left.\left. \theta|x_{p-1}|\xi_{p-1}\right\} \middle| y_{t-1} = x\right]$$

$$\leq c_{10} + \max\left\{\left[\max\left\{\sum_{j=1}^{p} |a_j|\frac{\xi_1}{\xi_j}, \sum_{j=1}^{p} |b_j|\frac{\xi_1}{\xi_j}\right\}\right]\right.$$

$$\left. \times [\max\{|x_1|\xi_1, \ldots, |x_p|\xi_p\}], \theta|x_1|\xi_1, \ldots, \theta|x_{p-1}|\xi_{p-1}\right\}$$

$$\leq c_{11} + \theta G(x), \tag{14.3.27}$$

where $A_j(t) = a_j I_t^{(1)} + b_j I_t^{(2)}$, $x = (x_i)$, c_i $(i = 8, \ldots, 11)$ are some positive constants, $I_t^{(1)} = I(y_t \geq y_{t-1})$ and $I_t^{(2)} = I(y_t < y_{t-1})$.

(ii) We consider the case when $p = m$. We define a function by

$$\sigma(z) = z\left[\frac{1}{\sigma_1}I_{\{z \geq 0\}} + \frac{1}{\sigma_2}I_{\{z < 0\}}\right] \tag{14.3.28}$$

for any z. Then given $y'_{t-1} = (y_{t-1}, \ldots, y_{t-m}) = (x_1, \ldots, x_m)$ and a set $A = (a_1, b_1) \times x_1 \times \cdots \times x_{m-1} \in \mathbf{R}^m$ with the condition $a_1 < b_1$, we can write

$$P(x, A) = \int_{\sigma(a_1 - x_1)}^{\sigma(b_1 - x_1)} g\left[v_t - r_0 - \sum_{i=1}^{m} r_i x_i\right] dv_t. \tag{14.3.29}$$

Let $\eta = \min\{1/\sigma_1, 1/\sigma_2\} > 0$. Because the density function $g(\cdot)$ is continuous and everywhere positive in $\mathbf{R}$ by our assumption, we can take a sufficiently small $\varepsilon > 0$ such that for some compact set C_1 we have $g[v_t - r_0 - \sum_{i=1}^{m} r_i x_i] > \varepsilon$ for any $(x_1, \ldots, x_m) \in C_1$. Hence given $y_{t-1} = x$ we have

$$P(x, A) > \varepsilon \eta (b_1 - a_1) > 0.$$

Also we take a set $A = (a_1, b_1) \times (a_2, b_2) \times x_1 \times \cdots \times x_{m-2} \in \mathbf{R}^m$ with the condition $a_i < b_i$ ($i = 1, 2$). Then

$$P^2(x, A) = \int_{\sigma(a_2-x_1)}^{\sigma(b_2-x_1)} \left\{ \int_{\sigma(a_1-y_t)}^{\sigma(b_1-y_t)} g \left[v_t - r_0 - \sum_{i=1}^{m} r_i x_i \right] \right.$$
$$\left. \times g \left[v_{t+1} - r_0 - r_1 y_t - \sum_{i=2}^{m} r_i x_{i-1} \right] dv_t \right\} dv_{t+1},$$

(14.3.30)

where $y_t = x_1 + \sigma(v_t - r_0 - \sum_{i=1}^{m} r_i x_i)$. Then by applying the same argument, we can take a sufficiently small $\varepsilon > 0$ and a compact set $\mathbf{C}_2$ such that for any $(x_1, \ldots, x_m) \in \mathbf{C}_2$,

$$P^2(x, A) > \varepsilon^2 \eta^2 (b_1 - a_1)(b_2 - a_2) > 0.$$

Hence by using the assumptions in (iii), for $A = (a_1, b_1) \times \cdots \times (a_m, b_m) \in \mathbf{R}^m$ with the condition $a_i < b_i$ ($i = 1, \ldots, m$), we have

$$\inf_{x \in C_m} P^m(x, A) > 0 \qquad (14.3.31)$$

for a compact set $\mathbf{C}_m$ in $\mathbf{R}^m$. These arguments show that the Markov chain for $\{y_t\}$ is ϕ-irreducible and $\mathbf{C}_m$ is a small set.

(iii)   By using the result in (i), we already know the growth condition in Lemma 1 is satisfied if we set $\mathbf{C}_m = \{\|x\| \leq M\}$ for a large M. Because the Markov chain for $\{y_t\}$ is aperiodic and ϕ-irreducible, as we have seen in (ii), we can apply Lemma 1. Hence we have established that $\{y_t\}$ is geometrically ergodic.   □

Proposition 5. *In the structural form of the pth order univariate SSAR model given by* (14.2.2), *assume* (i) *the coherency conditions given by* (14.3.20), (ii) *a sufficient condition for the geometric ergodicity* $\rho_4 < 1$, (iii) $E[|v_t|^k] < +\infty$ *for any positive integer* $k \geq 1$, *and* (iv) $E[|y_0|^k] < +\infty$ *for any positive integer* $k \geq 1$. *Then*

$$E[|y_t|^k] < +\infty. \qquad (14.3.32)$$

Proof: The method of proof is similar to the first part of the proof of Proposition 4. We take the criterion function

$$G(x) = 1 + \left(\max_{1 \leq j \leq p} |x_j| \xi_j \right)^k \qquad (14.3.33)$$

for $x = (x_i)$, where ξ_j ($j = 1, \ldots, p$) are defined as in the proof of Proposition 4. Then we consider the Markovian representation for $y'_t =$

$(y_t, y_{t-1}, \ldots, y_{t-p+1})$. For $k \geq 1$, we have

$$E[G(y_t) \mid y_{t-1} = x] \leq c_{12} + \theta G(x) \tag{14.3.34}$$

for some positive c_{12} and $0 < \theta < 1$. The rest of our argument is the same as the proof of Proposition 1. □

We should mention again that the above conditions given in this chapter are quite strong and sufficient, but they are not necessary and could be improved. Also, some of the results can easily be extended to more general cases. For an illustration, we will show the existence of moments for the univariate SSAR(p) model with the MA error.

Let $\{w_t\}$ be the i.i.d. disturbance terms satisfying condition (iii) with $k = 1$ in Proposition 5. We assume that the disturbance terms $\{v_t\}$ in the structural form of the SSAR(p) model given by (14.2.2) are a sequence of correlated random variables such that

$$v_t = \sum_{j=0}^{q} c_j^* w_{t-j}, \tag{14.3.35}$$

where $\{c_j^*\}$ are constants with $c_0^* = 1$ for the normalization. If we use a vector process $y_t' = (y_t, y_{t-1}, \ldots, y_{t-p+1}, w_t, w_{t-1}, \ldots, w_{t-q+1})$, then we have a Markovian representation for the vector process $\{y_t\}$. By taking the criterion function

$$G(x) = 1 + \max_{1 \leq j \leq p+q} |x_j| \xi_j, \tag{14.3.36}$$

where ξ_j $(j = 1, \ldots, m)$ are defined as in the proof of Proposition 4 and $m = p + q$, we have an inequality

$$E[G(y_t) \mid y_{t-1} = x] \leq c_{13} \left[1 + \sum_{j=1}^{q} |w_{t-j}| \right] + \theta G(x), \tag{14.3.37}$$

where $0 < \theta < 1$ and c_{13} is some constant. By repeating the above procedure and taking the conditional expectations, we have

$$E[G(y_t) \mid y_0 = x] \leq c_{13} \sum_{k=0}^{t-1} \theta^k E \left[1 + \sum_{j=1}^{q} |w_{t-k-j}| \mid y_0 = x \right] + \theta^t G(x). \tag{14.3.38}$$

Then by taking the expectation with respect to the initial distribution, we finally have

$$E[|y_t|] < +\infty, \tag{14.3.39}$$

provided that we assume condition (iv) with $k = 1$ in Proposition 5 and the condition $E[|w_s|] < \infty$ for $-q \leq s \leq 0$. We can use the similar arguments to obtain

$$E[|y_t|^k] < +\infty \tag{14.3.40}$$

for an arbitrary integer $k \geq 1$.

4   Estimation of the SSAR models

4.1   *Maximum likelihood estimation*

In nonlinear time series analysis the least squares method has been often used to estimate the unknown parameters of the time series models in the form of (14.1.2). Sato and Kunitomo (1996) have pointed out that there is a serious bias problem in the standard least squares estimation of the structural forms due to the simultaneity in the class of the SSAR models. The estimation problem of structural forms of simultaneous equation models has been one of the central issues in traditional econometric analyses.

Instead of the least squares estimation method, Sato and Kunitomo (1996a) have proposed to use maximum likelihood (ML) estimation for SSAR models. Given the initial condition y_0 and $|\Omega_i| \neq 0$ $(i = 1, 2)$, the ML estimator for vector SSAR models under Gaussian disturbances is defined by maximizing the conditional log likelihood function

$$\log L_T(\theta) = -\frac{m(T-1)}{2} \log 2\pi - \frac{1}{2} \sum_{t=2}^{T} \sum_{i=1}^{2} I_t^{(i)} \log |\Omega_i|$$

$$-\frac{1}{2} \sum_{t=2}^{T} \sum_{i=1}^{2} (y_t - \mu_i - A_i y_{t-1})' \Omega_i^{-1} (y_t - \mu_i - A_i y_{t-1}) I_t^{(i)}, \tag{14.4.1}$$

where $A_1 = A, A_2 = B, I_t^{(1)} = I(e_1' y_t \geq e_1' y_{t-1})$, and $I_t^{(2)} = I(e_1' y_t < e_1' y_{t-1})$ with the indicator function $I(\cdot)$. In the above notation we denote the vector of structural parameters by $\theta = (\theta_i)$.

We note that the numerical maximization in the maximum likelihood estimation should be done by using the conditions given by (14.2.5) and (14.2.6). Because the restrictions imposed by these conditions are not highly nonlinear, the surfaces of the likelihood functions are standard and smooth. As an illustration for the numerical optimization problem we give the concentrated likelihood function for the first order SSAR model with constant terms in Figure 14.3. In the SSAR(1) model $\theta' = (r_0, r_1, \sigma_1, \sigma_2)$ and we concentrate the likelihood function with respect to r_0 and r_1 such that $r_0 = r_0(\sigma_1, \sigma_2)$ and $r_1 = r_1(\sigma_1, \sigma_2)$ by using the likelihood equations.

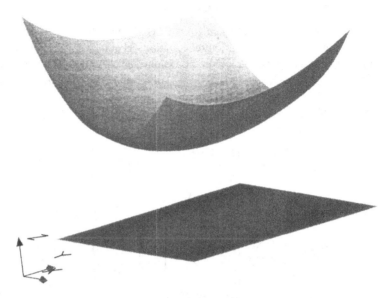

Figure 14.3. The surface of -1 times the concentrated likelihood function of the SSAR(1) model with constant terms when $a_1 = 0.2$ and $b_1 = 0.8$. It was constructed by simulations under Gaussian noise and $T = 20,000$. The Y-axis is σ_1, and the X-axis is σ_2.

As for the asymptotic properties of the ML estimation method when the underlying process is (geometrically) ergodic, under a set of regularity conditions and Gaussian disturbances the ML estimator $\hat{\theta}_{\mathrm{ML}}$ of unknown parameter θ is consistent and asymptotically normally distributed as

$$\sqrt{T}(\hat{\theta}_{\mathrm{ML}} - \theta_0) \xrightarrow{\mathrm{d}} N[0, I(\theta_0)^{-1}], \tag{14.4.2}$$

where

$$I(\theta_0) = \lim_{T \to \infty} \frac{1}{T} E\left[-\frac{\partial^2 \log L_T(\theta)}{\partial \theta \, \partial \theta'} \bigg|_{\theta=\theta_0} \right], \tag{14.4.3}$$

which is a nonsingular matrix, and θ_0 is the vector of true parameters.

The rigorous proof for the asymptotic properties of the ML estimator is the result of lengthy arguments on the (geometrically) ergodic SSAR models. Sato and Kunitomo (1996) have investigated the estimation problem and given a sketch of its proof. We also expect to have the corresponding results on the ML estimator for the scalar SSAR(p) models when they are (geometrically) ergodic.

4.2   *An instrumental variables estimation*

Because the estimation problem for the SSAR models is quite similar to the estimation problem of the structural equations as nonlinear simultaneous equations, an alternative estimation method is nonlinear instrumental variables (IV) estimation. Actually, this is a special case of the generalized method of moments (GMM) proposed by Hansen (1982). Given the initial condition y_0 and the observations for y_t [$= (y_{i,t})$], one type of IV estimators is defined by minimizing the criterion function

$$Q_T(\theta) = F_T(\theta)' H_T^{-1} F_T(\theta), \tag{14.4.4}$$

where

$$F_T(\theta) = \frac{1}{T} \sum_{t=2}^{T} \begin{pmatrix} v_{1,t}(\theta) \\ \vdots \\ v_{m,t}(\theta) \\ v_{1,t}^2(\theta) - 1 \\ \vdots \\ v_{m,t}^2(\theta) - 1 \end{pmatrix} \otimes \begin{pmatrix} 1 \\ y_{1,t-1} \\ \vdots \\ y_{m,t-1} \end{pmatrix},$$

$$\tag{14.4.5}$$

$$H_T = W \otimes \frac{1}{T} \sum_{t=2}^{T} \begin{pmatrix} 1 \\ y_{1,t-1} \\ \vdots \\ y_{m,t-1} \end{pmatrix} \begin{pmatrix} 1 \\ y_{1,t-1} \\ \vdots \\ y_{m,t-1} \end{pmatrix}',$$

and W is a $2m \times 2m$ nonsingular matrix. In this notation the random variables $v_t(\theta) = (v_{i,t}(\theta))$ and $y_{t-1} = (y_{i,t-1})$ are obtained from

$$v(\theta) = I_t^{(1)} D_1^{-1} [y_t - \mu_1 - A y_{t-1}] + I_t^{(2)} D_2^{-1} [y_t - \mu_2 - B y_{t-1}]$$

under the assumption of $|D_i| \neq 0$ ($i = 1, 2$). We denote the nonlinear instrumental variables estimator for the vector of the structural parameters θ as $\hat{\theta}_{IV}$.

Let

$$\Omega = E \left[\begin{pmatrix} v_{1,t}(\theta_0) \\ \vdots \\ v_{m,t}(\theta_0) \\ v_{1,t}^2(\theta_0) - 1 \\ \vdots \\ v_{m,t}^2(\theta_0) - 1 \end{pmatrix} (v_{1,t}(\theta_0), \ldots, v_{m,t}(\theta_0), v_{1,t}^2(\theta_0) - 1, \ldots, v_{m,t}^2(\theta_0) - 1) \right]$$

be the variance–covariance matrix. Then it may be desirable to use an estimator $\hat{\Omega}_T$ of Ω for the matrix W in H_T. But it seems that we should not use an

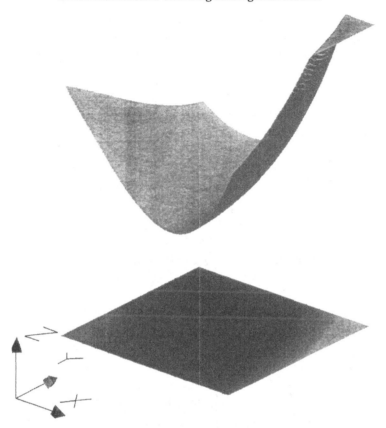

Figure 14.4. The surface of the concentrated criterion function of the SSAR(1) model with constant terms when $a_1 = 0.2$, $b_1 = 0.8$, and $\kappa_4 = -1.0$. It was constructed by simulations under Gaussian noise and $T = 20{,}000$. The Y-axis is σ_1, and the X-axis is σ_2.

iteration procedure for the minimization of the criterion function Q_T and $\hat{\Omega}_T$ in the estimation. This is partly because we can hardly obtain an initial consistent estimator for Ω, and we do not necessarily have good numerical convergence.

As an illustration of the numerical optimization problem, in Figure 14.4 we give the surface of the criterion function for the SSAR(1) model with constant terms when

$$W = \Omega = \begin{pmatrix} 1 & 0 \\ 0 & \kappa_4 + 2 \end{pmatrix}$$

as if it were known. The parameter κ_4 represents the kurtosis of the disturbances $[\kappa_4 = E(v_t^4) - 3]$, and we have concentrated the criterion function with respect to the parameters such that $r_0 = r_0(\sigma_1, \sigma_2)$ and $r_1 = r_1(\sigma_1, \sigma_2)$ by using its components. The surfaces of the criterion function can be flat in a direction depending on the parameter κ_4, which may result in difficulty in the numerical convergence of the estimation.

Also, we might use other orthogonality conditions such as $E[v_{i,t} v_{j,t}] = 0$ for $i \neq j$. Then the computation of the IV estimation would be more complicated.

For the asymptotic properties of the ML estimation method when the underlying process is (geometrically) ergodic, under a set of regularity conditions and fairly general distributions for the disturbances the nonlinear instrumental variables estimator $\hat{\theta}_{\mathrm{IV}}$ of unknown parameter θ is consistent and asymptotically normally distributed as

$$\sqrt{T}(\hat{\theta}_{\mathrm{IV}} - \theta_0) \xrightarrow{\mathrm{d}} N\,[0,\, V(\theta_0)]\,, \tag{14.4.6}$$

where

$$V(\theta_0) = (G'H^{-1}G)^{-1}G'H^{-1}(\Omega \otimes M)H^{-1}G(G'H^{-1}G)^{-1}, \tag{14.4.7}$$

where $H = \operatorname{plim}_{T \to \infty} H_T$,

$$G = \operatorname*{plim}_{T \to \infty}\left[-\frac{\partial F_T(\theta)}{\partial \theta}\bigg|_{\theta=\theta_0}\right],$$

and

$$M = \operatorname*{plim}_{T \to \infty}\frac{1}{T}\sum_{t=2}^{T}\begin{pmatrix}1\\ y_{1,t-1}\\ \vdots\\ y_{m,t-1}\end{pmatrix}\begin{pmatrix}1\\ y_{1,t-1}\\ \vdots\\ y_{m,t-1}\end{pmatrix}',$$

provided the quantities appearing are well defined.

The rigorous proof would be a set of lengthy arguments on the (geometrically) ergodic SSAR models. We also expect corresponding results on the nonlinear instrumental variables estimator for the univariate SSAR(p) models when they are (geometrically) ergodic. Sato (1999) has investigated the problems of statistical estimation and testing in SSAR models by using the instrumental variables method.

5   Concluding remarks

In this chapter we have discussed simultaneous switching autoregressive (SSAR) models. We have stressed the distinction between the structural form and the reduced form of such models. The reduced form has a Markovian representation, and it is as well defined as the probability model. However, we also use the structural form of the SSAR models, because it has often some theoretical justification and is intuitively appealing, as we have illustrated by the example of a disequilibrium econometric model in Section 2.2. We have adopted this distinction and the terminology from the traditional econometric modeling of simultaneous equations systems.

We have given several conditions for geometric ergodicity and the existence of moments for SSAR models. Some of our derivations and discussions in this chapter are free of technicalities, and we hope that they will be helpful to econometricians as well as to statisticians.

The SSAR model has been introduced through a disequilibrium econometric model, which can be classified as a Tobit type in the class of limited dependent variables models.[4] Amemiya (1974) has investigated the estimation method of a Fair–Jaffee model, and the estimation problem for SSAR models can be regarded as an extension in its dynamic aspects. Kunitomo and Sato (1996a, 1999) have discussed this issue in a systematic way. An interesting aspect of SSAR modeling in econometrics may be to shed new light on the possible applicability of limited dependent variables models, mainly developed for cross section data analyses, to nonlinear time series analysis.

Finally, we should mention that the standard SSAR process discussed in this chapter has been recently extended to a class of nonstationary SSAR processes by Kunitomo and Sato (1996b, 1999). For an illustration, in Figure 14.5 we give two sample paths of the homoskedastic SSARI(1) (first-order simultaneous switching integrated autoregressive) process and the SSARI(1) process with the first-order ARCH (autoregressive conditional heteroskedasticity) model. They are the integrated $I(1)$ processes defined by the structural form of the SSAR model given by (14.2.2) with $p = 1$ and

$$v_t = v_{t-1} + w_t \sqrt{h_t}, \qquad (14.5.1)$$

where $\{w_t\}$ are i.i.d. random variables with $E(w_t) = 0$, $E(w_t^2) = 1$, and $h_t = 1 + \alpha h_{t-1} w_{t-1}^2$ with the condition $0 \leq \alpha < 1$. The conditional heteroskedasticity is modeled by the volatility function h_t, and we have the homoskedastic SSARI(1) model when $\alpha = 0$ in this framework.[5] This type of time series modeling should be useful for econometric applications of financial time series data, because it gives a simple way to construct integrated processes with asymmetrical sample path as well as conditional heteroskedasticity. These aspects have been often observed in many financial time series, including asset price processes.

---

[4] Chapter 10 of Amemiya (1985) is a survey of this class of econometric applications, including some disequilibrium econometric models.

[5] The ARCH modeling for the conditional volatility functions of asset variables was introduced by Engle (1982).

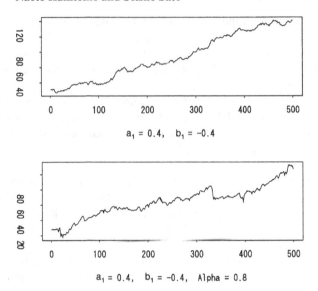

$a_1 = 0.4$, $b_1 = -0.4$

$a_1 = 0.4$, $b_1 = -0.4$,   Alpha = 0.8

Figure 14.5. Two sample paths generated by the nonergodic SSAR(1) processes: (a) a sample path of the SSAR(1) model given by Kunitomo and Sato (1999); (b) a sample path of the SSARI(1)–ARCH(1) model given by Kunitomo and Sato (1996b), where α is the coefficient of the ARCH(1) model for the disturbance terms. We have set a linear time trend function in the simulations.

REFERENCES

Amemiya, T. (1974), "A Note of a Fair and Jaffee Model," *Econometrica*, **42**, 759–762.
(1985), *Advanced Econometrics* (Oxford: Blackwell).
Chan, K. S. and Tong, H. (1985), "On the Use of the Deterministic Lyapunov Function for the Ergodicity of Stochastic Difference Equation," *Adv. Appl. Prob.*, **17**, 666–678.
Chan, K. S., Petruccelli, J. D., Tong, H., and Woolford, S. W. (1985), "A Multiple-Threshold AR(1) Model," *Adv. Appl. Prob.*, **22**, 267–279.
Engle, R. (1982), "Autoregressive Conditional Heteroskedasticity with Estimates of the Variances of U.K. Inflation," *Econometrica*, **50**, 987–1008.
Fair, R. C. and Jaffee, D. M. (1972), "Methods of Estimation for Markets in Disequilibrium," *Econometrica*, **40**, 497–514.
Hansen, L. P. (1982), "Large Sample Properties of Generalized Method of Moments Estimators," *Econometrica*, **50**, 1029–1054.
Kunitomo, N. (1999), "On Ergodicity of Some TAR(2) Processes," Discussion Paper CIRJE-F-55, Faculty of Economics, University of Tokyo.
Kunitomo, N. and Sato, S. (1996a), "Asymmetry in Economic Time Series and Simultaneous Switching Autoregressive Model," *Structural Change and Economic Dynamics*, **7**, 1–34.
(1996b), "Estimation of Asymmetrical Volatility for Asset Prices: The Simultaneous Switching ARIMA Approach," Discussion Paper 96-E-24, Institute for Monetary and Economic Studies, Bank of Japan.

(1999), "Stationary and Non-stationary Simultaneous Switching Autoregressive Models with an Application to Financial Time Series," *Japanese Economic Review*, **50**, 161–190.

Laffont, J. J. and Garcia, R. (1977), "Disequilibrium Econometrics for Business Loans," *Econometrica*, **45**, 1187–1204.

Nummelin, E. (1984), *General Irreducible Markov Chains and Non-negative Operators* (Cambridge, UK: Cambridge University Press).

Quandt, R. (1988), *The Econometrics of Disequilibrium* (Oxford: Blackwell).

Sato, S. (1999), "Estimation and Testing of the Simultaneous Switching Autoregressive Models by the Instrumental Variables Method" (in Japanese). *Journal of Japan Statistical Society*, **29**, 257–270.

Sato, S. and Kunitomo, N. (1996), "Some Properties of the Maximum Likelihood Estimator in the Simultaneous Switching Autoregressive Model," *Journal of Time Series Analysis*, **17**, 287–307.

Tong, H. (1990), *Non-linear Time Series* (Oxford: Oxford University Press).

CHAPTER 15

Some econometrics of scarring

Tony Lancaster

1   Introduction

If we have several successive durations for each of a number of individuals, we can consider the possibility that the distribution of any one depends on the values taken by earlier durations in the sequence. Such a dependence has been called lagged duration dependence.[1] If the durations are those of spells of unemployment, a briefer and more evocative phrase is *scarring*. This effect might work through a learning process (for example, the agent's beliefs might be dependent on the lengths of his previous spells); it might work through a signaling process in which employers use the lengths of previous spells in formulating their current job offers. Whatever the mechanism, it seems useful to be able to make a consistent estimate of the scarring effect, and this chapter aims to provide that.

In many potential applications (for example, unemployment) it is likely that the number of durations available for any individual is small. On the other hand, we may well have many individuals for whom the scarring effect, if it exists, might reasonably be assumed the same. This thought leads us to consider how to do inference about scarring with a sample of many individuals, each of whom contributes a small number of durations. So the problem is that of inference about autoregressive models for short, but broad, panel duration data.

It might at first seem a simple problem. If we have two durations for many people, why not look to see if there is any correlation between the two spell lengths? And if there is such correlation, then we could claim that it measures a scarring effect. The objection to this argument is that it is *the same person* who experiences both spells, and a correlation between their lengths might be

I would like to acknowledge helpful comments from Tiemen Woutersen, Richard Barrett, Cheng Hsiao, two referees, and participants at the Econometric Study Group meeting at Brisol, July 1998, and to thank the Department of Economics at the University of Hull for their hospitality.
[1] Heckman and Borjas (1980).

due to persistent unmeasured characteristics of each person. To counter this criticism it is necessary to allow for such effects as well as for scarring. The standard way to do this is to introduce person-specific time-invariant effects as additional unknown parameters in the model.

There is a very similar problem that has received much econometric attention: that of consistent inference in short autoregressive linear models while making allowance for agent-specific time-invariant effects. There are many solutions to this problem, all of which use an instrumental variable procedure.[2] But in a recent paper (Lancaster 1997) I have shown how to construct consistent, *likelihood-based* inference in such models. The present chapter follows the same approach, and with the same result. I shall show how to consistently estimate the autoregressive parameter in short panel duration data with fixed effects.[3]

Though, as in the linear model, there exist many consistent estimators in the autoregressive duration model, the method given here will be likelihood based. The advantage of such a method is that it uses all of the restrictions that are embodied in the likelihood function.

The strategy is to find an orthogonal reparametrization of the fixed effect for each individual, say f_i, to a new fixed effect, say g_i, which is independent of the scarring parameter in the information matrix sense. The g_i are then integrated out of the likelihood with respect to a prior distribution in which g_i is independent of the scarring parameter. The marginal posterior density of the scarring parameter is then shown to possess a mode which consistently estimates the true parameter as the number of individuals in the sample becomes large.

It should be emphasized that this method, though likelihood based, is not maximum likelihood (ML). The ML estimator is inconsistent in the scarring model, and we shall document this fact. This inconsistency is yet another example of the phenomenon described by Neyman and Scott (1948) in which the ML estimator is poorly behaved in the presence of a large number of incidental parameters.

In Section 2 I shall set up the model and provide a number of preliminary results. The model and the sampling scheme will be about the simplest one which allows for a scarring effect. The reason for this is partly expository (the argument will be simpler to follow in a stripped-down model) and partly because I do not know how to solve the problem in some more complicated settings. I shall indicate in the concluding section which extensions I know or believe

---

[2] See, for example, Hsiao (1986).

[3] Consistency here refers to the behavior of the estimator as the number of individuals becomes large with the number of durations for each agent fixed. The phrase "fixed effects" is shorthand for a quantity that is time invariant and agent specific and such that the likelihood is written conditionally on its value(s).

are easy and which extensions currently seem difficult. In Section 3 I derive the orthogonal reparametrization, and in Section 4 I calculate the marginal posterior density of the scarring parameter and show the consistency of its mode. In Section 5 I examine the maximum likelihood estimator of the scarring parameter and explore its inconsistency. In Section 6 I conclude the chapter with a brief discussion of extensions.

2   The scarring model

Consider the following model of scarring for any particular individual for whom we observe two[4] complete durations in the presence of persistent unmeasured individual specific effects. Let t_1 be exponential with hazard $v = e^f$. Given t_1 let t_2 be exponential with hazard vt_1^γ. The parameter γ measures the scarring effect and is common to all members of the population, while v is persistent, time-invariant, person-specific, unobserved heterogeneity, which I shall call the *fixed effect* for short. Observations for distinct individuals will be assumed stochastically independent given the values of f and of γ. If we have a sample of N individuals, there are $N + 1$ parameters in the model: N fixed effects, plus γ.[5] The joint distribution of t_1, t_2 given f, γ, for a single individual, is

$$p(t_1, t_2 \mid v, \gamma) = v^2 t_1^\gamma \exp\{-v(t_1 + t_2 t_1^\gamma)\}. \tag{15.1}$$

Since the conditional distribution of t_2 given t_1, f, γ is exponential, we readily find the conditional moments

$$\mathcal{E}(\log t_2 \mid t_1, f) = \psi(1) - \gamma \log t_1 - f, \qquad \mathcal{V}(\log t_2 \mid t_1, f) = \psi'(1). \tag{15.2}$$

So in terms of the log durations we have a homoscedastic linear autoregressive model with an additive fixed effect.[6]

It is worth emphasizing that the durations in this model are not, in general, contiguous in clock time. The clock time at which the first spell ends is not in general the clock time at which the second begins. The t's refer to times on clocks that are reset to zero each time a spell ends. A model for contiguous, autocorrelated, exponential durations exists in the statistics literature; it was apparently first considered by Wold (1948), and was mentioned recently by Engle and Russell (1998), who give further literature citations.

[4] The generalization to many durations per individual is given briefly in Section 6.
[5] Note that this is a first order autoregressive model. Higher order models may be treated in a similar way to the approach of this chapter but are, perhaps, of less practical interest.
[6] $\psi(\cdot)$ is the digamma function, and we have $\psi(1) = -0.5772$, $\psi'(1) = 1.645$.

3   An orthogonal reparametrization

The main procedure to be studied in this chapter is a Bayesian[7] method in which the prior is chosen with a view to consistent estimation of the scarring parameter from a large number of pairs of durations. The idea behind the construction of the prior is to find a reparametrization of the fixed effect f to a new effect g such that g and γ are as nearly as possible independent in the likelihood. We then adopt a prior in which g and γ are independent. We operationalize the idea of "near-independence in the likelihood" by asking that the information matrix for g, γ be diagonal. So the first step is to find such an orthogonal reparametrization of $f_1, f_2, \ldots, f_N$.

The log likelihood provided by a single agent is, from (15.1),

$$L(f, \gamma) = 2f + \gamma \log t_1 - e^f\left(t_1 + t_2 t_1^\gamma\right),$$

from which we derive the scores and the information matrix

$$L_f = 2 - e^f\left(t_1 + t_2 t_1^\gamma\right), \qquad L_\gamma = \log t_1 - e^f t_2 t_1^\gamma \log t_1,$$

$$L_{ff} = -e^f\left(t_1 + t_2 t_1^\gamma\right), \qquad L_{f\gamma} = -e^f t_2 t_1^\gamma \log t_1,$$

$$L_{\gamma\gamma} = -e^f t_2 t_1^\gamma \log^2 t_1,$$

$$\mathcal{I}(f, \gamma) = \begin{pmatrix} 2 & f - \psi(1) \\ f - \psi(1) & \psi'(1) + (\psi(1) - f)^2 \end{pmatrix}.$$

It can be seen that the information matrix is not diagonal. We therefore seek a transformation to new parameters g, γ whose information matrix will be diagonal. Write $f = f(g, \gamma)$. Then $L_g = L_f\, \partial f / \partial g$ and

$$L_{g\gamma} = L_f\left(\frac{\partial(\partial f/\partial g)}{\partial \gamma}\right) + \frac{\partial f}{\partial g}\left[L_{ff}\frac{\partial f}{\partial \gamma} + L_{f\gamma}\right].$$

Taking expectations using $\mathcal{E}(L_f) = 0$ and equating the result to zero gives

$$\mathcal{E}(L_{g\gamma}) = 0 = \frac{\partial f}{\partial g}\left[\mathcal{E}(L_{ff})\frac{\partial f}{\partial \gamma} + \mathcal{E}(L_{f\gamma})\right]. \tag{15.3}$$

Thus, to find g we must solve the differential equation

$$\mathcal{E}(L_{ff})\frac{\partial f}{\partial \gamma} + \mathcal{E}(L_{f\gamma}) = 0.$$

---

[7] Perhaps "Bayesian" should be in quotation marks, since choosing a prior to achieve consistent inference is not quite in the spirit of mainstream Bayesian econometrics. There is, however, a small Bayesian literature on consistent estimation in problems such as the present one involving infinite dimensional parameter spaces. See, for example, Diaconis and Freedman (1986).

Using the information matrix provided above, we find the equation

$$\frac{\partial f}{\partial \gamma} = \frac{f - \psi(1)}{2} \tag{15.4}$$

with general solution

$$f = \psi(1) + g e^{\gamma/2} \tag{15.5}$$

as a version of the required function $f(g, \gamma)$. The new fixed effect g has been introduced as the arbitrary constant that arises in the solution of the differential equation.

If we now think of the likelihood as a function of g, γ, the information matrix is readily found to be

$$\mathcal{I}(g, \gamma) = \begin{pmatrix} 2e^{\gamma} & 0 \\ 0 & \psi'(1) + (\psi(1) - f)^2 \end{pmatrix}. \tag{15.6}$$

Thus g, γ is an orthogonal reparametrization, and this is true for every individual. Thus the information matrix for $g_1, \ldots, g_N$, γ is itself diagonal.

In the next section we propose a joint prior density for $g_1, \ldots, g_N$ and γ in which these parameters are mutually independent. We then integrate out the new fixed effects to determine a marginal posterior density for γ. The mode of this density will be the proposed consistent estimator.

4   Marginal posterior densities

We shall now give a prior which leads to consistent inference for γ. This is motivated by the construction of the last section in which we showed that g, γ are information orthogonal and, therefore, asymptotically in the number of spells available for each person, independent. Assume therefore that, in the prior, $g_1, \ldots, g_N$, γ are mutually independent and that the marginal density of any g is uniform on the real line. The marginal density of γ will also be taken as uniform, but this is only for simplicity of notation. Since information accumulates about γ as $N \to \infty$, any nondogmatic prior will eventually be dominated by the data.

Then the marginal posterior density of γ may be developed as

$$p(\gamma \,|\, t_1, t_2) \propto \prod_i \int_{-\infty}^{\infty} e^{2f_i} t_{1i}^{\gamma} \exp\{-e_i^f \left(t_{1i} + t_{2i} t_{1i}^{\gamma}\right)\} \, dg_i$$

$$= \prod_i \int_{-\infty}^{\infty} e^{2f_i} t_{1i}^{\gamma} \exp\{-e_i^f \left(t_{1i} + t_{2i} t_{1i}^{\gamma}\right)\} e^{-\gamma/2} \, df_i$$

$$= \prod_i \frac{e^{-\gamma/2} t_{1i}^{\gamma}}{\left(t_{1i} + t_{2i} t_{1i}^{\gamma}\right)^2}.$$

The critical step in this development is the move from the first line to the second, where we change the variable of integration from g to f. This introduces the Jacobian term $e^{-\gamma/2}$.

The proposed estimator, $\tilde{\gamma}$, maximizes the log posterior density, say,

$$q(\gamma) = -N\gamma/2 + \gamma \sum \log t_{1i} - 2 \sum \log\left(t_{1i} + t_{2i}t_{1i}^{\gamma}\right) \qquad (15.7)$$

over the real line. It is easy to see that $q(\cdot)$ is globally concave and that $\tilde{\gamma}$ solves $q'(\tilde{\gamma}) = 0$.

To prove consistency we need to make some hypothesis about the variation of f in the population. We shall assume that the $\{f_i\}$ are independently and identically distributed with finite first two moments. Then the pairs t_{1i}, t_{2i} are themselves independently and identically distributed, and we may show that $N^{-1}q(\gamma)$ converges uniformly in probability to its expectation on any compact parameter space. The main element in the consistency proof then consists in showing that $\mathcal{E}q(\gamma)$ is uniquely maximized at γ_0. It suffices to show that $\mathcal{E}q(\gamma) \mid f$ is so maximized, that is, that $\mathcal{E}q'(\gamma_0) = 0$ and $\mathcal{E}q''(\gamma_0) < 0$. The algebra showing these results is given in the appendix to this chapter.

Exact finite sample Bayesian inference about γ may be carried out directly from the marginal posterior density – by plotting it, in the present one parameter model, or more generally by sampling from it using the Markov chain Monte Carlo method.

It should be noted that while uniform integration of an orthogonal fixed effect leads to consistent Bayesian inference in the present model and a number of others of econometric interest (Lancaster 1997), there is no guarantee that it will always do so.

5   The maximum likelihood estimator

In this section we shall show that the ML estimator is inconsistent for γ and characterize that inconsistency.

The ML estimator estimates $v_1, \ldots, v_N, \gamma$, and it may be found by first concentrating the likelihood with respect to the v's and then maximizing the concentrated likelihood. For given γ the ML estimator of v_i is readily found, from (15.1), to be $2/(t_{1i} + t_{2i}t_{1i}^{\gamma})$. Substituting these solutions in the likelihood then gives the concentrated log likelihood

$$l^c(\gamma) = \gamma \sum \log t_{1i} - 2 \sum \log\left(t_{1i} + t_{2i}t_{1i}^{\gamma}\right). \qquad (15.8)$$

Comparing this expression with (15.7), we see that this expression is the log marginal posterior density that we would have found had we assumed that f, γ were independently and uniformly distributed. It is the posterior density without the jacobian term $e^{-N\gamma/2}$.

The inconsistency of ML follows from the consistency of the posterior mode and the fact that ML maximizes the log posterior density plus $N\gamma/2$. The form taken by the inconsistency is interesting; it is independent of the true value of γ. If $f = \log v$ is iid with mean zero and variance σ_f^2, a first order approximation to the inconsistency is

$$\text{plim } \hat{\gamma}_{ml} - \gamma = \frac{1}{0.8 + 2\sigma_f^2/3}. \tag{15.9}$$

Whatever the true value of γ, even if it is zero, if there is no omitted heterogeneity, then the error in the ML estimator will be about $1/0.8 = 1.25$. On the other hand, if σ_f^2 is very large, the inconsistency will be small. Recall that the ML estimator is Bayes under a flat, infinite variance prior on f. So ML is fine when this prior is roughly right.[8] To get a feel for the magnitude of σ_f^2, consider the variance of the logarithm of the first spell length. This is $\psi'(1) + \sigma_f^2 = 1.645 + \sigma_f^2$. So if half the variation in (the logarithms) of first spell lengths was attributable to unmeasured individual characteristics, then $\sigma_f^2 = 1.645$ and the error in the ML estimator will be about 0.5, independently of the true value of γ.

6 Concluding remarks

In this chapter we have shown how to make consistent estimates of a scarring effect using two consecutive uncensored spell lengths for many people. Several extensions of the model used here are straightforward and have been omitted only for expositional clarity. Others are harder.

6.1 *Exogenous time-varying covariates*

It is straightforward to modify the approach taken in this chapter to allow for strictly exogenous covariates which modify the hazard in a multiplicative way. Specifically, we can allow the hazard for t_1 to be $ve^{x_{1i}\beta}$ and the hazard for t_2 given t_1 to be $ve^{x_{2i}\beta}t_1^\gamma$. No change to the orthogonal parametrization is needed as long as we center each pair of x's to have mean zero. Then g is orthogonal not only to γ but also to β. The criterion function (15.7) is changed to

$$q(\gamma, \beta) = -N\gamma/2 + \gamma \sum \log t_{1i} - 2 \sum \log \left(e^{x_{1i}\beta}t_{1i} + e^{x_{2i}\beta}t_{2i}t_{1i}^\gamma\right). \tag{15.10}$$

The mode of this log posterior density provides a consistent estimator of β, γ if, for example, we assume that x_{1i}, x_{2i} are iid with finite second moments.

---

[8] The inconsistency of ML in this model is yet another manifestation of its poor behavior in models where the number of parameters grows with the sample size, a phenomenon described by Neyman and Scott in their *Econometrica* chapter of 1948. Lancaster (1999) provides a recent survey of this "incidental parameter" problem.

Alternatively, a Markov chain Monte Carlo sampler which exploits the log concavity of the component conditional densities is readily constructed. This provides exact finite sample inference.

6.2   *Many spells*

Another easy extension is to the case where we observe two *or more* spells for each person, not necessarily the same number for each person. These spell lengths must, however, be stochastically independent conditional on the fixed effect and covariate values. The only change here is to alter the differential equation (15.4) whose solution provides the orthogonal parameter, and the new equation is also readily solved. Specifically, suppose we observe T conditionally independent durations for each agent such that $t_1 \sim E(v)$ and for $s > 1$, $t_s \mid t_{s-1}, \ldots, t_1 \sim E(v t_{s-1}^\gamma)$, $s = 2, \ldots, T$. The log likelihood is thus

$$L(f, \gamma) = Tf + \gamma \sum_{s=1}^{T-1} \log t_s - v \sum_{s=2}^{T} t_s t_{s-1}^\gamma - v t_1.$$

Define

$$b(z) = -\frac{1}{T} \sum_{t=1}^{T-1} \frac{T-t}{t} z^t. \tag{15.11}$$

Then an orthogonal parameter g is provided by

$$f = \psi(1) + g e^{b(-\gamma)},$$

which generalizes (15.5). The marginal posterior density of γ is then[9]

$$p(\gamma \mid t_1, \ldots, t_T) \propto \prod_i \frac{e^{-b(-\gamma)} \prod_{s=1}^{T-1} t_{si}^\gamma}{\left(t_{1i} + \sum_{s=2}^{T} t_{si} t_{s-1,i}^\gamma\right)^T}.$$

The function $b(\cdot)$ is the same function as appears in the orthogonalization of the dynamic normal linear model (Lancaster 1997).

6.3   *Right censoring*

Duration data, as is well known, is often subject to right censoring. The question then arises as to whether the method described above can yield consistent estimation with right-censored data. To make this question specific, let us imagine a situation in which the first spells are uncensored but the second spells are subject to right censoring at an exogenously fixed time c. In this case we can show

---

[9] The modification to allow for different numbers of durations for each agent is obvious.

that the transformation $f = \psi(1) + g e^{\gamma/2}$ does *not* orthogonalize the informa-tion matrix. The orthogonal reparametrization involves a differential equation which does not appear to have an analytical solution. On the other hand, some numerical calculations using artificially generated data suggest that consistency of the Bayes procedure is little affected even when the censoring fraction is as large as 50%. Further study is desirable.

6.4 *Other sampling schemes*

Duration data in economics does not often come in the form of pairs of condi-tionally independent spell lengths.[10] Typically, it is more appropriate to think of spells arising as part of a multiple state stochastic process observed for a fixed period of time. In this case the number of spells will be random and their lengths dependent. It might be useful to think about parametrizations of, say, alternating Poisson processes with a common time-invariant parameter.

Appendix

To show that $\mathcal{E}(q'(\gamma)) = 0$ at the truth, it is useful to work out the joint distri-bution of $z_2 = t_1 + t_2 t_1^{\gamma}$ and $z_1 = t_1$. Elementary calculations give

$$p(z_1, z_2) = v^2 e^{-vz_2}, \qquad z_2 \geq z_1,$$
$$p(z_1) = v e^{-vz_1},$$
$$p(z_2) = v^2 z_2 e^{-vz_2},$$
$$p(z_2 \mid z_1) = v e^{-v(z_2 - z_1)}, \qquad z_2 \geq z_1,$$
$$p(z_1 \mid z_2) = 1/z_2, \qquad z_1 \leq z_2,$$

where $v = e^f$. We may then deduce that, for example,

$$\mathcal{E}\left(z_1^s \mid z_2\right) = \frac{z_2^s}{s+1}, \qquad \mathcal{E}(\log z_1 \mid z_2) = \log z_2 - 1,$$
$$\mathcal{E}(z_1 \log z_1 \mid z_2) = \frac{z_2(2 \log z_2 - 1)}{4},$$

etc. Now $q'(\gamma)$ may be written as

$$q'(\gamma) = -\frac{1}{2} - \log z_1 + 2z_1 \log z_1/z_2,$$

and taking expectations using the above results establishes that this expression has mean zero. That this locates a unique maximum follows from the global concavity of q.

---

[10] Woutersen (2000) develops new, consistent, estimators for censored, dependent, panel duration data.

REFERENCES

Diaconis, P. and Freedman, D. (1986), "On the Consistency of Bayes Estimates," *Annals of Statistics*, **14**, 1–67.

Engle, R. F. and Russell, J. R. (1988), "Autoregressive Conditional Duration: A New Model for Irregularly Spaced Financial Data," *Econometrica*, **66**, 5, 1127–1162.

Heckman, J. J. and Borjas, G. (1980), "Does Unemployment Cause Future Unemployment? Definitions, Questions and Answers from a Continuous Time Model of Heterogeneity and State Dependence," *Economica*, **47**, 247–283.

Hsiao, C. (1986), *Analysis of Panel Data* (Cambridge: Cambridge University Press).

Lancaster, T. (1997), "Orthogonal Parameters and Panel Data," Brown University, Department of Economics, WP 97-32.

Lancaster, T. (2000), "The Incidental Parameter Problem Since 1948," *Journal of Econometrics*, **95**, 391–413.

Neyman, J. and Scott, E. L. (1948), "Consistent Estimation from Partially Consistent Observations," *Econometrica*, **16**, 1–32.

Wold, H. (1948), "On Stationary Point Processes and Markov Chains," *Skandinavisk Aktuarietidskrift*, **31**, 229–240.

Woutersen, T. (2000), "Essays on the Integrated Hazard and Orthogonality Concepts," Ph.D. dissertation, Brown University.

CHAPTER 16

A censored switching regression approach to evaluating the effect of sunk costs and firm-level disequilibrium on export performance

Seung-Jae Yhee, J. B. Nugent, and Cheng Hsiao

1   Introduction

Despite ever increasing recognition of the importance of manufacturers' exports to economic growth, economists have been nearly silent on the effectiveness of various specific export promotion policies and on how their effectiveness might vary across enterprises according to the relative importance of different constraints which these firms face. Indeed, trade models use equilibrium models and typically ignore firm-level variables in order to concentrate on macro- or industry-level factors such as exchange rates, tariff rates, and other general types of policies.

Recently, however, several papers analyzing firm behavior among both exporters and nonexporters have begun to emerge. For example, Bernard and Jensen (1995a,b, 1996, 1997) found significant differences between exporters and nonexporters among US manufacturing plants.[1] Similar differences have been observed among the firms in other countries, especially in developing countries where the interest is greatest (Roberts and Tybout 1997 for Colombia; Aw and Batra 1994 for Taiwan; Aitken, Hanson, and Harrison 1997 for Mexico, and Bernard and Wagner 1997 for Germany). In particular, Aitken, Hanson, and Harrison (1997) provided evidence that plant size, wages, and especially foreign ownership are positively related to the decision to export. They also examined whether spillovers associated with one firm's export activity reduced the cost of exporting for other firms, and then found evidence of spillovers from multinational enterprises but not from general export activity. Roberts

The authors express their appreciation to Linsu Kim and his students from Korea University for their efforts in collecting this data, to the World Bank for its financial support of the data collection effort, and to the National Science Foundation for research support.

[1] In particular, exporters were found to have more workers, proportionally more white-collar workers, higher wages, higher productivity, greater capital intensity, and a higher probability of being part of a multinational firm than nonexporters.

and Tybout (1997) showed that in the presence of sunk costs, a firm's prior export experience as well as some plant characteristics, such as size of capital, plant age, and ownership structure, are positively related to the propensity to export. Aw and Hwang (1995) found that the bulk of the difference in output between the groups of producers was explained by the larger size of exporters than nonexporters, and there were significant differences in productivity levels between exporters and nonexporters. On the other hand, Kim, Nugent, and Yhee (1997) analyzed the role of transaction costs as sunk costs in Korean small- and medium-sized enterprises' choice among alternative export channels, under the assumption that firm-specific transaction costs for a given channel are a function of the firm's characteristics.[2]

Among others, Bernard and Jensen (1996) and Roberts and Tybout (1997) more explicitly considered sunk costs in determining export performance, showing that such costs serve as barriers to entry into and exit from export markets. Both such studies tested for the effects of entry costs at the firm level by estimating the coefficient(s) of a dummy variable indicating whether or not a firm had participated in export markets in the previous period. None of these papers has examined the effects of specific trade promotion variables and their variation across firm types.

This chapter follows Bernard and Jensen (1996) and Roberts and Tybout (1997) in considering sunk costs as barriers to movement into and out of export markets, and also considering plant-level characteristics, in explaining variations in export behavior across firms. However, in this chapter a distinctive disequilibrium analysis is employed in which sunk costs play the crucial role of distinguishing between a firm's potential production and its potential marketing. Thereby, the sunk costs provide a source of disequilibrium internal to the firm rather than between supply and demand. A firm's actual exports are realized only when the firm's production potential (or technological capability) and (international) marketing capability are equalized and realized.[3] From this perspective, either its technological capability or its international marketing capability will constrain a firm's export performance. If a firm possesses neither or only one of these capabilities, it remains a nonexporter. If one capability is weak relative to the other, a firm's export behavior is constrained by the weaker of the two capabilities. Sunk costs, especially when combined with uncertainty, can impede adjustments of the two capabilities. Such problems are especially acute in small- and medium-sized enterprises (SMEs), since they are likely to be especially weak in one or the other or both of these capabilities. At the same time, SMEs become an especially important class of firms for evaluating the effectiveness of specific export promotion variables that are often focused on SMEs.

---

[2] Four channels were considered: direct exporting, foreign buyers, nonprofit agencies, and subcontracting.

[3] The definitions of the technology capability and marketing capability will be given in Section 2.1.

Therefore, in this chapter we use a switching regression model with censoring to identify which constraint – technological capability (T-regime) or marketing capability (M-regime) – is the binding one as far as export performance is concerned in a sample of Korean SMEs. Unlike Bernard and Jensen (1996) and Roberts and Tybout (1997), which use but one logit equation, our switching regression model consists of two equations, one corresponding to each regime type. This switching regression model has the flexibility of (i) analyzing a firm's export behavior in terms of both the T and M regimes, which relate directly to each firm's two main activities, production management and marketing management; (ii) identifying those plant characteristics which exert the greatest influence over each regime type; and (iii) capturing the role of sunk costs in terms of the estimated probabilities of excess marketing capability.[4] This is done for a sample of Korean SMEs spread over four specific sectors in which SMEs have been prominent in exports and where the Korean government has had SME export support systems in place for some time. For each type of support, we identify its effects not only on actual exports but also on each regime type (or constraint). In this way we analyze the role of sunk costs in export performance from a disequilibrium perspective.

The organization of this chapter is as follows: Section 2 discusses the concept, role, and sources of sunk costs, and provides a framework for analyzing SME export performance. In Section 3, a switching model is set up, and the data and measures used described. Section 4 reports the results. A summary of the findings and policy implications is given in Section 5.

2   Sunk costs and the analysis of SME export performance

2.1   *Sunk costs*

Sunk costs are investment expenditures that cannot be fully recovered through transfer or sale once undertaken. The extent of sunk costs depends on the difference in value between the original outlay less depreciation and its alternative use (salvage value, resale or transfer price). The larger that difference, the more sunk costs can distort a firm's optimal decision in a competitive environment.

Asplund (1995) collected information on salvage values of individual machine tools in Swedish manufacturing industries in both 1960 and 1990 to show that 47% and 78%, respectively, of the discarded assets were scrapped rather than sold on second-hand markets. This means that in both samples these investments are largely sunk costs. He also showed that for an average new machine, a firm can expect to get back from instant resale only 10–55% of the initial price. Sutton (1991) considered R&D and advertising costs as additional sources of

---

[4]   The probability of excess technology capability is just 1 minus the probability of excess marketing capability.

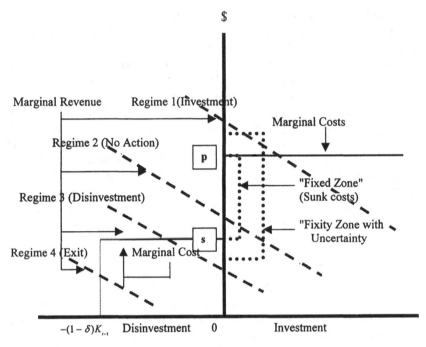

Figure 16.1. Investment behavior under sunk cost.

exogenous and endogenous sunk costs that can serve as barriers to entry and exit and thereby affect industry structure. Bernard and Jensen (1996) showed that, if a firm exported yesterday but not today, it would lose all the sunk costs spent for penetrating export markets. On the other hand, Roberts and Tybout (1997) showed that staying out of export markets more than 2 years makes a firm lose all the sunk costs spent to enter export markets. This is why sunk costs are believed to matter and are an increasingly common feature of economic analysis.

To explain the role of sunk costs, Barham and Chavas (1997) used Figure 16.1 after deriving an optimal investment rule in a dynamic framework. In this figure, there are two marginal costs on investment: One is the unit purchase price of capital, p, when there is a positive investment. The other is the unit salvage value, s, when there is a disinvestment. To avoid an arbitrage opportunity, p must be greater than s. The sunk cost is the difference between the two marginal costs. In regime 1, a positive investment occurs because the present value of marginal product of investment is greater than the marginal cost. In regime 2, however, if the present value of marginal product lies between the two marginal costs, a firm has no incentive either to invest or to disinvest. This is a *zone of asset fixity* wherein a firm's behavior would not be affected by small changes in the economic environment. Finally, in regime 3, the firm disinvests or exits from the market because the present value of marginal product is below the unit salvage value.

According to Barham and Chavas (1997), the distortions due to sunk costs are: (i) the zone of asset fixity in regime 2 where the firm fails to react to economic signals, (ii) the irreversible character of the effects after their original cause is removed, and (iii) the fact that when combined with uncertainty, sunk costs have adverse effects on investment. If a firm has a positive probability of exiting during its planning horizon, sunk costs act as the disincentive to invest. That is, sunk costs in connection with uncertainty act as entry barriers under very general conditions. On the contrary, if a firm has a positive probability of re-entry during its planning horizon, sunk costs reduce the incentive to disinvest and to exit. Therefore, the fixity zone becomes wider, as shown in the figure. In summary, sunk costs reduce resource mobility, particularly when they are combined with irreversibility and uncertainty, by acting as a barrier to both entry and exit. By limiting the mobility of a firm's resources, both a firm's technological and its marketing capabilities can be limited for a given period.

Kim (1997) defines a firm's technological capability as "the ability to make effective use of technological knowledge in efforts to assimilate, use, adapt, and change existing technologies." A firm's technological capability in any period consists of three elements: production, investment (including duplication and expansion), and innovation. For each firm, these three elements form the firm's technology capability for any given period and can be represented by various characteristics of each firm's internal and external environment, as explained in the following subsection on the sources of sunk costs.

The kinds of investment outlays needed for satisfying foreign demand are more site-specific, time-specific, and/or firm- or industry-specific than those needed for satisfying domestic demand. The physical features of such investments make them costly to install, remove, or relocate. For this reason the value of such investments can fall sharply over time. Such features make it costly to retrofit or transfer them to other firms, industries, or countries. According to Sutton (1991), a major source of such sunk costs is the costs of adaptive R&D expenditures, restructuring, and retraining to improve productivity promptly in the face of changes, either foreseen or unforeseen.

Similarly, a firm's marketing capability can be defined in terms of three parallel elements, namely, the maintenance of existing export markets, entry into new markets, and innovation in marketing techniques. Each entails sunk costs: a difference between the original value of such outlays and their value in an alternative use. Among these are (i) the costs of advertising, identifying appropriate trading partners, and obtaining information about market conditions in export markets[5]; (ii) the costs of constructing and maintaining marketing

---

[5] For some pioneering efforts along these lines see Keesing (1979), and Levy, Berry, and Nugent (1999).

networks; (iii) the costs of developing new marketing techniques; (iv) the costs of negotiating, writing, and enforcing contracts between the parties; and (v) the costs of information on government regulations and other policies in both foreign and domestic markets. These sunk costs are likely to be especially large for SMEs because of their concentration on rather specific niche markets.

Despite the obvious relevance of these kinds of costs in export markets, surprisingly few attempts have been made to use the sunk-cost perspective for testing hypotheses concerning alternative means of penetrating international markets and for deriving policy implications.

2.2   A disequilibrium framework for the analysis of SME exports

Our framework for the analysis of SME exports is a disequilibrium one based on the concept of strategic management. Strategic management can be viewed, as in Dess and Miller (1993), as a series of steps in which a chief executive officer (CEO) should accomplish the following tasks: (i) analyze the opportunities and threats or constraints that exist in the external environment; (ii) analyze the organization's internal strengths and weaknesses; (iii) identify the organization's objectives; (iv) formulate strategies (at the corporate, business unit, and functional levels) to match the organization's strengths and weaknesses with the opportunities and threats offered by its external environment; (v) implement those strategies; and (vi) engage in strategic control activities to ensure goal attainment.

Any SME possesses a specific internal environment consisting of a certain financial, technical, human, and organizational endowment of resources, as well as a certain size. The internal environment has been accumulated through the history of the firm and determines the SME's strengths and weaknesses as far as foreign markets are concerned. There also exists an external environment, which includes the existing as well as changing conditions in technology, in finance, labor, capital, and export markets, and in governmental and other support systems that maybe available to the firm. The various characteristics of this external environment can act as either opportunities or threats to a firm. At any time, the firm may be incompletely adjusted to these opportunities and threats. The internal and external environmental conditions specify the predetermined and/or exogenous structure that provides the basis for each firm to choose its optimal managerial strategies. In strategic management theory, the determination of a firm's internal environment and external environment is called *strengths, weaknesses, opportunities, and threats analysis* (SWOT analysis). The analysis identifies the particular factors in the exogenous structure that affect the technological or marketing capabilities or both.

The flow chart in Figure 16.2 summarizes an SME's strategic decision making process for exporting. By following the arrows in the diagram, the flow of an SME's decision-making process can be easily understood.

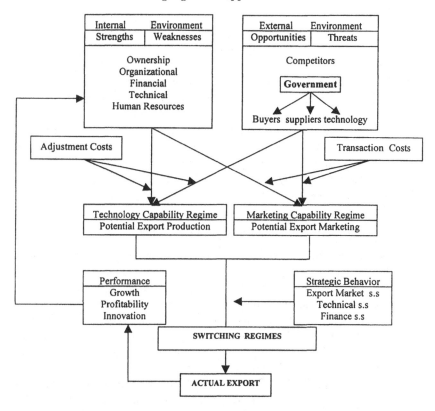

Figure 16.2. Framework for SME analysis.

The external environment includes those elements external to the SME that directly affect the formulation and accomplishment of its business objectives and, in turn, its success and failure. Major elements include: (i) foreign buyers, (ii) suppliers, including creditors, (iii) competitors, (iv) government as a regulator/facilitator, and (v) technology.

One of the most important elements in the external environment of an SME is the government. The government can enable a firm to draw upon opportunities and to mitigate the threats to it stemming from other elements in the external environment by providing various types of support. Since SMEs may be too weak to handle the large sunk costs in catering to export markets, public assistance in managing these sunk costs can be extremely important. The arrows in Figure 16.2 going from the government element to the suppliers element (financial support system), to the buyers element (marketing support system), and finally to the technology element (technical support system) represent the various ways in which government may act as a catalyst.

Since different SMEs may be at different stages in their life cycles, they may pursue different competitive strategies, each requiring a different combination of resources and capabilities. In this respect, the censored switching regression model developed in the next section can be useful in identifying the relative extent to which the technology constraint is more (or less) binding than the marketing constraint. This is measured in terms of the probability of an excess marketing (or technology) constraint, the time pattern of which is traced out, thereby identifying different stages through which SMEs may evolve. By averaging the probabilities by sector or industry, it is possible to find which sector or industry is booming or decaying in its business cycle and/or life cycle. From such a disequilibrium analysis, the appropriate role for government support to SMEs at different points in their life cycle can be better identified.

3   A censored switching regression model and data

To get some idea about how the concept of switching regimes can be applied to SMEs and their exports, turn to Table 16.1, which is based on a survey on Korean SMEs in 1989. The table shows several reasons why Korean SMEs suffer from bottlenecks in finance. Out of 941 firms in the sample, 34.6% identified the shortage of sales, the main source of a firm's internal finance, as the primary bottleneck. In other words, this large percentage of Korean SMEs sold less in 1989 than they could produce technologically, indicating the marketing constraint to be binding.

On the contrary, 39.8% of 941 firms could not produce more, though they could sell more than what they produced (the second and third reasons). This means that those SMEs were subject to a technological constraint, rather than a marketing constraint. To separate one constraint from the other, we use a switching regression model.

In this section, under the assumption that there exist considerable sunk costs in export markets, we develop a censored switching model consisting of a

Table 16.1. *Reasons for bottleneck in Korean SME finance*

Reason	No. of workers:	1–20	21–50	51–100	101–300	301–	Average
		Percentage					
Shortage of sales		34.9	35.7	29.7	38.0	35.3	34.6
Expansion of production facilities		17.2	20.7	27.2	22.1	22.1	21.6
Increase in operation cost		16.7	21.4	16.8	17.8	13.2	18.2
Other		31.2	22.2	26.3	22.1	29.4	25.6
Sum		100	100	100	100	100	100

Notes: Sample size of SMEs: 941. Year: 1989. Source: Park et al. (1992).

technology capability regime and a marketing capability regime. Subsequently, the likelihood function for estimating the switching regression, and data and variables used are discussed.

3.1   A censored switching regression model

We assume that SMEs treat export markets and domestic markets differently even if the products sold in the two markets are the same. Therefore, we shall ignore firms' behavior in domestic markets and focus on their behavior in export markets. Korean SMEs are assumed to act as pricetakers in export markets. For a given period, the quantity of goods sold in export markets was bounded by either its technological capability or its marketing capability. Moreover, neither its current technological nor its marketing capability can be adjusted flexibly and instantaneously from its existing level because of existing sunk costs. As explained above, sunk costs hinder resource mobility by creating a fixity zone, a hindrance which is reinforced when uncertainty and irreversibility prevail. Thus, a profit-maximizing firm will choose the level of exports q_{it} to

$$\text{Max}_{q_{it}} \Pi_{it} = [\text{TR}(q_{it}) - \text{PC}(q_{it}) - \text{MC}(q_{it}) \mid \Omega_{it-1}]$$

subject to $q_{it} \leq b_{it}, \quad q_{it} \leq m_{it}, \quad i = 1, 2, \ldots, N, \quad t = 1, 2, \ldots, T,$ (16.1)

where Π_{it}, TR, PC, MC, and q_{it} are the profit, total revenue, production cost, and marketing cost and the desired quantity of exports for the ith firm in the tth time period, and Ω_{it-1} is the internal and external environment of the ith firm at the beginning of time period t. The technology constraint of the ith firm at the tth time period is specified as

$$b_{it} = \sum_{j=1}^{J} \alpha_j X_{jit}^T + \sum_{h=1}^{H} \gamma_h^T X_{hit}^C + \varepsilon_{it},$$ (16.2)

and the marketing constraint is specified as

$$m_{it} = \sum_{k=1}^{K} \beta_k X_{kit}^M + \sum_{h=1}^{H} \gamma_h^M X_{hit}^C + \eta_{it},$$ (16.3)

where X_{jit}^T, X_{kit}^M, and X_{hit}^C, $j = 1, 2, 3, \ldots, J$, $h = 1, 2, \ldots, H$, $k = 1, 2, \ldots, K$, are technology variables, marketing variables, and common variables in the internal and external environment of the ith firm at the beginning of time t.

All possible adjustments are conditional on Ω_{it-1}. Because of sunk costs, each of the current technological and marketing capabilities varies over a very limited range around the technology and marketing capabilities determined by Ω_{it-1}. In other words, sunk costs prevent firms from balancing production and marketing capabilities without hindrance. Hence, we may view the excess of technology over marketing capabilities as due to the effect of sunk costs on the production side, and the reverse as due to the sunk costs on the marketing side. Therefore, we have either one of the following two cases for the solution of (16.1) for q_{it}^*:

Case 1: $q_{it}^* = b_{it}$ and $q_{it}^* < m_{it}$.
Case 2: $q_{it}^* = m_{it}$ and $q_{it}^* < b_{it}$.

The above two cases can be expressed as the following minimum function:

$$q_{it}^* = \text{Min}(b_{it}, m_{it}). \tag{16.4}$$

Then the actual export ex_{it} equals

$$ex_{it} = \begin{cases} q_{it}^* & \text{if } q_{it}^* > 0, \\ 0 & \text{if } q_{it}^* \leq 0. \end{cases} \tag{16.5}$$

The model consisting of only (16.1)–(16.4) is in the same form as a canonical disequilibrium model (Fair and Jaffee 1972, Amemiya 1984; Quandt 1988, Laroque and Salanie 1994), which is a switching regression model. However, the model becomes a censored switching model when (16.5) is added, which is the model estimated in this chapter. The negative values of q_{it}^* measure the degree to which a nonexporter is incapable of becoming an exporter. That is, the closer a firm's negative value of q_{it}^* is to 0, the more likely a nonexporter is to become an exporter.

According to (16.1)–(16.5), a representative SME's CEO decides on the planned amount of exports in two steps at the beginning of each period. In the first step, for a given demand conditions in export markets, he sees the possible production amount and the possible marketing amount respectively based on the firm's internal and external environments at the beginning of the period. He then tries to balance the two amounts by changing the adjustable variables. Finally, after balancing, he chooses the planned amount on the basis of the binding capability.

For variances and covariances among errors in (16.2) and (16.3), we assume that

$$\text{cov}(\varepsilon_{it}, \varepsilon_{js}) = \begin{cases} \sigma_\varepsilon^2 & \text{when} & i = j & \text{and} & t = s, \\ 0 & \text{otherwise}, \end{cases}$$

$$\text{cov}(\eta_{it}, \eta_{js}) = \begin{cases} \sigma_\eta^2 & \text{when} & i = j & \text{and} & t = s, \\ 0 & \text{otherwise}, \end{cases} \tag{16.6}$$

$$\text{cov}(\varepsilon_{it}, \eta_{js}) = \begin{cases} (0, \Sigma), & \Sigma = \begin{pmatrix} \sigma_\varepsilon^2 & \sigma_{\varepsilon\eta} \\ \sigma_{\varepsilon\eta} & \sigma_\eta^2 \end{pmatrix}, & \text{when } i = j \text{ and } t = s \\ 0 & \text{otherwise}. \end{cases}$$

When the switching regression model (16.2)–(16.5) is estimated, each estimated coefficient measures the marginal effect of each predetermined or exogenous variable on the potential production and the potential marketing amounts, b_{it} and m_{it}, in export markets. In order to know the marginal effect of each exogenous variable on the actual export ex_{it}, the equation for ex_{it} must be derived from the switching regression model.

First, the closed form equation for q_{it}^* given as (16.2)–(16.4) is given by[6]

$$q_{it}^* = E(q_{it}^*) + \vartheta_{it}, \tag{16.7}$$

where

$$E(q_{it}^*) = \Phi(\upsilon_{it})\alpha' X_{it}^T + (1 - \Phi(\upsilon_{it}))\beta' X_{it}^M - \sigma\phi(\upsilon_{it}),$$

in which Φ is the standard normal cdf,

$$X_{it}^T = \left(X_{jit}^T, X_{hit}^C\right) \qquad \text{and} \qquad X_{it}^M = \left(X_{kit}^M, X_{hit}^C\right),$$

$$\sigma^2 = \sigma_\varepsilon^2 + \sigma_\eta^2 - 2\sigma_{\varepsilon\eta}, \quad \text{and} \quad \upsilon_{it} = \frac{\beta' X_{it}^M - \alpha' X_{it}^T}{\sigma};$$

and where

$$\mathrm{Var}(\vartheta_{it}) = \sigma_\varepsilon^2 \theta_{1it} + \sigma_\eta^2 \theta_{2it} + \sigma_{\varepsilon\eta}\theta_{3it} + \theta_{4it},$$

in which

$$\theta_{1it} = \Phi(\upsilon_{it}) + \upsilon_{it}\phi(\upsilon_{it}),$$
$$\theta_{2it} = 1 - \Phi(\upsilon_{it}) + \upsilon_{it}\phi(\upsilon_{it}),$$
$$\theta_{3it} = -\upsilon_{it}\phi(\upsilon_{it}),$$
$$\theta_{4it} = \sigma^2 \upsilon_{it}^2 \Phi(\upsilon_{it})[1 - \Phi(\upsilon_{it})] - \sigma^2\phi(\upsilon_{it})^2 - 2\sigma^2\phi(\upsilon_{it})\Phi(\upsilon_{it}).$$

Since the actual export, ex_{it}, is the q_{it}^* that is left-censored at 0, the ex_{it} equation can be obtained by applying the standard Tobit-type expectation to q_{it}^* as follows:

$$ex_{it} = E(ex_{it}) + \varphi_{it}, \tag{16.8}$$

where

$$E(ex_{it}) = (1 - F(-\tau_{it}))E(q_{it}^*/q_{it}^* > 0),$$

in which

$$\tau_{it} = \frac{E(q_{it}^*)}{\sqrt{\mathrm{Var}(\varphi_{it})}}$$

---

[6] For a detailed derivation, see Quandt (1988) or Madalla (1990).

and

$$E(q_{it}^*/q_{it}^* > 0) = \frac{1}{1 - F(0)} \int_0^\infty q_{it}^* f(q_{it}^*) d(q_{it}^*)$$

with

$$f(q_{it}^*) = \int_{q_{it}^*}^\infty g(q_{it}^*, m_{it}) \, dm_{it} + \int_{q_{it}^*}^\infty g(b_{it}, q_{it}^*) \, db_{it},$$

F is the cdf of q_{it}^*, f is the density of q_{it}^*, g is the joint density of b_{it} and m_{it}, and φ_{it} is the error term.

Equation (16.8) is used to predict the marginal effect of each exogenous variable on actual export after the parameters in both regimes (16.2) and (16.3) are estimated by the MLE method. We do so by plugging the estimates of α 's, β's, and γ's obtained from MLE into (16.8) and differentiating it with respect to each exogenous variable.

If there exists a flexible mechanism to equate technological with marketing constraint, then q_{it}^* becomes the standard Tobit model:

$$q_{it}^* = \sum_{r=1}^R \delta_r X_{rit} + \xi_{it},$$

$$\mathrm{ex}_{it} = q_{it}^* \quad \text{if} \quad q_{it}^* > 0, \tag{16.9}$$

$$i = 1, 2, \ldots, n, \quad r = 1, 2, \ldots, R, \quad t = 1, 2, \ldots, T$$

Here, $X_{rit}, r = 1, 2, \ldots, R$, include all the variables of X_{jit}^T, X_{kit}^M, and X_{hit}^C, $j = 1, 2, 3 \ldots, J, h = 1, 2, \ldots, H, k = 1, 2, \ldots, K$, in (16.2) and (16.3). Then the equation for the actual export ex_{it} becomes

$$\mathrm{ex}_{it} = E(\mathrm{ex}_{it}) + \zeta_{it},$$

$$E(\mathrm{ex}_{it}) = \Phi(\kappa_{it})(E(q_{it}^*) + \lambda_{it}^e \sqrt{\mathrm{Var}(q_{it}^*)}),$$

$$E(q_{it}^*) = \sum_{r=1}^R \delta_r X_{rit}, \tag{16.10}$$

$$\lambda_{it}^e = \phi(\kappa_{it})/\Phi(\kappa_{it}),$$

$$\kappa_{it} = \frac{E(q_{it}^*)}{\sqrt{\mathrm{Var}(q_{it}^*)}}.$$

Although it can be easily derived, the variance–covariance structure of the error terms in equation (16.10) is not given here, because only the marginal effect of each exogenous variable on ex_{it} is of interest. By plugging the estimates of the parameters in (16.9), obtained by applying the standard Tobit method, into (16.10) and then differentiating (16.10) with respect to each exogenous variable, the marginal effect of each exogenous variable on the actual export ex_{it} is computed for each observation.

3.2   *Estimation: maximum-likelihood method*

The switching regression model consisting of (16.2)–(16.5) is of the same type as the canonical disequilibrium model except that ex_{it} in (16.5) is left-censored at 0. In applying the MLE method for the canonical disequilibrium model, it is well known that (i) there is a possibility of an unbounded ML function and perfect correlation between errors in two regimes, and (ii) the ML estimators may provide only local solutions. To overcome these difficulties, several estimation methods (such as the non-linear least-squares method, the moment-generating-function method, the EM algorithm method, and a modified MLE method) have been developed. The MLE method is adopted here because it is efficient. We try to avoid the aforementioned difficulties in estimation by assuming (as is commonly done) that there is no correlation between the two regimes and by starting the iterations from the estimate obtained by applying the standard Tobit to equations (16.2) and (16.3) with ex_{it} as the dependent variable instead of b_{it} and m_{it}.

Power (1993) dealt with various kinds of likelihood functions for endogenous switching regression models with limited dependent variables. One of his likelihood functions can be used for our purposes, but must be modified because our switching regression model consisting of (16.2)–(16.5) is censored and without known sample separation. There are four regimes for the likelihood function considered here.

Let $g(b_{it}, m_{it})$ be the joint normal density of b_{it} and m_{it}.

Case 1: $ex_{it} = 0$ and $b_{it} < m_{it}$:

$$L_{1it} \equiv \text{pr}(ex_{it} = 0 \mid b_{it} < m_{it}) = \int_{-\infty}^{0} \int_{b_{it}}^{\infty} g(b_{it}, m_{it}) \, dm_{it} \, db_{it} / \pi_{it}. \tag{16.11}$$

Case 2: $ex_{it} = 0$ and $b_{it} > m_{it}$:

$$L_{2it} \equiv \text{pr}(ex_{it} = 0 \mid b_{it} > m_{it})$$
$$= \int_{-\infty}^{0} \int_{m_{it}}^{\infty} g(b_{it}, m_{it}) \, db_{it} \, dm_{it} / (1 - \pi_{it}). \tag{16.12}$$

Case 3: $ex_{it} > 0$ and $b_{it} < m_{it}$:

$$L_{3it} \equiv h(ex_{it} \mid b_{it} < m_{it}) = \int_{ex_{it}}^{\infty} g(ex_{it}, m_{it}) \, dm_{it} / \pi_{it}. \tag{16.13}$$

Case 4: $ex_{it} > 0$ and $b_{it} > m_{it}$:

$$L_{4it} \equiv h(ex_{it} \mid b_{it} > m_{it}) = \int_{ex_{it}}^{\infty} g(b_{it}, ex_{it}) \, db_{it} / (1 - \pi_{it}). \tag{16.14}$$

Here π_{it} is the unconditional probability that the technology capability regime in the ith firm is binding at time t. That is,

$$\pi_{it} \equiv \mathrm{pr}(b_{it} < m_{it})$$

$$= \int_{b_{it}}^{\infty} g(b_{it}, m_{it}) \, dm_{it}. \tag{16.15}$$

Let d_{it} be the dummy variable, which is 1 if the ith firm is an exporter at time t, and 0 otherwise. Combining cases 1 through 4, we get the following unconditional likelihood function for the ith firm:

$$L_{it} = (1 - d_{it})(\pi_{it} L_{1it} + (1 - \pi_{it})L_{2it}) + d_{it}(\pi_{it} L_{3it} + (1 - \pi_{it})L_{4it}). \tag{16.16}$$

Taking the natural logarithm of equation (16.16) and summing over observations yields the log-likelihood function:

$$\ln L = \sum_{i=1}^{N} \sum_{t=1}^{T} \ln L_{it}. \tag{16.17}$$

This function is maximized to obtain the ML estimators of the α's, β's, and γ's under the assumption that there is no contemporary correlation between the errors in the two regimes. The independence assumption allows (16.11) through (16.14) to be written in much simpler form.

The probability that each firm is bounded by the T-regime, i.e., the probability of excess marketing capability, needs to be computed in order to figure out the effects of sunk costs on each firm's export behavior. The probability that each firm is bounded by the M-regime, i.e., the probability of excess production capability, is simply 1 minus the probability of excess marketing capability. For convenience, the probability of excess marketing capability will be used instead of the probability of excess production capability. The closer this probability is to 0.5, the less dominant will be either constraint. The closer it is to 1, the more dominant is the technology capability constraint, and the closer it is to 0, the more dominant is the marketing capability constraint. Instead of using the unconditional probability of excess marketing capability of equation (16.15), the following conditional probability of excess marketing capability, which is based on more information and provides a sharper discrimination between two regimes,[7] will be used:

$$\pi_{it}^c \equiv \mathrm{pr}(b_{it} < m_{it}/\mathrm{ex}_{it})$$

$$= \frac{(1 - d_{it})\pi_{it}\bar{L}_{3it}}{\pi_{it}\bar{L}_{3it} + (1 - \pi_{it})\bar{L}_{4it}} + \frac{d_{it}\pi_{it}\bar{L}_{3it}}{\pi_{it}L_{3it} + (1 - \pi_{it})L_{4it}}, \tag{16.18}$$

[7] See Burkett (1981) and Quandt and Rosen (1985).

where $\bar{L}_{3it}$ is the same as L_{3it} except that b_{it} is substituted for ex_{it} in the lower bound of the integral, and $\bar{L}_{4it}$ is the same as L_{4it} except that m_{it} is substituted for ex_{it} in the lower bound of the integral. Then the life cycle or business cycle of each sector or size group in export markets can be predicted by averaging the probabilities of excess marketing capability for all firms in that sector or size group.

Finally, the properties of ML estimators need to be mentioned. Hartley and Mallela (1977) proved the strong consistency and asymptotic normality of the ML estimators for the canonical disequilibrium model under the assumption that the variances of error terms in the model are bounded away from 0. This is still true for a local ML estimator. As we know, the switching regression model (16.3) is very similar to the canonical disequilibrium model except that q_{it}^* is left-censored. All the conditions for consistency and asymptotic normality of the ML estimators are unaffected by the left censoring of q_{it}^*. Thus, the same procedure can be used to prove the strong consistency and asymptotic normality of the ML estimators for the censored switching regression model (16.3).

3.3 Data[8] and variables

For Korean SMEs, reliable data on their exports, endowments, and other characteristics and on the means used for penetrating export markets are unavailable from official statistical sources. Furthermore, information on the use and evaluation of SME support mechanisms by SMEs themselves is virtually nonexistent. For this reason, Kim and Nugent (1994) conducted an in-depth survey of a sample of SMEs. In order to assure sufficient variety in the use of different export mechanisms and sources of support at minimum cost in terms of sample size, they selected four sectors on the basis of the following criteria: (i) the complexity of technology, (ii) the rate of technological change in products, (iii) the degree of subcontracting, and (iv) the number of years in which Korean firms have been exporting. They considered only sectors in which SMEs were prominent in employment and exports. The selected sectors are: woven textiles (WT), auto parts (AP), electronic parts and components (EP), and factory automation (FA). FA uses small-batch technology and has a high rate of technological change but relatively low export intensity and little experience in exporting. AP and EP use large batch production technology but vary in their rates of technological change, export propensity, and experience. On the other hand, WT uses virtually continuous production technology and has a low rate of technological change.

Having selected the sectors, Kim and Nugent (1994) sampled SMEs from each sector using the following rules: (i) the sample sizes in each sector were

---

[8] For more detail on the data and means of data collection, see Kim and Nugent (1994).

approximately proportional to the number of SMEs in the sector, and (ii) within each sector, a stratified random sampling procedure was used. This had the effect of making the probability of a firm's inclusion in the sample roughly proportional to its contribution to sectoral employment among SMEs. Through this procedure, 122 SMEs were selected: 42 in WT, 20 each in AP and EP, and 40 in FA. Although we have four years of panel data (1988 to 1991), the number of observations used in the censored switching regression model is 342 instead of 488, since some observations have missing values and for some variables their one-period lags are used in order to avoid simultaneity bias.

The value of each export support variable is evenly divided over the previous three years. For SMEs which had been in existence for less than 3 years, the value was distributed evenly over the years in existence. Table 16.2 summarizes the distribution of the observations by sector and size group, for all firms and for exporters and nonexporters separately.

Table 16.3 contains all the variables used in this chapter and their expected effects on both regimes. In this table, quantitative measures of various internal capabilities and external factors have been obtained through factor analysis,

Table 16.2. *Observation and percentage by sector and size*

Group	Size	WT Obs.	%	AP Obs.	%	EP Obs.	%	FA Obs.	%	Total Obs.	%
All	1	26	7.5	11	3.2	10	2.9	50	14.4	97	27.9
	2	27	7.8	19	5.5	17	4.9	35	10.1	98	28.2
	3	41	11.8	12	3.4	24	6.9	18	5.2	95	27.3
	4	25	7.2	13	3.7	8	2.3	12	3.4	58	16.7
	Total	119	34.2	55	15.8	59	17.0	115	33.0	348	100.0
Exporter	1	18	5.2	2	0.6	2	0.6	2	0.6	24	6.9
	2	18	5.2	11	3.2	11	3.2	11	3.2	51	14.7
	3	29	8.3	6	1.7	20	5.7	14	4.0	69	19.8
	4	19	5.5	13	3.7	8	2.3	11	3.2	51	14.7
	Total	84	24.1	32	9.2	41	11.8	38	10.9	195	56.0
Non-exporter	1	8	2.3	9	2.6	8	2.3	48	13.8	73	21.0
	2	9	2.6	8	2.3	6	1.7	24	6.9	47	13.5
	3	12	3.4	6	1.7	4	1.1	4	1.1	26	7.5
	4	6	1.7	0	0.0	0	0.0	1	0.3	7	2.0
	Total	35	10.1	23	6.6	18	5.2	77	22.1	153	44.0

Notes: Using L to represent the number of employees, size 1 means $L < 50$, size 2 means $50 \leq L < 100$, size 3 means $100 \leq L < 200$, and size 4 means $L \geq 200$. The percentages reported in all cells except those in the last column are of the number of observations in the cell relative to the total number of observations. The percentages reported in the last column are those in that row compared with the group total.

and each of several different types of SME support systems has been related to both the external and internal environment. The variable names are given in italics in the middle column of the table, and the expected direction of effects on the different regime types in the last two columns. In what follows we identify certain hypotheses concerning these results as indicated by H1–H14.

3.3.1   *Plant characteristics*

(i) Retrospective variables
(H1)   *The number of years from the establishment year to first export year (bfexyr) is expected to have a negative effect on a firm's export.*
(H2)   *The expected sign of the number of years from first export to the current year (afexyr) must be strongly positive.*

bfexyr and *afexyr*, which belong to this category, measure the degree of readiness for first export at the startup year and of the learning through accumulated experience in exporting, respectively. A firm with high *bfexyr* needed a long time until its first export, suggesting that the firm was less prepared for exporting at its startup. More experience in exports makes a firm's access to export markets easier by reducing its sunk costs.

(ii) Type of ownership
(H3)   *A firm with corporate-type ownership, equ = 1, exports more than a firm with private ownership, equ = 0.*

The former is generally larger in size than the latter, and so the former can more fully take advantage of economies of scale in export markets.

(iii) Labor, capital, and productivity [9]
(H4)   *More production workers (lpdw) increase the production capability of a firm for exporting.*
(H5)   *The expected effects of management workers (lmgw) are positive on both sides.*
(H6)   *However, the size effect of marketing (lmkw) workers on exporting is ambiguous.*
(H7)   *The capital size (lcap) is expected to have positive effects on both regimes.*

To avoid simultaneity bias, a one-time lag is taken for our measures, which are labor and capital (discussed here) and productivity variables (discussed

---

[9] The debate on the direction of causality between exports and productivity is rather heated (Aw and Hwang 1995).

Table 16.3. *Variables, regimes, and expected signs*

Category	Sub-category	Variable	Description	Expected sign	
				T-reg.	M-reg.
Plant	Retrospective	*bfexyr*	Years before first export	−	−
		afexyr	Years after first export	+	+
	Ownership	*equ*	Dummy on corporate form	+	+
	Labor and Capital:				
	Labor	*lpdw*	No. of production workers	+	***
		lmgw	No. of management workers	***	+
		lmkw	No. of marketing workers	***	− +
	Capital	*lcap*	Paid-in capital (billion won)	+	+
	Productivity	*lprman*	Labor productivity (billion won)	+	+
		lprcap	Capital productivity (billion won)	?	+
	Product change	*inn*	No. of new products	+	+
	Buyer concentration	*buycon*	concentration of first three buyers	***	+
	Manager's dummy:				
	Education	*gradedu*	Education above college	+	+
	Previous experience	*jobtt*	Manager's technology experience	+	***
		jobss	Manager's sales experience	***	+
		jobexx	Manager's export experience	***	+
Factor analysis	Internal factors	*cfac1*	Marketing and management capability	+	***
		cfac2	Financial capability	+	+
		cfac3	Technology capability	+	***
		cfac4	External relations	+	+
	External factors	*efac1*	Resource tightness	−	−
		efac2	Finance tightness	−	−
		efac3	Technical dynamics	−	−
		efac4	Market competition	−	−
		efac5	Market size	−	−

420

SME support systems					
Marketing:	Designation dummy	fdeg1	Promising SMEs	***	?
		fdeg23	Business or item in *Kairetsu*	***	?
	Dummy	mdeg1	Reserved business area to SMEs	***	?
		mdeg2	Item produced by collective contract	***	?
	Penetrating	pen	Penetrating export market	***	?
Technology:					
	Nonfinancial	tecsup	Technological supports	?	***
	Financial	ftesup	Tech. development	?	***
		fwcsup	Working capital	?	?
		exfsup	Export finance	?	?
		forsup	Credit guarantee systems used	?	?
Both:		mdeg3	Membership in KOTRA	?	?
	Financial	tesup	Tax exemptions received	?	?
		iesup	Income exemptions received	?	?
	Non-financial	trsup	Tax reductions received	?	?
	Tax	resup	Reserves received	?	?
		sdsup	Special depreciation	?	?
Sector dummy		Ap	Automotive parts sector	—	—
		Ep	Electronic parts sector	—	—
		FA	Factory automation sector	—	—
Time dummy		td90	1990	?	?
		td89	1989	?	?

Notes: All support variables except the marketing dummy variables denote the number of different sources belonging to the corresponding categories used by the SME. *** indicates that the corresponding variable is not included in the corresponding regime. ? indicates that the expected sign of the variable is ambiguous a priori, the sign to be determined empirically. All variables in monetary units are based on constant prices of 1990.

next). An increase in *lmkw* may not cause an increase of a firm's marketing capability in export markets. Instead, it may contribute to expanding the domestic market alone.

(H8)   A firm with high productivity exports more.

Productivity is one of the most important proxies measuring a firm's past success.[10] The firms that have succeeded in the past are the "good" firms with higher productivity. Conversely, a firm must have had high productivity to succeed in export markets. To avoid this causality problem, a one-time lag is taken for productivity variables.

A firm with high productivity can compete effectively in export markets. Labor productivity (*lprman*) and capital productivity (*lprcap*) are considered here.

(iv) Product change and buyer concentration
(H9)   The number of new products introduced each period (inn) has a negative effect for the T-regime, but a positive effect for the M-regime.

(H10)   High buyer concentration (buycon) will have a positive effect on the M-regime.

An increase in the number of new products introduced each period should help a firm attract more buyers by quickly satisfying changes in buyers' needs. On the other hand, it needs more sunk costs to adopt new technology and new facilities to replace the existing technology and facilities, which become obsolete relatively quickly. High buyer concentration guarantees more stable marketing through subcontracting and long-term contracts with LEs or foreign buyers.

(v) CEO's background
(H11)   The dummy for graduate education (gradedu) has positive effects on both regimes. The dummy for technology experience (jobtt) has a positive effect on the T-regime. The dummies for sales experience (jobss) and for export experience (jobexx) have positive effects on the M-regime.

To control for "unobserved" managerial abilities that may introduce permanent heterogeneity among firms,[11] several dummy variables describing a CEO's background are introduced. They are dummy variables for graduate education (*gradedu*), technology experience (*jobtt*), sales experience (*jobss*), and export

---

[10] Firm size is another proxy (Bernard and Jensen 1996b).

[11] Bernard and Jensen (1996b) and Roberts and Tybout (1997) show how and why managerial background is important in explaining persistent heterogeneity among firms.

experience (*jobexx*). Each CEO's previous experience is expected to lower adjustment costs and/or the transaction costs of penetrating export markets.

(vi) Sector and time dummy variables

(H12)   The dummy variables for other sectors compared to the woven-textile sector will be expected to show negative effects on exports, since WT has the highest export propensity.

(H13)   For the time dummies, the direction of their effects on export cannot be determined a priori.

Using sector dummies is the simplest way to capture the heterogeneity over sectors. The woven-textile sector (WT), which has high export propensity, is used as the reference sector, and the year 1989 as the reference year. On the other hand, the time dummies are supposed to catch not only the technology and marketing progress but also the effect of change in exchange rate over time.

3.3.2   Subjective variables

(H14)   In relation to the eleven factors derived through factor analysis, positive effects on exports are expected for the internal capability *factors and negative effects for the external* tightness *factors.*

Eleven standardized factors from CEOs' subjective evaluations of each firm on internal and external environment were derived,[12] which summarize the CEO's subjective SWOT analysis. The names of the internal capability factors were marketing and management capability (*cfac1*), financial capability (*cfac2*), technology capability (*cfac3*), and external relation capability (*cfac4*). The names of the external capability factors were resource tightness (*efac1*), finance tightness (*efac2*), technical dynamics (*efac3*), market competitiveness (*efac4*), and small market (*efac5*).

3.3.3   SME support variables

One of the most important features of SMEs in Korea is their weakness in technology, marketing, and financing capabilities. They depend largely on LEs and government-led institutions, explicitly or implicitly. As a result, support from external agents such as LEs and the government can have a big impact on their behavior. The support from LEs through vertical or horizontal integration helps SMEs strengthen their marketing capability but not their technology capability. Instead, the support from government has been the most reliable and important source for improving both technology and export marketing.

---

[12] To see the derivation of the factors and the corresponding factor loadings, see Kim and Nugent (1994).

Although they are divided into two groups of technology supports and marketing supports, SME support variables are further classified into four groups for convenience: supports for stable marketing, non-financial supports, financial supports, and tax supports. Dummies for designation as a promising SME (*fdeg1*), business or item in *kairestsu* (*fdeg23*), business area reserved for SMEs (*mdeg1*), and item produced by collective contract (*mdeg2*) belong to the supports for stable marketing. Penetrating export market (*pen*), membership in KOTRA (*mdeg3*), and technological training and supports (*tecsup*) belong to the non-financial supports. Technology development (*ftesup*), working capital (*fwcsup*), export finance (*exfsup*), and credit guarantee systems used (*forsup*) are the financial-support variables. Tax exemptions received (*tesup*), income exemptions received (*iesup*), tax reductions received (*trsup*), tax reserves received (*resup*), and special depreciation (*sdsup*) are the tax-support variables.

Table 16.3 shows the variables belonging to each of the four groups. The details can be found in Kim and Nugent (1994). We shall not make any conjecture about the effectiveness of each support variable. However, it should be noted that some support variables are only for exporters, while the others are for both exporters and nonexporters.

4   Estimation results

4.1   *Model selection and merits of censored switching model*

Our criteria for model specification are consistent with economic theory, statistical significance of included variables, and good explanatory power. An iterative general-to-specific specification search strategy is adopted. We started with a model with the largest number of RHS variables containing all the variables described in Table 16.3, then compared it with the same model without support variables to see whether any of the support variables was significant in SMEs' exports. According to the result of the LR test between the two specifications, the SME support variables appeared to be very significant even at $\alpha = 0.01$. Thus, the largest model was chosen as the maintained hypothesis to select the final specification. After estimation at each stage, the variables with t-values less than 0.5 were dropped, and the corresponding LR test between the previous specification and the new specification was carried out to detect any significant change. After four steps, the estimates shown in the second and third columns of Table 16.4 were obtained as the final specification.

We can compare and contrast the results of the two-regime censored regression model (16.2)–(16.5) with the standard Tobit model (16.9) having the same RHS variables as the final specification. The estimation result of Tobit model is given in the fourth column of Table 16.4. By plugging the estimates from both the censored switching regression model and the Tobit model into (16.8)

Table 16.4. *Censored switching regression model and tobit model*

| | Estimate | | | Mean | | | | | |
| | Switching regimes | | Tobit | Switching regimes | | | Tobit | | |
Variable	T-reg.	M-reg.	Tobit	Exp.	N-exp.	All	Exp.	N-exp.	All
Cont.	3.432***	−1.830***	−1.937***	0.923	0.077	0.551	−1.492	−0.237	−0.940
bfexyr	−0.216***	−0.046*	−0.103***	−0.115	−0.011	−0.069	−0.080	−0.013	−0.050
afexyr	0.052*	0.158***	0.118***	0.080	0.008	0.048	0.091	0.014	0.057
lpdw	0.010***	—	0.008***	0.005	0.000	0.003	0.006	0.001	0.004
lmgw	0.032**	0.015	0.014	0.020	0.002	0.012	0.011	0.002	0.007
lmkw	—	−0.095***	−0.047***	−0.034	−0.003	−0.020	−0.036	−0.006	−0.023
lcap	NS	1.524***	0.958***	0.541	0.055	0.327	0.738	0.117	0.465
lprman	10.753***	NS	5.193***	4.928	0.450	2.959	4.000	0.635	2.520
Lprcap	0.023**	0.101***	0.073***	0.046	0.005	0.028	0.056	0.009	0.035
inn	−0.103***	0.141***	−0.022	0.003	0.001	0.002	−0.017	−0.003	−0.011
buycon	—	0.020***	0.009***	0.007	0.001	0.004	0.007	0.001	0.005
jobss	—	2.858***	0.912***	1.015	0.103	0.614	0.703	0.112	0.443
jobexx	—	−1.160***	0.655**	−0.412	−0.042	−0.249	0.504	0.080	0.318
cfac1	0.390**	−0.300**	0.063	0.072	0.005	0.043	0.048	0.008	0.031
cfac2	0.391**	NS	0.170	0.179	0.016	0.108	0.131	0.021	0.083
efac2	0.530***	0.555***	0.256**	0.440	0.042	0.265	0.197	0.031	0.124
efac3	1.123***	0.922***	0.861***	0.842	0.080	0.507	0.664	0.105	0.418
efac4	—	−0.384***	0.068	−0.136	−0.014	−0.082	0.053	0.008	0.033
efac5	—	−0.340**	−0.096	−0.121	−0.012	−0.073	−0.074	−0.012	−0.047
fdeg1	—	−1.022***	−0.263	−0.363	−0.037	−0.220	−0.202	−0.032	−0.128
fdeg23	—	5.520***	0.743*	1.960	0.200	1.186	0.572	0.091	0.361
mdeg1	—	1.848***	1.339***	0.656	0.067	0.397	1.031	0.164	0.650
mdeg2	—	−6.584***	−6.286***	−2.338	−0.238	−1.415	−4.842	−0.769	−3.051
mdeg3	0.368	NS	0.497	0.169	0.015	0.101	0.383	0.061	0.241
tecsup	−0.160*	—	0.026	−0.073	−0.007	−0.044	0.020	0.003	0.013
forsup	0.268	1.140***	0.636***	0.528	0.052	0.319	0.490	0.078	0.309
ftesup	1.209***	NS	0.338**	0.554	0.051	0.333	0.261	0.041	0.164
fwcsup	−0.760***	−0.183	−0.446***	−0.413	−0.038	−0.248	−0.343	−0.054	−0.216
pen	—	0.421***	0.095	0.149	0.015	0.090	0.073	0.012	0.046
exfsup	0.311	0.619***	0.393***	0.362	0.035	0.219	0.303	0.048	0.191
tesup	−0.919***	0.435***	−0.356***	−0.267	−0.023	−0.159	−0.274	−0.043	−0.173
iesup	−0.838**	NS	0.012	−0.384	−0.035	−0.230	0.009	0.002	0.006
trsup	0.269	−0.909***	−0.120	−0.199	−0.022	−0.121	−0.092	−0.015	−0.058
resup	0.279*	NS	0.165	0.128	0.012	0.077	0.127	−0.020	0.080
sdsup	1.688***	−0.336**	0.486***	0.654	0.058	0.392	0.375	0.059	0.236
AP	NS	−6.645***	−0.985*	−2.360	−0.240	−1.428	−0.759	−0.120	−0.478
EP	NS	−2.991***	−1.298***	−1.062	−0.108	−0.643	−1.000	−0.159	−0.630
FA	NS	−4.154***	−1.869***	−1.475	−0.150	−0.893	−1.440	−0.229	−0.907
td90	−0.368	NS	−0.197	−0.169	−0.015	−0.101	−0.152	−0.024	−0.096
td91	NS	−0.400***	−0.177	−0.142	−0.014	−0.086	−0.137	−0.022	−0.086
σ	1.251***	0.534***	1.314***						
R^2	0.90804		0.86282						
R^2	0.89109		0.84545						

Notes: NS denotes that the corresponding variable was dropped in the final specification because of insignificance. The 5th to the 10th columns are the averaged marginal effects on actual exports. ***, significant at $\alpha = 0.01$; **, at $\alpha = 0.05$; *, at 0.1.

and (16.10), respectively, and then differentiating (16.8) and (16.10) with respect to each of the RHS variables, the marginal effect of each RHS variable on actual exports is obtained for each of the models. These marginal effects on actual export are averaged over all the observations, and they are separately reported on for the exporters, nonexporters, or both in the fifth to tenth columns in Table 16.4.

As shown at the bottom of the second and third columns in Table 16.4, unlike the usual application using cross-sectional or panel data, the values of R^2 and $\bar{R}^2$ are very high in both models. Notably, they are about 4% higher in the switching model than in the standard Tobit model. This is one of the advantages of the switching model relative to the standard Tobit model. Another advantage is the ability to more sharply discriminate in export performance between exporters and nonexporters. The averaged marginal effects of RHS variables on actual exports among nonexporters compared with those among exporters are much smaller in the switching model than in the standard Tobit model. Third, the effects of almost all the SME support variables except for *mdeg1*, *mdeg2*, and *mdeg3* are larger in absolute terms and more significant in the switching regression model. Finally, the switching model allows one to gain a deeper understanding of a firm's export behavior from both the technology and marketing perspectives, while the standard Tobit model focuses on only the realized data. The switching model allows decisionmakers inside firms (CEOs) and policymakers outside firms to balance and allocate efficiently the resources available between the technology and marketing sides.

4.2   *Marginal effects on two regimes and testing hypotheses*

In this subsection, the hypotheses on parameters set up in Section 3.3 are tested and the effectiveness of each SME support variable is evaluated. The marginal effects of the RHS variables on two regimes are given the first and second columns in Table 16.4. In the table, the estimates with three asterisks are significant at $\alpha = 0.01$, with two are significant at $\alpha = 0.05$, and with one are significant at $\alpha = 0.1$. The averaged marginal effects of RHS variables on actual exports are given the fifth to seventh columns in Table 16.4.

(i) Retrospective variables. As expected, the signs of *bfexyr* on both capability regimes are negative and those of *afexyr* are positive. Hypotheses (H1) and (H2) are verified in that *bfexyr* has a much stronger negative effect on the T-regime than on the M-regime, while *afexyr* has a stronger effect on the M-regime. The longer the waiting period to first exports is, the worse the technology and marketing capabilities on exports. In other words, the firm with a long waiting period to the first exports suffers from severe technological and marketing constraints in exporting, particularly from technological constraints. This is because the firms having longer waiting periods have depended largely on the domestic market in doing their business. Thus, their businesses tend to remain small and to be poorly equipped.

On the contrary, the period from first export to the current period has a very strong positive effect on exports, particularly export marketing capability. The length of the period can be used as a proxy for measuring the benefits of learning through the accumulated experience from the previous exports. The longer a firm has stayed in export markets, the more benefits it enjoys in terms of sunk costs. The positive effect of plant age on the propensity to export observed by Roberts and Tybout (1997) is not observed here. For exporters, the positive effect of plant age on the propensity to export is clearly verified, since *afexyr* has a strong positive effect on exports. However, for nonexporters, plant age has a strong negative effect on the propensity to export, since *bfexyr* has a strong negative effect.[13] When all the firms, including both exporters and nonexporters, are considered, there is no clear effect of age on export propensity.

(ii) Type of ownership. Although hypothesis (H3) states that a firm with corporate-type ownership (*equ* = 1) should export more than an individually owned firm (*equ* = 0), this dummy variable was dropped in the final specification because its effect was found to be statistically insignificant.

(iii) Labor, capital, and productivity. Again as shown in Table 16.4, both the number of production workers (*lpdw*) and the number of management workers (*lmgw*) have significant positive effects on the T-regime but not on the M-regime, and the number of marketing workers (*lmkw*) has a significant negative effect on the M-regime. Thus, this result is consistent with hypotheses (H4), (H5), and (H6), though the effect of *lmkw* on the M-regime appeared to be negative.

On the other hand, the capital amount turned out to have a positive and significant effect only on the M-regime. Greater capital increases export marketing, which is consistent with (H7) although it is not significant in the T-regime. According to the corresponding estimate, when capital increases by 1 unit, the export marketing capability appears to increase by about 1.5 times. This shows how important capital can be in determining a firm's export marketing capability.

By contrast, labor productivity has little effect on an SME's marketing capability but a very strong positive effect on technology capability. Indeed, when labor productivity increases by 1 unit, technology capability for exporting increases by more than ten times. Capital productivity has a greater effect on the M-regime than on the T-regime, although its effects are significant in both regimes. This result supports (H8).

---

[13] An increase in firm age increases *afexyr* for exporters, but decreases *bfexyr* for nonexporters.

According to the estimates, the productivity variables exert the greatest influences over both the technological and marketing capabilities of firms. High productivity of labor and capital makes a firm successful in export markets. Conversely, a firm that has succeeded in export markets has higher productivity. That is why CEOs and policymakers must focus on improving productivity, especially labor productivity, if they are to succeed in export markets.

(iv) New products, buyer concentration, and manager's background. As expected in (H9), the estimated numbers of new products developed (*inn*) have the same directions of effects on the T-regime and the M-regime. More new products every year add to the burden on a firm's technology capability for export markets; however, they also stimulate and expand the firm's export marketing capability. This is because the development of new products requires a lot of sunk costs, but also serves to help attract more buyers. On the other hand, the more a firm's sales are concentrated on the first three buyers (*buycon*), the higher its marketing capability appears to become. This phenomenon is related to SMEs' subcontracting relationship with small numbers of LEs or foreign buyers. A firm with a higher subcontracting ratio has higher buyer concentration and so enjoys stronger marketing capability. Thus, (H10) is confirmed.

A CEO's sales experience (*jobss*) turns out to have a substantial positive effect on the marketing capability of his firm, while his previous export experience (*jobexx*) has a smaller but negative effect. The latter implies that previous experience in exports makes him shrink from, rather than stimulate, exporting, perhaps because of difficult experience in exports. Clearly, the estimate for *jobss* is consistent with (H11), while that of *jobexx* is not.

(v) Sector dummies and time dummies. As indicated by the entries for the three sectoral dummy variables, firms in AP, EP, and FA lag substantially behind the (excluded) WT sector in marketing capability for exporting, while there are no differences in technology capability among them. Hence, although improvements in technological capabilities can increase exports in all sectors, the expansion of marketing capability is crucial only for the AP, EP, and FA sectors.

On the other hand, the time dummies, which can pick up the influence of time-varying influences like exchange rates,[14] show that marketing capability in 1991 was significantly lower than in the omitted year 1989 and in 1990. Except for this, however, there were no effects of the time dummies on either of the regimes.

(vi) Manager's subjective evaluations. The signs of the estimates for the manager's own subjective evaluation of the firm's marketing and management

---

[14] The exchange rate (won per dollar) was increasing during the period 1989–1991.

capability factor (*cfac1*) in Table 16.4 are positive in the T-regime and negative in the M-regime. Although the positive effect in the T-regime was expected (H13), the negative effect on the M-regime was not. The effect of *cfac1* on actual exports, however, which is determined by the interaction between the T-regime and the M-regime, is positive, as shown Table 16.4.

The positive sign of the financial capability factor (*cfac2*), and the negative signs of the market competitiveness (*efac4*) and small-market-size factors (*efac5*), respectively, are all as expected. A CEO's confidence in his firm's financial capability increases his firm's technological and marketing capability in export markets. When the CEO thinks that the markets are very competitive and small, the firm appears to be weak in export marketing capability.

However, the strong positive effects of *efac2* on both regimes, implying that the financial tightness yields positive effects on technological and marketing capabilities, were not expected. This seems to be the result of the firm's effort to solve its financial difficulties by exporting more, which helps the firm qualify to receive special export support funds such as *forsup* and *exfsup*. On the other hand, when a CEO thinks that production technology changes quickly, i.e., receives positive scores for *efac3*, it makes the firm stronger in export markets.

(vii) SME support variables. The measures of SME support variables for stabilizing SMEs' marketing include: designating a SME as a promising SME (*fdeg1*), fostering the horizontal and the vertical integration with LEs (*fdeg23*), reserving some business areas for exclusive use by SMEs (*mdeg1*), and improving bargaining power through collective contracts (*mdeg2*). The main purpose of these policies is to stabilize SMEs' marketing capability over time, since SMEs, particularly small-sized SMEs, are apt to go bankrupt even under a weak business cycle. According to Table 16.4, firms which are integrated horizontally or vertically with LEs (*fdeg23* = 1) or have their product areas reserved for SMEs have much greater marketing capability in export markets than others. On the other hand, the firms participating in collective contracts (*mdeg2* = 1) reveal poor marketing capabilities in export markets. This may reflect the fact that collective contracts are primarily used in domestic marketing. The negative impact on export marketing of the designation as promising SMEs (*fdeg1*) was unexpected, since this designation was given to those firms (mostly small) which were deemed promising in technology or exporting.

Not surprisingly, support specifically designed to help SMEs penetrate export markets and given only to exporters (*pen*) has a comparatively large effect on SMEs' export marketing capabilities. On the other hand, the effect of support received by the firm for modernizing or upgrading technology capability including the improvements in design and quality of the products (*tecsup*) has a negative effect on the T-regime. Yet, since both exporters and nonexporters are eligible for this kind of support, this negative effect on exports via the T-regime is not surprising.

Of the four kinds of financial support considered here (*forsup*, *ftesup*, *fwcsup*, and *exfsup*), only *exfsup*, financial support for export and overseas investment, is directly connected with exports. Since such support is often given to firms that are supposed to export in the near future, the direction of causality could be a problem in this case. Nevertheless, it is shown to have a very significant positive influence on export marketing capability but an insignificant one on technology capability. The variable measuring the use of credit guarantee systems for SMEs (*forsup*) has effects similar to those of *exfsup*, i.e., positive and significant for the M-regime, but not for the T-regime. The measure of financial support for technology development (*ftesup*) has a large positive effect on technology capability. On the other hand, the effect of support received from the fund for working capital or management stability (*fwcsup*) appears to be negative.

Among tax-incentive variables, the special depreciation (*sdsup*) on working assets, facilities for productivity improvement, and other facilities appears to have a strong positive effect on the T-regime, as does the that on investment for research and training (*resup*). As explained in Section 2, tax support through special depreciation lowers the sunk costs existing in both regimes by allowing a firm to recover quickly the investment for exporting. Both the use of tax exemptions (*tesup*) and the use of income exemptions (*iesup*) are shown in Table 16.4 to have negative effects on technology capability. However, the effect of *tesup* on actual exports is greatly weakened by the positive effect it has on the M-regime.

4.3   *Predicted means of T-regime, M-regime, and actual Exports*

By plugging the parameter estimates from the switching regression model into the respective α's, β's, and γ's in equations (16.2) and (16.3), the predicted values for both the technology capability regime and the marketing capability regime are obtained. Then, the predicted values are averaged for each group to get the mean of that group. It is of interest to test the sign of the average of the predicted values for the firms in each group. Table 16.5 shows the result of the sign tests by firm size and sector. In the table, a striking distinction between exporters and nonexporters is observed. The means of the predicted values for exporters are very significantly positive in both regimes, regardless of size and sector. However, those for nonexporters are significantly negative in the M-regime. They are also insignificantly negative in the T-regime for all groups except for those of size 1 and the FA sector, where the signs are significantly positive though the magnitudes are small. According to this result, although nonexporters are weak in technological capability, they are still weaker in marketing capability in export markets. This is why nonexporters

Table 16.5. *Sign test for mean of predicted values of each regime and predicted actual export by firm size and sector*

| | Exporter | | | | | | Non-exporter | | | | |
| | T-regime | | M-regime | | Predicted export | Actual export | T-regime | | M-regime | | Predicted export |
Group	Mean	p-value	Mean	p-value			Mean	p-value	Mean	p-value	
Size 1	2.796	0.000	3.152	0.000	2.484	2.497	0.960	0.002	−3.977	0.000	0.017
Size 2	2.602	0.000	3.354	0.000	1.806	1.663	−0.165	0.329	−3.058	0.000	0.144
Size 3	3.385	0.000	4.382	0.000	2.312	2.222	−0.675	0.103	−1.573	0.010	0.111
Size 4	4.908	0.000	4.747	0.000	3.521	3.754	−0.704	0.266	−2.180	0.002	0.002
WT	4.539	0.000	5.802	0.000	3.831	3.947	−0.730	0.063	−1.103	0.046	0.237
AP	1.146	0.000	2.456	0.000	1.110	1.058	−0.477	0.201	−2.196	0.003	0.044
EP	3.255	0.000	4.194	0.000	2.310	2.181	−0.399	0.259	−2.722	0.000	0.043
FA	3.480	0.000	1.401	0.000	1.020	0.913	1.085	0.000	−4.572	0.000	0.011
Total	3.506	0.000	4.057	0.000	2.517	2.510	0.261	0.118	−3.204	0.000	0.071

Notes: "Mean" is the mean of the predicted values in each of the regimes by size and sector. "Predicted export" is actual export predicted from the estimated T-regime and M-regime. Unit: billion won.

cannot export. Particularly, nonexporters belonging to size group 1 have technological readiness for exporting but cannot find a way to sell their products in export markets because of the insurmountable barrier of sunk costs. Even if there were considerable foreign demand for their products, nonexporters would be without a channel for connecting themselves with buyers. The situation is similar for nonexporters in the FA sector, because most of them belong to size group 1. Therefore, some effective policies for facilitating export marketing should be directed to nonexporters in the FA sector or in size group 1. More generally, policies for enhancing nonexporters' technology capabilities should be accompanied by policies designed to help firms to satisfy foreign buyers' needs.

On the contrary, exporters seem to have no problem in marketing capability relative to technological capability, except for the FA sector, where the mean of the predicted values in the M-regime is less than that in the T-regime. However, that does not necessarily mean that a firm or a sector whose technological capability is greater (less) than its marketing capability does not need to expand marketing capability (technology capability). For example, the firm or sector could be small, export little, and be subject to severe adjustment costs and substantial sunk costs in export markets. Thus, both firms themselves and government support policies should be aimed at achieving balance between the two regimes.

The predicted values of actual exports in Table 16.5 can be obtained by plugging the coefficient estimates from Table 16.4 into equation (16.8). Although the means for the T-regime and for the M-regime are both very different from the mean of actual exports, the predicted values for actual exports in Table 16.5 are very close to actual exports, which explains the high R^{-2} of 0.891 for the switching model in Table 16.4. In particular, the predicted values of actual exports for nonexporters are pretty close to zero, even though nonexporters have large negative scores for marketing capability. The reason is that these negative scores cause the excess-marketing probability, which is the weight for the mean of the M-regime in computing the predicted values of actual exports, to approach zero.

In the above discussion, it is implicitly assumed that the variances of the two regimes are similar. Under this assumption, the stronger of the two capabilities, i.e., the regime which is more binding in determining actual exports, can be identified by comparing the means of the two regimes. If this assumption does not hold, the variances of the regimes must be considered also. Indeed, according to Table 16.4, the variance estimates in the two regimes are 1.251^2 and 0.531^2 respectively, implying that the estimate in the T-regime is 6 times as big as that in the M-regime. Thus, even if the means of the two regimes are considerably different from each other, which constraint is more binding cannot be concluded definitely for each group of firms. To solve this problem, a measure reflecting the information on the variations of two regimes is needed. For this purpose, we use the conditional excess-marketing probability as discussed in the next subsection.

4.4 *Probability of excess marketing capability*

One of the purposes of this chapter is to examine the pattern over time of the excess-marketing probabilities by sector or size for exporters and nonexporters, separately. With knowledge of the time path of such probabilities by sector and size, the life cycle or business cycle of each sector or size group with respect to technological and marketing capabilities can be explained. To do this, a panel data set with a long time series would be needed. The data used here, however, is incomplete panel data with only three observations over time, implying that the inferences we draw are confined to this three-year period.

According to Table 16.7, the averages of the conditional excess marketing probabilities for exporters and nonexporters are 51.8% and 0.2%, respectively. The percentage of observations with average probability more than 0.5 are 47.2% and 0% among exporters and nonexporters, respectively. This means that exporters have little in the way of marketing problems compared to their technological problems, while nonexporters have no marketing ability in export markets. Table 16.6 also shows that the marketing capabilities of WT and especially AP firms declined from 1989 to 1991. On the other hand, the excess-marketing probability of EP firms increased steadily from 49.9% to 58.7%. Firms in the WT, AP, and EP sectors are much less constrained by their marketing capabilities than by their technological capabilities. Clearly, they need ways to overcome their technological constraints on exports. The time pattern of excess-marketing probabilities can also be very important for coping with the existing and emerging difficulties and uncertainties. As explained above,

Table 16.6. *Means of π_{it}^c and percentage of observations with $\pi_{it}^c > 0.5$ by sector and year*

Group	Sector	1991		1990		1989		Total	
		Cp	%	Cp	%	Cp	%	Cp	%
Exporter	WT	0.541	48.4	0.584	53.6	0.609	56.0	0.576	52.4
	AP	0.497	41.7	0.659	63.6	0.705	66.7	0.611	56.3
	EP	0.587	53.8	0.556	50.0	0.499	42.9	0.546	48.8
	FA	0.227	25.0	0.325	28.6	0.287	25.0	0.282	26.3
	All	0.487	44.1	0.536	49.3	0.533	48.3	0.518	47.2
All	WT	0.401	35.7	0.402	36.6	0.424	38.9	0.408	37.0
	AP	0.300	25.0	0.403	38.9	0.375	35.3	0.357	32.7
	EP	0.383	35.0	0.390	35.0	0.368	31.6	0.380	33.9
	FA	0.069	7.5	0.114	10.0	0.099	08.6	0.094	8.7
	Total	0.273	24.6	0.303	27.7	0.300	27.1	0.291	26.4

Note: "Cp" stands for conditional probability of excess marketing capability.

Table 16.7. *Means of π_{it}^c and percentage of observations with $\pi_{it}^c > 0.5$ by size*

Group	Size 1		Size 2		Size 3		Size 4		All	
	Cp	%	Cp	%	Cp	%	Cp	%	Cp	%
Exporter	0.440	33.3	0.499	43.1	0.587	56.5	0.481	45.1	0.518	47.2
Nonexporter	0.001	0.0	0.004	0.0	0.005	0.0	0.000	0.0	0.002	0.0
All	0.110	8.2	0.262	22.4	0.427	41.1	0.423	39.7	0.291	26.4

Note: If L is the number of employees, then size 1 means $L < 50$, size 2 means $50 \leq L < 100$, size 3 means $100 \leq L < 200$, and size 4 means $L \geq 200$.

the WT and AP firms are shown to have gradually lost their marketing capabilities in export markets. Some measures for stimulating marketing capabilities, therefore, will have to be undertaken.

The most problematic sector in export marketing is the FA sector. This is due to its lack of experience in export markets, and to the attributes of the products that have been designed primarily to meet the standards and needs of the domestic market. Only a few large firms in the FA sector export, while most small firms do not. However, according to Table 16.6, the FA sector is the only sector in which nonexporting firms have a significant technological capability for exporting. If the marketing capability of such firms could be increased, the prospects for exports in this sector could be greatly increased.

For other nonexporters, the prospects for exporting are less bright, since such firms face the more difficult barrier to exports of large sunk costs. While their technology capabilities are also very weak, their marketing capabilities are even weaker.

Table 16.7 shows the means of excess marketing probabilities and the percentages of the observations with probability more than 0.5 by size of firm. Size is one of the most important variables for representing a firm's technological and marketing capabilities and export potential. As noted above, exporters are typically much larger than nonexporters. While larger firms may have several advantages over smaller ones, of particular interest is the pattern of excess-marketing probability by size. According to Table 16.7, although the probability of excess-marketing capability is slightly lower in size 4 than in size 3, the tendency among exporters is for the average of the probabilities to increase as size increases. That means that size (measured by the number of workers) affects the relative marketing capability of a firm. However, after size group 3, the effect begins to fade away because the export fraction of total sales also begins to decrease.

5 Summary and policy recommendation

By using a censored switching regression model, we have analyzed Korean SMEs' export behavior on the micro-economic level and in the strategic management (disequilibrium) framework. Although the model is slightly more complicated than traditional ones, it provides results that can be firm specific. Although both switching and censoring problems are allowed for, the estimators from the model are still consistent and asymptotically normal. The R^2 and $\bar{R}^2$ of the censored switching regression model on actual exports were 90.8% and 89.1% respectively, demonstrating an excellent fit despite the few RHS variables used. On the basis of such estimates, the model sharply distinguished exporters from nonexporters. For exporters, the average predicted values of technology capability and marketing capability were naturally very significantly positive. In all size groups except size group 4 and all the sectors except AP, marketing capability was higher than technology capability. However, at the firm level, 47.2% of exporters have a probability of excess marketing capability less than 0.5, implying that a substantial percentage of firms was suffering more from insufficient marketing capability than from insufficient technology capability (Table 16.6). Furthermore, the values and signs of excess marketing capability vary over sectors and sizes (Table 16.5). Thus, policies for balancing the technology capability and marketing capability are desirable to promote the actual exports of SMEs efficiently.

On the other hand, for nonexporters, with the exception of firms in size group 1 and the FA sector, the technology capability is extremely low and in fact negative, implying that nonexporters are not ready to export from the point of view of technology capability. The reason why firms in size group 1 had a positive technology capability is that almost all nonexporters in the technologically sophisticated FA sector are in size group 1 and capable of exporting from the technological-capability perspective. Much worse than that, however, is that nonexporters' marketing capability was very significantly negative, implying that nonexporters are faced with very difficult-to-surmount sunk costs in penetrating export markets. This phenomenon is more serious for firms in size group 1 and the FA sector. Lowering their sunk costs in export markets is the most important and urgent task if those nonexporters, particularly in size 1 and the FA sector, that were ready to export on the technology side are to succeed in export markets.

According to the descriptive statistics,[15] SME exporters have had greater experience in exports, more workers, higher productivity (particularly capital productivity), more new products, greater buyer concentration, and higher CEOs' previous sales experience than nonexporters. These findings are consistent with

---

[15] See Kim, Nugent, and Yhee (1997) for details.

those of Bernard and Jensen (1995a, 1995b, 1996a, 1996b) and of Roberts and Tybout (1997).

Considering that Korea's SMEs compete with comparable exports of lower-wage countries, it is noteworthy that in this study the marginal effect of labor productivity appears to be the most important factor in promoting exports. Every unit increase of labor productivity increases actual exports by about five times. Thus, improving labor productivity is the most important factor for succeeding in export markets. More capital through factory automation, through development and adoption of advanced technology, through more productive training for workers, and through restructuring are among the best ways to improve labor productivity. According to the descriptive statistics, the capital productivity of exporters is twice that of nonexporters.

On the other hand, vertical or horizontal integration with large enterprises (LEs) seems to have helped SME exports very considerably. That is, almost all SMEs are related to LEs through subcontracting relationships. In our sample, the ratio of subcontract receiving to total sales in size 1 was about 68%, and the fraction of SMEs participating in the subcontracting (including both receiving and placing of orders) was more than 85% in Korea in 1990. Although such integration of SMEs with LEs can secure markets for SMEs, deep dependence on LEs can impede the development of SMEs' own internal marketing and technological capabilities. As a result, cyclical fluctuations in LE business activity can easily be transferred to SMEs. The recent financial crisis in Korea, which started at the end of 1997, has tended to make SMEs the scapegoats by forcing financial institutions to cut them off from credit, leaving many SMEs vulnerable to financial failure stemming from their shortcomings in technological and marketing capabilities.

With respect to the non-financial-support variables, the support to penetrate export markets by government or nonprofit agencies had a strong effect on SMEs' marketing capability in export markets. To help SMEs identify and connect with appropriate buyers is very important for lowering sunk costs in accessing export markets. More specific, reliable, cost efficient, and accessible forms of support for SMEs in penetrating export markets must be designed.

Among financial supports, while the credit guarantee system was the most effective in export marketing, the financial support for developing new technology was very effective in increasing technology capability, and the support for export and overseas investment also was effective for marketing capability. Financial support systems need to be sophisticated to meet international rules under the control of IMF and WTO, but the special conditions faced by individual SMEs must be given greater consideration.

For tax supports, special depreciation allowances appear to have had a strong effect on exports. The special depreciation allowances for facilities, asset investment, and restructuring for improving technology and productivity would appear to be especially useful for export promotion by reducing the sunk costs associated with particular foreign markets and niches.

Conditional on the sample, the averages of the conditional excess marketing probabilities are 51.2% for exporters and 0.2% for nonexporters, and the percentages of observations with excess-marketing probability over 0.5 are 48.8% for exporters and 0% for nonexporters. That is, the exporters have few serious problems in marketing relative to technology, while nonexporters have virtually no marketing ability in export markets. Since nonexporters had a considerably negative marketing capability and a zero technology capability, the excess-marketing probability for the nonexporters cannot but be zero.

It is of interest to examine the time path of excess-marketing probability. The marketing capabilities of WT and especially AP firms declined sharply from 1989 to 1991. On the other hand, the EPs' excess-marketing probability increased steadily from 49.9% to 58.7%. This pattern should be very important in deciding the timing, the magnitude, and the kind of SME support policies. With respect to size, the excess-marketing probability increased for firms in size groups 1–3 but declined slightly for firms in size group 4. On the whole, we conclude that larger SMEs have greater marketing capability.

When all SMEs are divided into two subgroups – one bound by the T-regime and the other bound by the M-regime – the use of excess-marketing probabilities can facilitate the design of more efficient support systems. The forms of support aimed at promoting technological capability for the groups binding to the T-regime and those aimed at marketing capability for the groups binding to the M-regime could improve the efficiency of resources used for SME supports by balancing technology capability and marketing capability.

REFERENCES

Aitken, B., Hanson, G., and Harrison, A. (1997), "Spillovers, Foreign Investment, and Export Behavior," *Journal of International Economics*, **43**, 103–132.

Amemiya, T. (1974), "A Note on a Fair and Jaffee Model," *Econometrica*, **42**, No. 4 (July), 759–762.

——— (1984), "Tobit Model: A Survey," *Journal of Econometrics*, **24**, 3–16.

Asplund, Marcus (1995), "What Fraction of Capital Investment Is Sunk Costs?" Working Paper Series in Economics and Finance RePEc: hhs: hastef: 0068, The Economic Research Institute, Stockholm School.

Aw, B. and Batra, G. (1994), "Exports, Firm Size and Wage Inequalities," mimeo, Economics Department, Pennsylvania State University.

Aw, B-Y. and Hwang, A. R. (1995), "Productivity and the Export Market: A Firm-Level Analysis," *Journal of Development Economics*, **47**, 313–332.

Barham, B. L. and Chavas, J.-P. (1997), "Sunk Costs and Resource Mobility: Implications for Economic and Policy Analysis," Staff Paper Series No. 410 (April), Department of Agriculture and Applied Economics, University of Wisconsin-Madison.

Bernard, A. B. (1995), "Exporters and Trade Liberalization in Mexico: Production Structure and Performance," Working Paper, Economics Department, MIT.

Bernard, Andrew B. and Jensen, J. B. (1995a), "Exporters, Jobs, and Wages in US manufacturing, 1976–1987," Brookings *Papers on Economic Activity, Microeconomics*, Washington.

(1995b), "Inside the U.S. Export Boom." mimeo, MIT.

(1997), "Exporters, Skill-Upgrading, and the Wage Gap," *Journal of International Economics*, **42**, 3–31.

(1996), "Why Firms Export," mimeo, Economics Department, MIT.

Bernard, A. B. and Wagner, J. (1997), "Exporters and Success in German Manufacturing," *Weltwirtschaftliches Archiv*, forthcoming.

Burkett, J. B. (1981), "Marginal and Conditional Probabilities of Excess Demand," *Economics Letters*, **8**, 159–162.

Dess, G. G. and Miller, A. (1993), *Strategic Management* (New York: McGraw-Hill).

Fair, R. C. and Jaffee, D. M. (1972), "Methods of Estimation for Markets in Disequilibrium," *Econometrica*, **40**, 497–514.

Hartley, M. J. and Parthasaradhi Mallela (1977), "The Asymptotic Properties of a Maximum Likelihood Estimator for a Model of Markets in Disequilibrium," *Econometrica*, **45**, 1205–1220.

Itoh, Motoshige and Shujiro Urata (1994), "Small and Medium-Size Enterprise Support Policies in Japan," Policy Research Working Paper 1403, World Bank Policy Research Department.

Keesing, D. B. (1979), "Trade Policy for Developing Countries," Staff Working Paper No. 353, World Bank.

Kim, J. H. and Cho, K. H. (1991), *Liberalization and Reorganization of Subcontracting System* (Seoul, Korea: KIET).

Kim, Linsu (1997), *Imitation to Innovation: The Dynamics of Korea's Technological Learning* (Cambridge: Harvard Business School Press).

Kim, Linsu and Nugent, J. B. (1994), "The Republic of Korea's Small and Medium-Size Enterprises and Their Support Mechanisms," Policy Working Paper 1404, The World Bank Policy Research Department.

Kim, L., Nugent, J. B., and Yhee, S.-J. (1997), "Transaction Costs and Export Channels of Small and Medium Sized Enterprises: The Case of Korea," *Contemporary Economic Policy*, **XV**, No. 1, 104–120.

Laroque, G. and Salanie, B. (1994), "Estimating the Canonical Disequilibrium Model," *Journal of Econometrics*, **62**, 165–210.

Levy, B. (1991), "Transaction Costs, the Size of Firms and Industrial Policy: Lessons from a Comparative Case Study of the Footwear Industry in Korea and Taiwan," *Journal of Development Economics*, 151–178.

Levy, B., Berry, A., and Nugent, J. B. (1999), *Fulfilling the Export Potential of Small and Medium Firms* (Boston: Kluwer Academic).

Maddala, G. S. (1990), *Limited Dependent Variables in Econometrics*, Econometric Society Monographs, 1990.

Morawetz, D. (1981), *Why the Emperor's New Clothes Are Not Made in Colombia* (New York: Oxford University Press).

Park, Y. H., Yang, H. B., Cho, C., and Lee, S. H. (1992), *Analysis of Actual Usage and Effect of Small and Medium-Sized Enterprise Systems* (Seoul, Korea: KIET).

Power, D. A. (1993), "Endogenous Switch Regression Models with Limited Dependent Variables," *Sociological Methods & Research*, **22**, 248–273.

Quandt, R. E. (1988), *The Econometrics of Disequilibrium* (Oxford: Blackwell).

Quandt, R. E. and Rosen, H. S. (1985), "Is There Chronic Excess Supply of Labor? Designing a Statistical Test," *Economic Letters*, **19**, 193–197.

Roberts, M. and Tybout, J. (1997), "The Decision to Export in Colombia: An Empirical Model of Entry with Sunk Costs," *The American Economic Review*, **87**, No. 4, 545–564.

Sutton, J. (1991), *Sunk Costs and Market Structure: Price Competition, Advertising, and the Evolution of Concentration* (Cambridge, MA: MIT Press).

Takeshi Amemiya

Born on March 29, 1935 in Tokyo, Japan
Married, has two children
Citizen of Japan, Permanent Resident of the United States

Affiliation

Department of Economics, Stanford University, Stanford, California 94305

Education

B.A. in Social Science, International Christian University, Tokyo, 1958
M.A. in Economics, American University, Washington D.C., 1961
Ph.D. in Economics, Johns Hopkins University, 1964

Positions

Research Associate and Visiting Assistant Professor of Economics, Stanford University, 1964–65
Assistant Professor of Economics, Stanford University, 1965–66
Lecturer, Institute of Economic Research, Hitotsubashi University, 1966–68
Senior Research Associate, Stanford University, July–September, 1967
Associate Professor of Economics, Stanford University, 1968–74
Professor of Economics, Stanford University, 1974–86
Senior Fellow, National Bureau of Economic Research, Computer Research Center, Cambridge, Massachusetts, April–July, 1975
Visiting Scholar, as a Guggenheim Fellow, London School of Economics, Department of Statistics, January–June 1976
Visiting Professor, as a Fellow of the Japan Society for the Promotion of Science, Kyoto University, Institute of Economic Research, July–October, 1981
Visiting Professor, International Christian University, Tokyo, 1985–86
Edward Ames Edmonds Professor of Economics, Stanford University, 1986 to present

Visiting Professor, as a fellow of Alexander von Humboldt Foundation, University of Kiel and University of Frankfurt, May–August, 1988

Visiting Professor, as a Fellow of the Japan Society for the Promotion of Science, University of Tokyo, February–July 1989

Visiting Professor, as a fellow of Alexander von Humboldt Foundation, University of Kiel and University of Frankfurt, May–August, 1990

Visiting Professor, Free University of Amsterdam, The Netherlands, April–July, 1993

Visiting Professor, Toyo Eiwa Women's University, Yokohama, Japan, September–December, 1994, April–June 1995, September–December, 1995

Visiting Professor, Center for Economic Studies, University of Munich, Germany, March–April, 1999

Fellowships and Grants

Ford Foundation Doctoral Dissertation Fellowship in Economics, Johns Hopkins University, 1963–64

Principal Investigator, NSF Research Project in Econometrics, Stanford University, 1965–66

Coprincipal Investigator, with T.W. Anderson, NSF Research Project in Econometrics, Stanford University, 1969–78

Guggenheim Fellowship, 1975–76

Principal Investigator, NSF Research Project in Econometrics, Stanford University, 1979 to present

Japan Society for Promotion of Science Fellowship, 1981 and 1989

Alexander von Humboldt Senior U.S. Scientist Award, 1988

Memberships

Phi Beta Kappa
International Statistics Institute
Econometric Society (Fellow)
American Statistical Association (Fellow)
American Academy of Arts and Sciences (Fellow)

Editorial Activities

Associate Editor, *Econometrica*, 1970–75
Associate Editor, *Journal of the American Statistical Association*, 1970–73
Reviewer, *Mathematical Review*, 1975–78
Coeditor, *Econometrica*, 1981–82
Coeditor, *Journal of Econometrics*, 1982 to present

Listings

Who's Who in America
Who's Who in Economics

Bibliography

Books

Studies in Econometrics, Time Series, and Multivariate Statistics (coeditor with S. Karlin and L. A. Goodman), Academic Press, New York, 1983.

Advanced Econometrics, Harvard University Press, 1985.

Collected Essays of Takeshi Amemiya, Edward Elgar Pub., 1994.

Introduction to Statistics and Econometrics, Harvard University Press, 1994.

Introduction to Aristotle's Ethics (In Japanese), Translation and Commentary on *Aristotle's Ethics* by J. O. Urmson, Iwanami Publisher, Tokyo, January 1998.

Published Articles

"On the Use of Principal Components of Independent Variables in Two-Stage Least Squares Estimation," *International Economic Review*, Vol. 7 (1966), 283–303.

"Specification Analysis in the Estimation of Parameters of a Simultaneous Equation Model with Autoregressive Residuals," *Econometrica*, Vol. 34 (1966), 283–306.

"A Comparative Study of Alternative Estimators in a Distributed-Lag Model," (with W. Fuller), *Econometrica*, Vol. 35 (1967), 509–529.

"The Correlation Study of the Residuals in a Multivariate Regression Model," *The Economic Review*, Vol. 19 (1968), 125–132.

"Methodology of Econometric Prediction," *The Structural Change and Prediction of the Japanese Economy* (I. Yamada, ed.), Shunju-sha, Tokyo, Japan, (1969), (in Japanese).

"The Effect of Aggregation on Prediction in the Autoregressive model," *Proceedings, 1971 IEEE Conference on Decision and Control*, 537–539.

"The Estimation of the Variances in a Variance-Components Model," *International Economic Review*, Vol. 12 (1971), 1–13.

"The Effect of Aggregation on Prediction in the Autoregressive Model," (with R. Y. Wu), *Journal of the American Statistical Association*, Vol. 67 (September 1972). 628–632.

"Generalized Least Squares with an Estimated Autocovariance Matrix," *Econometrica*, Vol. 41 (July 1973), 723–532.

"Regression Analysis When the Dependent Variable Is Truncated Normal," *Econometrica*, Vol. 41 (November 1973), 997–1016.

"Regression Analysis When the Variance of the Dependent Variable Is Proportional to the Square of Its Expectation," *Journal of the American Statistical Association*, Vol. 68 (December 1973), 928–934.

"Regression Analysis When the Dependent Variable Is Truncated Lognormal: An Application to the Determinants of the Duration of Welfare Dependency," (with M. Boskin), *The International Economic Review*, Vol. 15 (June 1974), 485–496.

"The Nonlinear Two Stage Least Squares Estimator," *Journal of Econometrics*, Vol. 2 (July 1974), 255–257.

"A Note on a Fair and Jaffee Model," *Econometrica*, Vol. 42 (July 1974), 759–762.

"Selecting the Optimal Order of Polynomial in the Almon Distributive Lag" (with K. Morimune), Review of Economics and Statistics, Vol. 56 (August 1974), 378–386.

"Multivariate Regression and Simultaneous Equation Models When the Dependent Variables Are Truncated Normal," *Econometrica*, Vol. 42 (November 1974). 999–1012.

"Bivariate Probit Analysis: Minimum Chi-Square Methods," *Journal of the American Statistical Association*, Vol. 69 (December 1974), 940–944.

"A Modified Logit Model" (with F. Nold), *Review of Economics and Statistics*, Vol. 57 (1975), 255–257.

"The Nonlinear Limited Information Maximum Likelihood Estimator and the Modified Nonlinear Two Stage Least-Squares Estimator," *Journal of Econometrics*, Vol. 3 (1975), 375–386.

"Qualitative Response Models," *Annals of Economics and Social Measurement*. Vol. 4 (Summer 1975), 363–372.

"L'estimation des Modèles à Equations Simultanées non Lineaires," *Cahiers du Séminaire d'Econométrie*, Centre National de la Recherche Scientifique, (1976).

"The Maximum Likelihood, the Minimum Chi-Square, and the Nonlinear Weighted Least Squares Estimator in the General Qualitative Response Model," *Journal of the American Statistical Association*, Vol. 71 (1976), 347–351.

"On the Estimation of Production Frontiers: Maximum Likelihood Estimation of the Parameters of a Discontinuous Density Function," (with D.J. Aigner and D. J. Poirier), *International Economic Review*, Vol. 17 (1976), 377–396.

"The Maximum Likelihood and the Nonlinear Three-stage Least Squares Estimator in the General Nonlinear Simultaneous Equation Model," *Econometrica*, Vol. 45 (1977), 955–968.

"The Modified Second-Round Estimator in the General Qualitative Response Model," *Journal of Econometrics*, Vol. 5 (1977), 295–299.

"A Note on a Heteroscedastic Model," *Journal of Econometrics*, Vol. 6 (1977), 365–370.

"Some Theorems in the Linear Probability Model," *International Economic Review*, Vol. 8 (1977), 645–650.

"The Estimation of a Simultaneous-Equation Generalized Probit Model," *Econometrica*, Vol. 46 (1978), 1193–1205.

"A Note on a Random Coefficients Model," *International Economic Review*, Vol. 19 (1978), 739–796.

"On a Two-Step Estimation of a Multivariate Logit Model," *Journal of Econometrics*, Vol. 8 (1978), 13–21.

"The Estimation of a Simultaneous-Equation Tobit Model," *International Economic Review*, Vol. 20 (1979), 169–181.

"The n^{-2}-order Mean Squared Errors of the Maximum Likelihood and the Minimum Logit Chi-Square Estimator," *Annals of Statistics*, Vol. 8 (1980), 488–505.

"Selection of Regressors," *International Economic Review*, Vol. 21 (1980), 331–354.

"A Comparison of The Box-Cox Maximum Likelihood Estimator and the Nonlinear Two Stage Least Squares Estimator," (with J. L. Powell), *Journal of Econometrics*, Vol. (1981), 351–381.

"Qualitative Response Models: A Survey," *Journal of Economic Literature*, Vol. (1981), 1483–1536.

"Correction to a Lemma," *Econometrica*, Vol. 50 (1982), 1325–1328.

"The Two-Stage Least Absolute Deviations Estimators," *Econometrica*, Vol. (1982), 689–711.

"A Comparison of the Amemiya GLS and the Lee-Maddala-Trost G2SLS in a Simultaneous-Equations Tobit Model," *Journal of Econometrics*, Vol. 23 (1983), 295–300.

"A Comparison of the Logit Model and Normal Discriminant Analysis When the Independent Variables Are Binary," (with J. L. Powell), in *The Festschrift Volume in Honor of T. W. Anderson* (S. Karlin, T. Amemiya, and L. Goodman, eds.), Academic Press, New York, (1983), 3–30.

"Nonlinear Regression Models," *Handbook of Econometrics*, (Z. Griliches and M. Intrilligator, eds.), North Holland, The Netherland (1983), 334–389.

"Partially Generalized Least Squares and Two-Stage Least Squares Estimators," *Journal of Econometrics*, Vol. 23 (1983), 275–283.

"Tobit Models: A Survey," *Journal of Econometrics*, Vol. 24 (1984), 3–61.

"Instrumental-Variable Estimation of an Error-Components Model," (with T. E. MaCurdy), *Econometrica*, Vol. 54 (1986), 869–880.

"A Comparison of Two Consistent Estimators in the Choice-Based Sampling Qualitative Response Models," (with Q. Vuong), *Econometrica*, Vol. 55 (1987), 699–702.

"Discrete Choice Models," *The New Palgrave*, (J. Eatwell, M. Milgate, and P. Newman, eds.), The Macmillan Press, Ltd., Vol.1 (1987), 850–854.

"Limited Dependent Variables," *The New Palgrave*, (J. Eatwell, M. Milgate, and P. Newman, eds.), The Macmillan Press, Ltd., Vol. 3 (1987), 185–189.

"Two-Stage Least Squares," in *Encyclopedia of Statistical Sciences*, John Wiley & Sons, Inc., New York, (1988), 373–375.

"An Application of Nested Logit Models to the Labor Supply of the Elderly," (with K. Shimono), *The Economic Studies Quarterly*, Vol. 40 (1989), 14–22.

"T. W. Anderson and the Estimation of Dynamic Models Using Panel Data," *The Collected Papers of T. W. Anderson: 1943–1985*, (G. P. H. Styan, ed.), Vol. 2, John Wiley, New York, (1990), 1577–1578.

"Risan Sentaku Model (Discrete Choice Model)," (in Japanese) *Suri Kagaku Jiten* (*Encyclopaedia of Mathematical Sciences*). (H. Hironaka, ed.), Osaka Shoseki, Osaka, (1991), 489–494.

"A Study of Household Investment Patterns in Japan: An Application of Generalized Tobit Models," (with M. Saito and K. Shimono), *The Economic Studies Quarterly*, (March 1993).

"Japanese Economy and Economics in the Postwar Fifty Years (in Japanese)," (with K. Asakura, K. Hayami, K. Tsujimura, T. Nakamura, and Y. Kurabayashi), *Toyo Eiwa Journal of the Humanities and Social Sciences*, (September 1995), 5–68.

"Structural Duration Models," *Journal of Statistical Planning and Inference*, (January 1996), 39–52.

"A Note on Left Censoring," *Analysis of Panels Data and Limited Dependent Variable Models*, (C. Hsiao, K. Lahiri, L.-F. Lee, and M. H. Pesaran, eds.), Cambridge University Press, (1999) 7–22.

Index